D0861476

Marriage, Morals and Sex in America

SIDNEY DITZION

MARRIAGE

MORALS *and*

SEX *in* AMERICA

a history of ideas

[EXPANDED EDITION, WITH A NEW CHAPTER BY THE AUTHOR]

The Norton Library

W·W·NORTON & COMPANY·INC·

NEW YORK

TO
MY FATHER
AND
MOTHER

First published in the Norton Library 1978
by arrangement with Twayne Publishers.

Books That Live
The Norton imprint on a book means that in the publisher's
estimation it is a book not for a single season but for the years.
W. W. Norton & Company, Inc.

Library of Congress Cataloging in Publication Data

Ditzion, Sidney Herbert, 1908-
Marriage, morals, and sex in America.
(The Norton library)
Includes bibliographical references and index.
1.   Family—United States.   2.   United States—
Moral conditions.   3.   Marriage—United States.
I. Title.
HQ535.D5   1978   301.42   78-628
ISBN 0-393-00890-8

1 2 3 4 5 6 7 8 9 0

TO GRACE,
A CONSTANT REFUTATION
OF THE ANTI-MARRIAGE THEORIES
RECORDED IN THIS BOOK

Introduction

Every inquiry into the nature of the human animal raises questions of perspective and bias. Each scientist, utilizing his own special examining instruments, embarks upon a limited research and straightway presumes to come into possession of the ultimate truth concerning the behavior of man. And, since the scientific views of man are almost as numerous as there are viewers, the ordinary citizen is beset by baffling problems of choice and distinction.

The innocent layman is at best confronted with a broad choice of smug analyses. There are experts who claim all human motivation to arise out of man's economic needs and arrangements. Other wise leaders champion an explanation wholly spiritual. Still others insist that the sexual drive, together with its social implications, constitutes the regulating principle of human activity.

Marriage, Morals, and Sex in America, while not assuming sexuality to be the determinant of all behavior, accepts the hypothesis that man's economic, political, intellectual, and social activities are inextricably enmeshed with his sexual activities. The smallest concession to the existence of such personality integration allows us to proceed to a view of total man within the sexual frame of reference. When the reader notes the inseparable association of all these life components, he may well wish to question Bertrand Russell's recent assertion that "in general the interest that men and women take in each other has little influence upon politics."

The exploratory path employed in the present work is an historical one. And, inasmuch as the approaches to history are several, this book will in a large degree confine its interest to American *thinking* on the sex question from colonial times to the present. Although the story is built around a series of movements and group associations, the overall plan is a chronological one in which each of these social movements is displayed at the zenith of its influence on the public mind. The earlier stages of this account receive more leisurely treatment than they may seem to merit. This was done altogether consciously, the intention being to provide a detailed elaboration of the root ideas from which later tacticians and idea manufacturers were to draw sustenance or ammunition.

Many will argue, as did Leonardo da Vinci long ago, that

wisdom in such matters must proceed from experience rather than from the thoughts of others. While this is fundamentally true, it is equally true that these thoughts, or ideas, are accurate indicators of events and social movements. For ideas may at times be the prime movers of events to come; or, they may be harbingers of nascent social trends, soon to be recognized generally as reality; they may on the other occasions be representative of fact or behavior already in existence, but not yet publicly acknowledged or socially accepted.

Diehard materialists insist that ideas and ideals are futile substitutions for what people cannot have or be. Such a notion must be conceded to be patently false when we note how influential the blueprints of social architects have been in framing newer habits of life. In this important sense the history we are about to relate consists of more than the fantasies that dreams are made of; it is life itself as described by those who considered themselves to be on the verge of improving life, provided they could secure the help of their fellow citizens to erect the proposed structure.

There are two main themes that emerge from this presentation of evolving thought. The first emphasizes the interaction of manifold *social* reform movements with those movements intent upon *sexual* reform. That is to say, man's efforts to achieve dignity and freedom for self-realization take the form of a multilateral attack. To be sure, there has not always been agreement as to what true dignity really is. At one extreme, it has been believed that the highest dignity comes from obedience to the commandments of a superior being. At the other, the natural impulses of the individual have been accorded supremacy. In the conflict of competing reforms, the reformers and their opponents have shown little respect for each other's motives, and little understanding. Many sincere individuals have experienced difficulty in distinguishing the libertarians from the libertines. The conservators of old moral ways have consistently labeled *all* reformers libertines and infidels.

The second and central theme of this book carries the notion of unity of reform one step further. Questions like marriage and divorce, the education of women, women's rights in the family and in society, birth control, and sex education will be seen to merge easily into one another as the story unfolds. This confluence of ideas is in itself a demonstration that the sexual-social problem is indivisible. Actually, the array of problems with which people concerned themselves changed character only slightly from one period of time to another. However, the disposition of people to think, write, and act upon various components of the sexual problem altered markedly as shifting intellectual and social currents redirected the drift of public attention. Strong American reform movements, in the realm of idea or of action, elicited new elements of interest in the economic, political, physical, or personal aspects of marriage. Events and social changes might also serve to illumine hitherto unseen facets of the sexual question. Then too, the mere accumulation of knowledge, plus the will and growing freedom to disseminate it, have been capable of creating sharp focuses of interest.

In every instance, actors on the reform stage made certain to connect their emphasis with some set of intellectual, social, or political principles. Many placed their ideological wares on sale in the public market, while they themselves lived privately in accordance with socially accepted patterns of sexual behavior. They wrote essays and lectured to audiences, but did nothing about their grievances and suggestions. The account of such persons will consist of placing their ideas in the context of the period in which they lived. Biographical details will cast light upon the circumstances attending the birth of their ideas. Alongside the theoreticians, there were the bold practitioners like the Oneida Perfectionists and free love anarchists who acted out the ideas they advanced. The pages devoted to these will naturally savor more of life and less of printer's ink.

One remarkable similarity about practically all of these reform movements was that a large portion of their efforts was directed toward creating an equitable balance of power between the sexes, plus a more satisfying expression of sexuality for both sexes. When apparently identical ideas appeared in the context of separate reform movements, they were in actuality distinct as to logic and flavor but related in that they pursued a common objective. In brief, whatever their political, humanitarian, medical, faddist or religious complexions, these many reformers have been contributors to the feminist cause. *Marriage, Morals, and Sex in America* is, therefore, a complete story of the woman's rights movement—of the struggle to achieve human rights for a sexual "minority."

Table of Contents

ONE

Reason and Nature

ADVICE FROM ABROAD

Americans were Europeans until well after the Revolution. It is not surprising, then, that our literate population during the colonial era was strongly European in its notions about many aspects of life. We imported ideas on marriage and family relationships much as we did other social and political formulations. The men and women of our reading classes were inclined to take their cue in many matters of mind, body, and soul from their upper and middle-class cousins abroad.

Thus, as we search the thoughts of first and second century Americans, we are forced, in drawing our conclusions, to depend more on what they read than on what they wrote. An examination of their reading matter shows that the gist of the new ideas on woman-in-marriage, imported at that time from Europe, was that the female of the species was more nearly human than she was generally supposed to be. She therefore deserved a little better share of the available knowledge and power than she was getting.

A few American intellectuals observed the new trend as early as the seventeenth century, but it was not until the eighteenth that bookshelves in this country supported a good many anthologies like Steele's *The Ladies' Library,* as well as a variety of single works on the subject of woman's place in the world. Among the more influential writers of this kind of literature were Lord Halifax, Archbishop Fènelon, Mary Astell, Daniel Defoe, Joseph Addison, Richard Steele, Jonathan Swift, Samuel Richardson, and Mrs. Eliza Haywood.

One recurrent theme in the works of Richardson and Mrs. Haywood was the desirability of relying upon the intelligence, virtue, and dignity of an eligible young lady in her choice of a husband rather than upon the disastrous penchant of her parents for men of wealth and social position. The prevailing motif, however, was a call for greater educational and social opportunity for women, especially in the married state. Voices ranged from whispered pleas to shouted demands, but never, as yet, with any intention of seeking equality of the sexes. Halifax, Fènelon, and other conservative writers seemed at times to be advocating the intellectual advancement of women in order to enable them to bear the onus of their natural inferiority more philosophically. A case could be made for spiritual equality, but very few would go beyond that. Modesty, meekness, compassion, and piety were solid feminine virtues. A "good" woman ministered to her husband's needs, catered to his whims, and submitted to his will and judgment. Halifax was ready to advise women on how to get around difficult husbands; he would even tell them how to dominate their mates through the use of shrewd psychology—but always as intellectual and social underlings.

This one-sided picture could not possibly help being modified in a shifting pattern of social thought concerning the role of women in society. Both the Protestant ethic and a growing spirit of democracy militated against a purely male point of view. Life in a Catholic world had allowed a choice of two roads to prestige for adult womanhood—marriage or the convent. The Protestant creed, by depriving celibacy of its honored status, left only one acceptable course for the female ego. Spinsterhood, then as now, was getting the universal frown. The alternative was to make the best of it in marriage

"Making the best of it" meant bucking the line of male contempt commonly held by opinion-molders like Robert Burton, the English philosopher and humorist, Sir Thomas Browne, the physician-essayist, and the libertarian poet and pamphleteer, John Milton. Democracy implied a broadening of the base of social participation. A few high-minded males and indignant women literati insisted on reading "ladies invited" on the sign-board of the public house. In effect, this was a challenge to the powerful male monopoly on the part of a self-conscious and somewhat militant splinter of female agitators, abetted by philanthropically inclined male partisans.

The early leadership of this movement, which started off with a bang and decrescendoed to a whimper, fell to Daniel Defoe and Mary Astell. These two were among the rare few who proceeded on the assumption that, other things being equal, a woman's brain was as good as a man's. Two circumstances make their ideas of special interest to us. First, Mary Astell's writings, though unsigned, were included in the much read *Ladies' Library;* and Defoe's *Essay on Projects* was read by Benjamin Franklin and seems to have had a pervading influence on Franklin's treatment of the woman question. Second, Defoe and Astell wrote at the turn of the eighteenth century, long before really advanced ideas on the subject had received serious and widespread consideration.

Defoe was concerned mostly with promoting the piety and

education of women and said little to upset prevailing ideas on the marital relationship. He wished, in fact, to make women more capable and companionable, but nevertheless subordinate, wives. He did, however, tread on fairly fresh ground when he accused his own sex of so designing women's training as to produce the very ignorance and superficiality with which men were in the habit of taxing women.

Mary Astell, intellectual pamphleteer and mover in prominent English circles, was violently opposed to any conception of woman's innate inferiority. Her works, including the outstanding *Some Reflections on Marriage*, were replete with denials and refutations of arguments which used religious sanctions, nature, or economic and social decrees as authority for assigning a minor role to woman. Mary Astell's approach to marriage from the woman's viewpoint was the ultramodern one for almost a century.

Her chief target was Lord Halifax. Halifax admitted that women were in an unenviable position; but such was the decree of custom. One could not do anything about it, nor did one want to. In his *Advice to a Daughter* Halifax made the case clear and simple. It might be a heartless thing to say, but facts were facts. Nature gave men the lion's share of brains because to them fell the job of making the laws. Nature had also arranged matters so that women could perform their assigned duties in life under male supervision. As compensation, woman's face, form, and tears made her more than an even match for man and his intelligence. This sort of balance of power would certainly be hard on the few intellectually gifted women. But this was the sacrifice demanded by the dictates of the sacred institution of marriage.

This was the kind of talk which—together with the behavior that went along with it—led many a nineteenth-century libertarian to attack marriage *per se*. Mary Astell, whose behavior was determined by a close adherence to orthodox religion, reacted with humility. While maintaining that St. Paul and other scriptural sources supported the idea of the mutual dependence of men and women, she admitted that one of the sexes had to lead. While rejecting theories of natural inferiority, she felt that every social group had to have an executive officer. In the family, the husband and father was the chosen one.

Mary Astell, accordingly, assuming woman to be subordinate to man in the sacred and indissoluble relation of marriage, set down her demands and prescriptions for improved status. The reader of her *Reflections*, having waded past a deceptive irony born of indignation, finds a program something like this. First and foremost, woman needed an improved education and training to prepare her for the correct choice of a husband with whom she could live forevermore in a pact based on mutual esteem. But, since this kind of reciprocity was impossible as long as men continued to look upon women with condescension and disdain, men themselves needed to be re-educated. Neither men nor women could expect to achieve real happiness in marriage unless men learned to respect women's intellect and ability, to use their law-given authority gently and rationally, and to consult their wives as ranking officers rather than chief servants of the household.

The charges of exploitation, slavery, and oppression, first hurled at men by Mary Astell, were to be repeated by practically every radical in the marriage reform business for over two centuries. The analogy of married women to a suppressed minority or social class was to serve as the basic link between social reform movements and attacks on the constituted laws of marriage. John Milton, as Mary Astell pointed out, was ready enough to urge the people to resist an arbitrary king, but there was no voice to "cry up liberty to poor *Female Slaves* or plead for the lawfulness of Resisting a private Tyranny."

Such was woman's lot. It was, however, a comfort to consider that patiently bearing the brunt of an unwise marriage in this life would bring rewards in the hereafter. Easy divorce, as advocated by Milton, was decidedly against Mary Astell's convictions. The correct choice of a husband remained the essence of a dignified career in marriage. Women, to whom were available none of the easy escapes from law and custom of which men took advantage, were passive agents throughout, and therefore needed extra safeguards for their happiness. Mutual respect and consideration were the first principles of a marriage choice. A decent man would not take advantage of a helpless, trusting woman. A really superior man would emerge as the natural guide and leader of a more democratically conceived family unit.

These were brave words indeed, but unfortunately they were not read as widely as the broadly circulated *Spectator and Tatler* in which Addison, Steele, and Swift held forth. These writers, for the most part sincere in their desire to raise woman to a higher social level, concerned themselves mostly with criticising the then prevalent "polite" education of women. If the middle class emphasis on sewing, singing, and dancing for girls was superficial in a very harmful sense, the treatment of the problem by these essayists was superficial in an unconstructive sense. The pleasant writings of these philosophers shied away from disagreeable speculation on the subject of a similar cultural environment for male and female. The interesting question of whether an equal chance would reveal equal ability was not tackled.

The unpleasantly satiric Swift, whose writing generally belittled woman's worth, tucked many a scoffing remark under his precepts for successful marriage. His "Letter to a Very Young Lady on Her Marriage" contained some advice and some devastating criticism in the guise of advice. Its inclusion in the 1750 and 1793 editions of Benjamin Franklin's *Reflections on Courtship and Marriage* was testimony to its popularity—in all likelihood chiefly with male readers. Be as modest and reserved in marriage, he cautioned, as you were as a virgin. Be completely undemonstrative toward your husband in public; there are enough private hours in the twenty-four in which to ape the behavior of a French romance. Don't be hysterically possessive, nor affect neurotic loneliness in your husband's absence. Don't make a fetish of fine clothes—especially if you wear them to cover up a dirty body.

A few of Swift's "don'ts" were well meant. There was little charity, however, in his advice on choosing friends. Said he, it didn't matter much about the choice of girl friends, since all women waste their time on silly ideas and catty remarks. A woman should, if she could, get away from the kind which is always hatching up ideas about how to get the best of a husband. As a matter of fact, a husband should put a limit on the number of female friends his wife has: half a dozen "fools" are enough. Male company was a *sine qua non* for serious conversation. Of course, the husband should select these, because, among other things, women have as little judgment in this realm as in others.

Improving women's minds was naturally a matter of deep concern for Swift, and he gave much advice on this subject too. For, he explained, "As little respect as I have for the generality of your sex, it hath sometimes moved me with pity, to see the lady of the house withdraw immediately after dinner . . . as if it were an established maxim, that women are incapable of all conversation." The average woman could educate herself—though never beyond the attainments of a schoolboy— if she spent her time wisely instead of in inconsequential prattling. "When I reflect on this," carped Swift, "I cannot conceive you to be human creatures, but a sort of species hardly a degree above a monkey; who has more diverting tricks than any of you [and] is an animal less mischievous and expensive. . . . " This genre of satire must have made many a reader unhappy; but it was still far less objectionable, and better reading, than the coarse, salacious literature on the subject which was available in quantity in colonial America.

Addison did better for his women readers. He was far more generous and genuine, and sometimes even attributed their difficulties and shortcomings to the foibles of men. His "Essay on Jealousy," included with the Swift item in the 1793 edition of Franklin's *Reflections,* in some respects shows him to be as discerning of the roots of male jealousy as are experienced mind-probers of our time. Jealousy, said Addison, existed in three types of men: those who are insecure because of their own shortcomings with regard to age, appearance, ignorance or the like; those who project their own deceitful thoughts and behavior on their wives; and those who judge all women by that "vicious part of womankind" with whom they have associated, and perhaps still do, in pre-marital or adulterous escapades. Fortunately for England, there was a geographic component in the jealousy phenomenon: it was inversely related to the distance from the equator. Were Addison acquainted with subsequent economic interpretations of social and personal relations, he might have added that an important factor in jealousy is a fear of losing the property interest in a wife. But even in this essay, Addison is not a strong fighter for woman's cause. His partiality to male interests is indicated by the remedy he proposes. His question was not how to cure or ditch a jealous husband, but how to get along with one. The answer: Be extra-cautious and voluntarily restrict one's movements so as not to give an evil mind any cause for seeing evil.

As we move to the latter part of the eighteenth century and examine the motherly and fatherly advice of writers in the parent country and in France too, we note that the picture has not changed very much. Americans were importing, reprinting, and excerpting for their own publications, new authors with old ideas. Apparently practical knowledge and skills for womenfolk had not yet won out against "polite" accomplishments. Judging by frequency of reprint and inclusion in "lady's" volumes, and using such evidence as Mason Locke Weem's book orders to his employer, the publisher and bookseller, Matthew Carey, a list of best sellers in the field of woman's place in the universe would include Dr. John Gregory, James Fordyce, the Marchioness de Lambert, Hester Mulso Chapone, Hannah More, and the Reverend John Bennett. The books of Lord Chesterfield might be added in a separate category, because, although they were read to some extent, they were for the most part rejected by a discerning and fairminded audience.

Feminine reserve as a requisite for woman's happiness in and out of marriage was generally agreed upon. Modesty and restraint of the feelings were a part of it. Hannah More wanted a girl's entire personality moulded from childhood onward in a framework of mild but firm restraint. The independent spirit, so appropriate to boys, must be discouraged in their sisters. A girl should think for herself, but must yield to male opinion when it does not agree with hers. The world was going to expect submissiveness and forbearance of her, and the sooner she learned it, the better.

A man wanted a girl with accomplishments to embellish the domestic scene, provided she exercised her virtues and accomplishments in the shade. This proposition was universally accepted in its first part, but not in its second. All writers decried the narrowly conceived preparation for music, dress, and fashionable amusements and recommended more emphasis on the belles lettres, practical arts, and even (as in the case of Bennett and Dr. Gregory) a smattering of the sciences. But, where one faction urged girls for their own sakes to hide their learning from men because men generally looked upon women of parts "with a jealous and malignant eye," the other proclaimed violent disagreement with this commonly circulated notion.

The conflict was over what women could and could not do. There was complete agreement on what women should and should not do. Nature, propriety, and customs had established a male and a female jurisdiction. The greatest mistake women could make was to try to invade the male bailiwick. Women excelled in the perception of human quality and sentiment. Men were strong in the realms of reason, nature, and the harsh open world of business and politics. Women were not cut out for science. In general literature, women made up for this lack by their lively imagination and subtle sensitivities, but "the lofty epic, the pointed satire, and the more daring and successful flights of the tragic Muse, seem reserved for the bold adventures of the other sex." Men were expected to excel in science, valor, and eloquence. Women were applauded for running their families well. The main reason for expanding woman's educational vista was to enable her to meet her husband on some common ground. Discussion on a variety of topics made a happy household and prevented marriage from becoming "insipid."

Conservative as these views were, they represented considerable progress over those of their predecessors. Even spinsterhood acquired here some form of status as a recourse for women who did not find a man they could love and esteem. Marrying for your own good and happiness was fine, "but heaven forbid you should ever relinquish the ease and independence of a single life, to become the slaves of a fool's or a tyrant's caprice." The broad view had it that there was nothing wrong in remaining single except for the unjust social and psychological penalties one had to pay. One's friends dropped away, indelicate remarks from foul mouths had to be expected, and a life alone was the basis of personal insecurity. Again, a married woman acquired a warmer, better-rounded personality. She grew by her association with an intelligent husband; she travelled in social circles which had previously been closed to her by the "ceremonious coldness of a virgin state."

The male writers who gave advice in the matter of selecting a mate warned against the idea marrying a rake in order to reform him; his thirst for variety would lead him to abandon the best of women. Men suffering from hereditary diseases, especially insanity, were also to be avoided. If a woman was religious—and Hannah More considered a female skeptic the greatest incongruity—she should never marry an irreligious man; he might ridicule her attempts to instill piety in the children. Marriage for money or power was out of the question. In fact(and here the Reverend Bennett anticipated many an eloquent reformer), marrying for reasons other than love was called by men of principle "legal prostitution." Mrs. More would, in all likelihood, have rejected this pronouncement; for she had said that very few people in England married for love.

Other subjects generally treated in these works were religion, parental authority, and the kind of books that young ladies should not read. It was generally agreed that "religion" and "women" were inevitably and inseparably paired. Men might on occasion swerve from the path of religion because of their reading in the ancient pagan philosophers and modern skeptics. But even such men sought pious wives. It was their guarantee of undeviating virtue.

There was also unanimity on the harmfulness of reading romantic fiction. Parents at the time felt that these imaginative works presented an entirely mistaken picture of the passions as well as an unpractical picture of marriage. What disillusionment was in store for the novel-reading bride when she found herself "commanded," not "adored," by an ordinary man rather than by a swooning gallant!

On the question of parental authority, opinions ranged from obedience-to-parents-till-it-hurts to the humble plea of the liberal-minded Dr. Gregory that, while he hoped he was counseling well, if his children did not agree with him, they were under no compulsion to take his advice.

Lady Pennington, who got a considerable audience for her "An Unfortunate Mother's Advice to Her Absent Daughters, in a Letter to Miss Pennington," attempted to provide a complete guide to her children in the process of their education for life. She unfortunately had been separated from her husband and daughters by what she described as the unjust force of public opinion. As she explained, her husband had become incensed because her father's will had left her with an *independent* fortune; and then his family had goaded him into a separation. In those times, when a husband's control of his wife's property was rarely questioned, it was an insult to have her inheritance put beyond his reach.

One might have expected the unhappy Lady Pennington to urge her daughters toward strength and independence. Quite the contrary was her approach. Apparently her spirit was so completely crushed that she urged her daughters to grin and bear any misfortune that might come upon them in marriage. If they did not protest in their earthly state, she said, rewards would be forthcoming in heaven. The idea was to find a virtuous man of good sense and good nature. But, "Should the painful task of dealing with a morose tyrannical temper be assigned you, there is little more to be recommended, than a patient submission to an evil which admits not of a remedy." Handle him with kid gloves, she cautioned. If your husband is guilty of an indiscretion, turn your head the other way. Indeed, it was a mark of respect for a wife's piety to keep her in ignorance of extra-marital affairs.

William Alexander said, in the introduction to his *History of Women from the Earliest Antiquity to the Present Time* (1779), that he had prepared his two-volume work for the edification and glorification of women readers. What he produced was little different from other writings of the time with regard to the position of women in society. The impression Alexander made on readers hardly derived from the author's scholarship. The essence of his successful writing lay rather in his sensational accounts of various conceptions of chastity in ancient and eastern cultures. Alexander's anthropological research, with its emphasis on sex practices, on the use of artificial stimulants by both sexes, and on courtship and marriage customs in many lands, aroused a good deal of interest in England and America.

THE DOMESTIC SCENE

The writings of Englishmen were a strong influence but not an exclusive one. Ideas from abroad were from the beginning being colored or modified by American beliefs and practices. For one thing, the Puritan colonists believed that some education—at least as far as reading the Bible—was requisite toward the salvation of the female soul. Again conditions of life in the new world did not permit the development of toy-wives in a leisure-bound society. On the frontier especially, the problems of sustenance and defense demanded a self-reliant woman who shared more or less equally with her man the burdens and rewards of the family. While the isolated frontier environment, to a degree insulated from the social ideas of Europe, did not achieve the liberation of women, it did serve to modify the inherited notion of absolute male dominance.

Nor was it true on the other hand, that (as a reader is likely to feel after reading Elisabeth Dexter's *Colonial Women of Affairs*), that the colonies were full of independent women engaged in all sorts of occupations and enterprises. The greater part of these active women were widows carrying on their husbands' businesses. Women in literature, religion, and the theater were exceptions. Most economically self-sufficient women were tavern hostesses, shopkeepers, nurses, and teachers. The real point in Mrs. Dexter's observations is that American society admitted women into the working world when necessity dictated. Necessity had much to do with an economy which could not afford a dependent class. In the courts and in the home men yielded as much of their power as they had to and little more. The single standard of opportunity, freedom, and equality in family participation is still far from being the rule a couple of centuries later.

∾ ∾

Intelligent readers in early America had read Mary Astell and Daniel Defoe and had been influenced by them. The impulse which had greatest effect in moving ideas forward, and away from accepted notions based on the Bible and tradition, was a powerful wave of deism and rationalism. The American synthesis, developed out of the combination of ideological and environmental torces, was a conception of man as ideally a righteous, benevolent ruler. Equality for women was frequently announced, but always in terms that maintained men in the position of dominance.

One of the outstanding seminal writers to whom men like Benjamin Franklin and John Witherspoon went for source material was William Wollaston. Wollaston, a well-to-do schoolmaster who had taken Anglican orders, was part of a movement (which also claimed the controversialists Matthew Tindal and Thomas Chupp) designed to "save" Christianity through reason. The central effort of this movement was to single out those elements of Christianity whose truth could be maintained in the open market. The objective was a Gospel based on reason and enriched by love. Wollaston's *The Religion of Nature Delineated,* first published in a limited edition in 1724, defined this religion as "the pursuit of happiness by the practice of reason and truth. . . ." Sin, in this system, was the outcome of bad logic. For those who followed the tenets of this belief in reason, and still were cheated of their proper rewards in this world, Wollaston promised compensation in a future state.

Amply documented with quotations from Cicero, Seneca, Plato, Aristotle, Moses, and St. Paul, the book was highly publicized, and read and quoted with respect by contemporary writers. It sold ten thousand copies within a tew years of its first publication in 1724. By 1750 it had gone into a seventh edition. Obviously its views were congenial to a large number of readers.

The section devoted to "Truths Concerning Families and Relations" offered the initial proposition that marriage has a twofold purpose: the propagation of the species and the mutual happiness of the couple involved. The latter purpose, Wollaston contended, could stand on its own as an end to be achieved. The couple might not be conscious of it, but the Author of Nature was using their "strong inclination they have each to the enjoyment of the other" to attain their cooperation in the continuance of the race. The male-female combination was one of complementary functions which served to supply the needs of both; for example, the male supplied the necessary labor-power for earning a living, and the woman performed her domestic duties.

Marriage, in Wollaston's formulation, was at the center of an expanding wave of human relations. Having established the family unit on rational grounds, he then proceeded to show how it was strengthened and made permanent by some form of solemn contract, oath, or vow designed to maintain its force no matter what feelings and events might try to weaken it. The union was further strengthened, he pointed out, by the very integration of persons and fortunes it represented. Finally, the birth of children, involving a new relationship, rendered the original "legal and moral relationship a natural one which can never cease, or be annulled." Considerations like these made marriage without some assurance of success an infamous generator of adultery and all kinds of infidelity. Marriage had to follow the formula of share and share alike in good fortune and bad.

The knotty problem of male authority in the family worried Wollaston. The makers of laws and writers on social subjects had favored men much too much. "I would have them live so far on a *level*, as (according to my constant lesson) to be governed *both* by reason. If the man's reason be stronger, or his knowledge and experience greater (as it is commonly supposed to be) the *woman* will be obliged on that score to pay a *deference*, and submit to him." Many a cynical reader must have remarked that that brought them back to the starting point.

Benjamin Frankin's *Reflections on Courtship and Marriage* took its major leads from Defoe and Wollaston. First published by its author at Philadelphia in 1746, it went through several editions, issued at Harrisburg (Pennsylvania), London, and Edinburgh under the same cover with related items by Swift and Addison. Although Franklin's name did not appear on the title page, we have it on good authority that he was referred to as the author in the third edition, which appeared in 1758.

As Defoe had done at the very beginning of the eighteenth century, Franklin chided men for inflating women's conceit and vanity by flattering their beauty and petty accomplishments. The misled girls were directed to unpraiseworthy goals and then ridiculed for their lack of solid attainment in the realm of reason. Franklin, somewhat presumptuously, in the framework of social ideas held by most of his contemporaries, declared as fact that the adult personality is a direct outgrowth of youthful environment. Even at the age of marriage, a young woman's mind was still capable of cultivation under the sympathetic, tactful, and intelligent guidance of the right husband.

When dealing with that *bête noire* of young married people, to wit, the husband's prerogatives and the wife's duties as a subordinate, Franklin quoted Wollaston directly. He had every reason to be intimately acquainted with that rationalist's work inasmuch as he had composed type on the second edition of *The Religion of Nature Delineated* while working for the London printer S. Palmer, in 1725. Reason and nature, according to America's most versatile mind, rejected society's then common error of endowing one sex with the power of tyrannizing over the other. On the other hand—and here entered the joker—"nature, and the circumstances of human life, seem to design for man that superiority, and to invest him with a directing power in more difficult and important affairs of life." Assuming this to be the hard-headed truth, then whence did so many marital wars arise? They stemmed from an inadequate preparation of women's understanding of the marriage relationship as well as from men's disinclination to use tender and reasonable approaches to their wives. The mutual respect which generally existed before marriage had to be maintained afterwards. If a wife's desires were to be opposed, her husband should "reason with delicacy, coolness, and good temper, supported by a solidarity and strength of judgment." The fault lay with small minds, which, unable to resist the exercise of their constituted authority, were outstanding generators of wedded discord.

So much for the question of male prerogative. But the broad vision of the omniscient Franklin could hardly have been expected to exclude the rest of the marriage panorama. As an outstanding representative of a virtuous, home-loving middle class, it was his duty to examine every facet of that social *summum bonum,* marriage. He had to defend "the sacred cement of all societies" against the army of cheap wiseacres who used their unrepeatable jokes to bring the blessed state of matrimony into disrepute. If one were to judge by such racy pieces as *Les Quinze Joyes de Matrimonie* which eighteenth-century readers knew as *The Fifteen Comforts of Matrimony,* there was a real need to speak up for the virtue of wives and the merits of married life. So it was that Franklin devoted his reflections to the points of view of both sexes, to all aspects of making the right choice of a mate, and to prescriptions for post-nuptial peace.

His common sense "do's" and "don'ts," though trite today, doubtless needed saying then. Readers were urged to choose a congenial mind and temper, and to deliberate before proposing marriage. The pair that married in the heat of romantic infatuation would find difficulty in recognizing each other in more normal temperatures. Those who hid their faults sedulously and exposed only a synthetic personality before marriage, would have a similar pseudo-amnesia afterwards. Those who made overtures with the "ridiculous bombast of novels" were in effect helping to create an empty-headed, conceited fool whom they would soon come to despise. If a person has made up his mind to marry a girl, then by all means, declared Franklin, he must start getting her accustomed to serious, sensible conversation. He must start by building a friendship held together by ideas and common sentiments, something that will last beyond the excitement of early married life.

Marriage for wealth and comfort was another symptom of degraded times that made money a symbol of merit, and men were guiltier of this "little, sneaking, selfish spirit," than women. Marriages of interest were offensive to reason and nature. "What abominable prostitutions of persons and minds" declared Franklin in unrestrained denunciation, "are daily to be seen in many of our marriages! . . how many play the harlot for a good settlement, under the legal title of wife! How many the villain, to repair a broken fortune, or to gain one!" There was, however, no harm in a realistic discussion before marriage about respective economic resources and expectations. Such discussion avoided trouble and disappointment later on.

Franklin subscribed fully to Ben Jonson's sage remark on conduct in marriage: "That love comes by chance, but is kept by art." Capricious and captious bickering was to be avoided at all costs. A reciprocity of deference had to be cultivated. With Swift, and the essayists in the *Spectator, Guardian, and Tatler,* Franklin stressed the necessity of remaining as well-groomed after marriage as one was in the courtship period. His picture of the slatternly wife descending the staircase in the morning is an outstanding piece of humorous writing. Modesty and decency were to be practiced by married people whether in public or in the privacy of their own bedrooms. Franklin found it difficult to write about the abuse of sexual privileges in marriage itself. He spoke of the commonly known paradox of indecent relationships between husband and wife, and warned against degenerative abuses that would dull or destroy the subtle joys of married life. The desirability of restraint in private situations, applied with just as much force to behavior in the presence of others. Franklin's feeling that true love was communicated silently and imperceptibly made him suspect the sincerity of couples who were even mildly demonstrative in public.

The rationalist tradition, with its marked concern for the elevation of woman's position in society, was carried on in eighteenth century America by men in widely separated paths of life. Outstanding exponents were Tom Paine, the freethinking revolutionary, the Reverend John Witherspoon, President of Princeton, Benjamin Rush, physician and patriot, and the clergyman Enos Hitchcock.

Of the four pieces attributed to Paine, three appeared unsigned in the 1775 issues of the *Pennsylvania Magazine* during the period of Paine's editorship of that magazine. The one called "An Occasional Letter on the Female Sex," was by far the most vigorous of the marriage selections in the Paine group. It made much of woman's anomalous situation, in which she was at one and the same time oppressed by man and worshiped by him for her beauty. Man was both her tyrant and slave, but particularly the former. Woman shared man's miseries and got no relief from her own. She was equal in virtue but could not expect to get more than the short end of praise. By right, the letter reasoned, women ought to receive universal acclaim not only for the domestic functions they performed but also for their sufferings connected with the loss of husbands and sons. However, it continued, American unjust practices in this regard were not universal. One did note that in some countries women had received their share of public honors, monuments had been erected to them, and other forms of social dignity had been accorded them.

Paine's "Reflections on Unhappy Marriages" followed the Franklin pattern even to applying the prostitution label to mercenary marriages. His description of the descent after marriage from carelessness to indifference, thence to ennui, to strife, to complete insensibility, and to seeking pleasure elsewhere, was a piece of acute observation for a bachelor. An injection of Paine's chronic skepticism was accomplished through the device of reporting an American Indian's view of Christian marriage. Said the heathen savage, either your God is not clever or else he doesn't concern himself with your marriages: not one in a hundred has anything to do with happiness or common sense. The Indian knew the value of mutual affection without the making and accepting of ceremonial statements. Again, among the Indians, married people were so free to separate that they never felt the inclination to do so. And if the match did turn out to be a discordant one, the pair usually had sense enough to break it up. Paine was so attracted to pagan spontaneity in the affairs of the heart that he found time and space in those exciting revolutionary days for a fantasy woven about the characters of Cupid and Hymen.

It is interesting to find this sentimental core inside the hardened, fiery agitator for America's political freedom. There was, however, no contradiction between his tender feelings for humanity and his fierce attack on governments, ideas, and forces which oppressed human beings. His letter to a recently married lady in New York, first published in the Boston *Galaxy* and later repeated in the *Free Enquirer* in 1832, was a sad apologia for his not having married and a reaffirmation of his friendship both for the female sex and for the institution of marriage itself.

The *Pennsylvania Magazine,* which offered Paine's "Occasional Letter on the Female Sex" in August 1775, followed up immediately with a series of four articles entitled "Reflexions on Marriages." The author, who signed himself "Epaminondas," turned out to be none other than the President of Princeton College, John Witherspoon (as was indicated when the articles were republished in the *American Museum* of 1787 and 1788). The last installment of the Epaminondas series appeared in the issue of July 1776 which also contained, in the back-page section called "Monthly Intelligence," the text of the Declaration of Independence. The relative position of these two items gives cause for wonder as to their relative importance in the mind of a magazine editor.

With the thoroughness of a scholar, Witherspoon acquainted himself with a wide variety of sources and points of view on the marriage relationship. His own orthodoxy in religion did not exclude the deistic approach of Wollaston and others. There was enough of the Wollaston and Franklin approach to certain phases of the problem to guarantee that he knew them thoroughly. Indeed, his references to "moral writers," "some writers of moral philosophy," and "some other writers" obviously covered a lot of territory.

Marriage, Witherspoon assumed, was the prime relationship as sanctioned by natural law. All other social connections took their root from it. It was therefore incumbent on responsible men to single out as the enemies of reason, society, Providence, and "public utility," those conversationalists and writers who treacherously mocked the blessed state. Serious minded people, Witherspoon insisted, had also to hold to account the sincere but inept defense and glorification of the marriage institution by Addison, his *Spectator* colleagues, and the writers of plays and romances. These writers of pleasant, sentimental pieces did a disservice by stressing outward appearances too much, by depicting the rare female character whom eligible men would never find, and by holding forth promises of unmitigated bliss. Marriage was a far more earthy business than these people made it out to be. It had its plus and its minus. The successful marriage started with a sexual attraction which later matured into devotion. Nature, supported by reason and prudence, yielded the maximum result. How smoothly this process worked out in the American middle class family, where husband and wife cooperated to assure the family prosperity!

The treatment of equality of the sexes necessarily took on a different complexion in the "Lectures on Moral Philosophy," which were delivered to his students at Princeton, as compared with that of the rather popular *Pennsylvania Magazine* articles. The professor, in the name of academic impartiality, carefully avoided committing himself to any clear-cut belief. He spoke of those who believed in separate personal and property rights for male and female, of those who thought these should be equal, of those who supported benevolent male authority, and of the definitely superior position which the laws of practically all states had given the male in the family. The young men who sat at his feet must have drawn great egotistical sustenance from this particular lecture.

How Witherspoon expanded in the lecture hall on the published outlines of his materials we do not know. His magazine audience probably got the less equivocal but more forceful statement on the critical matter of equality. The initial premise was harmless enough: ". . . Wherever there is a great and confessed superiority of understanding on one side, with some good nature on the other, there is domestic peace." If Epaminondas had stopped here, male readers would have assumed their own interpretation and come away with a feeling of being justified in preserving the status quo. They were in for a quick jolt, however, because Witherspoon's rational conception of human relationships was consistent and thorough. Why, he asked, have we been assuming that this superiority could not be woman's as well as man's? Could there be anything strange and unnatural about accepting a wife's superior "reasoning" as one would accept anyone else's counsel? For the frightened men who were likely to shout back angrily at this thought, there were immediate assurances that this statement of the dictates of reason left no place for the unfortunate subordination of a hen-pecked husband. Hen-pecked husbands were not subdued by reason but by passion and ill-humor, woman's irrational weapons. The reference here was rather to that inequality of husband and wife where the "judgment" or intellectual capacity of one was superior to that of the other. Moreover, paradoxical as it might seem, Witherspoon's observations had led him to the conclusion that women used their superiority more graciously than did men.

This championship of the cause of women dared go even beyond the subject of equality. It entered into a calculation which resulted in placing three-fourths of the blame for ill-fated matches on the male. The man had had an opportunity of free, active choice; the woman could choose only from among those few who had asked her for her hand in marriage.

Epaminondas was not one to pull his punches. Perhaps he realized that even an important sector of male readers was not hostile to his views. Certainly the editor of the important *American Museum* was not; for if we look into the 1787 and 1788 issues of that magazine we find the "Reflexions" series again, this time bearing the pseudonym and also a note ascribing the articles to the President of

Princeton College. Witherspoon's popularity with highly respected readers was also confirmed by the imposing list of seven hundred subscribers to the three-volume edition of his works which appeared in 1800, six years after the author's death. The list, headed by John Adams, President of the United States, was heavily weighted with clergymen, physicians, college professors, and merchants. The family names of America's elite occurred frequently.

The establishment of philosophically air-tight principles regarding the social rights of man and woman was fine for Witherspoon, who traded in universals. The practical Dr. Benjamin Rush preferred to make his observations in the here and now. Here was the United States, and now was the time for building independent economic and cultural fortunes. His *Thoughts Upon Female Education* was published at Philadelphia in 1787 and reprinted along with Chesterfield's *Principles of Politeness and of Knowing the World* and Dr. Gregory's *Father's Legacy* at Boston in 1791. It was a declaration of independence, aimed this time not against the king of England but against the education and mode of life of middle-class women in the recently disowned mother country.

Polite drawing-room conversation, perhaps with a French visitor from the Continent, was no common feature of American life. Here men had to work constantly and hard in order to build their fortunes. They depended on their wives to watch over their property, to take full charge of the children's education, and, in the case of the death of the husband, to manage his estate. Americans could not afford the luxury of a long-extended "finishing" process. Girls had to be educated quickly because they married early and early assumed the weighty responsibilities of a family. Again, in America there was no servant class that knew its place. The management of a household was therefore a difficult and complicated business. Even if it were possible to educate girls in the polite subjects of music, French, and drawing, these would soon be forgotten by disuse. Arithmetic, bookkeeping, and the principles of liberty and government were more to the point, and the educational process had to be both simplified and accelerated so that it could be completed before marriage. If the job of educating young women were done quickly and well, their husbands would be freed for their economic and political duties, and their sons, whose early training depended almost completely upon their mother's intelligence and ability, would double the pace of national progress. Rush knew that much of the liberal talk about raising the level of woman's intellectual ability was falling on unwilling ears. He was acquainted with the argument which insisted that the more educated the woman, the less useful she was for fulfilling her proper domestic role. It was up to the women, Rush declared, to notify the male sex "that the female temper can only be governed by reason, and the cultivation of reason in women, is alike friendly to the order of nature, and to private as well as public happiness." Again reason and nature came to the conclusion that it was easier to handle an *intelligent* minority group than an ignorant one. Rush, however, was clearly against the use of arbitrary and unlimited authority over the weaker sex. There was something in his militant, enlightened attack upon those who thought that only an *ignorant* wife was an obedient one, which promised to result in a very advanced position if Rush had followed through his own line of thought. Of the narrow-minded view held by most men of his time, he said: ". . . This is the prejudice of little minds, and springs from the same spirit which opposes the general diffusion of knowledge among the citizens of our republics."

The clergyman, Enos Hitchcock, with whom Rush corresponded and undoubtedly discussed matters relating to the education of women, covered a larger area than Rush did, and discussed matters in much greater detail. The lengthy title of his work, whose central interest was the care and education of children, made explicit his thesis. It was: "Memoirs of the Bloomsgrove Family. In a Series of Letters to a Respectable Citizen of Philadelphia. Containing Sentiments on a Mode of Domestic Education, Suited to the Present State of Society, Government, and Manners, in the United States of America: and on the Dignity and Importance of the Female Character. . . ."

Hitchcock, the liberal-minded pastor of the Benevolent Congregational Church in Providence, had gone to school to those English and Continental masters who were so popular with most colonial American readers. His ideas on woman's education and on her role in society therefore had much of the old-world flavor. He nevertheless made his own declaration of independence, and viewed the problems before him through the sights of a very modern educational psychology. He criticised the former emphasis on teaching "what to think" rather than "how to think." To him, the education of childhood was preparation for life in the present and future. It had therefore to accommodate itself to varying environmental conditions.

This was the road which led to his (and Rush's) ideas on the education of American girls for a cooperative role in the management of their families. The principles of equality in our country made hard work the only sure way to wealth. The blood and sweat of both husband and wife were involved in the family's success. If women were brought up in the European mode that encouraged vanity and misguided expectations, there surely would be trouble ahead.

Hitchcock seemed to be moving toward one position when he leaned on his observation of American social conditions and political principles, and toward another when he dipped back into such venerable authorities as Rousseau, Lord Kames, Mrs. Chapone, and Dr. Gregory. He refused to hear of the submission of women based on their physical or mental inferiority to men. Neither would he accept a definition of submission which meant "any inferiority of species, or a surrender of any natural rights. [For]. . . there cannot be any ground in nature, any reason in society, for the odious idea." On the other hand, every social unit, including the family, needed leadership; and nature had assigned that role to man. The good judgment of women would probably bring them to that conclusion too. Submission in this sense meant not a groveling obedience to capricious tyrants, but referred to the transcendent importance of that "restraint to which the humor of your sex, their security from numberless and nameless dangers, and, I will venture to add, the safety of the world, require they should be early habituated."

The firm handling of a matter like this, requiring ultra-delicate balance, was no more possible for Enos Hitchcock than it has been for thousands of professionals and millions of lay experts since. Willingness to please, delicacy of sentiment, and pliability in habits of life seemed to hold the answer to the problems of marriage when these characteristics appeared in both husband and wife. This writer's acute sensitivity told him also that the relationship of one's parents to each other, an atmosphere of secure affection, and the general congeniality of the household had much to do with children's subsequent success in their own marriage. Moreover, there was more involved here than mere domestic tranquility. The very orderliness of society (of which the family was a miniature), depended on the success with which family life produced law-abiding, cooperative citizens.

The attainment of a larger number of smoothly operating, happy families, then, was not a mere matter of creating individual joy and peace of mind. Philosophers of the eighteenth century were, to be sure, thinking in terms of the individual. Practical men in public life, on the other hand, had foremost in their mind the needs of the state. The colonies needed hands with which to build, or to bear guns against France and Spain at the mid-century, against England herself later on. The demand of the times was for frequent, early, fruitful marriages.

Editors of the periodical press were eager exploiters of the popularity of the marriage theme. Precious little was to be found in the magazines in discouragement of the matrimonial venture. The struggle for sexual dominance would hardly be featured when the entire citizenry was concerned with populating young America. Yet the male editors and contributors to eighteenth-century magazines had somewhat to unbridle their anxieties. The unpredictability of women and their thirst for power were exhibited repeatedly through thinly woven satire, for the amusement of worry-ridden readers.

Such was not, however, the general temper of American magazine articles, which, whether borrowed from European sources or contributed by native authors, were on the whole optimistic. Marriage was glorified, held to be the sublunary *summum bonum,* and the essence of virtue and well-being, to be encouraged in every manner possible. Its benefits were enumerated. They included the inevitable enhancement of joys and mitigation of sorrows, the promise of immortality through one's children, the charms of a greatly improved social life, and the sweets of intellectual and emotional companionship. They stressed, as insurance against failure to achieve the full benefits of married life, the importance of choosing a partner of equal intelligence, similar tastes, and congenial ways. They pointed out what to look for and told how to behave during the courtship period. One who signed himself "Hymenaeus Phyz" in the *American Magazine,* 1757, having himself been punished by his failure to keep his eyes open during courtship, offered his fellow-citizens a new science, one which he thought would have extraordinary appeal to utilitarians receptive to all ideas which tended to improve the common welfare. His facetious scheme was to use the available knowledge of physiology and physiognomy to determine if and how long a given match would last.

An occasional male wit considered it his duty to counsel against certain caricatured female types. Men were told to avoid the wife who took the credit for all good that befell the family, and the woman of wit and reading who was always reminding her husband of his ignorance. Also to be avoided were the high-bred lady, the celebrated beauty, the superannuated virgin, and the termagant. Obadiah Oliver, the tradesman, told of his overread wife who insisted upon reading aloud to him. Her language had become so hifallutin that even Johnson's Dictionary did not help him understand her any more. "Inconveniences from a Too-Loving Wife," who deprived a man of his freedom of movement, were also enumerated.

Another possible cause of unhappiness in marriage was parental interference in the selection of a mate. The requirements of democratic self-determination by rational individuals made it impossible to accept the traditional absolute power of parents. Writers were therefore pressed to a compromise between accepted practice and their own philosophical convictions. Wollaston had equated parental authority with guidance, and filial obedience with respect and gratitude. Franklin denied parents the right to make any marital choice for their children which would cause them unhappiness. Witherspoon leaned more or less to Wollaston's view. Hitchcock, on the other hand, counted on such complete *rapport* among the members of his ideal family that the great problem of the parent-child relationship caused him no great worry.

Naturally there were pitfalls to be avoided in an otherwise natural and reasonable state of social existence. Only shirkers allowed uncertainties of marriage to deter them. Franklin's reference to the useless half a pair of scissors was quoted by magazine writers to goad young people out of their state of single blessedness. His letter to John Alleyne on early marriages was also used to hasten the change of state. Both his logic and his sentiment were hard to refute. Early marriages were successful in proportion as the parties to them were more adaptable each to the other. If youth lacked the wisdom needed for family management, older people were around to advise them. By complying with nature's urging to early marriage, youngsters could avoid entanglements which were apt to leave their scars on the reputation or the physical constitution. Also, by starting the family early, a man could live to see his children grown and educated. "Late children are early orphans. . . . With us in America, marriages are in the morning of life; our children are therefore educated and settled in the world by noon: and thus our business being done, we have an afternoon and evening of cheerful leisure to ourselves."

A good deal of semi-serious writing was devoted to excoriating, poking fun at, or half-heartedly apologizing for bachelors and spinsters. They were on occasion regarded as enemies of the state. Plans were dreamed up to ease or force them into marriage. Humorous poems like "The Bachelors' Last Shift" and an "Epigram on an Old Maid, Who Married Her Servant" served as reminders of the unpopularity of unmarried persons of age thirty or more. The *Pennsylvania Magazine's* "Old Bachelor" series (later reprinted by the *American Museum* along with Witherspoon's Epaminondas papers) and the inconsequential comments and replies it provoked, constituted a milder treatment of the pro's and con's of bachelorhood.

A point to be raised in the bachelor's defence was that he justly feared marrying because of the expensive taste women in general had when buying clothing. This "reason," considered by most a weak excuse, provoked in some quarters serious thoughts about the economic state of the nation itself. If men could not see their way to marrying, raising a family, and having a little left over, Americans were either living beyond their means in an effort to ape the European Joneses, or the balance of trade was against them. The fact was that both of these things were true. Certainly the balance of trade was against Americans. It was also high time, ran the argument, that men and women disciplined themselves so that two could live more prosperously than one.

A bachelor's saving graces were few but he was not completely damned. He did not, it was conceded, knowingly undermine the state. His was a crime of omission. The number one target of public abuse was the libertine whose irrational behavior involved the ruin of others along with his own. No penalty was severe enough for the bachelor who contrived to acquire some of the benefits of marriage while avoiding its responsibilities. There was no rational defence of his mode of existence. He violated at one and the same time the moral sanctions of society and the personal happiness of those whose fall he caused. His victim could not even speak out to justify herself because of the social consequences which would ensue. Rarely indeed would a woman write in justification of her unacceptable conduct. Such a one was "Eliza," whose letter, "From a Fallen woman, still proud, to the responsible male who has been so vicious as to talk about her on the streets after having made his conquest," was published in the advance-guard *Pennsylvania Magazine* during the period of Paine's supposed editorship. This letter and another piece called "The Learned Lady's Soliloquy" were early symptoms of a movement on the part of radical-minded publicists to redefine standards of sexual morality as well as to reinterpret the current conception of chastity, and, in a much broader sense, to obtain for women a greater freedom of association. Ideas in this vein, whether expressed in isolated magazine articles or as a part of the equality-in-marriage literature, were received with apparent equanimity. They prepared the way for Mary Wollstonecraft's outburst of pent-up fury which was reprinted in the United States in 1792, the year of its original appearance in England.

TWO

High Individualism from Abroad

MARY WOLLSTONECRAFT AND THE RIGHTS OF WOMAN

Fresh, young, uncultured America received Mary Wollstone-craft's revolutionary document far more casually than did the author's own, sophisticated, country. Several of the new nation's most respected intellectual leaders had prepared the way and in most respects had anticipated the startling thoughts of this female agitator for woman's rights. The hold of the Fordyces and Gregorys on the American mind had been largely broken by revised ideals of society, working hand in hand with a society which itself had already been revised by events and circumstances.

Here in these United States "reason and nature" had slogan-value strong enough to impose itself on a variety of socially-minded people. Deistic rationalists were of course the most legitimate owners of this twin weapon. But it was not theirs alone. Men of orthodox religious affiliation and of fairly conservative views had come to form their opinions in various degrees against the background of a somewhat modified conception of "reason and nature." "Reason" might be interpreted as the result of scriptural understanding, and "nature" as the creature of a traditional God. Both reason and nature, however, were operative in a country where geography and economics required the exertions of a wife side by side with her man, and where political ideology, boasting a respect for the rights of man, carried woman upward in the process. Thus not only were Americans talking up the abstract rights of woman to a more equal share in the responsibilities and benefits of our culture, but they were also beginning to provide encouragements and rewards for her contributions to the cooperative family.

Such beginnings, though pleasant to behold, were far from rendering Mary Wollstonecraft's *Vindication of the Rights of Woman* a superfluous piece of literature.The cult of the dominant male had been slightly weakened but never defeated. In fact it recovered nearly all of its lost territory in the political reaction and religious

revival of the early nineteenth century. Revolutionary America offered promises to its womanhood—promises which another century
and a half would fail to bring to full maturity. Nevertheless, Mary
Wollstonecraft was a tremendous influence in the work of pressing
the movement onward. She gave women in general and women
reformers in particular a rational basis for self-respect and self-confidence when making their claims. She provided for all nineteenth-
century marriage reformers and woman's rights protagonists a source
of exciting and convincing quotations. Besides, some influential
writers, who did not cite her directly, showed many signs of famili-
arity with her work.

Yet, as one examines her ideas, it cannot be said that she initiated a philosophy. Mary Wollstonecraft (later Mary Godwin as
the wife of the English political philosopher William Godwin) was a
result and product of the mainstream of European rationalism. She
accepted its thesis that man and his institutions are capable of reaching perfection, that man has it within his power to arrange his environment in such a way as to help himself and his fellow men in
their climb toward the ideal.

Her *Vindication* was an exhortation to women to gain self-realization by bursting out of the shackles of the prevailing double
standard in the moral, intellectual, and social spheres. It was a brave
attempt to convince men that their own perfectibility was being
threatened by the enslavement of the opposite sex. Her message
was a simple one: The rate of human progress would continue to be
slow as long as mankind was half free and half slave. Women, she
pleaded, were not seeking an autocratic rule over men; they sought
only to develop a spirit of self-discipline, self-respect, and self-confidence. They wanted only to control their own persons and to
demonstrate the reality of their much-advertised share with men in
a rational nature and an immortal soul. Of what value was it to concede to woman the possession of reasoning power when man denied
her the opportunity to develop it through use? How was her soul
ever to earn its immortality when society prevented her virtue from
developing freely to its full stature?

The eighteenth-century conception of the moral woman, as
Mary Wollstonecraft analyzed it, recognized only one virtue—chastity. If a woman only preserved her "reputation" she could safely
neglect all of her *real* moral obligations. She could ruin her family
by extravagance and even gambling as long as she kept her honor
intact. She could and did turn over the suckling of her infants to
wet-nurses and the raising of her children to incompetent servants.
This kind of ethical system was not, as it should have been, grounded
in the nature of man. It was a rationalization on men's part, and not
a well-reasoned formulation. Men reasoned thus in order to justify

their prejudices; they might better have used their thinking power to root up these prejudices.

The searching mind of this lady philosopher found such morality both unnatural and discriminatory. Nature could never have intended the human personality to be so easily corruptible that one minor slip should produce a completely depraved character. And whence a standard of virtue so different for the separate sexes? A woman sacrificed every domestic role and duty to preserve her reputation, which, once lost, her society—especially the female part of it—would never let her regain. Men could preserve their virtue while wallowing in a mire of assorted vices. And the evil was greater even than this! By equating morality with sexual morality, society was succeeding in depraving both sexes.

Unlike William Godwin and his anarchist pupils of the nineteenth century who would rescue women by subverting the marriage institution itself, Mary Wollstonecraft was a strong believer in married life and the domestic affections that go with it. Her ideological enemies, both the contemporary ones and those of succeeding ages, with intentional carelessness attributed to her the ideas of the man she met, lived with, and married *after* the publication of the *Vindication*. They could also point indignantly at her previous illicit relationship with Gilbert Imlay, the American adventurer and free-lance entrepreneur. And there was also the illegitimate offspring of this union, the luckless Fanny Imlay, to serve as yet another target for scorn. Only long after Mary Wollstonecraft's death did scholars try to explain her conduct. Her behavior, apparently, was not only at variance with the current morality but also quite inconsistent with her own expressed sentiments. But it seems that these were not contradictions after all: The affair with Imlay, for one thing, took place at the end of the year 1792 in Paris, during the rule of the Convention, when a man thought twice before declaring his English nationality on an official marriage registration form. Would, in fact, any French marriage of this period be recognized later? In the last analysis, there was little philosophical justification for the idea that immorality becomes moral by an act of official registration. No rational philosophy ever had accepted or would accept such a proposition. Many an Englishman visiting revolutionary Paris at the time could enter into a similar friendly liaison without disturbing the equanimity of the folks at home. Wordsworth's temporary attachment to Annette Vallon in the same year did not, for example, undermine his sister Dorothy's lifelong respect and friendship for her brother's mistress.

The evidence is that Mary Imlay, as she was referred to by some of her American friends in Paris at the time, was conscious of her anomalous position, but not at all worried by it. As she explained the use of the pronoun "us" in a letter written in 1794 to Ruth Barlow, wife of the American poet and patriot Joel Barlow, "You perceive that I am acquiring the matrimonial phraseology without having clogged my soul by promising obedience, etc." In a letter written very shortly before this one, Mary had gloried in the ease of her recent childbirth and in the joy of being a mother, thinking that the new relation established by the birth of a daughter would bring Imlay closer to her. She was, however, facing the unhappy truth as she added: ". . . but that most exalted of all happiness which I have any conception of, (I mean conjugal felicity) I expect not ever to experience."

Clearly, then, she was on the side of formal marriage as recognized by society. Her big concern was to change the marriage relationship so as to make it a symbol of constructive friendship, a friendship which would at the same time advance the individual's growth to perfection and redound to the benefit of the social body as a whole. Unless there existed a common definition and practice of virtue for both sexes, the search for true happiness was a lost cause. As long as there were separate and parallel systems of male and female virtue, the male and female irresponsibles had a standing excuse for avoiding the obligations they should justly honor. Was it not preferable to teach a single standard of virtue? Or to go beyond that, would it not be desirable to underline the double harm caused by male violations of chastity—that done to himself and to the woman he ruined physically and morally? The physical consequences were evil; the moral were more frightening still. "For [under the double standard] virtue is only a nominal distinction when the duties of citizens, husbands, wives, fathers, mothers, and directors of families, become merely the selfish ties of convenience." Termites in the family (the foundation of society) would certainly undermine the social structure proper.

Mary Wollstonecraft's high respect for marriage did not lessen her understanding and sympathy for the plight of the prostitute. She asked justice, not the charity of Magdalen homes, for women whose descent began with a single misstep, one deviation for which they were cast out of society and forced to follow the one occupation available to women without physical strength or vocational training. This was the result of the prevalent training in idleness, and in women's dependent status. Pleasure had become an all-consuming purpose, and such was the abject slavery of women in the service of pleasing men that it was not unknown for men of otherwise good taste to debauch their own wives. Again the perennial note that Benjamin Franklin had sounded in a muted key. In time it became the blast with which free love agitators would attempt to destroy the institution of marriage utterly.

The relationship between the sexes was in a degraded state indeed. The sources of difficulty were legion, many-faceted, and subtle. They could, however, be reduced to a simple formula of environmental influences. If, Mary Wollstonecraft reasoned, the mind was the product of experience and education, as Helvetius had declared, then women's mental powers had little chance of enlargement. Their subordinate position in society, plus a kind of education that did not help them overcome their subordination, could never add up to much. They were being trained to be docile and to please; and, since pleasing was their major vocation, no wonder they were forced to find their happiness in their persons and in a life devoted to pleasure. No man, therefore, had the right to satirize women on the basis of their penchant for pretty clothes, for their being attracted to rakes, "or even for being rakes at heart."

An individual's employment and social position determined his outlook on life. In every calling, said Mary Wollstonecraft, in which power was fixed by rank or class—and soldiers, sailors, clergymen, and idle rich gentlemen were in this category—morality was injured. Women were weak because they were subordinate, not the reverse. Granted that men were born superior in muscular strength, there was no reason to suppose that this superiority extended to other traits as well. Writers from Rousseau to Fordyce, however ill or well they meant, had mistaken the prejudices of society for the distinctions of nature. It was time for some male philosopher to explode such piffle and make it go up in smoke.

Moreover the entire structure of marriage itself was constantly endangered by the traditional notions of sex differences. The habitual roles of both sexes prevented the highly desired transition in marriage from initial passion to permanent friendship. When a man's palate had been jaded by monotonous "pleasing," what would happen to the marriage relationship? Having no inner resources upon which to fall back, would our young wife not try to please other men? Would not her husband seek more stimulating company elsewhere? Was there not a danger that society would develop a group of intellectually gifted heterae to whom ennui would drive married men? Weakness might excite a condescending tenderness on the part of men, but it would not draw forth the respect a woman wanted. "Fondness is a poor substitute for friendship." Woman must strengthen her body and mind, perform her social duties honestly and well, and aim at being a companion rather than a dependent of her husband. The idea was to be capable of friendship so that when the accent on sex was lightened after the initial stages of marriage (Mary Wollstonecraft thought that a prolonged state of sexual ardor actually incapacitated a couple for efficient parenthood), there would exist a solid basis for continued happiness.

Writers there were aplenty who had advocated the revision

of traditional practices in the education and training of women. Such writers, when measured by Mary Wollstonecraft's demands, were offering mere palliatives. None of them had reached the root of the evil—inequality of position and educational opportunity between men and women.

The new conception of equality revealed two separate but related aspects, one relating to training for socio-economic and therefore personal independence, and the other to successful *rapport* in marriage. With respect to subordination in the areas of religion, property, and politics, the position of women was related to a much larger and perhaps more vital problem which was studied in the *Vindication* under the chapter title, "Pernicious effects arising from unnatural distinctions in society." The power of property and class was for this apostle of human benevolence a poisoned fountain from which flowed "most of the evils and vices which render this world such a dreary scene." True morality would gain ground with the achievement of equality but it could never really flower unless the female half of the world's population were released from the chains which bound them. Power would always corrupt the powerful, and the oppressed would reciprocate, heaping corruption upon corruption, and hastening the degradation of both.

Thus, upon foundations of human equality the theme of the *Vindication* developed. Independent women could serve society well in medicine, politics, and business. The capacity to be useful and self-sufficient might save many a woman from common and "legal" prostitution, that is, marriage for support and protection alone. Important as independence was to all women, it was salvation without equal for spinsters—who were wont to become a burden on unmarried brothers or sources of discord in the homes of their sisters-in-law—and widows, who, with their children, either became charges upon the community or fell victim to unscrupulous men.

But training for success in marriage required an approach more fundamental than a mere emancipation proclamation. The sexes had to begin to know themselves and each other long before marriage. The dynamics of interpersonal relations had to work themselves out over a long period of regular and normal contact. Boys and girls could better sense how to live together when married, by growing up together in the home and school. Father-mother, parent-child, and sibling relationships must first take on the genuine marks of give-and-take in mutual respect. The artificial restraints and tyrannies of the past must give way to reason tempered by the bonds of affection and gratitude.

So much for the informal education of family life. The formal education of the school had also to be organized in such a way as to promote one kind of training for both boys and girls, unhampered by the conservative demands and interference of parents. The solution lay in coeducational, public institutions run by the nation. Everyone knew the bad sexual attitudes and habits acquired by boys in boy's schools, and by girls in girl's schools. It was also evident that the private schoolmaster could not be independent so long as individual parents paid him directly for his services. A truly enlightened state would support its coeducational schools right through the secondary level—this in an age when secondary education was available only to the male standard-bearers of a small elite. If these schools were only to provide instruction in personal health and hygiene, they would justify their expense. Their very existence, moreover, could not help but instill in all that respect and confidence which are the pillars of friendship. Let the libertine shout that such education would unsex woman. A trial of the project would demonstrate enhanced beauty, dignity, and true grace in women. "Were boys and girls permitted to pursue the same studies together, those graceful decencies might early be inculcated which produce modesty without those sexual distinctions which taint the mind . . . But till more understanding preponderates in society, there will be ever a want of heart and taste, and the harlot's *rouge* will supply the place of celestial suffusion which only virtuous affections can give to the face."

Thus Mary Wollstonecraft of England, speaking out for the independence of women. What she lacked in learning was more than amply compensated for by personal experience and self-education. Quite early in life, with but a meager middle-class "female education" behind her, she became the moral and economic protector of her family. She had frequently to shield her mother from a dissolute, cruel husband, rescue a sister from a profligate husband, and make up for the failure of shiftless brothers to assume their share of the family burdens. Her words possessed the logic of reality. Ears on both sides of the English Channel and of the Atlantic Ocean were raised to listen. [1]

[1] American publishers showed immediate interest, and, if they were anything like their descendents of our own time, their eagerness to publish was an index of probable reader response. Immediately after publication in England, two independent American editions of the *Vindication* appeared in 1792, one under the Philadelphia imprint of William Gibbons, the other issued by Thomas and Andrews of Boston. Gibbons used his *Lady's Magazine,* which was supposedly edited by "A Literary Society," to announce in the form of a ten-page review —actually a tabloid version of the *Vindication* itself—the availability of this most important book. This was the review which the *New Harmony Gazette* copied in 1825. Thomas and Andrews included in their own *Massachusetts Magazine* a page or so of extracts when their Boston edition of the book was in the process of publication. Matthew Carey, the Philadelphia publisher and bookseller, printed the work in octavo and duodecimo sizes in 1794. A handful of American editions appeared in the course of the following century. Toward the end of 1796, John

It is impossible to be precise about the immediate response of American readers to Mary Wollstonecraft's work. The precariousness of magazine publishing may have made it difficult to announce a point of view which might offend a sizeable number of readers. Even the *Massachusetts Magazine,* whose publishers had themselves put out an edition of the *Vindication,* was extremely circumspect in its review of the book. This review, directing the readers to those of Mary Wollstonecraft's pages which described "the consumptive influences of monarchy and its appendages, a vicious noblesse, profligate army, and mischievous navy," pointed out that Americans were safe from such evils but nevertheless must be on their guard against the demoralizing social psychology of class and rank distinctions. The review also recommended the book's critical analysis of conventional writers whose works had hitherto been accepted at face value. By no means, it said, were all of the author's ideas practicable and, even if they were, it was doubtful whether they could be beneficial if put into practice. "But among a few thinly scattered weeds, there are many durable trees, which unite the beauties of Flora with the firmness of the elm."

There is no way of distinguishing between some ideas having their genesis in the *Vindication* and those bred on American soil. It is, however, fairly certain that a writer like Judith Sargent Murray, the poet, essayist, and dramatist whose discursive letters appeared monthly in the *Massachusetts Magazine* from 1792 to 1794 under the rubric of "Gleaner," was substantially influenced by Miss Wollstonecraft. There were a few direct references too. A "Letter from an old bachelor" in the *New York Magazine* of August 1795 yielded the point that woman's follies were the fault of men, who framed their superficial education and spoiled them with flattery. The same magazine some months later quoted Mary Wollstonecraft's idyllic picture of the young mother suckling her babe, with her gentle husband caressing both. The *Weekly Museum* of New York paid the English authoress perhaps the greatest tribute of the period by publishing a long rhyme called "Rights of Woman" to be sung to the tune of "My Country, 'Tis of Thee," better known to the English as "God Save the King."

Other evidences of a favorable reception consist of scattered reports of reader interest such as that at Mrs. Susanna Rowson's school in Medford, Massachusetts, where the book was known to some of

---

Harrison, the editor and publisher of the *Weekly Museum,* listed the *Rights of Woman* regularly among the books he had available for sale. The enterprising Parson Weems did not press his supplier for copies of the *Vindication* but apparently handled sixteen copies of its author's *Maria: or, the Wrongs of Woman,* published by James Carey in 1799.

the young ladies attending. Aaron Burr is said to have responded to his reading of the English edition with a spontaneous decision to educate his daughter Theodosia along the lines prescribed by Miss Wollstonecraft.

Unfavorable reactions to Miss Wollstonecraft were frequent enough to create the suspicion that the *Vindication* was being read widely enough to frighten the smug protectors of the family *status quo*. Such reaction was exemplified by the "Wanderer" in the *Columbian Phenix* of 1800 who enumerated three stages of the progress of the female race (sic) in what some people called civilization. These were the Iron Age, or the age of duty; the Silver Age, or the age of pleasure; the Brazen Age, or the age of rights which mankind was suffering through at the moment. Once Mary Wollstonecraft had followed up the successful "rights of man" with her "rights of woman," "The hint ran like wildfire through the nation; complimentary verses and mellifluous sonnets dropped from the pens of minor poets, girls quitted their samplers, housemaids threw aside their untwirled mop, and nothing resounded from shore to shore but Mary and the Rights of Woman."

Throughout the nineteenth-century woman's rights agitations, the Wollstonecraft ghost haunted the defensive male more than any other. Windows were closed at night against Mary's own disembodied spirit or against its later representatives and spokesmen. Thus Thomas Green Fessenden in his book-length poem of 1818 on women as educators of the next generation and as powerful motivating forces behind their husbands:

Dame Nature tells us Mary's rights are wrong,

Her female freedom is a Syren-Song;

   ❋   ❋   ❋   ❋   ❋   ❋

Those who give motion to such state machines,

Succeed the best when placed behind the scenes.

In the same vein was the Reverend Hubbard Winslow's *Woman as She Should Be* (1838), inveighing against Mary's disciples, who thought that they could gain equality by doffing their femininity and assuming the tasks of man. And there were also the later frightened effusions of male writers on the woman problem like John Abbot's *The School Girl* (1840), T. S. Arthur's *Advice to Young Ladies* (1866), and the Reverend Stephen Dana's *Woman's Possibilities and Limitations* (1899).

Poor Mary had to answer for greater sins than her female egalitarianism. She was a victim of guilt by association with her friend and her husband William Godwin. No matter that she disagreed firmly with him in matters of religion and marriage. She still had to bear the onus of his unsavory reputation as a deist, an opponent of institutional marriage, and a revolutionary. Even after she had changed her husband's attitude toward marriage, the stigma remained with her until her early death after the childbirth of Mary Godwin, later the second wife of the poet Shelley. True though it was that Mr. and Mrs. Godwin had come by their philosophies through similar influences—as, for example, the deification of the intellect, belief in the kinship of reason and virtue and in the perfectibility of mankind—there were fundamental differences between them. Where Godwin reasoned from the supremacy of mind to the abolition of all social institutions, Mary arrived at reformation. Where he vacillated between deism and atheism, she was a theist of non-Christian persuasion. Their first meeting at the home of the publisher, Mr. Johnson might have been their last, had it not been for the taciturnity of another person who was at the same gathering. The person in question, Tom Paine, was such an inadequate conversationalist that Godwin and Mary Wollstonecraft were gradually drawn together in a spirited discussion of their differences.

It is gross understatement to call it unfair of magazines like the *Anti-Jacobin* to lump her with Godwin and Tom Paine in a campaign of ridicule. She hardly deserved a share in bits of abuse like "Sceptical, schismatic, and disaffected writers of the age. . . the unprincipled disciples of Godwin and his wife . . . the spawn of the monster." And:

> Then saw I mounted on a braying ass
> William and Mary, sooth, a couple jolly:
> Who married, note ye how it came to pass,
>   Although each held that marriage was but folly.

Or:

> Fierce passion's slave, she veer'd with every gust,
>   Love, Rights, and Wrongs, Philosophy and Lust.

Americans, at that time accustomed to checking the record before uttering words of condemnation, probably welcomed a piece in the *Boston Weekly Magazine* of February 5, 1803 which demonstrated by reference to Miss Wollstonecraft's early writings that she was not the infidel Godwin made her out to be in his memoirs of her life. In reality she had supported a religion of faith and revelation before being corrupted in this respect by him.

GODWIN AND THE RIGHTS OF INDIVIDUALS

Godwin's *Enquiry Concerning Political Justice and Its Influence on Morals and Happiness* was first published in the United States in 1796 from the second English edition of the same year. The first edition had apeared in 1793. The pattern of his philosophy was complex but unified; the details were numerous, but well-defined and inseparable from the whole. With his wife he believed that the human personality was a product of forces outside of itself, changing as external circumstances moulded and remoulded it, ever influenced by its physical and social environment. The minds of children, like soft clay, were taken up in their original amorphous state, distorted in a straight-jacket of social and political institutions, and gradually hardened to suit the present rulers of men. Government was not simply a negative force as Locke had believed and as Tom Paine still believed. It was a positive force for evil, chaining the human spirit. Abolish government; then virtue, knowledge, and reason would carry man to the perfect state of being which was his destiny.

Man acted voluntarily, Godwin thought, on the basis of his reasoned opinions. He could therefore always be made conscious of his motives and argued into correct action without resort to governmental restraint or force. The open and judicious use of praise and blame by his fellow citizens would unfailingly bring him around to virtuous behavior. This uncompromising individualism in ethics (which was later borrowed by such philosophical anarchists as Josiah Warren, Stephen Pearl Andrews, Ezra Hervey Heywood and Benjamin Tucker) was soon recognized by Godwin himself to be rigid and naive. In the third edition of *Political Justice* as well as in his essays published under the title *The Enquirer* (1797) he substituted emotional and esthetic considerations for pure reason as the prime motivation for man's choice of action. "Reason" was transferred to the job of choosing among feelings and values offered up to the mind for selection.

Godwin's doctrine of "universal benevolence" as originally stated chose to overlook the good derived from observing sympathies and obligations among blood relatives and friends. Men must award first consideration to those whose social contributions benefit most the whole of mankind. Personal allegiances were a mark of selfishness and had to be discouraged. Property (by which he meant inequality of wealth), religion, and family loyalties, all supported by custom and law, were the roadblocks which stood in the way of man's advance. Justice, declared Godwin, exacts from us the application of our talents, time, and resources, with the single object of producing the greatest sum of benefit to sentient beings. From each according to his ability, and to each according to his needs. This ideal condition was not to be achieved through cooperative endeavor or by legal enactment.[2] Equality would come naturally when men had achieved virtue through education. Monopoly and the accumulation of wealth

[2] Note that a national system of education, Mary Wollstonecraft's pet proposal, was anathema to Godwin.

must come into general public disrepute before it could disappear.

This brand of political freedom was to be gained through the spread of knowledge, free from any restriction whatsoever. Candid criticism of each and all by each and all was very much in order. On the other hand, the conscious teaching or communication of ideas and values was destructive of free intellectual growth—whence Godwin's abhorrence of the apparent necessity for people to live together. Co-habitation, a form of cooperation, was an evil. It was one of those dependence-generating human relationships, Godwin's opposition to which accounted for his distaste for the institution of marriage. Marriage customs which assumed that people would live together were inconsistent with man's psychological make-up. "It is absurd to expect that the inclinations and wishes of two human beings should coincide through any long period of time." Make them live together and you invite bickering and unhappiness. Marriage, as Godwin knew it, was a romantic deception, entered upon in haste, and confirmed irrevocably by law in opposition to the light of reason. The very essence of the marriage contract was a mutual promise that was to be kept during a human lifetime. Now the nature of man was such that his environment controlled his will, and he who presumed to promise anything for a future period was operating under false pretenses.

Godwin's most pointed objection to marriage, the one which appeared most prominently in later socialist and anarchist pronouncements, was the one which related this institution to the worst kind of property arrangement—monopoly. "So long as I seek to engross one woman to myself and to prohibit my neighbor from proving his superior desert and reaping the fruits of it, I am guilty of the most odious of monopolies." The monopolist ever guarded his possession jealously, while his potential competitors worked their stratagems to take it away from him. This sort of arrangement undermined the foundations of the brotherhood of man that was to be.

Naturally there were those who would say that a removal of restrictions on sex relationships, such as those enforced by customary monogamous marriage, would result in passion gone wild. The pictures conjured up by irrational and sex-ridden minds were horrible indeed. Apply the reasonable virtue and moderation that Godwin looked forward to in the new civilization, and the reproductive function would be carried on in terms of good sense and social duty. One ate and drank not for the mere pleasure of doing so but because these acts furthered ideal ends. "Reasonable men then will propagate their species, not because a certain sensible pleasure is annexed to this action, but because it is right the species should be propagated. . . ."

Did men predict a confusion of paternity? What of it? Was not paternity a species of aristocratic prejudice and sheer selfish pride? What if surnames did disappear? People would then be recognised for their own accomplishments rather than for their family connections. Care of the offspring in infancy, and their education, would devolve upon the mother. If her share of duties became too great because of frequent births, her benevolent neighbors would assist her. Food, clothing, and shelter offered no problem because workers who produced material goods would keep for themselves only as much they needed. The surplus, or profit, would be available for just distribution.

This was the William Godwin who remained the target of numberless guardians of social stability during his entire lifetime. *Political Justice* remained the stick with which to beat Godwin because, although he watered down some of his violent language and objectionable references in the second and third editions, he did not alter his ideas essentially. His attack on marriage in these editions was directed against the institution as it was practised in his society. But the remarks about the "withering away of paternity" and about "engrossing" were dropped.

They were dropped more because they had been misunderstood than because Godwin wished to withdraw them. His references to the emphasis on paternity was not a green light to the licentious, but an ironic commentary on the nexus between the class, property, and certainty of paternity. With regard to "engrossing," one could say that Godwin was so intent at the time on achieving disembodied rationality, that carnal meanings were out of the question.[3] It is unlikely too that the same philosopher who was predicting an immortality on earth which would obviate the necessity for propagation, was also looking forward to the free play of the sexual function.

The effects of life with the entirely human Mary showed up first in the "Summary of Principles" written while the third edition of *Political Justice* was in press and published as a part of it. The solid changes resulting from Godwin's new family environment—and a change of mind was entirely consistent with his philosophy—began to show in his *Memoirs of the Author of the Vindication of the Rights of Woman*, where a passage turned up celebrating the domestic scene as a training ground for the individual's larger services to humanity. The preface to *St. Leon*, his novel of the same period, indicated an intense desire to revise parts of *Political Justice*, especially the materials dealing with the private affections. The subsequent years witnessed a gradual but complete change of face on this point,

[3] As the scholar F.E.L. Priestley has speculated, "He most likely had in mind the 'engrossing' not of the body, but of the social attractions and agreeable conversation of woman." There was, therefore, no inconsistency in Godwin's predicting in 1796 that monogamy had a secure future.

until, in Godwin's final collection of essays, we find: "Christ's requirement that a disciple hate his father and mother, wife, children, brethren, sisters, while allowed to show a noble and a gallant spirit, is held worthy of distinct and unhesitating censure." The short period with Mary Wollstonecraft's little orphan Mary, a second marriage, still more experience of family life, and age and maturity, modified his complete negativism with regard to the family, making him, in his novels and in the *Essay on Population,* almost a public-relations agent for 'marriage.

Reason compromised with society—but in vain, for both his enemies and disciples chose to remember his earlier views. It was easy for his detractors to discredit him by lumping anti-marriage with anti-religion and anti-property. It was convenient for many of his disciples and for their intellectual progeny to use him in advertising liberalized divorce laws or free love.

CHARLES BROCKDEN BROWN: AMERICAN GODWINIAN

The alacrity with which American publishers reprinted Godwin was some indication of his popularity. His influence, however, was more evident in an indirect channel of literary expression. His deviant tendencies reached the American public most through the democratic Charles Brockden Brown, America's first novelist. Brown stands out as a native amalgam of both Godwins, Mary Wollstonecraft and William. This seems clear in spite of the fact that the scholar David Lee Clark, who wrote on *Brockden Brown and the Rights of Women,* insists that Brown learned nothing from Mary Wollstonecraft and Godwin which he did not already know from reading political philosophers from Locke to Condorcet, together with the revolutionary writers of his own time. In any case, much of what he learned from Godwin matured in his hands. He was also more conservative. Unpopular sentences usually flowed from the mouths of villainous characters. Whenever they appeared on the lips of virtuous ones, they were swallowed or recanted before the end of the story.

Alcuin (1798), Brown's dialogue in Utopia, owed most of its perceptions to Mary Wollstonecraft. It was a slight novel whose locale was a paradise for women where sexual equality was the unobtrusive norm. Mrs. Carter, Brown's equivalent of Mrs. Godwin, described what transpired on earth (yea, even in that democratic heaven on earth, the United States) with regard to woman's rights. When asked about her political affiliations, she replied cynically that women who were denied the use of their own discretion in ordinary matters, who could own no property, who were completely dependent on men for food and shelter, who did not even govern their own persons—such women had no politics. Woman was, in her relationship to society, "regarded merely as a beast," existing only for "the convenience of the more dignified sex." Laws were framed to enslave wives and to encourage tyranny in their husbands.

Alcuin was the rare utopian essay which left the reader without a solution beyond the argument for liberalizing divorce laws. Brown was either assuming that his readers would recognize the road of reason as leading from our imperfect earth to woman's paradise, or, more likely, was too sophisticated to offer pat solutions like Godwin's. Obviously not satisfied with his own first treatment of love and marriage, he kept the subject on his tongue and went on to ruminate on it in later novels all written within a single three-year period. Brown had learned from the early Godwin that the greatest evil in institutional marriage derived from the fact that it had its roots in a property-framed social system. Mercenary considerations in sex relationships, in and out of marriage, were despicable. A spontaneous union based on the free will of both parties was the only kind of marriage that was acceptable. As soon as spontaneity, friendship, and personal fidelity ceased to exist, the marriage was no longer justifiable. The theme of the equal, rational woman was touched upon in *Jane Talbot*. The responsibility of the male for woman's shortcomings and the boomerang effect of female follies on the progress of man were both loudly hinted at in *Arthur Merwyn*. Constantia Dudley, in *Ormand,* could hardly have been expected "to vow an affection that was not felt and could not be compelled, and to promise obedience to one whose judgment was glaringly defective . . . Education, besides, had created in her an insurmountable abhorrence of admitting to conjugal privileges the man who had no claim upon her love." Problems of love, marriage, and society were apparently associated in Brown's mind with the novel as a prime vehicle. For not only did he himself eschew the essay medium for his ideas on marriage but he seems also not to have used his influence to have such material included in the several magazines he edited or helped edit from 1799 to 1810.

Perhaps his exciting speculations on the reactions of the new woman to male friends had not encountered an equally excited public. The version of *Alcuin* published in the *Weekly Magazine* of Philadelphia was probably more widely read than the book form, but even it did not elicit much public reaction. A second part of the dialogue, promised for early publication, did not appear till 1815.

THE COUNTER-OFFENSIVE

For a certainty, the highly religious, moralistic, conservative literature exported by Hannah More from England to be printed and read by Americans fared better in the consumer market than did Brown's novels. Miss More's multitudinous writings for the instruction and amusement of the female sex bore American imprints from as early a date as 1774. She was standard equipment in the "lady's libraries" imported or printed here. Her prescription for the education of girls asked for greater intellectual content—but not with a view to rearing independent women. Conceived in this spirit, her *Coelebs in Search of a Wife,* about a cautious young bachelor who inspects a series of young women, object matrimony, sold 30,000 copies in America by 1809.

Hannah More considered her literary efforts to be instruments of salvation for human beings whose natural state was one of sin and corruption. Her highly religious and moralistic works aimed in general at counteracting contemporary currents of rationalistic thought and revolutionary tendencies in politics. She led the movement in England which succeeded in negating the influence of Godwin and his friends at an early date. Her announcement that she had placed the *Vindication of the Rights of Woman* on her private *index librorum prohibitorum* must have influenced greatly the attitude of the general public toward that book.

Her own solution for the female-education problem was to expand the intellectual horizons of her own sex, but only for disciplinary purposes. As definitely set down in her *Coelebs,* she would have the average girl trained in whatever "inculcates principles, polishes taste, regulates temper, trains to self-denial, and more especially, that which refers all actions, feelings, tastes, and passions to the love and fear of God." Thus Mr. Stanley, the model father in this book, explains how he toned down an over-vivacious daughter by giving her a course in arithmetic with a "tincture of mathematics."

America was flooded as well with Miss More's collections and individual editions of cheap tracts originally published in England and designed to teach manners and religion to the unmonied masses. This and the political ballad were the media she used skilfully against her radical opponents. One of these tracts was *The History of Mr. Fantom.* Fantom, a London retail merchant, had read Tom Paine and had been infected with his accursed ideas. The doctrine of universal benevolence had so impressed him that he soon began to neglect his moral obligations to his intimates. He even stopped going to church. His servants absorbed this moral carelessness in their turn, and caused Fantom no end of trouble. Fortunately, his wife was able to preserve the family from destruction, for she was a good woman long before "the new philosophy had discovered that marriage was a shameful infringement on human liberty, and an abridgement of the rights of man."

The predominant manner of treating the woman and marriage questions at the turn of the century was far closer to that of Mrs. More than to that of Mary Wollstonecraft. It was also more English than American. *The American Spectator, or Matrimonial Preceptor,* published in 1797 by David West of Boston, claimed that it was omitting a lot of material which had appeared in an English work of similar title because of its inapplicability to the American scene. Actually, it left out only that literature of derision which the European woman might still tolerate but which American women would not. The only strictly American contributions in the book were a short foreword and a concluding section. Beyond these, this collection of "essays, epistles, precepts, and examples, relating to the marriage state" was the *Spectator* and *Tatler* all over again. Dr. Johnson, a relative newcomer to the province of the marriage essay, was copiously represented.

The American passages of the *Matrimonial Preceptor* boasted that our country had discarded class distinctions in the realm of marriage, that ours were alliances of virtue and affection. America had added the rights of women to the rights of men, and husbands here held their wives in the esteem of friendship and partnership. The rare exceptions to the husband-friend pattern could hardly be called American or republican. Most men and women in the United States married, and married early because all could rely on receiving a just economic return for their industry. The mood was one of optimism, an optimism appropriate to the new venture of an expanding and more or less egalitarian society. The concluding words were: "Here industry, crowned by the blessing of benignant Heaven, supplies the wants of all; and blooming youth are seen in every dwelling, smiling around their parents, like blossoms on a fruitful tree. Health glows on the cheek, innocence and contentment sparkle in the eye, and the voice of nature tells the traveller, 'Happiness Dwells Here.'"

Where would Godwin's gloomy views on marriage fit in here? More appropriate was Dr. Johnson's bitter accusations directed against the anti-marriage men who used reason to justify their "rage of licentiousness and impatience of restraint. And perhaps to the sober, and understanding, and the pious, it may be sufficient to remark, that Marriage and Religion have the same enemies." There was cause too to argue with those young libertines who avoided marriage out of fear of a headstrong wife, yet practiced servility to avoid "offending an infamous Strumpet." The vixen was rare among American women, but any man of courage who had got saddled with one by mistake would know how to handle her.

Reading the *Matrimonial Preceptor* from cover to cover, one could find the usual selections on how to comport oneself with a husband or a wife, on the tyranny of husbands, on the brutality of certain of them, on the resemblance of marriage to friendship with the difference that the former was legally binding, on match making, what to look for in a mate, and so on. A selection from the sagacious Dr. Johnson on "The Causes of Disagreement in Marriage" supplied fresh insights into the social psychology of marriage. An unhappy person made an unhappy marriage, said he. The personality, not the institution, was at fault. Those who cried out for the good old single days were not sure of what they wanted. This yearning for the past had little to do with the unmarried aspect of it, but sprang from the recollection of the health, vigor, and hopeful expansiveness of youth. It was also the man's habit to see greener grass in other pastures. If the married envied the single, the reverse too was true. Marriage on the whole, though, was successful. Look how many do it a second time! A wonder it was that the institution worked as well as it did, seeing that people married for land and money, in order to satisfy their parents, to beget heirs, to escape from themselves, or to imitate others.

The early nineteenth-century book and pamphlet coverage of marriage was in essence little more than a continuation of that which prevailed in the preceding century. New editions of older works kept appearing. *The Whole Duty of Woman,* an English book supposedly addressed to girls by a woman writer, had had nine editions between 1761 and 1797 but nevertheless appeared again in 1810. This array of trite bits had actually been assembled by William Kendrick, a London hack better known as a drunkard and practitioner of libel than as a creative thinker. His cautioning of young ladies to beware of man's cunning flowed more naturally from his experience than did his emphasis on chastity and virginity. A firm apostle of the double standard, he wrote: "Preserve thy vow inviolate, for the strayings of thine husband absolve thee not." On the divine right of the male to rule, he solemnly preached: "As rebellion lifts up its head against its sovereign, and thereby adds weight to the yoke it attempteth to shake off, so the subjection of a wife, when she usurpeth to govern, should be converted into servitude."

That part of the serious works on marriage not written directly for the popular reader market consisted largely of sermons like John Johnson's *The Advantages and Disadvantages of the Marriage State,* and A. Hyde's *The Conjugal Relation Made Happy and Useful.* The message they delivered was that religion and marriage produce true happiness when the pattern of life is cut along the lines of Biblical precepts. In some cases a special point was made to reaffirm the "weaker vessel" status of woman. "A letter to a Gentleman of New York, by a Lady," probably written somewhere in the first quarter of the century, told what could happen to an up-and-coming young man who married a girl without religion.

THE WORD OF GOD

Lorenzo Dow's *Reflections on Matrimony* appeared for the eighth time in about as many years in this Evangelist preacher's *All the Polemical Works of Lorenzo* (New York, 1814). "Polemical" was the precise word for the works of the man who pamphleteered against Whigs, anti-Masons, Catholics, and finally against those Methodists who had been tainted with popery. True marriage, according to Dow, was a union of hearts entered into with the sanction of divine grace for purposes of mutual happiness, procreation, and the education of the resulting offspring. Obedience to the legal requirement of a ceremony was desirable but not absolutely necessary. It did help to establish parental responsibility and property rights. It also was a convenient means of distinguishing between legitimate offspring and the other kind. Dow knew the many causes of unhappiness in marriage but allowed divorce only if one party had suffered gross deception at the hands of the other. Otherwise, following the prevailing interpretation of Christ's statement on divorce in the Scriptures, he considered remarriage by either party a species of adultery. Moreover, he was so convinced of the universal application of marriage by divine intention that he called all forms of "forbidding to marry a doctrine of devils." This included, as one may gather from other of his writings, monasticism and similar celibate practices undertaken for religious motives.

Timothy Dwight, congregational minister, author, tutor at Yale from 1771 to 1776, and its president from 1795 to 1817, was a dominant figure in the Connecticut of his time. He stood as a staunch Federalist in politics and a rigid Calvinist in religion. Whether in the role of theologian, administrator, teacher, or as a competent man of letters and prominent member of the Hartford Wits, he used his very considerable influence to counteract current tendencies toward democracy and irreligion. Indeed he considered these as one evil with double-faced manifestations.

Dwight's sermons on marriage, lewdness, and divorce were a part of a Sunday morning theology cycle which ran a four-year course during his presidency at Yale. Published in 1818-19 after his death, they achieved tremendous popularity both here and abroad. The texts of the talks were based on the Scriptures, and on observation (or what Dwight called "fact") where Scriptural authority was not available. The text with which he opened and closed the marriage question was, "Thou shalt not commit adultery." His basic assumption in morals was that sin, in a way, derived its existence from marriage. Curiously enough, this was the same assumption adopted by the socialists and anarchists who reasoned from it that to abolish sin we must abolish marriage. The theologian, of course, concluded that society, with the help of God, could stamp out sin by buttressing the marriage structure. He was the antithesis to Godwin, an antidote for rationalist poison, and an excellent source of inspiration for holders of the line against reform.

To the Federalist temper of Timothy Dwight and his brother

Theodore, the election of Thomas Jefferson to the presidency was a catastrophe to be attributed to the spread of Jacobin ideas like those of William Godwin. In a speech delivered at New Haven on July 7, 1801, Theodore Dwight, after denouncing Godwin's ideas on marriage at some length, predicted that "One among the measures which will successively be dictated by the spirit of democracy . . . is the abolition of surnames." Here then, he continued, we have a philosophical madman's (Godwin's) picture of the society which Jacobinism is trying to build. Timothy Dwight's sermons in the latter years of the eighteenth century failed to mention Godwin by name. But, to be sure, he joined the chorus of anti-Godwin propaganda after the turn of the century, when it became appropriate politically to link the democracy of Thomas Jefferson with the threat to property, religion, marriage and the family represented by the ideas of Godwin. The Federalist line of attack is exemplified in the following lines taken from a satiric rhyme called "The 'Enlightened Eighteenth Century;' or, The 'Age of Reason,' " *(Columbian Centinel,* Jan. 14, 1801):

> When *Godwin* can prove that thieving is just,
> That virtue is pleasure, and pleasure is lust,
> That marriage is folly, and wh-r-ng is wise,
> And Wollstonecraft pure in philosophy's eyes.

For his own analysis of the origin and nature of marriage, Dwight leaned completely on the New Testament. He demonstrated that the marriage institution was of divine origin, that it joined the contracting parties in perpetual union by virtue of a most solemn covenant. The benefits of marriage, which were to be derived from "fact" rather than Scripture, were numerous and attractive, and unquestionably were present in an overwhelming majority of cases. The first benefit was the "comfort" of the couple. Unhappy marriages, as any fair-minded person could observe, were the exception, and occurred only among people who were temperamentally unsuited for social contact of any kind, or who married for any reasons in the conventional long list of reasons other than those of love and mutual respect. Of course, the enemies of marriage had exaggerated the number of failures. "They have misstated facts; they have sophisticated arguments; and where neither would answer their purpose, they have endeavored to accomplish it by contempt, sneers, and ridicule." One expected this sort of thing from disreputable characters, but Dwight was surprised and hurt to find otherwise respectable "writers in the peculiarly enlightened kingdom of Great Britain" propagating these "wretched calumnies and falsehoods. . . . "

Marriage was responsible for social assets far beyond its important contribution to the happiness of adult individuals. It was obvious that the growth and well-being of children was a function of the loving care they received from their legitimate parents.

Man's industry and the prudent use of his earthly goods were both impossible of attainment without the conventional family. For industry and prudence were not natural to the human race and grew only through "education" and "habit" as instilled in the family. Only affectionate parents would suffer the expense of time and energy entailed in a long, difficult process of education. The virtuous but unrelated citizens of a world such as Godwin projected would never have the persevering parental drive to last through the entire process.

Furthermore, the marriage institution was the "source of all subordination, and government; and consequently, of all order, peace, and safety in the world." It was the best of all possible agencies of social control. Gentle but firm parents were able to teach obedience without risking revolt; and this habit of obedience would carry over to all aspects of adult life. Anyone other than a parent would "rule with a rod of power," and thereby build up a resistance in children not only to this but to all other authority. Religion, too, depended for its existence on the marriage system. Naturally, people living in sin were not themselves religious, and their children grew up in the same pattern. Moreover, none but married parents built churches, supported ministers, or were in the habit of worship. Divine wisdom had created marriage and marriage supported the divine scheme.

Unfortunately, society did not seem to adhere rigidly to the Biblical injunction against sex outside of marriage; so accordingly, it was the duty of the pulpit to abandon its shyness and speak out against lewd thoughts and practices. Reliance on poets, satirists, and moralists to do the job of keeping the nation pure was utter self-deception. These were usually ineffectual in persuading to virtue and sometimes even enlisted in the service of vice. Nor could you expect too much from religious instruction by parents. There were good writers on the subject, yes, but "how few persons read their books, compared with the number of those who are present at the preaching of the gospel! Probably two-thirds of a million persons hear the gospel preached, weekly, in *New England.* Not one in a thousand of these, perhaps, has ever read a book, seriously exposing this unhappy part of the human character. Even where their books are read, and read with attention, they are little regarded, and produce little effect."

The cause of America's moral descent, said Dwight repeatedly, lay in the failure of its clergy to speak out against lewd thoughts and practices. The prevalence of licentious thoughts, words and deeds demanded continuous strenuous opposition on the part of the ministry. Every social influence, including art, literature, and even business, was conspiring to stimulate the latent but easily reached passions of the people. Within Dwight's definition of sexual sin, there was every reason for him to worry about the high frequency of violating the commandment, Thou shalt not commit adultery. As he saw it, naughty thoughts and words were to be condemned along with the acts to which, as he thought, these inevitably led. The church's task was well-nigh a hopeless one when "Genius, in every age, and in every country, has to a great extent prostituted its elevated powers for the deplorable purpose of seducing thoughtless minds to this sin. . . . The numbers of the Poet, the delightful melody of Song, the fascination of the Chisel, and the spell of the Pencil, have all been volunteered in the service of Satan, for the moral destruction of unhappy man. To finish this work of malignity, the Stage has lent all its splendid apparatus of mischief; the Shop has been converted into a show box of temptations; and its Owner into a pander of iniquity. Feeble, erratic, and giddy as the mind of man is in its nature . . . can we wonder, that it should yield to this formidable train of seducers?"

Strong words indeed. But they could hardly be called over statement in the mind of a Calvinist of the brimstone school who was certain that unchaste thoughts led to that act which discouraged, yea prevented marriage, presupposed seduction, encouraged licentiousness,. and destroyed all moral principle. Philosophy dealt with such matters from its ivory tower, while it rarely chose to meet face to face the innocent victim of these ideas, the faithful mate whose soul was rent with anguish. What gave philosophy the right to prescribe how to live, when it had never met successfully the concrete problems of life?

There had been honest attempts by logical-minded theologians, Dwight conceded, to do something for the innocent parties to divorce in the way of justifying second marriages for them. There was no basis in Scripture for such arguments. Christ had declared, and St. Paul had affirmed, that incontinence was the sole ground for divorce, and that second marriage by either party was adultery. Admittedly this was hard on women sinned against or deserted. But allowing exceptions opens the way through loopholes and trumped-up divorces for the possible destruction of an institution "which is the basis of all human good." Better that a few innocents should suffer. This suffering might enhance the chances of salvation for the separated parties; second marriages could not wash away the sin of either. Some advocates of a liberalized interpretation had offered as equivalents of adultery, "obstinate desertion, gross personal abuse, incompatibility, and confirmed madness." Never. No sin matches that of adultery. No Scripture mentions equivalents. Justice might seem to demand relief, but the Divine Word has forbidden any escape save the separation from bed and board.

Divorce, continued Dwight, aggravated human suffering rather than alleviated it. The availability of divorce gave wives the idea of saving up against the day when they might be independent once more. Husbands then planned their own moves to frustrate their wives' machinations. A separation of interests of this sort led to a separation of affections which, in turn, led to an intolerable atmosphere of struggle in which the children suffered whether or not a separation occurred. If and when the split did take place (if divorce were permissible), the children had a devil's choice to make. If they stayed with the mother they must share her status as a social outcast. If they chose the father, they walked into the home of a proverbially cold-hearted stepmother.

The safety of human happiness lay in the stern, unyielding application of the Biblical limitation of divorce. Only so could you insure life-long unity of interest. The hopelessness of any separation would induce married people to make the best of it in compromise. Resorting to "fact," Dwight averred that it was "well known to every observer of human nature, that a prominent part of this nature is *the love of novelty and variety, in all its pursuits.*" Nowhere was the penchant for variety stronger than in the matter of sex. Let down the bars, and divorce would be a chief characteristic of our society. Even in God-fearing, law-abiding, home-loving Connecticut, divorce was increasing. Luckily, a campaign of opposition was in motion against the abominable Connecticut law which permitted divorce for desertion without making it mandatory to serve the deserter with legal papers.

The campaign to which Dwight referred had started back in 1785, when the historian and Congregational pastor of the Church of North-Haven, Benjamin Trumbull, had delivered to the Consociation of New-Haven "An appeal to the public, especially to the learned, with respect to the unlawfulness of divorces, in all cases, excepting those of incontinency. . . ." Trumbull, delivering a long, learned Biblical discourse, reenforced by the technique of a finished debater, proved that desertion was neither fornication nor adultery. Moreover, he exposed the tragic iniquity of a legal system which protected the defendant in the smallest property suits and completely neglected the rights of a partner in marriage. How many cases there were of husbands assumed to have disappeared, and who turned up later to embarrass a remarried wife. Many American husbands shipped on the high seas or went out to the frontier and were unable to communicate with their homes over long periods of time. Were these brave men to be victimized? The law was bad *per se,* and worse in its encouragement of collusion under the guise of desertion, as well as in its failure to punish delinquents. Perjurers and adulterers walked out of the courtroom scot-free.

MARRIAGE, MORALS AND SEX IN AMERICA

IN DEFENSE OF DIVORCE

Addressing the general public in those days with pro-divorce sentiments must have been a risky business. One gathers this from the scarcity of such literature before the end of the nineteenth century's first quarter. One extraordinary pamphlet did appear in 1788 from the press of Zachariah Poulson, Jr., of Philadelphia. The authorship of *An Essay on Marriage; or the Lawfulness of Divorce, in Certain Cases, Considered.—Addressed to the Feelings of Mankind* is unknown, although it is quite conceivable that it came from the pen of its printer. Poulson, best known in the annals of publishing for his journal, *Poulson's Philadelphia Advertiser*, learned the value of liberty during the Revolution, having spent the period of British occupation in hiding. He was associated at various times with such progressive humanitarian movements as those in favor of prison reform and the abolition of slavery.

The *Essay*, provoked by a newspaper article about a woman who committed suicide because of marital difficulties, asked all liberty-loving Americans to do something for those unhappy ones "who are frequently united together in the worst kind of bondage to each other." As opponents of all kinds of tyranny, Americans had not only driven their enemies from the country but had also shown friendship "in a great measure, even unto the African slaves." Successful marriage was undoubtedly the key to human happiness. How just, then, that the humane spirit should extend itself to alleviating the lot of those unfortunate spouses who had come to grief through entirely unforseeable circumstances.

There were many causes of unhappy marriage, argued the author of this pamphlet, for which you could not hold people responsible. Economic and emotional difficulties, the interference of parents and friends, the forced marriage—all these in their many variations produced unbearable domestic situations. The wise men in religion and morals insisted that people who had shown poor judgment must bear their punishment. But they were wrong; for if reason guided the affections, we should probably never marry or propagate. We would probably do nothing out of pure feeling or love, since reason always calculated the rewards accruing to an act. On the other hand, once an error of the affections had been discovered, reason indicated that a correction was in order. You could not force people to love each other. Sooner or later they would burst out of their bonds in ugly violence.

God never intended mankind to be unhappy, the Poulson pamphlet continued. Even its many sufferings had some good purpose. This, in essence, was the belief held by that great number of right-thinking Americans who were rising up against the detestable

58

practice of slave-keeping. Nevertheless, even the slave was in a position to reap the joys of love without the heartaches and fears which religion and morality had imposed upon freemen. "They marry with whom, and for as long as they please, and no longer." The slave in Pennsylvania and New Jersey could even get relief from a cruel master upon complaint. But where was there any relief for the henpecked husband, or the abused and insulted wife? How many were the methods used by incompatible mates to torture each other! For them there was less hope of release from punishment than for a criminal. Theirs was an incommutable life sentence.

It was simply not true, as the guardians of morality argued, that the possibility of divorce would make marriage less binding. A judiciously controlled divorce system would add strength to the natural forces (such as the instinct to protect one's children) which kept man and wife together. Those tempted to offend their partners would think twice. Fraud and deception in courtship would be discouraged. Parents would not become desperate upon contemplating what they considered an unfortunate marriage. More bachelors would take the step if they did not fear its irrevocability. Men who had "deceived" women would not forsake them if they were not afraid of perpetual bondage. "Every plea for unlawful commerce between the sexes would then be taken away." Religion would prosper with this new evidence of the benevolence of the Divine Being. Interpersonal relations would generally improve and war eventually cease.

SEEN IN THE MAGAZINES

Only the faintest echoes of this ultra-modern conception could be heard from contemporary writers. The fairly universal assumption in magazine literature was that marriage was as incorrigible as death. There was no way out. Widespread unhappiness was acknowledged. Advice on how to avoid conflict with a vicious husband was offered. Explanations for male imperiousness were given. The brutality of men was advertised. The *National Register* in 1816 reported a Zurich experiment in curing incompatibility by locking a couple up in solitary confinement for a fortnight; apparently, they would come out completely dependent on each other and cured of their incompatibility.

In a literature which bespoke hopelessness or facetiousness born of futility, there were a few sparks of rebellion and innovation. The *Boston Weekly Magazine* of the early nineteenth century printed the lion's share of these. The rationalist participants in a series of dialogues which it published under the rubric of "The Passenger," arrived at a solution involving legal redress. The suggestions which came out of these imaginary conversations added up to a series of steps starting with an attempt at community-sponsored arbitration by a married couple; this failing, the case would go to a matrimonial court where grievances could be aired publicly and solutions attempted; if this step turned out to be of no avail, the couple would then be permitted to begin a divorce action in which both parties would receive equal protection under the law. The open hearings of the matrimonial court were supposed to operate as a deterrent to future abuse. Fear of exposure would insure humaneness and decency. The system would work according to the principle of that school of criminologists which believed that if all robbers were caught, robbery would disappear!

But there was comparatively little attention given elsewhere to this negative aspect of marriage—if separation and divorce may be called that. The great effort of the more or less serious periodical literature on the marriage question was directed toward positive measures for the prevention or palliation of unhappiness. The general and ladies' magazines were full of advice on how to behave as a wife in order to get along with a husband, or how an unmarried girl should conduct herself with men, or what qualities to look for in a prospective mate. There were also related articles on how to educate children and develop their character, and on the proprieties of parental and filial devotion. Readers also found amusement and comfort in pieces on the difficulties of proposing and lessons were offered on how to go about making an offer of marriage. The bachelor theme received much more than its due share of attention.

The Weekly Museum known as the (*Ladies' Weekly Museum* after the turn of the century) offered rather spirited contributions on the rights of women, their education, and their position in marriage. This magazine, which regularly reported toasts to Tom Paine at meetings of liberal societies and did honor to Mary Wollstonecraft and the rights of women, was exceptional in its flouting of traditional thought patterns. One "Friend to the Rights of Women" dared even propose that women should have an equal chance with men to make the first advances in choosing a marital partner. More successful marriages would result from matches in which the woman's inclinations were consulted and given greater weight.

The Boston Weekly Magazine of the same period provided a medium for open-minded discussion of all human problems in its "Passenger" and "Gossip" columns. Troubles were aired and human weaknesses exposed. Love, ambition, marriage, children, health, temperance, mutual rights, personal charms genuine and superficial, female behavior—all these were touched upon. Tradition and superstition were attacked, and reason exalted. "The Passenger" doubtless succeeded in jolting readers by including a flat statement (October 29, 1803) to the effect that "Man has no more right to sin with impunity than woman." "The Gossip" (February 5, 1803) had his male character declare that women were vitiating their own dignity by turning over all family authority to their husbands; furthermore, men were suffering from their own short vision in not permitting women to make their full and highly valued contributions to society.

On the whole there was little reference to the old authorities, perhaps because they were so well represented in available ladies' books. There were scattered single appearances of citations from Laurence Sterne's *Sentimental Journey,* Dr. Gregory's *Legacy,* Mrs. Pennington's *Advice to Married Ladies.* Swift's *To a Very Young Lady on Her Marriage* appeared in the *Olio* of 1813. *The New York Magazine* of July, 1797, printed an excerpt on sex education from Lord Kames' *Loose Hints upon Education.* Kames' "Instructions Preparatory to the Married State" made the usual remarks about the education of girls to submissiveness, and boys to the considerate treatment of women. Moreover, it also advised on the guidance of adolescents in the premarital stages. Girls were habituated to restraint from early childhood and therefore needed no special watching. Boys were not so easy to handle after puberty. It was well to take them hunting and engage them in other vigorous exercises to take their minds off those compelling appetites. When this tactic wore thin, then talks on the blessings of marriage and the dangers of loose women were good procedure. This was a good time also to start advising youngsters about what qualities to look for in a wife.

On the whole, the prognosis for happy and wholesome marriages in America appeared to be good. Life was lived closer to reality than in the Old World, and extrinsic considerations in the marriage mart were assumed to have been reduced to a minimum. The most frequently expressed fear was that too much novel reading would give women false notions about what a future husband should be like. It was assumed that financial considerations would enter into the choice of a marriage partner only rarely; but the possibility that girls would be attracted by fictional heroes of handsome mien and romantic temperament seemed ever-present as a threat to the marriage institution. Said the *Boston Weekly Magazine* in its "Thoughts on Marriage" (March 26, 1803), "If he is not virtuous, there is an end of all reasonable hopes of happiness, and the woman who marries a man, knowing him to be vicious, is a wedded harlot, whose base motives, or incontinent desires impel her to a future and certain wretchedness."

Added to the frequent advice on how to choose and get your mate was an even more abundant output of precepts on how to keep him (or her). Naturally, marriage was an activity in which a mistaken choice made it more difficult to ensure a lasting relationship. It was risky for a man to marry a novel-reading girl or a know-it-all intellectual. This cliché must have placed the woman's-uplift advocates in a difficult position; but they stuck to their guns and advised girls to educate themselves to the level of intellectual companionship with their husbands. Writers generally conceded that this made for wholesome friendship, provided that a woman did not exhibit her learning in public to embarrass her husband. Under no circumstances was an educated woman to marry an uneducated man.

Throughout all of this "guidance" literature there was little of the flavor of anxiety concerning the future of the marriage institution. The chances of success were presumed to be high provided people observed small precautions in their personal conduct. Obviously, Godwin had failed to frighten many people out of their optimism. Political independence, economic opportunity, and rising nationalism all encouraged marriage, whether in a "Picture of Matrimonial Felicity," a "Panegyric on Marriage," or "Connubial Happiness." The battle against natural forces and human competitors in a two-fisted environment also added charm to the affectionate security of the domestic scene.

As a corollary to this optimism, the preoccupation with bogies like libertinism and polygamy dropped off. The earlier concerted attack on libertines was apparently a carry-over from European society. Polygamy was not yet a public problem here; that is, unless, with Timothy Dwight, one interpreted second marriages as polygamy, or sexual reveries as licentiousness. Even the bachelor menace was not made too much of after the early years of the new century. The *Weekly Museum* of the 1790's censured bachelors and old maids, duly presenting very weak apologies in rebuttal. A "Letter from an Old Bachelor" in the *New York Magazine* (August 1795) added little to the apologiae for bachelorhood beyond revealing a sour grapes attitude. For the rest, there were a handful of pleasant comparisons of celibacy with marriage, the latter always emerging in the more favorable light.

HYMEN'S RECRUITING SERGEANT

The classic exhortation to marriage appeared not in a magazine but in a pamphlet by the exuberant and prolific Parson Weems. "Hymen's Recruiting Sergeant: or, the Maid's and Bachelor's Friend" appeared in some fourteen editions and variants from 1799 to 1851, besides which, many abstracts turned up in popular almanacs of the time. Although a few social historians have ascribed qualities of wolfish uxoriousness to Weems' attitude on woman and marriage in this and other writings, it seems more advisable to accept at face value his nationalistic call to compete with England and France by building up our population. Weems set forth a long array of reasons for marrying, emphasizing the emotional, social, psychological, and economic benefits to be derived. A man not only got more pleasure out of spending his money on a family, but a family also changed his situation in such a way as to give him the desire and freedom to make more money. King Solomon, Benjamin Franklin, and common sense had been strong advocates of early marriage. It preserved youth from the harlot's clutches and kept him out of brawls and duels over women. Religious people should marry in order to beget worshippers; humane persons, to perpetuate our glorious race; patriotic citizens, to raise up soldiers to defend it.

Weems' address to his readers was a clear exposition of his purpose: "To all the singles, whether masculines or feminines, throughout the United States. Dear Gentles, I am very clear that our *Yankee heroes* are made of, at least, as good stuff as any the BEST of the beef or frog-eating gentry on t'other side of the water. But neither this, nor any our fine speeches to our President, nor his fine speeches to us again, will ever save us from the British gripe or Carmagnole hug, while they can outnumber us *ten to one!* No, my friends, 'tis population, 'tis population *alone,* that can save our bacon. List, then, ye Bach'lors, and ye Maidens fair, If truly ye do love your country dear;

> O list with rapture to the great decree,
> Which *thus* in genesis you all may see:
> *Marry, and raise up soldiers, might and main,*
> Then laugh ye may, at England, France, and Spain.

It will be noticed that Weems sensed the somewhat growing independence of women and therefore laid by the assumption that all women wanted to marry. He noted an incipient opposition on the part of a few women to the promise of double-standard tyranny in marriage. The American disciples of reason and nature undoubtedly influenced his own definition of the odious word "obey" in the marriage ceremony:

> Let none e'er say the fates ordain,
> That man should bear their sway;
> When reason bids—let woman reign,
> When reason bids—obey!

Symptoms of a female uprising were visible in the lengthy recriminations of "A Contented Old Maid" in her *Boston Weekly Magazine* article of July 14, 1804. In the same year Charles Brockden Brown's *Literary Magazine and American Register* carried what was practically a glorification of spinsterhood. It asked the question "Is Marriage or Celibacy Most Eligible? Or, Is the Matron or the Old Maid the Best Member of Society?" The answer was that old maids deserved at least equal consideration. True, the married woman raised sons for the army, but any other woman could have done as well in her place. Furthermore, the old maid had voluntarily limited her consumption of manhood and had left at least one unrequisitioned man for someone else. Such behavior must be accounted social benevolence. And—most telling of all—in view of the tendency of population to outdistance subsistence, the spinster deserved a large share of social honor for refraining from marriage and procreation. The author of these rationalizations obviously had heard of Malthus' *Essay on the Principles of Population,* or more likely, of Franklin's *Observations Concerning the Increase of Mankind and the Peopling of Countries.*

But resort to the lucubrations of population theorists in this manner was neither frequent nor intended to be serious. As the complaining 'Delia' noted in the *Museum of Foreign Literature and Sciences,* men were understandably scarce during the Napoleonic war; but now, seven years after Waterloo, they still didn't want to marry. You pressed them as to their intentions, and they coolly quoted a chapter from Malthus. The true reasoning behind exhortations to breed or to refrain from breeding was either Biblical in inspiration or else a function of nationalistic sentiments: Parson Weems was nearer the reality of human motivation than Malthus.

THE POPULATION PROBLEM

Many of the very Americans who had for a long time been urging early marriages and an increased population were acquainted with Malthus' basic principles. Franklin's already mentioned *Observations* had appeared forty-seven years before Malthus' first English edition in 1798. Moreover, it was Franklin himself who had so strongly approved early marriages in America. This almost in the same breath with an announcement of the American tendency to double its population every twenty-five years. Franklin was well aware that the old world had for the most part reached its saturation point in population. His optimism derived from the unusual opportunity presented by New World geography, where there existed, according to the best knowledge of his time, a limitless expanse of arable land.

Malthus took Franklin's estimate of the New World rate of increase, applied it to the world in general, and arrived at his gloomy formula according to which only war, famine, and disease could keep the population in check. This part of his work outlasted the rest by virtue of having achieved perpetual motion in textbooks from his time to the present. Actually, Malthus gave very little space to developing this thesis; moreover, finding it unpleasant for his own stomach, he proposed in the 1803 edition of his *Essay* a new canon of moral restraint which consisted of late marriage plus premarital chastity. But this was not his prime interest. His mission was to use the popular natural-law philosophy in behalf of the political counter-revolution against Godwin and Condorcet.

Throughout the *Essay* there runs a strong and repeated motif which declares that a system of private property is the only effective restraint on unbridled population increase. With great care he offers logical, psychological, and social evidence to disprove Godwin's basic tenet that man is on his way toward a perfect state in which sexual arrangements would take care of themselves without institutional marriage, in which the food problem would be eliminated through the universal benevolence of an individualistic community of interest, and in which, wonder of wonders, men and women would become passionless. For this, Malthus said, he could see little evidence; nor was his imagination active enough to foresee it; nor would any man with a spark of humanity and even a slight recollection of the earlier part of his life contemplate this as being a state of perfection. The intellectual aspect of life was important but not the only one. "The superiority of intellectual, to sensual pleasures, consists rather, in their filling up more time, in their having a long range, and in their being less liable to satiety, than in their being more real and essential." To Godwin's, "Strip the commerce of the sexes of all its attendant circumstances, and it would be generally despised," Malthus replied: "Nonsense."

However, assume Godwin's marriage system in his one-for-all, all-for-one society to be in operation—as Malthus did for the sake of argument—and what would happen? People would for the most part live in monogamous relationships. (Malthus conceded that promiscuity was unnatural and abhorrent to human beings.) Everyone would marry early, undeterred by the fear of being caught for life. Since it was not an immediate economic inconvenience to have children in such a society, women would have them in unlimited numbers. The population would probably double every fifteen years, but, even accepting the twenty-five year rate which applied at the time in the United States, not even the most exhaustive use of all the available soil could feed such a population. Some check would be sought. The first check at hand was to make a man responsible for his procreative activities. At this point, present-day standards of female chastity reappear, standards which exist precisely to prevent irresponsible women and the children born of their carelessness from becoming a burden upon society. Here reappear institutional marriage and private property.

In essence, what was Malthus claiming? That communism was impracticable because the population would get out of hand. That poor relief defeated its own purposes by encouraging further irresponsibility. That the working class could improve its conditions by limiting its numbers. How was this to be achieved? By marrying late.

Men of feeling and men of religion reacted violently to what they termed an ungodly, inhuman, wicked bundle of ideas. God could not have given man a choice of such alternatives—prostitution and other vices on the one hand, disease and misery on the other. For, as George Bourne said in his *Marriage Indissoluble: and Divorce Unscriptural* (Harrisonburg, Va., 1813), prostitution was in exact proportion to the number of unmarried people. Malthus was further refuted, according to Bourne, by the consideration of an imminent Utopia in which the world would be able to support many more families than now.

These were pious and sentimental objections to an argument eminently suited to the ideals and needs of the wealthy. To them Malthus had spoken the final word in the "distressing matter of the lower classes," and they played it up wherever they could. Not even the brilliant essays of William Hazlitt could destroy its popularity. Malthus was still going strong when Godwin's dull, ineffectual *Of Population* came out in 1820. Godwin used inaccurate American statistics to disprove Malthus' garbled and inaccurate European statistics. He, of all people, tried to buttress his statements with impressive Scriptural citations.

The analyses and conclusions of both Godwin and Malthus left plenty of room for positions to be taken within the extremes they represented or, again, outside of their limits. One could accept the premise of rapid population growth and reply with the simple expedient of birth control. This was Francis Place's great contribution to population theory as presented in his *Illustrations and Proofs of the Principle of Population: including an examination of the Proposed Remedies of Mr. Malthus, and a Reply to the Objections of Mr. Godwin and Others* (1822). It was also possible to draw upon a battery of the social sciences in disproof of previous premises and conclusions. This was the path chosen by Alexander Hill Everett, who while performing his duties as American Chargé d'Affaires at the Court of the Netherlands, wrote and published his *New Ideas on Population with Remarks on the Theories of Malthus and Godwin* (London, 1823).

Everett, whose book appeared in Boston editions in 1823 and 1826 as well as in translation in Paris in 1826, set out to show that the American example proved both Malthus and Godwin to be wrong. His disposed of Godwin by reducing the doctrine of perfectibility to an absurdity. To Malthus, whose position was that population increase caused all physical and moral evil, he demonstrated that population was the real and only active principle of national wealth and happiness. Upon it rested the levels of production and consumption. Human beings were the original producers. Human beings, again, bought the products of industry and agriculture. The more people, the more profitable production. Self-sufficiency was not necessary for any given area or nation. Prosperity was the attribute of an expanding world rather than of a static one. All of this was easily proved by specific contemporary examples, by reference to general principles, and by a backward glance at the history of civilization.

The extent of population, according to Everett, was directly proportionate to the degree of civilization. By "civilization" he meant favorable economic, political, and geographical position. The Americans had all of these. Note also, he said, that *all* of them had to be present. The Indians who had the geographical situation but not the social institutions and moral qualities of our people, were starving. Malthus was therefore all wrong about discouraging early marriage. He was misguided and inhuman in urging governments to repeal poor laws—a measure, which Franklin had long ago proposed for England. Everett felt that Malthus' cold reasoning was inconsistent with the social instincts of human nature. He himself, especially in the generous American environment, would lift all barriers to marriage and establish institutions for the relief of the destitute.

Now, Everett argued further, let us assume that the Malthus scare has something to it. What should we do? If we tried to legislate against early—or what Malthus called "immoral"—marriage in the absence of a clear and present danger to the *whole* of society, we should have a difficult time enforcing our laws. Should we make restraint voluntary, then? No. You could not leave a matter like this to the people—especially the poor and ignorant who have a strong, immediate drive to procreate and are incapable of looking ahead. We might, however, raise the legal marriage age. That, the democratic Everett explained, would place the burden equally on the whole population rather than on the poor only, as the aristocratic Malthus was suggesting. We might even follow the example of the kingdom of bees and choose by lot who were to breed while the workers supported them.

But neither Providence nor natural law indicated that we should leave such matters to legal enactment and moral suasion. It was intended that all should marry and marry early. If this was in accordance with natural law, the same law would adjust the population problem. Swallow Malthus whole, and you would be forced to let logic push you to contraception and infant exposure—both abhorrent and unnecessary. Common sense would delay marriage and childbearing in most cases where economics so decreed.

It seems, though, that neither Everett's common sense, nor his Divine Providence, nor his natural law settled the problem for all time even in bountiful America. For, a look around during his own time and afterwards reveals a host of religious and social experiments, ideas, and movements, all having as part of their design some attempt to solve the marriage and population problem. The Shakers had their celibacy solution; the Rappites their part-time marriages; the Perfectionists at Oneida their male continence, Charles Knowlton and Robert Dale Owen their birth control.

THREE

The Free Enquirers

SHELLEY'S SOCIAL PHILOSOPHY

The story of Robert Owen's influence started back in England in more than one sense. Owen the manufacturer and philanthropist, had migrated here for a period of years. His son, Robert Dale Owen, remained here and became active in American political affairs. Both had learned much from Mary Wollstonecraft and William Godwin. The elder Owen was so clearly indebted to Godwin that an American clergyman, attacking Owen for his free-thinking creed, could honestly remark that this was the old boy Godwin all over again. Both father and son had been influenced, especially in their agnosticism and in their ideas of marriage, by the poet Percy Bysshe Shelley, who in large part was himself a product of the two Godwins and their eighteenth-century kinsmen of the Enlightenment.

Shelley was probably partly responsible for the elder Owen's extreme iconoclasm and his semi-digested interpretations of the liberal *philosophes*. Owen seems to have known little more than the poet's *Queen Mab,* which was certainly not his most mature work. The revolutionary ideology and political republicanism of eighteenth-century France and England had made their impression upon the mind of Shelley before his seventeenth or eighteenth year. A large measure of his intellectual framework he absorbed through Godwin, whose *Political Justice* he read in 1809 and whom he worshipped as a saintly benefactor of mankind. Before he was twenty, Shelley had read Holbach, Helvetius, Rousseau, Volney, Laplace, Bacon, Newton, and Hume. Lucretius, Epicurus, Diderot, Condorcet, and Paine were not omitted. Nor did he confine his reading to such material. Among his vast non-philosophical readings, we find four of Charles Brockden Brown's novels, all read before the summer of 1813.

The earliest synthesis of what was stirring in the youthful but learned mind of Shelley was his *Queen Mab,* a revolutionary manifesto coming out of his youthful years of much reading and limited experience. In spite of its immaturity—or, the cynical might say, because of it—this was the poem which had the greatest influence on the Owenites and later radicals of socialist and anarchist hue. This was the early attempt whose text and footnotes won Shelley a good part of his unsavory reputation during his lifetime and afterwards. This was the piece apropos of which the poet himself said years after its publication that he was no longer the author "[of that poem] in most furious style, with long notes against Jesus Christ, God the Father, and the King, the bishops, and marriage, and the devil knows what."

Shelley thus disavowed ideas he had borrowed from Godwin. Godwin himself had changed his mind on the marriage question before Shelley had come to read him. But Godwin's ideas and Shelley's interpretation of them in *Queen Mab* were too congenial to the radical disciples of both to be overlooked. And so, in spite of the author's own dissatisfaction, *Queen Mab* retained its popularity for those to whom it made good sense or excellent reading, and its notoriety for those to whom it was "dangerous thoughts." Kings, priests, and property, the poem taught, were unnatural and uneconomic. They shared responsibility for war, misery, and all that blasted life's beautiful perceptions and experience. Reason and virtue would rout error and vice through a partnership between man and nature in some mystical, cosmic process. Every man's existence would be changed and perfected.

In this simplified and revitalized world, man would turn vegetarian and thereby free himself of disease and of evil passions and beliefs. Equality would reign; Bastilles and cathedrals would fall to ruin. Woman would be on an equal footing with man. Prostitution and "prostitution's venomed bane" would be obsolete. Was all this to happen in a sudden overturn of present civilization? No, this was a natural process which would take place as the result of gradual change. However, it is clear that the poet was conscious of the agitational nature of his own *Queen Mab*. The precautions he exercised about its publication in 1813 are indicative of this. He forwarded the manuscript to the publisher, Hookham, with a request to print 250 copies "if you do not dread the arm of the law, or any exasperation of public opinion against yourself." Copies were sent to carefully chosen friendly readers with the title page, dedication, and imprint removed from each copy. In the ensuing eight years only seventy copies were distributed. None were sold.

Shelley was not afraid of his own ideas but of the consequences of distributing printed copies. The poem would not have got around at all were it not for pirated editions circulated by enterprising "friends." However, not wishing some of his important ideas to die stillborn, the poet refurbished and published anonymously his beliefs on diet and religion. These appeared in 1813 and 1814 under the titles of *A Vindication of Natural Diet*, and *A Refutation of Deism, in a Dialogue*. In the latter pamphlet, Shelley converted his headlong

attack on Christianity in *Queen Mab* into a subtle, highly ironic discussion whose infidel character was discernible only to readers who
understood the irony. The defense of the vegetarian regimen took
up its stand on the grounds of social and economic reasoning. Eliminate domesticated meat animals; more productive land will be available; life will be easy and natural; crime and war will disappear. In
addition the pamphlet suggests humanitarian vegetarianism, and is
indirectly related to the thinking of those sexologists who claimed—
and still claim—that eating meat and condiments heightens the sexual urge.

But Shelley's conception of pure love was quite unrelated to the
effects of meat-eating. His conception of morality had little to do
with usual values placed either on the interpersonal behavior of men
and women, or on the social duties and obligations of married people. His was a philosophical compound of ethical, esthetic, and political principles. How presumptuous it was for legal machinery to
attempt to regulate matters that were natural and involuntary!
"Love is inevitably consequent upon the perception of loveliness.
Love withers under constraint; its very essence is liberty: it is com-
patible neither with obedience, jealousy, nor fear: it is there most
pure, perfect and unlimited, where its votaries live in confidence,
equality, and unreserve." Would any thinking person consent to laws
which kept friends together after their desire for friendship had disappeared? How much worse to regulate the more subtle and variable
emotion, that capricious love so "dependent on those delicate pecu-
liarities of the imagination"! Living in a society which applied such
regulation was living in "feudal savageness and imperfect civilization" aggravated by Christian morality.

Marriage was selfishness, a violation of personal liberty. It was
transformed into intolerable tyranny as soon as one or both parties
tired of it. Where the parties showed good manners and kept up
appearances, the results were insincerity and hypocrisy. Where the
level of conduct was lowered by irremediable conflict of interests,
open warfare ensued. In either case the social heritage of the children was ill-humor, violence, and falsehood. Prostitution was the inevitable accompaniment of marriage and the prevailing definition of
chastity. One instance of yielding to nature—one error—made woman
an outcast, spurned most by her own sex. Society permitted only one
recourse—prostitution, which accounted for one-tenth of the population of London. It destroyed the finer capacities for love in young men
and made their children heirs to disease. Abolish marriage and, (see
Godwin) a natural, moral, probably monogamous arrangement would
be worked out. Was happiness the object of morality? Then marital
unions ought to cease once the evil results exceeded the good. "Love

is free; to promise forever to love the same woman is not less absurd than to promise forever to believe in the same creed: such a vow in both cases excludes us from all enquiry."

The reader who took a look backward would recognize here Godwin's thoughts on "promises." Gazing into a crystal ball which revealed the future he would see Robert Owen attacking social institutions as destroyers of freedom and happiness, Robert Dale Owen and Frances Wright revising the marriage ceremony to eliminate "promises" and "obedience," the libertarian and the libertine political theorists mouthing Shelley's well-formed phrases. Looking around him, that is, in 1821, when the bookseller William Clarke issued the first pirated edition of *Queen Mab*, the reader saw Shelley's marital difficulties with Harriet Westbrook connected by the public with the ideas expressed in the book's notes on marriage; he saw the poet's every act and move either interpreted as immorality or embellished to suit the extravagant spirit of the poet's theories.

Shelley's loves and social ideas did more to color American evaluations of him than did the intellectual and technical aspects of his verse. It is still the grand sport of biographers and character analysts to speculate on why he ever married the "illiterate," vulgar, seventeen-year-old Harriet Westbrook to whom he had delivered lectures against marriage before their elopement in 1811. His own nineteen-year-old adolescent candor and unworldliness seems to be one good reason. His sympathy for an infatuated girl, hard-pressed by her father, seems to be another. A recent biographer, Newman Ivey White, points out that Harriet talked Shelley into marriage by giving him to read Amelia Opie's *Adelina Mowbray, or the Mother and Daughter*, whose hero violates his anti-marriage principles in order to protect the heroine from the persecutions of society. Shelley's views changed markedly after he had read this book, and he thereafter justified his marriage on the grounds that the sacrifice entailed in living with a man outside of wedlock was too much to ask of a woman. His subsequent desertion of Harriet, his connection with Mary Godwin, Harriet's despair and suicide, and the poet's other female interests have engendered a variety of explanations on the part of scholars.

SHELLEY AND THE AMERICAN SCENE

What interests us immediately, however, is the effect of Shelley's life and writings on the battle of ideas in America. As with so many other literary and political issues, Shelley's ideas were known only at second and third hand to many Americans who argued violently about them. A pirated *Queen Mab* edition turned up in New York in 1821, coming from the press of W. Baldwin & Co. The late twenties saw much more bootleg Shelley. His popularity grew rapidly in the thirties, and by the end of the decade, when Mary Shelley sponsored an American edition of his prose works, the Shelley controversy was in full swing. The liberal press of Frances Wright and Robert Dale Owen had published in 1831 a *Queen Mab* "from the original London edition," and had prefaced the poem with their own introductory appreciation. Gilbert Vale's Beacon Office, a sort of heir to the Owen tradition, put out another *Queen Mab* in 1842, including the notice by the first legitimate American publishers, Wright and Owen.

It may be guessed that the radical, atheist readers of the *Free Enquirer, The Beacon,* and a few other agitational organs bought their *Queen Mabs* and liked what they read. Most Americans who knew about Shelley got their opinions by the reflected light of religious and literary critics. Outside of the Owen-Wright circuit, little of significance appeared before the Emerson-Andrews Boston controversy which flared up in 1837. Small items, like the one in the *American Atheneum* of September 1, 1821, noting the indictment of Shelley's 1821 pirater at the instigation of the Society for the Suppression of Vice, had not created much interest. The *Atheneum's* comment was: "It is dreadful to think that for the chance of a miserable pecuniary profit, any man would become the active agent to disseminate principles so subversive of the happiness of society."

The first large-scale discussion of Shelley's merits was incidental to a crisis in the New England civil war between the conservative and liberal Christians. Ralph Waldo Emerson's address to the Harvard Divinity School's graduating class of June 1836 was an early border incident of the impending full-scale struggle. Andrews Norton, editor, man of letters, and retired Professor of Sacred Literature, who referred to Emerson and his followers as "The New School of Literature and Religion" because it had accepted Shelley, managed to keep his peace for a while. But when the *Western Messenger,* in its issue of February 1837 published an article by a socialistically inclined writer who attacked organized religion generally and Presbyterianism in particular, the Presbyterian Norton attacked the *Messenger* (supposedly a religious periodical) for quoting the atheist Shelley with approval. James Freeman Clarke, a New England Unitarian clergyman then residing in Louisville, Kentucky, where he edited the *Western Messenger,* replied in the *Boston Daily Advertiser.* While it was deplorable, he argued, that Shelley was an unbeliever, we must understand that the poet had been driven to that position by bigotry. Of course, he was truly to be condemned for his extravagances, but "we must say that he often exhibits more true Christian feeling, and even Christian Faith, than many who scoff at him as an Atheist and an Outlaw." Norton struck back with his own view of Shelley's *Queen Mab,* a book which he called "as openly and *shockingly* blasphemous as any to which the most perverted state of heart and mind ever gave birth—a work, it is said, which Shelley himself repented of and endeavored to suppress." And the views on marriage! Marriage represented as a hateful institution! The poet had struck at the roots of human decency and affections, at civilization itself. Whereupon, Clarke commented in his own paper: Since when do critics damn good poetry because its author is an atheist? With that the flames of war died down—but only to spring up elsewhere.

It was Henry T. Tuckerman, New England critic, essayist and poet, who next stirred up the embers with his review of Shelley's *Prose Works* in the *Southern Literary Messenger* of June 1840. The reviewer was a sympathetic Shelleyan and expressed admiration for the poet's principles while not openly subscribing to them. The November issue of the same magazine carried Mrs. Seba Smith's indignant regrets that the talented Tuckerman should have defended Shelley, that unholy, pernicious, and dangerous disrupter of respectable institutions. In December "A Friend of Virtue" expressed his fear that Tuckerman's defense would give comfort to the opponents of religion and marriage.

The critic Francis Bowen summed up a prevailing view of all the romantic poets: Egotism had caused them to impose on the public "their theatrical exposure of private feelings." Burns, Byron, and Shelley had, by offering in the same package their wicked personal example with their poetic genius, done far more public harm than good.

A few progressive-minded critics protested. Orestes Brownson complained in a long article in the *Boston Quarterly Review* (1841) that Americans had been unfair to Shelley because of British literary domination here. Shelley had been a victim of intolerance and oppression in England, and Americans who read his English critics had made him a whipping boy in their own country. Until these latter years students had read Shelley *sub rosa*. Curious adults read him too, but also kept his books well out of sight. Prejudice was still so deeply rooted that it was not yet possible to get an honest American evaluation of works the reading of which but yesterday was considered a criminal offense. If the poet had gone astray in some of his ideas on diet, marriage, and religion, it was only because his tremendous human understanding and sympathies had made him interpret Godwin in that way.

Who could afford to upbraid Shelley for his radical suggestions? All the political indifference of Coleridge and the Toryism of Southey could not erase similar enthusiasms of their own in bygone days. These very symbols of conservatism, Brownson revealed, had once planned to build a Godwinesque pantisocracy on the Susquehanna, where they could further the perfection of man and his institutions—a "Utopia in our wild back-woods." These models of social correctness would have carried out their plans had they not met and shown a "growing preference for the attractive charms of the sister milliners of Bristol." Politically, Shelley would have concurred with the Declaration of Independence; the British could never like him for that. In some respects Shelley was a conservative who even doubted the advisability of introducing universal suffrage in England. He was also religious in the best sense in that he had a great respect for the teachings of Christ while abhorring the practices of many Christians.

The Fourierist Parke Godwin tried to supply the needed impartial evaluation of Shelley's poetry in the *Democratic Review* of December 1843. With good intentions he brushed by the *bête noire* of Shelley's marital conduct and ideas; but, being socialistically inclined himself, he emphasized the value of the intellectual message contained in *Queen Mab* and in the *Revolt of Islam*. What Shelley wished to teach in these poems was that every struggle for the rights of man, whether or not immediately successful, would prove ultimately to have been worth the effort.

By 1845, Shelley was known in America for his literary merit. Poets read his lyrics for pleasure, and in order to learn how to write their own. Shelley's views on marriage stopped getting a rise out of readers and kept their importance only for the partisans of free love in the latter part of the century. *Queen Mab* continued to have a general liberating effect on alert minds; the later periodicals were generally better disposed to him. The *Nation,* for example, was almost completely on his side. His morals were rarely discussed but his political and social ideas began to get a more sympathetic hearing. His poetry was read and discussed as poetry.

OWEN AND THE NEW VIEW

The remark by Brownson on Southey's and Coleridge's plan to build a Utopia *á la* Godwin in America was but an echo of Southey's own sneer at Owen's New Harmony plan. The import of Robert Southey's belittling statement (made in a letter to John Rickman) was that Robert Owen was a mere latter day pantisocratist who wished to carry out hare-brained schemes already rejected by more mature men. But the maturation process in question had been well characterized by the satirical pen of Orestes Brownson. What happened was that, while Coleridge, Southey, and their associate Robert Lovell were making their plans at Bristol, Southey became engaged to Edith Fricker, one of six daughters of Stephen Fricker, an unsuccessful manufacturer. Lovell soon after married her sister, Mary, and Coleridge became engaged to a third sister, Sara. These were the "milliner sisters of Bristol." One thing led to another, until Southey renounced the pantisocratic idea. This outraged Coleridge, but later he too gave up the plan and its underlying theory.

Owen was more than a romantic pantisocratist. His decision to leave the uncongenial political environment of England in order to experiment with socialism in more open-minded America was made after much thought and experience in cooperative endeavor. His streamlined factory reorganization at New Lanark, Scotland, had given him some reason to believe that environmental control might work. The operation of Infant and Lancastrian primary schools there had stirred him to imagine what a more extensive educational system could do for the reshaping of human nature and social institutions. He had formulated and announced a labor theory of value which, together with his organizational and publishing activities, made a great and permanent contribution to the British labor movement as well as to socialist theory.

This was no vague disciple of Godwin. He had been known to visit the Godwin home and had been referred to by Fanny Imlay (Mary Wollstonecraft's daughter by Gilbert Imlay) as a later student of Godwin's ideas and a "great and good man." Miss Imlay also reported that Owen had expressed to her his regrets that her mother was not alive; she would have been an enthusiastic supporter of his plans. William Hazlitt predicted, in 1816, after Owens' *New View of Society* had appeared, that this new descendant in the utopian line of Plato, More, Harrington, and Godwin would soon be the victim of public abuse as Godwin had been. As Hannah More and her cohorts had denounced Godwin, Malthus would attack Owen with his favorite counterthrusts of "vice" and "misery"; Southey would nail him in the *Quarterly Review;* the newspapers would hang him; the labels "Jacobin," "leveller," and "incendiary" would be pinned on him. Character assassination would replace the reasonable examination of his ideas—ideas which had already passed before the critical eyes of James Mill and Francis Place, both friends of Owen's recently acquired business partner, Jeremy Bentham.

The *New View* was in reality a reaction to the gloomy tenets of Malthus whom Owen had met and whose works he had read. Luckily, Owen did not permit himself to publicize his professed admiration for Shelley at an early date, for in so doing he would have hastened the decline of his reputation. Shelley's friend and biographer, Thomas Medwin, tells of an occasion on which he and James Lawrence visited the Owenite Chapel and found displayed on the book-table Shelley's *Queen Mab* and Lawrence's *Empire of the Nairs,* itself an anti-matrimonial fantasy about a land where women had taken the initiative from men and were using it successfully. Owen must have known the *Nairs* which lay on his counter; if not, he certainly felt its effect through Shelley, who did read it. As Medwin's story goes, after he and Lawrence listened to a harangue which promised the "disciples a millenium of roast beef and fowls, and three or four days recreation out of seven, equal division of property, and a universality of knowledge by education," they had an interview with Owen. When Owen discovered Medwin's connection with Shelley, he delivered a long eulogy on the poet, and, picking up a copy of *Queen Mab*, read the passage which he claimed was basic to one of his chief tenets. The passage was the one which began with "How long ought the sexual connection to last . . . ?"

Owen neither lectured in England nor wrote there about his ideas on marriage until 1835, when he published unrevised his *Marriages of the Priesthood of the Old Immoral World*. It was in this period that the *General Baptist Repository and Missionary Observer* May (1839) declared that Shelley was responsible for all of the so-called originality of Owen. The *Quarterly Review* of March 1840 also pointed out that Owen had quoted with applause Shelley's footnote on marriage in *Queen Mab*.

Americans would not have been as cordial as they were if they had had wind of Owen's dangerous ideas on religion and marriage. Had they known all, the enterprising Rappites might not have sold him their 20,000 acre village of Harmony, Indiana, for the very reasonable price of £30,000. The religious Rappites, who practised a "limited" celibacy, might have found it hard to do business with an irreligious person of suspicious morality. Again Owen might not have come here had any other land bargain elsewhere as good as this one been brought to his attention in subsequent years. America, then, would not have experienced the provocative ideas and activities of himself, his family, and his friends. For, although, the New Harmony experiment in communism soon failed and cost Owen the larger part of his capital (the early failure was attributed to the poor choice of co-operators, who turned out to be intellectually and emotionally unprepared), Owen and his partisans made a significant impression on American thought.

Interest here in the social philosophy of Robert Owen dated back to the period 1822-23 when he was introduced to America's minister to England, John Quincy Adams. The American representative immediately asked Owen for enough copies of his *New View* to distribute to each governor in the Union. The result of this gesture was to give Owen entrée to some very important people when he got here. Even before he got to New Harmony, he was invited to Washington where he presented his "Two Discourses on a New System of Society; as Delivered in the Capitol of the United States on the 25th February and 7th March, 1825." Reviews of the published addresses and of the *New View of Society* (the latter belatedly noticed in the American press) were open-minded and very cordial.

The *Cincinnati Literary Gazette* was almost enthusiastic about the principle of environmental control announced by Owen. It said that Owen had placed before the world the desirable ideas contained in the "Republic," "Political Justice," and the "Houmousian System" without their objectionable insistence on community of women to go along with community of property. The *Gazette* tried to forestall the imported variety of slander by explaining that Owen's enemies in Scotland and elsewhere had committed sins of omission, distortion, and illogic to discredit this well-meaning philosopher. "He had been accused of admitting all religions in his System, and thus opening the way for Polygamy, when individuals professing the creeds that allow it, may be received; but we find no such regulation in his plan, and he must know too well the bad effects of a plurality of women—and that it is only allowed where men become tyrants of the female sex—to admit of this practice in his virtuous society of equal rights." Owen had also been charged with running a glorified slave establishment at New Lanark. But see how he has invited to his experiment people of all classes! There was a fair chance that a genuine Utopia was in the building in Indiana, United States.

The establishment of the New Harmony project itself also got a sympathetic press. It was scarcely realized that the great human qualities of Owen's economic proposals could be the harbingers of subversive doctrines with regard to religion and the family. By the end of 1825, editors of Eastern city newspapers, noting what was brewing at New Harmony, began their campaign of subtle ridicule— for which the *New Harmony Gazette* had a stock reply, to the effect that where reason is inadequate, the captious use satire. But this was just a warming-up exercise. The real battle began when Owen delivered his Declaration of Mental Independence speech on July 4, 1826. After this, opposition to him and to his project was not confined to conservative newspaper editors. Owen had challenged almost the entire American clergy, with whom he subsequently fought a battle that was entirely above board, and not too frequently marred by matters irrelevant to religion.

The master, it seems, was not relying entirely on his great manifesto for a revision of popular prejudices about women, marriage, and family duties. No sooner had the colony got under way when he called together the women cooperators of the new society in order to give them a first lesson. They must stop nagging and lecturing their husbands and substitute the silent force of example. A wife, he said, could by this means "gain an interest in some of his leading passions, and make them accessory to his reformation." This was a good theory, coming from a reformer whose activities in behalf of the whole of mankind caused him to neglect his wife, desert her for long periods, and, in general, take her existence as a matter of course. This, however, could be said for the man who was completely absorbed in his movement: he never lost rapport with his own children, except for the one who remained in England with her mother, and he always retained a great love for all children.

The second lesson came in the form of the reprinting of Owen's 1816 "Address, delivered to the Inhabitants of New Lanark" by the *New Harmony Gazette*. This time, under the heading of adult education, the reader was told that there was much he could learn about organizing his domestic affairs and about training his children. Some bad habits had been with us so long, that they came to assume the title of "human nature." Among such misconceptions was the belief that individuals form their own characters. Another was that the individual could mold and control his own affections. "Hence insincerity and degradation of character. Hence the miseries of domestic life, and more than half the crimes of mankind."

The climax of the course arrived with Owen's "Oration Containing a Declaration of Mental Independence, delivered in the Public Hall, at New Harmony, Ind. . . . at the Celebration of the Fourth of July, 1826." The dateline of the *New Harmony Gazette* which ran this piece was the conventional July 12, 1826; the reader also noted that it was the fifty-first year of American Independence and the First Year of Mental Independence. (Some fifty years later, the free love, anarchist organ, *The Word,* began dating itself Y. L. 1, etc., denoting the Year of Love starting from another declaration of independence). Owen professed to have no revolutionary program. He calmly stated that the men of 1776 had intended all he was about to say; that it had taken fifty years to sweep away the impediments which the founding fathers had left standing at the time so as not to endanger their immediate objectives; that "it is for you to carry on, using the benefits of my long experience and careful analysis of the causes of man's suffering."

Thus spake the disciple of Godwin and Shelley:

> I now *Declare,* to you and to the world, that *Man,* up to this hour, has been, in all parts of the earth, a slave to a trinity of the most monstrous evils that could be combined to inflict mental and physical evil upon his whole race.
> I refer to Private, or Individual Property—absurd and irrational systems of religion—and Marriage, founded on individual property combined with some one of these irrational systems of religion.

The country which had received and given citizenship to Owen suddenly began to wish it had looked England's gift horse in the mouth. Among an open-minded people, there was, of course, room for differences of opinion. But here was a man who saw as destructive of human happiness the very tripod which social leaders considered the prop of civilization. These leaders were startled to hear that religion was stultifying superstition and that property oppressed the working and the idle poor. They were even more startled to learn that "The forms and ceremonies of marriage, as they have been hitherto performed, and afterwards supported, make it almost certain, that they were contrived and forced upon the people at the same time that property was first divided among a few leading individuals and Superstition was invented. . . ." This, pursued Owen, was how wealthy families contrived to stay wealthy. The aristocrats invented marriage and its hocus-pocus ceremony in order to disguise their real motives. They kept their children away from poor company; they kept all learning for themselves. This they did so "that they might, through the influence of their wealth, learning, and power, select the most beautiful and desirable women from among all the people—and thus enslave and make them, in fact, a part of private property."

Woven into this revolutionary philosophy, which somewhat anticipated the anthropology of Lewis Henry Morgan and the sociology of Friedrich Engels, was an ideal dear to the hearts of American democrats—marriage devoid of obnoxious considerations of wealth, family, and position. The new equality of wealth and social status would necessarily lead to virtuous and happy marriages. These marriages based on "esteem, regard, and affection" would last longer and perform better the real purpose of marriage, that of securing the well-being of the men and women who entered it. Furthermore, argued Owen, the law should provide, on as equally reputable a basis as marriage itself, for the dissolution of marriages which promised more misery than bliss. The primary aim of this formulation was, if we place it in the context of Owen's temperament and logic, to ameliorate the condition of women. The minds of many of his opponents made it out to be a bid for a free-love system. Owen's prognosis—after Godwin—that in the new world of reason man would not make promises which were not within his power to fulfill, was received as a doctrine of irresponsibility.

The Declaration of Mental Independence, Owen's program in outline, was intended for public consumption as well as for the members of the New Harmony community. It was promptly supplemented by Sunday instructional meetings for local residents. The trilogy was once more exposed, revealing marriage to be founded on the two errors of property and religion. Present practices were made out to be productive of pre-marital deception, greed, pride, and "disappointment of the natural affections leading in many cases to disease, misery and death . . . and an endless catalog of private and public crimes and calamities." Moreover, the education and personality of the very children for whose benefit the family existed were frustrated and warped by property and marriage. The proper growth of children demanded that from infancy they should work, play, and learn with groups of children of their own age. Only in a community of common property would they acquire a feeling for the rights of others. The family atmosphere, with its pampering, lack of rational order, and competition and bickering, was inimical to desirable ends. School education was the cure for misdirected family training; and even the success of this was problematic with teachers "trained in old societies and under old methods." The entire social structure had to be revamped.

Previous social planners had rested their case on a philosophic plane for want of civic authority to carry out their plans. Robert Owen had the advantage of having high prestige in the community whose organization he himself had initiated. He was quick to use his advantage. Early in 1827, the *New Harmony Gazette* (February 28) published his proposals for improving "The Social System." The new marriage arrangements tried to overcome the difficulties of the old with reference to insincerity, extraneous considerations in the choice of mates, incompatibility, and so on. The couple in question were to give notice of their intentions in writing, over their signatures, to a weekly meeting of the community committee, which at the time consisted of twelve elected members. (Owen added that committee members should be over thirty-five years old, preferably over forty.) Three months later, the parties were to repeat their notice, this time signed by two witnesses as well. The secretary of the committee would call a community meeting on the following day, at which the parties would appear to declare themselves husband and wife. They were then entitled to a separate dwelling unit. If the marriage turned out badly, the same procedure could be used to undo it.

Although the proposal did not carry with it detailed explanations for the waiting period and committee action, it may be surmised that the purpose was to allow time for investigation or "cooling off." Another matter which remains unclear is how this system was to work alongside of the established legal provisions of the State of Indiana; for Owen said, in the very next breath, that the community form could not supersede established laws. The new procedure was offered more as philosophic consolation for reason-bent cooperators than as a competitor to the ways of the old immoral world.

The *New Harmony Gazette*, which scrupulously observed the liberal tradition of publishing opposing views—usually for purposes of rebuttal—printed no strictly local reaction to the Owen propaganda. The cooperators were either completely cowed, or lacked the confidence to state publicly their possible objections to the master. Only one, a regular contributor to the *Gazette* who called himself the "mutualist," wanted to raise questions. He wanted to know whether this was not a new kind of sectarian dictatorship which was ordering cooperators to abandon their religion, their freedom of thought, and their wives. Would this produce liberty or mental slavery? An editorial reply said that anyone who had read his Owen carefully would have seen that the new society aimed only at the happiness of the individual. It gave him the opportunity of release from any alliance which caused misery, "because he [Owen] thinks it a *more virtuous* line of conduct to part *in peace,* than to live together in discord." After which, Mutualist shifted his previous line of argument and asked if either party should have the privilege of discarding the virtuous and living other party. The editor, Robert Dale Owen at the time, said he could not give an official reply; but, as he saw it, the only one to suffer would be the less worthy partner who had separated from a treasure he was too blind to recognize. The "good" party certainly would not want to continue an unsatisfactory relationship. Reason would be the arbiter "and enlightened public opinion will confirm her dictates." The Mutualist—possibly Josiah Warren, who, with his family, was living at New Harmony in 1826—did not seem satisfied with any formula which smacked of imposition on the happiness of any individual. He felt that that cooperative endeavor should not be mixed in with irrelevancies like marriage and religion.

Discussion was by no means confined to a handful of interested parties. Where the *Gazette,* with its one-thousand-copy edition (as of 1829) and estimated five thousand readers, failed to reach, far-flung newspapers filled in. The *National Gazette* of Philadelphia, the *Trenton True American,* the Woodbury, N. J., *Village Herald,* and others all had their say about this threat to religion and morals. The *National Intelligencer* of Washington, D. C. was willing to grant that if, in short, "he is a visionary enthusiast, bewildered by waking dreams, he is at least benevolent." But this benevolence, though it followed a genuine religious principle, was subversive of general good conduct in that it blurred the distinction between right and wrong. It also advocated kindness to a point which advised against anger toward a child who did wrong, and toward criminals and drunkards.

The Natchez *Ariel* could foresee only the worst from Owen's incitement to promiscuity as revealed in both the "Declaration" and the proposed "mock marriage" ceremony. Human nature, with its characteristic overpowering emotions and its inveterate tendency to quarrel at the drop of a handkerchief, would run wild if freed of the restraints of social reprisal and well-reasoned law. Might it not be considered selfish, by a slight extension of the logic of cooperation, to withhold from the community the use of one's exclusive "wife on trial"?

An utter misrepresentation, replied the indignant *Gazette;* and since the matter of marriage was the one which drew the most lies from the press, the editor took great pains to make clear the position of the free enquirers in an article of May 2, 1827. He must have had

Queen Mab open before him as he wrote of law and the affections. It was time to break the embarrassed silence on a subject of which it was altogether possible to speak simply and clearly. Friends and lovers were responsible only to each other. No law was ever successful in stimulating love or extinguishing hatred. Should we attempt binding bodies by force where no affection existed in the heart, the inevitable result would be failure. Compulsion was all right under old world despotisms; but Americans prized freedom above all else, and freedom of the affections above all other freedoms.

Opposers of freedom, said the editor, argued the expediency of controlling human whims. When was oppression ever expedient? Was love so ungenerous an emotion that the law had to enforce loyalty to its object? Experience failed to show that freedom led to promiscuity. It demonstrated rather that prohibition multiplied the force of the very thing it meant to repress. Laws did not prevent inconstancy; they merely drove it underground. Moreover, there was room for grave doubt as to whether expediency ever justified the right of one individual to exercise power over another, whether that right derived from the "color of skin our fellow-creatures possess, or . . . some idle form that may have been recited over them." Yes, hasty public opinion had tried to silence Socrates, Galileo, and others; but people who had the courage of their convictions and acted in good taste and with good intentions have always won the respect of others. Those who refused to bow to prevailing notions of market place love would earn the respect of their fellow citizens too.

In the years 1828 and 1829 Owen engaged in two major encounters with public sentiment in the West, but on neither occasion was the marriage issue argued. He was at the time on his way back from unsuccessful negotiations with the Mexican government for a land grant which was made contingent upon the passage by Mexico's Congress of an act to establish freedom of religion in that country. The act fell through, and, with it, Owen's grant. On this lecture tour he was pressing a twelve point program for the liberation of the human mind and challenging the entire clergy to debate. The Universalist minister Alexander Campbell took up the challenge and met Owen in a tedious, fruitless debate at Cincinnati. The consensus was that Owen got the worst of it.

At New Orleans, where he lectured a few months before the Cincinnati debate, Owen had a surprisingly friendly press. The *New Orleans Courier* reported that his lecture was well attended by a courteous, respectful crowd. The group did not agree with the ideas presented but felt that he was sincere and his ideas provocative. There were few women in the audience. Most women had stayed away because the word had been passed around that Owen would speak on indelicate phases of sex and marriage. The truth of the matter was that nothing of the sort took place. In fact, any lady who attended balls and plays, and read novels, ran no risk of being corrupted by her attendance at Owen's lecture. The one thing which did frighten the reporter was the seriousness and cogency of Owen's logic. The general feeling of the New Orleans press was that he had handled himself with dignity and poise. His seriousness, honesty and friendliness were praised. As for his theme, it could hardly be fully explored in one afternoon on a public platform. Even the Natchez *Ariel* began to take him more seriously.

The elder Owen was not one to pass up the opportunity of a fair reception. He pointed out to the people of New Orleans in a *Gazette* article the unwillingness of their clergy to meet him in open discussion and then proceeded to pay the inhabitants of the city a very dubious compliment. Their morals compared very favorably with those of other big cities he had seen. Prostitution was not in evidence as it was elsewhere. Upon investigation he had found the cause of its disappearance a curious one. The female quadroon had by custom and tacit understanding fulfilled the function, without the flavor of immorality and pollution of prostitution as it was known in all places where population was concentrated. The quadroon suffered no sense of shame nor loss of whatever social status she had. A great deal of human degradation was thus prevented among the rest of the population.

The younger Owen sensed that Louisianians would not like what his father had said. For himself, he felt that the position of the quadroon did not conform to reason; that there was much in it that was revolting, especially the situation in which a white father would pass his woman and children in the streets and not acknowledge them. However, it was still preferable to prostitution "producing disease of body and callousness of mind" and leading to premature death for thousands of miserable women. And, as a parting shot, he observed how ineffective the clergy had been in improving *this* situation.

From New Orleans, the great apostle of cooperation went out to Cincinnati, and then to Washington, where he interviewed Secretary of State Van Buren and President Jackson. The discussions centered around producing more friendly relations between the United States and Great Britain. Owen was assigned the role of unofficial ambassador, and, according to him, international relations straightened themselves out soon after his return to England. Home again, he concentrated for many years on an infant and elder school, a lecture hall, and an establishment for the exchange of goods without the intervention of money. In 1835 he decided to give Englishmen the benefit of the thought he had given to marriage in America. Hence his *Lectures on the Marriages of the Priesthood in the Old Immoral World*, the fourth edition of which appeared in 1840. By this time the complaints against clerical control of marriage had snowballed to ever larger proportions. The marriage system now had to bear the burden of the class struggle, serious problems of population, and the absence of rationality in society at large. The discussions precipitated by these lectures constitute the beginnings of a hundred-year debate in which the issue of socialism was fought by attack and defense of marital doctrines associated with it. The issue of marriage reform was likewise debated under a cloud of accusations and denials of socialist propaganda.

A FEMALE FREE ENQUIRER

As long as Robert Owen was present or nearby, his son, Robert Dale Owen, more or less accepted his father's thinking. Even when he disagreed and said so, he always found some justification for the elder Owen's position. But when, with the failure of the New Harmony experiment and the official departure of the leaders for New York and points east, the two were separated, the influence lost its potency. Another as strong replaced it. Robert Dale Owen lacked the physical vigor and personal qualities necessary for lecturing and debating. His role in youth was always played in study rooms and editorial offices. He needed a strong, attractive personality to supplement his own. And so, when Frances Wright appeared on her second visit to the United States in 1827, she promptly took over. A dominant and aggressive personality, she had an age advantage of six years over Owen. Miss Wright, a Scotswoman of free-thinking convictions, had long before decided that she would not be trampled on. It was in her nineteenth year that she experienced the force of the materialistic philosophy of Epicurus. From this point onward her sympathy for all revealed religion waned and gradually turned into intolerance. She became so anti-religious that she even disliked Voltaire's deism because it too was flavored with religious preconceptions. Her philosophical outlook had a clear preference for the revelations of material nature as they were being interpreted by the observations and experiments of the physical sciences. Her idea of human nature assumed that mind and body acted as a unit. The separate existence of a soul was incomprehensible to her.

Such was the frame of mind of the girl who in her early twenties decided to tour the United States because of its promising democratic liberalism. Both she and her sister Camilla spent the years 1818 to 1820 doing a grand tour of America, visiting or interviewing some of its outstanding citizens. Her first published work, *Views of Society and Manners in America,* was a collection of letters she had written in the course of her travels. Frances Wright could hold her own with the best. Within a short period after her return to England she made the acquaintance of General Lafayette, an acquaintance which became so intimate that his plan to adopt her as his step-daughter was abandoned only because of tremendous family pressure. When in the early months of 1824 it seemed good for the General's political health—his fortunes had just taken a severe beating in France—that he accept an official invitation to visit the United States, the Wright sisters were persuaded to accompany him.

Visits with Jefferson, Madison, and other leading figures in the same year aroused Frances Wright's interest in several American problems, among which was that of slavery. The following year found her traveling about with the emancipationist George Flower, looking for a location on which to carry out a great experiment. The plan was to purchase slaves whose labor at the new colony of Nashoba in Tennessee would amortize the cost of their emancipation. Free white workers were also invited to join this planned society of liberty and equality. Novices were to live in the colony for six months before the entire resident population voted on their application for permanent residence. Admission of a husband or wife did not automatically permit the inclusion of the other, nor of any children past the age of fourteen. Each resident was to be accepted only on his own merits.

The experiment failed. The economic burden was insurmountable. The slave group, having been practically dehumanized by their previous state of bondage, proved more than passively useless; they were obstacles. The white inhabitants confirmed the New Harmony experience; they were not prepared mentally and physically for the exigencies of a transitional society. Robert Dale Owen joined the Nashoba group at Miss Wright's invitation in the Spring of 1827, when the failure of New Harmony was conceded. Disillusioned, he was glad to accompany Frances on a trip to Europe necessitated by her very poor state of health. In their absence, James Richardson, one of the three resident trustees, had sent extracts from the records of the society to the editor of the abolitionist *Genius of Universal Emancipation* with *carte blanche* to publish them. The editor, Benjamin Lundy, promptly did,—much to the chagrin of the absent leaders, for this broadcast of details concerning the principles of family life encouraged among the newly arrived slaves helped considerably to build public opposition to the experiment. Richardson's impolitic act hastened the blackening of Nashoba's eye.

On the trip back from Europe, Miss Wright wrote and then published in the *New Harmony Gazette* (February 6, 1828) her "Nashoba; explanatory notes, respecting the nature and objects of the institution of Nashoba, and the Principles upon which it is founded. . . ."

She apparently intended to win her way back to public grace after the unfortunate *Genius of Universal Emancipation* incident. What she suffered, for her effort, was a lifelong plague on her reputation. Whenever in the years following she protested that she had never attacked marriage on a public platform, her detractors could dig up the "Explanatory Notes." Nashoba made her *persona non grata* in the South because of its attack on the color line. The "Notes" brought her disrepute in practically all circles. A few liberal papers received the "Notes" cordially, remarking upon their daring and intimating that this sort of thing was good—in Nashoba only. James Madison summed up the public reaction in a letter to Lafayette saying, "She has I fear created insuperable obstacles to the good fruits of which they [her talents] might be productive by her disregard or rather open defiance of the most established opinion & vivid feelings. Besides her views of amalgamating the white & black population so universally obnoxious, she gives an éclat to her notions on the subject of Religion & of marriage, the effect of which your knowledge of this Country can readily estimate."

What had Fanny (the familiar name by which her enemies referred to her) said? Among other things she had openly declared that the marriage laws which were observed outside the pale of Nashoba were to be disregarded inside it. Under the new dispensation neither male nor female had any claim, right or power over any member of the opposite sex except what was freely offered on the basis of mutual affection. A woman could not forfeit her individuality even if she wanted to. Freedom of the affections had been usurped on the rather plausible ground that parents had to be kept together to care for their children. What of the terrible fate of children in discordant homes? What of the natural rights of children called illegitimate because their fathers were able to escape legal responsibility? These were but a hint of the evils to which irrational marriage institutions gave birth. Look at the distortion of the sexual relationship in general. Look into hospitals and asylums. Consider the anxieties of parents of young men. Witness the parental grief for daughters whose health languishes beneath "the unnatural repression of feelings and desires inherent in their very organization. . . ." See how the legal system condemned some women to vicious restraint and others to vicious excess, while men are consigned to "debasing licentiousness, if not loathsome brutality."

Prostitution had been regularly defended as the best available means of controlling population growth. Frances Wright called it nonsense. The way to keep population down is to educate people to a realization that they must bring into the world only as many beings as they can comfortably feed, clothe, and educate. Restraint born of fear and religious prejudice inevitably led to error and failure. A more thorough acquaintance with all forms of human behavior and their consequences would accomplish the desired result. So why not change our false conceptions of right and wrong, and set humanity on a direct course toward the judicious employment of its affections and appetites? Do not ask a father and mother if they are married, but rather if they can educate and maintain their offspring. Encourage youth to act on the basis of reason and after intelligent enquiry. For example, when you would restrain the passion of irresponsible youth, do not label their action "criminal"; point out that the children of young parents are very often (sic) weak and unfit. Previous attempts to frighten people into having small families have had an effect only on the cultivated classes who were capable of breeding superior children. There was no question but that, in England especially, it had been the educated, well-bred, independent woman who had avoided the shame of "unlegalized connection" as well as the slave state of matrimony. Education was the way to adjustment, not obeisance to an artificial, malignant morality.

If Miss Wright had controlled her pen this one time, things would have gone much better for her. Her anti-religious ideas, her labor activities, her plans for public education, and her defiant appearances as a lady lecturer in public theatres would in themselves have provoked opposition; but no one could have accused her of hawking sexual promiscuity. Only once had she spoken of marriage in a public lecture, and then in answer to an insistent clerical provocateur among her audience in Cincinnati. The published lectures (which she delivered in much the same form and words in city after city) show nothing on the marriage question. Yet critic after critic made reference to remarks she never uttered. She was even named by the *Wabash Telegraph* as the anonymous author of the birth-control treatise *Every Woman's Book*, a prospectus of which had come out of the Owen-Wright printing establishment without the knowledge of either proprietor. It turned out that the author was the English radical Richard Carlile, pirater of some four or five *Queen Mab* editions.

It was far from Fanny's wish to get mixed up in matters like these. Her real motives for taking to the lecture platform in the United States were twofold: to increase her waning funds and to counteract a wave of revivalist fanaticism. Three different sects were in the process of promoting emotional excesses, wrecking families, and milking poor frontiersmen of whatever they had in ready cash. She asked her audiences to figure up the monetary cost of clergies and the churches, hard-earned dollars put into "clothing and feeding travelling preachers, who fill your streets and highways with trembling fanatics, and your very forests with frantic men and hysterical women." Of course, once she warmed up to her subject, it was but a step to attack all ritualized religion and the irrational mysticism that went with it.

Her speeches must have been effective. The press of the big cities, which liked her appearance, bearing, and manners, gave her frequent notices in a tone which was very reminiscent of the elder Owen's reception: nice fellow—too bad he has such radical ideas. The local ministerial groups and solid citizen forces deplored the immorality of a woman appearing in public as she did. On occasion, vegetables and other missiles were hurled at her from the audience. In one city a group of social leaders tried to force the local press into meeting Fanny's appearance with silent neglect. Door-to-door visitations were resorted to in order to keep people from patronizing an announced lecture. Lights were turned out at Abner Kneeland's Second Universalist Congregation in New York, leaving an audience of two thousand in total darkness. A fire was started at the Masonic Hall in an attempt to smoke out an audience two-thirds of which were women.

Frequently protesting her innocence and sincerity, this latter-day Mary Wollstonecraft struck back whenever an opportunity arose. Her position of influence on the *Free Enquirer* (formerly the *New Harmony Gazette*) after she and the younger Owen had shifted their political and publishing activities to New York, gave her as frequent opportunity as she wished. The *Free Enquirer* was a medium for disseminating the ideas of all free enquirers, whether they originated in the Owen-Wright group or were abstracted from any congenial text upon which the editors happened. It is, indeed, somewhat difficult to say which of the ideas were her own, which were Owen's, and which were the common possession of the whole company.

She probably shouldered more of the responsibility—and credit—for the proposal of a national system of education than she should have. Her pieces "On Existing Evils and their Remedy," her "Lectures on Knowledge," and other items revealed a fully developed political philosophy proceeding hand in hand with a program of universal education. A nation's strength depended on the united force of its citizens. Their equality was a guarantee of united thought and action. But equality functioned best when people were homogeneous with regard to their patterns of culture. To achieve this homogeneity, our people "must be raised in national institutions as children of a common family, and citizens of a common country." Hence a national system of free education for all from the age of two through college age. Hence an educational program including board and clothing, paid for out of a common fund established by levying a tax on all, plus a property tax. There was to be no distinction at all among children in granting educational opportunities. Security for the next generation was thus secured regardless of the wealth or poverty of their parents. The *Southern Review* aimed a query at a sensitive spot: Would Miss Wright still talk of using taxpayers' money for the education and support of children (legitimate and otherwise) of paupers and shiftless people if *she* were the mother of children? Replied the undaunted Frances: The more so were she a mother; and did anyone want to argue further? Upon this, her Southern questioner remarked uncomfortably that he had meant no personal offense, that he had said all he wanted to say and was ready to drop the argument.

Free enquirers were not ones to have the next to the last word. If lying, misquoting journalists (this time in New York) said that Frances Wright sought to reduce the morality of women to a system of convenience, she came up with the answer that she desired to elevate the morality of men *and* women to a system of convenience. If a correspondent, "Vindicia," suggested that there would be no disposition to break the marriage oath if it were unbreakable, she responded with a lecture on the degrading effects of superstitious oaths upon morale. This she supplemented with a treatise on how the marriage law gives impunity and privilege to brutality, ill-temper, neglect, hypocrisy, and violence. This brought "Vindicia" into line, with the reservation that man's nature was still evil and required a corrective *system* suited to his ways.

"Vindicia's" reasoning powers were deserving of praise, but she had fallen into the same error as had other audiences. No one was yet proposing systems. Listeners were merely being urged to employ the tools of knowledge and science toward a more satisfactory human adjustment. The issues were being misconstrued, and frequently on purpose. The discourses on the nature of knowledge and on the first principles of the moral sciences had been interrupted by heckling cries of "She wants to abolish marriage," or, "She denies the existence of God." Red herrings, all of them. The marriage contract could not constitute a subject for separate discussion even if one so wished; and one did not in any case. Marriage formed "*only an item in a system of coercive law*" which needed investigation in its entirety. Confucius, Socrates, Epicurus, and Jesus had exercised the privilege of probing into the mainsprings of human life with good results. Frances Wright was asking the world to join her in sharing in the privilege and in the results.

The laudable penchant for following out an idea and tracking it down rarely got the fiery enquirers out of a hole. The more deeply they dug, the more difficult it was to climb out. Yet a few of the communications to the *Free Enquirer* were certainly selected for their provocative value. A letter from "Philanthropos" of Cincinnati drew from Miss Wright detailed replies to fifteen separate questions on God, the immortality of the soul, standards of virtue, and the marriage contract. One from "M. W." told of a weak husband who, though an intelligent mechanic, threw away the family income on drink. Married four years, with three children, the mother might have obtained a job to support the family; but unfortunately the process of family increase could probably not be stopped. The girl's father would not help out because she had married a mechanic against his preference for a minister or lawyer. Furthermore, the father claimed, the young mechanic was a habitual drunkard because he was a skeptic. An excellent frame into which Miss Wright could work education, class relations, faith, marriage, and birth control. And she did, pointing out among other things that the "immoral" French knew how to equate family size and income. Moreover, why should not a woman have the privilege of choosing only "a suitable father for her children, and to leave her companion when irreclaimably addicted to habits injurious to her and her progeny? . . . But I check my pen. To a corrupt generation truths such as these are unsavory. To the few who, like our interesting correspondent, have hearts to feel and minds to distinguish, the present hints are addressed."

With and without direct provocation Miss Wright took occasion to deliver light and heavy blows against the twin menace of religion and religiously sanctioned matrimony. It might be a moral derivable from a story about a respectable merchant who had been driven to drink by religious differences with his wife. It could be a retelling on the fable of the Fury, Erynnis, who, in the manner of Tom Paine's "Cupid and Hymen," tricked Cupid out of his power over love and transferred authority to the marriage imp, Hymen. Then again, a revision of the Massachusetts laws giving a woman some property settlement upon divorce would call for an article on the "Rights and Wrongs of Woman." The very lectures on knowledge opened the door wide to a commentary on the education of women toward independence as individuals, or on equality in the social relationship of marriage. Male readers were exhorted to try to understand that the old idea of woman as a high-class servant or as a plaything was undermining the efficiency of the social organism. It was a certainty that men would rise or fall to the level to which they educated women.

The opposition could not deny that. For a great part of the way, Frances Wright made obvious sense. Newspapers often reported that she had not said anything to bear out the shady reputation that had preceded her. They also reported what she was reputed to have said elsewhere, sometimes acknowledging that they were writing from hearsay, and sometimes not. The *Philadelphia Album*, speaking of her fine talk on equality, thought equality could be carried too far. There had been reports, which had been circulated without any word of denial, that she was for a merging on equal terms of the white and Negro populations. Of course, slanderers probably exaggerated her original statement. It would be well, "especially after listening to her intelligent and beautiful address," continued the *Album*, to have a clarification on this point from her own life. The last heard from her on this matter was that she was hastening to catch the Providence steampacket at the moment but would elucidate at her first opportunity.

Indignation was again the keynote when Niles' *Weekly Register* (January 24, 1829) editorialized on her lectures at Baltimore, Philadelphia, and New York, where she was supposed to have advocated giving free reign to the inclinations, and doing away with distinctions between natural and illegitimate children and their parents. Indeed, she had not mentioned anything like it and the *Free Enquirer* had to take this usually accurate if conservative journal to task for its carelessness.

A good example of popularization by notoriety was furnished by a series of *Twelve Letters to Robert Dale Owen by an Observer*. These letters were originally published in a Philadelphia newspaper over the initials "W. Y." and afterwards printed by Thomas Kite of Philadelphia. They constituted a call to arms against the poison of infidelity which, if unchecked, would undermine the foundation of national prosperity; for, linked to this prosperity was the security of law, liberty, prosperity, religion, and the family. The truth had to be made known. Look at the dreaming Epicureanism of her "Three Days in Athens"! Note her suggestions (actually Owen's) of a contract of parentage to replace marriage! See this piece of logic about her not being able to observe the difference between a legitimate and an illegitimate child! And the proposal of National Education—a saddling of the virtuous with the burdens of the careless. Too bad so talented a woman should have become associated with such as Owen, Jennings, and the others. She has run riot for the love of fame. "To be famous she has consented to become infamous in the estimation of the wise and the good. . . ." A woman's place was in the home. Her sphere was not necessarily inferior, but different. If a woman wanted to write for publication, that was all right; "but it is better to read a woman's thoughts, than to hear them from the pulpit or the playhouse. It is a vitiated taste which countenances female quixotism; and quackery in divinity or politics is as bad as quackery in medicine. These mountebanks in morals, and rope dancers in politics, are dangerous doctors when they are permitted to tamper with the body politic." Why could not the intelligent Miss Wright confine herself to the beautiful, sentimental writing of a Mrs. Sigourney?

If she had, she would have avoided becoming the caricature of feminine disrepute in the eye of the general public. As it was, when her marriage to the Pestalozzian educator, Phiquepal D'Arusmont, was made public, newspaper comment was marked by incredulity. *The Ariel* noted the event as a contradiction and went on to quote at length the *New York American's* tale of this modest, intelligent woman and her "fall." She had defied the conventions of the world and had, as was inevitable, lost her respectability. Her "strong but perverted mind had taken up some ridiculous idea concerning the position which woman ought to maintain in the world. . . ." This must be a lesson to other women who might contemplate breaking out of their proper sphere.

Reports like this one were vague enough not to bother a woman of Frances Wright's rugged temperament. Other incidents, like the unauthorized publication of a letter she had written to Robert Jennings urging him to come and help her at Nashoba, must have made her bitter. The letter had repeated "dear Jennings" more frequently than was necessary, and had urged him to settle his wife with her father before leaving his home to come South. But the damaging evidence had been published before she could explain that she had advised this because Jennings' wife's health was too poor to face the asperities of life at Nashoba. And this was neither the first nor the last of nasty intimations. There had been Lafayette, and again her fellow-traveler, Robert Dale Owen.

Nor did the press forget Fanny Wright after she had accepted marriage herself and had all but left the public arena. People found reason to recall her in many connections. In 1837, the pious *Advocate of Moral Reform* printed a letter with a lesson under the title of "Tendency of Fanny Wright's Doctrines." The story was about a married woman whose reading of Fanny Wright's works led her to stop loving her husband and finally to leave him and take up with another man. Again in 1845, the publication of Margaret Fuller's *Woman in the Nineteenth Century* brought back to the editorial mind of the *New York Herald* memories of Frances Wright's lectures in the Park Theatre and the Hall of Science in New York. An innuendo about Miss Fuller's remarks on eastern harems plus the *Herald's* wise-cracking technique in connecting the two provoked Miss Wright to a full statement of her views. The letter was reprinted in the *Workingman's Advocate* (March 8, 1845) which, at that late date, was doing a good deal of reporting on the activities of the Owen group.

The letter reiterated the claim that at no time had its author expressed any preference for a "free and easy" system of marriage. Nor had she advocated any change in or repeal of existing laws on marriage. Her one public statement had been made at Cincinnati where she had allowed herself to be taunted by a Boston clergyman into saying things which he and the perverted press thereafter garbled and distorted. What she had said was that marriage could not be discussed by itself, but only in connection with morals or law; that the current moral system was erroneous and the legal system utterly worthless; that she would do her best to rid society of both not by subversion, but by urging a system of education calculated to inspire women with self-respect and dignity, and men with honor. With women and men mutually independent, society would come under sane regulation. Children would be provided for in a contract of parenthood, the same contract replacing the present slave contract of marriage which held parents coupled in chains.

We might as well make ourselves clear, stormed the self-righteous Fanny, since the *Herald* asks for it. No one had any intention of educating the public on marriage and the relations of the sexes. "What the one does for the regulation and elevation of the other, may be seen in our streets, our brothels, our houses of private assignation, our judicial courts, and even legislative records. . . ." There was clear evidence also in the behavior of citizens in the most highly revered professions. Yes, a glance at the very columns of the *Herald* would provide samples of the habits of society! And when a social reformer wants to educate men and women to honest independence, the achievement of which would remove all social problems, sexual and otherwise, the cry about "corrupting morals" is raised.

But men would have to "keep" women as long as women were equipped for nothing better. Men themselves would suffer by the arrangement until they found out "that slavery is a losing game between the sexes, as between the colors, [and then] we may begin to look out—not for *abolition,* but for reformation, justice, and universal emancipation." The *Herald* had provoked it; here it was, albeit in slightly circumscribed form. Miss Wright never speculated in public, as she did in private correspondence, on the possibilities of solving the slavery question through miscegenation.

ROBERT DALE OWEN

As between Frances Wright and her partner in business, politics, and philosophy, Robert Dale Owen, it is likely that Owen did most of the digging and constructing while Wright exhibited the product to public view. When the two were co-publishers and co-editors of the *New Harmony Gazette* and later the *Free Enquirer,* it was Owen who spent long hours in the editorial offices answering critics, debating in print, and ranging far and wide in the contemporary press for printable materials in every new area of politics, sociology, and science. For a while the chief topic of discussion was theology, but not to the exclusion of materials on the reform of civil and criminal law, capital punishment, and the civil and property rights of women. New findings in physiology, phrenology (the psychology of the day), hygiene, medicine, and diet were also commented upon or treated at great length.

It most certainly was Owen's idea to print extracts from *Queen Mab* in 1829 and to publish the entire poem, including its footnotes, in 1831. The same may be said of the simultaneous printing in the

Free Enquirer of a tabloid version of the poem with a full quotation of the poet's views on the abolition of marriage. Owen did in fact remark that Shelley's picture of the future was perhaps too rosy. However, that was a poet's privilege; and who knew but that revolutions would not get us there more quickly than we thought. He noted, too, in his publisher's blurb, that "the notes . . .which constitute its [the poem's] chief value, occupy more than half the volume." "Gleanings from the Papers of Percy Bysshe Shelley" also carried on the acknowledgement of the free enquirer's indebtedness to the poet. For quotations against religion, d'Holbach and Shelley were drawn on most heavily. The *Free Enquirer's* series of biographies on apostles of skepticism and reason, treated Shelley fourth, after Voltaire, Hume, and Godwin. Henry D. Robinson's rather long-winded treatment of Shelley stressed his anti-religious feelings and belief in human perfectibility, and also defended Shelley's marital conduct and views on morals in general. Owen also took the opportunity through the columns of the *Free Enquirer* to urge his fellow publishers to issue such standard works as Wollstonecraft's *Vindication,* Godwin's *Political Justice* and Constantine Volney's freethinking *The Ruins; or, A Survey of the Revolutions of Empires.* He offered to exchange with any publisher who took up the suggestion copies of Frances Wright's and his own works, their edition of *Queen Mab and* of Tom Paine's *Age of Reason.*

The younger Owen entered upon his investigation of family questions rather reluctantly. He expressed himself with perfect candor in commenting on a communication from a gentleman in Illinois who fully agreed on the weaknesses of legislative interference in family relationships. He knew the subject to be an extremely ticklish one. He was acquainted with the social penalties of running counter to prevailing traditions and prejudices. He was aware that his initial assumption, that indissoluble marriage was an immoral institution, was a dangerous one with which to start. But this evil institution was high on the *New Harmony Gazette's* agenda and what had to be done had to be done. The struggle between expediency and duty is apparent in these words, that amount almost to an apology for sincerity:

> If I am in error, it is most conscientiously. I have adopted my present views not easily, not hastily, not willingly; but slowly and after many misgivings and much reflection. And even after my reason was convinced, my early feelings strove to repress the conviction.
> . . . And if I am to speak on the subject at all, I must speak honestly. If I lose the respect of any man by doing so, it will be proof, not of my demerits but of his intolerance.

No man, however mistaken I might think him, ever lost my respect, because of his honesty.

The anxious note in this editorial statement had reference to more than a future course of policy. In the very same issue of the *Gazette* there appeared Owen's essay "Of Chastity" and an article on the "Moral State of the Tonga People," furnishing extracts from Mariner's *Tonga Islands*. This was not the first use of the anthropological approach to problems of family behavior. The *Gazette* had previously included bits on Turkish marriages, and the African notion of matrimony. The anthropological Utopia of New Britain was introduced by way of "Recollections of Subjects Observed by the Author, and of Observations made by the inhabitants of New Britain during his residence among them." Early marriages, it was reported, were encouraged among the New Britons by guaranteeing a "portion" to each and every male and female, whether orphaned or with living parents. Where land was owned by women and young orphans, their neighbors cultivated it for them. The natives here boasted that, by eliminating sex and class privileges, they had diminished the problem of immorality.

These were casual pieces not designed to startle the reader. The Tonga article described an extraordinarily loose system of moral regulation under which several affiliations were possible during a lifetime without moral censure. The point was that people did not take undue advantage of their freedom. It was workable and unattended by hardship for the adults or the children, whose mothers, married or divorced, provided full and tender care. Boy and girl children were instructed on matters of sex somewhere between the ages of eight and ten; they showed no ill effects—for only when such matters were treated as secrets, were children likely to be overcurious.

The essential point of this story, a point which Owen was emphasizing in his "Ideas on Propriety," "Of Chastity," and "Of Constancy," was that a new standard of chastity would soon be available as a product of the anthropological approach. His hypothetical statement of it at the moment was that the standard should involve consistency "with public decorum and due order and regularity in the social state, without tending to enervate the mind or debase the character of man." Were the Turcomans right about their conception of female honor when they permit the murder of a betrothed girl by a jealous swain for an ever so minor infraction? Were we much better in our prudish ideas of female modesty and chastity? Finally, was there any direct relationship between propriety and public opinion? Indeed not! These wide variations of practice illustrated the lack of an exact correlation between decorum and real virtue, or even between decorum and good taste. "So far is this conclusion from the truth, that we frequently find the selfish veiling their vices under the most punctilious orthodoxy, and see in the unprincipled, the most zealous sticklers for the popular forms of virtue."

There seemed to be no principle of pure reason that could be universally applied. Sincerity, charity, moderation, respect for the feelings and beliefs of others—these things added up to propriety. There had been a confusion between *popularity* of opinions and actions and their propriety. This was a matter which needed clarification.

Tolerance of the other man's beliefs apparently did not extend in Owen's mind to celibate chastity. The reverence paid it in our society, he thought, was a holdover from "monkish asceticism" which held that pain was virtue. That sort of thing was no longer popular. The new idea of chastity was associated with innocence and praiseworthy self-denial. Granted that excesses were injurious, did it follow that deprivation or repression was beneficial? Certainly not. Purity was a positive aspect of the expression of affection. It had little to do with legal restriction. If chastity meant "the sincere expression and disinterested exercise of our affections," it was to be prized even in its rarity. If it meant concealment or loveless legality, Owen had little respect for the word, for it was "a sanctioner of vice."

Constancy in itself was no virtue. In a state of perfection, perhaps, sticking to what you had was a virtue. But in a world bent on progress, constancy was foolish. The rule applied very well to constancy in love. If one were thinking only of examples of perfect mating, or if one were prescribing for some godly race, constancy could do no harm. Where there had been, or could be, no error, there was little need for correction. But man has to learn from experience. Deprive him of a second chance and you withdraw the right of fallible man to correct his errors. In a hypothetical society where there was no legal bondage, there would probably exist a good constancy ratio. Certainly there would be more *real* and less *affected* constancy. Moreover, human variations and individual differences would have to be reckoned with. Some would be happy with constancy and remain so. Others might seek their happiness in change. In any case, the prudishness connected with the present system would disappear.

Marriage practices, new theories and policies, and the position accorded women in them, gave Owen and his fellow editors an index of the social ideas of community minded sects. The Moravian practice of having the elders select mates for young people seemed far from desirable in spite of the enthusiastic testimony in its favor. Owen liked the proposals of the St. Simonians who promised women a future of equality in politics, property, and marriage. He would not underwrite their hierarchic system and bureaucracy, but he indicated that

St. Simonian ideas should be disseminated for what they were worth. He also praised the Shakers for their pleasant, non-competitive personalities, but reproved them for their irrational celibacy. So forceful was he in his denunciation of this evil, which he felt more than tipped the balance against everything good in the Shaker system, that Warder Cresson felt constrained to write a full explanation of this aspect of Shakerism for the *Free Inquirer*. Shortly afterward, in 1831 (the year in which Owen looked over the St. Simonians and the Shakers), *The Free Inquirer's* editor of that period, Amos Gilbert, printed a portion of William Owen's diary concerning the Shakers to supplement the discussion which had already taken place. Of the Mormons, Robert Dale Owen had little to say except that this "infatuated people" were again on the move. Mormonism was a "strange superstition that is now springing up in our country." When Owen was writing, the Mormons had not yet adopted polygamy.

The prolific literary output of this politician, editor, and publisher was amazing. Owen's interests in human beings and their social institutions were as broad and varied as the situations and permutations that occurred in life itself. During the years of his active editorship, his initials were signed to innumerable columns. When it was not some problem he picked for treatment, it was an 'answer to some benevolent or malevolent critic of his own ideas, of his father's, or of Frances Wright's. She was away so much on lecture engagements, that he found himself fighting her battles as his own. Actually the two differed so little that he automatically assumed the greater share of the debate that appeared in published form.

When "Gama" of the *New York Correspondent* addressed Frances Wright on the subject of divorce, Robert Dale Owen was the one who rebutted. "Gama" took the view deriving from eighteenth-century natural law theory, that marriage was not primarily for the mere gratification of the parties concerned, but for the propagation and nurture of the young of the species. No arrangement could replace the natural love of parents for their children. Miss Wright's limited view of the matter was a sensual, selfish one. The equal incidence of males and females in the population indicated clearly that nature meant to pair one man with one woman. No woman of practical sense would agree to a system which gave a man of forty license to leave his mate and find a younger partner. Nor would a woman of delicacy like, while her husband was making love to her, to contemplate the prospect that he meant it for only two or three years more. This writer's dim view of women's competence also lent substance to his argument that a plan which made divorce available was bad. He reasoned that a man who had deserted his wife would desert his children too; the control of education would then be left in the hands "chiefly of the weaker and more incompetent sex."

Owen apparently did not notice the opening that "Gama" had left for him in this reactionary statement. Either that, or he chose to meet the central issue on its own merits. Wright and Owen, he said, were the last ones to preach the neglect of children. On the contrary they would bind parents by law, whether they were married or unmarried, to assume the burdens of nurturing and educating their children. The sexual connection for motives of immediate pleasure alone was a flagrant crime. The free enquirers would protect children even more than "Gama." They would insist that any pair of parents who could not set an example of harmonious living for their children *must* separate—for their children's sake. Now, with regard to the burlesque on promising love for only two or three years hence, man could be "rational and amiable at one time." An oath of constancy till death placed love in a perjured state. Wherein did the acknowledgement of possible failure in love foreordain or hasten failure in marriage? Only the ostrich shut his eyes to evil with the hope of avoiding it.

As an illustration of how neither legal marriage nor its correlate, prostitution, were necessary social institutions, Owen wrote an article for the *Free Enquirer* (May 28, 1831) on "Marriage and Placement." Placement was an alternative then practiced in Haiti. It was a tacit compact into which a woman entered, retaining both her name and her property. The agreement could be abrogated with but a day's warning. It was respectable, having received the sanction of both Petion, the Jefferson of Haiti, and his successor, Boyer. The experience was that ten placements took place for every one marriage. The children of placed persons had the same rights as all other children. Naturally, clergymen frowned upon this innovation; it deprived them of fees for performing ceremonies. But if constancy and harmony were the criteria of morality, "placement" was far superior to marriage. There had been ten separations of the legally married for one voluntary separation of the placed. Libertinism was confined to the married, as were tyranny and viragoism. The incidence of prostitution was also reduced. How did this happen? For one thing, the absence of pecuniary considerations and other extraneous motives guaranteed the Haitians against ill-assortment in these voluntary unions. Again, public opinion made it unpopular to switch mates often. Moreover, the desire for change was not too frequent because of the sincerity of the initial choices.

Somehow, out of the mass of printed pages that Owen had filled with his marriage views, the article on placement made the greatest impression on his contemporary enemies among the clergy as well as on the free-love agitators of later decades. It was the piece which stood out too for the very scant tribe of American marriage historians. His oversympathetic description of placement produced the impression that he was advocating its general adoption, so that, despite his many pronunciamentos in the past (on top of such well-rounded explanations of his and Frances Wright's views on religion, education, and marriage as the one published in the *Free Enquirer* as far back as October 14, 1829), he was called upon to debate, refute, and elucidate over and over again.

The placement article did not really start something new. It merely added a block to the tall barricade behind which some very clever opponents were hiding. The *Observer's Twelve Letters to Young Men,* dealing with the Wright-Owen philosophy, was amply supplemented by an abusive pamphlet from the pen of William Gibbons, a Quaker physician of Wilmington, Delaware, and a voluminous correspondence from the more generous Delaware Quaker, Benjamin Ferris. Ferris had checked Gibbons' facts and had publicly certified them to be true. Owen complained that this certification of facts had been a subtle endorsement of the original abusive motive. The exchange of remarks ran on for some time. And then, there was Thomas Whittemore, noted author, preacher, and editor of the *Trumpet and Universalist Magazine* (Boston), who had to be taken in hand for printing a series of misleading articles by the Universalist, Linus S. Everett, under the title "The Rise and Progress of Infidelity in America." These articles, whose first publication in the *Trumpet* was anonymous, appeared again in pamphlet form in 1831 under the signature of Everett, who was then editor of the *Gospel Advocate.* The title of the pamphlet edition was *Exposure of the Principles of the Free Enquirers.*

The charges which Owen had to dodge in his running defensive battle from 1829 to 1831 and thereafter included everything his enterprising enemies could dig up by careful investigation. Gibbons' *An Exposition of Modern Skepticism, in a letter, addressed to the editors of the Free Enquirer,* a pamphlet which went through three editions in 1829 and 1830, went straight back to James Richardson's maladroit releases to the *Genius of Universal Emancipation* from which the following was quoted:

> Sunday evening, June 10, 1827.—Met the slaves. James Richardson (one of the trustees) informed them, that last night, Mamselle Josephine (a Quarteroon, or coloured woman) and he *began to live together;* and he took this occasion of repeating to them some views of *Color,* and of the *sexual relation.*

Luckily the Nashoba experiment had failed, commented Gibbons. For, if the restrictions of law and social opinion were removed, no parent would feel secure about the virtue of his growing daughters. Gibbons asked his readers to remember what happened to Mary Wollstonecraft in her ill-starred affair with Gilbert Imlay. Worthy of special note were her attempted suicide, her taking up with Godwin, and their subsequent concession to marital convention. This was a life-story well suited to illustrate what could happen if people listened to the group which was currently spreading similar ideas of infidelity in America. The evils ascribed to marriage by Owen and his coterie derived from their personal shortcomings, and were not inherent in the institutional arrangement as they alleged. Allow your moral delinquents any number of tries at marriage, said Gibbons, and you reap a harvest not of harmonious living but of progressive immorality. If "you [Owen] and your female reformer" think that your style of illegal relationship is pure, holy, and firm, why do you not agree to bind them with "human ceremonies"?

Gibbons' fury continued unabated. Traditional arrangements, he stormed, satisfied all the physical, psychological, and social needs of civilized peoples. They divided society into families which acted as sub-agents of social control. They settled the question of which woman was to live a settled, secure life with which man. Think, Gibbons implored his readers, of the animal-like feuds over women in a society which does not rigidly regulate marriage. As for public systems of education, remove the father's obligation to pay for his children's education, rid him of this and other parental duties, and he will behave like an animal, gratifying his "passions at a cheaper rate." The males of such an irresponsible society would never consent to pay taxes to maintain educational institutions. No people morally corrupt and devoid of religion ever would support public schools. The more Gibbons thought of it, the more he was convinced that Owen's "Science of human life" was nothing but a crude melange of wild or obscene notions and follies, which, could they be reduced to practice, would be found to be equally subversive of morals, order, government, and Christianity.

How Owen retained his composure upon reading this is hard to imagine, but he replied calmly that his writing had been addressed to the pure-hearted, leaving his readers to draw the conclusion that Gibbons was not of that number. He reiterated that whenever he had undertaken a search for the universal attributes of a sound morality, he had been met with charges of sanctioning prostitution and licentiousness, and of encouraging every man to abandon his wife. Thereupon, Frances Wright directed an appeal to the members of Gibbons' Quaker group in Wilmington, asking them to do the fair-minded thing, to read Owen's and her own statements in the *New Harmony Gazette* and *Free Enquirer*, files of which were available in their home town. She would not answer for James Richardson's indiscretion in the *Genius of Universal Emancipation*; it would avoid trouble and misunderstanding to have him answer for himself. With regard to Nashoba, she explained that her address at the time was directed to the discriminating few. As a physician, Gibbons should belong in that select group and should understand her attempt to explain how existing social customs were at war with human nature. If he did not understand her point, he should not be a physician. If he did understand, his attack upon her was dishonest.

For some reason, possibly because he smelled disaffection among some of the local Friends, Gibbons had a jury of upright neighbors read his pamphlet and certify to its accuracy. Thereupon Benjamin Ferris, one of the signers, became involved in a verbal brawl with Owen. He had added to the original document a précis, or, as Owen termed it, a "hypothetical enumeration of our principles." The items referring to marriage read, in this latest interpretative formulation, as follows:

> That you reprobate the Marriage Institute, as tyrannical and mischievous, and its forms as idle and offensive.
>
> That mutual inclination and consent are the only necessary preliminaries to sexual connections, where competent support and education for the offspring are provided, and that such connections may at any time be dissolved when such inclination ceases.
> That the Law and public opinion constraining single persons of adult age to preserve their chastity are injurious and absurd.

What was there to reply to this extension of Owen's logic which Owen had not already said in his explanations made to previous maligners? The old argument about the irrationality and insincerity of swearing love unto death was repeated, as were the old attacks on prostitution and celibacy and the redefinition of chastity, this time bearing Benjamin Franklin's seal of approval. One solid change could be noted—a flat statement that he, Robert Dale Owen, would no longer recommend the abolition of marriage in the present depraved state of society. At some time in the future, when human nature had been trained by public schools to reason, a revision of the law could be contemplated.

The threat, mentioned above, of a schismatic movement among Gibbons' religious cohorts was vague and merely tangential to his quarrel with free thought. Linus Everett, on the other hand, had to contend with real fifth-column activities within the Universalist Church. Starting with small questions and differences, the Universalist minister Abner Kneeland had become a big issue in sectarian circles. He had finally bolted his church and had become an avowed agnostic. He was at the moment acting as sales representative for Owen's *Moral Physiology,* America's first treatise on population adjustment by birth control. Everett had taken up arms to stop the flood of subversive activity which was spreading in all directions. He dipped back into the elder Owen's Declaration of Mental Independence and its three evils—which Frances Wright had expanded to seven at Nashoba. He dug up and published the letter (which Miss Wright claimed had been stolen and distorted) to Robert Jennings urging him to leave his wife up North and join the sisters Wright at Nashoba. Every vulnerable spot was further attacked, including Owen's *Moral Physiology,* which alone, said Everett, entitled its author to unqualified censure.

The struggle took on features that were more than merely personal. It emphasized the free-love motif because at that time it was the fashion to attack one's enemies in economics and religion with moralistic epithets, even as, today, the label "communist" is applied indiscriminately to political opponents. He was indeed not misrepresenting the earlier intentions of the Owen-Wright trio when he charged them with a sinister plan to overthrow the economic system, organized religion, and institutional marriage. But, in 1831, his bill of particulars was quite inaccurate.

Robert Dale Owen's letter of May 1831 to Thomas Whittemore, editor of the Boston *Trumpet,* would have brought some distinctions home even to Everett. The Owen of this letter still clung to the argument of insincerity and potential perjury in the marriage oath. He still preferred the noble principle of moral obligation which, he claimed, oaths tended to weaken. Nor did he yet see the point of forcing unwilling couples to remain together. This time he cited the poet Milton as authority for the inevitable failure of such a course of action. But doubt had entered Owen's mind about the lot of children in broken families. He now declared emphatically that their happiness should come first. He would insist on parents remaining together under all circumstances if a separation would hurt the children. Naturally, the decision would vary in each case, although it was still difficult for him to see how much good could come out of any bad marriage. He had also given some thought to the matter of divorce economics. He now felt that, upon separation, the family fortune should be divided equally between husband and wife; and, moreover, since women had not yet been trained for independent economic careers, their former husbands should be required to contribute toward their comfortable support. One more idea had occurred to him. It concerned the cases in which only one of the parties desired a separation,

What had happened to the former positive assertions about union and separation on a basis of individual choice? Apparently

Owen was dropping from the heights of Godwinian theory, and finding on his way down new aspects of earthly problems. Possibly Milton's careful, extended treatment of divorce served to remind him that there was more to it than the glib formula he had been using. As an editor of the *New Harmony Gazette* in 1828, he had probably chosen, and had seen through publication, serialization in seven instalments of the bard's essay on divorce (originally published in 1643). It would be interesting to know if Owen realized that this impressive piece of argumentation on the poet's part had been directly motivated by an unsuccessful marriage. The pamphlet, written and published within three months of Milton's wedding day, was the result of real experience with incompatibility. The bride had returned to her father's house at the end of one month of married life. The title of Milton's tract gives a good indication as to its approach: *The doctrine and discipline of divorce: restor'd to the good of both sexes, from the bondage of Canon law, and other mistakes, to Christian freedom, guided by the rule of charity.*

It was impossible to pin the stigma of personal motivation on Robert Dale Owen as one could with Milton. A few of his co-workers did engage in questionable antics, but not Owen. His severest critics could find no concrete evidence of misbehavior with which to confront him. He could, and did, introduce many of his daring essays with an unqualified statement about the purity of his personal conduct. He married Mary Robinson in 1832, and their life together had all of the qualities of that pure affection he had so frequently advertised.

SCIENCE AND SOCIETY

A true accounting of Owen and his friends must present them as having been genuinely engaged in the search for a science of society. Every aspect of human inquiry was drawn upon for its possible contribution to the enhancement of human welfare. The goal of their investigations was very close to that of Franklin's essay, "On True Happiness," which the *Free Enquirer* chose for quotation from the *Pennsylvania Gazette* of 1735. True happiness was to be found in order, moderation, and the preservation of health through temperance. This was the meaning of the enquirers' struggle against the separation of body and soul by religious theory. This was the background of their insistence upon the unity of muscle and brain, of physiology and morals. Hence the extracts from the *Journal of Health* on physical education, designed to lift girls out of their traditional frailty and so remove their invidious distinction of being the weaker sex. The articles on gymnastics for women repeated this lesson specifically. Owen himself wrote a leading article on "Fashionable Incarceration" in which he held that this "immoral action" would prove injurious to offspring. "Fashionable Incarceration" referred simply to tight corseting, a practice which Owen, for the sake of emphasis, likened to the vice of "young men running the debasing and health destroying career of libertinism, then to become fathers of a puny and peevish offspring." As far back as 1826, the *New Harmony Gazette* had reprinted *Jameson on Exercise,* pointing out the relationship of the physical state of fathers to the health of their progeny.

The social meaning of genetics also interested this group. In 1828 there were two instalments of "Extracts from Gregoire's Enquiry into the Intellectual and Moral Faculties of Negroes." In the year following, there appeared a quoted piece on the "Nonexistence of Hereditary Disorders," arguing that people did not inherit diseases like consumption, gout, and insanity, but only a predisposition to contract them. Readers were told that with proper precautions these diseases could be avoided, or their effects minimized.

The attention given to health education, hygiene, and physiological knowledge was perfectly consistent with the philosophy of free enquiry. As far as Owen was concerned, nine-tenths of all money spent on doctors could thus be saved by exercising common sense with regard to hygiene. Doctors admitted this, Owen contended, even though their incomes stood to suffer. Honest practitioners would agree that the hush-hush of prevailing custom brought many an unmarried girl and boy into their offices for treatment? As physiologists, doctors must condemn a morality that doomed one sex to unnatural restraints and made drinking libertines of the other. Owen suggested that the schools, instead of teaching Latin and Greek to youngsters, should teach them to take care of their minds and bodies. Upon this, a physician commented that Owen was right, except that doctors were very necessary to treat the ailments that come of natural causes. Owen argued back that for every illness attributable to nature, there were hundreds attributable to man's ignorance.

From the well-being of man to his education was but a short step. Owen's quasi-psychosomatic approach to the problems of humankind involved speculations on whom to educate, when and how to educate, and what to teach. Thence "The Effects of Slavery on the Education of Free Children," the national guardianship and public education plans, the quarrel with the *Southern Review* about the project for equal educational opportunity, and the insistence on equal rights for legitimate and illegitimate children. The enquirers' interest in phrenology was also associated with Owen's eagerness to find out what makes people tick and how to make them tick better. His review of Spurzheim's *Principles of Education founded on the Study of the Nature of Man* showed clearly enough that he was not swallowing whole all the mental fodder he came upon, for he was highly skeptical of Spurzheim's craniology. In another connection he criticized phrenological science for breaking human behavior up into thirty or forty propensities or traits, when it was obvious that a human being acted as a unit. But he did seize upon Spurzheim's premise that the brain was the center of the nervous system. Morality, if this were so, was rooted in human physiology, quite contrary to the assumptions of the legal profession and the clergy. And if this nervous system was a part of the mechanism of heredity, how important it was to learn a good deal about the person one married? How important not to sacrifice the future of one's children to present pleasure!

At this point advice on handling infants and children became pertinent. The importance of nursing children was mentioned. Readers were also warned against rocking them. The possible influence of diet on personality made it appropriate to discuss vegetarianism, Grahamism, and other current dietary systems. And, finally, the subject of sex education was specifically treated. The laws of propagation, suggested a communication to the *New Harmony Gazette,* should be taught to the extent to which children could understand them—first by recourse to the example of plants, then of animals, and last with regard to man himself. Two important reasons were offered to justify bringing such matters to children: to relieve their anxieties and to give them useful information. Knowledge of the facts of reproduction would benefit the race. It would encourage care of the physical constitution that was to be handed down to one's progeny. Sex needed as much attention as hunger and thirst. All were drives not subject to the will and "their activity must therefore be directed." How could we expect young people to repress their feelings if we did not warn them of the consequences of their conduct?

The little group of agile minds at New Harmony (and later at New York) worked in good conscience and with sincerity. Sometimes they produced solid sense; at other times they blurted out half-truths and utter nonsense. They could not claim the maturity of modern social science, but they were working towards it. Nor did they overlook anything that might contribute to an honest solution. No one's word was taken at its face value; no hostile critics with good intentions were treated with disrespect.

On many questions, a clear developmental pattern ran through the pages of the *Gazette* and *Free Enquirer.* From 1825 to 1833 some differences of opinion were seen to resolve themselves; and fresh differences cropped up. The subject of woman's role in society, for example, had an interesting history. In the *Gazette's* early years, a good deal of space was given to clichés about woman's softening and polishing effect on man. There were regular fill-ins describing how a delicate, virtuous, accomplished woman could bring ease, con-

fidence, refinement, and mental expansion to a man. The free enquirers accepted Mary Wollstonecraft's proposals to give women
educational equality with men; but there was no quick assumption
that all women should assume equality in all the affairs of men. The
question had to remain in tentative form until a generation of female
education should provide objective data on whether or not women
were suited for politics. The editorial writer of this opinion—either
Robert L. Jennings or Owen's brother, William—would give single
women the ballot, and that in deference to Mary Wollstonecraft's
opinion. Marriage created a problematic situation. When a woman
married the man of her choice, her husband became her political
representative by and with her own consent; they had but one common interest. On the other hand, if the marital choice had been made
because of parental pressure, or for any reasons other than voluntary ones, what then? In 1825 there was room for debate on this
question. Eight years later, editor Amos Gilbert, an ex-Quaker with
strong attachments to his former creed, reprinted a speech "On the
Necessity of a Proper Choice of Magistrates" which ridiculed the notion of being represented by a husband. The speech, by a pupil of
the British radical Richard Carlile, declared that one might as well
argue that each family could elect one of its members to represent it.

The eight years between 1825 and 1833 saw a variety of items on
the woman question. The rude reception given to Frances Wright's
"female" lectures called for strong arguments on equality. John
Milton, who had done so well on divorce, was taken to task for his
degrading estimate of the female mind and character in the lines

> Not equal, as their sex not equal seemed,
> For contemplation he, and valour formed,
> For softness she, and sweet attractive grace.

Owen himself felt constrained to voice objections to Washington
Irving's *Sketch Book* story, "The Broken Heart." Irving had mistaken
environment for nature in stating that a woman's life is a history of
her affections. The story, Owen admitted, was an accurate representation of reality in that a man's varied interests did help him over a
love disappointment that could easily wreck a woman for life. But
the author should have used his art to persuade readers to destroy
the double standard of intellect and social efficiency. After the sexual
revolution, "Then will the monopoly of sex perish with other unjust
monopolies; and women will not be restricted to one virtue, and one
passion, and one occupation."

Amid serious discussions of the literary treatment of marriage,
of laws which made a husband responsible for his wife's asocial behavior, of the philosophical implications of ceremonies and promises,

of property rights, and human rights, there was time and space for humor. Fielding's "Modern Glossary" definition of marriage, a sample of what American rationalists decried as sacrilegious ridicule, called it "A kind of traffic, carried on between the two sexes, in which both are constantly endeavoring to cheat the other and both are commonly losers in the end." A report of supposedly authentic statistics from a Brussels paper listed as in the thousands cases of "wives who have abandoned their husbands for lovers," "couples living at war under the same roof," and "couples who hated each other cordially but are keeping up appearances." The story of "The Sabbath School Superintendent" proved that truth was stranger than fiction. It told of a female Sunday school teacher who tracked down an absentee girl to a brothel where she was being kept by force. While the moral young lady was berating the brothel-keeper, a male colleague from the Sunday school appeared. The accusing question put to him was: "I am here looking for a girl student; what are you doing here?"

Miss Wright apparently accepted as genuine the humorous "Speech of Miss Polly Baker" which later scholarship has attributed to the ingenious Dr. Franklin. The piece was reputedly delivered to a Connecticut colonial court where Miss Baker was being prosecuted for the fifth time for having her fifth illegitimate child. So convincingly did she demonstrate that her conduct had patriotic motives—insofar as she had added five persons to the community without burdening it in the least—that one of the judges married her the next day. Miss Wright saw merit in her claim in the context of the unpopulated colonies.

In reply to the perennial innuendoes and charges of libertinism or free love-ism, Owen would calmly remark that such tactics were generally a cover for the immorality of the censor himself. He would also point out that it was easier to gain popularity upon the ruins of someone else's reputation than on virtues of one's own. On one occasion an anonymous donor sent him a copy of the annual report of the New York Magdalen Society. The implication was that prostitution was associated with the kind of marriage morals that Owen espoused. He suspected as much, and so proceeded to write for the *Free Enquirer* (July 23, 1831) a full outline of the statistical report in his hands. The feeling of disgust aroused in him by this portrait of vice in New York made it difficult to do the job. But he saw it as his duty; besides, it provided a grand setting for an attack on religious and moral standards.

The figures most assuredly came on good authority since the sponsors of the Magdalen Society were orthodox leaders of high standing. Twenty thousand women were engaged in prostitution in 1830, ten thousand in groups and ten thousand as individual entrepreneurs. Owen would discount fifty percent and call the total ten thousand.

Each received three visits daily, or, in all, 10,000,000 annually. At fifty cents per visit, that made five million dollars a year, exclusive of the money spent for liquor, board, taxis, theatres, etc. in connection with the trade. A total of some eleven million dollars was spent for vice in New York City alone. The economic consequences, let alone the personal and social ones, were sickening to contemplate. And the effects on the health of the women engaged in the trade! They showed a life expectancy of from three to five years from the date of beginning this career. Statistically speaking, one of every three marriageable females in some way or other received the wages of prostitution; one out of every six was an abandoned specimen of promiscuity. An analysis of male visitations (making all allowances for strangers in the city, for the distorting effects of averages in statistics, and even for exaggeration) showed that more than one-half of the male population, married and unmarried, were customers thrice weekly.

It made Owen shrink from the company of his neighbors. He wanted to run away to a place where people were less sordid than in the New York described by this report. It was unthinkable that the priceless possession of love should be bought and sold in the common market. But no! This could not be true of the free human affections. "Love has no price; and that which is sold *for* love, is a foul counterfeit. . . ." This was the effect of a Christianity which controls bodies and souls. What a job it had done! Eighteen hundred years of sincere effort had failed to eradicate this evil. And, addressing Arthur Tappan, the pious president of the organization which had issued the report on prostitution, Owen quoted: "Out of thine own mouth do I condemn thee." Amos Gilbert, apparently feeling that Owen had not used his opportunity fully, proceeded to point out that the male population had never received its share of censure. It was always the poor women who were blamed, some of whom had been lured or seduced into the business, some of whom had been recruited through poverty and destitution. Others had fallen into it through sheer ignorance. The preaching of Magdalen societies was helpful, but the *Free Enquirer's* job was to bring to society a study of efficient preventive measures. Sex education, marriage reform, and divorce reform constituted the answer.

The editors at New Harmony and New York had not given extended attention to the reform of divorce laws. Their thinking had taken the radical course of reforming marriage to forestall divorce. But always implicit was the idea that a liberalization of divorce laws was important to the program. The need for available divorce was indeed their argument for marriage reform. As one "old bachelor" argued in a humourous interchange on dog taxes and marriage taxes, if you permitted the government to collect a tax from all desiring divorce, you could abolish all other taxes and pay off the national debt in three years.

∽　∽

What Owen the visionary agitator failed to do in the early period, Owen the practical politician in the liberal ranks, labored hard to do later. After 1836, a political career in the Indiana Legislature and in the Indiana Constitutional Convention of 1850 gave him the chance to speak up for the property rights of women. He also had a hand in modifying Indiana's divorce laws to a minor extent. But his muddy reputation from the *Free Enquirer* years had stuck so well, that even the palliatives he spoke for in Indiana were subjected to smear tactics by fellow legislators and others. As late as 1860 he was drawn out of retirement by one of Horace Greeley's *Tribune* editorials on divorce and women's rights. Greeley, who was considered a dependable liberal in politics, adhered firmly to the Scriptural command with regard to divorce. One cause was ground for separation, and that was adultery. He would agree to work for the liberalization of property and other legal rights of women, but he was adamant on the question of divorce.

On March 1, 1860, Greeley was using his powerful editorial pen to oppose a move to modify the New York divorce laws. What more convenient for the occasion than to call Indiana a "paradise of free lovers" where lax divorce laws, authored by the lax morality of Robert Dale Owen, left men and women free to carry out their unrestrained impulses. The unjustly accused Owen immediately asked for the privilege of a hearing. A duel in the *Tribune* ensued. Owen offered the information that he had been instrumental in adding only one cause for divorce in Indiana, i.e., drunkenness for a two-year period; and the law had been carefully worded in order to prevent abuse. Indiana had done very well with its marriage and divorce laws, while New England and New York, *because* of their legislative rigidity, were notorious for low sex morals. Their laws had in fact necessitated adultery by requiring it for divorce proceedings. If Owen differed from Greeley it was in his effort to purify marriage "as the holiest of earthly institutions" by providing for legitimate divorce where necessary.

Greeley explained that Indiana had not reaped the evils which normally came of lax divorce laws because it was a young, rural State. Moreover, its inhabitants had for the most part been educated in the morality of older States. They had not been exposed to temptations born of crowds, luxury, and idleness. Furthermore, said he, alluding to Owen's wish to revise the marriage laws, if people wanted to practice some other form of sexual union, they must not misrepresent it by calling it "marriage." Indissoluble, monogamous marriage had proved itself superior to polygamy, concubinage, easy divorce, and their close relative, free love. For women oppressed by drunkards, there was separation from bed and board. Why leave the brute free to take advantage of a second woman? To what temptations, to what travesty on marriage does your "bed and board" separation lead, responded Owen. Besides, the Biblical formula for divorce had been designed for other times and other places. Greeley countered by saying that the word of Christ was eternal and universal. Owen thereupon wanted to know if the many Protestant states which had modified the eternal law were un-Christian? Greeley had the last word in an almost two-month-long debate—which was joined midway by a rabbi who felt that Owen's interpretation of the Old Testament was incorrect. Greeley's view won out in the legislature. Local bar associations and welfare agencies in New York State are still struggling for divorce law reform.

MORAL PHYSIOLOGY

Owen's declaration that he liked popularity very well, but that he liked independence better, applied with significant force to his public statements on population problems and population checks. As late as 1828 the assumption that class oppression was responsible for underproduction was still accepted by the Owen group. His father's essay, a "New View of Society," assured the readers of the *New Harmony Gazette* (1825) that with the aid of science and education, each person could produce ten times his needs. Investigation would prove, he told them, that the fear of overpopulation, at least until the whole earth was under cultivation, was a "mere phantom of the imagination, calculated solely to keep the world in unnecessary ignorance, vice, and crime. . . ." An extract from a pamphlet written by the Englishman Abram Combe confirmed this opinion for *Gazette* readers in 1828. The essential problem of a depressed country was its undersupply of consumer power.

At this time, Owen came under the influence of neo-Malthusian thought. He was little acquainted with the work of the Benthamite philosophical radicals except for that of Richard Carlile. When in England, he apparently had not read Francis Place and James Mill; but Carlile's writings had reached him in America. His thinking, as it progressed, was influenced from several directions, but it was largely his personal history which led him to think the problem through. He had read Carlile's birth-control essay, *Every Woman's Book* and had published the opinion that although he found the language coarse in spots, this was not adequate reason to cast aside the basically good contribution it made. Some months later, in connection with the unauthorized issuance of a prospectus of the Carlile work from the Owen-Wright printing establishment, he felt constrained to offer a full set of facts concerning this work. He explained that the book had gone through several editions in England, and that it was to be considered along with the respected works of James Mill and Francis Place. It had been openly sold in the working-class districts of London—though not without arrests and court proceedings—and had been circulated secretly in the United States. Secrecy inevitably placed it in the hands of the wrong people instead of where it belonged—in "the hands of the philanthropist, of the philosopher, of the physiologist, and above all, of every father and mother of a family. . . ." Owen was eager to spread its message, having been deeply touched by what he considered a representative appeal from a woman for help in solving her problem of a growing family and an irresponsible husband. He would not, however, consent to publish the book (as had been announced in the unauthorized prospectus) for reasons of his own. These reasons he stated candidly: he lacked the necessary knowledge to judge the work with regard to its physiological accuracy; his printers were young boys; and, mostly, he feared that the immaturity and honest prejudices of readers would destroy the book's usefulness.

On top of this came his altercation with the *New York Typographical Society*. The row started with an attack by that group upon the educational proposals of the "Association for the Promotion of Industry and Promotion of National Education" of which Owen was corresponding secretary, and therefore the signer of all its public communications. One such communication, asking for an endorsement of principles, had been sent to numerous organizations, including the Typographical Society. This organization took offence at Owen's insinuation—in reality that of the group he represented—that the United States was the scene of poverty, unemployment, sectarianism in education, and inadequate educational facilities. It wrote to Owen telling him to go back to Britain whence he had come.

This was in 1829. In the course of the following year, Owen, in a friendly spirit, forwarded to the Society two unusual typographical specimens which he had received from England. The gift was rejected, and a committee was assigned to write Owen of the Society's decision. The framers of the letter took it upon themselves to give detailed reasons. As heads of families, responsible for instilling in their children's hearts reverence for a God whose existence Owen denied, they would have nothing to do with him. He was a foreign-born incendiary—as were all incendiaries—and more dangerous to society than an arsonist or highway robber. He was an advocate of promiscuity, a marriage destroyer, "one who unblushingly *recommends* his criminal projects in a public paper . . . the most filthy, obscene, and wicked publication that ever disgraced the American press; a publication which holds old inducements and facilities for the prostitution of our daughters, our sisters, and our wives."

One could understand, Owen remarked, how the typographers, many of them employed by religious publishers, would make a point of attacking irreligion. For the rest, they had shown bad manners and "intermeddling officiousness" on a matter which really needed more time for study. But since it had become a matter of honor and self-respect to Owen, he cound not "choose but speak plainly and if, in so doing, I too roughly touch the honest prejudices of some, my readers will bear me witness, that the occasion is not of my seeking." He would prefer addressing only the young and pure of heart to whom one could speak without fear of misunderstanding and prejudice. Unfortunately, though, the reading audience contained many profligate, evil-minded people, the kind that always overdid their protestations of chastity. When preparing to address such as these, he wondered whether or not he was wasting his time. But the honest, conscientious worker for the betterment of the world could not be stopped by considerations of this sort. He must go on. He would not carry forward discussions of the Carlile book for reasons already stated, but he would proceed with a treatment of his own on the subject of population.

The groundwork was already prepared. Owen had by this time engaged in a friendly, fruitful discussion of the population question with William Jackson of Harmony Grove. The materials had appeared in the pages of the *Working Man's Advocate,* the *Delaware Free Press,* and the *Free Enquirer.* The two were in substantial agreement most of the way. They differed only on the matter of which should be considered the chief cause of the workers' depressed condition: Jackson championed overpopulation; Owen, underpopulation plus competition among workers. At the point where the disputants showed signs of impatience born of exhaustion, Owen made a concession. He conceded that, whereas the course of social development would vindicate his view in the long run, under present conditions the only effective ameliorative was to induce workers to limit the size of their families. As a matter of fact, said Owen as he climbed on the bandwagon of the birth-control movement, he was already in very hot water with the Typographical Society for approving Carlile's pamphlet on the very subject.

Owen confirmed his change of direction in short order by a series of two articles entitled "The Population Question." The treatment was an eclectic one, indicating indebtedness to Malthus, Godwin, Ricardo, Thompson, Mill, Place, and others. Owen granted the essential truth of Malthus' analysis, modifying only the estimate of the length of time it took for the population to double itself. His belief was that the process would take twenty-five to fifty years as against Malthus' twenty-five or less. The big quarrel was with the disciples of this population theorist who posited the inevitability of poverty, class differences, and immorality. Owen flatly rejected the idea that only late marriages or celibacy could palliate the evils of the world. He denied also that to provide another solution would be in opposition to God and nature. A few groups like the Shaking Quakers (Shakers) might practice celibacy; but for the mass of the population, it was impossible—and hardly desirable—that they should want to give up those "dearest of social relations" during the ten best years of their lives to follow Malthus' prescription of marriage at thirty. While the population problem might be solved by a system of temporary celibacy, immorality would follow as a general way of life. The alternatives had to be faced.

The birth rate had to be curtailed not by avoiding family relations but by modifying practices within them. There were more reasons than the ones already alleged for discouraging propagation. For example, there were women whose health and very lives would be endangered by childbirth. Some people ought not to risk passing on hereditary diseases, especially those of a mental character; and there were the numberless families which were too poor to risk becoming larger—to say nothing of the ill effects of repeated childbirth on mothers when adequate nutritional, medical, and household care were not available. And bad situations worsened when a father died of overwork and left the entire burden of a large family to his widow. Charity and vice then became the children's careers.

The French, Owen continued, met the problem openly and successfully. Their logic was simple. If young men do not fear the responsibilities of imminent parenthood, they do not resort to the brothel. Nor do they involve their women friends in complications and then leave them high and dry. Women do not have to risk the dangers of abortion-inducing drugs; they do not contemplate child murder. Crime and wretchedness emanating from undesired pregnancy had to be stopped. James Mill, in his *Encyclopedia Britannica* article, "Colony," had written a masterful piece of circumlocution on the subject. Richard Carlile was more definite. For himself, Owen was interested in moving toward the solution of social problems through discussions of monopoly, taxation, trade, and commerce, but the exigencies of the situation forced him to consider population control. It were better to amend laws and customs, "but while the grass is growing, let us prevent the horse from starving if we can." The big question on the immediate agenda was: "Is there no alternative between the life of a rake or of a Shaker on the one hand, and the heavy responsibility of a dozen children on the other?" A little treatise on the physiology of the subject, to be published soon (as promised in the *Free Enquirer* of October 23, 1830), would throw some light on the matter.

The little treatise was Owen's *Moral Physiology; or, a brief and plain treatise on the population question.* There was good reason for the author's trepidation before publication. Even as the prospectus appeared, Owen noted an attack on his moral principles by one Paul Brown in a pamphlet on marriage. His opponents had been given to presenting disgusting caricatures of his ideas and the forthcoming work would add to their opportunity. He was counting on the common sense of the people to win him more friends than enemies after his *Moral Physiology* was read. He was confident of its usefulness. It would sell for twenty-five cents unembellished, and for about thirty-five cents with a frontispiece done by a leading lithographer from a beautiful French painting.[1]

The long introduction prefacing the discussion proper was an index of Owen's fear of criticism and reprisal. In it he repeated much of what he had already said in the *Free Enquirer* about his reasons for embarking on the population discussion. He advertised his own personal purity and boasted of an unimpeachable moral record. Then followed a statement of purpose specifying that what followed was a treatment of a strictly physiological subject although, as with so many subjects of this kind, it envolved "political economy, morals, and social science."

The text itself was mainly concerned with the sociological issues rather than with physiology. Of some eighty pages, only a half-dozen were devoted to the physiological and emotional aspects of contraception. Owen realized that his own *forte* was social science. His descriptions of three contraceptive methods, two of which were dropped in subsequent editions, were at best tentative. Readers were requested to report back and keep the matter under discussion. As a sociologist with a secondary interest in medicine, he was scientist enough to leave extended treatment of such subjects to physicians with a secondary interest in society. He probably had heard Dr. Charles Knowlton's "course of physiological lectures as connected with moral philosophy" at the Hall of Science in New York. Perhaps subconsciously he was yielding to the better informed Knowlton, who, influenced by *Moral Physiology,* published his more specifically physiological *Fruits of Philosophy* in January 1832. The latter summarized Owen's elaborate social essay, but presented a much expanded and corrected version of the practical science of population control.

Moral Physiology gave particular attention to a redefinition of chastity in marriage. It deprecated the emphasis placed by religious tradition on the propagative purposes of the marriage institution, and emphasized as an ideal the happiness of the two parties to the con-

[1] On the same page with this prospectus he solicited subscriptions to the publication of Frances Wright's Epicurean work, *A Few Days in Athens,* and Shelley's *Queen Mab.*

jugal contract. In doing so, it merely carried forward the rational doctrines of Franklin, Witherspoon, and the others. There was nothing revolutionary about its approach except the attempt to give open social sanction to practices already privately sanctioned and practiced by the American and British middle classes. The ideas, which had been explored in the *Free Enquirer,* were here systematized and enlarged for the use of a larger potential audience than the magazine had reached. While still refusing to capitulate to the Malthusian thesis that the western world was already overpeopled, Owen offered his chapter on population control—not necessarily limitation—as an aid to man's effort to reach perfection. One anticipated result was the eugenic improvement of the species. Other by-products were a bettering of the quality of the marriage tie, a lowered incidence of bachelorhood, and an effective reduction of prostitution. The work of raising the status of women would receive an added impetus. Children of poor parents, now being fewer, would find their chances of receiving a good education much improved.

The public reception accorded *Moral Physiology* was an agreeable surprise to its author. Considering that there were only two people, himself and his friend, the conservative Jacksonian statesman Nicholas Trist, to apply themselves personally to publicizing the work, the distribution figure of 1500 copies in five months was encouraging. The only papers which advertised it regularly were *The Free Enquirer* itself and the *New Harmony Disseminator.* A fourth edition, much revised with regard to the material on prudential checks, was announced on May 28, 1831, and a sixth on February 3, 1832. Thomas Skidmore, Owen's mortal rival in the labor movement, got out what may be called a fifth edition in 1831. Later in the decade, Gilbert Vale published a reprint and advertised it regularly in his Tom Paine organ, *The Beacon.* London imprints came off the presses in 1832 and 1841. Ezra Hervey Heywood issued and advertised the work in his anarchist *The Word* in the 1870's and 80's. Boston was the place of publication for a tenth edition in 1881. The spark set off in 1830 by Owen was responsible for a minor free-speech conflagration in England which appears in the annals of law as *"The Queen v. Edward Truelove for publishing the Hon. R. D. Owen's Moral Physiology* (London, Truelove, 1878). Moral Physiology had an estimated circulation of some 60,000 copies by 1874.

Few prominent figures of the time could be found to sing the praises of such a daring work. Trist, of course, applauded his friend's achievement loyally. Thomas Cooper, the liberal president of South Carolina College (in defence of whose academic freedom the *Free Enquirer* had already had occasion to speak), praised its bold approach and rated it above the work of Francis Place for public service. Ex-President Madison expected great things of a pamphlet which he had not yet seen; his judgement was based upon the known calibre of its author.

From Paris came Frances Wright's congratulatory note, telling Owen not to expect too much of an ignorant, hypocritical world. Naturally, she used the occasion to advertise her own pet ideas. Youth, she said, must be raised under a new, liberally conceived educational regimen in order to be better prepared for Owen's program of enlightenment. She also enlarged upon the necessity for people to "be individually independent in worldly circumstances" before they could act virtuously. Owen's apropos thought was: "Let me have the world's ears, and I know I can make it think *a little;* in spite of itself."

One correspondent, who signed herself "Mary," wanted to underscore for Owen the extent to which women's acts and thoughts were under the censorship. She herself was happily married to a very liberal-minded gentleman. She had emotional and financial security in a very high degree; yet even she had to maintain anonymity for fear of current public opinion. She did want to assure Owen that nine-tenths of his women readers would approve his work, though none would dare to say so openly. The fact that the author of *Moral Physiology* had done so very much for women would itself put a heavy clamp on their mouths.

The truth was even worse than one had suspected, Owen mused. But he could see that woman must win her political and legal freedom first before she could raise her voice in personal and social matters. And even then, he thought, after a day of victory more glorious than the French Revolution, it would take some time before women could use their power effectively.

A journeyman mechanic who wrote to Owen was far more sanguine about the results of the publication of Owen's *Moral Physiology.* He believed it to be the most useful book since Paine's *Common Sense.* It had opened for him (as a male) new vistas and brushed away the old nightmare of an uncertain future. "I found myself, in this all important matter, a free agent, and, in a degree, the arbiter of my own destiny."

Protests, on the other hand, must have been many. Fortunately for Owen, they did not reach the proportions of public furore. His old adversary, Linus Everett of the *Trumpet,* assumed the role of a father in his objections to "a plain physiological work." Owen struck back immediately with his "Linus Everett, Benedict Arnold, and Moral Physiology," saying that there were many fathers who felt differently. It was characteristic of renegades caught departing from orthodoxy, Owen explained, to overdo their religion and morality in an effort to convince the authorities of returning faith. Note how Benedict Arnold had nauseated even Tory friends with his zeal against former comrades. It was pitiable that Everett should find himself in this very position. Owen asked editor Whittemore for space in the *Trumpet*, was granted his wish, and delivered his by now standard essay on religion, social institutions, moral responsibility, and the rest. Another battle of the pens followed, with the usual failure to get anywhere.

Moral Physiology succeeded in reviving still another old struggle, this one with the agrarians in the New York Working Man's Party. This group, under the leadership of Alexander Ming and Thomas Skidmore, advocated an equal division of property among adults as against the free enquirers' preference for a program of public education. Skidmore's plan was to tax inheritances fifty percent and to divide the proceeds, as well as giving all who reached maturity an equal share in the available land. He would also grant full support and education up to a legal age of maturity, and would forbid the government to involve itself in commercial entanglements with other countries that might react harmfully upon the people. His group maintained, in brief, that the right of children to equal maintenance and education would be assured if their parents were equal in property. The Owen group reversed the process and declared that state effort must be put into education first, and then people would be intellectually and morally equipped to divide property justly.

To further its program within the Working Man's Party, the Owen group formed an Association for the Promotion of Industry and for the Promotion of National Education which succeeded in ousting the Skidmore agrarians from their position of leadership.

Skidmore had been waiting for a chance to stage a counter attack, and *Moral Physiology* provided the chance. He published an accurate copy of Owen's fourth edition, adding copious footnotes in rebuttal of the original. The title-page read: *Moral Physiology exposed and refuted. . . . Comprising the Entire Work of Robert Dale Owen on that subject, with Critical Notes showing its tendency to degrade and render still more unhappy than it is now, the condition of the Working Classes, by denying their right to increase the number of their children; and recommending the same odious means to suppress such increase as are contained in Carlile's "What is Love, or, Every Woman's Book."* The appeal was obviously to the moral sensitivities and class allegiance of the workers.

At appropriate points in the original text, Skidmore demonstrated that the workingman would encourage a reduction of the wage scale by limiting his family. Subscribing, apparently, to the axiom that wage levels always sought the level of subsistence, he maintained that an increased population would benefit the workers by enabling manufacturers to sell their mass-produced goods at cheaper prices. Moreover, workingmen were asked to note how

Owen, leader of the "sponge party" of America, was urging discrimination against the working class. Why should not these workers share in the privilege of other classes, that of having as many children as they wished? The author of *Moral Physiology* was an "aristocratical, sophisticated, self-contradictory, contemptible Jesuit."

The even-tempered Owen could only say that there was no reply to a "low sneer," and then go on to treat Skidmore's strictures calmly. He would not suppress the viciously footnoted edition; he would advertise it in his own paper and make a copy of it available in his own circulating library. At one point he did reply in kind, however, to the effect that Skidmore was pressing the equal division plan in order to benefit his own estate in Indiana. Moreover, the points at issue would be clarified somewhat in still another edition including a twelve-page appendix in which one could find the favorable opinions of a talented author, a physician and professor, and a mechanic. Communications from hostile sources and answers to them would be included along with new materials on heredity and physiology.

This was in August of 1831. Owen had at the moment little to be grateful for except a few laudatory letters concerning *Moral Physiology*. He was lonely. The Wright sisters were gone, his family was in England, and he felt as one fighting the battle single-handed. But early in the following year he met, fell in love with, and soon married Mary Jane Robinson, a frequent member of Hall of Science audiences and an open admirer of his *Moral Physiology*. So well was her heart attuned to his that she soon became a vegetarian in accordance with his dietary habits. He could now make definite plans for a trip back to England. His departure from active reform activities drew a hail and farewell for a job well done from his successor on the *Free Enquirer*: with both Wright and Owen now safely married, it was opportune to reaffirm the high ideals held by these two on connubial felicity.

Upon arriving in England Owen received an invitation from the great Francis Place, who had read and approved, with minor exceptions, the text of Owen's pamphlet. So pleased was Place, that he asked Owen to make certain revisions for an immediate edition. This young Owen did, against his father's advice to let sleeping dogs lie. The edition was prepared and printed. An interesting note on Place's views on both Owens appeared in a letter he sent to Harriet Martineau. The letter was a summary of Place's ideas on population and highly recommended Robert Dale Owen's book, a copy of which Place was forwarding to Miss Martineau. He explained that "Robert Dale is the son of my old and somewhat crazy friend Robert Owen."

Within a year after his departure for England, Robert Dale

Owen returned to settle at New Harmony with his family. Most of the old faces were gone and the intellectual tempo of this mid-western settlement had slowed to a walk. But Owen adjusted himself well to a less exciting career, and in 1836 was ready to run for the Indiana Assembly. His opponents might well have defeated him in spite of the upright stand he took on important issues; what they did was to awaken the slumbering *Moral Physiology* affair. Owen met the issue squarely by gathering up as many copies of the pamphlet as he could find and distributing them to respectable citizens of Posey County. A local Baptist minister pronounced the work moral and Owen was elected to the Indiana Legislature for three one-year terms.

When Owen decided to run for Congress in 1839, he was again charged with atheism, blasphemy, licentiousness, and with being against marriage, in a handbill prepared by Benoni Stinson and Jesse Lane, two clergymen with political pretensions. This time the time factor was against Owen. He was caught unawares, thinking that he had permanently squelched the character assassins three years before. He was held to account for every idea he had discussed or espoused in his radical period. Neither his emphatic denials, nor his attempt to distribute *Moral Physiology* again, nor the help and encouragement given by Vale and his New York *Beacon* were of any use. True, his vote was sizeable, considering the campaign that had been waged against him, but he lost the election. It was at this point that doubt began to creep into the mind of the politician grown practical. Disregarding what citizens thought of *Moral Physiology*, he declared, he himself had for some years been questioning the "wisdom or prudence of the publication." As things turned out, the harm was not irreparable; he was later elected to Congress on the Democratic ticket and spent the years 1843 to 1847 in the national legislature.

AN HEIR TO FREE ENQUIRY

Toward the end of the *Free Enquirer's* life, the publisher Gilbert Vale was invited to edit it but turned down the offer. Vale was a member of the loosely-knit coterie associated with Owen in his adult education activities, specializing in popular lectures on astronomy. Some three years after the *Free Enquirer* ceased publication, Vale started his own periodical, *The Beacon,* an organ which was known for its devotion to the memory of Tom Paine. This magazine preserved the breadth of interest of the older publication, but without some of its extremist tendencies. Articles on education, phrenology, eugenics, religion, women's rights, and marriage were scattered through its pages. It printed Owen's vitriolic essay, the "Influence of the Clerical Profession" and came to the defence of

Moral Physiology when it and its author were under attack in the Indiana Congressional election of 1839. Vale advertised regularly a list of books for sale which included Voltaire, Volney, Paine, Wright, Owen, Knowlton, and Vale's own *Compendium of the Life of Paine*. It will be remembered also that the Beacon Office got out its own editions of *Queen Mab* and *Moral Physiology*.

The items on women's rights and marriage were as variously slanted as the sources from which Vale borrowed his materials; for, inasmuch as editing and writing everything in such a magazine was too great a task for one person, items were picked up and printed without the exercise of too much selectivity. The results were of unequal value. The journal recorded toasts made at Paine celebrations, such as "Woman—Man's best companion and the choice flower of nature; cultivated by a liberal education, she will adorn the Age of Reason." Schiller, on "The Worth of Women," advertised the pacifying influence of the gentle sex on man's impatience, ambition, and warlike spirit. From Gaskell's *Manufacturing Population* came a description of moral debasement occasioned by the circumstance that entire families of factory workers lived in one room. "This condition," declared the article, "destroys all notions of sexual decency and domestic chastity—producing coarseness of habits and filthy indelicacy which are so disgusting and repulsive in women." Owen would never have missed such a chance for editorial comment on the nexus between economics, class, and morals; Vale was less alive to his opportunities. Another piece on "Woman in England" from the *Monthly Repertory* went through the whole panorama of the slavery of working-class wives, the superficiality of middle-class women, marriage for wealth and its relation to the "hirelings who infest the street," the harshness of marriage laws, and the horrible crimes that spring from marriage. All the editor would say to this was that current marriage laws presented advantages and disadvantages. "We think them disputable."

The reprinted "Advice of Patrick Henry to his Only Daughter" was in the tradition that once turned Mary Wollstonecraft's stomach. On another occasion, a masculine voice from the *Journal of Commerce* complained that man was an underdog who always deferred to woman and got nowhere for his pains. Mrs. Jameson on "Love and Legislation" called for an open discussion of sexual habits, customs, and laws more nearly in the spirit of free inquiry. Were not, she asked, sexual love and the consequent marriage choice too serious to be "treated with profaneness, as a mere illusion? or with coarseness as a mere impulse? or with fear, as a mere disease? or with shame as a mere weakness? or with levity as a mere accident?" These were lines worthy of the *New Harmony Disseminator;* but that journal was represented in the *Beacon* by a piece of male chauvinism which had appeared originally in the *National Intelligencer*. Vale noted his surprise that the *Disseminator,* published in Robert Dale Owen's home town and latest place of residence, should use the familiar and derogatory "Fanny" (for Frances Wright) and reprint "these blockhead views."

VICE UNMASKED

For all his lack of vigor as an editor, Vale probably did more than other editors or groups to carry forward an open-minded re-investigation of standards in marriage and morals. The great crusade of the Presbyterian minister John R. McDowall against prostitution did not look for causes. It sought rather to kill evil by the revivalist technique of applying religion vigorously. *McDowall's Journal,* later to become the *Advocate of Moral Reform,* urged early marriages on Testament authority and gave evidence of its views on polygamy, lewdness, and marriage, by reprinting Timothy Dwight in full. Frances Wright was *persona non grata.* In preference to her theories, the *Journal* subscribed to the notion that a girl should marry family and fortune.

One might suppose that the Reverend McDowall would be rewarded handsomely for his services. His tactics were, however, too vigorous for sensitive citizens—for the expressed aims of his earlier *Magdalen Facts* and of his *Journal* were, first, to expose the evils of houses of ill fame, theaters, and gambling establishments, and then to expose the New York City leaders in education, law, and religion who profited from these enterprises. His efforts were received with threats of mob violence, expulsion from the Presbyterian Church, and a verdict of "guilty" from a grand jury. His offence was that of promoting lewd and indecent journalism.

The *Journal* may have had some public influence by its promotion of sex education in home and school, but even that is problematical. The public did not like his brand of crusading. Even the *Working Man's Advocate,* which noted shocking disclosures of prostitution, white slavery, and seduction, found space for "No Libertine's" letter attacking "McDowall's Journal and its Female Pedlar." The writer had a just complaint. A female canvasser had entered his establishment to solicit a subscription to the *Journal.* When he had stated that he would not subscribe because he did not approve of the *Journal,* she promptly called him a libertine. "No Libertine" accounted for the woman's zeal and abuse with the suggestion that the lady was probably one of McDowall's reformed Magdalens.

MAGAZINES AND THE WOMAN QUESTION

To say that the literary output of the period contributed little new toward the positive forging of a new morality does not

mean that their observations of the old were without value. There
was much to be said for marriage as it was and even the radicals
had to admit it. Here and there among the pleasant writings of Mrs.
Sigourney, Mrs. Stanford, Miss Anna Marie Sargeant, and others on
advice to brides, on conduct in marriage, and on the benefits to be
derived therefrom, there were many thoughts and speculations which
revealed the effects of the questionings and insights of advancing
social thought. Women's magazines like *The Ladies' Companion*,
The Ladies' Pearl, and *The Ladies' Garland*, did their bit to keep
alive the questions of woman's education, her legal defences against
cruel husbands, and her functions in the education of children. The
old male assumption, that when marriage was the scene of unhappiness it was the woman's fault, was challenged with meek indignation. Match-making and parental interference in marriage was assailed.

Nor were the ladies' magazines without some allies in the
general periodical press. One finds among numerous pertinent but
inconsequential articles in the *New York Mirror* a strong statement
on the right of women to authority over their children and respect
from their husbands, the one being absolutely necessary to the other.
The American Annals of Education carried the banner for the greater
dignity and independence of a better educated womanhood.

An interest in the physical and moral effects of marriage had
been created by the spread of new medical and sociological knowledge. *The Ladies' Pearl* quoted Dr. Rush and others on the longer
life enjoyed by married persons. Authority was also cited for the
statement that too early marriage had the opposite effect. *The Ladies'
Garland* confirmed this view and also added that premature marriage
was a good preparation for divorce. *The Hesperian* dug into the
eighteenth-century statistical studies of Odier and Departieux to disprove the longevity claims made by protagonists of celibacy. *The New
Yorker* made a case for "The Moral Effects of Marriage" by quoting
penal statistics of a Pennsylvania institution: the great preponderance
of unmarried inmates was taken as proof of the effects of marriage
"in promoting good habits, morality, and virtue, among the lowest
classes of society."

The marriage literature of the period from 1825 to 1840 was
assuming direction. The issues were more clearly drawn. The comparative absence of miscellaneous collections of "prestige" writers
might be taken as one indication of this change. The reader who
was interested in that kind of literature had to depend on eclectic
magazines like the *Poughkeepsie Casket* to satisfy his taste. He could
find there small and frequently entertaining pieces on "Gretna
Green," "quickie" marriages, alienated affection, the sorrows of woman, and the authority of husbands. For those who preferred cynical

humor, the *Rural Repository* obliged with Sir Walter Scott's "Balance of Society in Marriage," the *Republic of Letters* with Bacon "On Marriage and Single Life," and Lamb's "A Bachelor's Complaint of the Behavior of Married People," and the *New York Mirror* with "Coleridge's Ideas of Married Happiness."

But the chief concern of this age and of those that followed was the question of equal rights. The egalitarians claimed it would solidify the the family; the upholders of benevolent authoritarianism replied that an organization without a leader would soon disintegrate. The real problem was: Does growing individualism produce social harmony by its characteristic freedom of thought and action? Or does it encourage aloofness, segmentation, and discord? More time, thought and discussion were needed. It remained for the numerous bands of individualists, mutualists, and socialists of the rest of the century to write, talk, and debate upon an issue which meant as much to the successful functioning of a democratic state as it did to the happiness of a small family unit.

FOUR

Ferment of the Forties

Ideas, like the minds which trade in them, never exhibit complete change. Nor do they spring forth full-grown, like Athene or Eve. They are born through the union of highly pluralized parents. Their modifications, even when they seem quite radical, are but minor changes of pattern. A slight reorganization of design, a small but significant addition, give them strikingly new meanings.

The rationalist philosophy which Godwin reshuffled to achieve his political justice was itself in a sense the modified aspect of St. Augustine's Heavenly City. Robert Owen's community socialism was Godwinism adapted to the social problems of a nascent industrialism. Those parts of the configuration which suited each artist's mind were retained; those which did not fit, did not survive. New elements, colors, and techniques were tried. Those which seemed to bring the canvas nearer the artist's conceived perfection were preserved; those which disrupted the harmony of the work were quickly erased.

Not all minds given to such creation produced ideas of sufficient novelty to attract popular attention. A few thinkers presented works that startled, but in an annoying way; the disagreeable was soon forgotten by all except the few who found satisfaction in it. The accomplishments of other theorists, again, had real merit but were not noticed because they merely acted as a bridge between more attractive designs. All, however, seemed to be striving toward the perfection motif. The search for truth, reason, God, harmony, or a millennium were variations on a basic theme. They were worked out in rationalism, individualism, socialism, transcendentalism, associationism, and social perfectionism, as well as in a multitude of religious permutations.

The decade of the thirties saw many of these patterns in their formative stages. During the so-called "mad forties," they were presented to the public through the medium of transcendentalism. The intellectual roads and bridges which converged upon this mode of thought are too numerous to map here. Many of the outstanding figures who walked in these circles were of a religious and conservative bent. To understand how they were able and willing to think in novel terms, pursuing ideas that led far from the beaten track, it will help to look at a few of the literary links which connected them with the unconventional minds of a former time.

William Ellery Channing, Bronson Alcott, and Orestes Brownson were three such links. Channing's impress upon the literary mind of mid-nineteenth century New England was unmistakable. His influence upon the social and religious leadership of his time is as clear. It was he around whom the Unitarian revolt against traditional Congregationalism was centered. It was his insistence upon man's essential virtue and perfectibility that built a religion of liberalism and humanity.

Preacher Channing could not express a direct intellectual obligation to freethinkers like Mary Wollstonecraft and William Godwin, but he nevertheless admired their performance. Channing's reading of these Jacobins during his post-collegiate years (1798-1800) certainly affected his theology and social philosophy. Upon reading Mrs. Godwin, he had acclaimed her the greatest woman of her age, and had bestowed upon her *Vindication* that highest accolade, "a masculine performance." While he was transported by her noble, generous, and even sublime sentiments, he turned a deaf ear to her ideas on marriage. These, he said, if carried into practice, would prove fatal to society.

He also had some praise for Godwin, whose *Caleb Williams* and *Political Justice* he had read. But his applause became considerably muffled as he remembered that Godwin and his friends were deists who refused to recognize the Hand of God. "The pride of human nature has been their source of error," he wrote. Yet his differences with Godwin were fewer than his agreements by temperament and intellectual training. He would not accept the power of the environment, as Godwin had, to the point of denying the freedom of the will. He did follow Godwin to the position that relaxing all governmental restraint over individuals must conduce to the common well-being; that the less power given to man over man, the better. The flavor of Channing's thought was pacifist, humanitarian, and social-minded—but individualistic in the best Godwinian sense. He was an outstanding forerunner of transcendental individualism. His service was to open the minds of his contemporaries so that strange thoughts, even those of Godwin, might affect their working-out of social change.

∿　∿

Amos Bronson Alcott was twenty-nine years old when he bought his first volume of Godwin. That was in the year 1828. His previous experience had consisted of peddling and school-teaching. No wall of theological or religious loyalty obstructed his view of the eighteenth-century deist. He found Godwin's reasoning fool-proof and in many respects a confirmation of conclusions which he himself had already arrived at. There was a good deal in the down-to-earth logic of Godwin on the interdependence of mankind, the idea of progress and perfectibility, and the spontaneous expression of the individual, that fitted well with Alcott's mystic transcendentalism. For what were the transcendentalists trying to do other than achieve many of Godwin's reforms, though on a vague plane somewhere above the reach of reason? Theirs was an amorphous philosophy and religion of reform. Somehow industrialism had exposed the failure of the rational approach to society; these thinkers were seeking that rationality in the nature of the universal which transcended human experience, but which would clear the road to the perfection of man and his institutions. Alcott was extracting from his reading whatever he thought would help in the search for this essence. His intellectual diet for a two-month period included Godwin, Owen (the similarity of whose sentiments to Godwin's he noted), the Gospels, and Shelley. He was much attracted to the latter's political and social theories.

The spirit of reform took firmer hold of Alcott during his residence in England at Henry G. Wright's school. The school, devoted to education through spontaneous expression, was conducted in a building appropriately named Alcott House. It was also the meeting place for a multitude of reformist and faddist movements which were aiding the search for perfection in England during the forties. Alcott did his bit to bring back with him to America a few of the new ideas which had not as yet been transplanted to his own country nor generated spontaneously there. In Wright's circle, Alcott met a leading apostle of novelty, the Pestalozzian enthusiast James Pierrepont Greaves. He also formed a lasting friendship with the ascetic Charles Lane, whose ideas on diet and education were close to Alcott's to begin with.

∽ ∽

Lane, editor of *The Healthian*, was a power in the True Harmonic Association, a reformist group which left hardly a social stone unturned. The report of a single meeting of these harmonists, a meeting which Alcott himself chaired, revealed the group's complete program. It consisted of three phases. The first, "reformation," looked to a revision of existing monetary arrangements, the corn laws, the penal code, education, the church, the legal status of primogeniture, and the divorce laws. A representative legislature was demanded. Educational improvement was desired, but racial improvement by eugenics was preferred. The divine sanction was to replace civil and ecclesiastical authority in marriage.

The second phase, that of "transition," apparently involved a by-passing of the priests and legislators in search of perfection. The priest, the harmonists decided, laughed at perfectibility because it threatened his dominion over the human spirit. "We, therefore . . . ignore human governments, creeds, and institutions; we deny the right of any man to dictate laws for our regulation, or duties for our performance; and declare our allegiance only to Universal Love, the all-embracing Justice." The goal was purity, not vengeance; positive targets for human welfare, not the prohibitions of governments and laws.

The third and most radical step was that of "formation." Its premise was that a complete reformation had to start at birth with the generation of a new race of men. Providence had ordained that a new Eden was to be built in New England, and the True Harmonic Association was a training school for "generators." The attention of the trainees was drawn to the basic questions of marriage and family life, including the breeding and education of children; to housewifery and husbandry; to the relations of the neighborhood; and to man's relation to the Creator. The breeding of pure beings, instilled with pure habits, would produce pure minds; these, in turn, would automatically reject tyranny and domination. Under the new program of eugenics and euthenics, "the outward frame shall beam with soul; it shall be a vital fact in which is typically unfolded the whole of perfectness."

Slogans of transcendent mysticism were not all the talkative pedlar brought back from England. He was laden as well with the persons of Wright and Lane, plus a trunk full of pamphlets representing most of the reform movements of English creation. Some of the organizations and titles were the Communist Apostles, Alists, Plans for Syncretic Associations, Pestalozzian Societies, Self-Supporting Institutions (manual labor schools), Experimental Normal Schools, Hydropathic and Philosophical Associations, Health Unions, Phalansterian Gazettes, and "Necessities of Internal Marriage Illustrated by Phrenological Diagrams."

Upon Alcott's return to this country in 1842, Lane joined him as a partner in their vegetarian paradise at Fruitlands. Wright came to Fruitlands later, but departed before long because he and Lane were engaged in constant bickering. Nor could Alcott himself get along very well with the dictatorial Lane, who did everything to extremes and made about-faces without blinking an eye. At first he urged the Alcotts to follow the rule of celibacy, and he sent his own son to the Shaker settlement at Harvard. No sooner had he done this when he himself remarried and in time raised a family of five. All of the Alcotts were happy to see Lane finally go off to join his son in the Quaker fold. An economic snake in the grass had marred the paradise at Fruitlands, and the Alcott family was soon to pack up and depart from Eden too.

Lane was a man of faith who had no patience with those who considered themselves circumscribed by external conditions. These scientists of society, he maintained, had overlooked the factor of "central artistic nature" (a new mystical conception of Lane's manufacture), and were therefore as visionary as those who would reform society without the aid of science. Educational, political, and religious efforts had failed, thus leaving the way open for cynicism, skepticism, and misanthropy. But as one contemplated the current efforts of a few men in New England to combine the spiritual and the practical in the work of social reform, one's hope was renewed.

> Creation, construction, generation, not of life itself, but of new, beautiful, harmonious modes of it, is now man's great work. He is to open a place, to clear an area for the manifestation of spirit under a new aspect. The precinct must be kept pure and unspotted from the world, free from old corruption in food, in raiment, in law, in commerce, in wedlock. Holiness, innocence, lustre must overspread all things, inspire all acts, permeate all beings. . . .

These were current "social tendencies," and the moral outlook was good. However, if the reformers were to overlook the centrality of the family in their plans, Lane believed their work would be in vain. The family owned the mechanisms of heredity and congenital and post-natal influence. From it emanated the springs of all human qualities and acts. The family might not yet offer the best example of harmony, but it could not be discarded. The Creator had used "two human instruments to produce a third," and this was an unchangeable necessity. But, as with other institutions, the family had to change its ways. Connubial, parental, and universal love were all the same thing; nor did the exercise of one detract from the other. When wedlock should be based on "moral sympathy," or "mental likeness," this harmony of being would be transmitted to the offspring in the same way as were physical characteristics. The effect was so strong, that the family tie would persist even if the children were separated from their parents at birth. Fitting marriage did not preclude a love for humanity at large (as Godwin claimed when he condemned the private affections). The family was no excuse for selfishness. The results of marriage were not more corrupting than those of any other social institution.

The truth, according to Lane, was that the family was then under the domination of other social institutions, and was, in its evil aspects, merely reflecting their image. The error of society was that natural relations had been reversed: where the family should have been giving character to the church, the state, and to commerce and industry, these badly oriented institutions were shaping the ways of the family. Man's most wholesome attitudes originated in the home. Family affection and economy would have very salutary effects on commerce and the state if only these dead externals would step down from their dominant position and let the family lead them.

The problem at the moment was to decide whether to work toward associations of individuals or of families. It was a question whether one could harmonize families without inculcating harmony in individual relations first. The answer seemed to depend on how quickly the whole process of regeneration got under way. Everybody was talking of association, but the mere association of families would not necessarily improve them. "In the scientific and artistic association of families, something may be attained, but success here calls for a skill, in handling human arrangements and materials, not yet attained." One aspect of the arrangements and materials needed immediate revision—woman had to be given her just place in the family as well as in society. Those men who feared that women would progress at men's expense had to be convinced that men had been doing too much of the world's work and that women should be allowed to assume their proper share of his functions.

❧ ❧

Some social technicians were seeking human elevation in political reform, some in economics, some through social reorganization, and still others in literature or religion. The omnivorous mind of Orestes Augustus Brownson partook of all these intellectual dishes. He was stimulus, colleague, and critic as he journeyed on his long pilgrimage in search of intellectual security. As he moved through the romantic upheaval of Fourierism, socialism, abolitionism, and the rest of the trials and errors of the thirties and forties, no one exceeded his influence among prominent intellectuals. The liberal theologian Theodore Parker attached himself to Brownson for a while and absorbed many of his ideas. Bronson Alcott, Margaret Fuller, and George Bancroft were contributors to the periodicals which Brownson edited. George Ripley had many a conversation with him before organizing the Brook Farm experiment in individual development through cooperative participation. Even Thoreau was touched by Brownson. The political philosophy of the sage of Walden Pond showed, implicitly, many a mark of the same Godwinism whose influence Brownson admitted.

Brownson could think and talk about a tremendous variety of political and sectarian doctrines because he had had experience of all and had temporarily embraced several of them during his extensive intellectual voyages. The long pursuit of spiritual truth started with a Presbyterian period, followed shortly by rebellion against its orthodox doctrines. In 1824 he joined the liberal Universalists, for whom he preached from 1825 to 1829. During this period he met and came under the sway of the dynamic Frances Wright, whose campaign for a system of popular education he joined. He also became a corresponding editor of the *Free Enquirer* but withdrew in 1830 because he found it impossible to work with a non-religious group. In the year following he embarked upon an independent ministry and published a periodical called *The Philanthropist*. Another season found him in Channing's Unitarian fold, where, though restless, he remained until October, 1844, when he retired into the Roman Catholic Church. During the years 1838 to 1842 he edited and wrote most of the *Boston Quarterly Review*. For another year or so he edited the *Democratic Review* in New York and worked actively at formulating the strategy of the Democratic Party. In 1844 he returned to Boston to edit his own *Brownson's Quarterly Review*.

His was a lifelong vacillation between the individualistic tendency of Godwin and the socialism of Owen and the St. Simonians. His first reading of *Political Justice* prefixed the switch to Universalism. The second prepared him for the Owen-Wright circle, since he was much impressed by Owen's environmental thesis as well as by his demonstration of the injustices of the world. Frances Wright stood halfway between, and would probably have retained a longer hold on Brownson were it not for her atheism. His appreciation of Godwin's statement of the marriage problem, along with the elder Owen's interpretation, probably softened him up for Miss Wright's thrusts against that institution. As he looked retrospectively upon his early days, he intimated strongly that he had once accepted the Godwinian conception of marriage as an obstacle to social justice. In trying to reconcile his later beliefs with his early reasoning, he began to find Christian truth in some of Godwin's ideas on justice, property, and marriage. Godwin's negation of religion eventually nullified his influence on Brownson, and partly explains his failure to reach the minds of the New England reformers of the middle of the nineteenth century. However, their faith in the cultivation of the individual as an instrument of perfectibility was Godwinian and also transcendental.

What we get by reading Orestes Brownson on marriage, morals, and the woman question, is an historical pattern representing the temporal sequence of his associations. When he reviewed Shelley in 1841 he said merely that the poet had gone "woefully astray in his

Queen Mab notes." Some half-dozen years later he wrote of Haw-thorne's *Scarlet Letter* that it was a glorification of sin and should never have been published. Back in 1836 he had been a member of the Transcendental Club; in 1845, he captioned his review of Theo-dore Parker's *Discourse on Matters Pertaining to Religion,* "Tran-scendentalism, or Latest Form of Infidelity." He compared the new religion of reform with every heresy he could remember from church history. Moreover, he linked it with Fourierist community efforts, and these with immorality. He pointed out that Margaret Fuller, in her *Woman in the Nineteenth Century,* had "patronized several re-nowned courtesans" and then went on in this context to report that Miss Fuller's chief argument with the masculine social order was that it inhibited the free expression of woman's natural sentiments and affections. There followed an unsubtle anecdote about the tricks nature was fond of playing on girls who practiced this freedom.

Brownson raged at the thought that he had entertained in his own home the purveyors of sacrilegious and immoral literature. At that very moment, he had in his possession an English transcenden-talist pamphlet (probably brought over by Alcott or one of his friends) which brazenly undermined "the Christian doctrine of chastity and marriage, and in the sacred name of God and humanity, universal brotherhood, and social progress, advocates a promiscuous sexual intercourse. . . ." But how the sagacious Brownson could connect such ideas with Parker, Emerson, Margaret Fuller, et al., is a mystery.

His treatment of the feminist movement yields a number of in-teresting ideas. A review of Lady Morgan's *Woman and Her Master* in 1841 accepted the thesis that a male civilization was but half a civilization. But Lady Morgan had gone too far. She had claimed certain superiorities for women. What this meant to Brownson was that man had better look out in these days of woman's rights lest he emerge as the underdog. As far as Brownson could tell, the truth was that spontaneity dominated in women, and reflection in men. Women were useful for stirring men out of their meditations and giving them the reckless courage to move onward. According to Brownson's treatment of St. Simonianism, written after he had en-tered the Catholic Church, the most striking thing about the system was its insistence on genuine equality for women.

Again in 1864 he declared himself on the feminist question, but this time as an open enemy of the movement. He used as his vehicle for this offensive a review of Bayard Taylor's *Hannah Thurston* which bore the running title, "Literature, Love, and Marriage." American fiction was "feminine," and Brownson deplored feminine literature regardless of the sex of its writer. Woman was gifted with flashes of inspiration, but without man she amounted to nothing. The quarrel he had with Taylor's story was that its heroine was too self-sufficient to fall in love with any man, and the hero was too well-bred to fall in love with a woman of such ultra-feminist convictions. Such women possessed no real sentiment nor the love that sends the glory of Christian womanhood in search of a lord. Woman's rights theorists married to get a servant and were "willing to pay him his wages." On the other hand, men of class and wealth of the stamp of the hero, Max Woodbury, would not fall in love with a woman like Hannah except "to get a housekeeper to cook, clean, and bring him his slippers." It was as abhorrent to a man of station to attach himself to a female who appeared side by side with men on a public platform, demanding all sorts of "political, social and domestic changes," as it would be for him to fall in love with a second-hand mistress or a notorious courtesan. Not that it was wrong for women to engage in activities for the uplift of their sex. What was bad was that, "when they go farther, and attempt to make her as independent of man as he is of her, they forget the respective provinces of the sexes, and simply attempt to reverse the laws of nature, and assign to the female of the species the office of the male. It is not conventionalism but God, that has made man the head of woman." Daily experience had shown that girls were not attracted to the men in the woman's rights movement. "A woman wants a man, not a woman, for her husband, and a man wants a woman, not a man, for his wife."

How swiftly do one's ideas on the freedom of the spirit and the affections undergo change! Back in 1840, when Brownson was still calling for a destruction of theocratic and state power, he railed against the social institutions which jailed man's very soul. These were the days when he wrote in his essay on "The Laboring Classes" (the excuse being a review of Carlyle's *Chartism*) that only out of an American class struggle could a virile native literature arise. The soul of man needed liberation from the priest who held his conscience, from the fashion which controlled his tastes, and from the society which invaded "the very sanctuary of his heart" and set bounds to that love which was man's only source of rapport with the essence of reality.

Such thoughts were more than fourteen years distant from the views expressed in the review of *Hannah Thurston,* where Brownson asserted unqualifiedly that love marriages were inevitably unhappy ones. Sentiment, he declared in his later years, was irrational, and, being so, could be removed or reversed by slight accidents like a rainy day, a headache, a chance remark misunderstood, a gesture, a look, or a host of irrelevancies. Sentiment was within ourselves, and therefore was hardly the instrument to measure external reality with the same validity as sense and reason. Love out of sentiment was momentary self-love, not the love of another. It was a feeling which could dissolve as quickly as it came—and then, where was your love and what happened to your marriage? The only love object which could lay claim to permanence was a flawless one: there was but one such in the universe, and that was God. Man and woman loving each other in God, and thus participating in perfection though not embodying it as individuals, were alone capable of true, indestructible marriage.

The Catholic philosopher had little sympathy left for contemporary woman whose stock in trade on public platforms, as he saw it, was male brutality, but whose aim was purely and simply to have her own way. Personal feelings had their place in marriage, but modern writers were pricing it too high. The old custom—still the current custom in the old countries—of letting parents choose mates for their children, worked much better. Marriages thus initiated, and having as their ultimate object a love of the perfect, complete, and infinite God, had a lifetime guarantee. "Marriage based on this love is sacred, holy, and can never, whatever the imperfections of the spouses, be utterly miserable, because it can never leave the mind utterly empty, and the soul to devour itself." The performance of marital duties insured the soul's peace even where perfect harmony did not exist between man and wife. Where a match was arranged for a girl fresh out of school and innocent, she might not like it at first; but assuming good will on both sides, affection would follow, "because nothing is demanded that, with God's Grace, it is not possible on either side to give." This lesson, said Brownson, was just a philosophical interpretation of every-day church teaching: that love in the Creator would make you happy, married or unmarried. "So take what I have said kindly; for if I am old now, I have been young, and remember too well the follies of my youth."

Brownson's receptivity to ideas promoted by various socialist movements showed the same changes, in time. When Albert Brisbane's *Social Destiny of Man* appeared, he was quite sympathetic to the Fourierist doctrines it interpreted. He approved its principles because it left individual property intact while proposing a system of associated labor. At the time, early in 1841, he gave an uncritical précis of the Fourierist belief that the evil man suffered was social and not political, that the character of society corresponded with the distribution of property, which in turn corresponded with the organization of industry. The solution of the problem lay in harmonizing industrial organization with the laws of human behavior and with the structure of the material world.

Later in the same year he reverted, in criticism of Fourier, to his old statement of the contradiction between coexisting individual and social drives. The two were irreconcilable and stood as an immovable block in the way of perfection. The human organism possessed a variety of behavior components whose contradictions precluded the satisfaction of all. Some of its "passions"—the term used by Fourier to signify traits, drives, and activities—would always be satisfied at the expense of others. Again, Nature did not exhibit an economical balance. She achieved her goals by an overexpenditure of means. For example, he said, take the passion of love, which was designed to insure the continuance of the species. Wherever its strength was sufficient to fulfill this purpose, it never stopped there. It demanded "more than the other elements of our being, without self-denial, can yield it."

The difficulties with Owen's system were of another order, thought Brownson. It denied religion, which was absolutely necessary to man; its environmental emphasis denied the freedom of the will, without which reform was impossible; it also denied the right of private property, thus subverting the basis of man's very existence. Man knew his being only when he could say "this is mine."

As apt an illustration as any of how minds receive new social formulae selectively is provided by a comparison of Robert Dale Owen's and Brownson's appreciations of the St. Simonians. Owen's was written at the height of his search for a science of society; Brownson's, when he had moved toward Catholicism. The two things which stood out in Brownson's eyes were the hierarchic structure worked out by the disciples of St. Simon and the argument between the leaders, Bazard and Enfantin, over acceptance of traditional marriage customs. These constituted to Brownson the usable residue of a short history of about ten years during which the followers of St. Simon had their greatest success in France. The effects on Brownson were, first, to divest him of the distaste for the Papal hierarchy normally entertained by his fellow Americans, and then to teach him the axiom that many promising social movements were bound to split on the question of sex relationships.

Brownson's analysis was along personal lines. He liked the general social and economic proposals of St. Simonism because he himself had already arrived at similar conclusions. To the doctrine of sexual equality his attitude had been one of acquiescence rather than approval. He was convinced that woman was the weaker vessel, but, since equality was accepted by his friends, he kept his peace. However, when Harriet Martineau and Margaret Fuller began to intimate female superiority, his blood was up and he promptly asserted his masculine dignity.

Owen, on the other hand, read the issues of the St. Simonian *Organisateur* with an enthusiasm which was dampened only by the proposal of a hierarchy to be headed by a Social Priest and Priestess. These were to constitute a court of last resort on questions which arose among the faithful. Such an office seemed to him very much

like that of a Pope. But he did give these French innovators credit
for the shrewd use of esthetic and religious bait to unite science
with labor in a modern society. For the rest—the disapproval of
conventional marriage contracts, the abolition of all laws which deprived women of political and legal rights which men enjoyed, the
sermons delivered to women about their tremendously expanded
opportunities, and, in short, the confirmation of Godwinian and
Owenite phrases—the movement which stemmed from St. Simon
had fine things to offer to a suffering world. Young Owen joyfully
reprinted mottoes and phrases like:

> All privileges of birth shall, without exception, be abolished.
> . . . All social institutions ought to have for their object
> the melioration of the moral, physical, and intellectual con-
> dition for the most numerous and poorest class. . . . To
> everyone according to his capacity: to every capacity accord-
> ing to its works. . . . [And, of typical marriages of the day]
> Thus two plants, scarcely rooted in the burning soil of some
> sandy desert, and abandoned to the tempest of a stormy
> heaven, cling to each other, choke each other's growth, and
> at last wither away, their strength destroyed, and their sap
> arrested, by their mutual convolutions. Love, then, in vig-
> orous minds, is a true disease, at those periods when all its
> energy is concentrated in a purely individual passion. . . .
> No, jealousy is then a brutal egotism which degrades what it
> loves, which menaces even in caressing and revenges in
> punishing itself. . . ."

The all curious Brownson went about tasting everybody's wares,
buying a few things but rejecting most. Not once in his long career
did he try his hand at an original reconstruction. The same cannot be
said for the transcendentalists whom he impressed so deeply. They
were not mere eclectics; they did not dress themselves with other
people's mantles. Nor did they, as a rule, consciously try to impose
their molds on others. Theirs was an energetic effort to achieve individual dignity through repeated re-combinations of sentiment, reason, and social science. Some of their thoughts may truly have dissipated themselves in the clouds. But there was nothing aimless,
vacuous, and inconsistent in sharing in such humane causes as
antimilitarism, abolition, temperance, prison reform, and associationism, the Fourierist brand of socialism. This last could not be
brushed aside by critics—Brownson among them—as dilettantist talk
about reform, for it launched a devastating criticism of the values
which underpinned the social structure. It sought a wholesale revaluation of the prevailing practice of individualism.

The task of the Fourierists was to erase all antagonisms among the groups which comprise society, among the individuals who belong to groups, and within the individual himself. The logic of their social arrangements would operate also to erase conflicts between the individual and the group, it was claimed. The problems of vocational education and guidance would be automatically solved in an harmonious industrial organization. Full employment was not to be achieved by an elaborate administrative and legislative paraphernalia; it would come into being inevitably through pursuit of the Fourierist program as a whole.

America in 1842 was emerging from the serious depression which had started in 1837. The reform market was buzzing with competition as it echoed a similar intellectual ferment in Western Europe. Fourier, in making his bid for supremacy, wrote at length on the error and charlatanry of what he called "*les deux sectes St. Simon et Owen.*" He accused them of holding back association, socialism, and progress. The elder Owen recalled in his autobiography that he had met and talked with Fourier; his version of the story was that Fourier had stolen his, Robert Owen's, ideas. On this side of the ocean, Albert Brisbane and Horace Greeley were interpreting Fourierism for Americans. Robert Dale Owen seemed sympathetic, but did not respond to Brisbane's request to write on the subject for the *Phalanx.*

Quite naturally the majority of American reform interests, whether of socialist, transcendental, or other persuasion, dipped into Fourier for what he was worth to them. The New England intellectuals first tried their own brand of collective endeavor at Brook Farm and later reorganized as a Fourierist phalanx. Many of them were intrigued by the scientific precision of the phalanx and exalted by its mystical properties. But Emerson, the diehard individualist, could not appreciate the collective life at all. He met with George and Sophia Ripley, Alcott, and Margaret Fuller, and listened to their plans for Brook Farm. He came to the conversations with an open mind, to hear what this social experiment could do to give more self-expression to the individual soul. Perhaps collectivism was indeed the medium for calling forth the greater individualism. But when all was said and done, the scheme left him cold. As far as he was concerned, the Universal Mind dwelled in individual breasts and not in communities. Naturally, Thoreau was deaf to the call of association. He wanted to be alone in Godwinian independence, for he was an anarchist.

For all their lack of uniformity, the Brook Farm collectivists and their Fourierist friends in New York showed far more direction than the other faddist reformers of the forties who are often mistakenly considered to be the norm of their generation. It was in terms of the competition of a multitude of ideas, mostly bad, that the failure of the Fourierist missionaries, sent out from Brook Farm in 1847, was explained. They could not hope to convince "people, who have not intelligence enough to discriminate between a true Constructive Reform, and the No-God, No-Government, No-Marriage, No-Money, No-Meat, No-Salt, No-Pepper system of community." Tragically enough for the conscientious, honest, and altogether moral dwellers in American Association, they had to answer not only for a few of the above-mentioned negativisms which they did not practice, but also for several speculative aspects of Fourierism which only experts like Brisbane and Parke Godwin had thought about, and which they were not certain they understood.

Nevertheless they used the technique best known to them, the written word, to explain the basic ideas and to clarify some of the refinements of the originator of the system. Greeley opened the pages of the *New York Tribune* to thrice-weekly contributions by Brisbane. Editorial space and a good deal more was used for comment and expansion. Parke Godwin, who worked for William Cullen Bryant's *New York Evening Post,* got out his *Popular View of the Doctrines of Fourier* in 1844, after Brisbane had published his more sophisticated *Social Destiny of Man* (1840), and his *Association; or a Concise Exposition of the Practical Part of Fourier's Social Science* (1843). Margaret Fuller made her *Dial* a free medium of discussion of all manner of social and literary problems from its first issue until she handed over the editorship to Emerson in April 1842. George and Sophia Ripley, Charles A. Dana, John S. Dwight, William Henry Channing, Parke Godwin, Henry James, Senior, and the others carried on the tradition of free discussion in the *Harbinger* which was published at the Brook Farm Phalanx, West Roxbury, Massachusetts, from 1845 to 1847, and thereafter by the American Union of Associationists whose headquarters were in New York City. During the whole life of the periodical, 1845 to 1849, issues emanated from Boston and New York simultaneously.

Fourierism was doubtless too strong a potion to be swallowed straight from the original bottle. Even Brisbane's explanations needed further dilution in the form of interpretation. The *Dial* lent a helping hand with an early article (1842) on "Fourierism and the Socialists," using Brisbane's words to announce the central purpose of Fourier. The new system—whose outstanding feature, as far as the *Dial* could see, was its neat mechanics—was to be a "means of effecting a final reconciliation between religion and science." In order to accomplish this, reason had to determine the true nature of the soul so that the two could work together. The practical means of providing a setting conducive to a successful research were twofold. First, the social lot of the vast disinherited majority had to be improved to a point where they would have the freedom, the will, and the energy, to participate in the quest for universal truth. Second, there must arise a great genius "to discover a theory of Universal Unity, a true theory of the Immortality of the Soul, the laws of Order and Harmony which govern creation. . . ." So far, Fourier was "it."

Parke Godwin, knew from his writing and editing for the adult public that any new thing must be introduced to them by a brief historical outline of its background. He therefore offered a schematic treatment of Fourierism in his *Popular View.* Social reformers, he posited, were divided into three categories: There were the pure theorists who made literature with their intellectual Utopias, as for example, Plato in the *Republic,* More in *Utopia,* Harrington in *Oceana,* and Campanella in the *City of the Sun.* Then there were the practical architects like the Rappites, Moravians, and Shakers, who constructed societies in imitation of the supposed communism of early Christianity. And lastly, a combination of the first two, the theoretico-practical architects like Robert Owen, Etienne Cabet, Charles Fourier, and Saint-Simon. Owenism, according to Parke Godwin, was a forerunner of Fourierism, as New Harmony was of Brook Farm.

In actuality, the Brook Farmers practiced Fourier's social philosophy even less than the New Harmonists lived according to Owen's. The former may have organized their economy for a brief period into industrial series and sub-groups, a logical organization for any kind of productive enterprise, but they seemed to have little success in their avowed purpose of freeing the passions for the sake of harmonious development. Nevertheless, the Fourierist "passions" (probably best compared with phrenology's "propensities," with the "faculties" of a later psychology, and with the "personality traits," "drives," and "behavior patterns" of our own time) were explained in full by Brisbane, who, in matters social and political, was the precise opposite of his son, Arthur Brisbane, editor and columnist for William Randolph Hearst in a later period.

The passions were created by God, according to this interpretation, but were judged good or bad in accordance with the ethical conceptions formulated by human reason. They were all beneficial in their original form but, distorted or "subverted" by the arbitrary demands of human legislation, they sought satisfaction in unnatural channels. Thus ambition, in its political subversions, became tyranny, oppression, usurpation, revolution, and conspiracy; in business it took the form of avarice, rapacity, and fraud; in social relations, it produced cruelty, arrogance, insolence, and the domineering spirit. Love had been forced into even more distasteful shapes according to Brisbane: "Love, in its subversive action, gives rise to prostitution, sexual excesses, adultery, rape, seduction, infanticide, jealousy, despair, insanity, and other disorders and crimes which cannot well be mentioned." Fourier apparently attributed more lawlessness to love than

Owen had. At least his list was longer, and stimulated the imaginations of converts with its references to the unmentionable.

The force which God had implanted in man to motivate these passions was technically known as passional attraction. This force could be described as a kind of gravitational pull which drew all urges toward the object of their gratification. The totality of these pulls impelled man to fulfill his destiny on earth. No rules, regulations, laws, customs, or social prejudices could stop the meeting of passion and object. They could only be "subverted" temporarily. As with the senses of taste, smell, hearing; as with the urge to friendship, each with its own purpose to fulfill, so with love, the "amatory attraction" in man. "It imparts a desire to form ties and relations of an Amatory character, and leads to the Sexual Unity of the Race, and to the procreation and continuation of the species."

The idea of "unity" was so vague that no two of the most discerning of the Fourierist oracles could agree on its meaning. When fused with the Swedenborgianism that Henry James, Senior, had absorbed abroad, it defied definition the more. To those who were flapping their wings vigorously in an attempt to soar aloft, unity was the essence of original creation, the principle which brought about the frictionless cooperation of the infinite number of parts in the universe. To cynical materialists and pious upholders of the ways of "civilization" (the Fourierist name for reactionary contemporary society), "unity" spelled "free love-ism."

For the time being, there were more immediate social problems for the solution of which American socialists and transcendentalists could borrow more realistically from Fourier. The emancipation of women was one of these problems. George Ripley's wife, Sophia, had heard enough about the subject from the lips of Margaret Fuller to write her own piece on woman in the *Dial* at the very beginning of the decade of the forties. The article, which she signed with the letters "W. N.," possibly because these begin and end the word "woman," was in the spiritual, sentimental vein, but it made a strong case against invidious discrimination, and for individuality and independence. It lacked, however, the learning and powerful rhetoric which made Miss Fuller's *Dial* articles, published in 1845 as *Woman in the Nineteenth Century*, the milestone it was to become in feminist expression. (The place occupied by this book in the lore of the woman's rights agitations suggests that it be treated with that movement rather than in the setting of New England transcendentalism.)

Male associationists also showed their breadth of interest by writing on the implications of association for women. William Henry Channing, a unitarian minister deeply influenced by his uncle, William Ellery Channing, wrote for the *Harbinger* on "men, women, and morals." His thoughts on "Woman's Functions in the Movement" were devoted almost entirely to an invitation to the other sex to get in at the bottom of the ladder in order to participate in determining the role of women in the new society. Channing urged them to a "full and free cooperation with man in advancing the interests of humanity." As he noted the activities of women in the humanitarian causes of temperance, abolition, and aid for the blind and insane, he could say: "The age seems to be preparing for an era of Woman's Restoration to her original co-sovereignty. . . ."

George Ripley advertised his movement by illustrating the "Influence of Association on Women." He could show that right in Boston, where the system of public education led the rest of the country, girls could get a classical and scientific education only by paying for it on a private basis while boys could get it at public expense. Admission to college was also among the unattainables for girls. Association, on the other hand, guaranteed to women "the benefit of a complete, thorough, and efficient education." The real superiority of women in certain branches of intellectual endeavor was yet to be brought out, and association would insure its emergence.

American associationists, as Ripley represented them, were committed to the elimination of economic considerations from the marriage choice, to the predominance of the spiritual over the material aspects of marriage, and to a system of equal education which would "bring about Nature's intention of a spiritual relationship between man and woman." They would take no responsibility for Fourier's speculations about the possible relations of the sexes in the vague and distant era of harmony.

The opposition press shed many tears for home and family, and their charges against Fourierism had just enough validity to make them seem convincing. The French architect of association had more than once expressed himself on the "Falseness of the Oppressive System in the Relations of Love." He had declared in his "descriptions"—as Godwin and Owen had intimated in their sensational indictments of institutional marriage—that "perpetual fidelity in love is contrary to human nature; that though we may induce a few simple characters of both sexes to adopt such a morality, we shall never bring the mass of men and women to it, and therefore that any legislation which requires tastes and characters so incompatible with the passions, can produce only theoretical absurdities and practical disorders."

The *Tribune* explained defensively that not even Fourier advocated any immediate change in the marriage system; that his theoretical essays were concerned with a future state of man when he should be purified back to his natural state by the new order of social relations. The opposition, in rebuttal, still claimed that the associationists were hiding their real intentions behind their glib verbalisms about harmonizing moral standards and laws with natural inclinations.

As far as the *Tribune* was concerned, this was a red herring being thrown across the trail. A defender of association in the *Democratic Review* concurred. The truth of the matter was that associationists were of all religious, political, ethical, and other backgrounds, and no one could say whether or not the movement as a unit believed in marriage divine and perpetual.

There was indeed a world of difference between the treatment Brisbane gave "Government, Church, and Marriage" and the treatment of "Moral Reform" by William Henry Channing. Brisbane, a member of a wealthy New York family, had behind him a long stay abroad during which he had sat at the feet of Fourier himself. So thoroughly steeped was he in the doctrines of the master that when he returned, he acted the echo, giving the sound of the original with but a lessening of volume. He listed the antagonisms of society both in their abstract and specific varieties. Opposed to reform, there was conservatism; opposed to liberty, order. Swedenborg had stated this prime contradiction as Love versus Wisdom; Fourier, as Attraction versus Series. The job of social science was to adjust one to the other to produce harmony. Concrete examples of discord were evident in class and sectarian struggle, in the conflict between faith and science. In marriage itself, there existed a long list of conflicts on the legal, economic, religious, and personal planes.

Institutions and human behavior were ever at war. Intelligent men must face the facts, said the social scientist Brisbane, anticipating Professor Kinsey by a century. Instead of studying human traits and emotions with the respect they deserve as productions of the Creator, Brisbane continued, people damned them as evil. Instead of adjusting society to the nature of its human constituents, we try to adjust the individual being to society. If musicians had condemned discordant sounds to begin with, they would never have been able to work them into harmony. Marriage was indeed necessary as the ordering process for regulating the desire for love and paternity. Marriage as then practiced was doing the job to a certain extent, but it was shot through with so many "subversions" that it favored the material and carnal aspects of the sexual union as against the spiritual ones.

The time was not yet ripe for going into the exact nature of marriage and divorce reform. Certain principles, however, could be immediately endorsed by associationists. The subservience of women in marriage and the absolute control of fathers over children were unjust and degrading. The consequences followed a logical pattern which could be stated thus: "Just in proportion as human nature is degraded, must government be tyrannical, the church superstitious, and marriage oppressive to the weaker sex." Another proposition which was readily acceptable was that the reasons for which married couples could obtain divorce meant public disgrace for the people involved;

the divorce laws were part of a conspiracy against human dignity. Swedenborg supplemented Fourier in the last and most important principle, namely that spiritual marriage must be rescued from the selfish and contaminating calculations which smothered it. The material must always be subservient to the spiritual. Marriage, as Brisbane knew it, sanctioned or condoned a variety of immoralities among which legalized prostitution was prominent. By legalized prostitution he meant the same thing as had Franklin and many others—wedlock for fortune, simply to gratify desire, and other motives which rendered the spiritual principle subservient to the material. Church, law, and public opinion stood behind this union of the bodies. Real marriage, as far as American Fourierists were concerned, meant a union of the souls.

Many of the attacks on Brisbane by New York newspapers were provoked by his slurs against the church. William Henry Channing was more circumspect, and also more religious. He chose to examine every contemporary problem, fastening on licentiousness as the social problem of prime importance. "The relations between Man and Woman are the very citadel of society; and the angels or devils who possess it, will easily command all outposts." Some said that the rising dignity of woman, the simplicity of manners in America, and our feeling as a people for home ties, kept the situation well in hand. Others maintained that our personal reserve, the absence of social classes, and our general restlessness made the question a grave one.

No matter which school was right, said Channing, the reform job was the same. One saw visible signs of a new dignity for chastity and sacred marriage in the physiological and other literature of the time. Unfortunately there was also a parallel tendency in the opposite direction. Prostitution was on the rise in the cities. Certain groups in society were playing tricks with moral standards; all too many had ruled out marriage and were substituting "chance connections." Immorality was as rife among the upper social strata as among the lower—the difference lay only in the means employed. The new wave of immigration, already beginning, would aggravate matters. Urbanization had created problems non-existent in thinly populated societies. "The poppy seed of light novels, scattered broadcast over our land for the last few years, are already springing up rankly, because the soul was ready for such a crop; and the next generation will be made drunk with the opium of voluptuousness, if we do not unite to kill the poison plant."

Extermination of vice needed the strength of all available social forces. Penalties and restraints were to be applied by law and moral conviction strengthened by a program of exhortation and appeal. Some tacticians were suggesting licensing laws for brothels. Would you license anyone to administer poison, Channing demanded. Charming picture: Elegantly dressed women entertaining gentlemen in their lavishly furnished houses of ill fame, and earning enough to send their daughters through college! Of course they protested that their personal liberty would be infringed if the practice of their profession were to be made a penal offense! And of course we may expect their clients, the lawyers and judges and other solid citizens who patronized them, to join in the protest. Receivers of stolen property were subject to conviction. How different were the receivers of these women, who were irretrievable once they got into this business? Likewise, Channing added, should adulterers and seducers be penalized as counterfeiters.

The *Harbinger* published several articles on marriage which deprecated unions of the hand without the heart. Harriet Martineau, the Englishwoman who traveled extensively, observed and participated in many reform movements, and wrote on a tremendous range of subjects, struck at the "divine institution" idea. As far as she could see, a good deal of it fell into the category of legal prostitution—a happy phrase which rolled on every radical reformer's tongue. An article reprinted in the *Harbinger* from the *Lynn Pioneer* called the defenseless submission of wives "Legalized Rape"—another phrase of which the radicals in the feminist and anarchist movements were tremendously fond. One J. H. Duganne introduced the class angle in his thoughts on "Unhappy Marriages." Marriages of the poor, he said, were likely to be more successful because fewer extraneous factors entered into their choice of a mate. Hasty marriages among them were rare, since their chronic insecurity made them more cautious in everything they did.

The rich, on the other hand, were rapid breeders of infidelity and immorality. The causes lay in the unreal education of both sexes, in the inculcation of disdain for people outside a given caste or circle, and in match-making and infant betrothals. The materialistic outlook prevalent among the middle classes, and their exaggerated adherence to the double standard, contributed not a little to the high incidence of marital failure among them. A clipping from the *Lynn News* supported the thesis that man was joining together many whom God would have preferred to have asunder.

❧ ❧

Association, then, was no very serious threat to the marriage institution. If it were, Horace Greeley for one would not have touched it with a ten-foot pole. What worried those who clung stubbornly to the past was the apparent weakening of family strength implicit in association's reorganization of the family functions. Quite in keeping with their promise to women of greater independence and opportunity, the strategists of association came forth with plans for a "com-

bined kitchen," or a "combined household." Isolated households
meant domestic servitude for women. The only available alternative
under the old arrangement was to emancipate women by letting men
sink to women's former level. Hysterical opponents of the project
immediately predicted "combined wives." More temperate ones, however, feared only that the family would be destroyed. If they were
thinking of the social and religious controls exercised by the family,
their uneasiness was perhaps justified. For meals in a dining hall,
common nurseries, and common schools surely invited a fresh interchange of ideas and beliefs. The critics of association, disregarding
possible advantages, responded intuitively with the same argument
that all critics of socialization proposals have used: The individuality
of persons and of families would be lost in the common mass.

But everyone, and especially the womenfolk, knew that there was
a lot to say for Fourier in his capacity of efficiency expert. The male
defenders of association said plenty in due time. First it had to be
made plain that nowhere in Brisbane's writings had compulsory combination been advocated. Everyone was to have a free choice of the
private domestic system, the public hotel arrangement, or any combination of the two. As for the possible monotony of eating at the
same table day in and day out, year after year, wherein did this differ
from the practice of the ordinary family. And in any case, one was
free to choose his company or change it if he pleased.

But the fear of compulsory association was hard to dispel; even
those already converted to general sympathy with the movement had
doubts about so unexpected a change in the traditional groupings.
The transcendental faction had a soft spot in its heart for home. One
of them had argued its merits in the *Dial* of 1841. Love at home had
the function of counteracting selfishness outside. All reform was
said to begin at home. The principles, motives, hopes, and fears
which grew out of home life would purify a man's social and business
life. Home was the transcendentalist retreat from the grating world
of industry and commerce. It was the place where self-improvement
flourished and the inner resources of the soul unfolded in accordance
with the idealist vision of the immanence of divinity in the individual.
Would the new order preserve all this? Even women hesitated to accept the proferred freedom if it meant losing that little authority they
exercised in their own homes.

Channing, Charles A. Dana, John S. Dwight, and other knights
of association, stepped forward to disperse the dragons which men-
aced home and hearth. Channing testified in *The Present* (January
1845) that no loosening of family ties had yet shown up in experimental communities. It seemed to him that, on the contrary, husbands
and wives were showing each other increased consideration and respect. The parent-child relationship had benefited too, since associa-

145

tion took over many correctional and disciplinary duties, leaving only affection, confidence, and virtue in the family environment. Charles Anderson Dana, that most versatile of Brook Farmers who was later to be associated with Horace Greeley's *Tribune*, loosed a whole battery of objections to the isolated family. Not that anything derogatory was aimed at the family itself. Association would not tread on it with a "profane foot." In fact, it would hold the family together against the forces of the age that were dispersing it to all corners of the country in search of economic opportunity. The present family system had many faults in practice which bore out criticisms implied in the theoretical structure of Fourierism. The isolated family was uneconomical. Think of the waste entailed in the preparation of food and in the heating of houses! Again, the present system engendered selfishness of the worst and most subtle kind. Think how family is pitted against family, and parent against child, in competition for the meager material goods available for sharing. And lastly, the isolated family failed to promote the healthy development of heart, mind, and body. Were not all housewives unhappy and perpetually annoyed by little things? Think of the monotony suffered by a woman cooped up daily to take care of cooking and cleaning, while the husband is off somewhere—not near his wife as he would be under the associationists' plan—wasting his strength away in uneconomic labor.

These irritations were subject to control in associationist society, in which the harmonious interaction of all life factors could be planned. Harmonious society depended upon the correct balance of all the social affections. The isolated family developed only two forms of affection—love and parental sentiment. Hence the antagonisms and aggravated individualism in a society of rigidly separated family units. Swedenborg (whose *Delights of Wisdom concerning Conjugal love: after which follow the pleasures of insanity concerning scortatory love*, had been published in Philadelphia in 1796, but passed up by American intellectuals as impossible to fathom) was called in as witness. "Families, in an internal sense, signify probity, and also charity and love. All things relating to mutual love, are in the heavens as consanguinities of relationships, consequently as families." So there you are! We shall all be one happy family in heaven. Association was near enough to Heaven to begin to rival it.

Heaven would come to earth in reality for the children of association, since they were going to get expert supervision in their moral and intellectual growth. They would work, play, and learn with large numbers of children of their own age. The graded school, difficult to achieve in most small communities of the time, was assured in the phalanx structure. Every opportunity, from that of mental-motor development in pre-school years to intellectual development in college, was feasible under association. It was impossible to secure competent teaching in practically every isolated household, but under association, trained teachers would do away with the problem of the spoiled children whom everyone admitted were being bred in seven-eighths of American families. Yes, seven-eighths of those who practiced parenthood were unfit to raise children, and society had to be protected against the product of their ignorance.

Dana's strong sentiments were supported and embellished by the very idealistic John S. Dwight, whose pastorate in the Unitarian church gave him prestige in matters of the spirit, and whose experience as a music teacher and critic enriched his appreciation of civilization conceived as an art and of the ideal life conceived as harmony. Dwight's highly charged article on "Home," written in 1841, prepared him for his articles on "The Children of Association" and the "Plan of an Associative Dwelling" in 1846 and 1848 respectively. His philosophical eloquence on the subject of the graded school soared as he spoke of the principle of *ascending progressive emulation* by whose capillary action children were drawn up to the next grade. In association schools, children were kept in the "true sphere with their equals" and "natural affinities of age and character" were consulted in the selection of attendants and teachers. Moreover, the same children would live in happy homes, secure in their emotions and economic status.

Licentiousness? There was no place for it to develop in the phalanx quarters where single males and females were lodged separately. And why would any girl surrounded by friends and relations, educated, and ultimately assured of a good marriage, be tempted to enter into a clandestine affair? (The untranscendent clergy might have said of this social logic that Reason supported it but Nature did not).

Thus far the associationists had been able to answer critics with a disavowal of some of Fourier's sex reforms or by disclaiming any intention of putting his ideas into practice at once. It was difficult to continue debating significantly with the proponents of some future state of harmony when men would be angelic beings who could do no wrong. If the attack grew more intense, the associationists could always retaliate with a phrase from Swedenborg or with a quotation from his American medium, Andrew Jackson Davis. Henry James, Senior—who had discovered Swedenborg during his voyage abroad with his family in 1844, and was now, advocating Swedenborgianism together with Fourierism—used this technique to his own honest satisfaction. His excellent prose and striking images frequently left him with the last word. It was impossible, however, to sidestep the *New York Observer*, the militant Presbyterian newspaper which was attacking the Catholics when not attacking the Fourierists.

Up until the end of 1848, James and his friends were engaged in an evenly matched polemical campaign against the *Observer*. The Presbyterian editors would impute all sorts of vice to "association," and James would reply that the Presbyterian church was confining its Christian charity to its own nest—and losing members swiftly for its pains. But finally, James ever ready to give his fellow men the benefit of what he had learned, translated and published anonymously Victor Hennequin's *Love in the Phalanstery*, a Fourierist pamphlet which outlined the plan for harmonizing sexual relations. Soon after the *Observer* wrote its initial blasts, James admitted his authorship of the translation and rolled up his sleeves for a finish fight. Naturally enough, the whole of the American associationist movement was involved. The ideas were those of Fourier, and, unfortunately, the inside face of the pamphlet's cover carried the advertisement of the American Union of Associationists and the *Harbinger*, appropriately presenting a list of officers. Horace Greeley headed the list as President; Ripley and Parke Godwin followed as Secretaries.

All the prefatory disclaimers in the world could not separate these names from their proximity to the contents of the pamphlet. Into the bargain, the American preface wanted to reject the book's contents and yet keep its conclusions. What else could James have meant when he said: "It is hard to see how any well meaning man can read it without cordially asserting to its *conclusions*. The present law of sexual relations clearly demands a revision." The criticism of the handling of adolescence by our present civilization was trite enough. The promise of wholesome outlets for youthful energies in the industrial and agricultural pursuits of the phalanx was new only insofar as it demonstrated how the phalanstery was in harmony with nature. The real novelty was to be found in an elaborate list of categories into which the female sex was to be divided in the Fourierist future. Much of the terminology was superfluous, and some, for American readers, was meaningless. A few of the definitions looked like respectable circumlocutions for categories of prostitutes. The New York *Observer* was not purely malicious when it used the adjectives "obscene" and "abominable." The assistant editor who wrote a book note on Hennequin for the prim *Godey's Lady's Book* obviously had not read the work, which he described as "A small tract, very interesting both to Fourierists and those who are not so, beautifully printed, and worth the reading." All this at twelve and a half cents! *Holden's Dollar Magazine* reported that the book was good in that it was informative, and bad in that it would corrupt the morals of youth. Moreover, Holden's reviewer added, the Hennequin tract, for the first time in the literature of Fourierism, made quite clear that the system was not based on universals of human behavior as claimed, but on the particular state of society under which the author of these ideas had lived.

The thumbprints of present problems and present expediency were everywhere apparent in this exposition of love in the phalanstery.

The Observer had the same interpretation but was not so kind or as calm in its expression of it. The *Harbinger* people were very much on the defensive. Ripley reviewed the book, emphasizing the anticipatory nature of Fourier's thinking. Parke Godwin also protested that neither the French nor the American associationists were thinking of the here and now. Fourier himself had reproved Owen and others for advocating immediate change. He always had maintained that the change must come about by a deliberate vote of legislators, parents, and the church. Both Godwin and a writer who signed himself "N" felt that Fourier had been somewhat precipitate in his analysis and conclusions with regard to sexual matters. "N" thought that the French social scientist had simply taken the current practice of the French lower classes and transplanted it to an elevated position in his design for the future. But notwithstanding the shortcomings of the plan, it still had the merit of being a sincere attempt to conquer promiscuity. That was more than could be said for the plans and activities of other contemporary social leaders.

Henry James had particular reason to be aggrieved at the *Observer's* review of his translation. The finger was, in the last analysis, pointed at him. Under the initials "Y. S." (a rather childish label of anonymity consisting of the final letters of his first and last names) James protested that the translation was meant "only to arouse public attention to the great question of a right ordering of sexual relations." The translator's preface had said so and it should have been clear that publication of the book implied neither endorsement nor rejection. Intelligent people, said James, must consult all available scientific literature in a field which interests them. There was little excuse for shunning this particular attempt to get the world out of the mess it was in with regard to that most bothersome area of human behavior, sex. The *Observer* and its friends hated to see their smug satisfaction disturbed. Hence this hysteria, hence these tears.

James' line of reasoning was this: Present society was based upon the family, and that was perhaps as it should be. But whence arise the family's imperfections? (And here James bared his neck for the axe.) Society recognized sex only in marriage, and hence drove many an unwilling party into a relationship he would not have entered otherwise. If Fourier could produce a society not based on the family, then his was the privilege and the obligation "to demand liberty in love." In a harmonic society, every human drive claimed similar freedom of expression. Marriage, James affirmed, was a divine institution; but divinity resided not in the thing itself, but in its ability to pass the pragmatic test. The individual was the most sacred unit on Earth.

What had to be asked was: How did the sacred individual fare in marriage?

Many would argue that God had instituted marriage as divine in an absolute sense, and placed an eternal ban on all "extra-conjugal" love. The answer to this argument was that such prohibitions were temporary ones designed to help man reach a state of perfection. Man needed divine negatives as long as he was on the road to improvement; but once he reached the perfect state and dwelled in a divine, or harmonic, society, negative man would be converted to affirmative man and the moral law, the negative expression of the Divine Will, would then become superfluous.

Marriage, moreover, was not the legal, conventional practice. It was a spiritual union of man and woman, an exclusively internal union, the union of understanding and will. This argument may have settled matters for James, but his audience was far from being convinced. The Swedenborgian clergyman, the Reverend Alfred E. Ford, disagreed with James' interpretation and use of New Church doctrine. Ford did not mind publicly expanding his own views toward resolving James "confusion."

Expand they both did. "A. E. F." (Ford did not sign his own contributions either) and "Y. S." kept up their controversy for about a year, covering pages and pages of closely printed folio sheets. At one point when they both seemed exhausted and were already writing postscripts a certain "G. F. T." interjected a remark that started them off again. Ford's initial comments on *Love in the Phalanstery* were sane, systematic, and lucid in contrast to James' effusions. "Association" had enough trouble with outside carping, he pleaded. Let us—for the Swedenborgian cleric was an associationist too—publically disavow Fourier's erotic principles. "A. E. F." declared that he was not alone in the association movement in his belief that the phalansteric arrangements described by Hennequin would increase the world's miseries instead of lessening them. What did the new system amount to? Those who married entered a stage of "constancy" which they could abandon without legal or other process, either by mutual consent, or on the simple initiative of either party. One left one's "constancy series" and entered another "series" with another partner—"not, indeed, promiscuously, but under regulations." This flitting about would lessen the social esteem in which one was held, but not irreparably. A similar lessening of public esteem was all that differentiated Fourier's series of loose-living *bayadères* from those registered in "constancy" series. By whatever name you called it, the Reverend Ford insisted, when a woman lived with someone other than her husband, it was adultery.

This was pandering to popular prejudices, replied James. He would agree that Fourier was immoral; he would express his own serious reservations; but nothing would make him give up his scientific study of society, nor would he seek to promote the prosperity of associationism by completely denouncing Fourier's speculations on love in the divine order. Like Robert Dale Owen, he refused to sell his soul for favorable public opinion. Moreover, the Fourier system was on the side of God and Swedenborg in its failure to impose legal and social penalties upon those who broke the human laws of an imperfect society. Where no law existed, there could be no transgression. In a truly divine society, there would be no basis for creating a dichotomy of good and evil. In answer, "A. E. F." did not think one could reconcile Hell with the Divine Order. Obviously, replied James, he had not heard that the New Church had hit upon the reconciliation of Heaven and Hell as the basis of a divine order. "A. E. F." should really catch up with his Swedenborg readings.

In essence, what emerges from the controversy with regard to James' views is that he was entirely too sympathetic to Fourier's proposal of complete release from manmade restrictions. He accepted the socialist analysis of the coincidence of marriage law with property law, along with the analogy of monogamy to monopoly. The time would come, he predicted—very much as if he had just been reading William Godwin—when men and women would "dispense with every outward or legal claim to the other's affections, and to assert an exclusively private claim, or claim based upon paramount individual worth. I suppose the time will come when both men and women will reject an enforced homage, a homage enforced by the danger of public ignominy; a time when they will utterly loathe an affection which is unwillingly rendered."

In defiance of Ford's pleas to James to renounce these evil ideas (as Greeley's *Tribune* had already done in its parallel controversy with the *Courier*), James pushed his position further. Weaving back and forth from the spiritual to the natural, from God to social science, and from universal law to manmade law, he fabricated a tapestry which depicted free love. He made sure, of course, to arm himself against personal abuse. Neither he nor his wife, he frankly explained, had ever been tempted to violate their strictly legal vows. His motive was not, therefore, selfish. His explanations had been undertaken because he could not live with himself unless he expressed fully and clearly his relations with God. His life had been a search for the divine will within the soul of man. His ideas on marriage were an important part of the conclusions he had formed.

∽ ∽

The forties produced so great a variety of compounds based on common substances that it was impossible to find two exactly alike. Even when two could be found with the same major ingredients in almost the same proportion, subtle differences in quantity were bound to result in wide disparities of a qualitative order. James, whose Swedenborgian content outweighed the Fourierist, would recognize the permanence only of a union of souls. Dr. Marx Edgeworth Lazarus, a Fourierist with not a little Swedenborg in him, would accept permanence in no union whatsoever. His book, *Love versus Marriage* (1852), was addressed "To all true lovers. To the modest and the brave of either sex, who believe that God reveals to the instinct of each heart the laws which he destines it to obey, who fear not to follow the magic clew of charm, but defy the interference of all foreign powers. . . ." In other words, one's inclinations were one's best guide. Some 325 pages of sociology, psychology, physiology, medicine, Swedenborg, Emerson, Tennyson, Byron, and Shelley amplified the theory.

The book provided extensive sex education in addition to furnishing a set of universal marriage principles. Instead of starting with the customary "harmony" of the flowers and bees, it went back to the source of all harmony, the sun. From the sun and moon which brought about and guided all conjugation on earth, it proceeded to natural phenomena nearer earth. The ocean and earth were conjugated, as were light and air. The rivers were conjugated with islands. "They fertilize them and modify their temperature." The same principle was then carried through the plant, insect, and animal worlds, where each obeyed his seasons and harmonies. Only man seemed to distort the grand harmonic picture of which he too was a part. He had violated the smooth interrelatedness of the whole by creating a marriage institution which had no connection with the principles of conjugal harmony as here described. There was no place for "exclusive and permanent property in the person or the soul of the being beloved. . . . I say exclusive possession of soul as well as body, for this is the source of confusion for those who, while they indignantly protest against that legal chattelism in persons which constitutes the arbitrary marriage of civilization, yet admit the idea on which its marriage law is founded, under the name of spiritual mating, or the marriage of souls."

Lazarus' analysis of the nature of the human heart led him to believe that there were many "conjugal affinities" for each one in several mortal stages of harmonic growth and in the metamorphoses of the infinite hereafter. For if, in our poor hemmed-in existence in this one-minute mortal career, "we have been able to form several true love relations, and realize much happiness and spiritual development from each, how many more may we not expect to form during our progressive development and numerous transitions, during the cycles of eternity, and in those aromal and spiritual bodies whose finer texture no longer subjects them to obstructions of gross matter, in following the lead of our passional affinities." From this obvious extension of Swedenborgianism he proceeded to a clear statement of his credo, which declared that one could love many, in series or simultaneously, without committing a breach of fidelity. Moreover, as it developed in his elaboration of phalansteric love, chastity was unrelated to virtue. In essence he was preaching Shelley's mathematics of love, namely that to divide was not to take away. *Love vs. Marriage* was, by any definition but a libertine's, an incitement to promiscuity. The language was explicit and frequently unrefined, especially when viewed by the critical eye of Henry James.

There were many things on which these two intellectuals could see eye to eye, but not enough to preserve harmony between them. This radical Fourierist physician had come out from behind the screen of "future application" with which the others had covered themselves. He had also snickered at the eternal union, or spiritual marriage, of souls—James' last refuge in the struggle for liberalized conventions of marriage and divorce. Lazarus' book got a very caustic review in the *Tribune* from Henry James, who was by this time a staunch supporter of the role of the family nucleus in society.

James' honesty in expressing his convictions was admirable, but it brought down upon him a rush of enemies coming from all points of the intellectual compass. The *Observer* affair flared up again, and its editors had to be reminded by James that they were only muddying the waters to cover up their pique at an attack on their religious conservatism. (James had previously published a line on "that fossil and fatiguing Christianity, of which the *Observer* is so afflictive a type, and its editor so distinguished and disinterested a martyr.") Why, James asked, did the *Observer* persist in its attempts to ruin his personal reputation when the philosopher had nothing with which to defend it but pure reason. His campaign against several church organizations had for its purpose the reinjection into religion of a living piety "attuned to the ministries of science." In short, he wished to strip religion of its mumbo-jumbo and make it an instrument for feeding the hungry, clothing the naked, and enlightening the ignorant. In the same way, he wished to purify marriage so that it would rest on "inward sweetness" rather than on legal bondage. Did the *Observer* think so little of human goodness as to believe that the most religious and refined of men would instantly rush into adultery if police restraint were removed?

But the *Observer* was really the least of his troubles. Behind him stood his friend Horace Greeley, berating him for looking beyond the word of Christ in the matter of divorce. Before him stood that eccentric reformer, martyred abolitionist, shorthand enthusiast, and preacher of individual sovereignty, Stephen Pearl Andrews. This experienced radical, whose ranging mind had carried him a step beyond the transcendental Fourierists, suggested that James settle the marriage question by answering a more fundamental one.

The crucial questions were: Up to what point shall man, by virtue of being man, be permitted to exercise his freedom without interference on the part of other individuals or their combined form, society? Who was to set the standards of propriety and morality? Do you leave it to the individual polygamist to decide on the goodness or badness of his way of life? Or is someone else to do the approving and disapproving? James had stated clearly that the conjugal, parental, and other social ties of man would be transformed into divinely beautiful relationships if relieved of the pressures of law and custom. Would marriage still be marriage by dictionary, law, or Bible in this liberated form?

The issue thus set, Greeley made space available in the *Tribune* until he thought the subject had been covered. But Andrews wanted to keep the argument going and chided Greeley in terms of the very brand of liberalism which the editor professed. Appealing to the superstitions of an uneducated majority in order to beat down the reasoning of an innovator was hardly in the liberal spirit. The analogy of his own lot to that of the unheeded Socrates and Christ occurred to Andrews as it had to Frances Wright and others. Greeley, who agreed with his worst ideological enemies on the privilege of disagreeing (and liberally opened the columns of the *Tribune* to give the other fellow a public hearing) began to have his reservations after a few exchanges with Andrews. The man's language verged on the indecent in the first place. Then too, why should an editor permit his paper to repeatedly advertise Andrews' notions about equating virtue with adultery? But if Greeley would not print an extension of Andrews' remarks, his opponent would and did reprint the entire series, including those items rejected by the *Tribune* as superfluous, indecent, and presumptuous.

Henry James was tired. His first contribution to the new debate was addressed to Greeley. Its tenor was that James had already answered Andrews' queries, and, besides, they were not pertinent to the James' quarrel with the *Observer*. He did not want to bother with Andrews at all. However, he soon reconsidered and made a statement for Andrews' benefit on the desirability of having society grant divorces to parties who had mistakenly joined in the conjugal union. But society had to enter the picture because it had an important stake in the individual's actions. Andrews' formula about individual freedom plus the willingness to take consequences had to include also a willingness to take the social consequences. Man was under subjection to nature, to society, and to God. "His appetites and his sensuous understanding relate him to nature; his passions and rational understanding relate him to society or his fellow-man;

and his ideas relate him to God." The social nature of man was beginning to stand out as the medium through which he was able to increase his individual stature. Society was the reservoir of the arts and sciences from which each drew his raw materials and to which each contributed his product.

With that James dropped out of the argument—only to turn up two decades later with a letter to "H. Y. R." in the *St. Paul's Press.* The occasion was a momentous one in the history of American morality. Preacher Henry Ward Beecher of Plymouth Church, Brooklyn, was defending himself in court against editor Theodore Tilton's suit for alienation of affections. Beecher was said to have had unholy relations with a worshipping member of his congregation. Victoria Woodhull, that fearless advocate of all nameable freedoms, had exposed the family quarrel, and by the time the trial came up, the matter had become a national issue. Beecher's friends and supporters tried to hush the whole thing up; the press and the public enjoyed the details of the scandal, and Beecher's enemies called him a freelover. James could not agree with that view. Beecher had merely yielded in a moment of weakness. The free love theorists were glorifying a merely instinctual drive and talking as if it were the flywheel of society. They were lowering the dignity of the human race. They might better concentrate on rewriting the law of divorce, and gain their ends in that way without tampering with what was great and beautiful in man. Was it not self-discipline and self-denial that differentiated man from the animal world? Again, if a man married a wife who to him symbolized perfection, and then afterward found liberty in conflict with wedlock, these were choices for the conscience to make. For himself, James would choose to stick it out and seek the sources of weakness within himself. But divorce should be available to others. James' view was colored by the fact that he recognized the divine in his wife. He had had experience of her sweetness, patience, and understanding. "Thus marriage is to me my finest divine revelation. I should simply have gone to hell long ago if my wife had not saved me . . . by unconsciously being the good, modest woman she is."

"H. Y. R." winked to Andrews, indicating that the dear old metaphysician had his heart in the right place but simply could not come down to earth long enough to handle practical affairs. Once woman had been liberated, said James' correspondent, she would "settle down under the cool, healing influence of modest restraint," and the whole issue of free love would be dead. It was true that much scullduggery went on under the name of free love, but James was exaggerating. Andrews intimated slyly that James himself may not have been on that spiritually higher plane which permitted individual sovereignty without abuse. Moreover, he denied that the free love advocates were thinking in purely physiological terms. "Individual sovereignty" was still a good slogan. As for James' metaphysics, it was so far out of this world that no one could make head or tail of it. The fact was that in one of his published letters of the debate dating back twenty years, Andrews had asked Greeley to leave James out of the discussion because he did not know how to take a clear position. Greeley's views may have been entirely backward and perverse, but they were definite. In that sense it was a pleasure to argue with him.

The position of the editor of the *New York Tribune* was indeed a clear one. He swept individual sovereignty out of the way immediately, pointing out that not even Andrews could be predicating a society in which a man could do *anything* he pleased. The state had to interfere to protect the overall welfare of the people. Now, granting that there were one hundred present cases in which divorce was individually indicated and socially desirable, if you made its facilities generally available, thousands would rush into careless or irresponsible marriages knowing that they could get out easily. The fellows who now lay intricate plans for the ruin of maidens outside of marriage would accomplish their ends legally and then skip out. Better to let the hundred worthy cases suffer than bring on an era of immorality such as liberalized divorce laws had precipitated after the first French Revolution. If it were left to Greeley, he would allow only adultery as cause, and not even that if Christ had not said so. Marriage laws may not yet have been perfected, but they were the best plan thus far proposed.

There were a number of sophistries on public sale, and they needed exposure badly, said the public servant, Horace Greeley. Many had already been duped by the one about a ceremony not being necessary as long as affection was there. "The free trade sophistry respecting marriage is already on every libertine's tongue; it has overrun the whole country in yellow covered literature which is as abundant as the frogs of Egypt and a great deal more pernicious." Stephen Pearl Andrews had glibly referred back to our liberty-loving Pilgrim fathers. Yes, was Greeley's retort, they could afford liberty because they practiced restraint. Our own contemporaries were not disciplined enough to judge themselves as strictly as they judged others. Why, even the most licentious fathers wanted their children to be moral. A curse on those who would distort the sexual function from its original propagative purposes! Also on those women to whom emancipation meant the freedom to choose a new father for each of their children! What a pandemonium of paternities they invited! And how they were going to cheat children out of their birthright, which included biparental protection and education!

Andrews had a ready answer, for he had listened carefully to the Owenites and Fourierists when they doubted the fitness of parents to raise the children they bore. Andrews had ready answers to more difficult questions as well, because he was an eclectic in doctrines of social upheaval.

The *New York Times* could also see the interrelatedness among the great variety of social reform ideas which had grown up in the United States. Its tirade on "Free Love Systems" had as its main target the doctrines of Fourier which the rival *Tribune* had helped disseminate.

But no movement under any name was overlooked if the *Times* suspected its connection with socialism or free love. It was all the same thing if one was smart enough to see behind the ruses. There were numerous disguises and forms; the tactic changed to suit the times. At the moment, argumentative literature had been abandoned in favor of the novel, the medical treatise, the biographical sketch, and the adroit literary notice. No matter how they organized it, in secret societies or in the "hundreds" of intellectuals, it was the same inducement to evil-doing running the gamut from elopement to divorce.

The seeds lay in Byron and Shelley, in the romances of George Sand and Eugene Sue—the last two being transmission belts for Fourierism. It had begun in this country with the Owens and Fanny Wright and was on current display in Victor Considerant, Albert Brisbane, Parke Godwin, and Margaret Fuller. There were also Horace Greeley, with his thoughts on isolated households, the associationists, and the preachers of the gospel that the law of attraction is as binding in society as the Law of Gravitation in physics. All blinds for free love and socialism, including the transcendental speculation upon social laws and woman's rights; including the reformist denunciations of all existing evils, and Dr. Lazarus with his translations from Fourier, St. Pierre, Toussenel and the St. Simonians. Included in the same camp were the distortions of Swedenborg, modern spiritualism, spirit-rappings and mediums, the Woman's Rights movement, and John Humphrey Noyes' Perfectionists at Oneida with their anti-marriage instigations.

The *Times* was well up on its radicals, though it emphasized vague similarities and overlooked important distinctions. It could see how Stephen Pearl Andrews was converting the individualism of his most recent mentor, Josiah Warren, into a philosophical justification of the popular free love trend. It was rather mistaken, as will be seen, in its interpretation of Warren's intentions.

FIVE

Free Land, Free Labor, Free Love

Josiah Warren has the distinction of having been the father of American anarchist thought. The ideas he developed were certainly not present in his early environment—Boston; nor did they come from his father, a distinguished general in the Revolutionary War. The family background of high Puritanism had scant connection with the economic and philosophical anarchism of his adult life. Warren married at twenty—that was in 1818—and went West to seek his fortune. Some five years later he invented and engaged in the manufacture of a cheap lard-burning lamp. However, it was not long before Robert Owen came through Cincinnati on a lecture tour, winning Warren to his plan for an ideal society, and paving the way for the subsequent removal of the Warren family to New Harmony. It was there that the intellectually curious lamp manufacturer made the acquaintance of some of the best scientific and educational minds of his time. And from these he learned to observe and question.

His search for the true principles underlying the happiness of man in a well-adjusted society started at New Harmony. But the Owens had injected too much environmental control into socialism for Warren's tastes. Freedom to him had to carry with it the right of an individual to do what he pleased with his own property and reputation, providing no one else suffered the consequences of his indiscretions. He did not want to be bullied into a new kind of life any more than he would wish to be inhibited by the forms of an old one. Two letters from "The Mutualist," which the *New Harmony Gazette* published during Warren's residence at Owen's frontier Utopia, could very well have come from his pen. The letters expressed a fear that inherent in the proposed road to freedom was a potential threat of bureaucratic domination. Robert Owen's own leader complex may have added to this fear. "The Mutualist" could not quite agree that a society should control anyone's preferences in the matter of religion, or even his desire to assume the obligations of marriage set by law and convention. There even seemed to be an intimation, in the New Harmony mores, that going into the marital state with a view toward permanence might be considered a social error. Naturally the editors of the *Gazette* told "Mutualist" that he had misconstrued both Owen and the system.

However, since dogma was dogma, Warren went back to Cincinnati to try his own little plan, the "Time Store." At the time store one exchanged the product of one's labor for a "note" which was valued according to the time spent at work and the "repugnance" of the job performed. Each product in Warren's store had a clock price —that is, the production-time value of the article plus the cost of distribution. Labor cost, not arbitrary value, became the measuring-rod for price. One important principle, that labor is the only acceptable kind of property, was established. At one stroke, the "time store" was to short circuit the whole paraphernalia of value controls. Those who labored would take over from those who owned and exchanged. This would bring man closer to his natural state of society, since nature recognized no ownership or control which was not the result of a man's own exertions. If one's property happened to increase in value through no effort of his own, then the state was to take over the surplus because surpluses of this kind are a social product. The scheme was an ancestor of Henry George's single-tax proposal. The larger system of governmental apparatus was to rest in the hands of a group of experts, a brain trust with technocratic authority.

Warren's own subsequent trials and errors in economic and community enterprise tended more to confirm his early opinions than to modify them. "Cost the limit of price" and "individual sovereignty" remained his watchwords. In "A Few Words to the Pioneers" written for *Woodhull and Claflin's Weekly* three years before his death, he transmitted two important lessons to the younger, fresher breed of reformers. The first was that the labor question constituted the pivot of society; the second, that many a noble reformer with fine ideas had been overlooked or rejected by society because the marriage bogey hovered nearby. Frances Wright had warned of a great civil war over the slavery question and, in her own way, had tried to forestall it with her experiment in emancipation. But no one had listened to her because she insisted on answering the test question on marriage in a manner consistent with her philosophy of freedom. "It mattered nothing that the great Robert Owen gave us the key to self-emancipation and to universal peace and to all the social virtues—this great, horrible spectre stood right across our path, threatening destruction to all who should attempt to pass him, even peaceably."

The apostle of individual sovereignty knew of this from personal experience too. He had been confronted with the loyalty test and had answered, he thought, well. He would leave marriage just as it was;

he would not meddle with it at all. But this had failed to satisfy his inquisitors and, from small beginnings, there grew up a Frankenstein who frightened even Warren's friends away. After a while, people became so fearful that they would not discuss the question in their own parlors.

To illustrate how the world is ready to believe the worst of any new social experiment, the public reaction to Modern Times (the community which Warren founded on Long Island in 1851) provided incidents aplenty. The community had fared well enough until the *New York Tribune* gave it its first publicity. From that point onward, all kinds of cranks and curiosity-seekers visited it and then spread malicious gossip about it.

The principle of the community had it that everybody was welcome on a live-and-let-live basis. One woman with a particularly bad figure had taken to wearing men's clothes of garish cut and cloth. Her neighbors claimed that the disgusting sight she presented was interfering with their own individual sovereignty but did nothing beyond pulling their blinds down when she walked by. But the word got around that all the women in the community dressed like men.

One member of the group had his children running around in the nude even in the bitter cold of winter. Another old man, almost blind, claimed he could see better when he took his clothes off, and his vision was very valuable to him. A woman with a diet mania starved herself to death. A foursome consisting of one man and three women took up house as a cozy family group and annoyed all their neighbors with their boisterous behavior; they went their separate ways in three months. Warren and his friends told them "that no four people, nor even any two people can govern one house or drive one horse at the same time—that nature demands and will have an *Individual* deciding power in every sphere, whether that government is a person, an idea, or anything else; it must be individuality or all will be confusion."

Here was Warren, a moderate who tried his best to meet society halfway, insisting only on the give and take of individuals. But people painted the community in the light of its worst members, giving it a reputation for nudism, faddism, polygamy, bohemianism and free love practices. Did Warren believe in free love as it was exemplified by the spiritualist groups and erotic irresponsibles who had confused the issue of marriage reform? He was uncompromisingly against that kind of irrationality, which, as he knew from experience, led to insanity and suicide. The horrible effects of promiscuity, he suggested, were to be seen at Dr. Jourdain's Gallery of Anatomical Specimens in Boston.

The venerable veteran of several reform movements and witness of many others postponed his own decision on the family problem for forty-five years, and even then would not speak with finality. The nearest he came to presenting a formula after decades of thought was a statement which itself was tentative: The principle of individuality as applied to marriage affirmed the generally accepted idea that *one* man for *one* woman was right. The only qualification he would make—and this one he claimed had been incorporated in the laws of several nations—was that the contract should specify a definite period of time, understood and agreed upon by both parties. The period in general use, he said, was two years, "renewable by consent of both parties."

Ezra Heywood and other pioneers of the sixties and seventies dissented strongly. They objected to any form of legally binding contract whatsoever. Warren maintained his position against his own disciples and fought them publicly on this difference. He objected first to terms like "thieves" and "robbers" which these headstrong youngsters were employing to describe people who clung to current practices. The point was well taken: "With regard to State marriages, I think you don't intend to make uncompromising war upon them when parties prefer to be married by State laws and ceremonies; yet your words may be so understood and certainly will be so represented by the mercenary press and all other obstructives to freedom."

Social institutions as they existed, said Warren, were indeed repressive and it was necessary to seek release from them. But, and this was his second dissent, in seeking freedom we must not revert to primitive promiscuity. Such behavior, he had observed, was leading to disastrous consequences. One of the results, which was being hushed up by the press, was an increasing incidence of venereal diseases. It was bad to rush to extremes. The real solution would come with the settling of the labor question. A thoroughgoing application of the principles of justice to *all* of the labor of *all* men, women, and children, would straighten out family relations just as it would settle so many other social problems.

Warren himself became a source of dispute among Heywood's coterie because of the stand he took on the Beecher scandal. He had declared that Beecher's individuality had been invaded by *The Word* and by *Woodhull and Claflin's Weekly,* both of which had revelled in their exposés of Beecher's alleged irregularities with Theodore Tilton's wife. Olivia Shepard, a Western free love advocate, took the lead. She held Warren to account for defending Beecher instead of Mrs. Woodhull, that paragon of outspokenness who had pressed the Beecher-Tilton exposure to avenge public attacks on her own character. Mrs. Shepard suggested that Warren apply the principles of "equity" to the relations of the sexes as he had in his "time" stores. The sculptor Sidney H. Morse stood by Warren and showed how the father of native American anarchy had been able to win over people from all walks of life by his intelligent moderation.

THE PANTARCH

Stephen Pearl Andrews, whose real claim to fame was that he digested Warren's ideas and prepared them for public consumption, did not participate in this quarrel openly. His debt to Warren was too great to allow his participation in a dispute in which he was definitely on Victoria Woodhull's side. The fact was that he had chosen Mrs. Woodhull to trumpet the anti-marriage notions he had been developing in the James-Greeley discussions twenty years before. For many years Andrews and Colonel Blood (Victoria Woodhull's current husband) had written Victoria's articles and speeches. They also edited for oral delivery or publication any ideas she might have thought of on her own.

Stephen Pearl Andrews was the philosopher-priest who directed the anti-marriage cult. The Tilton faction in the Beecher-Tilton controversy was eager to bring in Andrews as a witness. It could be shown that Andrews was a frequent enough visitor at Beecher's home to have infected him with the free love virus. A Beecher partisan wanted it to be known that the Pantarch (a title justly assigned to Andrews for it was the one to be held by the director of his own proposed pantarchy, or universal society) "has been the Woodhull's mentor—at least up to the point where the latter was required to submit wholly to the mental dictation and social mastership of the would-be Pontiff of Free-Loveism."

The Pantarch's brain could deal in nothing smaller than universals. He was attracted to Isaac Pitman's shorthand system because of its applicability to sounds in any language. He imported it into the United States and opened a school of phonology in Boston. An interest in philology led him to a new international language which he called "Alwato." His search for the global principles of society caused him to work Warren's ideas on economic anarchism into a *Science of Society* which he published in 1852, two years after he met Warren. The reconciliation of individual sovereignty with social requirements was *his* way of harmonizing the universe.

Human experience did not seem to play a strong part in his formulation of social ideas. As a hostile critic noted in a physical description of Andrews, he was "bowed of shoulder—from stooping over his study table, in all probability. . . . His complexion is 'sicklied o'er with the pale caste of thought,' but like his thought, the pallor is sickly." The same critic thought him "as remarkable a heresiarch as Brigham Young," and a man who had not achieved the fame of the Mormon prophet but was even more mischievous.

Andrews' special danger to organized society was that he argued so well. The *Tribune* exchange of the fifties revealed him as a man to be feared in a debate. All of the reformers of his period were accepting one version or another of individualist and social welfare doctrines. The Pantarch had a way of using his techniques of universal analogy to drive a hesitant opponent down the path of logical consistency. At the end of the path the opponent found himself faced with Andrews' conclusion—and it was hard to walk around it.

Henry James, Senior, found himself in this embarrassing position all too suddenly because in principle he was at one with Andrews about allowing perfect individual freedom to do its work in the love relationship. But James had wanted to preserve marriage, desiring only to remove its impurities by a chemical reaction with the science of Fourier and the theology of Swedenborg. Andrews tried to force James to state whether he meant by marriage the purest kind of union, or the institution as practiced in society. If he meant the first, he must join with Andrews in divesting the relationship of its religious and legal chains. If he meant the second, his lengthy and seemingly profound utterances were completely devoid of meaning. But James would not take a definite position, Andrews complained; when you get near to talking sense with him, "he cuttlefishes, by a final plunge into metaphysical mysticism."

It was for the benefit of the less elusive Greeley that Andrews used historical and political analogy in the systematization of his ideas. The story ran thus: Before the Protestant Reformation, the world was constrained by three superstitions—the ecclesiastical the governmental, and the matrimonial. These were, despite Andrews' failure to acknowledge the debt. Owen's three stumbling-blocks of civilization. But where Owen declared them all still to be operating in all their viciousness, Andrews found the church shaken by Luther, and governmental tyranny somewhat dislodged by the American Revolution. It remained only for modern socialism to revolutionize the sphere of domestic relations. If Greeley could accept Fourier's principle of attraction in the realms of free trade and labor reform (and he had done so), he was simply stubborn in his rejection of its application everywhere else. The world was at the dawn of a new era of freedom. New principles were in their formative stages.

According to Andrews, discriminating reformers were beginning to distinguish purity in the sexual union of loving souls from the sordid considerations of a marriage settlement. The issue of purity was even on the way to being separated in thought from the humane, prudential, and economical arrangements for the care of offspring. Horace Greeley was eager to retain the divine, or sacred, status of the family for reasons of sexual purity, the physical and cultural nurturing of children, and the protection and support of the weaker sex. Obviously Greeley was resisting the movement toward a greater freedom of the affections because he feared an enervating effect upon the family. This might or might not prove to be so. But it could be shown to Andrews' satisfaction, that the traditional functions of the family, as outlined by Greeley himself, would be strengthened by a greater freedom in love relations. The same beneficial results might be expected in this area from respecting individual sovereignty as had already been noticed in free trade, free enterprise, and freedom from state systems of religion and education.

Now, Andrews asked what was this thing called purity? Greeley said that it meant fidelity to the marriage relation. Greeley also declared marriage to be sacred because it was indispensable to purity. He seemed to reason in circles, or, as Andrews called it, he employed "a rotary method of ratiocination." Sexual purity, it would seem, should be defined with reference only to the mutual health and happiness of the parties concerned, and in consideration of future as well as present consequences. The answer was to be sought in new fields of scientific investigation in physiology, psychology, and economics. The scientists must certainly bring salutary change to the present sexual ethic which bred prostitution and the "solitary vice."

Andrews considered himself more sophisticated than most people by virtue of his reading in the up-and-coming sciences. He boasted the acquaintance of Dr. Thomas L. Nichols, the hydrotherapist, physiologist, sexologist, and sociologist whose *Esoteric Anthropology* (published in 1853) was "a comprehensive and confidential treatise on the structure, functions, attractions, and perversions, true and false physical and social conditions, and the most intimate relations of men and women." He also knew Nichols' wife, Mary Gove Nichols, who was entitled to acclaim in as many fields of knowledge and experience as her husband. She was, in fact, supposed to have diagnosed Andrews' irritability some years before as "excessive amative propensity," that is, as compared with his wife's "gravitational frequency." The prescription, as one historian's version goes, was to have the surplus absorbed elsewhere.

Mrs. Nichols was especially expert on that aspect of the marriage institution which had to do with the protection of women. She had also done much original observation on the subject of purity. The truly free woman, said Mrs. Nichols in a letter to Andrews, was one who had "health of body and spirit—who believes in God, and reverently obeys his laws in herself." Such a woman needed no law to guard her chastity. Virtue, to her, went beyond a rule of the game. "Such a woman has a heaven-conferred right to choose the father of her babe." Mr. Greeley, thought Andrews, had hard climbing ahead to reach Mrs. Nichols' level of purity. More and more intelligent women were recognizing that purity was not, as they had known it, nervous exhaustion born of fear on one side, and force on the other. Moreover, some of the physiological knowledge which caused thoughtful people to reconsider their notion of purity was on exhibit at the Albany Medical College in the form of uterine growths. Andrews accepted without question Mrs. Nichols' diagnosis of the cause of such woman's ailments. She had had much experience in such matters, and more than a decade before, in the late thirties, she had delivered and published her *Lectures to Ladies on Anatomy and Physiology.*

Andrews pointed to still another aspect of female protection which traditional marriage managed badly. This was the matter of self-sufficiency which Mary Wollstonecraft had discussed with telling effect. Quite contrary to the generally held misconception, marriage was the direct source of anxiety and insecurity in the female mind. Wives were constantly in dread of being cast adrift, unable to take care of themselves and their children in the case of a husband's death. And it went deeper than this. No human being needed or wanted to be taken care of; with "justice, freedom, and friendly cooperation" everyone could take care of himself. "Provided for by another, and subject to his will as the return tribute, they [women] pine, sicken, and die. . . . Our whole marital system is the house of bondage and the slaughter-house of the female sex." An intellectually, vocationally equipped woman, living in a combined household, as suggested by Greeley's own associationist friends, would not suffer from these deep-seated anxieties whether or not a husband was on the premises.

If, after reading a review of the disadvantages of marriage, Horace Greeley still thought it worth preserving for the sake of children, Stephen Pearl Andrews disagreed there too. For Andrews had read Owen and others on socialized nurseries and schools. He had also read and digested the eugenical speculations of his time. Having in view the most advanced knowledge of the time on heredity and child care, how could anyone be satisfied with the family's performance? One-half of the human family died in infancy. "Nine-tenths of the remainder are merely grown-up abortions, half-made before birth, and worse distorted and perverted by ignorant management and horrible abuses afterward."

For a social scientist who knew a great deal about environmental influence, Andrews attached surprising importance to the influence of heredity. If a woman were deprived of the privilege of choosing or refusing the father of her children, she was, he believed, knowingly perpetuating every bad trait that her husband possessed. And in many cases the worst crime a person could commit was to perpetuate himself.

Andrews may have been confused as to which effects were hereditary and which arose from early family environment, but he did appreciate the character disorders suffered by unwanted children. He also knew of the wounds an impressionable child could receive if his parents hated each other. Moreover, his declaration that intemperance, madness, murder, and all other vices were hereditary, that criminality started "back in the egg," was quite in keeping with what many responsible physicians and criminologists of his time believed.

This was how (as Andrews explained it step by step to Mr. Greeley) a free-lover came to his beliefs. He applied Josiah Warren's individual sovereignty—with the usual prohibition of encroachment on other people's rights—to this special area of activity, and left the rest to the mutual adjustment of two people sans interference from without. Free love was still in doctrinal form and had no application for people who were not prepared for it, did not understand it, or lacked the sense of principle and justice required for its successful practice. The free love advocate accepted with gratitude liberalized divorce laws or any other relaxation of social control over marriage. The ultimate goal, however, was that of the abolitionists—the destruction, not the amelioration, of a social evil.

Finally deprived of the *Tribune* as a medium for reaching the public by Greeley's refusal to publish more letters on the subject, Andrews, as has been mentioned, printed the entire correspondence—that which had appeared in the *Tribune* plus what Greeley had turned down—and let the matter go at that. He withdrew; but the anti-free love party, with its numbers, talent, and access to the press, continued the campaign of slander and abuse. Andrews took it good-naturedly for five years and then wrote a letter to the editor of the *Tribune* reaffirming the stand of his group on the abolition of the marital tie. He showed how scientific advance must amend old customs and beliefs; how even religion had progressed to the point where socialist millennialists and Swedenborgians were urging the adoption of practices that prevailed in Heaven, where, it should be remembered, there "is no marrying or giving in marriage."

Added to science and religion, there were the brilliant advances in sociology to consider in shaping public policy. Warren's principle of individual sovereignty had put a new face on the whole science of society. This principle applied also to the individual's choice of constancy or variety. It applied to his freedom from restraint in morals as much as it did to his freedom from state domination in religion. Those who predicted the worst outcome from this freedom were the ones who subscribed to a religious dogma that conceived man to be inherently bad. Man was essentially good, Andrews affirmed, good enough to deserve the very freedom which would allow his goodness to emerge. Freedom in any area always engendered some harm, but the beneficial growth it nurtured completely overshadowed any possible evil. Even if, as smart snipers had been whispering, free love heralded "free lust," the anthropologist of the future might find it preferable to the excesses and deprivations suffered by the present "victims of a moral marasmus."

The *Tribune,* showing its old liberal spirit, published Andrews' letter in full on November 8, 1858, and supplied full editorial comment in its reply. Greeley explained that the *Tribune* was again risking the onus of "free-loveism" because it preferred killing off the germ by exposure. He praised Andrews for his combination of acuteness and frankness and then went on to show how teachers, parents, and clergymen should combat the free love movement with a point-by-point refutation: Freedom to do right was right; freedom to throw an old or invalid wife out of the house to make room for a new one was wrong; no one had ever demonstrated that nature and science stood in deadly opposition to the Bible; Andrews' omission of the "at-his-own-cost" safeguard from the individual sovereignty formula demonstrated a sly shift away from the little responsibility free love advocates had formerly been willing to assume; the dogma of total depravity, denied by Andrews, was amply demonstrated by the existence of believers in free love, or would be if their desire for loose living were encouraged; the small matter of raising children under a system of plural fatherhood had still not been dealt with.

Social leaders behaved as if they were on the defensive in this struggle, and they were not, Greeley continued. Parents, journalists, and philosophers had to speak out, to address themselves plainly to children on the destructive consequences of licentiousness. The vice in question was more ruinous than alcohol. No child should pass his tenth year without having been fully informed and warned. The *New York Times,* which had spoken its mind on the role of the *Tribune* in spreading the Fourierist scourge, said "bravo" to Greeley's editorial. It could not, however, agree with the suggestion that children should be taught about sex in the home, in school, or anywhere else.

❧ ❧

As the decade of the fifties drew to a close, the interest in many social reform movements died down to make way for the great issue of the day—the struggle between the Northern and Southern sections of the United States for political and economic dominance. The woman's rights movement maintained its strength a little longer than other programs for reform, possibly because of its close association with abolitionism. The Andrews-Greeley exchange of November 1858 was the last major restatement of the marriage question, and, at that, had only a one-day stand in a single newspaper.

The end of the War between the States released reformist energies from the Great Cause and placed them at the disposal of reborn social movements. The old faces met again at meetings devoted to temperance, women's rights, labor, marriage, and the rest. Although the views represented were as many and varied as the number of participants, everyone seemed to meet everyone else at the meetings of the New England Labor Reform League, or in its broadened form, the American Labor Reform League. Alcott, Brisbane, Warren, and Andrews graced the platform. Among those who joined them were Colonel William Bachelder Greene, who had been a member of the Brook Farm Association; Edward Linton, who had lived at Modern Times; John Orvis, a reformer with socialist tendencies; and Sidney H. Morse, a sculptor. Among those who were destined to do a large part of the spadework in advancing future causes were Ezra Hervey Heywood and Benjamin R. Tucker. As was to be expected in this crowd of prima donnas, complete agreement on any issue was impossible except for a unanimous insistence on freedom of speech, press, and thought.

No longer did they have to worry about breaking into the big press in order to get their ideas disseminated. Heywood, joined for a time by Tucker, published *The Word* from Princeton, Massachusetts, and Heywood and his wife Angela ran the Cooperative Publishing Company which printed or distributed practically everything of interest to reform movements. Victoria Woodhull and her sister, Tennie C. Claflin, published their weekly regularly except for short periods when jail sentences, court proceedings, or lack of funds prevented its appearance. *The Word* indicated where it stood on most issues by its catchword captions: "free labor," "free land," "free love," "anti-monopoly," "anti-taxes," and (with the entrance into the picture of a spiritualist faction) "anti-death." It had no objection to property or capital if the claim to it were based on individual labor. It sought the extinction of interest, rent, dividends, and profit except as they represented work done. It also wanted to abolish railway, telegraphic, banking, trade-union, and other corporations which charged more than value given.

The publisher of *The Word,* himself an extreme representative of individualist anarchism, did not exclude contributions from mutualistic anarchists, socialist (or communist) anarchists, or from any other kind of sincere reformer. He promised to publish the views of Wendell Phillips, Henry Ward Beecher, Colonel Greene, Josiah Warren, John Orvis, Elizabeth Cady Stanton, Albert Brisbane, John Humphrey Noyes, Victoria Woodhull, Tennie Claflin, and many others. Actually he included some of them only by quotation from things they wrote elsewhere. Others he cited for purposes of arguing with them. Ample representation was also accorded the "opposition."

Heywood was one with Victoria Woodhull in his anti-slavery and woman's suffrage sympathies. He joined her in the Universal Peace Society and the Labor Reform League. He would favor any organized movement which respected natural rights and free contractual relations among individuals. He parted with *Woodhull and Claflin's Weekly* when it showed signs of Marxist stateism or majority-rule democracy. The *Weekly* did indeed favor a sane state sovereignty. Without it, it argued, the people were a mob of "savage individual sovereigns." Woodhull and Claflin, Heywood conceded, were among the bravest free love partisans in the country and deserved the highest praise for their work in marriage reform. But they advocated state nurseries for children; and this was a contradiction to the doctrine of freedom with individual responsibility. Mrs. Woodhull's Equal Rights Party also favored such despotisms as compulsory education and licensed prostitution, both abhorrent to freedom and individualism. Added to these complaints was a personal one. Heywood was giving space to Mrs. Woodhull's materials, but she was not reciprocating in her own paper.

The explanation for Mrs. Woodhull's inconsistency was simply that she was no one's disciple. She was frequently Andrews' or Colonel Blood's mouthpiece; but if anyone else's point of view looked spectacular enough to catch public attention, she was perfectly capable of affixing her name to it. If a juicy turn could be given to an idea, she would do so at once. She had no defined philosophy which might saddle her with consistency; the anarchists on the other hand —especially those who fabricated their structure out of one or two basic statements—had principles of universal applicability. Josiah Warren's "individual sovereignty" and "cost the limit of price" not only laid down a line, but could be proudly asserted to be a continuation of the principles of self-rule and self-support which Jefferson had written into the Declaration of Independence. The anarchists had but systematized traditional American individualism, and enriched it with the philosophies of Godwin, Bentham and Proudhon—and later John Stuart Mill, Max Stirner, and Herbert Spencer.

Such, indeed, was the boast of Ezra Hervey Heywood, an early Warren disciple who came into his own after the Civil War. Born in 1829 into an outstanding New England family which boasted several members in Congress and in the judiciary, Heywood asserted his sovereignty upon his father's death in 1848 by renouncing the family name of Hoar and adopting the one he was to bear thereafter. He was headed for the Congregational ministry, but was diverted through association with a wide assortment of radical reformers such as one was bound to encounter in those days. A meeting with William Lloyd Garrison was the probable beginning of his entrance into the reform arena. The Massachusetts Anti-Slavery Society found in him an active member. But when the abolitionist crusade culminated in a war, Heywood withdrew. As an ardent pacifist he could not countenance the use of force for any cause.

The natural shift of interest at this point was to the women's rights movement, which had been closely associated with anti-slavery. When the war was over, Heywood threw himself into the grand reform front and spoke on every question which lent itself to his individualistic principles. The greater part of his thinking, however, was specialized. All social problems that entered his mind came out integrated with the emancipation of labor, of women, or both. Heywood worked vigorously for woman suffrage and equal property rights; but neither of these was as important in his eyes as marriage reform. And, to him, reform meant abolition of the entire institution and its replacement by free love contracts. He was joined, encouraged and aided in his efforts by Angela Fiducia Tilton, whom he had married in 1865, and with whom, according to all accounts, he lived in constancy until death parted them. There were four children— Angelo, Hermes, Psyche Ceres, and Vesta.

His personal conduct must have been exemplary. The neighbors at Princeton, Massachusetts, where Mrs. Heywood ran a resort boarding-house to supplement the small family income derived from publishing pamphlets, defended him regularly and served as character witnesses in the several obscenity prosecutions which were brought against him under the Comstock Law of 1873. The guests at "Mountain Home" must also have impressed these neighbors with their earnestness and moderation. Their New England breeding would never have permitted them to testify in behalf of a family that entertained revolutionaries and libertines.

Anthony Comstock, for one, could not appreciate Heywood's moral sincerity or the purity of his motives. He had persuaded Congress to pass a law which made it a criminal offense to place indecent and obscene printed matter in the mails, and much of his career was devoted to decoying victims into shooting distance. But no one had to lure the freedom-loving Heywood into a fight. He had an active desire to meet book-burning drives head on. There was a strong flavor in his attitude of a bid for immortality through heroism or martyrdom on the marriage front. A few years after the first proceedings against him for distributing his *Cupid's Yokes* through the mails, he declared that seers in all ages had been persecuted for attempting to apply intelligence to the problems of love and parentage. Personal sacrifice for principle had been the rule from Stephen Pearl Andrews, Mary Wollstonecraft and Charles Fourier's time back to Jesus and Plato. If Comstock's laws were bent on prohibiting the dissemination of physiological information on contraception, it was the duty of citizens to shout their disapproval. "For, not superstitious Nescience, but. . . . Science is the right rule of faith and practice in Sexuality."

Cupid's Yokes or, the Binding Forces of Conjugal Life, appeared in 1876. Its subtitle described it as "an essay to consider some moral and physiological phases of Love and Marriage, wherein is asserted the natural right and necessity of Sexual Self-Government." Heywood's little work on sex, as we have seen, was not the first of its kind in America; nor was it the first that this audacious publicist had shipped from his arsenal at Princeton. From the early days of his publishing and bookselling venture, he had been selling Owen's *Moral Physiology* and John Humphrey Noyes' *Scientific Propagation* and *Male Continence.* His error consisted in not hiding behind circumlocution as Owen had, and in not floating a halo of religious mysticism over his intentions as Noyes did.

Heywood spoke in a language which went beyond clarity. It was designed to shock readers as well as to disseminate information. His first arrest, for mailing Dr. Russel Thatcher Trall's *Sexual Physiology* and his own *Cupid's Yokes,* came in June 1878. Comstock had started action against both Heywood and D. M. Bennett the preceding year for mailing the Trall book, but during the proceedings *in re Cupid's Yokes* denied that Dr. Trall's volume had anything to do with the prosecution. The Princeton anarchist was sentenced to two years at hard labor. His influential friend, the woman's rights advocate Laura Cuppy Smith, soon got President Hayes to pardon him on the ground that Heywood's health was in such a bad state that the jail term placed his life in jeopardy. (He lived twenty-five years longer.) Heywood was also vindicated by a statement of exoneration made by Attorney General Devens.

Comstock's latest victim was not alone in his struggle with the law and its investigator of vice. He had companionship in persecution and friends to defend him publicly. Parker Pillsbury was only one of the experienced reformers who stood by his side. Pillsbury, who had left the ministry because of its conservative opposition to the anti-slavery movement, and who had come out of the war as a woman's rights advocate, wrote Heywood a letter which was published immediately after the conviction. By an apt selection of passages from the Bible, he demonstrated that the Book "is now the *filthiest* book, in many parts, to be found in decent households. . . . If the Church is not ashamed of its book, you need not be ashamed of yours."

De Robigne Mortimer Bennett, editor of the free thought *Truth Seeker,* went to jail for thirteen months in 1879 for sheer honesty. Not a fellow-traveler of Heywood's in any sense, he did feel that *Cupid's Yokes* had a purpose to serve, and he did not hesitate to distribute copies. Comstock got him. The government rewarded him with time to write his letters "From Ludlow Street Jail Where Obscenity Is." Bennett had few ideas on the marriage question such as would involve him in legal difficulties. He admitted that women were better off in the United States than elsewhere, but he considered the thousands of unhappy marriages around him evidence enough of room for improvement. If *Cupid's Yokes* had suggestions, let every interested party have access to them.

Corrupting influence on youth? Youth would not much care to read this boring and academic pamphlet. Obscene? For "amorous, exciting" language and idea—as the law defined obscenity—*Cupid's Yokes* did not hold a candle to Boccaccio, Rabelais, much of Montaigne, Chaucer, Smollett, Swift, Fielding, Rousseau, and others. The Bible rated high in a competitive list. "It is certainly hard to send Mr. Heywood and myself to prison for the very thing that God set us the copy for." Moreover, the hand that fed had been bitten. After twenty-five years of service to the one-time progressive Republican party, Bennett now found himself in disgrace, a victim of his own party, which had but recently moved over to represent the "priestly tyranny." The same state apparatus, Bennett noted, had also fined the liberal Dr. Edward Bond Foote $3,500 for mailing legitimate medical and physiological advice.

Bennett's sentence failed both to expiate the crime of the liberals and to satisfy the Comstocks of the nation. Heywood was arrested again in October 1882, and brought to trial for a variety of counts in April of the following year. The subject of one of the indictments was that *The Word Extra* had contained two objectionable quotations from Walt Whitman's *Leaves of Grass*, namely "To a Common Prostitute" and "A Woman Waits for Me." The judge ruled that neither this nor *Cupid's Yokes* was obscene. Another point at issue was an advertisement which *The Word* carried for the "Comstock Syringe." It was explained in court that this was a hoax designed to tease Comstock, and to signify the intention of women to transfer the initiative for child-bearing from the censors' hands to their own.

The proceedings and testimony, later published at Princeton with notes and comments, gave the Heywood group a choice launching platform for their publicity. Their leader became the Luther of the nineteenth century. The Protestants of the present, it appeared, were exercising their legal and natural right of private judgment in morals. They sought the utter abolition of marriage, church, state, and every extant institution. The quotable Declaration of Independence was quoted. There was no question of treason because no overt act of violence against the government had been counseled or committed.

On the specific issue of birth control, Heywood, with quotations from Darwin, John Stuart Mill, Malthus, and Professor Fawcett, announced that it was time to take cognizance of a problem. As for contraceptive techniques, free lovers as a group were not ardent proselyters for their use. But again, it was a choice between government instruction or of abuses far worse than control by prevention. Besides, if one observed the size of the families of well-to-do Fifth Avenue churchgoers, he would find that these pious people were using the information whose dissemination they paid Comstock $4000 a year to prevent.

The difficulties generated by the reproductive instinct, said the defense, would continue until this instinct was "inspired by intelligence and placed under the dominion of the will." Suppression settled nothing, cured nothing. Comstock laws, anti-polygamy legislation, and liquor laws helped no more than the imprisonment of free lovers for their attempt to unmask the reality of social evil. You might as well jail the geologists as a preventive measure against the earthquake these scientists had predicted. The problems involved in love and marriage had to be turned over to reason, conscience, and moral order. You could not hide the all-pervading factor of sex. It cropped up even in religion as phallic symbolism, in monuments, in the cross itself. It was to be found throughout the sciences. The concept of Mother Earth itself had sexual significance. The defendant could not be judged obscene. And he was not.

But he was acquitted only to be hounded until he *was* convicted in 1890 and sentenced to two years imprisonment. His death in 1893 freed him of his obligation to find freedom.

At the end of Heywood's first year in the Charlestown jail, Julian Hawthorne, the novelist son of the more famous Nathaniel, wrote to the editor of the *Twentieth Century* in Heywood's behalf. He pointed out that this victim of censorship suffered from tuberculosis, a condition which incarceration would aggravate. He showed that Heywood had demonstrated a lifelong devotion to the ideals of freedom brought over by the Pilgrim Fathers and continued by the heroes of the Revolution. Moreover, many other writers and reformers had made proposals counter to accepted patterns and were none the worse for it. However much one objected to the use of a "severely Anglo-Saxon vocabulary"—as Hawthorne did object—in the discussion of the delicate subject of sexual physiology and obstetrics, one had to admit that Heywood's motives and accomplishments in *Cupid's Yokes* did not verge on the objectionable. The Princeton rebel, as Hawthorne described him, was an old eccentric who deserved consideration for his honest convictions—honest enough to make him pursue a course which landed him in jail once before. Hawthorne had no wish to associate himself with the theories of the man he was defending. He did not even know him. But as a carrier of the principle of freedom of thought and expression, inherited from a two-century line of patriot forefathers, he considered it a duty to defend a fellow American's right to publish.

Hawthorne could have added that Heywood had, during the twenty years or so preceding his conviction, published a varied list of works which showed him to be anything but a dealer in pornography. His own first published work (1868) had been a speech delivered before the Labor Reform League of Worcester in which he explained labor's objectives with reference to the distribution of wealth and other social measures. For the achievement of labor's aims he recommended the universal ballot plus trade unions, eight-hour associations, and cooperative societies. The last three means he later frowned upon as showing the marks of monopoly and restraint of the individual. His remarks with regard to marriage were intended to show how young, pure, and idealistic men and women, unable to marry because their income as workers placed marriage beyond their means, were tending more and more to remain unmarried and suffer the vicious and immoral distortions of the celibate state. Also, since Heywood had but recently thrown himself into woman's rights work, he recommended as a help to the solution of marriage difficulties that women be given the chance and inducement to work, the right to vote, and the right and means to pay their own bills.

Yours or Mine: Explaining the true basis of property and the causes of its inequitable distribution was printed at the office of the *Weekly American Workman* in 1869. Forty thousand copies were printed in less than a decade. *Hard Cash,* published in 1874, advocated a loosening of currency restrictions. It also purported to show how monopolies in finance capital were hindering free enterprise, hurting both labor and capital, and precipitating depressions and panics. *Free Trade* appeared in the eighties to warn of the danger of protective tariffs. *The Great Strike,* published originally in Benjamin Tucker's *Radical Review* (1878), attempted to define the claims of capital and labor in the irrepressible conflict that kept owner and producer constantly at each other's throats.

Social Ethics pleaded the cause of individual sovereignty in morals and religion. It showed that temperance and rational sobriety were to be attained by strengthening the individual will rather than by legal prohibition. Heywood claimed that the economic situation drove the workers to drink as their only escape from oppression, and the rich, relieved of the necessity for work, were likewise driven to intemperance of all sorts for want of better things to do with all their leisure time. The Women's Christian Temperance Union was doing good work, Heywood thought, but its tactics were the tactics of men—tyranny and coercion. The crusading ladies would do better, Heywood suggested, to urge all women to boycott drunkards, to "re-

fuse to conceive and bear drunkards." This type of boycott would teach men the lesson that wine and women were not to be coupled in thought in the sense that both could be bought with money. "The law of love which woman may personate towards man, in dealing with temperance, is stronger than courts, majorities, and armies."

Uncivil liberty, of which 80,000 copies were distributed between 1872 and 1877, might have been called "Ye Compleately Equal Woman." It was sub-titled "The Unsocial Heism opposed to woman suffrage, the political usurpation of men over women." This suffrage pamphlet considered the entire array of female disabilities, from babies to ballots. It told how only a prostitute could claim her own child; how married women risked fines and imprisonment for challenging their husbands' complete control over their children; how they could not choose medical care for their own bodies; how all these things were beyond their ability to improve because they had no voice in the choosing of representatives or in the making of laws. In return for yielding up human rights, women were supposed to get "protection." What kind of protection was it that always left the woman displaying her sin, while the male culprit enjoyed immunity from the law and from public opinion.

The male prerogative was in Heywood's eyes another ruling-class technique, an iron fist which withheld a "say" in social matters from more than fifty percent of the Massachusetts population. An arrangement, like that enjoyed by the Mormons, which made men the sons of God but women the daughters of men, might work in certain theocratic societies; but in these glorious, free United States —never! The resemblance of married women to slaves was all too evident. The Negro had been just whose "cuffy" he happened to be; the wife was still just whose "birdie" or "drudge" she happened to be. "As many slaves, so many enemies." So many beings whose potential creativeness was being lost to society. So many others whose irresponsibility to law leads them to rule by indirection, "to secure recognition by depravity and rebellion."

Heywood could connect almost any blot on the human record with the inferior status of womanhood. Women tried to rule men because they could not rule themselves: hence the double standard and the wickedness it bred. Females lacked independence; they were bullied by their husbands; they were insecure in their own home: hence divorce. The "shame of the cities" was itself a form of retribution for the irrational morality concocted by man. The ballot in woman's hands would not solve *all* social problems. But women, at least, were impartial about many issues. They would help to uplift labor and beat down both Wall Street and the government monopoly at Washington. They would tend to purify government in the same way as coeducation at Antioch College had produced a better behaved student body as compared with the "celibate" colleges of the East.

In a society guided by intelligence, science, the handmaiden of politics, would enter the home to free women and thereby solve some of the most difficult problems that families had to face. All the personal and human relationships connected with family functioning would come under the scrutiny of the physiological, sociological, and psychological sciences. Technological advances would shed their grace on the disagreeable aspects of ordinary domestic duties. Each member of the family would find his true place in the harmonious household. But before any of the benefits of science and the ballot could be fully realized, men would have to submit to the formula that "Constantly acknowledged twoness is indispensable to coincident oneness." No two intelligent beings could live together in wholesome peace unless the liberty of each was held inviolate.

Toward the preparation of *Cupid's Yokes,* the book which prodded the authorities to badger him for the rest of his life, Heywood gathered every bit of scientific and pseudo-scientific knowledge that had come within his ken. He called on reason to sustain the principles of liberal religion; on politics and sociology to throw governmental authority out of the house whenever the very individual and personal matter of sex was up for discussion. There was New Testament evidence to show that Jesus understood the natural right of woman to consort with whom she chose. The right of private judgement had already been conceded in politics and religion. Why should it be denied in domestic affairs? Why should priests and magistrates supervise one body function and not the others? It was barbarous and shocking to think that affectionate relations could be better governed by statute than by individual reason; that the performance of a ceremony should render "good" what before was "bad." Could it be that ministers or clerks could make people, naturally incapable of self-government, capable of the same by virtue of their pronouncements? All "a rude species of conventional impertinence," Heywood concluded.

Outspoken to a fault in its dragging of science and morality into the open, *Cupid's Yokes* was at times idealistically delicate in its definitions. It referred to a certain universal drive as "this mingled sense of esteem, benevolence, and passional attraction called Love, [which] is so generally diffused that most people know life to be incomplete until the calls of affection are met in healthful, happy, and prosperous association with persons of the opposite sex." Where sometimes he ordered nosey bodies away from keyholes in language which courts may *still* feel is contrary to postal regulations, elsewhere Heywood used the figurative language of spiritualism to say: "Love is induction of unity between two persons by Magnetic Forces. A third visible party who comes to seal the bond, interferes with these forces." All of which meant that individual, sovereign males and females could dispense with courts and churches.

Considering Heywood's busy life of publishing, editing, meeting with political groups, and raising a family, his researches into scientific authority and the subjects of population limitation and eugenics were pretty extensive. He cited as source and authority on the mental and physical dangers of celibacy George Napheys, R. T. Trall, and Dio Lewis, and even went back to the seventeenth-century English Hippocrates, Dr. Thomas Sydenham. For birth-control material, he drew on Owen, Noyes, Dr. Thomas L. Nichols, Trall, and the British *Elements of Social Science*. Heywood agreed with Andrews and a host of other theoretical reformers on the possibility of improving the world by breeding superior people. He noted that Noyes had embarked on a program of scientific propagation, or stirpiculture, on a practical level. Most of the physicians who had attached themselves to liberal movements saw great possibilities in eugenics. The element of mate selection for breeding purposes was in itself a social reform movement. The free love advocates could complain, with the responsible backing of Galton's *Hereditary Genius*, that the legal marriage requirement acted to prevent great people from reproducing. The new science of heredity, supported by the popular evolutionary principles of Darwin, was most congenial to reformers in the anarchist frame. Individual choice, unhampered by antiquated customs and laws, was the very essence of a program of race improvement.

In common with many socialists, anarchists were fond of comparing marriage with other business monopolies. Heywood tried to demonstrate in *Cupid's Yokes* how the evils of the economic system entered into the dealings of the sexes. He pointed out how male capitalists discriminated against women workers, excluding them from jobs and keeping their wages down, with the result that "men became buyers and women sellers of virtue."

The author of *Cupid's Yokes* was saying much the same thing as the most conservative marriage critics when he assailed economics for defiling the pure love relation. The anarchist innovation lay in its emphasis on abolishing marriage instead of trying merely to eliminate materialistic considerations from marriage. Heywood's analysis and cure for disturbing aspects of sex offered an even more novel suggestion:

> The usury system enables capital to control and consume property which they never earned, laborers being defrauded to an equal extent; this injustice creates intemperance and reckless desires in both classes; but when power to accumu-

late property without work is abolished, the habits of industry which both men and women must acquire, will promote
sexual temperance. In marriage, usury, and the exceptionally low wages of women, then, I find the main sources of
prostitution.

It could also be predicted that the profit system would "go down
with its twin relic of barbarism, the marriage system. . . ."

This was Heywood's platform. Wherever he had a hand in drawing up resolutions for an organization, some aspect of this theme
crept in. At the second convention of the American Labor Reform
League, he offered for consideration a statement that the first duty
of labor reformers was "to assist in delivering woman from the
degradation to which the ignorance, stupidity, lust, and avarice of
men have consigned her. . . ." The membership which accepted
this resolution also found itself moving to have nothing to do with
any individual or organization which did not support a program of
complete emancipation for women.

Heywood lost his influence in the American Labor Reform
League within a few years. But there was still the New England
Labor Reform League which was ever ready to pass similar resolutions. The practice of offering lower wages to women teachers than
to their male colleagues was assailed by the League. Other discriminatory tactics and legislation were denounced. Society was ordered
to take its feet off the necks of women.

It was not the business of the New England Labor Reform
League, wrote Heywood in a resolution which he prepared for the
fourth convention, to deal with love and marriage; but any friend
of male oppression was no friend of the Convention. Victoria Woodhull was welcome to the platform. So was anyone else who wanted
to fight the system under which men had the industrial and social
services of women at reduced monetary and moral costs. The convention would also disavow pussyfooting suffragettes like Lucy Stone
and Susan B. Anthony who were playing ball with the two standard
parties in government, a gang of male usurpers, rogues, despots, and
libertines.

The New England press looked upon these proceedings with
ill-assured equanimity. The meetings were dignified by the presence
of respected intellectuals and politicians. There was little agreement
as to program even among those on the platform. Moreover, the audience seemed to take the speakers' exhortations passively. The *Boston
Journal* thought the labor crowd honest, more or less sane, and
harmless. But by 1875 the New England conventions began to show
less respectability and more agitation. Epithets like "a feast of mad-

ness" and "a flow of filth" appeared in print as characterizations of the very group which the press but two years before had felt should be allowed to carry on its ineffectual activities unsuppressed and unglorified by notoriety.

One of the personalities who came to public attention at the meetings of the N. E. L. R. L. was eighteen-year-old Benjamin R. Tucker. Tucker had left the Massachusetts Institute of Technology in 1872 in order to educate himself more satisfactorily by listening to the intellectuals who spoke in the lecture-hall instead of the college classroom. His abiding interest was the development of various phases of philosophical anarchy. He had met Josiah Warren and Colonel William B. Greene at Heywood's meetings and had been won over. Two immediate effects on his conduct followed. He turned from the support of Horace Greeley for president and followed the political line developed by Warren and Greene. Then, on the suggestion of Greene he began a translation of Pierre Joseph Proudhon's *What is Property?* Although Warren had arrived independently at conclusions similar to those of this French anarchist-philosopher, he had not developed a formulation adequate for study by intellectually minded radicals. Proudhon's writings on the destruction of interest, of capital, and of the state itself filled the need. What most of the non-intellectuals learned from Tucker's translation was that "property is robbery."

Mr. and Mrs. Heywood helped form the New England Free Love League in February 1873, but L. K. Joslin was elected its president, and "Bennie" Tucker secretary. Tucker, a shy lad of nineteen, had read much about sexual problems, but, because of the drain of his heavy intellectual pursuits, was as yet unaware of the true meaning of the free love cause he espoused. He frequently protested that his prime purpose in the League was to fight the issue of civil liberties. Victoria Woodhull had been denied the privilege of the public platform in Boston. The League had been organized to see that she got it. Without doubt, his youthful enthusiasm for libertarian causes was being channeled carefully by the older and more experienced Heywood.

Free love was a principle with Tucker. Once one accepted it, he did not have to keep talking about it. As co-editor of *The Word,* he let Heywood and his friends exploit the sexual issue to their hearts' desire. In 1876, he sent Heywood a friendly letter of resignation, explaining that he did not want to remain with a periodical that stressed the free love theme at the expense of more serious philosophical, economic, and political matters. Free love might have been a burning question for Tucker back in 1873 when he had become involved in amours with Mrs. Woodhull, but within three years she had so clearly revealed to him the fraudulent side of her character that he no longer cared to engage in juggling the kind of ideas he had so closely associated with her. Yet he did remain faithful in a quiet way to the free love principle which she herself later abandoned. In his own magazines—the *Radical Review*, which lasted one year, and *Liberty*, which lasted twenty-seven—he devoted himself to the serious study of political philosophy. It is a fair assumption to say that Tucker had been drawn into free love circles because of the fatal attraction held for him by anything with the word "free" in it.

THE SISTERS CLAFLIN

With Victoria Woodhull (née Victoria Claflin) it was different. Born to parents who were completely devoid of character and social responsibility, Victoria had excellent preparation in her early home life for the stunts she later engineered as a politician, feminist, anarchist, socialist, and spiritualist leader. An affectionless diet provided by morally and economically impoverished parents left the Claflin children with a lifelong hunger for attention from whatever source they could get it. Victoria and Tennessie (later converted to Tennie) succeeded by their wits and unscrupulousness in getting just what they wanted. Even prosecution in the courts and prison sentences gave them a martyr's satisfaction.

The Claflin sisters ran a successful stockbrokers office in New York (set up with the aid of Commodore Vanderbilt himself). They also, with the aid of Victoria's second husband, Captain Blood, conducted their labor-supporting spiritualist, anarchist, and catch-all scandal sheet. Though they worked together, Victoria won far greater prominence through her ability as a speaker and her superior personal charm.

Free love on the part of the Claflin sisters appeared to be very free indeed. What distinguished the two was that Victoria operated subtly, selectively, and with finesse. Tennie was a ruder and probably more promiscuous trader in her stock of affections. She had failed with the reticent Tucker where her sister had succeeded. Victoria practiced what she preached, and probably boasted more than she practiced. Her way of securing audience attention was to make perfectly plain to her listeners just what she considered her sexual freedom to consist in. She would loudly celebrate the nature and extent of individual biological needs and ridicule any backward notion that would deny their satisfaction. If she were persecuted as a result of her gratuitously provocative outbursts, she would complain that she was being silenced just because she was a woman.

Were it not for her notoriety, Mrs. Woodhull might have wielded a powerful influence. Many minds much stronger than her own were won by her striking personality. Most of her admirers quite certainly did not know that ghosts were doing her writing and even part of her thinking for her. Benjamin Tucker knew all of this; he was all but positive that she did not even know how to write. Yet he admired her for understanding and believing in everything she said. It was more than mere parroting to use these ideas successfully in spontaneous debate. Victoria proved herself in this way more than once.

Whether she was repeating Stephen Pearl Andrews' ideas or anyone's else is a matter of small importance. She raised issues in the open forum and got people to discuss matters that needed an airing. In the post-Civil War period there probably existed a greater gap between private behavior and public morals than at any time in American history before or since. In proportion as one valued his reputation one was eligible to be a victim of blackmail. If the Claflin clan did not actually go in for blackmail, they could have. With their vast acquaintanceship among high and low, and their *Weekly* as a club to hold over possible prey, one might almost give them credit for preferring scandal to blackmail when confronted with a choice of action.

"Just because she was a woman," Mrs. Woodhull did not intend to allow the law and its vice agents to hound her, keep her off the lecture platform, and censor her newspaper. One of the big grievances she and her friends had against Beecher and his friends was that they treated Beecher's marital irregularity as a criminal act. For many months after Victoria heard the bit of scandal from the trustworthy Elizabeth Cady Stanton's own lips, she refrained from exposing Beecher because she still clung to principle and abhorred the *argumentum ad hominem*. But she was being harassed more and more by male adversaries at the same time that she was being deserted by male liberals. Beecher, whose pseudo-liberalism had given Victoria reason to think he was a friend of hers, had also failed her. He had refused to introduce her "Principles of Social Freedom" speech at Steinway Hall in November 1872. Tilton, who had for a while been closer to her than their diverse political views would warrant, reluctantly did the honors after a painful struggle between conscience and expediency.

According to Mrs. Woodhull, Beecher was an especially obnoxious ingrate. He had deserted her while he could still freshly recall a "friendly" relationship with her of the same order as Tilton's. Nevertheless she refrained from exposing him until it appeared that nothing short of a great public scandal could save *Woodhull and Claflin's Weekly* and her own economic and personal future from disaster. She then let the cat out of the bag and the whole country started to chase it. Tilton's mouth had been closed by the fear of losing his livelihood. He also thought it best not to say much because he had to admit to himself that he was as guilty of infidelity as his own wife had allegedly been with the Reverend Beecher. But he was now forced to save his face by bringing a suit against Beecher for alienation of affections. The Woodhull publishing fortunes were temporarily restored.

The anarchist-spiritualist-free love world was in a dither. All sorts of dividing lines appeared. All kinds of theories were offered. Some claimed that Comstock's activities had been paid for by those who wished to keep Beecher's reputation intact. To them it looked very much as if the ministers had formed a society for the prevention of vice in Boston as a blind to divert attention from their own immoral practices. Others said that Mrs. Woodhull's campaign against Beecher was designed to maneuver him into the free love camp. The tactic was to force him to preach what he practiced. The feminist commentators interjected that the whole controversy ignored the personality of Mrs. Tilton. It looked to them like a disagreement between two slave masters. The idealistic Olivia Shepard, pouring salt on the wound, berated Beecher for disclaiming a child born to Mrs. Tilton. A humorous letter, allegedly from Brigham Young, offered Beecher a place in the Mormon community, where polygamy would not be criticized as it was in Brooklyn.

Beecher's own brothers and sisters divided on the issue of Henry's character. That ardent woman's rights worker, Isabella Beecher Hooker, had sensed that her brother was not exactly honorable. The Reverend Thomas Beecher was inclined to have misgivings about his brother's advanced ideas. The Reverend William H. Beecher believed that Henry's conduct was unimpeachable despite his bad relationship with his own wife. If he were as wayward as people claimed, why would he pick an "old, faded, married one," when his position in the Plymouth congregation presented so many more attractive opportunities. Harriet Beecher Stowe, the rigidly moralistic author of *Uncle Tom's Cabin*, hated Mrs. Woodhull enough to add to her reasons for believing in Henry's innocence.

The loudest voice of dissent from within the Heywood group was that of the mutualist Colonel Greene. He accused *The Word* of tyrannizing over Beecher by demanding that he either refute Mrs. Woodhull's charges or admit their truth. The point was that no one, including Beecher, had any obligation to cater to public opinion. If Beecher did not want to employ his spare time in defending himself, that was his business. Warren joined Greene in taking exception to the scandal mongering tactics of *The Word*.

An impartial observer might have asked how much honest principle could be found in Victoria's declarations on the Beecher affair or anything else. Was it purely in search of justice that she shouted back characteristically to a heckler in her "Social Freedom" audience:

"Yes! I am a free lover! I have an inalienable, constitutional, and natural right to love whom I may, to love as long or as short a period as I can, to change that love every day if I please!" The speech itself, prepared by Stephen Pearl Andrews, would not have embarrassed poor Tilton, who stepped into Beecher's shoes to present Victoria to her audience; but the impromptu remarks caused a cyclone. And Tilton, into the bargain, was stumping for Horace Greeley in a presidential campaign! Such an opportunity to associate Greeley with the free love movement could not be overlooked. And it wasn't.

Adding to the confusion was the censorship issue raised by the arrest of the sisters Claflin, together with Victoria's current husband, Captain Blood. They had also exposed Luther Challis, a New York broker, in the same copy of the *Weekly* which broke the Beecher scandal. The language used was unsavory and the facts printed were open to question. But good liberals would not go into the details of the case. They had to make their protest vigorous, without qualification or hesitation. *The Word* called Woodhull's reporting "fair and chaste" as she saw the facts. Sidney H. Morse, of the free-thought *Index*, defended by the method of attack. He said that much of the prejudice against the maligned lady broker was itself vulgar. Furthermore, he had heard more obscenity uttered about her than had ever escaped her own lips. One had to admit that she was a little extravagant in speech; but she believed in her philosophy as consistently as Garrison had in his.

Wherein lay her consistency? At this distance from the events, the most strikingly consistent feature is the erotic note in Mrs. Woodhull's speeches. Her privately managed speaking engagements, seeking large attendance as they naturally would, banked on an audience looking for stimulation. In feminist groups she injected a word for woman's right to choose and change her male partner with the same freedom and equality which characterized her right to political representation. When speaking before the American Association of Spiritualists—who honored her with the presidency of their organization—or to other spiritualist groups, she enlarged on the relationship between sexual freedom and bodily health. In a speech called "The Elixir of Life; or Why do we die?" Victoria seemed to promise the elimination of disease and possible immortality, contingent upon the achievement of a freely operating "magnetism". She promised the best results if operator and subject were of opposite sexes. At the Spiritualists' Camp Meeting at Vineland, New Jersey, her theme was "The Scare-Crows of Sexual Freedom." Her listeners were taught to recognize the horrifying symbolic word "License" as a scarecrow used to frighten them out of their freedom. A person had a right to be promiscuous if he so chose. "What is it to you whether I live upon fish or flesh?" she queried rhetorically.

FREE LAND, FREE LABOR, FREE LOVE

The sex fixation was not without public profit, for it dramatized the importance of introducing youth to the facts of life and broke partly through the prevailing morbid reticence. The nature of these attacks on marriage may also have stimulated wholesome adjustment in disturbed households. But Victoria drove her popularity too far. By 1876 most people were past the stage where they would trust her. She had already started to write reinterpretations of the Bible, much to the disgust of her radical friends. The symbols were still erotic. "A speech on the Garden of Eden; or Paradise lost and found" demonstrated that readers of the Bible failed to recognize the allegorical character of the story. In reality, the Garden of Eden was the human body, and the rivers referred to were the blood, the bowels, and the urinary and reproductive organs. Sigmund Freud and his followers could not have offered a better analysis of literary symbolism.

When, finally, monogamy became a supreme ideal in Mrs. Woodhull's writings, Tucker could take it no more. He sat down to write what he thought was the truth about her. The weary Victoria gave up the struggle for freedom and left for England with her sister Tennie. There, after a short rest, she resumed her lecturing, but in a vein that was chaste, or allegorical. The Garden of Eden theme pleased her new audiences in England more than it had her old ones in America. Whenever she dipped into her other American materials, they were cleaned up before being exposed to public view. Her personal conduct was also revised along lines straight and narrow. John Biddulph Martin, the son of a highly respected banker, married her after a long campaign to overcome the objections of his family.

FREE LOVE: OUT OF THIS WORLD AND IN IT

Back in America no significant changes had taken place among the libertarian radicals as a result of her apostasy. The only organizational pattern which had changed as a result of her arrival and departure was that of the spiritualists. They split up on the free love question, the *anti's* gathering around the *Banner of Light*, a conservative spiritualist paper, and the *pro's* around the *Crucible*, whose editor was the lively Reverend Moses Hull.

The spiritualist "leftists" had expressed their appreciation of the candor with which Moses Hull and his wife Elvira revealed the details of their own amatory relations. No one thought too much of a subsequent announcement that Moses Hull and Mattie Sawyer had joined forces. The purist sons and daughters of liberty attacked the practice of making a public announcement of something that was no one's business but Hull's and Mattie Sawyer's. But unanimity was not to be had among anarchists. Publicity, it seems, could be justified as a form of defiance of social regulation, and that in itself was worth something. Leo Miller and Mattie Strickland published the news of their union as well. The readers of *The Word* were also notified that the son born to these spiritual mates would go by the name of Strickland-Miller—the mother's name first since she had most of the responsibility of childbearing. There was speculation about the complete disappearance of the male parent's surname in a society devoted to free love. Probably not with tongue in cheek either, for Stephen Pearl Andrews predicted that within a few years anyone who lived any differently would be ridiculed.

Moses Hull's Doctor of Divinity degree must have given him a special prestige in spiritualist circles. Hull seems to have made his entrance into the world of revolt through his experience as a compositor and editor for D. M. Bennett's *Truth Seeker*. His early publications, namely, *Which: Spiritualism or Christianity?* and *That Terrible Question*, came off Bennett's press. The latter examined the marriage problem, recommending the "wonderful uniting of two matched souls." A mistake was to be immediately rectified by divorce, since, if the parties remained married, their mis-mating would lead to all kinds of physical and mental deficiencies in themselves, in their children, and in their children's children.

The versatile and spirited Hull inaugurated his own journal, *The Crucible*. We find his imprints moving from Boston in the late seventies to Des Moines in the late eighties, and thence to Buffalo in the nineties. The Nonconformist Publishing Company and the Progressive Thinker Publishers also put their imprint on Hull's materials, which were largely devoted to solving economic depressions and to elevating spiritualism as a competitor to conventional Christianity. The summation of his work may be found in his *Encyclopedia of Biblical Spiritualism* (1895).

Free love leaders organized their forces on regional, national, and tactical lines. Hull, the Heywoods, Tucker, the pacifist L. K. Joslin, and Francis Barry were generally delegates—no doubt self-constituted—to the conventions. The New England Free Love League, organized in February 1873, met in Boston. The Western Woman's Emancipation Society had its headquarters at Ravenna, Ohio, which was also the site of the National Free Love Convention in December 1873. The first set of officers of the national organization included Orson S. Murray as President, Addie Ballou and Francis Barry as Secretaries, and Jenny Leys as Head of the Executive Committee. Parker Pillsbury, the rebel cleric, was elected President for the following year but declined "positively." Other prominent workers in the cause were Seward Mitchell from Maine, Parma W. Olmstead from Vermont, A. Briggs Davis, Warren Chase and Heywood's sister-in-law, Josephine Tilton, from Massachusetts.

The New England group may have organized originally to insure Victoria Woodhull a hearing. But at its first convention, held
four years after its paper existence had been announced in 1873, it
revealed iconoclastic tendencies of the most radical kind. Joslin, its
president, announced that the free love movement sought to abolish
marriage, and he asserted the natural right of making and dissolving
contracts as the parties to them thought best. Mrs. M. L. Burton
declared that marriage laws were a mere patchwork, unfit for the
purpose of holding society together. The relations of the sexes were
governed by an inflexible natural law which could not be changed,
but only distorted, by manmade expedients. Heywood presented a
set of eight resolutions which embodied his pet agitational clichés:
(1) Marriage laws denied the natural right of association and improvement. (2) Chastity by law was ridiculous; all laws penalizing
infractions of chastity must be immediately repealed. (3) Marriage
restrictions, usury, and exceptionally low wages were the chief causes
of prostitution; the social evil would disappear only after its nourish-
ing sources, legal and economic, had been swept away. (4) Intelligence and reason must replace religious sanctions in the regulation
of male-female relations. (5) The Reverend Henry Ward Beecher
had every right to commit adultery, but no right to lie about it; Tilton's prosecution had been that of a slavemaster in that it used the
courts to protect a husband's property interest in his wife. (6) Male
legislation made women dependent underlings. (7) The insinuation
that there was danger in allowing women to meet and do business
with men was a lewd falsehood. (8) The revolution begun by Mary
Wollstonecraft and carried on at present by the agitators for women's
rights and sexual freedom, was fashioning order out of social chaos;
soon marriage would join slavery, piracy and other obsolete abomina-
tions.

The resolutions passed at the National Convention at Ravenna
were prepared by Francis Barry. They emphasized the natural right
of woman to *herself* along with political and economic equality. Tribute was paid to forerunners in the cause, including Mary Wollstonecraft, Frances Wright, and, to a lesser degree, Dr. Thomas L. Nichols,
his wife Mary Gove Nichols, and "their compeers whose pioneer work
in behalf of sexual freedom made it possible for later workers to
achieve, with a less degree of danger, self-sacrifice, and ostracism,
much greater apparent results."

The most important result of the 1873 meetings was that they
inaugurated a series of similar meetings of the same leaders and followers. The Western Woman's Emancipation Society met at Ravenna
in August 1874, and pointed its guns at legalized prostitution—that
is to say, marriage. A facetious resolution read that it would take
less to make unlegal prostitution a satisfactory life for woman than

187

to convert conventional marriage into a sane institution. With this resolution, it became more disgraceful to enter into or abet the marriage relation than to be an habitué of a red light district.

At the "Social Freedom" convention called in 1875 by Moses Hull and Mattie Sawyer, resolutions were presented by both Hull and Heywood. Hull stressed the need for sweeping aside legal obstacles in order to permit experiment. Heywood repeated his favorite resolutions and asked his hearers to note that they were merely extending American principles already realized in politics and religion.

In 1876, Boston was the scene of the Sexual Science Association meeting, with Joslin presiding and Hull presenting the resolutions. A new danger had appeared on the free love horizon and had to be resolved against. Several people had published their articles of agreement to live in connubial relations with each other. Rank heresy! For one thing, such people were in essence declaring that they did not trust each other's honesty. For another, this was "marriage" by another name; the old crime was still there. Again, by admitting the interference of church, state, and society, these reformers were effectively erecting another dead structure which future abolitionists would have to labor to remove. Mattie Sawyer delivered a talk entitled "Love a Law Unto Itself." Replying to the accusation that she was being "kept" by Moses Hull, she declared: "I am not kept by him nor by any man; I am self-supporting and divide my time between the kitchen and the rostrum."

The Boston press laughed, then railed, at the ideas and language which came out of these conventions. Brick Pomeroy of the *Democrat* decried the capture of the spiritualist convention of December 1874 by the likes of Hull and Chase. The free love movement was a transparent cloak for promiscuity, he wrote. Its principals were "Long-haired men, short-haired women, drowsy boozers who see visions, grass widows who go hell-pestling over the land for affinities, bleary-eyed old roués, who claim to be pillars of the new Jerusalem, luscious-lipped virgins in training for the new church, and discarded husbands." The *Saturday Evening Express* was not as picturesque in its comments but it certainly concurred in the feeling that this was a "free-lust" movement. The partisans were called "lecherous loafers who live by and on their unhallowed liaisons" and who should be in jail. The *Express* was surprised that persons of the intellectual calibre of the Heywoods would lend "their influence to such corruption and rottenness."

The Heywoods were surprised for their own part that otherwise discerning people could not recognize the stark purity of the doctrine they were promoting. They did not "lend themselves." They led. They would join with right-thinking people whether or not they were in agreement on all issues. Their sense of humor permitted them to print the *New York Daily Graphic's* version of the free lovers' maxim: "Beget and forget." They would publish the opinions of those who differed from them and of those who opposed them. They would even print the nasty remarks made by puritanical newspaper reporters. The building of a *science of morals and marriage* required the experience of defamation as well as that of affirmation. As Lois Waisbrooker, a signer of the resolutions placed before Hull's Social Freedom Convention, remarked:

> The social question is under investigation, and we have no standard except the standard of authority—we must have the standard of nature and science; to this end, personal experiences are in order; every person must not only be permitted but induced to come forward and give his or her personal experiences; and in this free inquiry those who are as chaste as ice should have no precedence over those whose fires are irrepressible.

Alas, no wealthy philanthropic foundation was available, in answer to Mrs. Waisbrooker's call, to bring in psychologists, zoologists, and statisticians for the purpose of making a study of the subject. The next best thing was for *The Word, The Crucible,* and Moses Harman's *Lucifer* to print theoretical essays (which were, of course, colored by personal experience) and to present revelatory case histories.

The Word specialized in theoretical disputes whose inevitable occurrence was conditioned by the nature of Heywood's anarchistic temper. There could be no authority, he declared authoritatively, on the definition and practice of free love because of its premise of individual sovereignty and independence of authority. And therein lay a multitude of quarrels. The Beecher-Woodhull-Greene-Tilton debate was one of many provoked by events, by outsiders, or by the editors of *The Word* themselves.

The arguments with *Woodhull and Claflin's Weekly* were many. Its attitudes on free love were satisfactory, but, to the dismay of the anarchists, it had been praising socialist ideas like that of a state currency, state schools, state nurseries, state transportation, state land tenure, and state industrial establishments. Tucker's boyhood friend, William B. Wright, was horror-struck by the proposal that the state take responsibility for the children of free love matches. An infringement of the rights of individuals who have no children! Taxation without consent! Tyranny!

Mrs. Woodhull had years before advocated the licensing of prostitution and, although she had since half-admitted her error, she had never completely recanted. There were several objections to licensing. Was not marriage reform and the achievement of equality for women going to eliminate that profession? The idea also ran counter to the ideals of liberty of congregation without state interference. Addie Ballou of Terre Haute, Indiana, wanted to organize a Magdalen's Protective Union. No other occupational group, she explained, was so largely patronized by social and legal dignitaries, and so frequently encroached upon by trespass and unjust laws.

Curiously enough—or not so curiously if one accepts the laissez-faire philosophy in all areas of government—*The Word* lumped Victoria Woodhull's licensing idea with her favorable attitude toward free state schools. Both were evidences of social oppression. When *Woodhull and Claflin's Weekly* pointed to compulsory schools as a mainstay of civilization, *The Word* charged, it supported the most revolting kind of dictatorial government then being urged by socialist aggregations like the Marxist International Workingmen's Association. The *Weekly*, in fact, was more than vaguely Marxist at this point in its history. It was the first American publication to print a complete English version of the Communist Manifesto.

❧ ❧

The problem of education was a chronic dilemma with individualists from William Godwin onward. They all leaned on education as the means of "leveling upward," yet they feared government enough to refuse its assistance to the cause of education. They ultimately reasoned themselves into a preference for channeling state funds in such a way that they might uplift individuals in the mass to a point where each could take care of his own education. William B. Wright offered the crisp axiom that educated thieves were as objectionable as ignorant ones. The compulsory school was likened to the compulsory church. Gerrit Smith, the abolitionist and temperance reformer, favored voluntary contributions for public education. He carried his thought into action by donating funds to start a free public library at Oswego, New York.

The Word persisted in its rationalizations. So also did the American Labor Reform League, whose fourth annual convention in May 1874 protested the passage of a compulsory education act in New York State "as impertinent and wicked, an unwarrantable violation of the sacred rights of parent and of child, an injury to the cause of education, an added insult to the laboring man and woman. . . ." Woodhull and Claflin shrugged their shoulders. They failed to see how the cooperative efforts of a political group to organize and manage educational agencies constituted tyranny over any individual. "Is organization despotism?" they asked. In their view, *The Word* spoke too much as if children were the property of their parents, and as such to be denied an education if the parents were too poor to pay for it. There were distinctions between the position of individuals in free love and in free education.

A disagreement with Victoria Woodhull was not too serious a matter for *The Word* because she was a free-lance radical with no obligation to be consistent. Nor were Moses Hull's ultraist deviations too troublesome either. But Colonel William Bachelder Greene was a challenge. Greene let common sense temper the strait and narrow logic favored by his anarchist associates. His West Point education and army experience had taught him the need for at least some regulation of individual whims. Studies at the Harvard Divinity School, and several years as a regularly ordained Unitarian clergyman, made it difficult for him to take an atheistic or spiritualist view of religion, as did various anarchic free love groups. Moreover, his affiliations were too numerous and varied to permit of a rigid sectarianism in politics. Brook Farm saw him in the forties. He was a representative —in the anomalous shape of an abolitionist democrat—to the Massachusetts Constitutional Convention of 1853. The post-war years found him active in the labor movement, and in the woman's rights and other reform movements.

Greene's scholarship also made it hard for him to accept the superficial generalities of his friends. His knowledge of Hebrew and Egyptian antiquities was profound. He published in fields as widely separated as mathematics, religious philosophy, history, and Freemasonry. Among the titles were *The Sovereignty of the People* (1863), *The Facts of Consciousness and the Philosophy of Herbert Spencer* (1871), and *New England Transcendentalism* (1872). Heywood advertised and distributed Greene's works. Greene, however, was under no obligation to follow the policy of *The Word*.

William Greene admitted that the muddled free love doctrine of his contemporaries was beyond his full comprehension. What was more, he had little interest in it. Before a man was justified in changing any institution, he had to have a grievance. Certainly the Heywood crowd had no grievance against those who wanted to marry in the legal way. What, then, did they want to accomplish? Greene reviewed their aims: They wanted a contract which would be terminable at will. They wanted property to remain with the woman at the termination of the contract. The children should likewise remain with the mother, with satisfactory legal status guaranteed to mother and children. Greene showed that they could accomplish their first aim by the repeal of a single chapter of the General Statutes of Massachusetts. The rest could be done through the normal channels of agreement between husband and wife, provided that all inheritance matters were taken care of during the lifetime of the parties.

He saw no reason for free lovers to abolish marriage unless

they contemplated polygamy or "complex marriage." In fact, the abolition of marriage was an unconstitutional impairment by a State of lawfully undertaken contracts of marriage. With but one change in the State law, young men and women could undertake almost any private arrangement they wished, and, by their praiseworthy conduct, gain acceptance in the society of their neighbors. The greatest risk anyone would run in that case was a small fine. And did anyone hear of the State ever invoking its laws against a man for living with a mistress? Greene had another suggestion to make which was probably generally understood to be facetious. He told the free love advocates to organize as a denomination which required its members never to enter a contract which they could not also sever. Amendment XI of the Massachusetts Constitution said that "No subordination of any one sect or denomination to another shall ever be established by law."

Francis Barry of the Western emancipationists was impatient with Greene's obtuseness. How could the man fail to see that abolishing marriage interfered with no rights, no contracts? Free love was directed, like the Garrison agitation, against a form of chattel slavery. But Greene thought this analogy more inspirational than rational. No one could ever convince him of the similarity between marriage and slavery. The Barry formula, according to Greene, was reminiscent of animal-like promiscuity wherein the "parties can live together in any way they please, and so long as they please." Heywood himself seemed to expose to derision anyone who adopted Barry's idea of free love.

Greene sought to define marriage, or any form of it by the purpose it achieved. If you included the procreation and care of children, then you had to see to it that one or both of the parents could not abandon the youngsters at will. If you agreed to that, you had marriage again. No true liberal would deny women the right to have children just because the means of prevention were at hand. If you argued that the state would take care of the children, then what of the rights of childless taxpayers? So, then, it was marriage reform and not abolition that women really desired. They wanted federation with their husbands in place of consolidation into the supreme male orbit. Mutualism, therefore—Warren's and Greene's great compromise of the individualist and cooperative principles—was what would work best in marriage as it did in banking and insurance. Changes in the laws to give women separate property rights (and such were currently being effected in Massachusetts) were prefatory to the status of equality in marriage which American women demanded. What they wanted was not license but a relationship on fairer, more nearly Christian grounds.

What side was he on, queried *The Word*—at great length, as usual. Greene had brought society back into the picture, and had set a trap thereby. Liberty in love seemed to be an unclean word in his language, whereas it was perfectly proper in law, religion, or trade. Those who, like him, gave the idea of free love a lascivious connotation were really expressing their own moral condition. *The Word* would have had more to say had it chosen for analysis Greene's critical comments on Dr. Edward H. Clarke's book, *Sex in Education*. For here the mutualist criticized an overemphasis on woman's physiology to the neglect of her soul and spirit. Said Greene, woman had a life of the body, of the soul, and of the spirit. The first was the province of the physiologist, the second of the moralist, and the third of the clergy. The hope for woman's emancipation, thought Greene, was in her religion. It was well to keep physiology treatises out of school-girls' hands. Under no circumstances should girls be permitted to see the "damnable" illustrations in these texts.

This was quite a falling-off from *The Word's* insistence that pure people had nothing to hide. Liberation, as *The Word* understood the term, carried with it the free distribution of knowledge pertaining to all matters of interest to human beings. Greene's reservations also pointed up a difference in approach to the problems of female emancipation. His recommendations were those of the more vigorous faction in the woman's rights movement: legal and economic equality was to be achieved first. Equal status in marriage would follow. Touch property and you touch marriage, said Greene. Elizabeth Cady Stanton and her militant friends agreed.

The ultra-radicals accepted this proposition too. But the fulfillment of its promise was too slow and uncertain for them. They would shock society by urging women to immediate revolt against male domination, and against imposition in marriage and outside of it. With regard to that aspect of liberation which lay in economic equality, they recommended dressing more like a man so that freedom of movement on the job would increase women's efficiency and consequently their earning power. In regard to the sex role, woman was told to learn all about her physiological functioning and to defend her body against abuse. It was for her to determine the number of children she should bear. The Owen barrier methods and Noyes' control by male continence did not meet with approval everywhere, but were accepted for the part they played in helping woman to freedom. Heywood at times seemed somewhat revolted at the practices current among those who desired to limit the number of their children. He acquiesced because he had no substitute to offer, and did his part by advertising available knowledge of contraceptive techniques.

MARRIAGE, MORALS AND SEX IN AMERICA

THE ORDEAL OF MOSES HARMAN

The clique that operated from Valley Falls, Kansas, knew neither reticence nor revulsion. The core of the Valley Falls rebellion consisted of Moses Harman, an anarchist in spirit but not in name; his daughter Lillian, generally referred to by *The Word* as Miss Dr. Harman; and Edwin C. Walker. It stood thus: Walker had been divorced from his wife and was living with Miss Harman as man and wife with Moses Harman's blessing. The illegal spouses were caught in the net of the law in 1886 and rewarded by jail sentences —two and a half months for the male culprit and one and a half for the female. Benjamin Tucker, hitherto a close friend of Walker's, deserted him now because the latter had tried to prove in court that his marriage to Lillian Harman was legal. Tucker declared that he would contribute neither money nor moral support toward vindicating the right of men and women to enslave themselves.

The marriage, incidentally, was nicknamed the "Lucifer match" because the radical organ of this coterie was *Lucifer, the Light Bearer*. From 1880 onward, *Lucifer,* carrying the banner of sexual freedom, directed a high-wattage spotlight on sex. Although firmer in its resistance to personal promiscuity than the Hull-Woodhull axis, *Lucifer* was looser in its verbal candor. When it spoke of the "next revolution" it meant the revolt of woman from her present condition of sex slavery. Political and social ideas were mentioned in a subsidiary manner. Woman's slave status, it was agreed, was truly connected with her position of economic dependence, but the substance of the *Lucifer*-led revolt was sexual not financial. Economic equality was an acceptable road to freedom but not the only one. *Lucifer's* "Penelope" dreamed of a state of independence not in a society where financial rewards were equal for men and women, but in one where the state would support women as a reward for bringing up children to the age of eighteen. The children, from their nineteenth year onward, would repay the state for its outlay.

"Emancipation" referred to liberation from disease and male brutality. Education in health and "family sociology" was the unvaried theme. The shocking personal history was considered an excellent educational device. One of its purposes was to dramatize the importance of having parents teach their children the facts of life. Probably uppermost in Harman's mind was his eugenic obsession—his belief that the personalities of future members of the race were profoundly affected by the circumstances surrounding conception. His notions on the subject were not much tempered by his close association after 1900 with the scientific eugenics movement.

Moses Harman's two pet fanaticisms put him in prison for five years in April 1890: He wished first to test his right to print anything he pleased; he also thought that the more shocking his case histories, the quicker his readers would be shocked into changing shocking conditions. Many broadminded readers of *Lucifer* were themselves disgusted with the offending material which sent Harman to jail. The first piece that reaped the wrath of the law was the so-called Markland letter which told of a wife's suffering submission to her husband's "abnormal" approaches. The letter (which had been received and forwarded to Harman by W. G. Markland, a correspondent for *Lucifer*) could have used medical terms with safety but the writer had preferred translating them into the layman's language. The publisher of *Lucifer* was sentenced and then released on appeal. While still out of jail he received and published a case report which a Dr. R. V. O'Neill of New York had submitted as a good match for the Markland contribution. Back to jail Harman went on a second indictment and conviction for printing obscene material.

A reputation for sincerity of motive won the martyr's crown for Harman but did not yield him his freedom. The anarchists, of course, stood behind him. He was their representative in the eugenics movement and a fellow victim of censorship. At his death in 1910, Emma Goldman's *Mother Earth* printed two separate eulogies. Outside of the circles of extreme individualism, the best protests in his behalf came from the Liberal Club in New York and from the progressive-minded magazine, *Twentieth Century*.

The editor of *Twentieth Century* felt that some of the things in *Lucifer* were in poor taste—Heywood's defenders had felt the same way about him—but the magazine was certainly not immoral or obscene. It was absurd and disgraceful that such a man should be hounded by the government's paid spies. It was equally foolish to suppose that such a man could ever be suppressed. "For the government, that is rotten to the heart, that licenses so many social immoralities, to persecute Mr. Harman is to wash the outside of the cup that is all filthy within." It was not Harman's disgrace, but the government's. It was not Harman's obscenity, but that of the judge who sentenced him. The social leaders who suppressed disclosures of outrages against women were, in essence, working to retain the privileges of male domination for themselves.

In the eyes of the New York liberals, the trial had been an inquisition whose disposition of the case was tantamount to saying:

You have been guilty of publishing the facts concerning an affair of private life which ought not to be made known. We recognize that by the present marriage institution woman is the slave of man, and he has the right to do as he wills with her. "Wives submit yourselves to your husband in all things." If such outrages occur we mean that they shall *not* be published. You would arouse a spirit of revolt among women. They would no longer be willing slaves. This must not be. We propose to keep them subservient to our will and pleasure, and any man who moves to relieve women from this abject slavery shall be sentenced to five years imprisonment.

Liberals who stood up to be counted as being against censorship were very careful to specify precisely what they were defending. Certainly few of them were ready to be associated publicly with Harman's special line of thought, which linked evolution with eugenics to produce the free love solution. Darwin had described a race as improving gradually through a process of natural selection in which the fittest tended to survive and reproduce. Harman, in common with other eugenics enthusiasts, proposed to accelerate the pace of improvement by a practice of mate selection. Each woman (that is, after the sexual revolution) would choose the father of her child with reference to the hereditary qualities he had to offer. The children of such preferential mating would also benefit from the harmony in which they were conceived and reared.

Heredity, by this eugenist's definition, meant everything that preceded birth, including the tone of parental relationships as well as impressions received during the nine months of gestation. Little wonder, then, that so much emphasis was placed on social reform through marriage reform. How all-important marriage reform must have seemed to those who believed that nine-tenths of all learning took place before birth; "that is, that the training he gets through suggestions made upon the maternal mind during the period of embryonic growth tremendously outweighs all the work of teachers, and of environment generally, after he enters upon the stage of postnatal existence, or of independent life." Hence the strongly worded admonition to the male to make his contribution to the child's endowment by being extra-considerate toward its mother after conception. Who did not know of cases in which a child's mental and physical character was definitely shaped by some shock received by the mother when the embryo was passing through a phylogenic stage in its evolution corresponding to the shocking phylum? For example, there were children who resembled birds of prey because their mothers had been frightened by such a bird just at the time when the embryo was in the bird stage of development.

Institutional marriage was sadly lacking in all possible eugenic advantages. The right of children to be born well was almost universally denied them. Born in deception and strife, they perpetuated a world of lies, competition, and war. Harman knew these things not from superficial observation, nor yet from mere reasoning. He had spent twenty-five years of his life "boarding around" with families, as a rural schoolteacher generally did at the time. Outpourings from the hearts of husbands and wives about their marital maladjustments and sufferings had convinced him of the utter failure of marriage as a social institution. He had also had experience as a confidential adviser to both parties in family quarrels as a Justice of the Peace. There had also been a period of itinerant preaching undertaken for the Methodists. Whatever criticisms Harman had in regard to marriage had come to him at first hand. They were not the derivative notions one got from reading Byron, Shelley, Tom Paine, Rousseau, or Voltaire.

The institution, as Harman knew it, was an instrument by which the ruling class and the clergy could keep the subject classes in subjection. Given the right and the technique of reproducing scientifically and in limited numbers, the downtrodden would in short order become a threat to the superior position of their masters. That was why legislators, judges, lawyers, and ministers maintained their prohibitory laws against open discussion, the free spread of knowledge, and the practices of family limitation. The silencer on sex, originally invoked because of the moral abuses engendered by ancient forms of phallic worship, was retained to avert revolt fathered by knowledge.

Harman's indictment of marriage was reenforced by the triad of beliefs by which he lived—the belief in freedom, or the negation of all enslavement; the belief in love, or the negation of all hate; the belief in knowledge for use, or the negation of all ignorance. He was a good Warrenite, trusting to liberty plus responsibility to produce a true morality. As elaborated in his *Love and Freedom*, the love choice was to be made for a limited time with opportunity for the rectification of mistakes. In *Institutional Marriage*, Harman used the device of a fictional Martian who, during a ten-year exile, had a chance to observe marriage on earth. The whole experience was strange to this visitor whose homeland knew no propagation—perpetuating itself instead by a process of periodic rejuvenation. The Martians were immortal, somewhat after the pattern of the perfect, sexless world predicted by William Godwin. Nevertheless, the man from another planet had an earthly sense of the ridiculous. He scratched his head vigorously when he noted husbands suing their wives' lovers for alienation of affection, or "loss of services." As a rule, thought Harman (in the person of his fictitious stranger on earth) the wife's affections had been alienated long before her new male interest appeared.

Much of Harman's psychology and eugenics, though widely accepted by discriminating minds of his time, would be ridiculed today. Yet, the effects of his pseudo-science were beneficial even if they were based upon an immature and fallacious body of biological knowledge. Surely there was little harm in teaching that superior children were born to fathers who treated their women tenderly, and to mothers who idealized their mates during pregnancy.

Many of Harman's dicta may also have been inspirational in effect. For he too, like Robert Owen and Ezra Heywood, had a touch of the saviour-martyr complex. He too dated some of his works after a new calendar, using the death of the martyred philosopher heretic Giordano Bruno as his starting-point. His *Right to Be Born Well* had its dedication datelined "Chicago, U. S. A., July, 305—Brunonian Era, Mythical Era, 1905." But there was more than egomania in this man whose work in behalf of sexual adjustment was known far beyond a local coterie of radicals. Expectant mothers in general were indebted to him for popularizing knowledge of diet, clothing, and health care during pregnancy. The woman's rights people knew him for his bold writing and speaking on the equalitarian aims of the feminist movement.

Harman's greatest claim to public praise was his perennial battle with the censors, a struggle which he carried on in the face of certain punishment. As George Bernard Shaw wrote to Lillian Harman upon her father's death:

> It seems nothing short of a miracle that your father should have succeeded in living for seventy-nine years in a country so extremely dangerous for men who have both enlightened opinions and the courage of them as the United States of America. It is certainly no fault of the Americans that he did not die before; the last imprisonment of his was really an outrage to political decency.
>
> I am glad to gather from your letter that he escaped the illness and pain that often trouble a good man's end; and I hope that now that he is dead, and can no longer shock Mr. Comstock and the rest of the American idols, some little sense of shame at the way he was treated may find expression in America.

The militant revolutionary, Eugene V. Debs, wrote his humble tribute for the *Appeal to Reason*:

> One of the sweetest, purest, and bravest men of the present generation breathed his last on earth a few days ago when Moses Harman fell into his dreamless sleep. . . .
>
> He was completely forgetful of self as any mortal ever was on this earth. He was brave enough to face without fear all the world's cruel opposition and tender enough to forgive even the enemies who so relentlessly pursued him.

FREE LAND, FREE LABOR, FREE LOVE

As the editor of *Lucifer,* Harman's life was a continuous round of poverty, privation, and persecution. . . . He was a purist in the most rational sense of that term, and the sexual ignorance and slavery of his age appealed to all his boundless sympathies and stirred to their depths all the vast energies of his splendid intellect and his sturdy manhood. He was an apostle of freedom and light, a warrior in the cause of human regeneration, but all his methods were the methods of sweetness, gentleness and peace. . . .

HARMAN'S EPIGONES

Many an independent radical in nineteenth-century America had supported himself by publishing and bookselling. Robert Dale Owen, Gilbert Vale, and Ezra Heywood, and Moses Harman were notable examples of the same combination of talents. They all wrote, lectured, edited, published, and distributed periodicals, pamphlets, and books. Their specialty—though not by any means an exclusive one—was the forward-looking pamphlet or book treating of those sciences which more directly affected human relationships. Among those whose works bore the imprint "M. Harman," (or its variants, the "Light Bearer Library" and "Lucifer Radical Tracts"), were of course, Harman's coadjutors, his daughter and Edwin C. Walker. The same press also issued pamphlets by Dr. Juliet H. Severance, Hulda L. Potter-Loomis, Orford Northcote, and others who preached that each individual must determine his own moral behavior.

The frame of reference of these writers was consistently anti-clerical and pro-evolution in both biological and social areas. Titles like "Social Freedom the Most Important Factor in Human Evolution," and "Ruled by the Tomb; A Discussion of Free Thought and Free Love," are a clue to the points which Harman's crew was belaboring. The whole position was summarized by Miss Harman in her talk on "The Regeneration of Society" which she delivered in 1898 before the Manhattan Liberal Club. This speech offered nothing new; there was little room for novelty in an area which had already been minutely explored by minds like her own. The relations of love and parentage, she declared, had been frozen by church and state. The evolutionary progress of humanity demanded the natural selection of the best human qualities. This was impossible while the law held mismated people together and prohibited the right of reproductive association to those who were best adapted for parenthood.

Edwin Walker, more versatile and more prolific than his unofficial wife, carried his share of the burden of proving that law, religion, and conventional education were stifling the spontaneity of human affections. He not only wrote for Harman, but also had a press of his own and edited the magazine *Fair Play* from 1888 to 1908. In *Love and the Law* he asked his readers to compare the solicitous, respectful, conduct of the courting male, with the abuse and display of unamiable traits once the marriage ceremony had been performed and the law forbade the wife the privilege of saying "No."

Variety vs. Monogamy made two points: First, that the hypocritical world was praising proscriptive monogamy while following many practices that were in flagrant violation of it. Second, that after the attainment of liberty, i.e., the free practice of free love, society would have the opportunity to observe whether monogamy or variety was superior as a sexual policy. Walker would bet on variety. Even within the current restrictive customs and regulations he could point out several forms of varietism. There was the practicing monogamist and theoretical varietist—one who wanted variety but found the environment unfavorable. Then came the theoretical monogamists and practical varietists—the hypocritical Philistines. Next came the contemporaneous varietists who maintained many connections at the same time, and then the consecutive varietists, who pursued one affection at a time.

Although Walker called for a division of labor among reformers in his *Religion and Rationalism,* his own work was an object-lesson in the indivisibility of reform. In his *Our Worship of Primitive Social Guesses,* and in *Vice; Its Friends and Its Foes,* he illustrated the connectedness of love, law, politics, prostitution, parentage, religion, anthropology, economics, psychology, divorce, fear, freedom, and more, at fifteen cents per pamphlet. *What the Young Need to Know* was a "primer of sexual rationalism" in which Walker urged his readers to stop being ashamed of the facts. Basically, the whole philosophy could be summarized in a simple recommendation that each individual be given as full information as possible on all social topics and be left to the guidance of his conscience thereafter. The understanding was, according to anarchist theory, that this individual must be ready to shoulder the full consequences of a poor choice in thought, conduct, or action.

LATTER-DAY ANARCHISTS

The New York distribution center of anarchist propaganda was the Mother Earth Publishing Association. *Mother Earth,* its periodical, was published from 1906 to 1918 by Emma Goldman, a Russian immigrant who had arrived in America in 1886 at the age of seventeen. Her twentieth year found her in New York City, where her vague but nevertheless ardent ideals of personal freedom were helped toward definition by the anarchists Johann Most and Alexander Berkman. She also met many other leaders in both the socialist and anarchist movements. Although many of her friends were of foreign birth, she soon came to meet or read about the Heywoods, the Harmans, and other lights of native anarchy.

Miss Goldman's first public exposition on birth control was given at the Sunrise Club in New York at the invitation of its president, none other than Harman's unofficial son-in-law, Edwin C. Walker. This was in 1915. She had been interested in the subject before the turn of the century, had attended the Neo-Malthusian Congress in Paris in 1900, and had followed with interest the trials and tribulations of Moses Harman, and later of William and Margaret Sanger. Emma Goldman's initial interest arose from a humanitarian wish to relieve the poor women on New York's East Side, many of whom she had attended in childbirth. The Sunrise Club audience was composed of some six hundred professional people and middle class sophisticates who applauded her matter of fact treatment of contraception. But she was not satisfied with her reception, despite her listeners' cordiality. The complacency of her audience indicated that they were already acquainted with the practices she advocated. No raid interrupted the meeting, no arrest took place. The good word had to be delivered to more innocent minds. She therefore decided upon a series of her own Sunday meetings at locations of her own choosing.

In one important respect the lectures in that first series were a failure. Miss Goldman was confronted by vigilantes and police; but nary a Comstock, or an arrest. The only censorship came from her own comrades. This was the story: The approval of several sympathetic physicians bolstered her own conviction that she was an expert sexologist. Thereupon she promptly enlarged her scope to include lectures on homosexuality. At a time when few persons spoke publicly of such matters, it was anybody's free territory. Some of her friends begged her not to add to the ugly reputation anarchists already had by lecturing on such unnatural themes. She harkened to her friends' advice as cordially as she listened to enemies who sought to curb her freedom—the lectures went on. Members of her audiences uncovered the secrets of their nature to her and got comfort for their "unnatural" affliction. This gave high satisfaction to all. So, probably, did her long awaited arrest in New York, which resulted in a Carnegie Hall protest meeting and an opportunity to lecture the court for an hour on controlled motherhood. On principle, Emma preferred fifteen days in the workhouse to the hundred dollar fine imposed by the judge.

Mother Earth printed articles criticizing marriage and agitating for sexual freedom, but it did not exploit the subject with the frequency and fury of *Lucifer*. Miss Goldman lectured and lived upon her principles of free love. Although she abhorred the use of crude language—an exhibition of erotic suggestiveness by Billy Sunday nauseated her—she was inclined, especially in the early years, to use the sex stimulant on her audiences. When Prince Peter Kropotkin, the Russian scientist, sociologist, and anarchist, suggested to her that the paper *Free Society* would increase its influence by giving less space to sex, a heated discussion arose. Kropotkin argued that woman's emancipation lay in the direction of raising her to the intellectual level of man. Equality had nothing to do with sex. Neither Kropotkin nor his adversary would yield an inch until Miss Goldman broke the deadlock with the remark that at Kropotkin's age, perhaps her interest in and emphasis upon sex would decrease too. "But it *is* [important] *now*, and it is a tremendous factor for thousands, millions even, of young people." The great anarchist theoretician abandoned his position. "Perhaps you are right, after all," he wrote.

In America, anarchist tradition looked for an emancipation of woman which would give her the same individual sovereignty it was seeking for the male. So that when Miss Goldman took account in 1906 of the achievement of the feminist movement, she pronounced it a failure. If woman really wanted to be free, by Miss Goldman's standards, she had to emancipate herself from emancipation. To date she had merely moved in large numbers from the constricting environment of the home to the equally intolerable factory, sweat shop, department store, and office. A curious thing had happened. Many "emancipated" women had come to prefer the chains of marriage to those of industry. Such women obviously had not the courage to free themselves from the bonds of moral and social prejudice. The birth control lectures of 1916 pointed up a promised emancipation from perennial childbearing and diaper washing. They also showed how women could prevent capitalist wars (there was one going on at the time) by refusing to replenish the supply of cannon fodder.

Marriage, said Miss Goldman, was more insult than protection. It was degrading to human dignity and made parasites of its female participants. It incapacitated woman for life's struggle, erased her social consciousness, paralyzed her intellect, and then threw her the bone of "protection." The really emancipated woman must defy all her potential slavemasters—Mrs. Grundy, Comstock, the bosses, the boards of education, and the rest. She must listen to the voice of nature; she must take her privileges of love and motherhood with the serenity of a truly free individual.

Writers for *Mother Earth* supplied articles in a similar tone from time to time. John R. Coryell discussed the artificiality of marriage and the home, wherein sex was inevitably treated as a "nasty mystery." To those who were proposing "trial marriages" and "free unions," he replied that any form which interfered with freedom was objectionable. These innovations were equally unsatisfactory inasmuch as they called the attention of society to the union itself and to the paternity of the resulting children. Trial marriage met his requirements during the trial period, but then became as oppressive as any marriage. If one had to abide by a system of formal union, then complete freedom of divorce must accompany it. In an examination of "Motherhood and Marriage," Henriette Fuerth reported these two feminine roles to be distinct phenomena; the first a constant, the second an evolutionary accident. Ada May Krecker condemned marriage as an obsolete institution whose job was already being performed better by other social agencies. As witness to the kind of sanctity that current morality attached to marriage, W. S. Van Valkenburgh drew the attention of his readers to exhortations to young men to "sow the seed for a war baby before going to the front" (1915). He called his piece "Posthumous Babies."

One of the leading literary figures of the *Mother Earth* coterie was the Michigan-born Voltairine De Cleyre, whose character, name, and political views are explained in large part by her father's religious gyrations. At the time of his daughter's birth in 1866, De Cleyre was a rebellious freethinker; hence the given name in celebration of Voltaire. When it came time to decide on Voltairine's education, her father had already become a Catholic, and he chose the life of a nun for his daughter. Hence to a convent for her education. But the precocious child refused to be directed from without. Her first significant political experience was the affair of the Haymarket anarchists in 1887. On first impulse, she cried out for their hanging. Soon after, having lost faith in the justice of American law and trial by jury, she changed her mind about the convicted Haymarket demonstrators and took a definite radical turn herself. A lecture by Clarence Darrow led her to socialism. From there, Miss De Cleyre, a born iconoclast, moved easily to anarchism.

The literature of protest and revolt acquired a considerable body of effective eloquence from this "priestess of pity and vengeance." Among her poems were "Mary Wollstonecraft," "The Wandering Jew," "The Suicide's Defense," "The Cry of the Unfit," and "Bastard Born." The last, forty-six indignant quatrains, was the prayer of an illegitimate child who asked:

> Am I not as the rest of you,
>   With a hope to reach, and a dream to live?
> With a soul to suffer, a heart to know
>   The pangs that the thrusts of the heartless give?

Anarchists of the period naturally had an intense interest in children born out of wedlock. "Bastard Born" might almost be considered a companion piece to Miss De Cleyre's "They Who Marry Do Ill," which appeared in *Mother Earth* in 1908.

Her contribution to Moses Harman's defense was a lecture on "Sex Slavery" at the end of which she invited her audience to sign a petition for a pardon to be sent to President Harrison. Harman was in prison, she declared, just because "he called a spade a spade," because he gave the parts of the body their right names. "Why? Why, when murder is stalking in your streets, when dens of infamy are so thick within your city that competition has forced down the price of prostitution to the level of wages of your starving shirtmakers . . . when debauchees of the worst type hold your public offices . . . why then sits Moses Harman there within his prison cell?" Because, she answered, he looked squarely at this thing called "morality" and called it a liar and an enslaver of women to the whims and selfish gratification of their husbands. Did anyone want to know exactly what the notorious Markland letter contained? Miss De Cleyre would tell him if he came up to the platform at the end of the protest meeting.

Not everyone who attended a sexual freedom meeting was necessarily of anarchist persuasion. Many a highly respected and well-to-do citizen came, so it was said, to get comfort for his innermost desires or clandestine practices. Libertarians of every political color came in the cause of freedom. There were physicians who were seeking materials for their science of sex. There were sociologically minded students whose purpose was similar.

Non-anarchist and near-anarchist literature was also full of searchings for permanent harmony in the sexual sphere. Such a treatment could come even from so impersonal a source as the American News Company, which published a general pamphlet on "Marriage and Divorce" (1870). Its view was almost puritanic as it called for the generation of a cleaner, smoother, better-adjusted society through a bursting of the bonds of the mismated. Again, the projector of "A Sex Revolution" might be a spiritualist like Mrs. Lois Waisbrooker who had on many an occasion written communications to Heywood's *Word*. Mrs. Waisbrooker sometimes fictionalized her messages and sometimes presented her ideas in more formal pamphlets like *The Occult Forces of Sex*. Others, like R. D. Chapman and Elizabeth Fields, sought to combat polygamy and prostitution by discovering the "natural law" of human relationships. Once found, this natural way of life could be taught to children. In time the whole of society would come out into the sunshine of love, unfettered by law or artificial codes of morals. Sam Atkinson, in his *Science and a Priest* urged that the questions of sexual morals and marriage be taken out of the hands of the clergy because it was signally unqualified to deal with such matters.

So many were the suggestions for marriage reform or abolition, and so varied their source and direction, that there developed a number of specialized students of sexology. C. L. James, an anarchist whose writing career spanned some forty years, was printed by many publishers including himself, Moses Harman, and the Mother Earth Publishing Company. He wrote on the origins of anarchism, on its relationship to the population problem and Malthusian doctrine, on woman's rights, and, of course, on marriage.

His *Future Relation of the Sexes,* whose publication coincided with the launching of Ezra Heywood's career, surveyed the field of sexual reformation and offered a comparative analysis of the many doctrines and practices available. The Shakers, said James, had not yet proven that celibacy was possible for all men, and doubtless would never prove it. They had, however, by glorifying the spiritual element of human love, influenced the extreme free love school in its agitation against male animality and selfishness.

"Varietism," a self-explanatory practice carried out in isolated community experiments, was self-defeating to C. L. James' way of thinking. It bred license, jealousy, and disappointment. It gave the desired freedom to women, but produced intemperance in men. James felt, as he sought generalizations in his science, that fully emancipated women would drift naturally to monogamous choice. In this stage they would prefer constancy in their men. In the last analysis, an equalitarian monogamous system would develop once women had attained complete freedom of choice and rejection.

Some form of Oneida communism, with an element of community regulation, seemed ideal to James. His objection to complex marriage at Oneida was that such self-denial and loss of individuality as it required was possible only for people with a deep religious feeling. For that reason, Noyes' community, James predicted, would not last more than a hundred years. He saw good in all theories and practices which permitted change where desired. It all came to the same thing, whether in the *Future Relation of the Sexes,* or in an earlier exposition, *The Law of Marriage:* The best in available ideas moved toward the conclusions of "free love" advocates. Free love, plus physiological and birth control knowledge for women, would achieve their emancipation, together with a truly ideal existence, side by side, for male and female alike.

∽ ∽

The measure of public acceptance of the ideas of James, Heywood, and Harman was reported in Dora Forster's treatise on *Sex Radicalism* which came off Harman's press in 1905. The scientists of social affairs had been so thoroughly intimidated by religious authorities, said Miss Forster, that the sex radicals had to pursue the subject unaided. The doctors were at the moment muted by the fear of social and economic sanctions, but would probably cooperate with the sex radicals if given enough encouragement to publicize their physiological findings. Some help could also be expected from social movements which were anti-clerical. Such movements—to be counted on for the task of removing social obstructions rather than for constructive work in the specialized field of sex—were the forces of secularism, spiritualism, anarchism, and socialism.

There were many questions to be asked and answered by science. It would be well to know more about sexual precocity, its correlation with the mental calibre of children, and how it should be handled when found. Vast human enrichment would come out of research into the physiology and psychology of the brothel, of male and female celibacy, of habits and practices in marriage. Many answers were already at hand. Too often convention had opposed science with the expected results of repression, distortion, perversion, and a train of other psychological disturbances. Our Puritanical society had kept women in ignorance. Their lack of knowledge had shut off all roads to fulfillment in marriage save one: nature, less cruel than society, often gave women the satisfactions of maternity. By virtue of rewarding motherhood, women's seething caldron of unhappiness was kept from boiling over.

The elements in Dora Forster's program for ironing out the rough spots of sexual life were numerous, specific, and well elaborated. Worked into the framework of free love doctrine were the ideas of equality evolved by the feminist movement, the physiological and birth control knowledge contributed by medical science, and the dominant role of sex in the human personality as advertised by a few bold psychologists. This last may have been a new light shed by contemporary scientists, but many a social reformer must have assumed it long before as an underlying truth. Otherwise it would be difficult to explain why Utopians of a religious or rational caste, radical reformers of the social structure, all included some plan to modify sex arrangements.

Dora Forster did not mention as possible allies in the liberation the sects which emerged from religious revivals and the millennialist currents of the nineteenth century. This was not an oversight on her part. For, by 1905, when she wrote her *Sex Radicalism*, the religiously inspired communal groups, whose prescriptions for family life included everything from total celibacy to polygamy, had already passed out of existence. Social pressures, legal prohibitions, the decline of religious zeal, and economic misfortune had already played their part in destroying these innovations in economic and family organization which for almost a century had attracted the curious and shocked the conventional.

SIX

Spiritual Wives

Religious Communism in America during the first part of the nineteenth century attracted many a professional traveler and reformer to observe briefly and then write about what he had seen. What incited his curiosity was probably the combination of notable characteristics held pretty much in common by such communities. Life was simple. The inhabitants were industrious, self-denying, and generally under the control of a strong leader. Their efforts were frequently rewarded by an economic prosperity not shared by people in nearby communities. In reviewing the histories of these communal experiments, John Humphrey Noyes, himself the organizing genius of one of them, hinted that this kind of success came only to such communities as were dominated by a strong religious motif. He also hinted, in justification of his own rigid rule at Oneida, New York, that an iron hand at the spiritual helm was necessary.

For rational reformers like Robert Dale Owen and his friends, the no-marriage feature of many of these communities was explanation enough for a prosperous economy. Without marriage there were no children. Without children the population remained static or declined. Surpluses were obviously easier to attain where new mouths were not appearing more rapidly than the capacity to feed them could be enlarged. The population level was maintained by the entrance of able-bodied converts. Celibacy, moreover, was a kind of birth control whose practitioner was not liable to reap a harvest of public abuse as had Robert Dale Owen when he published his prescription for limiting the population.

For reasons that are not apparent, the younger Owen, who found time to write about every unusual sexual morality that came to his notice, said nothing about the Rappites from whom his father had purchased the New Harmony land site. The followers of George Rapp, a dissident German Lutheran who brought his group from abroad to live in simple New Testament communism, renounced marriage after they arrived in America. Couples who had already been married were asked to renounce their vows. Nonconformists were asked to leave the community. Except for those young couples who escaped from the community by eloping, plus a few people so lacking in faith as to continue having children—much to Rapp's disgust—the Harmonists obeyed. Expecting to enter the Kingdom of Heaven momentarily, the pietistic Rappites uncomplainingly threw their worldly assets—material and emotional—into a common lot, and followed their leader implicitly. Rapp himself reminded his followers at intervals that his own life had one purpose, that of presenting them to God at the second coming. Uncharitable critics intimated that Rapp lived only to get the community assets signed over to himself.

Adverse commentaries on the "unnatural" asceticism of the Rappites were not wanting. That romantic defier of convention, Lord Byron, celebrated the community in one of the cantos of his *Don Juan*. He wrote:

> When Rapp the Harmonist embargo'd Marriage
> In his harmonious settlement which flourishes
> Strangely enough as yet without miscarriage,
> Because it breeds no more mouths than it nourishes,
> Without those sad expenses which disparage what
> Nature most encourages. . . .

Gilbert Vale, successor in spirit to Robert Dale Owen's position as chief publisher of progressive literature, visited Rapp's settlement at Economy, Ohio (the settlement to which the Rappites moved after the sale of Harmony) in 1837. He reported that the settlement was run like a monarchy with Rapp as king. Things ran quite smoothly, rations being drawn from a common stock. Many of the taxing household functions, like baking, had become public enterprises. "But," continued Vale, "that unfortunate 'but' perpetually comes in to mar perfect happiness—but they have some very foolish, unnatural, and inconvenient regulations; besides the necessity of doing even what is right *by rule.*"

The most absurd of their regulations, thought Vale, was their form of marriage contract. They had apparently made a small concession to nature. The contracting couple lived together for one year and then parted for six. The arrangement was such that there was never more than one family member at a time who was completely dependent. Now, this may have insured a population of producers only, but it hardly redounded to the good of the married pair, Vale reported. It placed man and wife in "peculiar situations" and encouraged vices that would bring the worst of evils in their wake.

Under the circumstances, it is surprising that only one schismatic movement developed among the Rappites. It was in 1831 that Bernhard Muller, alias Count Maximilian de Leon, wormed his way to popularity in Economy. His rather popular heresy consisted in announcing the joys of marriage, of a livelier life, and of other earthly temptations. The obvious success of his campaign shook the confidence of Father Rapp and his adopted son, Federick. The technique of calling for a vote of confidence before mutiny could spread too far was used by the Rapps and with success. The vote was five hundred for Father Rapp, and two hundred and fifty for the count. The minority seceded, only to be duped and later deserted by their leader. The Rappite venture itself started to disintegrate for want of leadership and fresh blood almost immediately after the death of George Rapp in 1847. The community aspect disappeared. The property was finally sold by the trustees in 1903 to a group of Pittsburgh capitalists.

Other colonies of religious communists were formed back in the thirties and forties with the same high consciousness of the need to define their sex regulations. Bethel, in Missouri, was started in 1840 by a group of Rapp's disillusioned secessionists under the leadership of Dr. William Kiel. The Prussian-born Kiel was in search of a sect which he could lead back to Bible simplicity when he met and joined forces with the rebel Rappites. Their new society and its offshoot at Aurora retained enough of the heresy of Count de Leon to accept the marriage institution and the family unit of society.

The settlers at Zoar, Ohio, were Separatists like Rapp's cohorts. They had followed their leader, Joseph Michael Bimeler, here from Germany. Being very poor, they found it highly desirable to socialize their property. The group of 53 men and 104 women who incorporated in 1832, agreed to give up marriage and thus to limit their population until they had paid the debts incurred in the founding of the colony. It was believed also that a division into family units would tend to a division of interests among the brethren. They chose to be bachelor communists for reasons that were clearly more economic than religious.

The similarly humble and economical Amanites made their first settlement near Buffalo in 1842. Herr Metz, their contact with God, went into daily trances in search of divine spirit, caught some of it, and brought it back to share with his comrades. But women were deprived of their just share of communal equality. They were denied an opportunity to voice their opinions. They ate separately and kept pretty much to themselves. Marriage was more tolerated then welcomed. Wedding ceremonies were as gloomy as funeral services. With the years, the farming community of the Amanites, which moved to Iowa in 1855, became more progressive in its social outlook. Women were admitted to the councils, and educational and social services were expanded. Church and state were separated in 1931 and the economic and social lives of the faithful came under secular jurisdiction.

MARRIAGE, MORALS AND SEX IN AMERICA

MOTHER ANN LEE

The feminine outlook was infinitely better in the United Society of Believers (better known as the Shakers) from its very inception. Mother Ann Lee, who received her doctrinal instructions from James and Jane Wardley in England, led her flock to America in 1774 after much legal and social persecution in her native country. The feminist part of Shaker religion, as developed by Mother Ann, was woven into the fundamental creed. The Shakers believed that just as the Holy Spirit had appeared the first time in the male form to redeem the original sin of man, the second appearance would come in the shape of a woman to rescue women from their original fall in the Garden of Eden.

Ann Lee was convinced that she was the current embodiment of the Holy Spirit sent to earth to prepare the faithful for the millennium. And the believers believed. She could recall being favored with heavenly visions as far back as her illiterate, poverty-stricken childhood. Maturing into womanhood, she sharpened her vague religious experiences of youth into a focus which clarified the picture of human depravity. The highlight of sin, the most impure feature of life on earth, she concluded, was the sexual relationship. Salvation must come through a renunciation of the flesh by the elect. The greater the struggle against the demands of the body, the more evident the advance toward divinity—the better the preparation for entrance into Heaven. Far from denying their conflicts, the Shakers advertised them as proof of the tremendous spiritual strength they had to exert in order to overcome their instinctual urges.

To be sure, spiritual elevation through celibacy was not peculiar to the Shaker sect. It had long since been adopted by monastic orders and other ecclesiastical bodies. The big difference was that in the case of the Shakers marriage was forbidden to the entire civil community. But the distinction was not as sharp as it might seem. For the Shakers never really expected everyone to rise to their own heights. They indicated that most of the world would and could continue living as it had done. It would remain for the Shakers to finish the job of salvation in the great beyond. They, as experts in saving, could expedite the task of Universal Salvation in Heaven, where everyone would be secure from earthly temptations. For the time being, they recognized an "Outer World" where property and marriage were not to be considered as bearing the taint of sin.

The self-discipline of Shakerism, rigidly applied by full-fledged members of the sect, never did operate to destroy tolerance and understanding of other people's psychological needs. New entrants were allowed to subscribe to Shaker principles while remaining with their own families. While communal ownership of property was the accepted pattern for Shaker communities, some people were admitted to the labor exchange without being required to give up their private property. Though chastity was demanded of all permanent residents, if boy and girl Shakers happened to fall in love, they would be sent off with a blessing, plus cash enough to get a start in the "Outer World." The Shakers admitted, with quiet charity, to large numbers of such defections from the faith.

During the early part of the nineteenth century, the many American Shaker settlements received and graciously welcomed all sorts of visitors. Some of these were travelers from abroad. Others were native observers. There were holiday travelers and professional reporters. Those interested primarily in economic reform went to see how communalization of property was working out. Large numbers were naturally curious about the ritual dances in which the deep emotions of the soul manifested themselves in violent agitations of the body. This was the aspect of Shaker worship which led people originally to use the derogatory term "Shaker," the name which the United Society later adopted as its official calling. The brothers and sisters would—separately to be sure—swirl in a wheel-dance circle, stamping sin underfoot. Or, a phalanx of one sex would face one of the other, all shaking their hands violently downward so as to toss sin out of the body through the finger tips.

Visitors like De Tocqueville and De Beaumont, both Catholics, witnessed these exhibitions and swiftly concluded that the Shakers were demented. Others were more charitable, and conceded that such goings on were well suited to the poor, ignorant people who made up these communal groups. Ignorant they were, for the Shakers, in their early days, shared none of the intellectual leanings of the Amanite sect. They were said, in fact, to have actively discouraged reading even of the Bible. Their education was almost purely vocational, a partial explanation for their late economic success and their bequeathing to our culture a native American craftsmanship examples of which are sought feverishly by collectors of our day.

There was general praise for the friendliness, simplicity, and charity which Shakers actually practiced after preaching. The apparent material success of these people, whose principles forbade more than a just profit on articles sold, also impressed many distinguished travelers. Harriet Martineau declared that if the bare material things of life were a measure of success, the Shakers were successful. However, she commented, a more enlightened group of people could really have done wonders if they chose to use the same principles of association, and to grace them with a more liberal idea of culture and education.

As one would expect, there were many comments about the meaning and consequences of strict chastity. Robert Dale Owen found much to praise in the social economy of the Shakers but eloquently damned their glorification of celibacy. He described it as a perversion of human nature, saying that if everyone joined this sect, the species would become extinct in one generation. He would certainly agree with anyone who found fault with marriage customs and ethics; but the remedy was not to deny expression to the reproductive instinct altogether. Hinting that the Shakers were applying an economic measure in the guise of religion, Owen declared that it was possible to have successful socialism and mating too. He would forward a copy of *Moral Physiology* to the chief elder of the Lebanon Society. This book, he clearly implied, contained the blueprint for harmony of sex, science, and society.

The elder who replied to Owen in vindication of Shaker doctrines forgot the customary mild manners of his sect. He was most ungracious about acknowledging the gift copy of *Moral Physiology,* pointing out that the non-Shaker world was quite willing for humankind to expire. Its murderous wars and advocacy of birth control techniques were obvious indications that the human race wished to destroy itself. "Were it not for the pleasure connected with the act" by which the race was perpetuated, he elaborated, the earth would be unpeopled in no time without the help of the anti-propagation doctrines of the United Believers. The evil was not in laws and customs, as Owen would have it, but in the fleshly desires which caused violations of laws and customs.

Several of the visitors who wrote about the Shakers were negative or hostile to the grim, joyless life they lived. Those, including Charles Dickens, who were not specifically oriented to the sexual roots of Shaker conduct, noted the humorless character of their activities and let it go at that. William Owen, Robert Dale's brother, attributed the cause of Shaker joylessness to their misunderstanding of the values of sex. He explained that they hoped to replace the usual fervent attraction for one object of desire with a diffuse affection for a hundred sisters or brothers. Moreover, the Shakers had failed to produce, with their synthetic version of family love, a substitute for the charm of "brotherly confidence and sisterly freedom." The result, Owen concluded, was inhibition—the blocking of channels of free communication between male and female. Hence the aspect of restraint noted by visitors. Hence the physical operations of the rituals which rose to such feverish heights in the 1840's (when an added infection of the spiritualist revival set in) that the Shaker ministry had to exclude all visitors from religious services.

Analysts of Shaker society have almost always focused on its sexual aspects. This is to be expected, if only because the practice of total chastity is likely to provoke the interest of a world which lives otherwise. John Humphrey Noyes, leader of the revolutionary marriage and eugenics group of Perfectionists at Oneida, singled out the "leadership of women" as the distinguishing mark of Shakerism. Speaking for his own sex, he declared that *men* would never have been inspired to erect a socialism in which male and female cooperated side by side without forming the final union. It was a symptom of female ascendancy when the courtship stage (which stage of love women prefer to the culminating stage of marriage) was perpetuated throughout life. Said Noyes: "Women like to talk about love; but men want the love itself. Among the [earlier American] Perfectionists the women led the way in bundling with purposes as chaste as those of the Shakers. For a time they had their way; but in time the men had their way."

Shakerism was also explained simply as the expiation of original sin. One theory, which accepted the obvious, explained Shaker chastity as Ann Lee's personal revenge against those life forces which first gave her four children and then took them away by early death. Abraham Stanley, the man she had married, reacted to his misfortunes in quite another way. When Ann took to the self-contained sexual life, he ran away with another woman.

Theodore Schroeder, so able in his defense of unpopular causes that American anarchists embraced him as their own, read deeply in the imported literature of an incipient psychoanalysis and arrived at a novel exposition on the Shakers and other religious groups. His lack of sympathy for revealed religion, when added to his recently acquired knowledge of the mind in its subconscious operations, and then mixed with history and anthropology, produced a conclusion that all religion was built around a nebulous core of sex.

Probing back into Ann Lee's early childhood, as analysts still do with their patients, he found that she was a "wild creature" from the moment she was born. Every attention-seeking device—including hysteria and convulsions—had been in her repertory. She had not been a normal, playful child. Her contemplative, serious nature was a sure sign, according to Schroeder, "of precocity and subjectivity such as are a usual accompaniment of sexual precocity, and sexual shame." In short, the founder of American Shakerism could never resolve her religious, social, and sex motivations. She therefore felt inferior. She was afraid of impulses from which she wanted to be protected. Her marriage she never welcomed; for it failed to divest her of her guilt or sin complex. Such a pattern usually resulted, Schroeder explained, in exhibitionism, prudery, or an anomalous combination of both.

The shoe fit Ann Lee perfectly, the analyst declared. She had been arrested at the infantile stage of fantasy and could therefore never make herself socially useful on a mature level of practical achievement for the benefit of mankind. Her lust for power, in conflict with her unquenchable lust for things of which she was ashamed, led her to "exhibit" celibacy as the highest form of life. Affirming the common sense explanation that Robert Dale Owen had offered long ago, the learned Schroeder phrased it thus: "Having a psychological inhibition against normal gratification, she must make a virtue of her deprivation, which will be commensurate with the sorrows thereof."

A personal conflict of this kind, the psychologist explained, could result either in great egotistic exaltation or in morbid depression. Some people just went crazy. Others became saints and martyrs. To Ann Lee, as she watched visions during her first jail sentence, it had occurred that she was the Christ of the second coming. When asked about her presumptuousness in thus elevating herself, she replied simply that she had stepped in to head the family of Christ in exactly the same way as any woman assumes the family helm when her husband is away.

Turning away from carnal love, said Schroeder, it was "normal" for Mother Ann Lee to embrace a fantasy. From childish things to godly things was a path well known. And there was doubt too that Mother Ann confined herself to supernatural beings. For repression, even with the best of religious formulae, did not always leave the sex-obsessed subject satisfied with a "purely spiritual outlet." One could if he wished (and Schroeder was capable of this kind of wishful thinking) believe the many tales told about Ann Lee's escapades.

There were cynics who wanted very much to believe that the Shakers were not beyond welcoming clandestine affairs. But witnesses to such there were none. David Lamson, who with his wife lived among the Shakers for two years, had no proof that they failed to live up to their professions of total abstinence. He did remark that the ministry and elders had every opportunity to cheat, inasmuch as they lived privately, apart from the rest of the community. It would be miraculous, he mused, if they were able to restrain themselves entirely.

Among the Shaker laymen, he testified, young men and women stole interviews regularly. This was the first step in the series of events which generally led to their departure from Shakerdom. Mrs. Lamson, as the story went, became a confidante of some of the younger sisters. These unburdened themselves to her, revealing the trials and excitements of their courtship activities in the lower part of the Shaker residence at times when the rest of the "family" was asleep above.

According to experts on religious communism, the Shakers' chance of community survival was high because they had eliminated family jealousies and competition. They also had the advantage of centralized discipline. For a long time during the nineteenth century, appointments to the eldership were made from headquarters at New Lebanon. In somewhat the same way as the monastery at Cluny set an example for the reform of monastery life in the tenth century, the group at New Lebanon in New York State exerted its influence on other groups scattered throughout New Hampshire, Maine, and Massachusetts.

Notwithstanding its economic and organizational fitness for survival, Shakerism at present can muster interest in itself only as a dying sect, once prosperous and well known for its craftsmanship and peculiar religious beliefs. To the *Life* reporter (March 26, 1949) who wondered why all the male Shakers died off first, one might suggest two possible explanations. There were more women Shakers in the first place. The males, moreover, were inclined to seek security elsewhere as they noted the disintegration of their sect.

Why the disintegration? In the first place, the non-perpetuating Shakers depended on certain important community features to gain converts; and these features lost their force in the Civil War era. Women who sought the greater dignity accorded females in Shaker communities began to find comparable dignity in industry and the professions. Those who chose Shakerism as a refuge from too much childbearing had their desires fulfilled in the increased spread of birth control information. The prosperity of Shaker communities must also have attracted many of the economically insecure. But this prosperity depended largely on small-scale handicraft industries which rapidly lost ground before low-price, large-scale manufacturing. And, again, the inspiration of religion could and did lead many to more satisfactory sexual solutions in the polygamy of the Mormons, or in the "complex marriage" of Noyes' Perfectionists.

PLURAL WIVES

The maverick psychologist Theodore Schroeder connected Shaker celibacy with salacity. He felt the same way about the Mormons. It was, in fact, his experience among the Mormons that gave him his first conviction of the blood relationship "between religion and lust." Known to liberals of his active period as a fearless progressive, Schroeder offered his legal talent to anyone deprived of civil liberties or human rights. Although from early youth, when he first was influenced by the belligerent agnostic, Colonel Robert G. Ingersoll, Schroeder's life was ruled by science and reason, he would always defend the right of people to practice a religion of their choice. He had traveled to Utah to live among the Mormons so that he might defend them against persecution and legal sanctions. He had assumed that the charges against them were grossly exaggerated. But a period of observation changed his mind. He then turned about and fought them with every weapon at his command.

One of these weapons was psychological exposure. Using the same kind of analysis with which he later measured up the Shakers, Schroeder convincingly demonstrated that a standard set of facts—the conflict between sex drive and moral restriction, the emotional upsurge of religious revival, and low intelligence—could produce precisely opposite effects. In one case it was "nonogamy," in the other, polygamy.

What first made Schroeder believe that all was not strictly spiritual among the Mormons was his witnessing their revival meetings. The parties most subject to "deliriums," he noted, were the younger folk whose emotional disturbances could best be ascribed to sex repression during adolescence. Further research turned up materials which jibed with the findings of previous students of the psychology of revivals. Mormon history indicated that during periods of spiritual upsurge (especially the one at Kirtland, Ohio, where their leader Joseph Smith held court in the thirties), many of the prominent figures had practiced adultery. According to some critics, Smith's first revelation of "the eternity of the marriage covenant" came during one of these spells of moral chaos. The plurality of wives was a part of the revelation.

The doctrine had worked its way up from the "kiss of charity," a symbol of brotherly and sisterly love, through the many theories of spiritual wifery—a German invention—to the high point of multiple unions of the flesh. The moral justification for the doctrine of spiritual wives started in Heaven where souls were being propagated in vast numbers. These souls had to find bodies on earth where they must serve a period of probation before they could be eligible for a permanent abode in heaven. Accordingly, the highest service one could perform was to manufacture bodies in large numbers, so that all available souls could find habitations on earth. The more mortal bodies one produced, the better qualified one was to take his place among the soul-multiplying saints in the hereafter. Women were limited in their capacity to breed; men were not. Ergo polygamy, at first limited to the upper echelons of the privileged ministry, and then extended, upon complaints of undemocratic discrimination, to all male Mormons.

A further consideration was that a woman could not win salvation unless her soul was "sealed up" to her male affinity on earth. The interpretation of the Mormon elders was that each woman had to be sealed to an elder in order to get into heaven. Nor could a man get into Heaven without his sexual complement. Brigham Young, the leader of the Utah settlement, declared, "as no man can be perfect without the woman, so no woman can be perfect without a man to lead her. I tell you the truth as it is in the bosom of eternity; and I say to every man upon the face of the earth, if he wishes to be saved, he cannot be saved without a woman by his side." And so it came to pass that if a woman complained that she had mistakenly married A instead of her affinity B, a ceremony would be arranged to "seal" her to B. If A felt he also wanted to be "sealed" to her, the church would perform a ceremony to cover his needs. The complications were evident. They were resolved as well as they could be in a formal adoption of polygamy.

According to the best accounts, the movement started with Joseph Smith, a barely literate and not very intelligent boy, whose early life showed marks of instability closely resembling that of the Claflin sisters. Shiftless Father Smith used his visions to bolster his prestige where Buck Claflin exploited his legal talent. The mother organized her life around a neurotic religiosity. She was on the constant lookout for new religious sects that might satisfy her peculiar needs. Where other mothers looked forward to a successful business or professional life for their sons, she hoped that one of hers might blossom into a Messiah. The one unusual hereditary gift she handed on to her children was a strain of epilepsy. But this was not to be passed by lightly. One recalls that epileptic seizures stood Ann Lee and even Mohammed in good stead in getting their divine credentials accepted.

It was to young Smith's credit that he capitalized on his defects and became one of the outstanding administrative organizers of his time. His dull mind, which made him the butt for the practical jokes of his boyhood friends, was later cited by the faithful as proof that he could neither have delivered the Book of Mormon nor performed his other feats without divine inspiration. Even before he came into the limelight with his revelations, he had built up a following among the superstitious with his alleged powers of magic. His fond mother helped him a lot, for she was not averse to broadcasting her son's very special talents. Smith's salesmanship improved until he was able to sell the millennium to large masses of willing believers whom he finally corralled into the Church of Latter Day Saints.

One might well be skeptical of post-mortem analysts who attempt to psychologize sexual motivations into successful leaders of the past. But the presence of solid biographical data in Smith's case is convincing. His youth and manhood were stormy. His moral code was irregular even in the eyes of the very tolerant. Marriage failed to curb his philandering ways. The fact that his marriage yielded only one child, who died at an early age, may explain his maladjustment. At any rate, his habits became so well known that he had to legitimatize them with a revelation. Realizing what opposition he might arouse, he let the new light seep out gradually at first, using the trial balloon device to see how far he could get. Of course, his first wife, Emma, would not relish the idea either. To get by her, he resorted to having a number of "sisters" around the house in the guise of celestial tenants. When she found out why those angels really were there, she complained bitterly, but finally compromised when he promised to dispossess all but two. It took nine years, from revelation in 1843 to publication in 1852, to infiltrate the minds of the faithful with the new doctrines in their pure, unadulterated form.

By a most curious coincidence the spiritual-wife doctrine, as worked out in the early days by Smith and his fellow leaders, included a system of social categories arranged to harmonize women in the Mormon society. It is hard not to think of Fourier's list of ladies' series as one reads of Smith's. Working from earth upwards, there were the Cyprian Saints, the Cloistered Sisters of Charity, and the Cloistered Saints. A girl got into the lowest order if she was reported for indiscretions. The Prophet maintained a spy system whose business it was to help build up the Cyprian category. Upon confession, the accused was entered into her group, thereafter to become public property subject to call by "any of the Elders who had been initiated into the mysteries of the new order." The Cloistered Sisters were licensed by the Prophet to select a private clientele. The Cloistered Saints were allocated to individual members of the Mormon aristocracy, that is, those who stood high in the Church Councils.

Highly conscious of the role of sex in human behavior, the Mormon leaders were eager, as apostles of a new society, to work out a sexual *modus vivendi*. Their religious breeding instilled in them a horror of adultery, a sin which could be cleansed only by the blood of the guilty one. The Mormon husband could easily justify the murder of his adulterous wife. Her soul had to be saved. Smith and his friends were also appalled by prostitution, the price, they said, Christianity was paying for its ill-conceived monogamy. The male and female souls could then insure their salvation only through polygamy—which was officially adopted on August 29, 1852.

Polygamy, though confined to a few Western areas, was a national issue. Libraries of theological treatises were produced in support of both sides of the question. The Mormons were very fond of referring to Old Testament heroes with their multiple spouses. Their enemies rebutted with contrary citations in impressive numbers. Protestant elements were held to account for their loose constructionist tolerance—most of the Mormons had, after all, come out of Protestant sects. The Protestants protested that most of the Mormon membership was of foreign birth. They did have to admit, however, that the ringleaders were of American stock.

The drive to outlaw polygamy by national legislation stimulated a good deal of thought on marriage and divorce laws generally.[1]

[1] Leonard W. Bacon wrote in the *Princeton Review* of 1882 on "Polygamy in New England," showing that Puritans were practicing polygamy with legal and

At least one question seemed to be clarified by the struggle—marriage had to be under the jurisdiction of the civil authorities. The affair of the Mormons had provided an example of the immoral inventions that came of entrusting marriage to religious authority.

Horace Greeley, who could favor no marriage practice but the one outlined in the New Testament, naturally objected to the Mormon way of doing it. He was able, moreover, to hang his argument on the feminist cause. His visit to the Mormons had convinced him that their women were worse off than American womanhood in general. They were being treated as mere childbearing machines. As far as he could determine from his observation, Mormon women were never asked their opinions on any matter of political or social consequence. Greeley had visited many Mormon homes but could not remember any family head ever mentioning his wife. Never had a single lady of the house been introduced to him. Perhaps such introductions were omitted because of the time needed to perform them.

Susan Young Gates, one of Brigham Young's fifty-six children, gave quite a different picture of woman's lot under polygamy. According to her story, reciprocal love and respect was at its best in Utah. It was most "thrilling," "divine," and "intense." The Mormons were above the average in health and intelligence. Quite to the contrary of the tales brought back by the like of Greeley, Mormon women were making unusual progress in settling the feminine problem of the nineteenth century. They were beginning to move out into independent careers in business, art, and the professions precisely because their marital relations facilitated their freedom of movement.

President Grover Cleveland's views were much the same as Greeley's. He declared in his first annual message to Congress that the American mother had the right to be "secure and happy in the exclusive love of the father of her children, [to shed] the warm light of true womanhood, unperverted and unpolluted, upon all within her pure and wholesome family circle. These are not the cheerless, crushed, and unwomanly mothers of polygamy." Nor could a man be stimulated to loyalty and service to his country without the spurs of conjugal and parental affection. Polygamy was un-American. It must therefore be made illegal.

Few if any non-Mormon commentators on polygamy have been willing to accept the system as a workable form of family relationship for our society. But where none has condoned, many have explained its reasons for existence. Here and there an economic deter-

religious sanction. The only difference between them and the Mormons was that they had only one wife at a time. Bacon was putting the unpopularity of polygamy to crude use in a campaign against liberal divorce laws .

minist has ascribed the tremendous impulse to beget to the need for cheap labor to work the vast Western lands. Many wives and a larger number of progeny was a simple and direct way of finding workers. Seen from the viewpoint of woman's rights, the invention of plural wives has been associated with woman's revolt against overbreeding, gynecological difficulties, and shortened lives. The presence of male vigor, it is claimed, combined with ignorance of contraception to make the social mind develop a way of distributing the burden of childbirth.

Notwithstanding his opposition to Mormon polygamy, Theodore Schroeder was against using the law of the nation to suppress it. His libertarian principles watered down his intense antagonism to a point where he advocated letting the Mormon evil die a natural death. By 1906 he could maintain with truth that more and more of the Latter Day Saints were conforming to local injunction. The Mormons had received a new revelation telling them to conform to the ways of the world, and there were very few left who wanted to remain unreconstructed.

Schroeder's real fears about the Mormons had little reference to their marrying habits. It was his psychological analysis of the ultimate consequences of their preoccupation with sex that frightened him into the fight. This continual thinking, talking, acting, and worshipping of sex and procreation in revival excitements was certain to result in a population of hypersexed individuals—the males especially. This exaggerated drive, according to acceptable biological theory at that time, would be transmitted to the next generation, which, in the case of the Mormons, was quite a sizeable one. The prospects were indeed terrifying when one considered what might happen when the normal channels of gratification had lost their capacity to satisfy. A race of degenerates would roam the streets and fields. No home could be safe from sadism, incest, pederasty, and all those other abnormalities which were in the process of receiving their technical names as Schroeder wrote about the Mormons.

COMPLEX MARRIAGE

In combing the field for examples of the sexual origin of religion, Schroeder seems to have passed by that most revolutionary experiment in the complete socializing of the personality at Oneida, New York. Such an oversight may be laid to one of several circumstances. In the first place, Noyes' Perfectionists at Oneida had already given up their communism of wives along with their communism of property by the time Schroeder became interested in the subject. The practice of complex marriage had been given up in 1879 in response to one of the greatest pressure campaigns that has been waged against any religious group in history.

Another possible explanation may lie in the observance of diplomatic courtesies among radicals—for Noyes qualified as one by virtue of his reputation for being a moral incendiary and political anarchist. Ezra Heywood had treated with great respect Noyes' scientific contributions to sexology. Any friend of Heywood's must have found a friend in Schroeder. Again, though Noyes' original ideas had their roots in religion, the leader of the Perfectionists was more than mildly interested in tearing down the structure of propertied churches. Moreover, his inventiveness in the marriage field had as much or more background in empirical considerations as it did in the spiritual realm.

John Humphrey Noyes did not fit Schroeder's formula at all. He possessed neither the background of poverty nor that of ignorance which gave some of the other sects their first leaders. His forebears were of hardy, wealthy, and respectable New England stock. His father was economically, politically, and personally successful. The children had had a secure and affectionate family life. When not yet twenty years old, Noyes came home to Putney, Vermont, with a Dartmouth diploma under his arm. His intention was to enter the legal profession.

But the revivalist excitement caught him up almost immediately and the ministry quickly displaced the bar as Noyes' life goal. Accordingly, he went back to Andover and Yale for three more years of schooling, which yielded a license to preach. The license was soon withdrawn because of the unorthodox tendencies displayed by the reformist Noyes. The remainder of the thirties was spent in looking around for a mould that would contain a religion of Biblical simplicity.

The period was crowded with studying and participating in various reform movements. In March 1837, Noyes visited William Lloyd Garrison, demanding that the freedom-loving interests of the North challenge the slavocracy that controlled the national government. The exhortation was said to have had its effect on Garrison's later strategy. Soon after, the plight of the working people in the severe depression that lasted from 1837 to 1842 claimed Noyes' attention. He read the elder Owen and Fourier. He became interested in the foundations of Shaker community life. The experiment at Brook Farm also came to his notice. Some combination of religious revivalism and socialist economics appeared to him to promise the best solution for human maladjustment. The ultimate goal of perfection, or the establishment of the Kingdom of Heaven on earth, was to be sought through the life of Bible communism.

The vision of heavenly love seems to have suggested the idea of socialized mating to Noyes. The thought was that a man should not embrace one woman exclusively any more than he should hold on to private property. All men in the community should ideally be potential husbands of all women; and all children the pride and joy of all the adults. The end-product, as subsequent events reveal, was not the working-out of a divine blueprint. It was to be the result of knowledge, logic, and personal experiences.

Most of the pertinent experiences were to become part of Noyes' biography. William Hepworth Dixon, editor of the London *Atheneum* and author of the book, *Spiritual Wives,* claimed that Noyes left a long trail of promiscuity behind him when he blossomed forth with the bright idea of complex marriage. Noyes denied these allegations, and asserted his strict adherence to the accepted moral code up to the moment when he and his wife both entered the new dispensation. He also insisted that he had refrained from proposing either complex marriage or "male continence" (Noyes' contribution to birth control) until he felt that his group was fully prepared for these practices.

Events seem to have had approximately the following sequence: At some time late in 1836, Noyes lost out in love to a rival. In January of the following year, the debris of his disappointment found itself neatly arranged in a new conception of love. Feeling the need to express his thoughts to someone, he put his ideas on paper and sent them in a letter to his friend, David Harrison. This "Battle-Axe Letter," so called because it got out of Harrison's hands and was printed in the Reverend Theophilus Gates' rabidly anti-marriage paper, *The Battle-Axe and Weapons of War,* was later to force Noyes to reshape his life as well as his theories.

"I will write all that is in my heart on one delicate subject," said Noyes, "and you may judge for yourself whether it is expedient to show this letter to others. When the will of God is done on earth as it is in heaven, there will be no marriage. The marriage supper of the Lamb is a feast at which every dish is free to every guest. Exclusiveness, jealousy, quarreling, have no place there. . . . God has placed a wall of partition between male and female during apostasy for good reasons, which will be broken down in the resurrection for equally good reasons; but woe to him who abolishes the law of apostasy before he stands in the holiness of the resurrection. The guests of the marriage supper may have each his favorite dish, each a dish of his own procuring, and that without the jealousy of exclusiveness. I call a certain woman my wife, she is yours; she is Christ's and in Him she is the bride of all Saints. She is dear in the hands of a stranger, and according to my promise to her I rejoice. My claim upon her cuts directly across the marriage covenant of this world and God knows the end."

History proved that it was not very politic to reveal the contents of this letter. Its publication drew forth such a hue and cry that Noyes found it necessary to enter into conventional marriage to prove that he was not as wicked as people were saying. Hepworth Dixon charged that Noyes married for money. Noyes replied that his funds, as it happened, had been low, and that his marriage had given him a needed boost, but that the motive of the match with Harriet Holton was love. At any rate, five children were born with little time between births. Four of them were stillborn. It was time for a revaluation of the mating and propagation problems.

His wife had suffered much. The rewards were small. Should she not have had more of a choice in the matter of propagation? As Noyes examined the store of available ideas toward a solution of the problem of human rights, he began to question the right of men to dominate women through the mechanism of law and the routine of custom. He studied several of the marriage revisionists of his time and rejected them because of their denial of religion. Upon the urging of Professor George Bush, who later championed Swedenborg in his lectures at the College of the City of New York, he studied the Heavenly Doctrine, only to find fault with its theoretical foundations as well as with its implications for marriage. A reading of Swedenborg's *Conjugal Love* convinced him that the New Church had been infected by middle-class ideals of male supremacy. Paramours were apparently allowed for husbands, but there was to be no comparable privilege for mere wives.

The divine dictates seemed to Noyes to require an entirely new marriage form, the one to which he gave the name "complex." Equality was now assured. The procedure and ceremony were described by Dr. John Ellis, who visited Oneida and set his observations down in *Free Love and Its Votaries,* a book which condemned all the practices in Noyes' community, making free love synonymous with socialism and calling both anathema to civilized society. Dr. Ellis obviously exaggerated his account because of his critical hostility to the entire sexual innovation. As a physician he could testify that the population control technique which went by the name of "male continence" had been ruinous to the health and morale of Oneida's population.

The regulation for "complex marriage" permitted any male and female, regardless of previous attachments, to come before the central committee and apply for the right to live as man and wife. Each would declare that he had found his affinity in the other, and wished to consummate the union which the Divine Will had ordered. The committee, by questioning and conference, would decide upon the validity of the claim. If they affirmed it, the couple could adjourn immediately to private quarters.

Noyes' reply to the critics of his plan was that science was proving so useful in controlling nature in the material realm that he could see no reason for overlooking it in the sexual realm. Frequent pregnancies were highly undesirable to women. It would certainly be a boon to women to transform wifehood from an "ominous" experience, fraught with fear and emotional distortion, to one of exaltation as it was intended to be.

A free choice in motherhood had to be added to a free choice in wifehood to make a reality of sex equality. The Yankee saint's insistence upon equality was contradictory to his unconcealed opinion about woman's inferiority. His equalitarian ideas seemed to many to rise out of his own spiritual and personal drives rather than out of a feminist rationale. Wherever the idea came from, the result was good. For, according to the best testimony, women under the system of Bible communism did achieve much of the status for which they were campaigning in the woman's rights movement.

The uncharitable critics of the Oneida Perfectionists' leader would credit him neither with good will nor originality. Hepworth Dixon, and also those who used his data as ammunition, stated that Noyes had received his inspiration for his birth control ideas from Owen's ungodly *Moral Physiology*. Noyes admitted that the reading of Owen's population treatise had strengthened his convictions, but insisted that it had contributed little to the adoption of the method of "male continence." On the contrary, said Noyes, his method had been more nearly influenced by Shaker abstinence than by Owen's system of "Male Incontinence plus Evasion." It used none of the mechanical means advocated in *Moral Physiology*. It was based on self-control through training rather than on the self-indulgence of Owenism.

Notwithstanding medical skepticism about the general workability of "male continence," it seems to have worked. Upon it depended the successful operation of the third part of Noyes' reformation —"stirpiculture," or controlled eugenics. Noyes assailed Darwin and Galton, charging them with failure to advertise the social possibilities of their findings on natural selection and heredity. They had overlooked the grand possibilities, he complained, of reforming the world by controlling the qualities of future generations. Had Noyes waited a while before uttering his accusations, he would have seen his own contribution in better perspective. In effect, the only difference between him and the social Darwinists of his own century was the authority he possessed in guiding the mating combinations of his own flock.

The experiment in stirpiculture was not to be accompanied by a lessening of human liberty. The voluntary members of his cooperative experiment joined in the spirit of scientists, willing "to make themselves eunuchs for the Kingdom of Heaven's sake." The resolutions signed by fifty-three women and thirty-eight men who joined in 1869, the first year of the experiment, read in part:

> That we do not belong to ourselves in any respect, but that we do belong first to God, and second to Mr. Noyes as God's true representative.
>
> That we have no rights or personal feelings in regard to childbearing which shall in the least degree oppose or embarrass him in his choice of scientific combination.

Except for a period of fifteen months during which a Stirpiculture Committee passed on mating applications, a cabinet of central members of the community decided who was fit to reproduce and in what combination. Those whose requests were vetoed—and there were some—were steered to other combinations satisfactory to all concerned. What this meant was that Noyes himself, who held the deciding vote in the cabinet, had full power to direct the breeding activities of his volunteers. The satiric Bernard Shaw wrote of this arrangement: "The existence of Noyes simplified the breeding problem for the Communists, the question of what sort of men they should strive to breed being settled at once by the obvious desirability of breeding another Noyes."

All observers were agreed, including the principal himself, that Noyes was an absolute dictator over his people. If successful religious communism needed a powerful theocrat, successful conduct of the eugenics experiment needed unquestioning obedience to a firm administrator. If physical well-being and longevity are an acceptable test, stirpiculture and communal child care did prove themselves worthy. Sickness, disease, and early death were infinitely less common among the residents of Oneida's Children's House than elsewhere in the nation. Out of the fifty-eight live births during the stirpiculture period, only six had died by 1921, when the age range of these eugenic babies was from forty-two to fifty-two years. The calculated norm for the country indicated forty-five deaths for a comparable group.

Such demonstrations were not yet available when the whole world was opposed to the New York Perfectionists and many a special investigator was engaged in exposing Noyesism. The Reverend Hubbard Eastman tried to demonstrate that Noyes was in the business for his own benefit, that he would destroy the family, "sap the foundations of civil government . . . and erect upon the ruins of republican institutions and the relics of morality, a petty monarchy, with a head as dogmatical and merciless as the Papal Throne." Dr. John Ellis uncovered the menace of a socialist conspiracy to foist free love upon our country. William Hepworth Dixon traced the theory of spiritual wives from its origins in Germany, through the revivalist irregularities of the wild American sorceresses, Mary Lincoln and Lucina Umphreville, directly to Noyes' Perfectionist paradise.

All of the hostile critics found their text in the leader's own statements. Noyes did in fact supply Dixon with much of his material. In 1867 Noyes described the development of his theories as follows: Revivals, generally theocratic, tended to bring some form of socialism in their wake if they went beyond religion. Religious love and sexual love were very much akin; and in the excitements and intimacies of revivals, these related loves were inclined to get shuffled. "The next thing a man wants, after he has found the salvation of his soul, is to find his Eve and his Paradise. . . . Hence these wild experiments and terrible disasters." That is, unless these divine revivals were accompanied by some divine organization of society. It was at the moment of organization that a prudent Mother Ann or an unbridled Joseph Smith stepped in to give shape to "the more morbid products of revivals." Noyes, you could be sure, gave a healthier form to the theocratic principle than did the other leaders. Did anyone object to dictation of the form of family life? The justification was that God seemed to like dictatorship. He had showered his favors even on Mohammedanism and Popery. In time, republican institutions would be pushed out of existence altogether.

UNSOCIAL SECTARIANISM

So common was the combination of Bible socialism and freedom from conventional moral standards, that ventures like Adin Ballou's Hopedale Community were at times afflicted by spontaneous displays of shocking conduct. Hopedale, established in 1841, was, like many of the other communal experiments, a distinctly religious movement looking back to the teachings of Jesus. The leaders sought to regenerate society so that it would conform to human needs. A regeneration of man's character was also in the program. The agenda was set, but the line of action and organization was left open to suggestion. Except for a single point: the Hopedale people were open-minded about many things, but marriage morals was not one of them. One of the principles set down in their "Constitution of the Practical Christian Republic" was a pledge "Never to violate the dictates of chastity by adultery, polygamy, concubinage, fornication, self-pollution, lasciviousness, amative abuse, impure language, or cherished lust."

The only acknowledged scandal in Hopedale's history involved a married male cooperator and a young lady who resided in his household. The miscreants were called in for a hearing and they promised to mend their ways. They did not. At their next hearing before the Council, they admitted their free love design and were expelled from the community. They packed up and moved, according to the official version of the story, to a "settlement of kindred *Individual Sovereigns.*" Their new home was Josiah Warren's Modern Times where, said Adin Ballou, residents laugh at the idea of constancy in love and make it extremely uncomfortable for anyone who does not believe in bartering spouses.

Minor indiscretions had been handled quietly up to the time of the free love incident. But now, to forestall future trouble, Hopedale's position on sex was announced to the world by a public resolution to the effect "That, with our views of Christian Chastity, we contemplate as utterly abhorrent the various 'Free Love' theories and practices insidiously propagated among susceptible minds under the pretext of higher religious perfection, moral exaltation, social refinement, individual sovereignty, physiological research and philosophical progress. . . ."

This statement of what Hopedale deplored was a good summary of the rationalist, spiritualist, anarchist, and perfectionist attempts to solve the marriage problem without placing the individual in chains. Hopedale's pronunciamento was typical of the attitude of clergy and lay leaders in the major religious sects. However, in the eyes of Jeremiah O'Callaghan, whose book, *The Holy Bible Authenticated,* represented a Catholic view in 1858, the onus of responsibility for non-believing infidels like proponents of free love, socialists, and spiritualists, lay on the Protestants; had not their insistence on civil jurisdiction in marriage and divorce left the road open for the many variants of immorality? Lack of consistency and discipline among the Protestants was accountable also for Mormonism, Shakerism, and other sectarianisms which were eating away the foundation of Protestantism itself. Infanticide and bastardy, according to O'Callaghan, were the natural result of Protestant marriages. Protestantism also led to divorces, and divorce was un-Christian.

The Right Reverend Dr. Amat, Bishop of Monterey, California, was also vehement in his condemnation of secular marriage. Matrimony, as an institution of God, had to conform to three conditions: unity, sanctity, and indissolubility. No human legislation could dissolve a union. Dr. Amat declared in his *Treatise on Matrimony According to the Doctrine and Discipline of the Catholic Church* (1864), that the only civil laws on marriage by which Christians need abide were those sanctioned and approved by the Church. In case of conflict, the civil law must be disobeyed. Moreover, the Church had a right to prohibit marriages or annul them if contracted under certain conditions. Among such impediments were: marriage to a slave if one did not know at the time of marriage that the other party was in bondage; marriage to one who had made a vow of celibacy; marriage to a relative within four degrees of kinship; marriage to one baptized in another religion.

❦   ❦

Catholic writers were obviously stretching a point when they imputed moral laxity to the Protestant clergy. The truth was readily available in a mass of sermons, books, and pamphlets from clerical pens, which applied the strict view of the Timothy Dwights and Lorenzo Dows of an earlier time. There were restrictions pronounced even on divorce for adultery if the husband were the guilty one. The difference was one considered to be inherent in the natural law: If the wife is unfaithful, "she confuses her husband's blood" and thus destroys her own family. If the husband is unfaithful, he does not thereby "vitiate her blood." He therefore had done nothing to dissolve the contract.

This obviously unequal consideration of the rights of women was typical of the general attitude of the clergy. They insisted upon woman's remaining a subject being, devoted to prayer, housekeeping, childbearing, and obedience to her husband. The many gift books, sermons, and works offering advice to the newly married reflected the anti-feminist stand of the clergy at large. On reading the remarks of such as Orestes Brownson and the Reverend J. D. Fulton on the woman question, the infidel *Word* printed the headline, "The Almighty against Woman's Rights." The opposition of the Almighty dated from a long time back. It was, in a real sense, responsible for starting the woman's rights movement in America. For it was at the time when the ladies were asked by clergymen to cease their activities in behalf of the anti-slavery movement, that the ladies started a movement of their own.

The attitude of the Protestant orthodoxy on the questions of marriage and divorce (among larger social questions) was crystallized in the National Reform Association. The original purpose of the eleven denominations which comprised the group at the time of its formation in 1864 was to amend the United States Constitution so as to make the will of God as revealed in the Scriptures the supreme authority in civil government. The members dedicated themselves to promoting what was Christian in national life and to opposing what was un-Christian. Their periodical, first published in 1867, was to devote itself to propaganda for the said constitutional amendment and carry the banner for the "Christian Law of Marriage," legal and moral enforcement of the Sabbath, and temperance reform.

The National Divorce Reform League (later known as the National League for the Protection of the Family) was composed of representatives of leading Christian groups, including the Catholics. Its object was "to promote an improvement in public sentiments and legislation on the institution of the Family, especially as affected by existing evils relating to marriage and divorce." Lobbies were sent to the legislatures of States whose divorce laws were considered to be lax. Connecticut, Massachusetts, and Maine responded almost immediately by tightening the provisions made for divorce within their territory.

Public sentiment was stirred up by reports of alarming increases in the incidence of divorce. Theodore Dwight Woolsey, the ex-President of Yale College who had been trained for the clergy, lent the weight of his position, learning, and descent from Timothy Dwight, to the movement by making speeches and writing for the magazines. The Reverend Samuel Dike, corresponding secretary of the League, wrote a great number of articles for the newspapers, made speaking tours of the largest cities in the country, and gave short lecture courses at major educational institutions. The family was declared to lie "at the root of nearly all that is dearest in property, education, morals, law and religion. . . . The Christian people of the country certainly cannot fail to recognize its Divine mission, and the call it thus makes for their generous support."

THE SOCIAL GOSPEL

Nevertheless, as was charged by Catholic spokesmen, the Protestant clergy in America was far from unanimous in its adhesion to this view. There had always been a considerable number of divines who concentrated on socializing Christianity in preference to Christianizing society. Some had exhibited their leanings by bolting to rationalist free thought groups. A few became independents. Others settled in spiritualist camps where Christianity was distorted beyond all recognition. There were examples of these among the friends of Owen, Warren, Heywood, and Harman. Many a renegade had "abused" his ministerial privilege by agitating against the structure of Christian marriage and divorce regulations.

Also to be reckoned with was that faction of the Unitarian church which had a strong preference for the human need as against the Godly command. The approach of this group dominated the Brook Farm scene. Among the humanitarian notables on the New England stage at mid-century was Theodore Parker, the rationalist Unitarian who held forth at West Roxbury, a Boston suburb.

In Parker's scheme of things, the supernatural had but a small role. The plight of the poor, the ignorant, the criminal class, drunkards, and prostitutes, received more consideration from the humane Parker than did prayers and exhortation. His early interest in the sexual question seems to have been stimulated by the abolitionist Wendell Phillips' address at the National Women's Rights Convention of October 1851. Meeting Phillips after the convention, he had intimated that it was foolish to waste one's breath on an issue such as the rights of women. Soon persuaded to the contrary opinion, within the year he gave several sermons in service of the cause.

Engaged as he was in serious thought directed toward the solution of several social problems, he soon came to see that there were elements of kinship in all of them. One examined the prostitution problem and found that it was linked both to the general feminist question and to social attitudes about sex. A visit to Charles Loring Brace, founder and superintendent of the Children's Aid Society of New York, added to Parker's knowledge of how slum life affected the moral behavior of girls and boys. He knew too that the poverty which kept young men from marrying helped make prostitution a going concern. Economic and vocational rehabilitation would help, but it was not a complete solution.

The grand subject of the Woman Question—which was only hazily defined in Parker's mind—was fundamental. A saner approach was needed in order to throw more light on the subject of sex. The conspiracy of silence had to be broken. "A history of the gradual development of the sexual element in mankind would be a notable theme," said Parker. The bodily instincts were there; they exerted an influence impossible to overcome or turn aside; no imposing Scriptural text could prove otherwise. The suppression of these instincts, Parker maintained in a long controversial correspondence with the Shaker dignitary Robert White, was productive of the worst of mental, moral, social, and psychological disorders. Parker admitted that neither the Shakers nor the Catholic Church was uniquely at fault in encouraging unwholesome attitudes. The whole country was obsessed with the equation of sin and sex.

Many a marriage landed on the rocks of this and other psychological hazards. Parker recognized this. He was also aware of the personality distortions that grew out of incompatibility, distortions which were aggravated by New England's morbid harping on morality. More lenient divorce laws were desirable but could do nothing more than act as palliatives. Nothing less than a thoroughgoing revision of the current evaluation of womanhood would clear up the marriage-divorce confusion. But Parker's idea of woman was far from revolutionary. He too subscribed to the cliché that "man will always head in affairs of the intellect, of reason, imagination, understanding; he has the better brain. But woman will always lead in affairs of emotion—moral, affectional, religious; she has the better heart."

There was no one position which could be ascribed to the liberal clergy of the last century on the question of marriage morals. There were those among the humanitarian religionists and Christian socialists who followed closely the position announced by their more conservative colleagues. Although Charles Loring Brace and others named "respect for woman" as an important achievement of Christianity, that respect was not always in evidence. The double standard of morals seems to have been universally accepted by clergy. The duty of personal purity and the sacredness of marriage had stronger application to women than to men. Henry Ward Beecher, an ardent feminist in more than one sense, and an avowed believer in intellectual equality between the sexes, nevertheless apparently acted on the assumption of male privilege in his relations with female members of his flock.

CLERGY AND LAITY ON MODERN MARRIAGE

The preachers of the social gospel in the late nineteenth and early twentieth centuries were extremely uneven in their interest in problems of crime, war, imperialism, international arbitration, divorce, socialism, populism, and the like. But in circles like the "Social Problems Group" which was begun in 1906 by the Reverend Richard H. Edwards, Congregational Pastor at the University of Wisconsin, there was good assurance that study and discussion were free enough to admit the newer points of view. Specialists were called in to lecture, but most of the questions to be discussed were suggested by group members themselves. "Divorce" was among the topics considered in the very first season.

The "Social Creed" of the Federal Council of Churches declared in 1912 "for the protection of the family, by the single standard of purity, uniform divorce laws, proper regulation of marriage, and proper housing." This declaration was an official acknowledgement that problems of marriage and the family had left the realm of Biblical prescription. In its commentary on the "Creed," the Federal Council noted that women-at-work meant hastily or badly cooked meals, which implied disgruntled husbands, and the possibility of waywardness and intemperance among male spouses. Also singled out for special attention was the heroism being displayed by working girls in preserving their moral integrity in the presence of both low earnings and "human wolves who go around seeking whom they may destroy."

Another Christian socialist, William Dwight Porter Bliss, seems (on the evidence of material included in his *Encyclopedia of Social Reform*) to have accepted the secular point of view. His contributor on family matters was the socialist George Elliott Howard, author of the standard *History of Matrimonial Institutions*. Howard recommended a discarding of both church and tradition in favor of the lessons of experience expertly interpreted. He predicted that more good would come from a rational education than from legislation. His position, as he summed it up, was that

First of all it is needful to free the mind from hamper-
ing traditions, and to accept the judgment of history. The
guiding light will come, not from authority, but from a
rational understanding of existing facts. The appeal to theological criteria, born of primitive and very different conditions, is in vain. The vast literature which seeks to solve
social questions by juggling with ancient texts is largely a
monument of wasted energy. Much of it is sterile, or it
serves but to retard progress and to befog the issue.

Voices of protest against clerical interference in the social regulation of family life had come from individual clergymen for several
decades. Octavius Brooks Frothingham, a Unitarian and Independent
considered to be the intellectual heir of Theodore Parker, was one
of them. His sermon on "Elective Affinity," preached in 1870, urged
a relaxation in divorce laws in the name of marital happiness and
more secure unions. With less law to rely upon, it was more likely
that marriages would follow the highly desired pattern of extended
courtship. The advance guard of many sects, including, of course,
the spiritualists, echoed the sentiment. Indissoluble marriage was
a good goal to be reached by moral means in distinction to legal
ones.

The more "independent" the clergyman, the more the scientific
and rational elements of thought entered into his judgments in the
family field. Moncure Conway had started his religious pilgrimage
in Methodism, had chosen the Harvard Divinity School for his professional education, had emerged a Unitarian, and was later called
to a Congregational Church in Cincinnati. His views on marriage
were written in a wholly non-religious mood, strongly reminiscent
of the Owen brand of opinion.

"Love," he asserted, "is not quite willing to accept the judge's
mace for his arrow. . . . Love, from so long having bandaged eyes,
will be all eye. . . . When the conserve becomes fatiguing, it will
be refreshed by a new flavor, not by a certificate. From the hour
when thought of obligation influences either party to it, the marriage
becomes a prostitution." Marital contracts, Conway thought, should
resemble business partnerships. When the partners no longer provided the kindliness, thoughtfulness, and mutual assistance for which
they united, they should dissolve the union. If women were afraid
of easy divorce in our society, they had reason. But guarantee them
respect, protection, and equality, and their fears would evaporate.

Colonel Robert G. Ingersoll went one step further in the direction away from revealed religion. Although his father was a clergyman, he himself had always had his doubts about Revelation.
Darwin's *Origin of Species* confirmed them. His marriage to the free

thinking Eva Amelia Parker confirmed him the more. A lawyer by profession—and with the richest clients—he gained most of his popularity with liberals by his zealous agnosticism on the lecture platform.

On the theme of woman and marriage, he was very close to the sentiments of Moses Harman and his group. The big hope of the future was for science to make woman the mistress of her own childbearing destiny. For it was Ingersoll's thought that ignorance, poverty, and vice were filling the world with unwanted and superfluous children whose affectionless, comfortless youth bred vicious adults to continue the cycle. The preaching, coaxing, praying, threatening, and charitable works of many centuries had proven themselves incapable of breaking the chain. Ingersoll looked "forward to the time when men and women, by reason of their knowledge of consequences, of the morality born of intelligence, will refuse to perpetuate disease and pain, will refuse to fill the world with failures."

The last decade of the century was highlighted by Ingersoll's published debate with highly placed representatives of the Catholic and Episcopalian churches. The Reverend Samuel W. Dike, of the National Divorce Reform League, introduced one exchange of ideas among Cardinal Gibbons, representing Roman Catholicism, Bishop Potter, representing the Episcopalian Church, and Colonel Bob (as Ingersoll was known to his audiences), the Agnostic. Another discussion with Cardinal Manning was published under the title, *Rome or Reason.*

The clerical defenders of the classic position claimed that Christianity had given marriage dignity and status by its regulations, which were, after all, essentially abstractions from human experience. The only divorce reform they could view with equanimity was the abolition of divorce altogether. Protection from abuse had been afforded injured parties in lesser forms of separation and had proven themselves sufficient. But Ingersoll would not be moved. He claimed that marriage was an arrangement between a man and a woman for their own purposes. The attendant ceremonies were a form of announcement to society that two souls had of free choice been joyfully united. It was also a protection for the married, their children, and for society itself. If the spirit of the contract were broken, separation should ensue. The happiness of an Infinite Being was not involved. The happiness of a wife who had married a brutal man was more to the point. The right of self-preservation had not been abrogated by the marriage contract. Nor was it in society's interest that children be born out of hatred and disgust.

There was a strong resemblance between Ingersoll and the rationalist liberators who preceded him. He glorified human love, the sexual union, and motherhood, keeping his ideas entirely on a naturalistic plane. Marriage reform with him had many points of identity with the movement to give women equal and rational consideration with men in all social relationships.

The impression Ingersoll and his confreres made on their opponents could not have been very deep. At this very moment legislators in many States are still unconvinced of the illogicality and unworkability of present divorce laws. All the clinical evidence of maladjustment which divorce lawyers uncover in their practice is unable to dislodge the hold of organized religion on the legislative mind. Nor are the angry voices of the chained, plus those of friends and sympathizers in principle, of more avail.

Curiously enough, the many rationalistic, radical, and agnostic emancipators were rarely sought as allies by organized feminism. Perhaps the women were wary of the political commitments they might have to make to their liberators. The prospect of wearing the badge of fellow traveler might have frightened them away. It is possible also that the truth lay with those who described women as creatures of sentiment, and therefore more subject to pious exhortation than men. Many explanations are possible. An excursion into the politics of feminism may throw more light on the validity of these speculations.

SEVEN

The Woman's Point of View

When and where the struggle for sexual dominance began is a question which excites one's curiosity but which is not very important towards an understanding of the long history of the war between the sexes. There is a strong likelihood that it all started the moment our species observed that it had somehow been divided into two varieties, distinguishable by body structure and propagative function.

In matriarchal societies about which anthropologists tell us, men were doubtless dissatisfied with the submissive role they had to play. In our own "man's world," women continue to carry on, often in alliance with humanitarian, sex-conscious males, their struggle against the injustice of their subordinate position. Tradition, military and economic considerations, the much exhibited physical superiority of the male, and his claim to "natural" dominance, have served to keep the battle from reaching a crisis and thus to postpone a decisive outcome.

But, however weak has been the weaker vessel, it has always asserted itself enough in one way or another to constitute a challenge or a threat to the sex in power. The Adam and Eve story may well be, as some have supposed, a literary invention designed to support the male claim against the permanent undercurrent of feminine revolt.

As in other areas of politics, the party in power in the republic of the sexes has never given up its privileges easily. The most democratic of male minds has on many an occasion sought a plausible justification for the comfortable benefits of inequality. Philosophers and scientists, using the tools of fact and reason, have in impressive numbers come to the conclusion that "whatever is is right."

Plato's idea of equality was that men and women should perform the same social functions, but it must be understood beforehand that women would perform neither as well nor as much. Though it had to be acknowledged that there were many superior women, as a rule the females were inferior to the males in social usefulness. Rousseau, reverting to the state of things in nature, found that man's strength gave him natural dominance. Woman was here to render life pleasant for him.

The philosopher Schopenhauer, reasoning again from nature,

developed his own rationalization of the double standard from the premise that woman's capacity to reproduce was finite, man's infinite. Hence, male constancy was unnatural. Darwin, on the other hand, worked outward from the theory of evolution to prove that men derived their privileged position not from nature but from experience. The male's preoccupation with the struggle for existence helped sharpen his mental powers and maintain them at a level above that of the non-competing females.

For a brief moment at the beginning of our era, it had looked as though woman's fortunes were on the rise. Jesus, a man of strong humanitarian impulse, strengthened possibly by what was observable in the rising status of Roman ladies, came close to a pronouncement for sexual equality when he challenged a group of conventionalist males with his "let him who is without sin cast the first stone." The implication here is that at least the privilege of immorality should be ruled by a single standard. Certainly his dicta on divorce and adultery have been interpreted too rigidly by Christians who prefer the elaborations of the disciple Paul to the original views of his master.

Paul's formulations, which set the cause of women back a millennium or two, were made more in response to the practical needs of building his sect than to the best ideals of charity, human and divine. If he would build and keep a following, he had to cater to the prevailing sentiment, which considered women to be decidedly second-class people. It is quite conceivable also that a too independent womanhood might have lessened the emphasis on childbearing at the time. The implications for the then current drive to populate the earth with Christians are clear.

A circumstance which aggravated woman's lot was the insistence of early Christianity on the merits of asceticism. What started as a reaction against the dissolute morals of a decaying civilization ended by bringing marriage itself into disrepute: Men who expressed themselves disparagingly of the institution which brought together male and female, would naturally not think of their own part in the arrangement as evil. It was woman's fault of course. There was also a strong intimation that woman's initiation into marriage was not different enough from her loss of chastity outside of marriage to relieve her of moral guilt. Again, males who relinquished the joys of marriage might easily be led to develop aggressive feelings against people whom they associated with their self-denial, thus adding to the tendency to belittle women.

But there was a limit to how far men could go in their negativism toward marriage. The institution remained acceptable insofar as it served its procreative purposes. Dignity was likewise accorded women insofar as they fulfilled the role of motherhood. The Protestant Reformation, with its accent on individual worth, lifted women somewhat in the social esteem, but Martin Luther himself concurred in the common belief in their inferiority.

A DIVINE CONTRADICTION

Such was the general framework which the women of democratic America inherited from earlier times: The chief purveyors of ideas relating to woman's place in society were males whose political, intellectual, and religious backgrounds confirmed their own title to dominance in all aspects of life. . Conveniently enough, one of woman's outstanding social assets was her religious activity; and both text and sermon only convinced her anew of her inferiority.

So deeply intrenched was this standard conception that many who were sincere supporters of the feminist cause in post-Revolutionary America could not bring themselves to follow Mary Wollstonecraft's teachings. For instance, whereas Thomas Green Fessenden was ready to admit in his poem "The Ladies' Monitor" that women were the motive force for an advancing civilization, he insisted that nature itself rejected the Wollstonecraft program. Although he would measure whole national cultures by the role they had accorded women, he insisted that the power of women—power he judged to be even greater than that of men—be exercised indirectly through the male leaders of society.

Mrs. Hannah Mather Crocker, who may be credited with writing the first feminist treatise by an American woman, also turned aside Mary Wollstonecraft's powerful plea for women's rights in favor of Hannah More's humble piety. While admitting that Mary Wollstonecraft had energetically and honestly struck out for the truth, and had in doing so given utterance to many an inspiring thought, Mrs. Crocker found it impossible to agree with her ideas on female independence. "Her theory is unfit for practice," said Mrs. Crocker, "though some of her sentiments and distinctions would do honor to the pen even of a man."

Mrs. Crocker, a minister's daughter, a minister's wife, and the granddaughter of Cotton Mather, made clear in her *Observations on the Real Rights of Women* (1818) that these must be "agreeable to Scripture." Woman, she admitted, had indeed fallen in the Garden of Eden. But the restoration of her original rights had taken place with the beginnings of Christianity, as symbolized in the elevation of the Mother Mary.

Notwithstanding the clear proof of woman's claims to equality as demonstrated by her historical role and contributions to culture, Mrs. Crocker's demands were modest. Equality, she prescribed, must start at home in woman's family status. The recognition of mutual rights of husband and wife was the very "touchstone of the matrimonial faith." It was the light which ultimately illuminated the road to national happiness and security. Some balance of power between the sexes had to be reached on the basis of their respective strengths and weaknesses, else "society must soon become a mere nuisance to itself." Experience would tell which rights and duties woman might justly share with man, and where she must leave the field completely to him.

No prophecy could have been more mistaken. Only a handful of true liberals, some of them foreign-born, could be found to support the application of the principles of American liberalism to woman's position in society. The orthodoxy regularly opposed what Mrs. Crocker had termed the real, orthodox principle of equality, and they could count on American womanhood for wholehearted support. Women stayed away in droves from Frances Wright's lectures. In the bitter days of her fight in 1828 against "The Christian Party in Politics," Miss Wright could justly say that her enemies depended on gullible women for support. Likewise, no amount of praise for the civilizing influence of women by the *New Harmony Gazette* and the *Free Enquirer* could win women away from their religious leaders.

Avoiding affiliation with organized progressive movements, and being still unorganized themselves, women depended for the advancement of their cause upon the signal feats of unusual members of their sex in the fields of education, literature, politics, and popular science. In 1821, the spirited agitation for higher education of women bore fruit in Emma Willard's seminary for girls at Troy, New York. Catharine Esther Beecher followed in 1828 with her Hartford Female Seminary, and Mary Lyon opened her Mt. Holyoke Seminary less than a decade later. But educational progress, however much it might improve the female mind, did little in those early days to stiffen woman's resistance against her male oppressors. However, the female seminaries did train many young women for active roles in the later movement for women's rights.

A few women leaders tried scientific lecturing by way of exploring woman's place in the larger scheme of things. In 1838 Mary Gove Nichols, to whose water-cure establishment in New York City many men of note flocked during the furious forties, gave public lectures on anatomy. Paulina Wright Davis, later to issue the call for the first national feminist convention, followed Mary Gove Nichols with lectures on physiology in 1844. Her use of a mannikin for purposes of illustration shocked prudish audiences. She was later fond of telling how, when she dropped the drapery from her mannikin, some ladies would veil their faces and others would make a hasty departure. There were even cases of fainting at the disclosure of this simulated state of naked nature. However, when in 1849 Elizabeth

Blackwell graduated at the head of her class in medicine from Geneva College, feminine pride seemed well on the way to overcoming feminine delicacy.

At that, the number of women in science and higher education was not large enough to make an impression on the superior male. It was not until the ladies showed a strong hand in public life that they could get the attention they wanted.

∾ ∾

That the *Communist Manifesto* and the "Declaration of Sentiments" by the leaders of America's female revolutionary elements should both have been issued in 1848 was little more than coincidence. The first was incidental to a revolutionary upsurge felt all over Europe. The second, which had been brewing in many minds over several decades, resulted from an afternoon tea conversation among a few of the leading temperance and anti-slavery lights.

The first woman's rights convention at Seneca Falls, New York, though held by a small, informal group, was really the culmination of a long series of activities and indignant statements of revolt by articulate women. Among the first to become aware of the strength of their sex were a handful of wives and sisters of leaders in the War for Independence. Remembering that their assistance and counsel had been sought and appreciated in crisis years, they pressed—behind the scenes, of course—for a permanent improvement in their status. Abigail Adams, the wife of John Adams, was quick to suggest that the principles of the Revolution should apply to woman too. She lost no time in writing to her husband, demanding that he keep the ladies in mind when helping to make the laws of the new nation. She warned:

Do not put such unlimited power in the hands of husbands. Remember, all men would be tyrants if they could. If particular care and attention are not paid to the ladies, we are determined to foment a rebellion, and will not hold ourselves bound to obey the laws in which we have no voice or representation.

But, alas, the male authors of the laws went on their way to construct a male democracy; and nowhere was there to be found a well-organized army of women to carry out Mrs. Adams' threat. Much writing and lecturing were used instead to wage a perennial war of persuasion. Fanny Wright did more than her bit but failed to carry much weight because of her drastic solution to the woman problem, to wit, the abolition of marriage. Mrs. Lydia Maria Child's *History of the Condition of Women in All Ages* (1832), the first

American storehouse of information on women and their contributions to civilization, got a much better hearing and actually succeeded in stirring up agitation. Eliza Woodson Farnham's *Woman and Her Era* did not fare as well, possibly because it intimated that women were more than equal to men. No one was ready for a doctrine of female superiority.

A weak battle line here, or a defeat there, however, was hardly cause for surrender. For the war of woman's rights was fought on many fronts and with a great variety of weapons. While the women writers, scientists, and educators were hammering away on their front, women lecturers and politicians maintained fire elsewhere for equal rights in property as well as in other fields of social participation.

An apt successor to Frances Wright after her retirement was the Polish-born reformer, Ernestine Louise Sismondi Potowski Rose, whose stay in England from 1832 to 1836 gained for her, among other contacts, an instructive acquaintance with Robert Owen and a congenial husband whose wealth and status assured her security from social pressures. Mrs. Rose's political complexion is best described by her position of leadership in the Association of All Classes of All Nations. The platform of this English organization was anti-discrimination for-any-reason-whatsoever.

The Roses' transfer to New York City in 1836 produced only a minor interruption in Ernestine's reform career. Steeled against general hostility to her ideas by her husband's money, Mrs. Rose toured the country in behalf of a many-faceted humanitarianism, lecturing on the "Science of Government." Free schools and the anti-slavery theme were both within her scope. Her campaign from 1837 to 1848 for the married women's property bill in New York State was joined by such worthies as Paulina Wright Davis and Elizabeth Cady Stanton.

Of the many movements which accounted for the funneling of a variety of reformers into the woman's rights movement—and these included temperance, education, and socialism—the drives for spiritual dignity and against slavery seemed best adapted to produce leaders for the feminist cause. Frances Wright struck hardest when attacking the Christian party in politics. Ernestine Rose's first thrust for liberty was her rejection of the Hebrew orthodoxy inherited from her father, a rabbi. Paulina Wright Davis, an eager participant in the religious revivals of her youth, revolted because she could not understand why her spiritual competence during a revival did not carry over, as far as the ministry was concerned, into post-revival seasons.

No combination of circumstances was better adapted to fashion women rebels than that of a ministerial conspiracy to prevent women from being active in the anti-slavery movement. In this way, Sarah Grimke and her sister Angelina discovered that before they could speak up for the freedom of the Negro they had first to free their own throats from the constricting fingers of male masters.

The Grimke sisters, born into an aristocratic, slave-owning family of Charleston, South Carolina, were highly sensitive to the gross inhumanities of their native environment. Theirs was more than a romantic sympathy for the downtrodden Negro. They persuaded their mother to turn over to them their share of the family estate's slave holdings, and promptly liberated their inherited human property. The cold reaction to Angelina's *Appeal to the Christian Women of the South* (1836) to "overthrow this horrible system of oppression and cruelty" was conclusive evidence that the sisters' efforts would be wasted in their Southern homeland.

New England was more receptive, but the welcome mat was so arranged as to make the girls stumble frequently as they toured the Northeast. From small audiences of women only—for men could not at first be persuaded to listen to an address by their inferiors— grew large audiences, chiefly of men. The Grimke girls were eloquent; and, despite the unpopularity of lady lecturers, large numbers of men came to listen to them as they had come some years before to hear the unconventional Frances Wright.

A few men might come to listen to words which reenforced their belief in a cause, but the majority was far from ready to yield an equal voice to women in any public cause. Sarah Grimke met the male adversary in the summer of 1837 when she was touring Massachusetts as an abolitionist speaker. She was informed in unequivocal terms in a published pastoral letter of the General Association of Congregational Ministers of Massachusetts that woman preachers and woman reformers were out of bounds. At this point the link in Sarah's mind between woman's rights and human rights was forged.

She established her argument with the telling logic of Mary Wollstonecraft and the solid facts gathered by Lydia Maria Child in her *History of the Condition of Woman*. So then, the duties of women are "unobtrusive and private, but the sources of mighty power"! "Ah!" she exclaimed, "how many of my sex feel in the dominion, thus unrighteously exercised over them, under the gentle appellation of *protection*, that what they have leaned upon has proved a broken reed at best, and oft a spear."

Of the marital relationship, Sarah Grimke could only speak with apologies for presumption, since she was unmarried. Miss Grimke could write on this subject relying only on the word of God, on observation, and on a modest knowledge of human nature. Thus gracefully excusing her limited information, she went on to declare that, for women, marriage was a fraud, an imposition, and a device of spiritual debasement. If the intention was that woman should be elevated by the association with a superior being, man, then the opposite had been accomplished. In law, in social life, and in morals, women had been ground into dependence and then declared incompetent for roles demanding individuality.

All of which, God's ministers claimed, was in accordance with divine intention. But what purpose could have been served, argued Miss Grimke with some originality, by providing man with one more obedient creature in a natural world already swarming with inferior animals and insects? No, this was not the reason for placing woman at the side of man. The reason was in truth to give him an equal partner and ally, "a free agent, gifted with intellect and endowed with immortality; not a partaker merely of his animal gratifications. . . ." The Creator never contemplated that women, when asked to sign petitions against slavery, should beg off with a "My husband does not approve."

The Northern abolitionist clergy and their large lay following would not see the point. And so, to all appearances, the anti-slavery struggle sired the woman suffrage movement of nineteenth-century America. The battles against the tyrannies of color and sex were fought simultaneously, the armies of the one being drawn upon for recruits by the other. Strength mustered for the war against the slavery of man by man was available for the war against the slavery of woman by man, both before and after the truce at Appomattox.

The rights asked by or in behalf of women covered the ground from helpless entreaties for sympathy to demands for complete equality; from the lily-livered literary innuendoes in male-sponsored ladies' magazines to full-blooded polemics on the part of earnest woman's rights advocates. The historic line of religious and moralistic writing continued to address itself to the feminist cause by reaffirming its faith in marriage as the best, and possibly the only, form of self-realization for women. The education of girls was to be slanted in the direction of sacred matrimony. But radicals in the movement, like Elizabeth Cady Stanton, sought—in addition to the ballot, equal property rights, education, and entrée into the professions—a complete, unhampered freedom for women in and out of marriage. Such freedom meant, of course, that divorce must become freely available to women who felt that their personalities were being violated in marriage. Also attached to the feminist cause were the ever-present political groups which sought to rally women and men behind their causes under an anti-marriage banner.

❧ ❧

However vociferous the leaders of the female revolution may have been in their own circles, they created only mild reverberations in society at large. The ordinary reader was at most times unaware of the real issues because they were quietly ignored in books, pamphlets, and periodical articles on woman's role and the marriage question. Writers, many of them clergymen, went on repeating the clichés about spiritual unions. Husbands were requested not to act as tyrants; wives were advised not to play the slave. Equality for women was rarely mentioned seriously.

The pseudonymous "Melva" nodded approval of this state of affairs in behalf of her sex. Writing over the imprint of the American Female Guardian Society, whose business was the honor and virtue of exploited womanhood, Melva, in her *Home Whispers* to husbands and wives, to husbands and fathers, and to wives and mothers, asked only for a slightly fairer deal for overburdened women. It was preposterous to seek equality with men in public life when the energies of women were already overtaxed. Women, declared Melva, were more crushed by their unmitigated cares than they were by the iron heel of male despotism.

This seems to have been the equality to which most American women aspired, or one to which they aspired under the persuasion of their male guardians. This was, at least, the temper of opinion reflected by stories and editorials in the cheaper magazines which claimed mass readership. The direction was clearly for more participation and consideration in the home, and definitely against full participation outside the home.

The magazines of somewhat more limited circulation went on writing in the tradition of satirizing the character of wives, emphasizing the disagreeable aspects of marriage on the one hand, and glorifying the institution on the other. The women's magazines themselves were, on the whole, not given to crusading for woman's independence and absolute equality either under the marriage contract or in her other contacts with the world. In fact, they printed surprisingly little on a subject of such deep concern to their readers. *Godey's Lady's Book*, the most widely read of all, was apparently designed by its enterprising publisher, Louis A. Godey, to give the ladies pleasing thoughts rather than disturbing ones. Fashions and tear-jerking romantic tales were more suitable than social problems. Accordingly, the few articles on marriage that appeared in the early volumes of *Godey's* had mostly to do with the ideal aspects of choosing a mate and living in constancy with him. The desired behavior of wives was discussed from what resembled the current male point of view. The male reader, however, was entreated not to trifle with a girl's affections, for whether or not a formal declaration of intention had been made, once a man had succeeded in winning a maid's love, he could retreat only with irreparable emotional damage to her and to himself.

Though politics were eschewed in Louis Godey's code, Sarah Josepha Hale, the editor Godey acquired when he bought Mrs. Hale's *Ladies' Magazine* in 1837, was permitted to editorialize lengthily on female education and on medical training for women. Nor could Godey prevent Sarah Hale from an occasional feminist outburst which might have cost the magazine a sizeable number of subscription renewals did not the rest of the items printed cover up her indiscretions with sugar-candied romance and other pleasant but inconsequential stuff. One such piece, unsigned, was written in 1837, during Mrs. Hale's first year with *Godey's*. It concerned itself with a bill then pending in the New York State legislature—a bill designed to protect the property acquired by a wife in her own name before or after marriage. It also provided that a husband have the same dower in his wife's estate if she died before him as she would have in his if he died before her. Mrs. Hale applauded the New York State legislature's attempt to establish a form of sexual equality which thus far only Louisiana had achieved.

The current law, which gave husbands full control over their wives' property, Mrs. Hale explained, had been introduced into jurisprudence "by some of the Northern pirates who conquered England . . . and it well corresponds with the manners of that savage period, when men lived by rapine and the sword, when physical strength was the measure of right. . . ." The injustice this worked upon women had been so well advertised by earlier agitators like Frances Wright that Sarah Hale had only to give a dramatic summary of the salient points.

This was an old story which everyone knew. But there was much to be said for the pending legislation from the male view as well. Under present laws, a bankrupt husband lost his wife's property—which had become his by marriage—as well as his own. Under the proposed law, the wife's property was a buffer against complete ruin and offered the failure a second chance.

Both wife and husband stood to gain by the new law both as individuals and as members of a happier, more secure family. When both were permitted to add equally to the "common stock of domestic comfort and worldly prosperity," then mutual confidence, esteem, and affection were truly increased. For those inclined to question her logic, Mrs. Hale followed up in the November 1837 *Godey's* with a highly contrived story called "The Love Marriage," a tale clearly designed as the Q.E.D. of her "work together—build together" thesis.

With this frontal attack on the male prerogative, Sarah Hale announced a central theme of the opening act of the "rights" drama, and bowed out as a leading player. For she was essentially a most conservative woman whose early widowhood, with five young children to care for, had made her favor woman's financial independence. The open war of the sexes was too much for her conventional view of things.

Thereafter, she contented herself and the subscribers to *Godey's Lady's Book* with safer forays. "Delicate women," that genre of middle-class parasite which cultivated debility to avoid responsibility, were a special object of disdain. Fresh air, exercise, and sensible dress for growing and grown girls made good feminist subject matter; although one wonders how a reader could take Mrs. Hale's advice against tight corseting and still attempt to wear the styles illustrated in her magazine.

The problems of marital infelicity and divorce did not much concern the unreal world of the *Lady's Book*. Readers learned from very pretty stories that, no matter how dark things looked, all would be well in the end. If they could live the lives of the stories and take the sugary advice of Mrs. Hale as she gave it in "A Whisper to a Newly Married Pair," all would be well for them too.[1]

It took the *Lady's Book* almost sixty years to emerge from its rose-colored vision of family life. But even its earliest views were thought by some religious leaders to be too worldly. Perhaps it was Mrs. Hale's vigorous statements toward the end of the thirties that prompted Samuel Williams, a Methodist leader in Cincinnati, to found in 1841 the *Ladies' Repository,* a magazine more suited to the needs of Christian women. Apparently such women did not need the stories of silly love affairs and the fashions direct from Paris which one found in Godey's magazine. They needed instead the highly moralistic provender dished out by the ministers who wrote most of the *Ladies' Repository* items. They needed idyllic pictures such as the prolific and ubiquitous Mrs. Lydia Howard Huntley Sigourney could paint. A poet and essayist of religious flavor, Mrs. Sigourney was eligible to contribute to the *Repository* pieces like her "Chapter for Old People, or Two Old People Together" in spite of her literary

[1] Toward the end of the century, after the science of post-Darwinian physiologists, plus the sophistications of city life, had forced things a little more into the open, an article in the *Lady's Book,* by Helen Campbell (1880) urged mothers to tell their daughters the actual facts of life. Many a marriage failure, according to this article, stemmed from the roots of parental secrecy and shame. "Ignorance," declared the writer, "is not innocence; the child whose knowledge of natural phases in the life of the body comes from servants, or is, perchance, acquired through some chance encounter in the streets, has lost something that no after effort can replace." Marriage, Helen Campbell declared, certainly meant more than current attitudes admitted. It would become a healthier institution if parents taught a saner view of sex physiology, and of the social responsibilities that went with it.

associations with the *Lady's Book,* the *Ladies' Companion,* and a host of other worldly magazines.

On the whole, the *Repository* was satisfied with ideas and institutions as they were. It traveled in a century-old literary rut, advising against marrying "unawakened sinners" and reformed rakes. It waxed satirical about tricky, disloyal wives and their vixenish mothers, the traditional mothers-in-law. It published "Letters to My Daughter" on meeting with the opposite sex, and on courtship, wifehood, and related subjects.

In the immediate post-Civil War period, the *Repository* opened its pages to a few of the new women leaders. The December 1869 issue carried Mrs. Mary A. Livermore's "Why Woman Demands the Ballot." In 1869 it was quite in order for this moderate—the radicals called her a traitor to the cause—suffragist, wife of the Universalist minister, the Reverend David Parker Livermore, to repeat the property arguments which had been so novel and disturbing when Mrs. Hale wrote them thirty-two years before. Opinion had so changed that one no longer had to be on the extreme left of the feminist movement to declare that it must be made respectable for women to work, and to say that social equality could be won by women only if they gained the right to vote. Henceforth, the essential difference between the center and the left of feminist politics was one of limiting or extending demands for liberation. The center gave exclusive attention to the attainment of the ballot; the left fought for immediate equality with men in every respect, asking for a single sexual and social standard before marriage, in marriage, and in divorce privileges.

To such a development in the relationships of the sexes the editor of the *Repository* was violently opposed. There were other avenues to increased equality and dignity for women. It could be shown that their position with respect to property and family rights at the very moment was better in the United States than anywhere else in the world. The *Repository* could ask, using an excerpt from Harriet Beecher Stowe's society novel *Pink and White Tyranny* to dramatize the point, what these woman emancipators hoped to accomplish by liberalizing divorce. Did they want a situation in which men would have their wives bear children and leave them helpless while they sought pleasure elsewhere? Christ had shown himself to be woman's great protector, the author of *Uncle Tom's Cabin* testified, in making the law of marriage irrevocable. Clearly she did not reckon with the possibility of having a Simon Legree in one's bed as well as in one's cabin.

Again, argued the *Repository,* there was evidence of a change in people's attitudes in the way pregnancy was no longer concealed as a social disgrace. There was a growing pride in the having of children. Julia Ward Howe, the abolitionist, suffragist, and peace crusader, was the authority for the prophetic statement that woman, in this Western Christian world, was well on the way to full self-realization. The author of the "Battle Hymn of the Republic" herself had declared: "If woman in America knows what she does, and why, she will place the maternal dignity at the foundation of all others." *Ipsa dixit.*

THE SHIFTING BACKDROP

There is a danger, as we review the arguments concerning the balance of personal and social power between the sexes, that we shall come away with the feeling that ideas, at least in this realm, never change. We may get the impression that this ideological wrangle goes on for centuries, *ad nauseam,* without getting anywhere. It is well, accordingly, to stop for a moment to note that not only have ideas on the nature of family relationships changed from period to period, but that subtle distinctions have developed in response to the broad context of political movements, religious innovations, community experiments, as well as reform drives of many sorts.

True enough, the aims have usually been shades of the same basic objectives—to raise the status of the wife toward equality with her husband, and to render the marital unions real rather than merely formal and legal. At each stage the reform ranks moved up to new objectives as old ones were gained. But the movement in idea and action was by no means uniform all along the front. It varied with the spirit and intention of individual leaders; it varied with the long-term objectives of each allied force as it made its contribution to the common effort. Those who came later were not necessarily more vigorous attackers than their predecessors. Moreover, it was not uncommon to find the allies fighting among themselves, the pious against the agnostics, the individualists against the socialists, the morally indignant against the amoral and immoral, those of one sect against those of another.

∽ ∽

A glance at the period that intervened between Sarah Josepha Hale's early work in the *Lady's Book* and Mrs. Livermore's similar ideas in the post-bellum years, points up telling developments in the social environment which explain why Mrs. Livermore confidently demanded the ballot in 1869 while only the boldest had dared to think of it before. Her strength did not derive from her own character. It was a strength backed by events, by an accumulation of impressive lectures and writings operating to mold public opinion, and, lastly, by a "rights" organization which men had learned they must reckon with.

The great event which strengthened the hand of women in politics was the Civil War itself.. The woman's rights agitators suspended meetings during the war period but increased their activity in the anti-slavery cause. They did their political bit for the party of Lincoln, seeking signatures for emancipation petitions, and engaging in relief work, supply packing, and bandage winding. For all this, and from the talk about a people's government, they expected the ballot as a reward. They did not get it. A Constitutional amendment designed to grant suffrage to women was defeated in the House of Representatives in 1869. Legislation introduced for the same purpose in succeeding decades fared likewise.

Women should have known that volunteer work would yield them momentary plaudits, their service soon to be forgotten by the superior male. Where they did gain in social status, they gained by virtue of having demonstrated competence in tasks left for them to do while the men fought at the battle-front. They worked farms, taught in schools, and tended store-counters. Girls had already been drawn into American factories whose period of rapid growth had started long before the Civil War. The war drew them in in even larger numbers. It provided them with opportunities to fill jobs requiring greater skill. Delicate women found new strength in their nation's hour of need. Those in comfortable circumstances even learned, because of a servant shortage, to do their own housekeeping. Moreover, the post-war period showed an unprecedented growth of economic activity, and all the available hands were needed.

The spokesmen for sexual egalitarianism had been saying for several decades that women had it in them. A check-list of the more vocal figures in the quest for educational opportunity reveals that it was not uncommon for well-educated, unmarried, comfortably situated women coming from cultured families to be prominent in the movement. The motivations of these talented ladies were humanitarian rather than political. They were seeking for others what they already had for themselves: education and self-sufficiency.

Catherine Maria Sedgwick, a novelist whose many works were issued over a span of several decades, falls into this category. Her novels emphasized the virtues of the home, where, obviously, woman was at her best and where the qualities supporting national stability had their origin. Among her non-fictional works were essays designed to help the less-favored to help themselves. *Means and Ends; or Self-training* was addressed to the young women of America, aged ten to sixteen. "What is education?" asked Miss Sedgwick rhetorically. It is, she explained within the framework of phrenology, the development and improvement of all the faculties with which one is born. It refers to the training of the intellect and the emotions, and the formation of habits and manners. Education starts at birth and ends with death. Its most effective form is self-education; its best direction, toward independence.

Girls, advised this spinster of fifty winters, don't let your parents rebuff your questions about marriage. You were made for marriage—and that has to be faced. Marriage is more than an occasion for parties and gifts, more than an occasion which resolves all the uncertainties, fears, and joys which precede it. It is an assumption of serious responsibilities; and it is for these that you must educate yourself. And to this end she offered many pages on health, exercise, fresh air, cooking, the sick-room, manners, dress, conversation and reading, and the rights of women.

"Might makes right," Miss Sedgwick declared. Women will be recognized and appreciated if they know things and know how to do things. None of the demands for property and family rights are preposterous if women qualify themselves by developing their abilities. They must also have the right to leave husbands who mistreat them, and still retain the custody of their children. The more self-sufficient a woman is, the more rights she is fit to exercise. Miss Sedgwick had learned this from her own experience, and she never faltered in her conviction. At sixty-eight, she wrote *Married or Single?*—a novel which flayed the notion that unmarried women are useless.

Catharine Esther Beecher, the eldest of preacher Lyman Beecher's family of thirteen children (which included the famous Henry Ward Beecher of Plymouth Pulpit, Brooklyn, and Harriet Beecher Stowe), suggested that it was better to spend money on education to prevent evil than on so many of the religious and humanitarian measures which were designed to remedy it. Her analysis of the cause of woman's low status pointed to the caste principle which tabooed woman's participation in healthful and productive labor; to the exodus of men to the West which left a surplus of women in the East; to the unavailability of prestige professions for women (without which it was hard to resist loveless marriages); and lastly, to the frustrations that came of having a productive mind whose exercise was restricted by social disapproval.

The remedy for Miss Beecher, an anti-suffragist in the feminist ranks, was far from constituting a headlong challenge to male supremacy. She urged that women concentrate on their proper sphere, the education of children. If all women sought honor and respect as teachers, mothers, nurses, and domestics, there would be none left to swell the ranks of marginal workers on the industrial labor market. Further, she suggested, a corps of missionary women teachers should be endowed for work in regions that needed them. By this highly philanthropic device, the extra women in the East could be "freed from the oppressions of the capitalists" by being drawn off into the West. Charles A. Dana, reviewing Catharine Beecher's *The Evils*

Suffered by American Women and American Children for the Fourierist *Harbinger* (1846), was very unhappy about this solution. He felt that nothing short of a complete social reform, rendering woman independent in every respect, could achieve a satisfactory solution for the problems facing American womanhood.

WOMAN IN THE NINETEENTH CENTURY

Indeed, no socially minded liberal in the Northeast could be satisfied with part-way measures after he had read Margaret Fuller's *Woman in the Nineteenth Century*. Margaret Fuller had been given a liberal education of the sort generally planned for precocious sons of intellectual families of her time. Her father, a lawyer-politician in Massachusetts, arranged for his bright daughter's schooling. She came into contact at a very early age with seminal minds of her time. The transcendentalist group around Ralph Waldo Emerson received her not patronizingly or chivalrously, as a charming lady of inferior intellect, but admiringly, as an equal. For all her manifestoes on sexual equality in some distant future, she really had not herself experienced much male condescension.

One of Margaret Fuller's biographers has drawn up an uncanny list of parallelisms between her and Mary Wollstonecraft. But the fact that they were both unmarried and thirty-three years old when they wrote their feminist tracts is the only real coincidence. That both should have written within the intellectual frame of reference of their times is hardly remarkable. Mary, reading and listening to the "rights of man" and "age of reason" discourses of the Paine-Godwin group would doubtless use the rationalist approach. Margaret, devouring the glory of the individual and his unfolding soul along with the Fourierist talk about association and the stimulus of attractive industry, would somehow inject at least the vocabulary of her world into her appeal for woman's self-realization. The differences between these two flame-throwers for the female militant were greater than the similarities. Nor were their effects on later thinkers comparable in extent. Mary Wollstonecraft's *Vindication* attracted wide popular attention and remained for many a decade the scriptural text of the woman's rights movement. Margaret Fuller's book mentioned most of the issues to be argued in the future feminist movement and was a powerful moving force for the "rights" leaders of the feminine fifties; but, with the beginning of the Civil War, mention of her name and quotation of her words practically disappeared.

The first version of Miss Fuller's manifesto was published as an article in the *Dial* of July 1843 under the title of "The Great Lawsuit—Man vs. men; woman vs. women." The article was revised and printed in book form in 1845. In 1855, five years after her death in a shipwreck off Fire Island, Margaret Fuller Ossoli's (she had married the titled but penniless Angelo Ossoli in Italy sometime in 1848) book was re-edited with an introduction by Horace Greeley, for whom she had worked as literary editor of the *Tribune* from late 1844 to 1847.

In her writings, Miss Fuller avoided categorical demands for full equality. She began by reviewing the well-known theme about the havoc abusive men worked on their whole families while wives stood helpless in the absence of independent property rights and rights with regard to children. Instances could be cited, she said, "that would startle the most vulgar and callous." But men, real men, could be depended upon to "take care of" the villains of their own sex. Woman in the nineteenth century was neither requesting nor insisting upon particular rights. She merely wanted a statement of principles so that she would know where she stood. The particulars would straighten themselves out in time. Investigate and establish the limits to which woman could aspire, Miss Fuller demanded, ". . . give her legitimate hopes, and a standard within herself; marriage and all other relations would by degrees be harmonized within these." Tear down all artificial barriers, try giving women the same opportunity for free development as you give men, she pleaded, and the skeptics would see that "no discordant collision, but a ravishing harmony of the spheres" will follow. Woman's freedom must be not a grudging concession but an unqualified right. Just as every good Negro emancipationist asserted that no man can own another, so everyone well disposed with regard to the cause of woman must insist that man cannot restrict the life of woman even with the best of intentions. If, when given full opportunity, it turned out that woman's ability was in fact inferior, she would be happy to live within her limitations.

Truly a disarming proposal. Many a man might have been tempted to vote for the experiment did not the learned Miss Fuller proceed to a detailed history of the glories of woman and her accomplishments from ancient mythological eras to modern times. There was too strong a hint in this part of the book that if individual women had been capable of such achievements on so many occasions, they might as a group, if given the opportunity to rise unhampered to the upper limits of their capacities, turn out to be the rulers of men.

Sensing this feeling of insecurity in men, the author of *Woman in the Nineteenth Century* teased the male for his vanity while appealing to his better sense. Man's immaturity and fondness for power, she explained with Wollstonecraftian shrewdness, made him forcefully suppress woman's efforts lest she eventually usurp his position. Actually, by not allowing her to develop her own potentialities, he left her with the sole alternative of seizing what she could of man's domain. The analogy to a slave stealing from his master and playing tricks on him must have appeared spontaneously in the minds of those of Miss Fuller's contemporaries whose moral zeal was focused on two emancipations at one time—that of the Negro and that of woman.

In a sense, Margaret mused, Negro women had better comparative status than their white sisters. "In slavery, acknowledged slavery, women are on a par with men. Each is a work-tool, an article of property, no more!" Analogously, (and here the learned Margaret Fuller could inject what she knew of New Church doctrine), "In perfect freedom such as is painted in Olympus, in Swedenborg's angelic state in the heaven where there is no marrying or giving in marriage, each is a purified intelligence, an enfranchised soul—no less."

Strengthened by the stimulus of her own brilliant writing, Miss Fuller got increasingly bold. At times she advocated equality with such finality that half-sympathetic and wholly unsympathetic readers could easily charge her with having forgotten her proposal to give women's abilities a mere try-out. Her handling of the transcendental theme on the self-sufficiency of each soul in its meeting with the central soul, ended in a declaration that woman must be led by herself, not by man. Her exposition on evidences of "better marriage in our time" was elaborated in detail, starting with the cooperative household partnership in which the husband and wife each did his part, and building up to intellectual companionship in the highest form. This last and best phase could be described as a pilgrimage toward a common shrine. As a good example of intellectual companionship, she named the much-frowned-on combination of Mary Wollstonecraft and William Godwin. Godwin had, after all, honored her spirit in spite of the way the world condemned her affair with Gilbert Imlay.

Lest anyone think that Miss Fuller had not read everything there was to be read on her subject, she presented an impressive catalog of ideas and authors, summarizing and criticizing the contribution of each. Her judgment of Swedenborg was that he had some half-baked, trite, and untenable ideas in his system; but, to his credit, he gave woman her chance at moral development. His idea of marriage was therefore a move in the right direction, allowing man and woman to share one "angelic ministry." Quakerism, on the other hand, stood for sexual equality, but was too confining to permit the development of the individual. Fourier was superficial. He saw only the outward institutional arrangement of society and he did not sufficiently take into account man's spirit, his individuality. Goethe's view was preferable. He saw the individual as capable of transcending institutions, and his treatment of women was also satisfactory. Fourier's industrial plans for giving women increased opportunity were, however, infinitely promising.

The Fourierist doctrine of attractive industry promised that people would work at jobs they liked. The choice was a free choice. It did not allow exclusion from a particular occupation because of sex. "Let them be sea-captains if they will!" Miss Fuller demanded in all seriousness. Fourier had actually expected that one-third of all women workers would want to take up men's vocations. Educate women to work and give them the chance to do so, prophesied Miss Fuller in "The Wrongs of American Women," and fewer of them will resort of prostitution.

Modern women, said the most modern of women disapprovingly, spoke too much of feminine modesty without demonstrating it in their behavior. Modesty was to be preserved "by filling the mind with noble desires." The usual idleness of woman was a corrupting influence; it begot demoralization, witness the unnatural curiosity for gossip, developed for want of something better to do. There was more filthy language used in New York boarding houses than in Five Points, New York's red-light district. Miss Fuller would prefer that these ladies went to *see* what went on before they fabricated their glib condemnation.

These were not idle words, for Margaret Fuller was soon to survey New York's institutions for the pariahs of society and to recommend measures for human rehabilitation. Upon actually speaking to women outcasts, she found them unhappy about their condition and eager to change it. The thought occurred to her, and she did not suppress it in her writing or conversation, that the distance between the fallen woman's behavior and the standard of respectability was not very great. "I have known few women," said the very proper Horace Greeley, "and scarce another maiden, who had the heart and courage to speak with such frank compassion in mixed circles of the most degraded and outcast portion of her sex."

Indeed, it would have been hard to find another maiden so uninhibited and so versatile as to be able to celebrate in detail as she did the facets bright and dull of both bachelorhood and marriage. There were glories in either state. Old maids and bachelors, who had not taken root in the earth the natural way, were a boon to society in many respects. For instance, they could develop independence and establish their unity with God without interference. Again, they had, as aunts and uncles, a fine influence on children with regard to matters about which parents, for want of time and talent, could not provide the necessary guidance. American spinsters were especially blessed. They lived in a country where their development was not as circumscribed as it was elsewhere. They had time and opportunity to read, think, and write.

Miss Fuller must have realized that male and female scoffers alike would single out her hymn to single blessedness and call it an *apologia pro vita sua.* She might even have expected critics to intimate that her whole book was composed of vaporous rationalizations from the pen of a frustrated old maid. They did.

Had these same critics a knowledge of the subtleties of a later psychology, they would have attributed her pages on sexology to frustration too. Perhaps so. But Miss Fuller's opinion was that an unmarried, educated woman of thirty-three should be able to write as unrestrictedly as a single man doing the same job. Besides, she felt very strongly that the dealings of women with men were too serious a matter for women to toy with in displays of vanity and coquetry. How could a man locate his proper soul-mate through the dense surface trappings with which women bedecked their personalities? How could women adjust properly in marriage when the whole subject of sexuality was hidden from them in a haze of secrecy?

The privilege of taking care of one's body was a symbol of independence, Miss Fuller declared. The privilege of knowing one's body and having the complete say over its disposition in marriage had as yet not been sufficiently discussed. It was a matter that sorely needed exposing to the light. Margaret Fuller was very skeptical about one point in particular with regard to sexual convention, and she expressed it thus:

> As to marriage, it has been inculcated in women, for centuries, that men have not only stronger passions than they, but of a sort that it would be shameful for them to share or even understand; that, therefore, they must "confide in their husbands," that is, submit implicitly to their will; that the least appearance of coldness or withdrawal, from whatever cause, in the wife is wicked, because liable to turn their husband's thoughts to illicit indulgence; for a man is so constituted that he must indulge his passions or die!

This, though, was to become a strong point in the platform of many a woman's rights champion. It was, as we have seen, to mean a jail sentence for Moses Harman, who dared print case histories in point. It was to become an ample justification, in the eyes of some, for free love doctrines. On the occasion when the birth of Margaret's child in Italy was whispered about in America before her secret marriage to Count Ossoli had been announced, people could refer back to her questionings of conventional marriage. They could speak of socialist marriages without benefit of clergy.

In reality, this child of transcendentalism had simply spoken out in the name of individual dignity for the right to stand on one's own and to make a bargain as an equal. Independence was at the top of the agenda for the feminist cause at the middle of the nineteenth century. Not that the sexes could dispense with one another; but the nature of woman's inculcated devotion had blighted love and degraded marriage. Self-realization had been impossible for *either* sex.

The critical response to *Woman in the Nineteenth Century* was prompt and vigorous. Reviews on the friendly side, like that in the liberal *Christian Examiner,* thought that the author had not been extravagant in her claims. They emphasized her renunciation of any wish to poach on male territory. She had been delicate and fearless; beyond the reach of petty caviling. Few critics, on the other hand, however sympathetic to her text, showed any enthusiasm for her style. The work was disgustingly disorganized, "rather a collection of bright intimations and clever sayings than an organized treatise."

Orestes Brownson, recently converted to Catholicism, found a most useful wedge in her stylistic weakness. He could begin his demolition at this obviously vulnerable spot. Miss Fuller was the "chieftainess" of the Transcendentalist sect, he said. She had a high sense of artistic appreciation but little artistic skill. She was a genuine woman; her book talked on and on without saying anything. She was a true transcendentalist—all confusion.

What was the lady driving at? What did she want? Surely she herself did not know. She and her whole Protestant infidel crowd were fighting an inner sickness. They sought a solid rock of certainty, but never found it. They were irrational; therefore not to be reasoned with. Their illness called for sympathy and nursing. "Take care," Brownson warned his readers, "not to heed what they say, and especially not to receive the ravings of their delirium as divine inspirations."

Did Miss Fuller want recognition for woman's immortal soul? It had already received more than its due of recognition from poets, "philanthropists, abolitionists, Fourierists, Saint-Simonians, dietetic reformers, and other reformers of all sorts and sizes, of all manner of things in the universe. . . ." See how men have adored their Goddesses! Who has not heard of the "divine Fanny" [Wright]? And men worship more than women's souls—their bodies too!

As to the complaint that woman's choice of worldly action had been limited, Brownson replied with authority "So had man's." God had assigned appropriate tasks to each sex and neither had more cause to complain than the other. But they should be *equal,* the querulous feminists were crying. Man *is* not the head of woman. *Dixit* Brownson, "We, on the authority of the Holy Ghost, say he is." Was not St. Paul's word at least as authoritative as Miss Fuller's?

Our lady philosopher had also fallen into the error—one which prevailed among non-Catholics—that human nature was perfectible, that the true moral society would be attained through the free, harmonious development of this nature. Brownson could not repeat too often the axiom: Nature is inherently corrupt and not to be trusted. Nor was there any reason to assume that the good aimed at by anyone would come in this world. "The earth is cursed." Restrictions on the social intercourse of men and women were designed to prevent the greatest evils brought on by accursed flesh.

Nothing personal, of course, Brownson hastened to interject. It was just that the reformer's assumptions were wrong, and therefore led to evil conclusions. Miss Fuller was mistaken, but there was no reason for the innuendoes that were being circulated about her and about her book. She had done nothing, some remarks in the press notwithstanding, which Protestants would consider a sin.

The *Southern Quarterly Review's* reviewer found fault on other grounds. He claimed it as a simple fact that women were born with muscular weakness and therefore destined to be dependent on men. Without going into the question of female mentality, it was obvious that mathematics, astronomy, or political science were not the feminine forte. When a woman crosses the line, she is, by virtue of her crossing, unsexed. In her new role, she may achieve "power as a *litterateur*," but she loses her power as a woman. Now, friendly spirits thought that Margaret Fuller "should have been by nature a woman among men, but by intellect she was a man among women." The difference was that where friends said it largely in praise of her intellect, the Southern reviewer was voicing a vague and pervasive fear among men of a reversal in sexual roles. If women became dominant, would they not treat men as the latter in their heyday had treated women?

ON THE MARCH

A reformer's life was not a happy one. When not plagued by enemies, he was badgered by fellow reformers. Into the bargain, the business of reform never kept a single pattern long enough for its devotees to know where they stood. Those who pledged themselves to one or more causes for humanitarian, religious, or selfish reasons were as likely as not to fall away from their erstwhile comrades because of differences in objectives which developed as their movement progressed. And there was always the fear of incurring guilt by association with persons who were connected with other, "less desirable" causes.

Thomas Wentworth Higginson, himself a frequenter of abolitionist and feminist meetings, told how prominent reform men had time and time again to account for the lunatic fringe in their own company. That very Christian abolitionist, William Lloyd Garrison, had, for instance to explain his previous association with John Humphrey Noyes, who transferred his early abolitionist energies to the free love experiment at Oneida. Wendell Phillips, that multiple-threat man on the All-American reform team, had on occasion to eject an obstreperous "adherent" from his meetings.[2]

◇ ◇

The clerical anti-slavery leadership of the early forties had its own version of exclusiveness in reform and was quite willing to create a split in the ranks rather than admit women to prominence in the movement. When the American Anti-Slavery Society met in May 1840, it found itself irreparably divided over the appointment of the Quakeress Abby Kelly to a business committee. Later in the same year, Wendell Phillips made a vigorous but unsuccessful attempt at the World's Anti-Slavery Convention in London to convince his fellow workers in the cause that liberalism and the exclusion of women were incompatible. Garrison, arriving late, was apprised of the state of affairs, and refused to participate in the convention debates.

Sitting in the gallery with the unyielding Garrison were Ann Green Phillips, delegate Elizabeth Cady Stanton, and delegate Lucretia Mott. The first two were wives of delegates. Mrs. Mott had come with her husband James; both were Philadelphia Quakers. Mrs. Stanton and Mrs. Mott found a common bond in indignation, and formed a friendship which provided the nucleus of the Woman's Rights Convention at Seneca Falls in July 1848. The kettle had been simmering since the earliest days of the Republic. It came to a boil in the late forties, the fire fed by Margaret Fuller's theories and Fourierist feminism.

Robert Owen had ushered in his revolution with a Declaration of Mental Independence written in the manner of the American Declaration of Independence from King George. The militant women of '48 modeled their own *Declaration of Sentiments* after the same document, directing their statement of grievances to King Man. "We hold these truths to be self-evident: that all men and women are created equal," they declared. People tolerate abuses and do not revolt for trivial causes,

> But when a long train of abuses and usurpations, pursuing invariably the same object, evinces a design to reduce them

[2] By means of the "guilty thoughts" and "bad associations" technique, the white-supremacy democrats injected the miscegenation issue into the election campaign of 1864. The whole thing was a well-organized hoax. In expounding the "theory of the blending of the races," the perpetrators craftily baited Phillips, Theodore Tilton, Henry Ward Beecher, Horace Greeley, and other leaders in the Republican campaign. The implication was that the Lincoln party would promote racial mixture if elected.

under absolute despotism, it is their duty to throw off such government, and to provide new guards for their future security. Such has been the patient sufferance of the women under this government, and such is now the necessity which constrains them to demand the equal station to which they are entitled.

The history of mankind is a history of repeated injuries and usurpations on the part of man toward woman, having in direct object the establishment of an absolute tyranny over her. To prove this, let facts be submitted to a candid world.

He has never permitted her to exercise her inalienable right to the elective franchise.

He has compelled her to submit to laws, in the formation of which she had no voice.

He has withheld from her rights which are given to the most ignorant and degraded men—both natives and foreigners.

Having deprived her of this first right of a citizen, the elective franchise, thereby leaving her without representation in the halls of legislation, he has oppressed her on all sides.

He has made her, if married, in the eye of the law, civilly dead.

He has taken from her all right in property, even to the wages she earns.

He has made her, morally, an irresponsible being, as she can commit many crimes with impunity, provided they be done in the presence of her husband. In the covenant of marriage, she is compelled to promise obedience to her husband, he becoming, to all intents and purposes, her master —the law giving him power to deprive her of her liberty, and to administer chastisement.

He has so framed the laws of divorce, as to what shall be the proper causes, and, in case of separation, to whom the guardianship of the children shall be given, as to be wholly regardless of the happiness of women—the law in all cases going upon a false supposition of the supremacy of man, and giving all power into his hands.

After depriving her of all rights as a married woman, if single, and the owner of property, he has taxed her to support a government which recognises her only when her property can be made profitable to it.

He has monopolised nearly all the profitable employments, and from those she is permitted to follow she receives but a scanty remuneration. He closes against her all the avenues of wealth and distinction which he considers most honourable to himself. As a teacher of theology, medicine, or law, she is not known.

He has denied her the facilities for obtaining a thorough education, all colleges being closed against her.

He allows her in church, as well as state, but a subordinate position, claiming Apostolic authority for her exclusion from the ministry, and, with some exceptions, from any public participation in the affairs of the church.

He has created a false pubic sentiment by giving to the world a different code of morals for men and women, by which moral delinquencies which exclude women from society are not only tolerated, but deemed of little account in man

He has usurped the prerogative of Jehovah himself, claiming it as his right to assign for her a sphere of action, when that belongs to her conscience and to her God.

He has endeavoured, in every way that he could, to destroy her confidence in her own powers, to lessen her self-respect, and to make her willing to lead a dependent and abject life.

Now, in view of this entire disfranchisement of one half the people of this country, their social and religious degradation; in view of the unjust laws above mentioned, and because women do feel themselves aggrieved, oppressed, and fraudulently deprived of their most sacred right, we insist that they have immediate admission to all the rights and privileges which belong to them as citizens of the United States.

In entering upon the great work before us, we anticipate

no small amount of misconception, misrepresentation, and ridicule; but we shall use every instrumentality within our power to effect our object. We shall employ agents, circulate tracts, petition the State and National legislatures, and endeavour to enlist the pulpit and press in our behalf. We hope this Convention will be followed by a series of Conventions embracing every part of the country.

With the Declaration and pertinent resolutions accepted, the convention adjourned to Rochester where it was reconvened two weeks later. There were questions to be thrashed out, matters of strategy and tactics to be discussed. Little difficulties cropped up almost at once. Reporting the Seneca Falls Convention for the *North Star*, the great Negro abolitionist Frederick Douglass had expressed bewilderment at the stubbornness of some men about the woman question. They would—and did—leave the movement to give the Negro his rights rather than give women the right to participate in the work of liberation. The causes of this paradoxical sentiment began to appear in the open at Rochester.

Some of the men were agreed on equality, but with reservations. They found it easy to accept the principle of equal pay for equal work, but equality in the family was another matter. "When the two heads disagree," queried a Mr. Sully, "who must decide?" Had not St. Paul made obedience obligatory upon the wife? Lucretia Mott replied that Quaker families practiced mate equality without trouble. The one who was right by reason made the decision. Moreover, St. Paul also advised these opponents of women's rights not to marry. Why did they follow his precepts in one respect and not in another? Mrs. Stanton then added facetiously that the suggested rule of superior will or reason was not an innovation; she could think of many a household where the woman wore the trousers.

When the first official National Woman's Rights Convention got under way at Worcester on October 23, 1850, there was one area of unquestionable unanimity. The law had arbitrarily deprived woman of her right to her own property and to her children. She could not independently manage her material goods by contract or testament: her husband was in full control. His power as a father went so far that he could arrange to have his wife separated from her children in the event of his own death.

But the only note of real militancy at this first convention was a resolution offered by Mrs. Ernestine L. Rose in the spirit of Margaret Fuller's formula: the fight for political, legal, and social equality would stop only when woman had attained the full realization of her capacity for development. In addition there were resolutions presented by William Henry Channing and Wendell Phillips. The one stated that women should demand and secure some superior court of appeal to which they could have recourse in cases of marital outrage. The other bade the convention keep in mind that "most grossly wronged and foully outraged" group, the million and one-half slave women in the South.

The second convention, held at Worcester in October 1851, continued the property and family rights theme. Phillips found a solution in giving woman a voice in determining future laws regulating property in the marriage state. He demanded that women be given a freedom of movement in the ·labor market equal to that of man. Women's labor was cheap, he explained, because of an oversupply in the few occupations to which they were admitted. Thus was laid the groundwork for their recruitment into prostitution. Phillips' case for relieving women's sufferings by granting them civil liberties and privileges seemed to strike a note of truth for all time. It was reprinted by the Equal Franchise Society of Pennsylvania in 1910 and again by the same group in 1916.

Antoinette Brown, who had fought her way into a theology course at Oberlin College, and was having more trouble in trying to secure ordination as a minister, translated the temper of the convention into religious terms. She informed her audience that while the Bible did instruct wives in obedience, "it also beseeches the husband to be in subjection to his wife." On the other hand, Abby Kelly, now Mrs. Foster, brought forward the materialist view: Independence was purchaseable. A woman ought not marry, she said, until she could support a family.

Lucy Stone, veteran lecturer for the Anti-Slavery Society and a former schoolteacher, declared that women must share responsibility with men for existing conditions. Instead of kow-towing to their male masters, instead of asking "May I have this, and may I have that?" they must get up and take what they want. It was not mere bravado with Lucy Stone. When in 1855 she married Henry Brown Blackwell, an ardent believer in woman's rights and a brother of America's first girl medical school graduate, Elizabeth Blackwell, the couple drew up a joint protest against the current legal disabilities of married women and published it in connection with their wedding ceremony. Also symbolic of Lucy's determination to retain her individuality in marriage was her transition from Miss Stone to Mrs. Stone, by this act contributing to our language the term "Lucy Stoner."

The usual galaxy of stars met again in 1852 and repeated, this time perhaps in more florid style, the things they were agreed upon. There were present Clarissa Howard Nichols, organizer of the women of Vermont and lecturer for the cause the country over, and Elizabeth Oakes Smith, preacher, lecturer, author of *Woman and*

Her Needs, and writer of larger quantities of poetry, fiction, juveniles, and history. Paulina Wright Davis, who had moved delicate women out of their seats with her anatomical illustrations, was President of the Central Committee. The Reverend Samuel J. May, active in movements for peace, abolition, temperance and woman's rights, read the prayer and was one of the four official secretaries of the meeting. Gerrit Smith, also to be found on all reform fronts, was a vice-President. Lucretia Mott was President. Of course, there were among the old faces, Lucy Stone, Ernestine Rose, Susan B. Anthony, and Elizabeth Cady Stanton. Greetings were received and read from absent friends; among these were Channing's and Greeley's.

Angelina Grimke Weld, not knowing whether she would be able to attend the convention, sent ahead her letter of greeting—actually an apostrophe to the world and its habit of accommodating itself quietly to change. The point she wanted to make was that, in contrast to the rest of human nature which welcomed change so gracefully, the world of human organization resisted change with all its might. All social organization, she claimed, had tended historically to stifle human growth and change. But the organization of women to which she was addressing herself was different. Its purpose was *change;* and fortunately, its movement was beginning in a period of resurgent civilization when readjustments of human need seemed to be favored by so many.

Among the more stimulating speeches delivered to the third convention was that of Mrs. Matilda Joslyn Gage, a newcomer to conventions but hardly a novice on the public platform. Mrs. Gage painted the whole picture of woman's degradation with eloquence and fervor. As she described the iniquities of men and their laws, as she spoke of woman's great capacity to cope with the trials of life, even giving up her virtue to avoid starvation, Mrs. Gage's indignation rose until she exhorted her listeners to battle:

> We need not expect the concessions demanded by women
> will be peaceably granted; there will be a long moral war-
> fare, before the citadel yields; in the meantime, let us take
> possession of the outposts. . . . Fear not any attempt to
> frown down the revolution already commenced; nothing is
> a more fertile aid of reform, than an attempt to check it;
> work on.

Matilda Gage's sincerity was beyond question. She herself worked on for many a decade, speaking, organizing, writing, editing, and researching for the cause. The year of her death, 1898, found her preparing a paper to be delivered at a meeting in commemoration of the half-century of America's woman's rights movement.

The casual listener at Syracuse in 1852 doubtless came away feeling that the meeting had been one of joyous unanimity. Individual speakers had set their own emphases and had used a variety of terms and expressions; but to all intents and purposes, their meaning was the same. Nevertheless, the listener with his ear to the ground would have felt the vibrations of approaching dissension. The impatient agitational temperaments and the children of rationalist, socialist doctrines seemed to be lining upon one side; the mild, polite ones, the children of well-mannered persuasion and those bred in the logic of religion, gave indications that they were moving in a different direction.

Mrs. Rose was first to show irritation. She disliked being introduced as a "Polish lady, educated in the Jewish faith." She immediately announced that the place of a person's birth made no difference. More important were the questions: Did his ideas stand the test of reason? and Did he behave in a way calculated to add to human happiness? "Yes," she said, "I am an example of the universality of our claims; for not American women only, but a daughter of poor, crushed Poland, and the downtrodden and persecuted people called the Jews . . . pleads for the equal rights of her sex."

Mrs. Rose agreed with the resolution on which she was speaking: women were insensible to their own degradation; they were as sick as the drunkard who could not do without his drink, as the tobacco addict who could not break the habit; their nerves had become so paralyzed that they felt no pain. "Woman is a slave, from the cradle to the grave." So depraved was public opinion on the subject, that the reasonable American husband earned himself the derogatory label "hen-pecked." Woman's rights involved man's rights as well. Reason was indivisible.

Mrs. Rose was obviously piqued by the language of Biblical-minded participants like Antoinette Brown, who persisted in using the Book of Books as authority for woman's claims to equality. It was just after Miss Brown had offered Scriptural support of her position in a learned address that the spirited Ernestine Rose remarked sarcastically that the "able theologian" should have been at the recent Constitutional Convention in Indiana. For there she might have been able to counteract the minister who put an evil spell on one of Robert Dale Owen's pro-feminist proposals.

There were grave objections, said Mrs. Rose at a later meeting, to having the religious interpretation broadcast as the sense of the convention. Such were the differences in theological interpretation that finding a correct one was out of the question. And had not the intrigues and squabbles over the meaning of the Scriptures produced so much strife and suffering among innocent people? "Here [on the question of sexual equality] we claim human rights and freedom, based upon the laws of humanity, and require no written authority from Moses or Paul, because those laws and our claims are prior to even these two great men."

Nevertheless, for the time being, the woman's rights advocates found the authority of prominent ministers very useful. The Tract Series, published after the Syracuse Convention, included outstanding sermons alongside speeches and communications to convention audiences.

Appropriately enough, Tract No. 1 was a sermon on *The Rights and Condition of Women* preached by the Reverend Samuel J. May in Syracuse in November 1845. May, who stood high for righteousness, integrity, and moral courage, had braved local opinion whenever he saw fit. An invitation to Angelina Grimke to preach abolitionism from his own pulpit was an act of real courage on his part. As principal of the Normal School at Lexington, Massachusetts, he escorted his students to an anti-slavery rally and was promptly reprimanded by his superior Horace Mann, for mixing politics with education.

The sermon on women was far more temperate than May's conduct in either of these two instances, but it made its point: The family was the most important institution on earth. The children and the household needed the energies of both parents equally. Neither could be spared from domestic duty until that duty was performed completely. The contribution of a wise and virtuous mother to family welfare was as great, if not greater, than that of the father. Women, therefore, as well as men, should guide and control the community with the energies left over from their family ministrations.

Several of the early woman's rights tractarians, noting the effectiveness of the step-by-step appeal, used a logical framework similar to Samuel May's. The fighting Unitarian transcendentalist, Theodore Parker, who, according to Lucy Stone's story, was converted to feminist enthusiasm after the 1851 convention, contributed to the tract series his sermon *The Public Functions of Woman* (delivered on March 27, 1853 at the Music Hall in Boston).

Parker spoke of much the same things as had the Reverend Samuel May. But his superior sense of the practical, plus his understanding of social values, produced a clearer, more forceful statement of the issues. He also proved that all transcendentalists did not, as the sneering Orestes Brownson claimed, have their heads in the clouds. His first assumption was that "the domestic function of woman . . . does not exhaust her powers. Woman's function, like charity, begins at home; then, like charity, goes everywhere. To make one-half of the human race consume its energies in the functions of housekeeper, wife and mother, is a monstrous waste of the most precious material God ever made."

Marriage weighed heavily in Parker's index of civilization. The fact that so many men and women were unmarried was, according to him, a great defect in Christian society. The Catholic Church was somewhat to blame for this situation because of its consecration of an unnatural evil, celibacy. Note, said he, the vice and the degradation of women that prevails in Catholic countries.

Parker saw the status of women in his time as a transitional one—between that condition in which she had been subordinate to man but having marriage for protection, and that in which she would be an independent equal. He distinguished three types of married women: The Drudge, whose life was housekeeping and no more; the Doll, who was good to look at and listen to, but no more; and the *Woman* who could run the house and play the doll and have energy for more. Science, by contributing its labor-saving devices, was fast increasing the numbers in this last category. Society had to accommodate itself to the available energies of the women in category three.

There remained the women who needed social opportunity in order to fill out their lives. There were those who had no talent for domestic duties. Keeping them in the home, regardless of whether or not they had talents in other directions, was, by Parker's now trite expression, equivalent to putting a born sailor on a farm. Then, consider the young women who would some day marry. What shall they do with their spare time now? The Middle Ages had its way of drawing non-domestic women into the church, bringing "a curse on man" by their experiment. In nineteenth century America, things should be better for women, declared Parker. But every sixth woman was a slave! "Sold as a beast; with no more legal respect paid to her marriage than the farmer pays to the conjunctions of his swine." Moreover, there were in democratic America unbelievable contrasts between women, rich and poor, well-bred and wretched. "Look," the preacher commanded his shocked audience, "at the wild sea of prostitution, which swells and breaks and dashes against the bulwarks of society—every ripple was a woman once!"

The Reverend Thomas Wentworth Higginson addressed his *Woman and Her Wishes* (1853) to the Massachusetts Constitutional Convention. His quotations from the writings of Margaret Fuller and others were attractive but, by this time, too well known to startle legislators into action. Mrs. Elizabeth Oakes Smith's tract on the *Sanctity of Marriage* gave a new turn to Samuel May's reasoning. Marriage, whether sacred or civil, was too serious a matter to risk possible uncongeniality between the parties to it. Mrs. Smith suggested that a qualifying examination should be undergone by those about to marry. If not that, one could at any rate take measures to insure that woman entered the marital state of her independent choice and will, thus partly insuring a firm basis for the initial relationship. Social and economic opportunity, and freedom to marry or not, were prerequisite to independence.

The fall of 1853 produced two conventions, one in New York City and the other in Cleveland. The New York Convention was largely devoted to ridiculing absurd provisions of current law with special attention to the legal disabilities of wives. Mrs. Rose pointed out, for example, that the New York State law forbade making of wills by idiots, lunatics, infants, and married women. Thomas Wentworth Higginson reasoned from the male theory of jury competence that it was improper to impanel a jury of men to decide on the claim of a divorced mother to the custody of her child. Mrs. Nichols climaxed the meeting with a riot-provoking statement on the textual command "to obey." If a woman must obey her husband according to Scripture, she said, must she also obey all the bachelors and other women's husbands in the community? The convention adjourned amid shouting and confusion.

The Cleveland meeting, officially the fourth national convention, started with the usual speechmaking and resolutions. There was little excitement until the reading of a letter from Channing suggesting that it was time for direct action. It was Channing's idea that the Convention should adopt a Declaration of Women's Rights and that the Declaration be implemented by petitions to state legislatures on specific points. All was well, except that one of the points asked that habitual drunkenness of either party be considered grounds for divorce. At once the spectre of religious circumscription rose and stirred up latent antagonisms. Antoinette Brown said she would agree if the word "separation" were substituted for "divorce." Mrs. Rose asked what the essential difference was. Miss Brown explained that "separation" meant no remarrying. Mrs. Rose failed to see why what was sufficient cause for separation was not also cause for *complete* divorce. Sensing the tenseness of the atmosphere, she hastened to add that this was not the time for a discussion of this question and deftly turned the talk to an examination of the fallacies of the double standard. She took the rationalist position that what was wrong for one sex was wrong for another, while others vaguely pinned the blame for marital messes on men. After another go at the property-rights routine, the meeting ended.

The affairs of the feminists ran with fair unanimity for several years following. When, in 1856, a Virginia theological student inquired of Thomas Wentworth Higginson whether the basis of the woman's rights movement was natural or derived from Revelation, the entire group on the platform stood firmly together against the obvious attempt at disruption. At all times the Biblical talents of Antoinette Brown could be relied on to justify woman's rights against the verbal onslaughts of men of religion. Mrs. Rose refrained from too-frequent innuendoes aimed at the ministry; she did, however, let people know that she was present by irritatingly pricking the bubble of their optimism. In 1856, when Lucy Stone introduced a note of self-congratulation to the effect that every Northern state had mended for the better its laws pertaining to women's property rights, Ernestine Rose chimed in with footnotes on all the disagreeable qualifications in these laws. For one thing, no state had yet granted women rights over their children. For another, rights pertained only to property acquired before marriage. Mrs. Stone agreed that married women lacked moral independence because they had not been granted the right to keep their own earnings. It was explained that this privilege had been withheld because legislators feared that wives might bill their husbands for domestic services rendered. Their fear was not wholly a product of the imagination, for Wendell Phillips had stated on more than one occasion that women did more than half the work that produced material rewards. Who knew but that one day they might not sue for their pay?

A favorite talking-point during the middle fifties was the improvement of *rapport* between husbands and wives by reenforcing women's spiritual, moral, and personal independence. Greeley, Higginson, and Blackwell (Lucy Stone's husband) favored the program. Mrs. Rose dramatized the theme by showing how, by limiting women's activities, men were forcing them to a devil's choice of selling themselves in matrimony or out of it. The argument was an old one in radical reformist circles, but fairly fresh in the woman's rights movement: Man—by his very protectiveness, by his concern for preserving woman's modesty—was undermining her virtue and forcing her into prostitution.

The opening of new vocations to woman and the extension of her education were considered the chief bulwarks against her particular perils. These measures would prevent her downfall if unmarried. They would bolster her self-respect and gain the respect of her husband in marriage. Wendell Phillips was prominent among reformers who held the conception that material circumstances strongly conditioned moral behavior. At the ninth woman's rights convention, held in New York City in 1859, he struck hard at the evils of urban-industrial civilization. "Your city starves the laborer," he charged; "starvation drives him or her into the ranks of vice; the man becomes a drunkard, the woman a prostitute." In New York

City, 10,000 women needleworkers were competing for 2000 jobs. How do you remedy such a situation? You can neither preach it nor reform it out of existence. "Natural economic laws are the remedy."

But Phillips' extremism in political and social matters was of a paternalistic kind. It was not born out of a sense of wrong done to himself or his own patrician social group, and he could therefore not be depended upon to follow straight through with his co-workers. Just as he had his differences with Garrison in abolitionism, there was a point in the woman's rights movement beyond which he refused to go. The limiting factor began to operate when, in the Convention of 1860, the female leadership in the feminist movement called for the organization's approval of liberalized divorce laws. Although Phillips fought on grounds of procedure and expediency, there is little doubt that he was prompted by ideals of chivalry as well as by less worthy traditions of his social set.

The long smoldering volcano of differences among the woman's rights leadership erupted after Elizabeth Cady Stanton had presented and spoken in favor of a set of ten resolutions written in support of the New York State legislature's pending divorce bill. The same legislation for liberalized divorce, it will be remembered, was occasion for a bitter newspaper debate between Horace Greeley and Robert Dale Owen. Mrs. Stanton's phraseology and logic revealed her acquaintance not only with the thinking of the Owen school, but also with the good arguments of Fourierist and anarchist spokesmen.

Mrs. Stanton's initial premise was that an individual can no more waive his freedom by signing a marriage contract than can a whole people swear everlasting allegiance to a bad government. The next resolution established women as the equals of men in their natural right to the pursuit of happiness. Therefore it was right, and obligatory, to abolish any agreement between human beings that failed to promote happiness. A *true* marriage could be known only by its results; so that, if it is said that no man can put asunder what God has united, it is likewise true that man cannot force the continued union of what God and nature had not joined together. In other words, if a married man and woman found themselves in conflict, then they were not true affinities by divine selection and should therefore be divorced.

A travesty on heavenly truth and holy law it was, said the fifth resolution, that physical impotence should be cause for divorce but not "mental, moral, or spiritual imbecility." Unhappy unions were, in a very serious sense, illegitimate; not to speak, with the authority of a currently accepted brand of eugenics, of the hereditary defects that descend to the children of partners who are badly mated. For reasons as compelling as all these, Mrs. Stanton was asking the convention to resolve that that most important of all contracts, the marriage contract, be no more binding than, for instance, a partnership in business.

For the benefit of those on the platform or in the audience who would argue the good of the whole community against the suffering of individuals, Elizabeth Stanton demonstrated the error of supposing that a law which oppresses the individual can promote the best interests of society. The idea of man's total depravity had also to be repudiated. Man was above all institutions, ecclesiastical and civil. Cheers for those heroic women who had defied opinion and the law by breaking up their loveless marriages!

Was it said that "separation" was available? What an uneasy, undercover life separated people lived! Again, separation favored the male. For—and here Mrs. Stanton used a cliché which no good feminist would accept—man had more in life than marriage; woman had only marriage. *That* marriage had to be a good one. Everyone was aware, she said, of Horace Greeley's recent fulminations on the eternality of the holy sacrament. But who ever said that all wisdom lived and died with Horace Greeley? Greeley himself would certainly have found Scriptural arguments against "unions forever," especially where incompatibility existed, if he had been married to the *New York Herald* instead of to the Republican party.

Greeley had stated toward the end of his correspondence with Owen that the subject of marriage and divorce had been completely explored down through the ages. Only half the ground had been surveyed, Mrs. Stanton reminded Greeley; and *that* half not by disinterested surveyors. There was one kind of marriage that had not been tried; that was "a contract made by equal parties to live an equal life, with equal restraints and privileges on either side. Thus far, we have had the man marriage, and nothing more."

As if by prearrangement, the Reverend Antoinette Brown, a dependable objector to divorce, was the next scheduled speaker. She was now Mrs. Samuel C. Blackwell, having married a brother of Elizabeth and Henry Blackwell, and the more assured of her authority in speaking of matters concerning marriage and divorce. If Mrs. Stanton could state her side of the question and Mr. Greeley his, Mrs. Blackwell was prepared to present her own views in thirteen resolutions and a supporting speech.

Her first assumption stated a conclusion much as had Mrs. Stanton's initial "whereas." But Mrs. Blackwell's proceeded in an entirely different direction. "Resolved," it read, "that marriage is the voluntary alliance of two persons of opposite sexes into one family, and that such an alliance, with its possible incidents (sic) of children, its common interest, etc., must be from the nature of things, as permanent as the life of the parties." Just as the parent could not annul his obligations to a child, so no married person could withdraw from obligations to a mate "no matter how profligate that other's conduct." Devotion of the one partner to raising the level of conduct of the other—*especially* if the other was sinful and guilty—must certainly exalt the character of the devoted one.

Now, this did not mean, continued Mrs. Blackwell, that a modern, independent, "equal" woman must sacrifice herself and her children to a degraded husband and father. If such a man could not be lifted to a level of decency, then legal separation was desirable. But even such a separation could not set aside the marriage contract completely. Actual divorce was out of the question; not because of Scriptural mandate (which had exhausted its usefulness at these meetings years before), but because of the nature of the social organization. Guard as well as you can against hasty, improper marriages; let your young woman wait until she is sure of her own mind at twenty-five or thirty (Miss Brown married at thirty-one); but once the step is taken it cannot be retraced.

Ernestine Rose did not need Scriptural quotations to draw her fire. She knew what she was *against* and what she was *for*. She was *for* divorce and was on her feet telling the audience so as soon as Mrs. Blackwell had uttered her last words.

The American mind of 1860 was just as likely as not to equate belief in divorce with advocacy of free love. Mrs. Rose knew, from her experience in the Owen reform movement of the thirties, what divorce advocates were up against. She therefore forestalled a name-calling session by anticipating the name-callers. While maintaining that love was not love if it were not free, she stood by the marriage institution. What Ernestine Rose demanded, as did Mrs. Stanton and some of the others, was a divorce law that would prevent violence being done to the human personality.

Poisoning one's mate had been resorted to all too often as the only available means of release. Did the advocates of strict laws prefer that? Was it unreasonable to ask that the list of "causes" be extended to include personal cruelty to a wife, wilful desertion for one year, and habitual intemperance? Moreover, proceeded Mrs. Rose in her best rhetoric, "I ask for a law of Divorce . . . to prevent free love, in its most hideous form, such as is now carried on but too often under the very name of marriage, where hypocrisy is added to the crime of legalized prostitution."

Mrs. Blackwell's "sermon" about equality in marriage was all very well and good. But the equal woman she talked about was a myth. Her remarks were hardly pertinent to the divorce law under discussion. If equality, so highly prized by the Reverend Antoinette Blackwell, was the essence of real marriage, and if, therefore, very few people were really married, why object to a law that would be consonant with the fact?

The circular logic of debate up to this point may have been edifying to some and amusing to others. But to the dignified Wendell Phillips it was totally irrelevant. This was not a Marriage Convention, he declared, important though such a convention might be. It was a convention whose purpose was to secure for women equality before society and the law. Divorce laws weighed equally upon women *and* men. It therefore seemed to him that the theory of marriage and divorce could not be discussed at a woman's convention. He, as a man, had the right to protest lack of representation at a discussion where the needs of his sex were not adequately represented. Even were he to admit, as everyone had to admit, that present marriage regulations were more unsatisfactory for women than for men, he could not see that statute books were the source of evil. Nor was it evident that you could change the unequal nature of the relationship by modifying its period of duration. Further, Phillips warned, such speeches as had been delivered about the marriage question were more than a waste of time; they were dangerous. It had been his very recent experience—in the anti-slavery movement —that added isssues were added sources of conflict. Experience had shown that because of totally extraneous matters the success of reform movements had been long postponed. For the reasons given, Phillips moved that the resolutions as read be ruled out of order and removed from the proceedings of the convention.

Antoinette Blackwell, believing, doubtless, that her own antidivorce resolutions were more to Phillips' taste, asked if he had meant hers too. Upon being informed that Phillips would want all resolutions deleted, she commented that she was not sure of the tactical advisability of the resolutions and discussion, but was sure of their relevance in the convention. As far as she was concerned, the marriage relation was the center of all human relations.

The convention was obviously against Phillips' silencing tactic. Garrison's view was that, whereas he would agree that the meeting had not been called to settle the marriage question, this question was indeed relevant to the rights of women. Mrs. Stanton, said Garrison, had offered resolutions as a part of her speech. Mrs. Stanton's words were her own; they had not been read into the record as recommendations of the Business Committee. In the name of a free platform, all speakers must be allowed their say.

When, after some discussion, a vote was taken on Phillips' motion to table, it lost. The resolutions reported by the Business Committee were then offered and adopted. A rallying speech by Mary Grew, first president of the Pennsylvania Woman's Suffrage Association, revived the spirit of the occasion, and the convention was adjourned *sine die.*

But Mrs. Stanton was unwilling to accept her success and relax into silence on the divorce issue; Phillips' obstructionism had provided her with an excuse for a "letter to the editor." The missive was, naturally, sent to the editor and the paper which was most liberal with its discussion space. It went to Greeley of the *Tribune* and was printed. Greeley, of course, agreed with Phillips; and, as expected, he was shocked by Mrs. Stanton's likening marriage to any other business contract. Mrs. Stanton insisted that both Phillips and Greeley were begging the question. Small doubt that she was right.

There was a question, however, as to whether the women militants should have tried to overwork the good will and intentions of men of breeding and prestige. Should the movement have risked alienating these magnanimous souls who were genuinely puzzled—partly because of their breeding—about the motivations and objectives of the feminist *avant guard?* Greeley, for instance, could believe in Margaret Fuller and publish her, while being slightly bewildered about her direction. Here she was shouting, "Let her be a sea captain if she will," and insisting at the same time that Greeley hold the door for her as she passed through!

In the same way, Emerson published *Woman in the Nineteenth Century* while anxious about retaining the old romantic ideals of womanhood. He sympathized with the movement but feared its tactics and results. When, in the very earliest stages of organization, the Massachusetts women leaders sought his support, he wrote Paulina Wright Davis:

> If women feel wronged, then they are wronged. But the mode of obtaining a redress, namely, a public convention called by women is not agreeable to me, and the things to be agitated for do not seem to me the best. Perhaps I am superstitious and traditional, but whilst I should vote for every franchise for women . . . I should not wish women to wish political functions, nor, if granted, assume them.

Emerson was so set against *organized* reform movements that it was a painful process to get any kind of open support from him. He would not sign petitions even when the persuasive Phillips asked him to. He delivered a lecture on "Women" (1855) before a Woman's Rights Convention, inwardly wishing that the feminist demands for equality would be qualified in many ways.

It was fortunate that the women developed their own leadership instead of depending on male humanitarians. They could not, however, say that the men had held them back. For the decade of the fifties showed great strides and the impetus lent by male public figures had counted. The year 1860 ended auspiciously for the woman's rights people, despite their grave differences on the divorce question.

AFTER THE WAR

Then intervened the Civil War, in which larger political and military issues swallowed up all the energies of the reformers, whose first thought became the solution of the slavery question by entrenching the national power of the Northern States. The successful outcome of the war found the woman question narrowed down but in sharper focus. The former slave came out with the ballot and full social rights written into the fundamental law of the land. The woman whose professional, domestic, and industrial skills had contributed so much to the success of the war, came out exactly where she was before in the eyes of the law.

The great and almost exclusive demand made thereafter by the woman's rights movement was for the franchise. Other problems were acknowledged to exist, but would be solved at the polls once women had the ballot. Except for rare excursions into peripheral matters, the line was adhered to closely.

Nevertheless the subject of divorce occasionally turned up in feminist meetings. Some public figure would declare that the divorce rate was highest where the number of suffragettes was highest. It was also suggested that family unity would be endangered if husband and wife added political differences to the other inevitable domestic dissensions. The feminists replied with facts. Neither in New-Jersey, where women had had the ballot during that State's first thirty years of independence, nor in any other State where woman suffrage was currently in effect, was the divorce rate higher than anywhere else. If anything—the "if anythings" were rarely substantiated—the opposite was the case. On rare occasions it was tentatively conceded that there might be a period of high divorce rate after the ballot was granted in order to straighten out the mess created by male-favored marriage relationships. With the exception of such minor incidents and an occasional piece of writing by some hardy woman warrior, the feminists lost interest in the marriage-divorce problem. After the Civil War that delicate subject became the property of the anarchists and spiritualists, of the socialists, of social-minded journalists and free-lance writers, and also of sociologists, psychologists, and physicians.

Those who expected the internal rumblings of the movement to be quieted once the uncomfortable divorce issue was eliminated, learned quickly that the old rift was still there. In May 1869, the militant group led by Elizabeth Cady Stanton and Susan B. Anthony, organized the National Woman Suffrage Association, whose objective was a suffrage amendment to the Federal Constitution. For thirty-five years its meetings were held in the nation's capital as a constant reminder to Congress. In November 1869, the American Woman Suffrage Association was organized around the Blackwell clan—Antoinette, Lucy, and the brothers. Thomas Wentworth Higginson, Julia Ward Howe and Mary Livermore, the last a successful lady editor and reformer, were among the leaders. Henry Ward Beecher was its first president. Its plan of operation, the ostensible reason for a separate organization, was to secure action through the States. Julia Ward Howe and Mary Livermore edited the *Woman's Journal* for their group. Susan B. Anthony, Elizabeth Stanton, and Laura Curtis Bullard, helped by Theodore Tilton, published *The Revolution.*

The affairs of the National Association interest us more because of the curiously exciting though short-lived alliance it had with the shameless Victoria Woodhull. It so happened that she had connections which got her a hearing on the suffrage question before Congressional committees when those inside the ranks of the movement had no entrée. There was also the coincidence that the third annual convention of the National Association was in session in Washington when Victoria appeared before the congressmen. Miss Anthony, Paulina Wright Davis, and Isabella Beecher Hooker, a latecomer into Lyman Beecher's brood, went to see her in action and were impressed.

The Claflin sisters were immediately invited to grace the platform of the Association's convention. The rival "American" group in Boston made the most of its rival's indiscretion. Mrs. Stanton replied with a standard defense formula: "When the men who make laws for us in Washington can stand forth and declare themselves pure and unspotted from all the sins mentioned in the Decalogue, then we will demand that every woman who makes a constitutional argument on our platform shall be as chaste as Diana."

Despite the unkind remarks from the Bostonian suffragists, the Washington movement took on a great impetus thanks to Victoria Woodhull. But the union was of short duration. The constant nagging of both branches of the woman's rights movement, plus Victoria's attempt to seize power by the unauthorized use of the names of some of her best partisans, soon broke up the friendship. Besides, Victoria was one for larger ventures; her movements from that point on were her own.

In any case, no lady of refinement could work along with Victoria and her sister Tennie for very long. The language of their public lectures was an outrage to even the liberal view of decency. Their conduct kept pace with their language. Where women could steel themselves against the label "unsexed" they were reluctant to have added that of "oversexed," which came with the public reaction to the Claflin sisters.

Obviously, the more delicate and fundamental points in the realm of feminist thought could not be explored within either organization. But the militant leaders of the old movement were reluctant to give up their ideas even if these lacked the support of a movement. They were willing to drop their promotion of the Bloomer costume because the gain involved was too little to warrant the journalistic ridicule thrown at women who adopted the "reform dress." But the promise of freedom through easier divorce was not lightly relinquished.

The alternative to organizational activity was to lecture and write on one's own; and this had its advantages in that it obviated the necessity of catering to the religious or other traditional sensitivities of members of a movement. Whereas official spokesmen had to assure legislators and churchmen that they envisioned no great family change in their new plans for woman's freedom, Mrs. Stanton could declare on her own that the family organization would be revolutionized under the new dispensation. She was free to hold the church responsible for woman's present low condition. These were thoughts that free-thought publishers were happy to print for women of distinction.

In days of low printing costs, words were cheap, and even writers with the most unconventional ideas got a hearing. Yet, without an organized movement to address, the idea promoters must have sensed the lack of influence of their writing. Such thoughts must have been passing through Mrs. Stanton's mind when, in 1890, she chose a most inauspicious gathering at which to present a resolution on divorce laws. The occasion was the convention which marked the re-cementing of friendship between the National and American suffrage groups.

It was an emergency situation. The National Divorce Reform League, that united front of the ministry of all religious denominations, was gaining strength. It was currently asking Congress to pass a uniform divorce law to fill the loopholes provided by lax laws in a few States. Mrs. Stanton, comparing the refuge value of liberal divorce laws for wives to what Canada's territories had been for the slaves, offered resolutions to the effect that no further divorce legislation be enacted in either Nation or State until such time as women had a voice in government. She further demanded that women get an equal voice with men in all church councils so that they might contribute their view to the interpretation of traditional religious law.

The National-American Convention gave these resolutions the silent treatment. Speaker upon speaker delivered loyalty orations, and Mrs. Stanton was elected first President of the united bodies, but that was all. The undiscourageable Elizabeth Cady Stanton tried again in the Convention of 1901. This time, as Honorary President, she sent her letter of greeting to her associates, a letter delivering her final blast at the church for its hindrances to the woman's rights movement. There was some comment, but none of the officers or other prominent members of the organization wished to be quoted as agreeing with Mrs. Stanton's views.

Matilda Gage too lost all hope for support from the suffrage organizations. Her *Woman, Church and State* was issued first in 1893 by C. H. Kerr, a Chicago publisher of socialist writings, and again in 1900 by the free-thought organization, the Truth-Seeker Company. She threw her political lot in with the Woman's National Liberal Union, formed in 1890 to combat what was called—as Frances Wright had called it in her time—"The Christian Party in Politics."

The Catholics and Protestants, according to the Liberal Union, were conspiring to effect a union of Church and State. Since suffrage was useless without liberty, progressive women were urged to oppose that arch-enemy of freedom, the Church. Temperance, the ballot, and the capital-labor struggle were within the scope of the Convention. Especially in need of consideration was the growing aggressiveness of the Catholic Church, particularly in matters pertaining to education and family life. Mrs. Gage herself spoke on these questions. She elaborated on the evils of church control of schools, and declared that educational systems were inferior wherever such control prevailed. Wherever the church took over, she added, women got the short end of education.

As the last decade of the nineteenth century arrived, it could be seen that agitators like Mrs. Stanton and Mrs. Gage had accomplished one important thing. They had suceeded in tearing large numbers of tradition-bound women loose from the mental bonds that held them. Both the liberals and conservatives in marriage and divorce questions were trying to *reason* their way through to an opinion instead of accepting established authority.

Symposia and panel discussions were encouraged and printed in the magazines of general distribution. Benjamin O. Flower's *Arena* was very generous with the space it gave to the marriage question. The *North American Review* printed Mrs. Stanton's arguments against uniform male-made divorce laws. It also carried the more or less conventional views of Mary A. Livermore, Amelia Barr, Rose Terry Cooke, and Elizabeth Stuart Phelps.

The official study, made by U. S. Commissioner of Labor Carroll D. Wright, showed that divorce had increased 150 per cent from 1867 to 1886. No one gloated over the increase, but interpretations varied with the other views of the interpreters. Some said that the nation could use more religion, others more education. Edward J. Phelps, from his vantage point as a professor of law, indicated that divorces were most frequent where churches and schools were most numerous. The remedy for the divorce situation, he recommended, lay in the prevention of remarriage by either of the divorced parties. Other experts suggested that the evil be checked in its root stage, urging that marriage itself needed more effective barriers and delaying apparatus. Mrs. Livermore was deeply concerned with the preservation of the family but would allow divorce under circumstances such as infidelity, cruelty, and desertion. Most were agreed that an absolute prohibition of divorce courted disaster.

FEMINISM IN OUR TIME

The American feminist movement of the twentieth century contributed little to the development of thought on the marriage relationship. It was left to a few foreign writers like the South African Olive Schreiner and the Swedish Ellen Key to inject novelty into public discussions of the subject.

The point made by Mrs. Schreiner was that the quantity and quality of women's functions in the social universe were decreasing as fast as civilization was advancing. Women were actually being prevented even from raising large families. If women did not win back their right—the essential right of the woman's rights movement —to a full share of honored and useful work, civilization itself would deteriorate. For as woman's mind and muscle weakened in this parasitic state, her offspring (male and female) would inherit the weakness, and the whole of mankind would follow a course of progressive enervation. Mona Caird, one of the "wild women" in British feminism, elaborated the idea of sexual parasitism along similar lines.

Anti-suffragists of the 1890's, like E. Lynn Linton, who wrote studies of the feminists entitled "The Wild Women as Politicians" and "The Wild Women as Social Insurgents," were yet to meet the outstanding woman proponent of moral anarchy of their time. It was not until 1909 that the first of Ellen Key's Swedish works was translated into English and made generally available to her Anglo-Saxon cohorts in the woman's rights movement. *The Century of the Child* was published in America in 1909, *Love and Marriage* in 1911, *The Woman Movement* in 1912.

These books were soon to become the focus of discussion on sex morals. Their lessons seemed to add up to a *laissez-faire* system of morality in which voluntary marital fidelity would replace regulation by law and church. The pamphlets of the Heywoods and the Harmans must have disappeared from circulation by this time; Ellen Key's critics seemed unaware that there was little new in this feminist's emphasis on high individualism in the land of love. Her special danger lay in the fact that she wrote clearly, boldly, and without reference to radical politics.

The uppermost purpose of the state was, Ellen Key explained, to insure the continuity of the race by insisting on the permanent union of two procreative parents. Wherever the *Liebesgluck*, or love-happiness, of the individual conflicted with social demand, the individual must be sacrificed. If one accepted the logic of this position, then voluntary motives in marriage and easy divorce were out of the question.

The position of state primacy, said Miss Key, following the individualist principle, was fallacious because it depended on the assumption that the whole could be benefited by the sacrifice of its parts. With but a slight change in emphasis, this apparently inevitable contradiction could be eliminated. Society could and "must render it possible for the erotic happiness of the individual to serve and foster the enhancement of the race, the ennobling of life." When you substituted the ultimate welfare of humanity for the demands of current society, it became quite feasible to satisfy the part and the whole—the individual and the race—without sacrificing the needs of either. Few "respectable" women would accept such ideas presented in the context of Fourierist or anarchist philosophy. But Miss Key, free of the taint of "isms," had quite a following. She could show very clear distinctions between her own program and that of all the free-thought upstarts who saw only two alternatives: "to be a slave to seminal appetite or a slave to duty."

The voluntary principle needed only one concession from society, namely that love be made an end in itself instead of a means to an end. Granting this, it would soon become clear "that not the marriage service, but the will of two people to bear the responsibility of their children, not the 'legitimacy' of the children, but their quality [should] be the standard of value for the morality of parenthood; that the dissolution of marriage [should] depend upon the will of one of the parties to the marriage contract, and the contractors be equally entitled in the union to equal privileges."

The Key doctrine, though divorced from politics, had elements which satisfied all political factions. For the left parties there were thoughts of individuality, equality, and cooperation. For conservatives, Miss Key used harsh words to condemn women who spoke at peace conferences while their children ran riot in the nursery. Mothers should stay at home, she directed, to be educators of souls. Feminists who might take offense at this were soothed with phrases about women's needing the same human rights as men in order to fulfill her two great life tasks: man-creation and soul-creation.

While many of these items were individually palatable, the whole dish savored strongly of free love. In the last analysis, only love and parental responsibility were to constitute the moral condition of sex relationships. Under the new code, one could have as proper a relationship outside of marriage as within it.

Even anarchists like Emma Goldman could find reason to praise Ellen Key's feminism. It was in line with what a writer for *Mother Earth* described as the thesis of the very early rights agitators, that women had to free their bodies before they could fight effectively for economic, social, and political freedom. And it was high praise to be accepted by anarchists who had stood on the sidelines of American feminism from its earliest days and had jeered at it for catering to convention and capitalism.

The anarchists had their own program for sex and marriage which was built on high individualism and resistance to all forms of oppression. The feminists based their movement on the grounds of reason and human equality as expressed in the Declaration of Independence and the Constitution. On the other hand, the socialist species of thought, though enriched by cross-breeding with native strains, can hardly be called characteristically American. This is not to say that it was better or worse, or more or less effective than competing ideologies. It means simply that socialism arrived here later and continued its connections with ideas at home longer and more consistently than did the others. In any case, the nature and impact of socialist conceptions of marriage on the American mind are impressive enough to deserve separate treatment.

EIGHT

The Socialist View
of the Family

Only very recently have critics of socialism and its communist form ceased to link these political radicalisms as a matter of course with immorality and the destruction of the family. The two notions are still to be seen as an inseparable couplet in moves to discredit persons or movements. No matter how many instances of marital infidelity among the capitalist rich are advertised in mass communication channels, communism and sex aberration may still be declared to be naturally mated without too great fear of contradiction.

Reasonable people of our own day find it hard to see the unavoidable connection between socialism and loose morals. However, it cannot be denied that there has been enough smoke connected with the socialist outlook for women to cause opponents of both feminism and socialism to cry "fire." Almost very leftist movement in our history has attempted, in one way or another, to demonstrate how its program of economic reform would accomplish the liberation of womanhood; and the liberated woman was an implied threat to existing standards which favored the male.

The Illinois Association Opposed to Woman Suffrage demonstrated the nexus in its publication called *Socialism vs. Legal Marriage*. The authors of this pamphlet could not say at the time of writing (1910) that every suffragist was a socialist. The leadership of the woman's rights movement was obviously ultra-conservative. They could in all honesty say, however, that every socialist was a suffragist and that woman suffrage stood high on the socialist platform. The next step for anti-suffragists was to show that the equality of classes, state nurseries, and secularism—all a part of socialist thinking—were anathema to inheritance laws, parental affection, and family life itself.

The founding fathers had established the Republic upon the social unit of the family, argued the pillars of society. The socialists would undermine the mainstays of our culture by treating us as individuals regardless of sex. A woman's inalienable work was the breeding of children. The establishment of equal work, equal pay, and equal political privileges, as demanded by the socialists, would deprive her of an important birthright. Burdened with all these equalities, a woman could not possibly care for her children. Hence the state nursery; hence the loss of parental care and affection. Even the radical Ellen Key would agree on this point with the opponents of feminism.

∽ ∽

Those whose business it was to damn socialism for its ideas and intentions were not given to separating one brand of socialist from another. Socialists were socialists. The errors and misdeeds of one were the responsibility of all. Socialism as a whole was involved in an attack on the *status quo;* no matter what the variation of tactic and purpose, any one or group associated with the movement was equally worthy of condemnation with all the others. Moreover, the public mind, by virtue of its having been trained to fear and hate socialist principles, got accustomed to attributing the misdeeds of all social critics to socialism and the socialists.

In our own time, few discriminating minds fall into this confusion. On the other hand, socialists make distinctions among themselves which are frequently too subtle for lay minds to grasp. For our own purposes—getting a full view of socialist proposals on marriage and related subjects—it seems best to adopt a somewhat liberally interpreted version of what most socialists call socialism. Accordingly, we shall look at two broad categories of thinking: those of "Utopian socialism" and "scientific socialism." The Utopians attributed the evils of society to "man's inhumanity to man" and proceeded to offer imaginative blueprints of better organized societies where the evils of present civilization had been eliminated. The scientific socialists claimed that fault lay in the inevitable inequities produced by an economic system which was out of keeping with man's worldly needs. The solution was to be sought in some form of communal state where economic equality was the ruling principle. The achievement of this end depended for its success upon the overthrow of currently ruling classes. All good socialists agreed that mere economic reform was not enough; the promised land of the ideal society had to show changes in the realm of education, ethics, and even aesthetics.

THE UTOPIANS

When dealing with Utopian recommendations for changes in the relationship between the sexes, it is neither feasible nor fruitful to separate the true socialists from those who simply did not like the complexion of things in the life of their time and were therefore provoked to draw, in fictional or essay form, the picture of better-planned societies. Most Utopians who looked at the marriage question saw similar defects in the current conventions, and may conveniently be treated as a group.

Utopians, whether socialist or otherwise, literary or practical (in that they attempted to set up actual communities), were equally agreed on the proposition that improving the health and welfare of the whole people depended on improving the condition of women. Closely associated with this idea was the observation that the disadvantages of oppressed classes weighed more heavily on women because they had inferior status with respect to the males within their own downtrodden group. Remembering how large the woman question loomed in the writings of Saint Simonian socialists, and of Fourierists and Owenites in Europe and America, one is convinced of the identity of this interest among early socialists. Again, the heavy emphasis placed on reorganizing the family structure in favor of women in both the New England and backwoods Utopias of the nineteenth century, may be recalled from earlier chapters.

Because of the time sequence of their operations, the literary Utopians did not find it necessary to compete with their experimental counterparts. The community experiments had pretty well spent themselves before the literary Utopians flowered. Indeed there is good evidence that the frustrated attempts to build actual communities in the earlier part of the century served as warning signs for later Utopians and persuaded them to sublimate their social drives in the writing of books. In the latter period, the Utopians were not compelled to argue with hard social and economic facts, but only with other ideologists. Of this phase Charles Bellamy wrote in his Utopian romance, *An Experiment in Marriage:*

> There was the spiritualist and the theosophist, the materialist, and loudest of all the agnostic, the old fashioned atheist, too, and the Darwinian, the Swedenborgian, the humanitarian, the positivist. Each one said many true and suggestive things, but all were extravagant in their intolerance, and furious in their confidence that if the world would but open its eyes to the truth, as theorized by its expounder, the millennium would be at hand.

In the field of Utopian writing, a competition among projected paradises replaced real-life rivalry among practical social projects. The first of these paradises, one recalls, was the locale of Charles Brockden Brown's *Alcuin,* the book which offered a long rationalist dialogue along the lines of the Godwin-Wollstonecraft argument on man's inhumanity to woman. But *Alcuin* fell short of the maturer

Utopian approach; it criticized marriage as it was, but provided no indication of a remedy in its land of make believe. Later Utopian theorists pointed up the defects of the world around them by contrasting it with their own perfected societies.

A few, like John Adolphus Etzler in his *The Paradise* (1833), inveighed against the curse placed on love and marriage by economic insecurity. Want of money kept true lovers apart. The possession of it, on the other hand, led to lifelong but loveless marriages. Etzler's paradox sounded a novel note. Most of the other Utopians dwelt upon that favorite theme of the feminists—the degradation suffered by married women because of their economic and legal subordination to their husbands.

Lawrence Gronlund offered to exorcise the evil spirit of economics in marriage by making economic equals of both sexes in his socialist tract, *Cooperative Commonwealth* (1884). Knowing well the standard cries of the opposition that socialism would destroy the family and that woman's rights would make her behave like a man, Gronlund framed his proposals so that they would answer these objections. He would have a division of labor in society that took physiological differences into consideration. There would be equal pay for equal work, but neither sex would compete in the labor market for the other's wages.

The economic bases of marriage itself would be modified in the Cooperative Commonwealth. The marriage market, with its supply and demand features, was to disappear. The new order would afford marriage opportunity for every interested young man and woman. Socialists had no wish to destroy the family. On the contrary, they would make it a happier one by removing it from its central position in society. Education would lead the way to a new order. It would teach how to achieve the best for each and the best for all at the same time.

Not all Utopias promised happy marriage as an automatic consequence of socialism. Charles Bellamy's Grape Valley residents would teach people living elsewhere on the planet a thing or two about personal conduct in marriage. The law made man and wife too sure of each other, that is, outside of Grape Valley. The result was a relationship marred by jealousy and suspicion, because, for lack of incentive to remain attractive to a legally bound mate, one of the parties was driving the other into the arms of a more attractive third party.

The Venusians, who came to criticize earthbound mortals in Henry Francis Allen's *The Key of Industrial Cooperative Government* (1886), had difficulty in understanding why their planetary neighbors did not use modern knowledge about heredity and eugenics in the planning of marriage. Science, they claimed, had it within its power to make mismating an impossibility. William Simpson's *Man from Mars* (1891) also promoted the eugenic path to perfect happiness.

The concern of Utopian writers over reforming the character of sex relationship in marriage extended itself quite naturally to the extramarital phases of that relationship. Rape was explained in S. Byron Welcome's *From Earth's Center* (1894) as the sex violence which had been accumulated by generations of late marriage. Marriage for expediency rather than love was also blamed. Nor was the possibility of an inherited tendency ruled out; for it was altogether conceivable that large numbers of descendants of raped Southern slave women could have been born with the tempestuous habits of their ancestors, the white masters.

The fallen woman and the prostitute had also to be accounted for in the erection of ideal societies. The nationalist socialist, Albert Chavannes, took care of the problem of the fallen woman in his nonexistent Socioland by teaching the facts of life to young people. In both his *The Future Commonwealth* (1892) and *In Brighter Climes* (1895) he advertised scientific sex education at an early age for youngsters of both sexes.

The troubles of young girls who slipped but once could be avoided by the spread of knowledge in Utopia because these troubles were normally the result of ignorance in our present civilization. Prostitution, however, was to be traced to deeper social causes which, when known, could be remedied in a well-planned world. Gronlund, for one, saw only a technical difference between the respectable wife of a wealthy citizen, whom she could not have married for love, and a prostitute who sold herself outside of the protective cover of marriage. In the capitalist system of private enterprise, he thought, marriage was just one more business. Prostitution was an institution based on the degradation of poor girls who had been forced into its clutches by the low wage system. Edward Bellamy, brother of Charles, and the most widely read Utopian of them all, considered prostitution to be a form of exploitation arising from class inequality.

As leader of the "nationalist" movement (that is, socialism through the nationalization of property and the maximum use of technological improvements), Edward Bellamy showed himself to be extraordinarily sensitive to the many disadvantages of being a woman in the nineteenth century. Discrimination in employment and drudgery in the home were conspicuously absent in his imaginative portrayal of Boston in the year 2087. Many were the acid comments of the characters in *Looking Backward* who discussed the lack of social wisdom in the leaders of 1887.

Bellamy did not dwell much on problems of love and marriage, but he did wonder at times just how ideal a relationship could be hoped for in a society which made a woman the object of humiliation with regard to her husband and master. He deprecated the demoralizing effects of all forms of personal dependence—including dependence of the poor upon the rich, the worker upon the boss, children upon parents, and woman upon man. As Dr. Leete, Bellamy's sage in the perfected society of the future, looked back at the woman's rights protest of the nineteenth century, he mused at the lack of insight of his humane male ancestors. They had deplored the lot of women without ever realizing "That it was robbery as well as cruelty when men seized for themselves the whole product of the world and left women to beg and wheedle for their share."

The analysis of the woman movement which Bellamy put into Dr. Leete's mouth was close to Marxist thought. It was so close that Marie A. Shipley of London charged him with plagiarism in a letter which appeared in Benjamin Tucker's magazine, *Liberty*. [1] The leaders of the feminist movement, said Dr. Leete, had been completely unaware, as were the early leaders of the working class, that they were going through the initial stages of a revolution. These leaders had mistakenly attributed the oppression of the masses to the wickedness of men rather than to class forces. "The secret of the sexual bondage and of the industrial bondage was the same—namely, the unequal distribution of wealth power. . . ." The system, not the individual, was at fault. Women had worked toward the goal of reforming their masters; they had not been sufficiently mature politically to think of abolishing the master class.

Civilized woman, according to Dr. Leete, had borne a triple yoke. The first yoke, subjection to the class rule of the rich, she bore in common with the mass of working-class men. The second was her personal subservience "not only in the sexual relation, but in all her behavior to the particular man on whom she depended for subsistence." The third and worst yoke was that of tradition and convention which so retarded her development that they made of her the inferior being men said she was. The heavy hand of convention weighed not only on her but indirectly on all mankind. Degrade the mother of men and the effects would show in those she nurtured.

The difference between "Utopian" and "scientific" socialisms was obviously not in their definition of society's problems. Both based their criticism of industrial capitalism on the mistreatment by the ruling classes of the less fortunate majority of the population. The soil and climate of American democracy was, in the nineteenth century, infinitely congenial to Utopian solutions, and the reasons are

[1] The book she charged Bellamy with paraphrasing was August Bebel's *Woman in the Past, Present, and Future*.

not far to seek. Frontier lands were still available to paradise planners. The masses and the classes were not yet as irretrievably separated as they had been in Europe. The classes, moreover, were so extensively engaged in philanthropic enterprises that there was still hope that they themselves, if aptly prompted, would lead the transformation to a perfect state.

Bellamy's socialism may not have had the endorsement of the more intellectual "scientific" socialists, but it had greater mass readership than their writings ever achieved. *Looking Backward* was a best seller in its time, with a distribution of a million copies. Its charm and simple logic caught the imagination of the many and for a time vitally influenced their political direction. Not so with the more sophisticated and more radical socialists, the limits of whose influence rarely reached beyond small groups of the faithful. Further limiting the spheres of operation of early non-Utopian socialists was the fact that they frequently addressed themselves to groups of foreign-born adherents, and propagandized in languages other than English.

THE SCIENTISTS

The arrival of scientific socialism upon the American scene was coincidental with the failure of revolutionary movements abroad. The carriers of these new notions were often the exiled leaders of those movements. There was no uniformity of revolutionary doctrine among the forty-eighters who fled to America after their failure at home; there were among them intellectuals of all sorts, representatives of the upper and lower strata of the middle class, as well as a sampling of the European working class who had fought their feudal oppressors under the banner of socialism.

Among the most extreme of non-socialist intellectual radicals was Karl Heinzen, whose criticism of existing conditions first got him into trouble in his student days. In 1827, Heinzen was expelled from the University of Bonn where he was studying medicine. He made his first trip to the United States in 1848 to escape legal pressure in Germany, only to return to his native land in the same year to help in the revolutionary struggle. The year 1849 found him back in New York, a political exile energetically fighting for every democratic reform mentionable. Naturally, he was available for carrying the anti-slavery and feminist movements to his German immigrant groups.

Unlike other German leftists who formed leagues and societies for the purpose of setting America on its ears, Heinzen neither advocated the abolition of marriage nor suggested state care and rearing of children. For the most part, his position was that of the American woman's rights movement: the low status of women in society and in the family was irrational and unscientific. Heinzen therefore used his newspaper, *Der Pionier,* to present the philosophical arguments

287

for equal dignity of the sexes. Nowhere, declared *Der Pionier* in 1851—drawing on the current popularity of phrenological psychology —could one discover a greater development of the organ for *Unterwurfigkeit* (obedience propensity) in the female than in the male. The old cliché that woman could not achieve independence because of her origin in Adam's rib would have carried more meaning, said this German organ of liberalism, had she been carved from the first man's heel. This part of the human anatomy was more symbolic of her relative standing in the social world.

By the time Heinzen had collected his ideas in a book entitled *The Rights of Women and the Sexual Relations,* and had them published in 1891 by the anarchist Benjamin Tucker, he had become utterly cynical about the American feminist movement. Moreover, the original intellectual snobbery which he and his fellow-immigrants of 1848 exhibited toward American culture had become exaggerated. The great liberal ideas brought over from Germany, he said, had been wasted on the crass, superficial American mind. As Heinzen contemplated the shallowness of humane understanding around him, he declared that he felt like "a prisoner in the midst of liberty."

If American women, for example, were to win the ballot, would they be a liberalizing force? Surely not. They would only help tighten the stranglehold of moral police and clerical power over social freedom. German women must counterbalance these tendencies. They must join with German men in resisting "temperance tyranny and religious fanaticism." The woman's rights movement must think more in terms of *common rights*. The women must learn that they had identical class interests with other disinherited people of both sexes. The question of whether women had come to understand the nature of their cause would be answered when women's groups came to the support of every radical cause. With regard to the marriage relationship itself, Heinzen offered little beyond his restatement of the principle that true marriages cannot keep separate accounts. Property had to be communal within the family lest financial barriers rise on what should be grounds of ideal mutuality.

Wilhelm Weitling, whose early visit to the United States in 1846 was interrupted like Heinzen's by the magnetic call to revolution in 1848, was closer to the scientific variety of socialist thinking. His career as a whole was of an essentially different order. Born the illegitimate son of a poor woman, he came to the radical frame of mind from his experience in the tailor's trade rather than in the intellectual atmosphere of a university. Likewise, Weitling's field for agitation was the working-men's organizations in contradistinction to Heinzen's journalistic approach to intellectual audiences. Weitling also had the benefit of some association with the priests of the new socialism, Karl Marx and Friedrich Engels. In spite of the fact that his rivalry with these leaders was keen enough for them to brand him with their choice derogatory epithet, "Utopian," he was close to their point of view on many a social question.

Not having the intellectual bent which normally leads to putting one's ideas into print, Weitling's influence was largely personal and organizational. His ideas on the marriage question therefore come to us only indirectly, through American republication of German imprints like *Des seligen Schneiders Weitling Lehre von Socialismus und Kommunismus* (New York, 1879). Like most other Utopians, Weitling felt that, if marriage was to be a happiness-producing human institution, it should last only so long as it served its function. But his "love, if you are able to love" did not in the least mean that he was proposing the dissolution of marriage. The socialist state, he asserted, would strengthen marriage by guaranteeing equal educational and social opportunity to boys and girls; the mating choice would then be freed from extraneous, distorting pressures. The sexual union would still further be strengthened by rendering married couples free of material cares.

∽ ∽

Karl Marx and Friedrich Engels, the architects of scientific socialism and the dominant segment of its brain trust, saw the family as a part of the pattern of economic relationships. In this view, it was meaningless to speak of marriage and the family without reference to a specific historical milieu. One also had to look at these institutional arrangements as they worked in each social class. It was one thing, said Marx and Engels in their *Communist Manifesto,* to examine the crass property relationship in the bourgeois family; it was another to see how the unpropertied working-class male dealt with his wife and children.

The *Communist Manifesto* protested loudly against the charge that socialists intended to do away with the family. The notion that communists would make common property of wives was but a figment of the bourgeois imagination. The misconception arose in the minds of bourgeois critics because the bourgeoisie treated its women as owned instruments of production; the communists proposed common ownership of the tools of production; ergo, the communists would socialize their wives. It was ironic, said the scientific socialists, that those who fashioned this logic were the same people whose factory system had destroyed families by separating mothers from their children and children from their families; the same people who had contrived to destroy the affectional family ties, replacing them with property relationships; the ones who were most guilty of marital infidelity and winked at prostitution.

As early as 1845, three years before the publication of the *Com-*

munist Manifesto, Marx announced his acceptance of the formula that human emancipation in the broad sense could be measured in terms of the status achieved by women. Engels elaborated the point in his ardently pro-feminist work, *The Origin of the Family, Private Property, and the State* which, published in 1884, soon went into several editions. American socialist readers got their first translation in 1902 from the Charles H. Kerr Press, an establishment cooperatively owned by some two thousand workingmen who subscribed ten dollars each to assure themselves of a literary output agreeable to their political tastes.[2]

Engels' treatise, using as a base the anthropological researches of the American Lewis H. Morgan as set down in his *Ancient Society,* was aimed directly against the usurping male rulers of the world. It wove its historical and sociological data into the Marxist design, demonstrating that both the form of the family and woman's status in it were dependent upon economic relationships. The family was shown to be a product of specific cultures rather than a divinely ordered institution. As the mode of producing material wealth changed, said the Marxist theorist, it induced changes in every aspect of social relationships, including the family. In primitive societies, where men and women had not yet divided community labors along sexual lines, male and female had very nearly equal power and prestige in society. The appearance of the first productive property—domestic animals—upon the economic scene, placed men in the dominant position. It was their task to manage and increase the family property, and preserve it for future heirs. The identification of heirs required a "one husband one wife" family. Hence the monogamous family and the father supreme.

Now, except for the time-lag when the family adjusted to changes in the productive machinery as well as to other social modifications resulting from these changes, the relations of the sexes were functional with relation to the prevailing economic system. The patriarchal family, according to the Marxist theory, not only prevented women from acquiring prestige in the economic world, but it also put them at a disadvantage in every other respect as well, producing the double standard of morality and all sorts of marital deception on the part of wives as well as husbands. True sexual attraction, a phenomenon requiring personal independence on both sides, could hardly be the controlling factor in marriage in a society that kept its women out of economic activity and prized the inheritance of family property so highly.

According to Engels, two major social changes would have to

[2] The influence of Engels' book on English language-readers in America antedated its appearance in translation by many years. The gist of Engels' thinking on women and the family came to this country by way of an 1886 translation of August Bebel's *Women in the Past, Present and Future.*

take place before women could really be emancipated from household slavery. First, the scale of production would have to become large enough both to demand the participation of women in industry and relieve them of domestic drudgery. Once they spent most of their time in a socially productive capacity, equality in all other aspects would not be far behind. This was already happening to some extent under capitalism, Engels noted, but there were too many conflicting claims upon women's energies under this contradiction-laden social system. The second change, the one to which socialism's enemies responded with greatest anger, was to be the social ownership of the means of production, plus community responsibility for education and the day-to-day care of children.

Women, relieved of constricting housework, would again be capable of an unhampered life of the affections. The elimination of the family as the basic unit of society meant the disappearance of the inheritance factor in family life. Young men and women, under socialism, would then marry for love alone. This type of marriage, the bourgeois, or middle class, ideal, would be socialist actuality for every one in a socialist society.

Nor did the original Marxists overlook the possible argument that economic security and independence might result in sexual irresponsibility and marital insecurity. Even economic determinists among the socialists could see the possibility of a free and unobligated woman philandering just as the male in contemporary society was wont to do. But there was a "scientific" answer for this fearsome prospect too. It was this: The very nature of sexual love produces a monogamous marriage form. Women had to tolerate erring husbands only because of their dependent status. The equal and financially secure woman under socialism would never play the multiple-mating game. Rather, her independence would make her husband toe the mark, with the result that monogamy would be the rule in accordance with nature's laws.

WOMEN UNDER SOCIALISM

If we were to measure the influence of Marx and Engels on the American view of family relationships by the number of Americans who were acquainted with *The Origin of the Family,* we should find such influence to be small indeed. For even if this text had been available in large numbers in the English language, it is questionable whether many readers could be found for it even among the adherents of the socialist International. The effect of this work must be traced through less sophisticated versions of its message and its implications. Such fare was supplied in magazines, pamphlets and popular books got out to keep the followers informed and to proselytize likely sectors of the bourgeois mentality. The nearest thing to Marx and Engels' masterworks were the writings of August Bebel, leader of the Marxist Social Democratic Party in Germany.

Bebel's reputation in America spread far beyond the circles of his comrades. He was without question the most powerful personality among the German socialists, even more influential than his co-worker, Wilhelm Liebknecht. American journalists knew him for his leadership of the opposition in the Reichstag before World War I. One magazine called him "The Red Pope," another, "The Red Napoleon." Bebel, who started his career as a turner, or lathe mechanic, became one of the leading figures of the communist movement, winning the reverence of no less a pair of revolutionaries than Lenin and Stalin.

The first American appearance of Bebel on the woman question came about through the agency of Lovell's Library of works of high social meaning. It was a translation of *Die Frau in der Vergangenheit, Gegenwort und Zukunft* (*Woman in the Past, Present, and Future*), by Dr. H. B. Adams Walther. The same work was published in later German editions as *Die Frau und der Socialismus* which was translated in 1904 from the thirty-third edition under the title, *Woman under Socialism*, by the American socialist leader Daniel De Leon. Another translation by Meta L. Stern from the Jubilee Fiftieth edition, appeared here as *Woman and Socialism*. At least two additional versions have been available to American readers—one a San Francisco edition, published by G. B. Benham in 1897, the other issued by Boni and Liveright in 1918.

The so-called woman question—actually the whole problem of family adjustment—became, in Bebel's hands, one more argument for doing away with the capitalist system. This area of human relations was, according to him, impossible to adjust under existing social and political institutions. The idea (one which American authors had already presented) that women must be dependent upon men because of their biological functions had been so ingrained in the permanent culture that servitude took the form of a habit which not even the slaves wanted to break.

Like all social revolutionaries who had the wit to know that it is bad to break completely with current customs, this interpreter of Marx and Engels accepted marriage as the basis for social development. But one had the choice of two kinds of marriage and it was best to see which was the more moral before making a selection. There was the compulsory, self-defeating form based on the bourgeois idea of property. Again, there was marriage such as would be possible only in a socialist society.

The moral superiority of the second choice was clear, especially if one considered the existence of prostitution as an accepted component of the capitalist sexual ethic. Along with the anarchists and militant feminists, Bebel made the point that loveless unions, perpetuated by law, were the equivalent of houses of ill-fame. He also called the attention of his readers to the manner in which society hypocritically averted its eyes and tolerated a moral code tailored to suit the male.

Marriage under socialism would be a private contract entered into by two parties without third-party intervention. Socialism, said Bebel, was not presenting an innovation in this respect. It was merely resurrecting a practice which prevailed before property relationships began to dominate social institutions, and it was adapting this practice to an advanced form of society.

The standard of morals envisioned by Bebel resembled that of the anarchists enough to negate all the protestations of the socialists about their belief in the marriage institution. Full democracy, equality, and education were, in Bebel's view, sufficient preparation to enable a responsible human being to live in a "love-and-let-love" society. Thus the formula: "Under the proviso that he inflict injury upon none, the individual shall himself oversee the satisfaction of his own instincts. *The satisfaction of the sexual instinct is as much a private concern as the satisfaction of any other natural instinct.*" All would go smoothly under the new dispensation. The very fact that intelligence and candor were to banish prudery and shyness in the future augured well for the adjustment of cases of strained relations between the sexes. "If incompatibility, disenchantment, or repulsion set in between two persons that have come together, morality commands that the unnatural, and therefore immoral, bond be dissolved." It is small wonder, then, that with socialist thought running on such themes, Karl Marx's daughter and her husband Edward Aveling should have been prompted to prepare lectures on Shelley's socialism.

∽ ✦ ∽

It was fortunate, in a sense, that socialist literature did not circulate too widely among non-socialist readers. For then it would have been the more difficult for followers of the International to talk their way out of charges of incitement to libertinism. American socialists, in any case, preferred to confine themselves to working within unions for better pay and conditions for women in industry. The reader of a paper like the *National Socialist* in the late seventies did indeed find articles on just such themes. But he also found that the editors of this paper, in their struggle against the ruling class, consistently defended anyone whose freedom had been infringed. Ezra Heywood's conviction for publishing obscene literature was condemned as "Another Stab at Liberty." *The National Socialist* also published a subscriber's letter in defense of John Humphrey Noyes' persecuted Oneida communists. The members of this community had violated no statute, this letter claimed. "These statutes do not make adultery a crime, nor prostitution; and even if they did, the practice of the Communists can be called by neither name." The editors of the paper added by way of comment that the character of the Oneida colony was one of fair play and honesty, and that the people were industrious, efficient, and capable. They were queer, but not wicked. As to their sexual practices, the editors did not, nor did they wish to know anything. If the Oneidans were satisfied, it was well. It was a case of "Judge not, lest ye be judged."

Socialists were indeed in a difficult position. They had, on the one hand, to uphold the freedom of minorities to behave according to the dictates of their own conscience. They had also to avoid offending the principles of morality accepted by the vast majority of potential converts to socialism. Moreover, their difficulties were frequently increased both by their iconoclastic allies and their fiendishly dishonest enemies. They were repeatedly assailed by an opposition literature which demonstrated the immorality of socialism by quoting unrepresentative passages out of legitimate socialist writings as well as by citing cunningly combined statements of socialists and anarchists. It was not hard to mix a little Bebel with Marx and Engels, then to fold in a sentence or two from the English socialists William Morris and Ernest Belfort Bax, season adeptly with Benjamin Tucker, cook in a well-heated oven until one got the following attractive product: "Socialism stands for free and irresponsible intercourse between the sexes, according as love or desire may dictate." This was exactly what the intellectually curious mechanic P. H. Scullin did in his *Socialism Means Slavery for the Working Man* (1910).

No doubt the expositors of socialism for the masses would have preferred to remain silent on a question which inevitably made everyone feel uncomfortable. But silence was an impossible tactic for workers in a cause which in so many ways could be made attractive to those working men and women who accepted the capitalist code of sexual morals. Popular alternatives to silence included an oath of allegiance to monogamy plus elaboration on what socialism could do to raise the status of women. This tactic was employed to advantage by Starkweather and Wilson in their pamphlet, *Socialism*, published in Lovell's Library in 1884. Written for the Pacific Coast Division of the revolutionary International Workmen's Association, the central theme of the work was that revolutions needed guns and dynamite —not votes. No sooner did these writers explain that society was composed of irreconcilable classes, than they hastened to assure readers that the social, sexual, and religious questions were not identical. Socialists were primarily interested in the first. The second and third were of consequence only insofar as they affected one's thinking about the first.

It was, for instance, the duty of socialists to let women know that the feminist movement was leading women into the same "delusion and snare" into which men had fallen, the delusion that the ballot can advance the cause of social equality. Socialists would have nothing to do with those "long-haired, mush-headed, sentimental idiots," the suffragists. As far as they were concerned, women's right to vote was "their right to join with the priest and the politician in completing the enslavement and utter degradation of themselves and the man also." Without a thoroughgoing change in the economic structure of society, even the male citizen could not use his vote to advantage. Socialism came first, then suffrage.

The relationship between the class-struggle and problems relating to family, home, marriage, and the status of women soon became a favorite theme of party writers. It was their job to win women to socialism and, at the same time, to remove the stain of libertinism from the socialist banner. May Wood Simons made her contribution in *Woman and the Social Question,* published as the first volume of Kerr's Pocket Library of Socialism (1899). A careful selection of passages from works of Marxist and bourgeois scholarship demonstrated with ease that capitalism was not a respecter of sexes; it exploited women equally with men in utter disregard of chivalric ideals. The publisher Charles Kerr himself took pen in hand to write a materialist study of ethical conduct which he called *Morals and Socialism.* To his own contribution, which deliberately avoided the question of sexual ethics as being too individual a matter for philosophic treatment, he appended an extract from Ernest Bax's *The Ethics of Socialism.* Bax's purpose in this passage was to answer the accusation that socialists neglected the "higher ideals of Humanity for the affairs of the stomach and of still more despised organs." There were two possible roads to the attainment of the higher things in life—one through a denial of the basic needs, and the other through an opposite course, their satisfaction. The ascetic method, it seemed to him, drew undue attention to these lower functions because of ever-present deprivation. On the other hand, provide food, housing, clothing, fuel, freedom of movement, and adequate sexual satisfaction—and then you put humanity in the way of establishing and attaining ideal goals of existence.

DE LEON AND WOMAN SUFFRAGE

Socialist spokesmen were under compulsion to explain or rationalize the implication in their social theory that all institutions which had developed with capitalist blessing had something wrong with them. Once informed by Marxist theoreticians that monogamy had been adopted to suit the needs of private property, it was altogether reasonable to expect the uninitiated to inquire what marriage form, if any, the socialists favored. If bourgeois marriage was a failure, what then? Responsible spokesmen for American socialism replied that monogamy itself was fine, but that the capitalist system had put a blight on it. The bourgeois mind had made narrow materialistic interests paramount in marriage and had thereby foredoomed it to failure.

One of Bebel's translators, the erudite, stormy labor leader Daniel De Leon, wrote a preface to his translation to air his disagreements with the original. He would agree with Bebel that women of all classes were oppressed in modern society and that therefore the woman question was the weakest link in the capitalist mail. But he refused to accept Bebel's prediction of absolute freedom of sexual expression under socialism. Bebel's prediction, though unacceptable, was yet understandable, for De Leon recognized that a society in a state of decomposition would take to extremes of conduct.

> On the matter of "Woman" or "The Family" the divergence among our rulers is most marked. While both extremes cling like shipwrecked mariners to the water-logged theory of private ownership in the means of production, the one extreme, represented by the Roman Catholic church-machine, is seen to recede even further back within the shell of orthodoxy, and the other extreme, represented by the pseudo-Darwinians, is seen to fly into ever wilder flights of heterodoxy on the matter of "marriage and Divorce." . . . The former seeks to assuage her agony with the benumbing balm of resignation, the latter to relieve her torture with the blister of libertinage. Between these two extremes stand the gathering forces of revolution that are taking shape in the militant Socialist Movement.

Although De Leon had little confidence in the potential liberating force of woman suffrage, he supported the feminist movement in favor of it as he would support the demands of any other political minority. The same people who charged socialism with the intent to destroy American family life were also saying that woman suffrage would break up the home. De Leon's strategy was to answer in court for both suffrage and socialism. This he did in "The Ballot and the Class Struggle," a lecture which was still timely for republication in 1933 although it was originally delivered in 1909.

If the home was threatened by socialism, reasoned this dialectician, then it must be safe and sound under the wing of capitalism. But was it? Was it not capitalism that forced women into factories in search of subsistence while their babies were entrusted to charity nurseries? Was it not the same economic system that drew men far away from their families in search of jobs, and children from the security of their homes to earn a small contribution to the family's small income? Was it not under capitalism that the marriage rate was declining while the divorce rate rose—especially in capitalist circles? Was this the protection the capitalist system provided for the sacred American home?

"The ballot would render woman sordid," they said—the same ones who said that the working class thought of nothing but their bellies. What indeed, asked De Leon, had started the woman's rights movement if not the spontaneous indignation of one sex at the state of subjection to which manmade law had reduced her? If the revolt of the women had shown evidences of sordidness it was probably because unorganized womanhood had seized upon retaliatory weapons in order to make dramatic demonstration of the cruelty inflicted by the privileged male. The infamous state of morals attributed to workers in the cause of independence for women was really a reflected image of the features of current class rule.

Neither the male bourgeois nor his female counterpart was capable of advancing the cause of womanhood a single step. The first opposed woman suffrage, as De Leon put it, "gallantly, theologically, judicially, sociologically, biologically—according to the angle of his mental strabismus." His female partner and opponent made all sorts of wild sacrifices to gain her end. Both provided ammunition for the anarchist frame of mind which derided the ballot altogether. The quest for the ballot was not to be derided. Women had a common cause with other struggling groups like carpenters, teachers, and Negroes. They must all unite in working-class solidarity. "The Sex line disrupts—as craft, color, creed, or nationality lines disrupt; the class line solidifies the revolutionary forces of our generation."

RED KATE

Not as rigid as De Leon in her interpretation of the class struggle, but no less a thorn in the side of capitalist defenders, was the woman known to the press as "Red Kate." Kate Richards O'Hare, a popular Socialist propagandist whose career included an international secretary-ship in the Socialist Party of America, described herself as a *stir-rerupper*. In recounting her agitational life to a court which was trying her for intent to interfere with the enlistment and recruiting service of the United States, she boasted participation in many a reform movement. As a high-school girl somewhere around the turn of the century, Kate O'Hare had been involved in the temperance movement. As a young woman she had campaigned against the combine of politicians and vice interests. Her mature years were occupied with stirring up the working people to demand their proper share of the national income and the amenities of life. She had finally been arrested at Bowman, North Dakota, for making a speech on "Socialism and the World War." The same speech had been made around the country some one hundred and forty times without trouble from the law or from the audiences. The arrest at Bowman was but a single incident in an epidemic of arrests which caught many prominent Socialists, among them Victor L. Berger, Scott Nearing, and Eugene V. Debs. Mrs. O'Hare's identification with "the movement" is indicated by the names—Eugene and Victor—which she gave to her twin boys. She paid for her loyalties and affiliations with a five-year prison term in a Federal penitentiary.

The National Ripsaw, which changed its name in 1917 to *Social Revolution*, was Kate O'Hare's prime medium of self-expression. This monthly paper advertised and reported on her lectures. It published her editorial articles alongside those of the great Debs, Oscar Ameringer, and the Socialist poet H. M. Tichenor. *The National Ripsaw* spoke to the ordinary worker rather than to intellectual and parlor socialists. Its motto was "Blind as a bat to everything but right." It symbolized the force that "will never let up till the plunderbund is ripped to pieces." Addressed to the man in the street, it carried advertisements of the kind which have since been banned from consumer-minded radical publications. The "ads" offered a full line of nostrums for complexion troubles, wrinkles, ruptures, fits, piles, bed-wetting, and tuberculosis. A new eight-tone hearing aid was featured; remedies were offered for gray hair and obesity. The heavyweight champion, Jess Willard, testified that Nuxated Iron was the secret of his victories over Jack Johnson and Frank Moran. "John's Wife" told how John quit drinking after she slipped a few shots of Golden Treatment into his food.

Amid this array of cures for popular ailments, Mrs. O'Hare held forth as a roving reporter, as commentator on all matters pertinent to socialism, and as a specialist on suffrage and other subjects near to the hearts of women socialists. Her longer writings appeared in the *Rip-saw Series*, a set of tracts devoted to various reform causes. To this series the socialist correspondent H. G. Creel contributed his *Prostitution for Profit; a Police Reporter's View of the White Slave Traffic;* Scott Nearing wrote one on *The Germs of War;* Tichenor wrote on *Woman under Capitalism;* James O'Neal on *Sabotage.* Kate O'Hare's pamphlets reflected her interests past and present. Some titles were *Liquor Traffic, The Church and Social Problem, Common Sense and the Few Abnormally Sexed,* and *Law and the White Slaver.* Her big point throughout was that prostitution was a product of the economic system which kept women in a state of dependence. To those moral physiologists who thought in terms of hypersensuality, Mrs. O'Hare offered the information that there were mighty few oversexed children in evidence, most of them to be found in the upper classes whose children were reared on pleasure.

The grand treatment of marriage and sex, the one which covered, according to *The National Ripsaw,* "the whole field of human interest and stands today as the greatest Socialist propaganda book in the English language" at one dollar bound and fifty cents with paper covers, was Kate O'Hare's *The Sorrows of Cupid*. Based on the same author's *What Happened to Dan*, a book which had been published in 1904, *The Sorrows of Cupid* was Mrs. O'Hare's elucidation of economic determinism, using the sex question as her vehicle.

The method was to develop each aspect of the sex problem in such a way as to lead up to a cumulative indictment of capitalist economics, law, and morality. Under "Life's Annals" she taught that the primal urges of sex attraction and reproduction were being opposed in our society by late marriages. An increasing number were not marrying at all. Marriages were falling apart under the corrupting influence of a badly organized society, and the remedy, that is, the divorce court, was "proving to be a cure worse than the disease." Net result: Fewer babies were being born.

The capitalist system was unquestionably responsible for decreasing marriage and increasing divorce. A young man preferred the prostitute to the bride because he abhorred subjecting the girl he loved to a life of poverty. Rather resort to a prostitute than drag another being down with him, to say nothing of the risk of rearing children destined to share their parents' hunger pangs. The social and economic environment of capitalism produced marital unhappiness which in turn was the cause of divorce. Divorce was a makeshift and a disgraceful method of dealing with so fundamental a part of life as the problems of marriage. The guilt, again, lay at the door of the capitalist system. It alone was to blame for broken ties and the fettering of Cupid.

When Mrs. O'Hare looked for "A rift in the lute," she found several. If one accepted the reasonable assumption that marriage had to be based on a sharing of ideals and on intellectual equality, one had to admit that the very foundation of marital happiness was missing in our society. For one observed that the domestic balance usually had a pretty thing on one side and a bank-book on the other. But suppose that male and female did start off at parity. They soon grow apart. Their development is unequal. The wives of the rich are chained to social obligations; the wives of the poor, to stoves and washtubs. Then what happened? The menfolk started looking elsewhere. If there is no divorce, then two prostitutes materialize where only one stood before—one legalized, one not.

There were other disturbing influences that made the sweet bells sound out of tune. One was bad health, another the lack of sex education, and still another, the teaching of fallacious ethics. Boys were indoctrinated with the double standard; girls with a horror of matters sexual. When the two married, misunderstanding was inevitable, with divorce following not far behind. All this was the fault of the social system. Intemperance was another cause for divorce. So was the fact that girls were ill-prepared for homemaking. These evils too were traceable to poverty and the labor system of capitalist society.

Added to capitalism's gifts to humanity—gifts of frustration, divorce, and prostitution—was race suicide itself. There were, according to Red Kate, two drains upon the race, thanks to which population was quickly disappearing. Not only were economic conditions forcing women to means—sometimes desperate means—of preventing motherhood, but the industries and mines were killing off children almost as fast as they were born. Poor housing and unemployment were adding their contribution to the debacle.

Mankind, therefore, and most particularly womankind, had all to gain by supporting a transition to socialism. The working class, among whom alone the practice of monogamy was a reality, would set the fashion in the new society. A perfect equality of the sexes, plus reeducation toward a single standard, would place love on the throne again. When a woman wanted to bear a child under socialism, she would have the whole of society behind her; that is to say, the full product of her husband's labor would be available to meet the family's needs.

This was socialism from a woman's point of view, a point of view which Mrs. O'Hare injected into her attempts to stir people up to do something she wanted them to do. Some of the most objectionable sentences in the pacifist speech for which she was jailed had to do with the debasement of motherhood in Western civilization by capitalist warmakers. If any of the men in her audience, this female orator challenged in the summer of 1917, thought that Socialism was going to degrade women, they ought to look at the lust and rapine that ran riot in war-torn Europe. Not only had Europe's womanhood to endure the filthy embraces of enemy soldiers, but they had also to suffer greater degradation at the hands of their own leaders in church and state.

> When the governments of Europe, and the clergy of Europe, demanded of the women that they give themselves in marriage, or out, in order that men might "breed before they die," that was not a crime of maddened passion, it was the cold-blooded crime of brutal selfishness, and by that crime the women of Europe were reduced to the status of breeding animals on a stockfarm.

The host of illegitimate children of battle-scarred Europe had been born out of war—not Socialism. These children, who would never know their fathers or even their fathers' language, had been born out of and into conditions so unnatural, that they could never grow up to be normal human beings. Physicians operating at the front had already described the situation as a nightmare. Children had been born with every conceivable mental and physical deformity. They were monstrosities destined ever to be a curse on society. And remember, cried Kate O'Hare, "remember, you dear old, rock-ribbed, hidebound, moss-backed democrats, these are not socialist babies—they are war babies."

There was much that capitalism would have to answer for to women, and Mrs. O'Hare did not overlook the theme when delivering her farewell address in twenty-four cities before giving herself up to the United States Marshal in March 1919. By this time, the Russian revolution had been accomplished and the O'Hares had stayed with the left wing of their party. The farewell address therefore had to do with *Americanism and Bolshevism,* emphasizing the revolutionary tradition in American history as well as in the origins of Christianity itself.

Women were now to be reckoned among the great revolutionary forces. They had had a great awakening in the war, which, by the way, had been started without women's consent. They had sacrificed their menfolk—sons, brothers, husbands, and lovers. They had accepted wheatless, meatless, heatless, and eatless days. They had filled men's places in the factories in order to keep the battlefront well-supplied. And, now, having helped make the world safe for democracy, the Congress of the United States had refused to give them a vote in American democracy. More than that! Women had had their first taste of decent wages during the war. Now the veterans were taking their jobs away and working women were being recommitted to the slavery of some other woman's kitchen or to the drudgery of sweatshops. Women would revolt rather than go back!

SOCIALISM FROM THE GREEN MOUNTAINS

While the O'Hares were crying out for social justice to women and children from their headquarters in the Middle West, another voice, more patient and more reasoning, was emanating from Vermont. This was the voice of the English-born socialist, John Spargo. *Rip-Saw's* Allen W. Ricker was probably more concrete in his elucidation of the Socialist position on love and marriage, but Spargo was published by the regular press and his works were widely reviewed in magazines of mass circulation. Ricker, in his *Free Love and Socialism; the Truth as to What Socialists Believe about Marriage,* named the names connected with the bourgeoisie's sex scandals, quoted statistics on marriage, divorce, and prostitution, and (having himself been a minister) gave specific instances of the church's inability to deal with such matters. Spargo reasoned sweetly and vaguely about socialism's spiritual values and about making the world safe for motherhood. Spargo was sure that socialism would usher in unvarying monogamy.

A contemporary book-reviewer was in the right when he characterized John Spargo by his "frantic desire to appear more levelheaded than other Socialists." Spargo's technique was more effective; his works drew warmth rather than fire from critical readers. His early books on humane subjects were well received. His *Bitter Cry of the Children* had great effect on the child welfare and anti-child labor movements. The *Review of Reviews* called his *Socialism and Motherhood* a "very sane and wise book." Spargo's *Applied Socialism* and *Common Sense of Socialism* were also generally acclaimed.

It was the custom of this practicing socialist, who was for several years on the national executive committee of the Socialist Party, to devote some part of his popular treatises to banishing the ghost of free love from socialism's abode. He never tired of restating the fact that the socialist fold enclosed no greater percentage of promiscuous members than the Republican or Democratic party, and that as great a proportion of professed Christians as of Socialists believed in free love. The difference lay in the amount of publicity given by the press to a socialist involved in such matters as against that given other citizens. Spargo could cite two parallel cases, both from the year 1908. One was that of a socialist who obtained a legal divorce and then remarried: there followed hundreds of editorials and sermons attacking socialism. The other was that of an Episcopalian clergyman who left his wife to live with another woman, neither the leaving nor the living with benefit of clergy. Did any one attack the Christian religion on that account? Indeed not. The whole affair was given the quiet treatment.

As many times as Spargo protested the injustice done socialism on the subject of sex relations, never did he devote his scholarship and rhetoric to the theme as effectively as in *Socialism and Motherhood* (1914). The best possible explanation for the extensive and separate treatment given here was that women seemed on the verge of gaining the ballot and therefore needed to be addressed as a distinct group on this much misunderstood and highly controversial matter.

Now, what was the promise of socialism to working-class women? The promise was equal rights with men in all life functions shared with men, plus the right to enjoy motherhood in health and safety. Motherhood was woman's holiest mission and socialism would give her triple-A priority to do the job of body- and soul-building for the young. "Nothing," insisted Spargo, "can take the place of maternal affection and attention. From time to time amiable theorists—generally childless!—have propounded plans for supplanting the individual mother in the rearing of children. All sorts of communal nurseries with 'scientific management' have been advocated. . . ." In reality, science supported Socialism in its claim the women had to be freed for the practice of motherhood.

Socialism from Robert Owen's day onward, Spargo continued, had thought in terms of the environmental influence on personality growth. Mothers were key figures in the child's environment.[3] Socialism, said the Green Mountain socialist, must make a powerful appeal to the mother instinct. It carried a message of security—of Life and Liberty and Love. It promised the mothers equality with the fathers of the race. "Socialism comes to the mother as an Angel of Light and Life, bearing the torch of a great hope. . . . And the mother yearns to take the Angel's gifts, but does not. Fear holds her back. She is the Slave of Fear."

What was this fear that kept mothers from accepting the angel's gifts? It was the myth that socialism's adversaries had taught them to believe, the fear that socialism would rob them of the security of husband and family. Whence did this myth arise and how did it grow? There was no difficulty in placing the origins of the rumor that socialism would abolish the family. It came from Plato's *Republic,* which had the elements of property communism in it along with its outré notions about community of women and state care for children. Spargo, speaking for modern socialism, held nothing in common with Plato but the broad aspects of public ownership of productive property. Those who would associate Plato's ideas on marriage with socialism, or even with modern anarchism, did not understand either the Greek philosopher or modern social philosophies. Plato prescribed a system of state regulation of mating—the very opposite of free love doctrines as currently understood. As far as most socialists were concerned, legal marriage seemed best adapted to produce greater stability of the sexual relationship. But law, representing social authority, could work only when it was abetted by personal loyalty and affection. One would not, therefore, want to abolish marriage but would improve it by social and economic adjustment.

But Plato had only started the disease. Socialists had been tagged with every existing kind of deviation from Christian marriage, including Shakerism, Noyesism, and Mormonism. This was in truth a tribute to the popularity of socialism, since almost every great popular movement in history had been charged by its enemies with plotting to abolish marriage. Catholics made this charge against Protestants, and fanatical Protestants viewed Catholic celibacy as an entering wedge

[3] Spargo explained that socialism did not reject the idea of hereditary influence in favor of the slogan that all were born with equal ability. The socialists argued with eugenists only when the latter claimed that you must improve society genetically. Socialism desired to see improvement for all through equal opportunity. It wished to model society after the family itself, giving opportunity to all members to use the household goods in common.

against marriage. The charge was levelled against the Chartists in early nineteenth-century England. This convenient fabrication had been used as well against American abolitionists, against the pioneers of the woman's rights movement, and against the founders of the Republican Party in 1856. The preposterousness of the accusation was best illustrated by an anti-Lincoln cartoon of 1860 which showed Lincoln riding into a lunatic asylum astride a rail carried by Horace Greeley. The members of the entourage were identified by the legend above their heads. One short-haired woman, obviously a Fourierist, was saying: "Oh! what a beautiful man he is. I feel a passional attraction every time I see his lovely face." Then followed long-haired men, one of them saying "I represent the free love element," and another, "I want religion abolished and the book of Mormon made the standard of morality."

If the socialists had to dispose only of these irresponsible accusations, said Spargo, things would be simple. But there were, unfortunately, individual socialists, who espoused foul ideas whose odor clung to the socialist cloak. There were the self-styled socialists like the poet Oscar Wilde and the biologist statistician Professor Karl Pearson. Wilde had written wildly in his *The Soul of Man under Socialism*, published in the United States in 1911, that socialism would annihilate the present form of the family. What did he know of socialism, who, throughout his book on the subject, spoke more like an anarchist communist than anything else? Pearson, for his part, had proposed planned mating on the order of Plato's system, adding the feature that childless women could take marriage or leave it in accordance with their emancipated inclination. Pearson, the population engineer, was a combination of anarchist and bureaucrat. Perhaps one in a thousand socialists would accept his ideas.

And what of August Bebel? Yes, Bebel was a socialist, one smart enough to know that his words would be distorted and used in the continuing war against socialism. He therefore made sure to say in the preface to his *Woman under Socialism* that his ideas were his own and not those of the party. As he predicted, the dishonesty of socialism's foes was general: in the six hundred books, pamphlets, and magazine articles where Spargo found Bebel's words quoted to prove that socialists advocated free love, there was not one mention of Bebel's dissociation of his own ideas on marriage from those of socialists as a party. Of the Englishmen William Morris and Ernest Bax, there was little to say except that they were atypical. Bax was so atypical that he even opposed woman suffrage on the ground that women were organically inferior to men. The ideas adopted by this handful of otherwise good socialists had been borrowed from anarchist teachings. Socialists believed in stable monogamy and were confident that it would be achieved once women had been emancipated economically. The socialism of the future was not more of a threat to marriage institutions than was the collective ownership of streets and highways at present.

The intelligent woman of the twentieth century, Spargo believed, would readily see that socialism was as incompatible with anarchic free love as it was with Pearson's directed mating. An effective socialist government might indeed encourage breeding of the fit and discourage the contrary, but it would never compel. Such a government would institute education for parenthood. It would fully educate all women so that they could make better decisions and abandon distracting fears. So then, ladies, concluded the persuasive Spargo, do not be afraid. Come one, come all, into the socialist fold.

Until 1917 the O'Hares and the Spargos were operating each in his own medium but nevertheless in the same camp. In the inner party struggle over America's entrance into World War I, Spargo parted ways with the left-wing socialist elements because their pacifism rubbed his patriotism the wrong way. The successful Bolshevik revolution shifted his literary efforts into the anti-Soviet mould. From 1918 to 1921 he wrote prolifically of Lenin's unfree Russia. At this point the direction of his interests changed suddenly. He now became a specialist on early American pottery and confined the outpourings of his pen to the role of Benningtonites (of Bennington, Vermont) in the American Revolution. His earlier role as a dignitary in the Socialist Party was replaced by honorary public posts and trusteeships. When asked in 1945 how his political thoughts ran, he replied that he still felt as he had for a long time that the problem of socialization was a spiritual one, and that spiritual methods had to be employed to bring about results in kind.

THE PARTY LINE

The revolutionary socialists, it is well known, became the American Communist Party, whose line on marriage and the family—and on many other issues—slowly but surely came to follow the shape of things in the Soviet Union. The era of theorizing was over. When asked how the communist would work out a given social problem, a finger was pointed eastward to *the source*.

The answer to the woman question was not broadcast to America from the Soviet Union until the early 1930's. The reasons were twofold and complementary. For one thing, society in Russia and its companion countries was still making its own very radical adjustments in the twenties. For another, the woman and marriage problem in America did not reach the critical point until the depression of the thirties, when women found themselves losing in the competition for jobs in industry and were also deprived of the safety of marriage. The economic wall which separated men and women from marriage was well-nigh insurmountable. The position of women in society was truly in a stage of crisis.

Naturally, this was a favorable climate for introducing Lenin's *Women in Society* as well as for distributing descriptive pamphlets on family life and woman's status in the Soviet Union. The collective story told by these pamphlets was that the Communist revolution was slowly but surely liberating women from the shackles which bourgeois maledom had placed upon them. The revolution had exposed the economic and political roots of inequality. Full emancipation was to be realized as soon as the whole of society had been reorganized. On November 19, 1918, Lenin promised the first all-Russian Congress of Women Workers that the Soviet Republic would establish complete sex equality. He announced that his government had already "abolished the source of bourgeois filth, repression, and humiliation—divorce proceedings." Marriage, free of the imposition of churches, could now be registered and unregistered with ease. It might take the backward ruralites time to shake themselves loose from the past, but they would learn.

Neither women nor children would have to endure the handicaps of capitalist civilization. There was to be no difference between children born in wedlock and out of it. The state would care for all mothers and all children. Women would also be liberated from kitchen slavery. The tendency of capitalism to foster corporate activities had produced such things as public dining-rooms, kindergartens, and nurseries on a small scale. The Soviet Republic would adopt these ideas on a large scale. Publicity, propaganda, and education were to spread the word of womanhood's new dignity and teach the way to accomplish it. Opportunities for women were to have as little limit as those for men. Some fifteen years later the Stalin Constitution wrote political and social equality for women into its articles 122 and 137. The right to work for the same pay as men received became a constitutional right, as did the rights to rest, leisure, social insurance, and education.

Nowhere in the depression thirties was the party position on sex more fully aired than in *Health and Hygiene,* the magazine published by the Daily Worker Medical Advisory Board. Here, amid advice to the masses to be on their guard against fake cures for colds and constipation, the editors served a lavish sprinkling of articles on marriage and sex hygiene. It was one thing to advertise the excellent appointments of Soviet abortoria—a letter from a recent patient testified to the fine care she got in one of them—but it was something else to advise the American proletariat what to do about their problems in the family way. Not only did the fake morality and censorship of capitalism deprive the masses of services and information (purposely to keep them in ignorance and slavery), but some capitalists were also growing fat on sales of abortifacient pills which *never* succeeded in disposing of a really and truly fertilized ovum.

There were problems enough in attaining sexual balance, in the eyes of the *Daily Worker* medicos, without the complications caused by capitalism and its moral arm, the church. For, however personal these problems may seem to the afflicted, they were in reality very closely connected with the social situation. It was, for example, popular in the thirties to attribute frigidity in married women almost wholly to their husbands' untutored approaches. This was admittedly partly true, but, according to the best in socially conscious psychiatry, it was only a very small part of the truth. The larger picture was one in which full, uninhibited self-expression had been so completely denied girls and women in our society that they were incapable as wives of responding with spontaneity to their husbands.

The very manner of their reception at birth—with the fuss made over boys and a "never mind, the next will be a boy" for girl babies —was a symbol of their inferiority. Now, girls reacted very early in life to this unfavorable treatment; and, although their repressive mechanisms were efficient, they bore the scars of resentment in the subconscious. Without really wanting to, they avenged the wrongs of womanhood by not participating fully in the joys of marriage. Adding to the difficulty were the scars left from an improper sex education in childhood, an education which sanctified and vilified sex alternately leaving the youngster unprepared to meet it squarely and honestly. The cure for mass female frigidity was social, although individual male tenderness, affection, and encouragement would help build the self-confidence necessary to accomplish a cure.

If the economic origins of male privilege were by chance unconvincing, the economic implications and consequences of male rule certainly became manifest in social crises. The women's rights that had been won in a century of struggle were obviously not permanent. The earliest victims of the world depression of the thirties were the women careerists. They were the first to lose their jobs to make room for unemployed men. In the last analysis, there was a direct relationship between the degree of exploitation of the masses and the status of women. Fascism merely exaggerated the picture by destroying woman's status completely.

Sex was awarded perhaps more than its just share of space by the editors of *Health and Hygiene*. The cynics were doubtless thinking that the communists used it as political bait. The editors, in stating the objectives of "A Healthy Sex Life," implied that they were catering to the needs of an anxious, insecure people whose social isolation led them to crave love and attention in its sexual forms. The fight for economic and social security was by inference a striving for a more wholesome and richer mode of sexual expression.

For the time being it was the duty of the communists, as the masses' best friend, to help alleviate their emotional discomfort. "Advice" covered the full span of problems, from the solitary vice—

no longer a *bête noire* let loose on the young in the form of religious scare stories, but a lesser evil than celibacy—to "change of life."

The knottiest advice problem of the depression decade was what to tell young couples whose family responsibilities stood in the way of marriage. The staff psychiatrist who essayed an answer started with the premise that unfulfilled stimulation over a long period of time was positively harmful. Diminished potency, even partial frigidity, were possible consequences. Nor was the psychiatrist, though he thought little of conventional morality, ready to advise living in sin. Couples, he said, who had been brought up to respect legal marriage, would develop nagging guilt feelings such as would surely interfere with their relationship. The male member might even start harboring a disrespect for his wife who had done something which (as his super-ego whispered to him) no respectable girl would do. He therefore suggested marrying and living each with his own family for the time being. The response from readers was indignant. A doctor who had only this to advise was certainly over sixty and therefore beyond the age of understanding. Nor could he be much of a Marxist who thought the economic situation was temporary. The capitalist world, everyone knew, had entered its permanent, and last, depression.

America did not have to depend entirely upon "red pamphlets" to get the proper slant on the developments of marriage and morals under socialism. There were several competent—by non-socialist standards—observers who went to see the experiment and who subsequently reported in book form both on what they had seen themselves and what they had learned from reading. Among the earliest of such books was Jessica Smith's *Woman in Soviet Russia* (1927). Then, in 1929, the rebel publisher Haldemann-Julius issued Anna Louise Strong's *Marriage and Morals in Soviet Russia*. In the years 1933 and 1934, two attractively written works gave considerable authority to favorable reports already known to Americans. They were *Red Virtue* by Ella Winter, wife of the famous "muckraker," Lincoln Steffens, and *Russia, Youth, and the Present-Day World*, by Dr. Frankwood E. Williams. Miss Winter had among her credentials a good training in economics and psychology plus long experience as a journalist. Dr. Williams was a prominent psychiatrist and a leader in American mental hygiene circles.

The most attractive note struck by these books, which found many eager readers in America, was that one of the most disturbing features of marriage in other societies was being quickly eliminated from Soviet marriage. That factor was fear. The point had great propaganda value in depression-bound America. Couples here refrained from marriage because they feared the prospect of unemployment and starvation wages. Under Socialism this fear had been removed. Young people who braved marriage in the depression economy feared pregnancy and the possibility of another mouth to feed. In the Soviet Union, information on contraception was supplied by public agencies and abortions were performed upon application to a state clinic. There were still minor hitches, but they would be remedied in time. But at present, for instance, unsophisticated women, especially those of peasant origin, might not understand their instructions. An obstacle even more difficult to surmount was a shortage of materials. The question of abortions looked simpler, except for the fact announced by one Moscow citizen (not quoted in the current literature) that "the child is twelve years old before you can get admission to the hospital." Besides, physicians tried to discourage women on medical grounds. But these deficiencies of a material order would be rectified by planning.

The entire concept of love, so the predictions went, would undergo a process of change in adaptation to collective ownership of the tools of production. There had been a tendency in the earlier post-revolutionary years to deride every old concept of sex ethics as bourgeois, and, in consequence, to discard moral barriers completely. The leaders of the revolution were rigid in their discouragement of this tendency. Lenin's "muddy glass of water" theory covered the subject. The point was: take your sex clean; you would not think of drinking a muddy glass of water.

Lenin, it is reported, once said to his fellow-revolutionary Clara Zetkin that the movement wanted neither monks nor Don Juans. It wanted people who could satisfy all their appetites in moderation. Many of the leaders of the liberated proletariat had interpreted their liberation too generally and had soon demonstrated their inability to keep their minds on the revolution. As a consequence of reform, it seemed to an observer of the thirties that a Puritan attitude prevailed in Moscow. The Soviet leader had to be careful. He could be purged from the party for personal as well as political deviations.

All seemed to be going well on the love line of the socialist revolution—so well that many a reviewer of these reports remarked that they sounded like chamber of commerce literature. Of all the subsidiary problems that arose in connection with the doings of male and female, only one seemed not yet on the way to solution. What would happen to the family under the new dispensation? To the leaders who were shaping the new society, it had seemed necessary to eliminate the worst aspects of bourgeois morality such as the restrictions on woman's freedom, the difficulty of divorce, marriage of purses, illegitimacy, and the legal ban on abortions. This they did. But then what?

Was it desirable at all to preserve the blood-related family now that all economic, educational, welfare, and recreational activities took place outside of the home? At one time it seemed to some that life in the commune had become so enriched that no one would miss the family unit. They spoke of the plausibility of adapting family feelings to the wider group, thus preserving the good features of the family form. It was probably the observed needs of children that changed this view later, for very soon one heard that monogamy was not being advocated for itself but because it was best for a child to have one mother and one father. In 1944 a *New Masses* writer described the Soviet family as a biological and spiritual unit.

With matters taking such a direction, the old provision for merely registering oneself out of a marriage with as little trouble as one contracted the marriage originally, had to be changed too. The earliest device used to reduce the number of divorces was the institution of stringent alimony laws. Later it was required that both parties appear before the registrar upon the application of one party for a divorce. Reconciliation was attempted and only when divorce seemed unavoidable was it granted—on the payment of a sizeable sum by the applicant. In 1944, the problem of population entered the picture. With war casualties reaching enormous proportions, every inducement for building families had to be offered; every move to destroy them had to be discouraged. A tightening of divorce procedures was decreed alongside of tax and subsidy rewards for large families. The new regulations required the divorce-seeking couple to appear before a people's court whose function it was to urge them against their plan of action. This failing, the case went before a higher court which heard the appeal for divorce. Costs rose from 50 rubles to from 500 to 2000, plus a hundred ruble fee to accompany the application. It began to look as if those antiquated, degrading, and insincere bourgeois divorce regulations might be easier on a man and wife seeking release from each other than were the new socialist laws.

But the final word had not yet been said. On April 24, 1948, the *Nation's* correspondent, Alexander Werth, reported from Soviet Russia that a still greater stiffening of divorce laws was in the offing. The public was being prepared from the lecture platform, said Mr. Werth, who had only recently listened to a very well attended talk by a Professor Kolbanovsky on "Love, Marriage, and the Family in Socialist Society." All was not as pure in socialist society as the surface indicated, the lecturer declared. Socialist leaders were still being haunted by the ghosts of certain "Marxist" theorists who claimed that the family was a bourgeois institution ready for the refuse heap. The fact was (by this time the refrain was familiar) that monogamy had its best chance under socialism. Love indeed had a biological basis, but communists abhorred *mere* biology. They believed in "the complex structure of spiritual, mental, and social processes that constitute love proper."

A happy combination of all these elements was now possible

under the rational arrangements of socialism. Besides, the family could grow to any size without fear of economic repercussions. Everything was planned to enhance the marriage comradeship of husband and wife. Then why think about divorce? Did jealousy enter the picture? Jealousy was an old bourgeois plant with property instincts at its roots. Jealousy led to disgusting situations unbecoming to socialists. Divorce was bad—especially because of the disastrous effects it had on a child's mind. "The sound family," the lecturer was reported as concluding, "was a vitally essential institution for the state, for the education of the young, and for the country's productive capacity."

Surely American communists, and those who read their literature in the depression thirties, ceased now to be struck by the simplicity of socialist solutions. They could, however, still point to successes in the areas of sexual equality, freedom of choice in marriage, and the banishment of the curse of illegitimacy. They could also recall another sexual project that had been brought to a successful conclusion, namely the eradication of prostitution.

The fight against prostitution received its loudest plaudits from Dr. Frankwood Williams. The socialist thesis that this most ancient profession stemmed from economic causes was dramatically demonstrated by the success of the Soviet technique of eradication by vocational retraining. The prostitute was not penalized by law; the entrepreneur and his salesmen were—and heavily. Institutions called Prophylactoria were set up to achieve the rehabilitation of Russia's *filles de joie*. Here they received medical care, food, and lodging. Not charity! For socialists ridiculed bourgeois philanthropy. Each girl earned enough by working to pay her way. She earned while she learned to read and write as well as to become a qualified worker.

To the American psychiatrist, all this seemed a humorous commentary, by contrast, on professional methods at home. In the Soviet Union they did not use words like *ego*, *libido*, and *sublimation*. They merely went ahead to restore the self-respect of maladjusted girls. They treated their physical ailments, taught them a trade, and gave them a sense of their own personal value and place in the normal scheme of things. From this point on, a system of personal conversion was used to advantage outside of the prophylactoria. In the manner of our Alcoholics Anonymous, a saved sister would go out and start the conversion of an unregenerated one.

The results, statistically, were amazing. Moscow before the Revolution counted 25,000 prostitutes. There were 4000 in 1924; 3000 in 1928; Dr. Williams reported some four to five hundred in 1932 and expected the problem to be "liquidated" within a year or two. Apparently it was. For Miss Winter reported the existence of a mere handful, patronized mostly by foreigners.

Doing away with prostitution had been easy. It proved that socialism could use its rationale in coping with a few of the evils besetting bourgeois society. The eyes of guilt-obsessed and fear-obsessed people were opened wide to the possibilities of socialism for themselves as individuals. Would the ever-present worries about family size and population control be managed as satisfactorily by the Communists as had these cognate problems?

The best in Marxist theory had as yet found no key to population management. Of a few things, however, theorists were certain. One of these was that overpopulation in capitalist countries was not a matter of there being too many people, but one of poor distribution of income. Marxists also knew that Malthus' theory—that population outdistanced the capacity to grow food—was patently untenable in an age of phenomenal technical progress. They knew that under socialism the equalization of income should enable the mass of the population to buy back what it produced; this balance would eliminate unemployment and solve the problem of overpopulation. Beyond this broad formula for an ideal society, the best generalization that could be arrived at was that the institutional variations in each society would set the pattern of its population problem.

The concrete situation that had to be faced by Communist leaders was little related to industrial production and employment. It was more a question of pressing the needs of the state against the wishes of its human members. An unexpressed plank in the woman platform of socialist movements had always been the relief from an ancient burden —that of bearing and raising large families. The early Soviet state, therefore, felt obliged to sacrifice principle to reality in the field of family limitation. All of its facilities for sex education and for the dissemination of information on the prevention of conception failed to prevent large numbers of undesired pregnancies. Women were led to decide in favor of abortion because of the straightened circumstances of life in the years following the Civil War. And, as the authorities put it, "the moral heritage of the past prevented women from making full use of the opportunities and rights the revolution had given them to perform their duties as mothers and citizens without any fear of the future."[4]

[4] Propagandists for communism in America failed to emphasize the element of expediency. The point to be made was that Soviet women had their abortions in state clinics without the dangers of secrecy and unsanitary conditions. This was 1921. Then the state machine instituted its campaign to discourage the practice, and in 1936, after a period of improving conditions, numerous meetings of working women (according to the official explanation) asked for a law prohibiting abortion in all but exceptional cases. Their wish was granted, and since then both the performer of the illegal operation and the patient are subject to sanctions. The doctor is liable to imprisonment. The patient is open to public censure. In cases of repeated violation, she may be fined in place of censure or may suffer both fine and censure. There were rumblings of dissent from the distaff side, despite the government's claim that the new regulation was a response to popular demand. As seen by the parties most interested, however, this was a form of unsocialist coercion in any woman's country.

SOCIALIST VIEW OF THE FAMILY

PLANNED SOCIETY AND PLANNED PARENTHOOD

Socialists of every variety had participated in American birth control thinking since the days of Robert Dale Owen. Voluntary limitation of family size appealed to them as it had appealed to other political groups which proceeded from rational and humane premises in their search for human happiness. Socialists generally answered to this description and were therefore fairly consistently to be found in the anti-Malthusian camp.

The outstanding socialist propagandist for population control after Robert Dale Owen was Annie Wood Besant, an Englishwoman who at one time described herself as a scientific socialist like Marx. Actually she was more closely related, during her socialist phase, to the gradualist group led by Bernard Shaw and Sidney Webb. Although Mrs. Besant did not visit the United States until the last decade of the century (by which time she had abandoned socialism for theosophy), her publications on marriage and birth-control were reprinted here and sold by the tens of thousands. Her fame began to spread when she and her freethinking colleague Charles Bradlaugh were haled into court in 1876 for publishing an old American birth control pamphlet, Dr. Charles Knowlton's *Fruits of Philosophy*. The prosecution failed and the principle of general dissemination of birth control information was established for England.

Soon after the trial, two of Mrs. Besant's popular works were printed in America and received numerous reprintings before the end of the century. The first, *Marriage; As It Was, As It Is, and As It Should Be*, sketched the story of marriage radicalism from Shelley, through Owen and the free thought heroes, then to free love advocates, and finally to her own thoughts on the question. These thoughts amounted to "monogamy for the children's benefit, but with divorce more available." The second work had sold thirty-four thousand copies by 1891. It was a thirty-cent pamphlet (cheap edition, fifteen cents) called *The Law of Population; Its Consequences and Its Bearing on Human Conduct and Morals*.

Here too the reader got a popular presentation of the population problem. Mrs. Besant attacked the class character of cruel, rich men's philosophies, from Malthus to the social Darwinists among her contemporaries who taught that the struggle for existence was necessary for the improvement of the human race. She pointed out that the race would actually deteriorate if the prudent, or fit, curbed their family size by late marriage and other means while the reckless, or unfit, married early and engendered children in large numbers.

After answering the main objections to birth control, she proceeded to demonstrate how each fighter for birth control had also been on the side of religious and political freedom. Some had argued on political and nationalistic grounds, having in mind the strength and wealth of their country side by side with utilitarian goals. Others had presented economic arguments, pointing out that the smaller the labor supply in a given trade or locality, the higher would be the wages of labor. For still others, the welfare of individual families was at stake. Individualistic protagonists of the population check had spoken in behalf of the physical and moral health of women. Finding these arguments unanswerable, Mrs. Besant next outlined the known techniques of contraception, indicating her preferences as she did so.

Although Mrs. Besant was not officially in the socialist ranks at the time she worked most vigorously for birth control, her credo contained many bywords of the movement for uplifting the disinherited. Said she: "We work for the redemption of the poor, for the salvation of the wretched; the cause of the people is the sacredest of all causes and is the one which is most certain to triumph, however sharp may be the struggle for victory."

The very same credo might also have been uttered by the mother of the American birth-control movement, Mrs. Margaret Sanger. However, it would be pressing a point very hard to say that Mrs. Sanger undertook her work of teaching the poor to limit their families because she was a socialist. The fact was that she was moved to adopt her career by her experiences as a nurse among the poor of New York's lower East Side. It was a coincidence that the living-room of the Sangers, William and Margaret, was a rendezvous for the best assortment of radicals America could offer in the years preceding our entrance into the first World War. Among the visitors could be found Bill Haywood, leader of the violent International Workers of the World, Emma Goldman's colleague Alexander Berkman, and John Reed, fresh from Harvard, and soon to write an on-the-spot report of the Bolshevik victory in his *Ten Days That Shook The World.*

Many of the Sangers' intellectual friends were parlor radicals; some were the practicing kind. People of every sort and class were "flocking to enlist under the flag of humanitarianism." Although Margaret claimed in her autobiography that she became involved in radicalism while innocently serving cocoa to her guests and arguing, for the sake of argument, on all sides of all questions, she was certainly ripe for participation in some one of the left-wing groups. By her own testimony, her intellectual sympathies were with the anarchists, but there seemed to her no practical way of attaining desirable human ends except socialism. She accordingly joined one of the socialist locals, an independent one, to be sure.

Mrs. Sanger's "assignment" was fashioned to fit her special qualifications. She was to do an organizational job among women's groups, teaching them the whys and wherefores of their grievances. They had so many questions to ask, most of them of a personal nature, that a friend suggested to Mrs. Sanger that she write down the answers in good form and try to get them published in the Socialist *Call.* The series was accepted, and appeared in the *Call* under the title, "What Every Mother Should Know." The success of this writing venture prompted its author to start another series on "What Every Girl Should Know." The U. S. Post Office stepped in by virtue of the authority vested in it by the Comstock Law of 1873, and the series died with its third or fourth installment.

But this was only one phase of the courageous Mrs. Sanger's essay in the field of journalism. In March 1914, the first issue of her short-lived *The Woman Rebel* came off the press, edited, managed, financed, and circulated by Margaret Sanger. *The Woman Rebel* was the essence of left feminism. Its slogan was: "No Gods, No Masters." Its objective, "to stimulate working women to think for themselves and to build up a conscious fighting character." Woman's rights and the Birth Control League were publicized alongside of the I. W. W., Mother Jones, and other symbols of radicalism. "Rebel thoughts" presented the words of Emma Goldman, Voltairine De Cleyre, Ellen Key, Olive Schreiner, and Helen Keller. Among the heroines whose biographies appeared before the law arrived to extinguish Mrs. Sanger's literary conflagration were "Mary Wollstonecraft: A Great Rebel," and "Louise Michel: The Red Virgin (1830-1905)."

However much Margaret Sanger may have wanted in later years to forget the episode of *The Woman Rebel*, she seemed never to forget the class significance of her struggle to free the channels of communication so that she might freely spread the science of planned parenthood. Her *Woman and the New Race*, which appeared in 1920 with a preface by the psychologist Havelock Ellis, was replete with references to the special meaning of birth control for the working class. It was the ignorant women of unskilled laborers' families who found themselves most frequently at the mercy of the abortion racketeer.

Workers, in fact, had everything to gain from keeping their family size down. The principle of fewer mouths to feed was immediately obvious to all. Then too, as Mrs. Besant and others had suggested, a scarcity labor market could be caused by a low birthrate in working-class homes. To date, the owning class had been able to hire labor aplenty at a wage calculated to insure bare subsistence and procreation. The *modus operandi* of the craft union must be adopted in the homes of all workers, Mrs. Sanger urged. Control the labor supply, and thereby control employment and wages to your own advantage.

∾ ∾

Socialists, as we have noted, were neither unanimous nor consistent. Their views on aspects of marriage and family life accommodated themselves to particular brands of political belief and tactic. On this, however, they were agreed always: Wherever the share of family functioning weighed oppressively on women, there was leveling to be done. They would relieve them of household functions by socializing these in a collective system. They would relieve women of childbearing that was detrimental to them as individuals or as members of working-class families. Outside the home, they would raise women to a position of equality with men in every respect.

Nineteenth-century theorists who questioned the values of monogamy, did so partly because they felt that woman had been the victim of the property system on which the monogamic family rested. By noting the connection between family relationships and the larger system of economic relationships, they clarified the linkage between woman's subordinate position in society and in the home. The ideological effect of socialist marriage literature has probably fostered the evolution of an inherently stronger family rather than caused the breakdown of this ancient social institution as was prophesied. If there were nothing else of benefit to society in the socialist and anarchist discussions of marriage reform and sex ethics, they at least did much to raise the level of treatment of these subjects to a more serious plane. The inconsequential talk and facetious advice of an earlier period were by no means obsolete at the beginning of the twentieth century. But the signs were that it was being overshadowed by the attempts of men and women of good will to apply swiftly accumulating scientific knowledge towards establishing a healthy balance between the rights of male and female.

NINE

Science Looks at Love and Life

The reader might legitimately conclude from what has gone before that only leftists, the advance guard in politics, and crackpots, have shown an abiding interest in the adjustment of sexual problems. This was definitely not the case. If one had to make a generalization, it would be closer to the truth to say that the problem was on almost everybody's mind most of the time. This state of anxiety on the part of each individual about his own thoughts and conduct—and everyone's else—remained inarticulate because of a grand social inhibition imposed by religious and moral codes. Only those who had the backing of a movement dared invade these restricted thought areas. Naturally such backing was to be sought and found only in movements which questioned the assumptions of the existing social order.

Other individuals who dared enter the no-man's-land of sexual ethics were members of the learned professions. Prestige could be relied upon somewhat to protect an outspoken professional, but even he often had to associate himself with some organized group for safety's sake. Without some mass following, even the most respected member of a community was in danger of losing his neighbors' respect, and possibly his very membership in the community. The only possible strategy for highly individualistic reformers was to play the humanitarian with all their might. The American mind often accepted otherwise suspect ideas if they marched in the humanitarian uniform.

Professionals who entered the battle over sex and the sexes almost always stood on the side of tradition. The ministry, except for a handful of freethinking renegades, was the mighty bulwark against all modifications of old mores. They defended their position with Biblical platitudes, resting on the authority vested in them by God at an earlier date. The lawyers, dependent by trade on older legal pronouncements, found it hard to look forward. They quoted Blackstone and the other legal worthies on all questions of social importance.

With all their opportunities for insight into human maladjustment, even doctors preferred to close their eyes—and, of course, those of their patients—to the host of urgent problems that arose from nature's sexual scheme. Such was the resistance of the medical profession to drawing the curtain aside that eager citizens considered themselves lucky when they had access even to fragmentary information. Permission to think, read, and perhaps talk about limited aspects of the sexual problem was sufficient relief for the time being.

The eighteenth-century physicians who wrote manuals of advice for brides and grooms supposed that their expert moralizing could quell a good deal of the unpleasant sound emanating from domestic frictions. Their common-sense suggestions on interpersonal relationships probably had a good effect on readers. But their refusal or inability to tackle sources of irritation of a more delicate order placed a severe limitation on their success in uprooting unwholesome aspects of marriage and family life.

The nineteenth-century physicians and hygienists who cared and dared were men—and less often, women—who came to their task out of a variety of motives. There were those who felt they must teach what they knew; perhaps they might also supplement their incomes by didactic writing. A few were led to study medical subjects by their own personal anxieties. Having been helped somewhat by their own acquisition of scientific knowledge, these self-cured doctors felt an obligation to pass their knowledge on to others. There was, of course, that large category of professionals who belonged to some social movement, serving it in the capacity for which they were best equipped. The mind of a freethinking, anarchist, Fourierist, or socialist doctor would naturally gravitate to speculation on matters that combined social with physiological interest. In the view of the nineteenth century German pathologist, Rudolph Virchow, a doctor's medical creed had of necessity to merge with his political and social creed. "As a natural scientist," he declared, "I can only be a republican, for the realization of the demands, which arise from the nature of man . . . is possible only in a republican state." Medical reform was, in his philosophy, to be postponed pending political victory by democratic forces.

FRUITS OF PHILOSOPHY

The backwoods Massachusetts physician, Charles Knowlton, liked to think that his fellow citizens persecuted him for sharing ideas with Robert Dale Owen, Frances Wright, and Abner Kneeland, the well-known Boston freethinker. Knowlton was right insofar as his troubles with the clergy arose out of his physiological approach to the study of the mind, an approach which ruled out the existence of a soul. But Knowlton's unpopularity was caused at least as much by his interest in birth control, an interest rooted more in his private life than in religious philosophy.

Knowlton's adolescence had been a stormy one—especially in its sexual aspect. He was chronically sick and depressed; and both his hypochondria and depression were connected with constant worry about sexual urges and their satisfaction. His formal education had been meager, but it was enough, when supplemented by what he learned for himself, to lead him to undertake a short-lived teaching career. He left the teaching profession because work in the schoolroom interfered with his main occupations of being sick, seeing doctors, and taking all sorts of medicine prescribed by them and by himself.

In 1821, shortly before he turned twenty-three, his health was restored. He had married Tabitha Stuart and made his first medical discovery, one that he emphasized throughout his medical career: early marriage was good medicine for youthful worries. At this point Knowlton's earlier difficulties disappeared, but new ones, connected with science and economics, beset him. With a wife on his hands, Knowlton decided to learn a trade and get a job. The vocation with which he had had most contact quite naturally appealed to him and he decided to become a doctor. By 1824 he had had enough apprenticeship, in addition to formal training at Dartmouth College, to permit him to hang out his shingle.

His student years were hardly the carefree kind. Young Knowlton was poor. To pay his way he went into the rather novel business of supplying anatomical specimens to the medical school. In consequence of his resourcefulness he had to face charges of grave-snatching. He was never convicted of this crime, but he did spend two months in a county jail for illegal dissection.

Medical practice did little towards making Knowlton solvent. He therefore decided to increase his income by writing a book on the physical basis of the mind. The product, *Elements of Modern Materialism,* appeared in 1829. Its contribution to psychology was considerable, but its sales were not. The author decided to "push" the book himself and went off on a sales expedition. Not only was the attempt a financial failure, but the young doctor was arrested at Amherst for peddling without a license.

Within a few years, Knowlton found himself the father of three, with prospects of solvency more distant than ever. When his practice should have been increasing, it fell off because he had earned the reputation of being a deist and an infidel. His old interest in sex revived. Charles Knowlton knew from his own experience the meaning of having too many children too soon. He was also witness to the economic despair into which his young married patients fell when their families grew faster than their bank accounts. His convictions were strengthened by his awareness of what happened to women's physical constitutions in these cases. Such were the conditions under which he set about to gather further information—from Owen's *Moral Physiology* and other works—toward preparing a little brochure for those of his patients most in need of advice on bearing fewer children.

Fruits of Philosophy; or the Private Companion of Young Married People appeared in January 1832. Its author was fined at Taunton and sentenced to three months at hard labor in Cambridge within the same year. The charge was "immorality." Abner Kneeland published a second edition the following year and thereby put himself in the line of fire. Although the book was met by a press conspiracy of silence, it sold well. The first edition was apparently read to pieces since nowhere in present-day libraries is a copy to be found. A tenth edition was published by private subscription in 1877. There were also numerous French, Dutch, and English reprints, the most famous of which was the one printed in England by Annie Besant and Charles Bradlaugh. This one, as has already been noted, sold over 300,000 copies in three years.

Whether or not it was the *Fruits of Philosophy* which invited public rage against its author is a moot question. Knowlton himself pointed out that copies of Carlile's *Every Woman's Book* and Owen's *Moral Physiology* were being printed and sold without exciting legal reprisals. He also said that a certain New York preacher had cribbed wholesale from his *Fruits of Philosophy* and had published a work just like it. No law was invoked against the preacher's book; why, then, against his? The answer was that the title page of Knowlton's work stated that it was by the author of *Modern Materialism*. This was in reality the book which the old guard really feared.

Knowlton protested time and time again that his book was intended to improve health and reduce immorality. The prevention was much more important than the cure which the McDowalls and Tappans were trying to effect in prostitute-ridden New York City. If any one of these pious gentlemen had written the *Fruits of Philosophy*, he would probably have been celebrated as a great benefactor of humankind by the selfsame people who were damning Knowlton so roundly.

The word had gone abroad that (in the words of the lawyer who prosecuted Kneeland in Massachusetts) *Fruits of Philosophy* was the "Complete Recipe how the trade of a Strumpet may be carried on without its inconveniences or dangers." With knowledge of contraception in the hands of all, female virtue was on the way out. To such charges, Knowlton replied indignantly that no girl should ever speak to men who had so low an opinion of women as to intimate that fear of pregnancy was the only thing which kept them virtuous. All fathers of young girls—and Knowlton qualified in this class—must also resent these innuendoes. Men who felt this way about women must have had a rather restricted sort of female companionship. Or, Knowlton added, "they must, methinks, have seen their younger days in times of 'bundling' memory."

From book to author was the logical transition. Knowlton had often to defend himself against character assassination. When accused of selling his book to young boys, he replied that he had kept its price high so as to keep it out of the hands of youngsters. He was branded "licentious" and was accused of being unfaithful in marriage. In answering his persecutors on one occasion, he indulged in a bit of self-revelation, saying that his slate was absolutely clean "with the exception of a trifling dalliance with a young lady so long ago that with me it was wholly out of mind, and under such circumstances, too, as clearly show that nothing objectionable was intended. . . . I make not, nor did I ever make any pretensions to angelic purity—indeed I am suspicious of those who do—I am flesh and blood, and bones, somewhat like other folks in all probability; but owing to my physical organization and to my studious habits, rather than to anything meritorious in me, I verily believe that there is not a man of my age in the town of Ashfield more *monkish* than I am."

Circumlocution was obviously not Dr. Knowlton's way. Perhaps that was what was so objectionable in the argument of *Fruits of Philosophy*. The sexual desire, he had written, was just another of the normal body appetites and had to be honored as such. Indulging it within reason resulted in health and satisfaction. Denial was probably harmful in itself; certainly denial did harm when it led to prostitution or the solitary vice. Celibacy was unquestionably an unwholesome state.

Birth control was positively necessary from many points of view. It was socially desirable inasmuch as it was the best way to counterbalance the population tendencies described by Malthus—famine, war, and disease were unthinkable as solutions. Birth control was on the side of individual welfare. It diminished the anxiety of fathers with regard to the financial support of their families. It guaranteed better training and greater opportunities for children born into small families. Women who bred fewer infants would enjoy better health and live longer. Their children would less frequently be weak and diseased. Marriage itself would come at an earlier age, thus lessening irregularity and immorality (chiefly among men). Marriage for love would become more common as the economic pressures were somewhat mitigated. There were eugenic values in birth control too. People with known undesirable inheritable tendencies, both physical and mental, could prevent the birth of unfit children. The possibility of positive eugenics—improving the species through controlled child-bearing—was also worthy of consideration.

These were the values, some of them borrowed from Owen's *Moral Physiology,* which Knowlton had in mind as he presented his discussion on the process of reproduction and the techniques of its prevention. His description of contraceptives was excellent for his time. His explanation of the physiological structure had its shortcomings, but it certainly lifted the subject of sex hygiene out of the realm of mystery and superstition. For superstition was his great enemy, the enemy which he chose for attack in his *Two Remarkable Lectures delivered . . . on the day of his leaving the jail at East Cambridge, March 31, 1833, where he had been imprisoned, for publishing a book.*

Even after he had cooled down and made his compromises with respectable society, Dr. Knowlton continued to argue the case for the free dissemination of ideas. His address to the Friends of Mental Liberty, a library association at Greenfield, Massachusetts, was a plea for the freedom of expression of new ideas without fear of community retaliation.

THE HEALTHIANS

It was really not the newness of unpopular ideas which incited people to violence against their purveyor. It was rather the threat of the new ideas to old ones. The liberal who presented his ideas on sex hygiene within the old framework could actually thrive on his books. This Knowlton's contemporary, William Andrus Alcott, proved by his prolific and successful authorship. Alcott was as eager as Knowlton to spread the gospel of health and hygiene, but his books had a pious cast and never tampered with the work of God.

At that, there was an unusual parallelism between the early careers of Knowlton and Alcott. William Alcott, who had gone to school with his more famous cousin, the transcendentalist Amos Bronson Alcott, later taught school, just as Knowlton had. But the pedagogical virus stayed in Alcott's system, and long after he qualified for the medical profession he worked hard for popular education—especially that phase of it which dealt with the development of physically sound citizens.

Though Alcott's interest in physical welfare seemed less personal than Knowlton's, he had experienced much anxiety during his teaching days because of repeated pulmonary ailments and attacks of rheumatism. His thesis at Yale in 1826 was on the prevention of consumption, the disease he thought he had. For such afflictions there was no simple and sudden cure, like Knowlton's marriage therapy. Alcott's ailments were so severe that he finally abandoned both the teaching and medical professions for educational editing and the writing of instructive popular books.

In 1826, Alcott met Sylvester Graham, that health crusader and vegetarian who combined business with faith by becoming a baker of whole wheat (Graham) bread. In the year following, Alcott and Graham were among the leading spirits in founding the American Physiological Society, whose membership counted more sick people than scientists. In his address before the first meeting of this group, Alcott demonstrated seriatim how people in each and every walk of life, however humble, however exalted, could benefit from knowing more about the science of life. The essence of the address was "Know thy body and preserve it well." With Knowlton, he recognized the intimate relationships of the senses, the brain, the nervous system, and the body functions. But unlike Knowlton, Alcott left religion in its traditionally superior position.

Physiology had very definite moral implications. Alcott came to this conclusion early in life and affirmed it in almost all of his writings. The lesson which ran through the *Moral Reformer*, the magazine he edited in 1835 and 1836, was that people overdid everything, living too fast and in too hysterical a manner. The *Moral Reformer* supported anti-corset societies, anti-gambling societies, and other "anti" movements. It was against ladies' dram shops, fermented liquors, smoking, late parties for young people, and even coffee, tea, condiments, and confections when not taken in the greatest moderation. The *Moral Reformer* favored bathing, drinking cold water, breathing fresh air, wearing sensible dress and taking regular exercise.

Dr. Alcott had much to say about what he apologetically called "physiological vice; that is, vice consisting in the depraved indulgence of the *three appetites*, or in the moral feelings brought immediately into action by their means." The three vices were intemperance, gluttony, and licentiousness.

Intemperance in this context meant more than the drinking of intoxicating beverages—although alcohol was the greatest offender, causing a national waste of $100,000,000 a year. Coffee and tea were included, their toll on the public pocket-book being estimated at $10,000,000 annually. Alcott had intimate knowledge of the use of stimulants. He had, during his schoolteaching years, tried alcohol and then opium pills in search of the stimulation he needed to carry on his daily work efficiently. His great discovery was that, though he taught better while under stimulation, the aftermath was depression, inefficiency, and the need for additional dosage.

The vice of gluttony likewise meant more to Alcott than mere overeating. It was the duty of the physiologist to bring home to people that they must stop swallowing "all sorts of improper excitants" like condiments, gravies, and the like. The eating of these overstimulating foods, it was claimed, led to a waste of $3,000,000,000 yearly in medicine, medical care, and loss of working time. Furthermore, there existed, according to this new school of physiology, a close connection between gluttony and sexual unrestraint. This theory, with refinements and modifications, has held its own among medical scientists down to our own times.

Of course, only a handful of nature faddists persist in going the same lengths as did the preachers of salvation via the gullet a century ago. Alcott's advice on plain cooking, given in his *Moral Philosophy of*

Courtship and Marriage, and elsewhere, made the point plainly enough. Cooking, he said, had a profound effect on the health, virtue, and vice of mankind. "Simple cookery promotes health, and virtue, and purity; just as complicated cookery has a reverse tendency. No man has ever become an adulterer, or a fornicator, or an idolater eating simples, such as plain wheat, corn, rye, potatoes, rice, peas, beans, turnips, apples . . . without any addition. Whereas the addition of butter, lard, sugar, eggs, pepper, ginger, spices . . . and even common salt to our dishes, has led thousands and millions of every age not only to vice and premature disease, but to that .bourne whence no traveler returns." Alcott felt too that suggestive literature, pictures, and songs did their part in inciting to licentiousness.

Intemperance and gluttony were costly to the purse. Licentiousness was costly to life itself. It killed millions each year and caused other millions to live a life of misery. This form of vice was all-pervading. It came in two forms—the solitary and the social. To those young people who were guilty of the solitary vice, Alcott, echoing the authoritative opinion of his day, promised every affliction from the common cold to idiocy, with St. Vitus dance, epilepsy, palsy, and blindness well within the realm of possibility.

The practitioners of social vice—that perpetrated in the company of one of the opposite sex—could expect horrible things to happen to them also. Threat number one, to be sure, was venereal disease. But no one who started sexual indulgence too early or indulged too frequently was safe from the dangers of begetting sickly children, and of himself declining in vitality at a premature age. Even marriage before the age of physical maturity—twenty-five or twenty-six for the male; twenty-one or twenty-two for the female—involved the danger of depleting one's supply of vital juices. For every year of precocious indulgence, one would decline three years earlier. This was reason enough for deprecating the newfangled (sic) doctrine of early marriage—for some misguided theorists were saying at the time that youngsters ought to marry as soon as they felt the impulse.

While much of this teaching was rooted in Puritan tradition, it was also backed by enough scientific quotation to make it carry weight with Alcott's broad reading public. This teacher-physician also reinforced his text with a crude polling technique, the primitive ancestor of better developed statistical studies of our own time. He asked men of his acquaintance how often they thought the sexual union should occur. Unfortunately Dr. Alcott prejudged his interviewees as well as the results of his entire investigation. The man who gave his estimate as twice weekly, Alcott doomed to an early death. Expert testimony, he declared, held that for men in sedentary occupations, the time pattern set by the lunar cycle was healthful and natural. The proof that this was Nature's dictum had been revealed in the physiological cycle set for the female of the species.

The religion of physiology, as preached by early disseminators of hygienic information, was greatly at odds with free enquiry on many points. One objective, however, all these writers had in common, and that was to lift the cloak of secrecy from the sexual question. Children, the science of phrenology taught, were all born with a good share of "causality," that is, curiosity. Their inquiring ways were to be encouraged. They were not to be deceived when they asked how babies were born. Telling them the truth was far less dangerous than telling fables. If parents could not bring themselves to give a forthright reply to questioning, it was preferable to tell children that they were not old enough to understand, and that the answer would be deferred until such time as they were capable of comprehending. The convenient lie served only to confuse youngsters and prepare them inadequately for marriage. Moreover, children in time developed morbid curiosities and began to distrust their parents when the truth came to them accidentally.

Sex education in the home and physiology in the schools promised a remedy. Marriage had to be prepared for; the preparation was to start at puberty. Alcott encouraged early social contacts (under supervision) between the sexes, and carried through his argument by recommending coeducation for the schools. Courtship could start at a very early age. Ten years of courting were not too long for gaining a thorough acquaintance with the qualities of a prospective mate. Certainly this approach to necessary knowledge was better than that obtained from popular literature, which, in addition to giving schoolboys a confused notion of physiology, left them with badly mistaken ideas about the nature of women. These books, written by the irresponsible Byron and his kind, made it appear that women were as sensual as men. They would have readers believe that female modesty was a ruse, a tactical measure. Alcott taught that all of this was an outright lie, for women were "constitutionally" pure until perverted or seduced by "our sex or hers." Bad women, it had to be said, were worse than bad men.

Robert Dale Owen's group propagandized for sex education in the belief that such knowledge, as with all other knowledge, would have a liberating effect on people and give them a potential resource for happiness—regardless of the use to which they chose to put it. Pious educators like Dr. Alcott, when they advocated the spread of such information, were thinking mostly of preparing the young for marriage as currently understood in law and Scripture. Marriage was a duty to be assumed by all who would serve God and humanity; it was not an optional undertaking—as preached by the free enquirers—designed primarily for the pleasure of the contracting parties. The nature and design of marriage, always permanent, was to train up a new generation, and to provide for the physical, moral, and intellectual growth of the partners and their children. Alcott accordingly spoke with great disdain of a certain New England physician (obviously Knowlton) "of much greater practical skill than integrity, especially towards God, [who] became the author of a small pocket volume, with a very inviting title, whose avowed object was to teach people both in married life and elsewhere, the art of gratifying the sexual appetite without the necessity of progeny. His book had a wide circulation. I have found it in nearly every part of our wide-spread country."

If one's duty to God was indeed involved in the commandment to propagate, it was surely mandatory to insist upon the indissolubility of marriage. For Protestant Christians, born and bred in puritan New England, the New Testament was clearly against divorce. Women, praise be to them, were retaining their piety in this respect more visibly than men. Women were upholding marriage morals in other respects too. For instance, it was not they who reprehensibly chose marriage partners of a much younger age than themselves. It was the men who had this strange preference. "Our own sex," the doctor admitted, "are exceedingly fond . . . of being wedded to very young women; and, as far as I have observed, this fondness has its principle origins in motives which neither admit of palliation or apology."

The general position adopted by many of the pious physiologists was that woman's role in the world was to help Christ redeem sinful mankind. This role was to be filled by women, as mothers, in training a generation of people with moderate appetites; as wives, in reshaping eating, drinking, smoking, sexual, and other undisciplined habits of the male.[1]

∽　∽

It was at the third annual meeting of the American Physiological Society that baker Graham, (fountainhead of the new hygienic religion, whose own poor health had persuaded him to abandon the ministry for a career in practical physiology) gave theological force to the above principle. This he did when speaking in support of the Reverend Mr. Thompson's resolution "That woman in the character of wife and mother, is only second to the Deity in the influence which she exerts on the physical, the intellectual and the moral interests of the human race, and that her education should be adapted to qualify her

[1] As Dr. Alcott remarked in his *Letters to a Sister*, the companion volume of his *Young Woman's Guide*, it was not desirable that women take to the public platform like Frances Wright, nor turn cavilling philosopher like Mary Wollstonecraft. Nor should "she become a mere Hannah More, and attempt to fulfill her mission wholly at the point of a pen." There were bigger things for her to do.

in the highest degree to cherish those interests in the wisest and best manner."

This resolution, said Graham, deserved unhesitating support inasmuch as it took cognizance of "all the constitutional relations which God in nature had established between woman and the physiological and psycological (sic) interests of the species." Woman's appointed position as executive secretary to God made her the all-powerful shaper of moral character on earth. Her bailiwick was the family cell. It was she who could interpret the divine ordinance for the improvement of mankind. Thence, through neat logical transitions, the health convention could conclude that man's upward course depended on diet control.

By every known principle of reasoning and religion, Graham and Alcott should have been compelled by their stand to declare woman the superior member of the marriage partnership. Graham's writings gave no indication that the problem of comparative status and power in the family ever bothered him. His lectures on sexual matters (published in 1834 as *A Lecture to Young Men on Chastity*) showed the baker's awareness that man lived not by bread and vegetables alone. They were scientific discourses on prevailing evils like the solitary vice and illicit relationships. Graham spoke at length about abusive and intemperate sex practices in marriage, hinting strongly that it was the wife who suffered most often from the evils described.

Dr. Alcott exceeded his co-worker in versatility and tact. His audience was the more appreciative for the humane understanding he gave them in place of Graham's strictures and reproaches. And it was not by accident that he was more lenient with his listeners and readers. The wise doctor, though he worshiped the revealer of whole wheat flour, saw clearly through the public's hostile reaction to Grahamism. While the butchers and bakers were crying for the blood of this purveyor of anti-fine flour and anti-flesh eating doctrines, they were, in reality, most upset by his morbid harping on the sex indulgence theme. They wanted to crucify him for broadcasting ideas so inimical to everybody's way of living.

The people who patronized writers and speakers wanted to be told how to adjust better in marriage, but they were hardly ready for uncomfortable and revolutionary suggestions. Discussion and advice on the power struggle in the household was nearer their tastes. William Alcott, the doctor who lived by his pen, tried to give them what they wanted. The question of physical gratification, which so successfully won enemies for Graham, Alcott handled deftly by stressing the exalting moral and educational values in marriage. He was ahead of his time on matters of courtship and social contact between boys and girls insofar as he advised a more natural, rational, coeducational growing-up process, albeit under strict supervision.

The subject which taxed Alcott's tact and subtlety to the utmost was the age-old and everlasting battle of the sexes on the home front. The tricky passage between Scylla and Charybdis he negotiated as follows: The Biblical mandate was for woman to be man's helper. Pious people had to accept that. But those who were storming the male bastions in behalf of sexual democracy had God's law on their side too. There were certain equalities—or similarities—upon which everyone agreed. For example, it was well to marry someone near oneself in age, wealth, interests, and intellect. One of the first activities to be shared by men and women was the decision as to what was woman's proper right and what was not. Intelligent and mature women would, Dr. Alcott was certain, arrive at the conclusion that their duties and influence were not identical with men's in all respects.

Alcott agreed that a wife should be as "independent" as her husband. "But is not woman more dependent than man, at least, in the married state?" Again, matrimony could not exist without concessions on both sides. But, on the face of it, woman was making greater concessions—or submitting to man—by leaving her home and assuming new family obligations and responsibilities. In any case, did reasonable submission really deprive a woman of her independence? Alcott thought not. Reason, nature, and revelation affirmed the balance of concession. The wife was happy who submitted voluntarily and cheerfully. Woman's role as domestic scientist was a glorious one. Her education must prepare her for it, but not to the exclusion of intellectual and physical training. William Andrus Alcott was the compromise modern of his era. Actually his program for female exercise, physical well-being, and the rest was uncommonly close to the radical thoughts of Mary Wollstonecraft, who had shocked her contemporaries not too many decades before.

∽ ∽

The years intervening between the careers of these philosophers of sexual equality had changed morality considerably. To agree with Mary Wollstonecraft in her own time was to have questionable morals. To agree with Alcott was to participate in a movement which promised to save the world from moral disruption. For healthianism was an ideological "ism" like any other, fully conscious of its social aims. Alcott himself once suggested that the physiologists join forces with the Fourierists so that both might work in harmony to produce harmony. Before long, the vegetarians, phrenologists, water-cure doctors, and anti-tobacco, anti-corset, and temperance people were to cross paths so frequently that they began to look like participants in a single reform movement. In a single symposium on the effects of tobacco on body and mind, published by the phrenology specialists Fowler and Wells, one read contributions by Alcott, Joel Shew, a prominent hydropathic physician, and Dr. Russell Thatcher Trall, specialist in all medical innovations.

In an age when every movement published its own magazine, the Grahamites had theirs. It was called, appropriately enough, *The Graham Journal of Health and Longevity* and was published from 1837 to 1839 with David Cambell, corresponding secretary of the American Physiological Society, as its editor. Having as its motto St. Paul's dictum, "He that striveth for mastery is temperate in all things," this journal served as a forum for diet and health disciples. It advertised the lectures and published writings of Graham, Alcott, and other leaders, featuring all and sundry in the struggle against dietary and other physiological vices. A favorite target was the typical contemporary doctor who fought the spread of popular health knowledge and preventive hygiene. In following this policy, *The Graham Journal* was reflecting a widespread antipathy toward the medical profession, which was at that time experiencing its all-time low in national prestige. One by one, the States were repealing the laws establishing certification requirements, until, in all but three States, almost anyone could practice medicine.

The doctors were having troubles with their public, and so were the Grahamites. Opposition from enemies in the sex-diet war was natural, but very soon, dissidence appeared from within. All too often a convertee began to have trouble with his unconverted wife and family, and they with him. Male partisans looked for girls who would promise to love, honor, and cook by Graham. Young ladies added a new kind of deception to their repertoire. When being courted, they feigned Grahamism in order to win a Grahamite. After marriage they would serve meat, butter, and spices. The faithful became so wary that they categorically refused to marry. The *Journal,* to counteract this tendency, quoted: "It is not good for man to be alone," and "Man should have a helpmeet for him." The correlation between marital status and longevity for both sexes was cited.

Then too, several inspired followers had other serious reservations. Among the earliest and most ardent of the female adherents-with-modification was Mrs. Mary Sargent Gove. The new health arts were very important to Mrs. Gove, for, having informally parted with her unintellectual husband, Hiram, she had to earn a living for herself and her young daughter. Raised in a home where Voltaire, Volney, and Tom Paine were read, she gained more ideas about learning than learning itself. She decided to equip herself to teach a subject close to her interests—the human body. When Dr. Alcott reported that his lectures to mixed audiences were meeting with embarrassment, complaints, and non-attendance, the American Physiological Society went in search of a lady lecturer. Mary Gove, humble but eager, was their **woman.**

MARRIAGE, MORALS AND SEX IN AMERICA

The courses of lectures to ladies on anatomy and physiology were given with gratifying success in Boston, Lynn and Haverhill. In New York, which heard Mrs. Gove in the spring of 1839, journalists and editors denounced the talks as obscene. Who were these newspaper upstarts, queried *The Graham Journal*, to speak against the respectable Mrs. Gove merely because she taught women how to take care of their bodies? Were not these the same editors who printed pictures of dancing girls and indulged in blatant pornography?

This public notice probably pleased Mary Gove very much, for she needed to bolster her self-esteem. As she noted in the biography of her first ten years, she was born with the disease of humility. "I longed for approval with limitless longing," she confessed, "and my parents starved the desire from a sense of duty."

Despite Mrs. Gove's friendly reception in Massachusetts, she decided to move to New York. The decision was made under compelling circumstances. In the first place, her reputation back home had suffered a death blow because, in the absence of Hiram Gove, Mrs. Gove had struck up an unconventional acquaintance with Henry Wright, Bronson Alcott's liberal-minded friend recently arrived from England. As the story goes, the curtains on the Gove windows were thin, and the eyes of neighbors had strayed in the direction of these windows at inopportune times. Hiram, the outraged husband, lent his willing tongue to the outraged neighbors, and their combined efforts made Lynn, Massachusetts, uninhabitable for Mrs. Gove. Wright had, furthermore, liberated Mary Gove from the Grahamite conception of morality, and left her with the need to re-form her physiological premises. The water-cure, or hydropathy, was gaining in popularity by leaps and bounds. Mrs. Gove left for New York carrying with her a letter of introduction to Dr. Joel Shew, the master of wet-sheet therapy, a copy of whose *Water Cure Journal and Herald of Reform* she had chanced to read.

An apprenticeship at the Shew establishment was tantamount to a full-scale liberal education. Here one met and conversed with the foremost New York reformers. One learned the latest phraseology of New England transcendentalism along with the incomprehensible but suggestive jargon of Associationism, the American translation of Fourier's doctrines. No less than the wealthy, brilliant, and attractive young Dr. M. Edgeworth Lazarus was present, spouting phrases like "attractional harmony" and "passional hygiene." Lazarus had not yet developed his Fourierist critique of conventional marriage, but his language showed the tendency even at this early date.

Mrs. Gove's experience with marriage had truly prepared her for such ideas. She was, in any case, of a naturally eclectic mind. She had learned much from her distant cousin, the writer John Neal, who championed woman's rights and freedom in love very convincingly. Phrenology and mesmerism were also a part of her new education. Mrs. Gove was quick to learn. After a short training period at Dr. Shew's, she started a practice of her own. Medicine and lecturing did not exhaust her talents. She also sent literary contributions to the most respectable magazines, and they were accepted.

Through intensive contact with so many high-calibre minds with related interests, it was inevitable that Mary Gove should find someone with whom to share strong "attractional bonds." Doubtless her eyes and heart had been in search of a truer affinity than the one to which she was still legally tied. At any rate, her meeting with Thomas Nichols set up strong sympathetic vibrations, and in July 1848—when she was allowed by law to shed her old, erroneously formed affinity —they became Dr. and Mrs. Nichols.

Nichols, who had interrupted his medical studies many years before, went back to school so that Mary Gove could collaborate with him in a licensed medical practice once the two were legally married. Mrs. Shew was practising hydropathy by virtue of Joel Shew's medical degree in this very way. Nichols got his degree from the University of the City of New York in 1850, some fifteen years after he had left Dartmouth to become a journalist. After a brief period of newspaper work, he had became editor and part owner of *The Buffalonian,* a vigorous sheet published in Buffalo, New York. The crusader in Nichols came to the surface almost immediately. He used his paper to fight a clique which had arrayed itself against one Benjamin Rathbun. The *Buffalonian's* editor soon found himself the defendant in a long series of libel suits. He was successful in all but one, and this one netted him a jail sentence extending from June 18 to October 15, 1839.

Thomas Nichols had played the role of reformer, and, once in jail, discovered that he had won recognition as a full member of the reforming profession. The abuse and character assassination in which his townsmen engaged were more convincing than a title or a diploma. On June 22, four days after he moved into his temporary abode, he wrote in his journal: "But of all these stupid slanders, the most absurd is the one now most industriously circulated—that I have been the calumniator of female virtue! As well might I try to quench the light of my existence, the sunshine of my prosperity, and the mildly beaming effulgence that throws a halo of hope over the darkest hour of despondency." Man fickle, false, and treacherous? Yes. But woman? Never. The "angelic sex" was guilty of none of man's perfidy.

If this thought lay lightly on the prisoner's mind at the moment, his prison experience secured it there forever and laid the groundwork for future sexual reform campaigns. For however harshly men were treating Thomas Low Nichols, women, some of whom he had met casually and a few of whom he was meeting for the first time, treated him with kindness and affection. To many he was a hero. Miranda, Julia, Constanza, and Rosalie wrote to him regularly. Some of these letters expressed emotions stronger than those of friendship. The prisoner was flattered. He failed to comprehend what made him so attractive to "the gentle and lovely sex." He had none of the qualities of a lady's man. But for all his shortcomings, he had acquired the reputation of an accomplished rake. Anyone who really knew him, he mused, would attest that he was the very essence of sugar-plum goodness.

What bothered him above other things was that more married than single women attached themselves to him. They persisted in writing to him, often in language which disturbed his peace of mind. "When the devil wishes to ruin a woman," said Nichols, "he puts a pen in her fingers." The man obviously protested his innocence too much; but his overpowering ego exposed him soon enough. On the same day when he whimpered about being slandered, he wrote revealingly in his journal:

> An incident, savoring of the romantic, occurred to me today. A *petite* and very pretty *brunette,* with beautiful black eyes, a rich color, and pouting lips, with a most enchanting "How d'ye do my dear?" expression, came to see me. My cell door happened to be open, and she looked in upon its arrangements. She knew me—as everybody does—but I had never seen her; and spoke so pityingly of my imprisonment— said that it was such a shame, such an outrage, to treat me as they did; and spoke so feelingly, that my arm stole gradually around her—I drew her imperceptibly nearer—I looked in her bright eyes, as I thanked her for her sympathy, and assured her, that with her, I could be happy anywhere—what in gallantry could I have said beside?—Our cheeks approached each other—then our lips and. . . . Now what else could I have done? After going so far, there was surely no retreating. And a kiss—such a pure, chaste, Platonic kiss as that, is as innocent as apple dumpling. Her husband might have been jealous, had he seen us; but it would have arisen entirely from a misapprehension.

Ladies had sent flowers and food delicacies to Nichols, but this, he noted, was the first kiss in prison. Three days later a pair of sparkling eyes peered once more through the bars—the same brunette. But this time the cell door was locked!

The journalist reformer's loyalty to the gentler sex grew stronger as he had more time to think things over behind bars. On July 5, he wrote: "No lady has come to see me for two days,—none that I know and love. I have had no letters." How horrible to be shut up with a lot of men—and without women! What a cutthroat existence this life would be without women! It was wrong and unnatural to separate the sexes at any time. Schools for boys and schools for girls were detestable arrangements. Boys and girls must grow up together, he concluded.

Female correspondence and visitors were a source of supreme comfort to the persecuted Nichols. He enjoyed their sympathy. But one day a dark shadow crossed the rays of cheer shed by thoughts of his kind lady friends. It came in the form of a letter from a girl seeking Nichols' sympathy. Apparently, her morals had slipped just once; and despite all efforts to rehabilitate herself, the door to respectable society was shut tight. Here indeed was a serious shortcoming of the other sex. Women were just and fair to men, but not to each other. If one of them, driven by a strong impulse, happened to overstep the conventions, they drove her from society. There was no forgiveness, no attempt to retrieve her for a virtuous life. It mattered not that the unpardonable impulse had been given her by God. It mattered not how beautiful, how accomplished, how good she was; nor how hard she yearned for pardon. ". . . She is hunted to her lonely and dishonored grave. Do women right in this? Is chastity in one sex no virtue, and its violation in the other the only vice that cannot be forgiven?"

Impressed by his own eloquence, the journalist declared himself converted to a career of writing sermons and lecturing on reform. During the remainder of his prison term, the reform horizon broadened. Lack of fresh air and exercise made him ponder on the subject of stimulants like coffee, tea, and spices. The prison fare led him to a consideration of the question of diet. A headache on July 15 led him to think of tobacco and opiates, neither of which he liked. A visit by two temperance ladies—"one married, the other single"—on September 18 made him ponder a new definition of intoxicating drinks, a definition which included "extracts and tinctures of intoxicating vegetables, especially of the narcotic species." Coffee and tea must be taboo. And, come to think of it, concluded Mr. Nichols, "I got as tipsy on strong coffee as I ever did on champagne."

The fifteen years following his jail term were occupied with much reading, writing, and speaking about physiology, Grahamite vegetarianism, Fourierist associationism, and other interests attractional and passional. He also studied Josiah Warren's anarchist ideas and John Noyes' Perfectionism. By way of concrete accomplishments there were his marriage to a true affinity, the medical degree, voluminous contributions by both affinities to diet and water-cure periodicals, the inauguration of a journal of their own, and several books on woman, free love, marriage, religion, and whatever else could be related to these eternally fascinating subjects.

It surprised no one that Nichols' first major work, published in the year after his union with Mary Gove, should have celebrated that divine species of humanity, woman. The book, whose abbreviated title was *Woman, in All Ages and Nations,* was encyclopedic. Its historical coverage was complete; its geography was universal. The author found his subject a labor of love in more ways than one. "No intellectual employment is more delightful than the study of human nature," said he, "and, in the female sex, we find humanity in its fairest and more exquisite developments."

One heard much in Nichols' day about moral reform and of the various movements and cults organized to accomplish the regeneration of a sick society. Why had not the reform philosophers seen the obvious workings of destiny? The future of civilization was in the hands of American womanhood.

The signs were clear. In the first place, female education was being taken more seriously. Anatomy, physiology, and the laws of health were fast becoming popular considerations in educational programs for girls. Women themselves were quick to see the value of this kind of study in preparing them for their most important occupation, that of caring for the young. The benefits would accumulate with each generation until "the physical and moral renovation and reformation of the world" would finally be effected as the Grahamites predicted.

The second hopeful trend could be seen in the disappearance from American courting customs of those upper-class formalities and ceremonies which prevented a couple from really getting acquainted. Social science in America—the Fourierist type, for instance—promised to obliterate artificial distinctions of wealth and class, thus allowing much greater liberty in the matter of choosing a mate. Besides which, the current "sex freedom and candor" commonly exhibited by contemporary women made good marriages more possible. The more barriers removed from male-female contact, the more spontaneous, the purer the marital choice. Those who shouted that such freedom would promote licentiousness were entirely mistaken, declared Nichols as he followed the free love line of his harmony-bent friends. On the contrary, freedom would curb vice by removing the temptations and excuses which inharmonious social arrangements produced. Down with sex slavery! Away with your double standards in education and morals! Marriage stood to gain in strength by greater freedom of choice; society would gain by stronger marriages.

The first step in a scientific approach to the problem was to ask what constituted the best kind of marriage. Nichols asked the question repeatedly as he examined the great divergence of acceptable practice among societies and social groups. The best generalization he could form was that one custom was as bad as another. All one could say was that the union of two sexes in love equaled marriage; every other type, of union was something else. What more could be said? Society was in an imperfect stage, and the time for passing final judgment was not yet at hand. Certain it was that the insistence of religionists on indissoluble marriage was riddled with contradictions. *With* love, there was no desire for separation; *without* it, there was no marriage.

The battle around Henry James, Senior, and his translation of *Love in a Phalanstery* was well known to the Nichols-Gove group. So was the free love debate as a whole, for it occupied the best brains among New York intellectuals of the forties. The science of behavior and the science of society were leading the progress parade. Thomas Nichols and his wife were near the front. They were friends and allies of practically every group represented in the march.

Actually, *Woman, in All Ages and Nations* was a document of the feminist movement. It belonged side by side with books like Lydia Maria Child's *History of Women* from which it quoted extensively. But property rights and domestic equality were myopic objectives when compared with Nichols' plans and promises. The day was coming, he predicted, when woman, having achieved the position which was her destiny according to God's design, would "preside over a beautiful planet, and worthily receive the homage and adoration of the sex that now treats her with ingratitude and, too often, with ignominy."

The new order of harmony was to manifest nearly all of the characteristics sought by reformers of the thirties. Health was to be at its best; and sound minds in sound bodies could accomplish any reform. Healthier women would beget healthier children—and painlessly. For, where women lived in accordance with the laws of life, they were freed from the dangers and pains of parturition. Social reorganization would do its part by eliminating hatred, jealousy, and competition. A new religion, purified by the wisdom of men, would banish the perversions and superstitions under which women, *because* they were especially pious, suffered. Next, present business methods, big profits, and other economic evils were to be abolished. And finally, the sphere of woman's usefulness to the world would be infinitely enlarged. This last part of the program, the one which would make all the difference in the world, depended chiefly on the Associationist promise to liberate women from kitchen slavery. The unfettered female, devoting surplus time to mental and physical development, would soon reach her true level. There was a growth potential for men also in the new society. A foretaste of heaven on earth was in the offing for women, for men, and for both in lasting wedded bliss.

Thus far, Dr. Nichols had not denied outright the value of marriage as it was practised. He had dwelt on its imperfections and possibilities for improving it in a reshuffled social system. A few years of moral support from his broadminded wife, plus an extended airing of the free love question by a few of his philosophical acquaintances, made him utterly sceptical about the serviceability of permanent marriage. In 1853, his *Esoteric Anthropology* disclosed its author as a confirmed free love advocate, besides furnishing the data of sex physiology in a manner so direct that even Nichols described it as a work intended only for *private* consumption. A thoroughly descriptive subtitle translated *Esoteric Anthropology* into "A Comprehensive and Confidential Treatise on the Structure, Functions, Passional Attractions and Perversions, True and False Physical and Social Conditions, and the Most Intimate Relations of Men and Women. Anatomical, Physiological, Pathological, Therapeutical and Obstetrical; Hygienic and Hydropathic."

A year later, Nichols wrote, in collaboration with Mary Gove Nichols, an up-to-date, all-inclusive treatment of the eternal problem. It was called *Marriage: Its History, Character, and Results; Its Sanctities, and Its Profanities; Its Science and Its Facts. Demonstrating Its Influence, as a Civilized Institution, on the Happiness of the Individual and the Progress of the Race. . . .* The real claim to distinction of this work was that it brought together summaries and extracts from the outstanding marriage literature of an age clogged with subtle contention. Moreover, this mass of material had been skilfully selected and interpreted by people of prestige—the medical team of Nichols and Nichols. These two doctors, one with a degree and the other without, both with experience in marriage and a knowledge of the latest in physiology and psychology (having added phrenology and spiritualism to their former repertory of diet and water-cure) offered their lengthy, expert opinion on the sex problem.

The sexual mores had come before a competent court and had been found wanting. Everyone, declared the court, was entitled to love plus its "ultimations and results." The system in operation was forcing unnatural celibacy on vast numbers of people. If one took the State of Massachusetts as an example, he would find that in that State there were twice as many women as men between the ages of twenty and forty-five. Half the women were doomed by statistics to a life of affectional starvation. Again, if one looked at the plight of the wives of sailors in the seacoast towns of Massachusetts, he would find an added discrimination against the women. Thousands of them were living in a state of virtual widowhood for many months each year while their husbands were at sea. These women either did or did not love their husbands. If they did not, they lived in chronic anxiety against the day of their spouses' safe return. If they did, what untold suffering by deprivation, without the possibility of compensation by another love.

The authors provided a formula to be followed by those who would realize love in its fullest fruition. It was, as Mrs. Nichols put it in her part of the marriage manual, "Fidelity to the Law of One's Life." Mrs. Nichols provided ample illustration of her point by drawing from her vast "clinical" file of cases and correspondence in point. One such case was of a Swedenborgian girl who, luckless woman, found her true affinity in a man married to another—unhappily, as usual. He, faithful to his real conjugal partner, the young girl, left his wife to live with her. The question was, how was one to cope with the un-Swedenborgian world which considered the girl not his spiritual wife but a kept woman? Mrs. Nichols spoke from experience when she advised her patient to be faithful to the law of her own life and to face the world with the support of her faith.

Citing Swedenborg, Shelley, God, and the medical profession, the Nicholses showed that love and procreation had little to do with legal marriage. Helped by the complicated vocabularies of the latest religions and philosophies, they forestalled, to their own satisfaction, charges of libertinism and promiscuity. The number of fathers acknowledged by a woman's children respectively was not a matter of importance to them. The question was rather: Were they born of healthy and loving parents? Were they reared under conditions conducive to health? Were their separate individualities respected?

These factors were not present in conventional monogamic marriage, which was therefore to be condemned as a system. The usual supporting statements about the misery of children, husband, and wife in a loveless marriage were offered in support of the argument against monogamy. It was shown, in the manner of Fourier, how the isolated family and the careful separation of male and female, were the destruction of society itself. Coldness, distrust, and restraint were everywhere. "Having but one woman, and the legal right to only that one . . . [man's] poverty makes him stingy. Women, in the same condition, are distrustful and jealous of each other. . . ."

The indictment was complete. It covered all counts. A tree was best known by its fruits, and, declared Dr. Nichols, as he introduced the "theoretical and scientific" section of *Marriage: Its History, Character, etc:*

> The fruits of the marriage system are bondage; isolation; perpetuity of error; sacrifice of health and all the conditions of happiness; compulsory and disgustful intercourse; com-

pulsory and unwelcome maternity; voluntary and involuntary abortions; deformed and diseased offspring; terrible infantile mortality; generations born into physical and passional discordance and perversion; compulsory chastity of surplus male or female populations; seduction and prostitution; the falsehood and hypocrisy of a pretentious moralism; rapacity of the higher, and oppression and poverty of the lower ranks; general reign of fraud, treachery, and social Ishmaelism.

If all the items in this catalog were even partly true, the world of 1854 was ready for a revolt of the masses and the classes—this time fighting behind the same barricade. The struggle for sexual power would be short, since everyone, except a few men of religion, would be fighting in a common cause. But, only very few accepted this prophecy. Even the friendly editors of the health journals to which Dr. and Mrs. Nichols had been contributing copiously felt that the dose was too strong. In 1853, the cause of freedom of the press was abetted by the start of *Nichols' Journal of Health, Water-Cure, and Human Progress*. The couple moved to Cincinnati in 1855 and there, for three years, published *Nichols' Monthly*, a journal which set forth the doctrines of free love, spiritualism, health reform, and individual liberty. They also ran a water-cure establishment at Yellow Springs in 1856 and 1857.

Quite suddenly, at about this time, both the Nicholses were converted to Catholicism and began to spend much of their time lecturing on hygiene in Catholic institutions in the Middle West. The early part of 1861 found them back in New York. Dr. Nichols made an unsuccessful attempt to get a weekly newspaper under way. Then, at the outbreak of the Civil War, both left for England. The ostensible reason was that the doctor believed in the individual sovereignty of the States and would not stand by to see the Northern section of the country impose on the South. Much time and many mental gyrations had intervened between 1834, when he witnessed a mobbing of Garrison in the liberator's own Boston office, and 1861, when he declared that the sympathy of Northern hearts might better be lavished on something nearer home than the slave in the distant South.

As Thomas Wentworth Higginson said of the reformers of his time, it was hard to find two who thought alike. Thomas Nichols' reservations extended beyond the abolitionist movement. There were nuances of his own free love position upon which he always insisted in face of the intricate caviling of other leaders. He even opposed a prominent phrenologist on one of the most crucial questions of all time: Was there an Organ (a common tendency to behave in a given way) of Union for Life? Professor Orson Squire Fowler had made a great discovery when he claimed to have located the said Organ on a woman patient's skull. The Associationist Doctor M. Edgeworth Lazarus denied the validity of the discovery. Nichols joined him in the negative, pointing out that, assuming the existence of such an organ, four-fifths of mankind—including every Turk and most other Orientals—had been born without it. He could have offered evidence nearer home in the form of his twice-wed wife, Mary Gove Nichols.

THE AMATIVE PROPENSITY

Fowler's experience and fame as a phrenologist was of long standing. It dated back to the early thirties, when, as a student at Amherst, his brilliant schoolmate and friend, Henry Ward Beecher, had stimulated his interest in this new and popular science of the mind. Phrenology, with the "sciences" of Pathetism, Mesmerism, and other methods of mental investigation, was the rage of the middle third of the last century. It absorbed the public interest—and income— in the way that psychiatry and psychoanalysis do today. Unlike psychiatrists and psychoanalysts, however, the phrenologist needed no special educational training. Hard work and ingenuity were the prime requisites. Fowler qualified; but, having no background in physiology or medicine, or anything else remotely related to his chosen profession, could not be called "doctor."

Fresh from college, he moved to New York with his younger brother and pupil, Lorenzo Niles Fowler, and immediately plunged into practice and publishing. As a surgeon adds to his reputation by using new operative techniques, so did Orson Fowler glorify his name by discovering new mental faculties, thereby ridding his clients of their personal problems. For phrenological diagnosis consisted in locating the ailing bump (or organ) and massaging the affected faculty back to health. The first handbook of phrenological self-analysis by the brothers Fowler was published in 1837. The sixty-first edition included eighty-three new organs added to the science by the elder Fowler alone. It was obvious why his reputation should have grown. He was the discoverer of the organs of Money-making, Money-saving, Good Manners, and dozens of other desirable mental assets. Patients naturally flocked to a therapist who could stimulate such beneficial bumps to greater growth.

One with such talents could not remain a general practitioner for long. Fowler soon began to specialize in the faculty of Amativeness and all directly relating thereto. Lorenzo took over the bulk of his psychotherapeutic practice while Lorenzo's wife Lydia, a distinguished leader in the Woman's Rights Movement, assisted in the work of marriage counseling and curing. Brother-in-law Orson was doubtless deeply influenced by his assistant. The numerous editions and revisions of *Fowler on Matrimony; or Phrenology and Physiology Applied to the Selection of Suitable Companions* all contained a powerful note on the education of women and the necessity for their gaining social equality. At twenty-five cents per copy, large editions sold quickly.

The book, which included directions to the married for living affectionately and happily, became a household necessity. It contained more practical advice than the Nichols offering, was less sentimental and more interesting than Alcott's works, and lacked the ominous Puritanism of Graham—for, though Fowler was a Grahamite in many respects, yet he was conservative enough to cater to social habit. All the books written by the Fowler brothers celebrated the institution of monogamic marriage and the virtues of the American home life that developed under its aegis.

While shrewdly translating the conventional "advice" literature into phrenological language so as to draw on a wide reading audience, Professor Fowler accommodatingly wove in phrases from the lips and pages of his reform confrères. Here and there (but rarely in the first and most-read portion of the book) the reader came upon ideas which would, if thought through, vitiate the earlier praise of monogamy. Readers made acquaintance with a thinly disguised doctrine of spiritual affinities, affinities over which the law had naught but rubber-stamp jurisdiction. Editions which appeared in the feminist fifties and thereafter carried this manifesto:

> I call upon woman to pause, and consider the oppressive evils under which she groans, and to rise and shake off her chains, and follow the dictates of her nature; to assert and maintain her independence; to rise from her abject servitude; to assert and maintain her rights and her freedom, and be herself.

Male customers who resented this outburst were probably more than smoothed over when they learned that the Union for Life factor was more active in woman than in man, the fact which accounted for the far greater power and intensity of woman's love than man's. Also likely to win approval from men was an exhortation to marry a mate with strong inhabitiveness, inasmuch as the cost of moving frequently was so large. Such advice was very important to middle-class New Yorkers who—a hundred years before the current housing shortage—found themselves moving every May first because the womenfolk wanted a change.

Then, too, for all his woman's rights verbiage, Fowler conceded male supremacy. He urged his readers, and women especially, to choose a mate with large moral faculties so that one's own would be "continually and agreeably excited." The importance of this principle for the woman lay in the circumstance that "she is mueh more under the power and subject to the caprice of her husband than he is to hers, and therefore *her* happiness depends more on *his* being a good-feeling man than his happiness depends on her good feelings; but what is more, man is less likely to be moral and virtuous than woman."

More practical still was the warning not to marry anyone the back of whose head showed too much Amativeness. On the other hand, a certain amount of development in a particular area behind the ears was very important. Without it a mate would prove unsatisfactory as a companion and parent. One should also select a companion whose phrenological developments resembled one's own. The one big exception to the rule was in the organ of acquisitiveness, which, if small in yourself, should be compensated by a large development in your beloved. Care had also to be exercised when caressing propensity-laden areas of the cranium. One misstroke might cause moral disaster.

Many readers gathered sufficient knowledge from *Fowler on Matrimony* and *Phrenology Proved, Illustrated, and Applied* to suit their intellectual needs. But thousands went on to read *Love and Parentage, Applied to the Improvement of Offspring, including Important Directions and Suggestions to Lovers and the Married concerning the Strongest Ties and the Most Momentous Relations of Life,* and its sequel, *Amativeness: or, Evils and Remedies of Excessive and Perverted Sexuality, including Warning and Advice to the Married and Single.* Such self-descriptive titles, and the books which they represented, came from the pen of no mere theorist. Orson married three times without destroying his Union for Life thesis, since he remarried each time upon the decease of a current affinity. The last wedding took place in 1882, five years before he died at the age of seventy-eight.

The contribution of the brothers Fowler to the popular health movement was by no means confined to their own writing and medical practice. Their publishing business, carried on in partnership with S. R. Wells from 1844 to 1863, was the central distribution point for universal reform. An enormous quantity of inexpensive pamphlet material poured forth from the press of Fowler and Wells. The firm also published, under Dr. Joel Shew's editorship, the *Water-Cure Journal and Herald of Reform.*

H₂O AND HEALTH

This important periodical was everything its title promised. It offered cures for all diseases through drinking water, bathing in it, douching with it, and wrapping oneself in wet sheets. It proscribed smoking, inoculation, self-pollution, early marriage, and eating animal foods—except half a glass of milk at mealtimes if desired. It railed at New York women who did not nurse their own children. It advised mental exercise as a cure for insanity. Notes on physical care during pregnancy were provided, and the possibility of making oneself cholera-proof by eating cracked wheat bread was explored. Mrs. Gove, later Mrs. Nichols, contributed regular clinical notes on water-cure.

The *Water-Cure Journal* counted among its correspondents a name which was to overshadow those of Graham, Alcott, and Nichols in hygienic circles. Dr. Russell Thatcher Trall came to New York City in 1840 to practise hydropathy. In 1843 he founded a water-cure establishment. Ten years later he opened for students of both sexes a medical school which was chartered in 1857 as the New York Hygeio-Therapeutic College. In 1863, Dr. Trall reached the height of his medico-literary career when he took over the *Water-Cure Journal* from Fowler and Wells and renamed it the *Herald of Health*. Coincidentally, this was also the title of Dr. David Mallison's magazine (devoted to "electrical medicine"), to which Trall sent some of his earliest writings in 1842 and 1843.

Dr. Trall's first love in the field of reform was the temperance movement for which he wrote in the forties. Early in the following decade the population problem drew his attention to the sexual arrangements of the human family. His reaction to Malthus' theories and remedies was violent. The Malthusian doctrine, said Trall in his introduction to the reprint of an unsigned *Westminster Review* article on physiology and population, "shocks our reason, insults the moral sense, and blasphemes Deity. . . ." The unsigned article which Trall heralded as a statement of the law of progress itself, was written by Herbert Spencer. The theme of this highly learned treatise was that the nervous and the reproductive systems competed for body energies. As the human race developed its mental mechanism to meet the demands of complex civilization, its breeding capacity would be reduced. Concretely, Spencer believed that intense brain work was accompanied by a drastically lowered rate of sperm production. This proved, according to Spencer, that the universe possessed an inner logic and harmony. The state of perfect existence in a world governed wholly by reason—the same world predicted by William Godwin in the previous century—again moved into the range of man's vision through Spencer's intellectual spy glass. Mind was destined to conquer matter, immortality to obviate the necessity for reproduction.

Either the prospect of harmony was too far off, or Dr. Trall was too practical to allow his own enthusiasm for this dream to overshadow a more pressing obligation to his clientele. As a consequence, his *Hydropathic Encyclopedia* advised women on the merits of the "safe period" and seemed to approve the idea of voluntary parenthood. Such inconsistency, as must have become apparent to discriminating readers after a while, was characteristic of his treatment of the birth control question. On one page of his *Sexual Physiology* (1866) he would piously announce in true Grahamite style that abstinence was the only acceptable method of controlling the family size. On another, he would discuss the methods used by certain tribes and national groups to induce abortion. Elsewhere the reader found a discourse on sponges and plugs which, when properly used, had the effect of preventing a meeting between sperm and ovum. Douches and drugs were treated briefly and in matter-of-fact fashion. Everybody, remarked Trall, seemed to be using them.

While this humane doctor certainly contradicted himself on some delicate subjects, on others he was entirely consistent. At the same time that he preached moderation and restraint in the frequency of sexual indulgence, he argued against prudery and secrecy. In fact, he would glorify the pursuit of sexual pleasures. His theory was that things treated in a matter-of-fact way rarely become the object of exaggerated and morbid preoccupation.

Trall was particularly consistent and emphatic on a point which might properly be called the focus of his attention. In all matters relating to marriage and the sexual relationship he insisted that woman have her freedom of choice. Would any man like it, he asked challengingly, if someone were to tell him how many children he was to have and when he was to have them? No woman liked it either. And there was more reason to leave this option with women: they were the ones who suffered from women's diseases and the hardships of pregnancy. No propensity, declared Mr. Trall in the language of phrenology, was more abused than Amativeness. In no other conflict of sexual interests was the male more at fault. Indeed, woman's equality in this particular matter implied her right to absolute supremacy.

The woman's rights movement had made a deep impression on Dr. Trall's social thinking. He eventually began to doubt whether there were fundamental differences between the sexes in such things as muscular structure. He suspected that most observed differences were caused by the nature of life activities. Were there not examples of masculine women and feminine men, he asked? And did we not make a mistake in separating boys from girls in play, school, and other activities? Then, too, was there any good reason for perpetuating our cramped style of conventional courting, the boy to pursue and the girl to have no more than the privilege of accepting? If anything, women were better at choosing mates than men. So impressed was Dr. Trall with the great role of woman in marriage, that he advised parents to send their daughters to his Hygeio-Therapeutic College as preparation for their careers as wives and mothers. There was more to successful marriage, he begged to state, than the alleged organ of Union for Life.

Nowhere, in the Civil War period and after, was the success of the popular health movement more apparent than in the *Herald of Health* under Dr. Trall's guidance. While North was fighting South on the battlefield, Trall and his cohorts were fighting alcohol, tobacco, meat, and male dominance in the *Herald of Health*. Men of prominence were invited to contribute articles in any field in which they felt competent. Horace Greeley wrote on "Alcoholic Liquors and Drugs," "Buildings for the Poor," and "Medical Ethics." The Reverend Henry Ward Beecher sent in pieces on "Athletic Sports," "Amusements," "The Law of Human Development," and, in keeping with his profession, "The Human Body as Temple of the Holy Ghost." The Reverend Octavius Brooks Frothingham wrote "Woman at Home," and "The Sacredness of the Body."

Dr. Diocletian Lewis (best known as "Dio") who had had some medical education but actually held his title by virtue of an honorary M. D., did a variety of pieces on woman's dress, normal schools, and physical training. The conservative Lewis, notorious for his annoying temperance agitation, was celebrated for his development of gymnastics and physical culture. Moreover, his writing talents were devoted as well to feminine hygiene, the digestive system, dress, and sex. Many a household knew his *Five Minute Chats with Young Women, and Certain Other Parties* as well as his *Chastity, Our Secret Sins.*

SOCIAL HYGIENE

Another contributor, also part owner and editor of the *Herald of Health*, was Dr. Martin Luther Holbrook, whose interests varied from "Hygiene in Ladies Seminaries," to "Shall We Eat Meat?" (an article on the parasitic diseases people contracted through pork and beef). Another article called the "Voice of Abused Childhood" raised the cry against child labor. Holbrook had come to New York City from an agricultural and medical education in Ohio. Publishing activities were not the only evidence of his enterprising nature. He also bought a part interest in a sanatarium of which he later became manager and sole proprietor. On the professional side, he was a professor of hygiene for fifteen years in the New York Medical College and Hospital for Women, did research in several medical areas, studied hypnotism and psychic phenomena with deep interest, and wrote many books which were printed by his own press.

Like most of the other pamphleteers for social progress through better physical health, Dr. Holbrook added marriage, eugenics, and sex hygiene to his literary output on liver complaints and nervous ailments. Such apparently different fields of medical interest were probably closely linked in his own mind under the general heading of gynecology. Holbrook's first full-length book provides a good index to his pervading humanitarian interest in women's health. It was his *Parturition without Pain; a Code of Directions for Escaping from the Primal Curse.*

What stirred the imagination of scientists most in Holbrook's time was the hypothesis that the race was destined to reach its perfect state through the processes of natural selection and sexual selection as described by Darwin. Throughout Holbrook's popular books on marriage and parenthood, the emphasis on human improvement through evolution was a strong one. He disagreed somewhat with Darwin on the proposition that the quantity of children born to a family governed their quality. But with regard to natural selection he was in full accord: "Let the strong, the capable, and the good," he declared in his *Stirpiculture,* "rear as many children as they can without overburdening themselves in any way, and let the weak, the imperfect and the bad raise few or none, but devote their lives to perfecting their own characters. In this way the future race will be modified for good and not for evil." The use of contraceptive methods was implied; but nowhere did the doctor describe these and their use.

Writing at a time when Anthony Comstock's anti-vice brigade was ever on the hunt for fresh prey, Dr. Holbrook was even more cautious than Dr. Trall. *Marriage and Parentage and the Sanitary and Physical Laws* (1882) and *Chastity, Its Physical, Intellectual, and Moral Advantages* (1894) revealed him to be of the Alcott stamp. One clear indication of where his allegiances lay in healthian circles was the name he gave to his only son—Dio Lewis Holbrook.

The information on birth control which Holbrook was loath to give and which Trall gave only sketchily and begrudgingly was very much needed and wanted by American women, judging from medical writing of the time. Even doctors who were not much interested in social reform took part in the fight against secrecy in sex. Naturally, some of these men were specialists in gynecology, and one subject most likely to provoke their interest in marriage and its implications was the frightening prevalence of abortions. In 1865, a one hundred dollar prize and a medal were awarded by the American Medical Association to the Boston gynecologist, Horatio Robinson Storer, for his essay on "Physical Evils of Forced Abortions." Storer was further rewarded in 1867 with a vice-presidency of the A.M.A.

Because of the reception given his treatment of this delicate theme, Storer published next a popular anti-abortion tract which appeared under the provocative title, *Why Not?—A Book for Every Woman*. The response to this book was equally gratifying. And since many of the testimonial letters sent the author by married women urged him to say something about the same subject to their husbands, Storer published, in 1869, a companion to *Why Not?*

This time it was *Is It I?—A Book for Every Man,* a plea to married men to give up absolute male rule and to consider the rights of their wives. It was a companion volume, the author explained, in the sense that it taught the male his sexual privileges and obligations. Much was made of the need for sex education to prevent some of the shameful practices engaged in by young people. In Dr. Storer's opinion, the best preventive medicine was marriage.

The fact of the matter was that this doctor hoped to counteract vicious tendencies through education. It worried him that "of late years, many have advocated the so-called doctrine of Free-love, in accordance with which, by some alleged process of elective affinity, every positive would seek its negative, every male its female, and this whether or no each of the parties were already legally the property of some other person." Subversive as such notions were to family solidarity, said Storer, the preachers of these beliefs had unfortunately found all too many proselytes.

As proof of the intellectual honesty and good faith of Ezra Heywood and his free-loving anarchist friends, it must be related that *The Word,* that avowed enemy of marriage, advertised and even distributed Storer's books, as it did Trall's and those of other writers on health for the people. *The Word* likewise found Dio Lewis' *Chastity* an excellent and useful volume while heartily disagreeing with the author's conservative views on marriage and with his cheering of the Comstock Laws. Readers of *The Word* were also made aware of the works of a newcomer in the field, who, though conservative, was in favor of telling the unsophisticated populace what it needed to know. The name of this humane physician was George Henry Napheys.

Perhaps it was because Napheys had had to struggle upward into medicine from humble beginnings that he felt so strongly about helping ordinary folk with their health troubles, especially those personal ones about which few experts were ready to speak freely. Having lost his parents when a boy, he learned shorthand and began to earn his living as a secretary. Some medical experience in the United States Navy and some post-Civil War schooling at Philadelphia's Jefferson Medical College brought him his medical degree in 1866. The new doctor devoted himself to a small private practice, to work in the Medical College's charity clinic, and, thanks to his shorthand skill, to writing up reports of medical meetings for the *Medical and Surgical Reporter.*

One of the first things his practitioner's eye noticed was the lack of works on sex hygiene written by responsible scientists. Napheys wrote his *The Physical Life of Woman* in 1869, submitting it in manuscript to physicians, clergymen, educators, and writers for their approval. The book was published in 1870, and counted among its sponsors the Reverends Henry Ward Beecher and Horace Bushnell as well as the Surgeon-General of the United States Army. In the following year, a companion volume for males was published under the title of *The Transmission of Life*. Napheys knew what opposition he could expect from guardians of public purity but decided—sustained as he was by the approval of many important people—to take his chances. "Ignorance," he declared, "is no more the mother of purity than it is of religion." Students of medicine, male and female, were apparently not the worse for their knowledge; the rest of the community would benefit just as doctors had.

Dr. Napheys treated his themes exhaustively, following organic development from youth in the premarital stages through parenthood with its duties and responsibilities. The physician's point of view was preserved throughout. "Plainly, yet delicately," in the words of the author, "the rules that should govern" a couple's relations were set forth. There were some married couples to whom no children came. There were others who had too many. Both situations were mentioned as needing corrective measures—"natural" measures of course. The inheritance of parental characteristics was also discussed, together with prenatal and child care.

Owing no allegiance to reform movements, Napheys found no fault with accepted marriage practices. In fact, he predicted that the sanctity of marriage would be observed more rigidly as civilization advanced. As he observed young men and women of his time, he found a mounting desire for genuine old-fashioned marriage. His own reason for writing was to increase the chances for happy marriage by furnishing a knowledge of proper sexual behavior.

In one important particular Napheys followed the pattern of popular health writing of lesser scientific pretension. Women, he thought, wielded a greater influence if they were beautiful. They therefore had an obligation to be beautiful—and had little reason not to be in view of the vast progress that had been made in the cosmetic arts. Together with D. G. Brinton, an army doctor, he wrote a handbook on the subject called *The Laws of Health in Relation to the Human Form*. Questions of overweight, skin care, pleasing breath, depilatories, and the use of garters were discussed with utmost candor. Brinton and Napheys had naught but scorn for those who called a leg a "limb" or an "extremity." The overdelicate in speech were strongly suspected of harboring unbecoming thoughts in their minds.

PLAIN HOME TALK

Whether they were originally so intentioned or not, most of the doctors who engaged in the popularization of sex knowledge entered at one point or another the territory of social reform. Their involvement ran from mild feminism for the gynecologists to radical extremism for some of the eugenists. But, however much social meaning may have been implicit in their writings, few doctors were highly conscious of their politics and still fewer joined organized movements to achieve their social purposes. In this respect, the Doctors Foote, father and son, were an outstanding exception.

The elder Edward Bliss Foote was born in 1829 to a family of small means. Having completed the meager education one received in those days in a Middle Western academy, he apprenticed himself to a printer. From printing to journalism was a short step. In three years Foote was near the top of his new vocation, holding a position as associate editor on the staff of a leading Brooklyn paper, the *Morning Journal.* A physician of his acquaintance provoked his interest in medicine. Foote's ability with the pen suggested his next occupational shift. He became secretary and assistant to his physician friend, studied medicine, and got his degree in 1860.

Nor had he laid aside his pen during the years of professional preparation. Two years before he was graduated from Penn Medical University in Philadelphia, he wrote and published the amazingly popular *Medical Common Sense* which sold 250,000 copies. In 1872 this early work was incorporated bodily in a new encyclopedic book of which a half-million copies found their way into up-to-the-minute homes. The new work was known as *Plain Home Talk about the Human System—The Habits of Men and Women—The Causes and Prevention of Disease—Our Sexual Relations and Social Natures,* etc.

Dr. Foote, and the son who followed in his footsteps, boasted of the best of motives for their interest in writing about sex. They wrote to help the many good people who were injured, lost to society, or completely destroyed for want of knowledge. They earned, true enough, large sums of money from the output of their Murray Hill Publishing Company. But they devoted this income unselfishly to the causes of human freedom. There lay before the Footes an easy road to wealth through writing and selling "safe" popular health manuals; for they had the skill of writing in a language "comprehensible alike to the rustic inmate of a basement and the exquisite student of an attic studio." Instead they chose the path lined with opposition, misunderstanding, and defamation. They were associated with political reform parties that never won an election and threw large sums of money into movements for human betterment. Their assumption was that no one was so wicked that he could not be improved by knowledge and affection in a friendly environment.

Starting their reformist activities under the influence of the liberal Unitarian, the Reverend Octavius Brooks Frothingham, the doctors Foote traveled to the religious left of complete anti-supernaturalism. Their *Health Monthly* ran from 1876 to 1895, giving space to every controversial subject of current interest. The reader was informed about Henry George's single tax agitation, about spelling reform, free thought, dress reform, prison reform, suffrage, women's property rights, greenbackism, cremation, birth control, and the relation of economics to crime. Medically significant reforms included pure food ideas, vivisection, the problem of venereal infection through the drinking cup, and the application of medicine and surgery to the prevention of crime.

Hardly onesided in their faith that controlled environment could better the race, the Footes, ardent readers of Darwin, Huxley, and Spencer, believed that the children of unfit parents were a liability to the species. The time had arrived, they declared, when thinking people should be interested first and foremost in the *quality* of reproduction, which of course meant encouraging the superior to breed and informing the rest about the desirability and the means of limiting their offspring. They advised, as important for the welfare of the next generation, that conception take place "when the respective progenitors are in a healthy condition of body and an elevated condition of mind. . . ." The young Edward Bond Foote summarized these views on breeding for quality in his *The Radical Remedy in Social Science; or Borning Better Babies through Regulating Reproduction by Controlling Conception.* Foote Junior practiced what he preached. His late marriage was a childless one because he considered himself physically unfit for fatherhood.

Both father and son were in the fight against the legalized bigotry of Comstock from its very inception, the former paying $8,000 in fines for a single act of defiance. The father's pamphlet, *Words in Pearl,* taught the technique of contraception and justified it on economic, eugenic, and medical grounds. The customary "decoy" letter requesting a copy was sent to him by a Comstock agent. He mailed one to the person who had asked for it and found himself under indictment, with bail set at $5,000, in the United States District Court of New York. This was in January 1876. The case was heard in June and July. The legal costs ran up to some $5,000 and, the verdict being "guilty," a fine of $3,000 had to be paid.

But the bold crusader had to concede a good deal to his adversary's strength. According to the table of contents of the 1881 edition of *Plain Home Talk,* pages 876 to 880 were supposed to be devoted to the prevention of conception. Instead they contained a discussion of Noyes' "male continence" method, because, according to Foote, of a "piece of meddlesome impertinence on the part of hasty law makers."

The cause, however, was not abandoned. The author of *Plain*

Home Talk prepared his *A Step Backward,* a pamphlet which explained his view on the Comstock Law of 1873 and on similar legislation enacted in New York State. The advances of science, both physical and social, said Foote, had made Malthus' checks undesirable even where necessary. Injurious methods of preventing conception were being practiced widely. Foeticide and baby farming were rampant. It was time that courageous spirits in America organized against the vestiges of "Romish asceticism of the fourth century" which were in the 1870's enjoying a recrudescence on the free soil of America.

It was hardly necessary, the pamphlet asserted, to cite the tremendous number of insane, blind, and otherwise defective people to demonstrate the need for birth control. Readers were urged to keep their minds open on the subject of scientific propagation and to consider the prospects for making the survival of the fittest a reality. Like Dr. Trall, the author suggested that the decision on having children be placed in the hands of the child-bearers. His own invention of a mechanical preventive device, designed by him for this purpose, had been refused patent rights some years before on the grounds that it would encourage immorality. Had the patent been granted, inventors would have been encouraged to improve and perfect it. As it was, doctors were prescribing inadequate and harmful devices to their patients with most unfortunate results. More than this he could not say without danger of legal reprisals. He could only recommend a few inexpensive pamphlets which as yet had not been banned from the mails.

Outside of the forbidden area of planned parenthood, he did what he could to beat back ignorance, that awesome enemy of mankind. "How many," he asked at the beginning of *Plain Home Talk*, "know the essential conditions to bring into the world a healthy child?" A boy and girl are in love. Or they think they are. Or maybe they are not. They marry. Soon the wife becomes pregnant. By design? Of course not. Probably by accident. And so "this botchery of human procreating machinery goes blindly at work turning out babies." Babies are born, and not one in a thousand mothers knows how to take care of them. Hence the necessity of that vast body of information presented by *Plain Home Talk*, on the causes from youth onward of nervous derangements, blood diseases, and whatever else ailed the reader.

Foote believed that sexual and marriage disturbances played a large part in causing disease. The section for married people therefore delved into every facet of married life, however minor it seemed. Snoring, sleeping in separate beds, jealousy, sexual indifference, and sexual moderation were discussed. Equality for the wife in marriage partnerships was advocated in true progressive fashion. There was little of the light humor which characterized many of the marriage manuals. The failures of monogamic marriage were a serious matter, and Foote was not averse to giving his full critical estimate of the problem just as Dr. Nichols had two decades before. He was, in fact, every bit as bitter as Nichols when he wrote:

> In every State in the Union, men and women can rush into matrimony *ad libitum,* but when once caught, they can wriggle and twist like a pig in a fence, but cannot get out. The result is that monogamic countries are filled with adulterers and illegalized polygamists, who sustain the health and soul destroying institution of prostitution; support in splendor thousands of fashionable courtesans; destroy the peace of the home circle; people our cities and villages with moral and physical lepers; fill our almshouses with paupers; our jails and prisons with criminals; our hospitals with cripples, and our asylums with lunatics. This is so, and every physician in extensive practice knows it.

For Thomas L. Nichols the inevitable logical consequence of such a state of affairs was to abolish legal marriage altogether in favor of a free love society. Dr. Foote's solution was of a different order. He agreed with the social scientists who were pressing for better-written divorce laws, but dismissed divorce as a mere palliative. a measure which would never remedy the causes of mismating and might even encourage lightly contracted sexual unions. He spoke against the suggested uniform national divorce law, arguing that the monopolists and bankers of our era could easily seize and wield the power once held by kings, nobles, and priests. Our State governments, he said, were big and strong enough to take care of our morals.

A scientific plan of regulation was conceivable. Dr. Edward Bliss Foote offered an outline of it as a basis for discussion before the Manhattan Liberal Club, one of the libertarian organizations in which he was a leading spirit. The scheme was so authoritarian that several of the members, among them the aged Stephen Pearl Andrews, rejected it immediately. It called for doing away with the prevailing system of legalizing marriage and substituting for it a Board of Physiologists composed of men and women in equal number, all well versed in psychology, phrenology, and physiognomy. The Board, a State body, was to be empowered to pass on the mutual suitability and congeniality of couples applying for marriage licenses. The same group was to grant divorces to the "miserably mated." A Federal cabinet department was to be given an advisory role. Its authority was to be so delimited as not to interfere with States' rights. Foote, like many other nineteenth-century liberal democrats, saw many objections to overexpanded welfare activity on the part of the government at Washington.

One feature included in the Foote plan was obviously designed to cater to the group which was lukewarm to regulated monogamy. It was this: Youngsters were to be encouraged to marry at a very early age—a provision meant to combat the vices—solitary, social, and homosexual. But the raising of a family *had* to be postponed until the parties had reached their maturity—thirty years for men, and twenty-five for women. The couple was to be given an opportunity to seek divorce before entering the "mature family" stage. "There would (under such regulation) be. a tolerable degree of certainty that the couple would carry through and raise a promising family of children before any serious matrimonial differences arose to poison the atmosphere of the home circle." An Institute of Heredity was provided for the purpose of educating the public on the subjects of hereditary and prenatal influence.

The liberals, along with their anarchist and socialist fellow travelers in common causes, felt that the humane Dr. Foote and his son had gone too far in their effort to right a grievous social wrong. They nevertheless continued to have the kindest thoughts for the family which had poured its funds into the Free Speech League and had contributed lavishly to the defense of freedom seekers who had run afoul of the law.

Upon the death of the father in 1906, and of his son six years later, the editors of the *Truth Seeker, Lucifer,* the *Freethinker, Mother Earth,* and the *Malthusian* added their eulogistic testimonials to the words of Theodore Schroeder, Moses Harman, his daughter Lillian, and Dr. Juliet H. Severance (anarchist-oriented worker in every important reform movement of her time). Tributes also arrived from Elizabeth Cady Stanton, "Bob" Ingersoll, and a host of clergymen, lawyers, and authors who had followed the Footes' active struggle against censorship.

The careers of Edward Bond Foote and Edward Bliss Foote should theoretically have frightened future medical experts on family limitation into some other form of specialization. Events and needs, however, were too compelling for twentieth-century doctors like William J. Robinson to give up their vigorous campaigns for population control. Moreover, it became fairly common, especially during the first World War, for medical magazines to publish views favorable to birth control. The arguments were largely gynecological and eugenic, the emphasis in the eugenics field being largely on the curbing of certain hereditary diseases or dispositions to disease. Doctors at this stage were rarely molested and were even applauded for their efforts by social-minded leaders, radical and conservative alike.

Liberal weeklies like the *Nation* and the *New Republic* did their part to publicize the movement as did also more "popular" magazines like the *Pictorial Review* and *Physical Culture.*

The war brought new reasons for adopting birth control, reasons which appealed in one way or another to pacifists and militarists, socialists and capitalists. The peace partisans contended that the menace of war would be reduced when overpopulation, fear of famine, and the consequent scramble for land were ended. If a nation *had* to fight a war, moreover, its defensive powers would be increased by a higher quality of men produced by controlled and selective procreation. The nation's aggressive patriots liked this notion well enough for military reasons. There was also a current fear, whipped up by yellow journalism, of the menace of an overpopulated Far East. Birth control was an idea for export, especially to the lands beyond the Pacific.

Partisans of the wage-earning sector of the population hoped to lessen serious social and economic evils by decreasing the population. Theirs was a prospect of fewer people unemployed, higher wages, and better jobs. On the other side of the picture were the more fortunately situated members of society who stood to gain at taxpaying time from decreasing state costs for the care of the unfit. The feminists approved because birth control would help maintain the gains in sexual equality which had been won during the war.

How well these social ideas have corresponded with social reality is still difficult to measure precisely. Of a certainty, the demand for knowledge of contraceptive methods has been greatest in times of economic depression when low incomes dramatized the advisability of having small families. Wars, on the other hand, with all their threat to personal and family security, have produced an opposite psychology. The phenomenon of war-baby breeding points clearly to a wholesale relaxation of marital prudence during periods of military emergency.

These are elements of the complex problem which has occupied the attentions of serious students of human affairs in our own century. Among those prominent in the scientific study of man in his sexual role have been sociologists, anthropologists, educators, psychologists, physicians, philosophers, and statisticians. This may be said of all of the scientists, that their job has been not only to explain prevailing sexual behavior, but also, in a sense, to justify much of what the currently accepted ethic would not countenance.

TEN

Female vs. Male in the Twentieth Century

"I dedicate this book," wrote Lester Frank Ward at the beginning of his *Pure Sociology*, "to the twentieth century on the first day of which it was begun." The time had come for social science to consolidate the scientific findings of the nineteenth century and to incorporate them into the permanent body of knowledge. Darwin and his followers had led the way with a thoroughly biological view of life; the anthropologists and historians had studied a great variety of cultures, thereby upsetting standards long maintained by powerful religious forces; pragmatic doctors and practical social scientists had used some of the available new learning in valiant movements to improve the circumstances attending man's sojourn in this life. It remained for devoted and intelligent investigators to synthesize the knowledge gained.

Among those who undertook this Herculean labor were large numbers of academicians who followed separate tendencies to the point where they merged into what has aptly been called social Darwinism. The new approach, briefly described, was to apply the basic notions of "survival of the fit" and "natural selection" to the study of society, and to attempt its improvement within the limits set by biologically determined factors. The more ruthless and ruggedly individualistic of these social architects placed their emphasis on the "survival of the fit" aspect of Darwinism, proposing that race improvement would profit by a discard of those who did not rate high in the struggle. The more humane, and those who adhered to the basic assumptions of democracy, sought an interpretation of natural selection which did not logically imply the extermination of the mass of their ordinary fellow men.

As so often happens when minds of differing mold speculate on the social meaning of a scientific hypothesis, the logic of social biology worked equally well for both sides. The "survival" faction claimed that man stood at the point of greatest development in his evolutionary march; existing conditions, therefore, were not only the best possible but were irremediable. The other side asserted that human intelligence had evolved to a maturity capable of rectifying nature's erratic ways. The latter position was best represented by Lester Ward. For his extensive experience and reading in biology and in sociology, gave him extraordinary qualifications for estimating nature's direction. The best and latest in anthropology, social history, and biology were drawn upon in his *Pure Sociology* to help demonstrate the existence of spontaneous life forces, and to show how these forces were largely, but not completely, responsible for the shape of social arrangements past, present and future. The other side of the picture, that is, the use of human intelligence to direct nature's energies into a more orderly pattern, he presented as *Applied Sociology.*

THE EQUAL HALF

It was lucky for sexual democracy that this brand of social Darwinism appeared when it did. Already it was being said that science confirmed the ancient assumption that woman was the weaker vessel. The female physiological organization, as this interpretation had it, was such that if woman attempted to go beyond her accustomed sphere in the world, she would certainly deteriorate and drag the whole of hereditarily determined future humanity down with her. The nineteenth-century feminists replied that if woman's biological services at home had not already destroyed her, not even the most arduous of men's tasks outside the home ever could cause physical deterioration. But conscientious and timid feminists needed something more solid than the spectacular and politically tainted proofs of a Moses Harman or an Ezra Heywood. They wanted a philosophy more universal in its groundwork than that of amateur eugenists. They wanted unanswerable proof that women were at least men's equals.

Ward's theory of gynaecocentricity satisfied their wish. It showed that the female principle was the source of perpetuity for the race in somewhat the same way as the sun was the source of planetary energies. The "other" sex, in short, held priority and superiority throughout nature. Anthropologists had studied primitive societies, and concluded that women had had the upper hand in a more "natural" period of civilization. The gynaecocentrist went back beyond that. He peeled off all the layers of life in evolution until he reached the single cell. In the beginning, there was one female cell and one male cell, and these joined as equal partners in the process of reproduction. As beings rose in the scale of complexity, the female took the lead as the principal form of life and carried with her a male appendage whose sole business it was to supply germinating particles when it came to be time for the female to reproduce. At the next stage, as exemplified by certain insect forms, the female did the necessary work to insure survival of the species, while the male stood by parasitically to wait for his one purpose in life, the act of fertilization. After that, he was destroyed. In the higher animal species, where the balance was modified, the power of sexual selection still belonged to the female. Males were endowed with more attractive forms or plumage supposedly in order to catch the attention of the females.

This situation, so the theory went, persisted in the earliest of human societies. Women were dominant as the life-bearing and life-maintaining half of society, while the men devoted their time to field sports and applied primitive cosmetics to enhance their appearance. This gynaecocratic stage, said Lester Ward, lasted only as long as the male was ignorant of his very definite contribution to the procreative process. While men were still unaware of their role in parenthood, women retained the privilege of sexual selection. But once they realized their family stakes, having increased their originally superior muscular endowment through generations of leisurely exercise, the men seized power. Thus the andocratic regime had been started. Jealous of their newly acquired paternity rights, men relegated their women to the "safety" of the household and assumed the work of the everyday world for themselves. With the shift of the privilege of sexual selection to the male, the female became preoccupied with her superficial attractions, and her original physical endowment atrophied through centuries of disuse. The male power of selection only intensified the downward process because men liked their women beautiful but weak. The highpoint of feminine frailty had come in the nineteenth century, when women competed in the struggle to be selected by fainting and otherwise feigning illness.

This was only one example of man's penchant for distorting nature's meaning. Our philosophers, in their efforts to glorify the human mind in its spiritual and religious attainments, had acquired the habit of deprecating the physical aspects of love. Some of the more advanced of these wise men had even predicted a millennium in which immortality would render sex unnecessary. It remained for new trends in scientific philosophy to restore the dignity accorded sex in ancient practices of phallic worship and other sexual rituals. Intellectual snobbishness finally made its peace, in the latter part of the nineteenth century, with the psychophysical fact that sex was necessary to humankind for spiritual as well as physical reasons. Backed by the exalted statements of a Condorcet, a Haeckel or a Schopenhauer, the sociologist of the twentieth century no longer needed the martyr's or the erotic's drive to celebrate the beauty and compelling power of natural love.

SEXOLOGY

Moreover, philosophical justifications were supplemented from the very beginning of the twentieth century by a plethora of sexologic writings. Available to the masses, who could purchase them at bookstores as well as through the mails, was a plentiful supply of popular pamphlets and books produced in the latter part of the preceding century. The works of the Foote family were kept in print. Dr. Alice B. Stockham, author of *Tokology, Karezza,* and the type-written *Wedding Night* (for distributing which she had been arrested and fined $300) remained active in the field of sex ethics and birth control. New American writers appeared to swell the publishing output in this field to some hundred items in a decade.

The larger part of the advanced scientific material, usually sold to professional men only, came from abroad to be republished or translated under American publishers' imprints. The list for 1901-1902 included Richard Krafft-Ebing's *Psychopathia Sexualis* in two authorized translations from the German. Another edition was printed in 1906. Six of the seven volumes of Havelock Ellis' *Studies in the Psychology of Sex* appeared between 1903 and 1910. Volume one, on *The Evolution of Modesty,* seems to have been enough in demand for its publisher, Frank A. Davis of Philadelphia, to issue a new and enlarged edition in 1910. The decade also saw an English adaptation of Dr. Auguste Henri Forel's *Sexual Question.*

Sex education, heretofore the province of a handful of politically oriented doctors and self-styled social scientists, received its first wholehearted academic recognition from the pen of Granville Stanley Hall, then president of Clark University. Hall's qualifications as a scientist were beyond question. Long years of laboratory experiment both here and abroad had prepared him for the presentation of his treatise on the period of sexual maturation. Including a comprehensive study of all that had been written on his subject, Hall published in 1904 his *Adolescence; Its Psychology and Its Relations to Physiology, Anthropology, Sociology, Sex, Crime, Religion, and Education.* The ideas presented were hard to refute, the manner of their expression beyond rebuke. Even Hall's plea for teaching science without religious restriction found the religious defenders of morality disarmed because the president of Clark had been fully educated and trained for the ministry before he turned to psychology. Hall even employed language derived from his earlier theological schooling. As the educator Edward L. Thorndike observed with marked disapproval, the language of *Adolescence* was a "highly complicated amalgam of medicine, erotic poetry, and inspirational teaching." An example of Hall's sexologese will show the point of Thorndike's criticism:

Every gemmule is mobilized and the sacred hour of heredity normally comes when adolescence is complete in wedlock and the cerebro-spinal rings up the sympathetic system, and this hands over the reins to the biophores and germ cells, which now assert their dominance over those of the soma. In the most unitary of all acts, which is the epitome and pleroma of life, we have the most intense of all affirmations of the will to live and realize that the only true God is love, and the center of life is worship. . . . Communion is fusion and beatitude. It is the supreme hedonic narcosis, a holy intoxication, the chief ecstasy, because the most intense of experiences. . . .

Luckily the unsophisticated public did not have to depend on Hall's effusions because it could not have learned much without the aid of an interpreter. The prestige of a college president and eminent teacher of psychology did a great deal to restore natural love to respectability but ordinary people went to dozens of plainer texts to get practical help for pressing problems. Those who could afford twenty-five dollars as the price of bolstering their self-confidence might purchase Webster Edgerly's five hundred page *Private Lessons in the Cultivation of Sex Magnetism; Teaching the Development and Wonderful Enlargement of those Powers and Influences that Nature Has Implanted in Every Life.* The generation born in the first decade of the twentieth century was more fortunate than its parents in that the price of Edgerly came down to seven dollars to compete with numerous subsequently published books on the art of love. For the time being, there were less pretentious lovers' manuals at twenty-five cents and upward.

The five-year period before the first World War provided a good market for fairly sound, inexpensive books from the pens of the prolific Winfield Scott Hall, Margaret Sanger, and William J. Robinson. Hall wrote, in addition to his *Biology, Physiology, and Sociology of Reproduction,* many family instruction pamphlets like *Father and Daughter, Father and Son,* and *Daughter, Mother, and Father.* At about the same time Mrs. Sanger offered *What Every Girl Should Know* and *What Every Mother Should Know.* Dr. Robinson, who built the Critic and Guide publishing house on the foundations of sex information, wrote his *Never Told Tales* about the consequences of sex ignorance, and then dedicated a series of small books to removing that ignorance. Among the first were *Sex Knowledge for Men, Sex Knowledge for Women and Girls,* and *Woman, Her Sex and Home Life.*

Winfield Scott Hall and his collaborator, Jeannette Winter, were warmly praised for expressing the great truths of life (learned from research into hundreds of personal histories) in just the way a parent would want to present these truths to his own children. Sanger and Robinson met with public resistance because of their birth control associations, and also, in all likelihood, because of their unwelcome, overspecific instructions to women and girls. The man who won universal acclaim from parents and professionals alike was Professor Maurice Alpheus Bigelow of Teachers College, Columbia University.

A disciple of the social hygienist Prince A. Morrow, Bigelow spent many years in the study of sex hygiene before presenting his *Sex Education* in 1916. The cordial reception given this book, which is standard reading to this day, had much to do with its author's skill in presenting scientific truth in a manner sufficiently conservative to avoid offense. Bigelow's vagueness in appropriate places added to his reputation so that few critics pronounced the book strong medicine for adolescents. Also to his credit was the fact that he set down specific criteria for good sex teaching, namely "a balanced and thoroughly qualified teacher and a judicious amount and selection of teaching." *Sex Education* was, in a sense, intended to stem the tide of current interest in sexual subjects, a tide which, according to Professor Bigelow, had pushed the doors open for too much instruction. The tide, of course, had been battering the dikes, though not too successfully, for several generations. A few of the factors which added impetus to it at this point were the increasing strength of feminism, an intensification of the perennial marriage crisis, and a visit to America by Sigmund Freud in 1909.

AS IN A DREAM

Freud visited this country in the autumn of 1909 under the most favorable auspices. Both he and his disciple Carl Jung (not yet at the time in revolt against Freud) had been invited by President G. Stanley Hall to participate in the program of Clark University's twentieth-anniversary celebration. Hall apparently had no idea of the stir he was about to create. He had not himself found Freud's contribution to psychology earth-shaking. The lengthy and heavily footnoted volumes of *Adolescence* contained but three citations of the work of the great Viennese psychoanalyst. The conservative Hall hardly anticipated that the American press of 1910 would be full of a new excitement which had caught the imagination of the American people, that his guests would provoke a struggle over a "belief," and that this "belief" would steadily gain adherents and sprout sectarian factions to accommodate differences of opinion among the believers.

Hall had prefaced his *Adolescence* with an exhortation to readers to do something quickly about the restlessness and undisciplined character of American youth. After Freud's visit (which Hall himself had arranged) the younger set got completely out of hand. At least that is what Freud's enemies among the intellectuals charged. It is reasonable to suppose that the Freudian description of a struggle between the libido and social restrictions provided an arsenal of self-justification for youth in revolt. But it was hardly reasonable to blame

Freud for starting a revolution which a great variety of movements had been instigating for an entire century. A reading of magazine literature around the turn of the century proves that America considered itself to be in a moral crisis many years before Freud became the whipping-boy of frightened Victorians. Before 1910 the causes of rapidly increasing divorce and moral laxity were sought in economics, urbanism, and woman's rights. There were those who found it simpler thereafter to blame the loosening of sexual controls on psychoanalysis.

Granting that Freud set people to thinking dangerously by his insistence on the conflict between sex and society, he cannot be said to have advocated directly the scrapping of conventional morality. Nor could he be held accountable if people gave freer rein to their latent behavior because they could now explain that "Freud says it is best not to inhibit." In simple fact, when the doctor announced his findings on the sexual roots of human conduct—as many others had more than hinted previously—most informed people accepted his hypothesis without emotion. The violent public reaction to Freud must therefore be attributed to other factors such as his manner of presentation, his theory of infantile sexuality, and his explorations into the nature of parent-child love relationships. There had always existed in the discussion of sexual matters a subtle separation between the sacred and the obscene. The line was not only vaguely drawn but it also shifted unpredictably from time to time. A writer of Havelock Ellis' stamp was able to present in print much of the content of his "restricted" *Studies in the Psychology of Sex* by translating it into delicately written literary essays. He could be clear without violating the inviolable. An attractive prose style successfully beclouded the discomforting meaning of what he said. Freud, on the other hand, had no regard for the sacred aspect of his subject, spoke too plainly and descriptively, and thereby incurred the opposition of his maturer—or older—audience. The doctors who stood with him at first soon drew back. Those who accepted the importance of examining overt sexual behavior, shrank from delving into the exposed subconscious. Otherwise balanced citizens were disturbed at the prospect of what might turn up if they looked beneath the placid surface.

Freud's objectionableness to his critics did not chiefly reside in the all-powerful role he assigned to the libidinal urge when applied to adults; that was tolerable to the open-minded. But few could accept the notion that an innocent babe got more from its nursing than milk, and that infants engaged in a variety of activities of a basically sexual nature. Moreover, when Freud plotted the constellation of love relationships among the blood members of a family, the resulting picture was so ugly that all averted their eyes. It was unthinkable that Oedipus and Electra, those beautifully tragic characters of ancient Greek drama, could be metaphoric symbols for all the Jacks and Jills of twentieth-century America. Many preferred to believe that clinical reports in a book like Freud's *Interpretation of Dreams* merely revealed "a seamy side of life in Vienna which might well have been left alone."

From 1910 to 1916 the American Dr. A. A. Brill published translations of *Three Contributions to the Theory of Sex, The Interpretation of Dreams, The Psychopathology of Everyday Life,* and *Wit and its Relation to the Unconscious.* Reviewers were sufficiently awed by Freud's reputation to credit him with good ideas and intentions. However, they quite commonly summed up their evaluation with a remark about the distortions produced by his emphasis on erotic influences. The *argumentum ad hominem* was not entirely overlooked by an occasional angry reviewer. One such commentator went so far as to remark that "Professor Freud writes with a degree of introspection which betrays his Oriental heredity and often leads him into pure mysticism."

Carl Jung too came off with his share of public disapproval as well as with some applause. When his *Psychology of the Unconscious* appeared here in 1916, some were impressed while others relegated it (especially that portion of it which dealt with the Oedipus complex) to the library of the pathologist. Warner Fite in the *Nation* described the book as presenting "some five-hundred-odd pages of incoherence and obscenity in the form of a psychoanalytic interpretation of the experiences of a sentimental young American woman. . . who wrote verses and believed herself to be inspired." On the whole, however, Jung made a positive impression on Americans in their early tasting of psychoanalysis. He left them with a two-word vocabulary with which they could glibly describe the universe of personality types. From that time onward, one could dismiss an acquaintance as an "introvert" or "extrovert," indicating by the inflection of the voice whether one approved or disapproved.

So far as the lay public was concerned, the net effect of the first ten years of Freudian influence was high receptivity on the part of irresponsible youth, rejection by the older representatives of social stability, and much debate over the importance of instinctual sex drives. The discussion itself was the most profitable aspect of the period since, in the process, the veil of conversational inhibition was lifted a little. The professional sociologists, finding Freud's science too subjective for their current aspirations to scientific status, were highly suspicious of psychoanalytic techniques and turned their backs on them for an entire decade following their presentation in America. Not that they were uninterested in problems of sex, love, and marriage. Problems of family structure and solidarity had been major concerns since the first years of professional self-consciousness. The statistical compilations and analyses of United States Commissioner of Labor Carroll D. Wright had further stimulated their interest in marriage and divorce. The years before Freud entered upon the scene found several sociologists preempting the province of sex by combining data from the disciplines of biology, psychology, anthropology, law, economics, ethics, statistics, and whatever else was pertinent, into a grand synthesized science of love.

SOCIAL SCIENCE OBJECTS

Psychoanalysis was disqualified on many counts. Not only was there a widespread aversion to explaining all behavior in terms of sexual behavior, but there was also an aversion on scientific grounds to explaining social phenomena in terms of any single factor. This was an era of pluralism, and Freud had designed a monolithic structure. Social science liked to group a variety of cultural items, particularly of the kind susceptible of direct observation, and then to build a theory by fitting the particles together inductively. Psychoanalysis found its data in mysterious recesses of the mind which could not be visited by the sociologists for purposes of verification. Freud claimed to work on biological foundations, but it was difficult to put one's finger on the organs he studied.

As nearly as could be determined, Dr. Freud was dealing with instinctive behavior as he had observed it among his patients. A good scientist, the sociologists felt, should integrate his work with that of other instinct specialists, Freud did not. The lists of instincts publicized by psychologists like William James, Edward Lee Thorndike, and William McDougall were worth considering. It was easier to think of complicated life patterns as being rooted in groups of competing instincts rather than in a single, overmastering one like sex. Sociologists too were contributing their lists. Albion W. Small of the University of Chicago spoke of six basic "interests." William Isaac Thomas, who taught at Oberlin until the turn of the century and then went to Chicago, listed four fundamental "wishes." [1]

Small wonder then that the American academic world developed a temporary blind spot for Freudianism. In the scholars' search for certainty and for solutions to social problems, the new, mysterious method of investigation might serve only to complicate their findings to date. A few pioneers were already beginning to challenge the

[1] Lester Ward, however, came close to Freud in his theory of the elaboration of all forms of love—romantic, conjugal, maternal and kinship—out of one basic "natural" love. Natural love was curiously like sex drive, but, in the context of Ward's larger system of psychic forces, it sounded more reasonable than it would if an entire sociological system had based upon it alone, as was Freud's. The exposition on natural love was but a section of *Pure Sociology* (there is a suspicion that Ward put it *there* for reasons of personal security); pure sociology was itself part of a larger treatment of social phenomena.

existence of instincts as such, hinting that what appeared innate was really custom-built behavior, and therefore subject to change, however slow. The long-term view of scientific sociology was toward human improvement through benevolent professional guidance. Instincts, innate drives, and the like were products of scientific observation, but they were troublesome, and there were many scientists who would have preferred for psychology to "undiscover" or learn how to control them.

∽ ∽

Particularly distressing to feminist-minded scholars must have been the implications of the castration complex, a Freudian invention. If it were true that women universally envied the male's special sexual equipment and felt inferior for the lack of it, then the dream of equality could only be a male dream. Lester Ward, in particular, was headed for disillusionment; for it was he who noted that there had been a reversal of trend in the balance of power and that "under the growing power of sociogenetic energies of society" the world was moving toward gynandocracy, or an autonomy of the sexes. Perhaps it was wish fulfillment that made him see the scale pans coming to rest at the same level. "I am tired," he protested, "of this one-sided civilization, this half-built society, of this false chivalry, this mock modesty, this pretended regard which one sex assumes for the other, while loads of putrid prejudice hang upon woman's neck."

Society was indeed moving toward a stage of equality for women *vis a vis* men but only scientists of Ward's optimistic bent and moral indignation could regard as imminent the final transition to that stage. The more objective view, that held by the equally competent William I. Thomas, was that the gap between male and female achievement still yawned wide; and there were reasons to suppose that it would never close. Men seemed to enjoy inherent advantages in their greater strength, restlessness, and motor aptitude. Such differences in physical traits must certainly produce parallel differences in social status and activity, not to speak of the variations in personality and mentality between the sexes.

The law of "greater variability of the male," a scientific generalization attributed to Darwin, was not the property of sociologists alone. The psychologists, mainly those working to improve educational practices, tested the law by newly developed research methods and affirmed the fact that the average woman is about as intelligent as the average man but that the males weighed more heavily on the genius and idiot ends of the scale. From the point of view of social engineering, the male idiots did not detract from the leadership and inventiveness of the geniuses, so that it appeared imperative to promote the education of male genius. G. Stanley Hall, building upon this hypothesis, offered a scheme for adolescent girls savoring of nectar and lilies. He would minimize the intellectual in his pedagogical heaven for girls, and concentrate on the development of the soul, the body, and the intuitions.

Professor Thorndike, though he objected to Hall's poetic bent, arrived at approximately the same conclusions. Practically speaking, the now accepted difference in range of ability meant that women should be educated for what they could do and probably would do in their adult lives. The probability of marriage and children cast its shadow on Thorndike's page. Moreover, calculating that the need for highly gifted individuals in highly intellectual professions was quite small, he decided that there was no point in educating women for leadership in such fields; it was, in any case, above their abilities. Society needed more nurses, teachers, doctors, and architects—professions well within the intellectual grasp of women and more suited to their emotional and artistic nature.

Rare was the male student of sex differences who concluded otherwise. Argue as he would that women inherited as much from their fathers as they did from their mothers, Havelock Ellis was forced to the standard frame of logic: woman's special physiological endowment must somehow devalue her equal heredity. Perhaps it was glandular differences, especially for childbearing functions, that played tricks on woman's brain. Certainly muscular factors were involved. How else could one explain the fact that female performance in the workaday world did not measure up to that of the male? Even in the arts, Ellis added, "to play a violin requires muscular strain, and only a robust woman can become a famous singer." To further elaborate, he pointed out that girls exhibited a precocity of both bodily and mental development at about the age of fourteen, racing ahead of the boys for a couple of years, and thereafter marking time while the boys moved ahead onward and upward. A few psychologists explained this phenomenon on the grounds that boys were emotionally blocked at the age of fourteen and that their later superior opportunities elicited full development, while girls were brought to a halt by worldly restrictions. Ellis countered the suggestion with an example from the animal world. One could not say "that the female giraffe leads a more confined and domestic life than her brother." Yet she was less agile in the battle for survival.

Few would have desired a change if the assumption of sexual differences were not used so consistently to perpetuate woman's minority status. There was a difference between distinction and discrimination. The feminist world favored retaining differences designed to coordinate the sexes. As it happened, the argument was used to subordinate one to the other, educationally, economically, and in every other way. For example boys remained the better social

365

investment and continued to get a more than equal chance to develop their latent genius. Women wanted a chance "to draw for genius" now that it had been announced that they were on the average as intelligent as men. They asked, as had Mary Wollstonecraft more than a century before, that cultural restrictions be removed—and then the world would see. It took time for a minority which had just entered its period of liberation to show what it could do. There was indeed a predominance of male names in *Who's Who,* but men had had a head·start to be reckoned in millennia. Intelligence tests affirmed male superiority. It remained to be seen whether the items tested were not favorable to boys because of their social roles, which gave them early practical training. Time and the refinement of testing mechanics would tell.

In the meantime the country had to cope with more immediate problems. After many decades of industrial exploitation of her labor—at which she was supposedly inferior to the male—the weaker vessel was most imperatively in need of governmental protection. Investigations by social agencies added weight to statistical compilations by official bodies, surveys which dramatically demonstrated that women were being overworked and underpaid even as compared with their exploited brothers, sons, and husbands. At the beginning of our century the health and welfare of American womanhood was still getting the lion's share of attention from purveyors of popular health knowledge. The physical culturist, Bernarr Macfadden, had joined in celebrating—with profit—the *Power and Beauty of Superb Womanhood* (1901). Diet and hydropathy for middle class-women were far from forgotten. But somebody had to have a care for the underfed working class woman to whom Macfadden's advice on fasting would have been superfluous even if she had had the wherewithal to buy his books and magazines.

A movement to organize women into trade unions did not meet with signal success. The socialist literature of Bebel and Kate O'Hare was a stimulant but not in revolutionary proportions. Scott Nearing and his wife, Nellie Marguerite Nearing, contributed pamphlets of the same kind, issuing in 1912 a compilation of their writings under the title of *Woman and Social Progress; a Discussion of the Biologic, Domestic, Industrial, and Social Possibilities of American Woman.* Mary Van Kleeck and other social workers carried out studies of the industries in which female employment was high.

Partly as a result of these researches and agitations, and partly because of a worldwide movement in that direction, State legislatures passed laws establishing a floor for women's wages and a ceiling for their hours of work. Outstanding as counsel for the defense in cases where ten-hour and minimum-wage laws were being challenged in the Supreme Court was Louis Brandeis, who was himself appointed to that court by President Wilson in 1916. The constitutionality of these laws was consistently upheld.

Protection from economic exploitation was all to the good, but, while acknowledged with gratitude, it bore no marks of the feminist goal of equality. The principle of equal pay for equal work was absent. Factory work had been added to housework without any upward adjustment of rewards for the performance of two jobs instead of one. And, with all the burdens they had assumed in order to supplement the below-subsistence wage brought in by their husbands, women were still not accorded their full share of social power in the community and family power in the home.

THE LITERATI

The situation at the beginning of the century was still safely under male control, but not comfortably so. The dictum that as man earns his living so does he think was valid enough to establish a case for the women, a case which sensitive literary men and women dramatized in their writings. Moreover, the astounding increase in the divorce rate could not remain unheeded. For what may have been an alarming statistic to social science was a symptom of faulty marriage doctrines and of the uncompromising war of the sexes to perceiving dramatists, novelists, and essayists. Magazines and newspapers catering to mass approval closed their eyes to this situation. They exploited the salacious and spectacular while branding the divorce-suit procedure immoral. A wholesale revolt against marriage led by disaffected womanhood was under way, but media of mass communication chose to treat it as an amusing local skirmish.

Feminine unrest, stimulated by educational and wage-earning opportunities as well as by the reduced scope of family life itself, was further inflamed by provocative books and plays. Curiously enough, the stimulus came not from reputedly infidel and immoral French literature, but from Scandinavian and Germanic sources. The prime instigator was the Norwegian dramatist, Henrik Ibsen, a most pronounced individualist and social anarchist in literary garb.

It was more than a literary whim of Ibsen's to have the heroine of his *A Doll's House* suddenly discover that her domestic happiness was specious, that her personality had been circumscribed and smothered by society's conventions. Her solution—to explore the world alone in search of selfhood—was of questionable wisdom; but in a time of change in women's status, few could be wise enough to reach adequate solutions.

Ghosts attacked family forms from another angle. It pictured the horrible hereditary effects created by an unfit father who fulfilled his procreative obligations to society. The product was a degenerate son. The story, as woven around the tragic life of a victimized mother,

367

was a pointed plea to change laws and customs which chained either marriage partner to a repulsive relationship. The case for a single standard was thus supported by one additional witness.

The Swedish feminist Ellen Key extracted from this tragedy the affirmation of her own principle—and that of Mary Gove Nichols—that a woman must be faithful to her own personality rather than to conventional morality. Miss Key hailed the progress made in her own era, when women acknowledged that they had erotic lives of their own, and men were beginning to discover that women were in possession of individual souls. People were beginning to demand of the male-female nexus that it exhibit mutuality in both the emotional and intellectual spheres. The rule of monogamy was being tempered rather than deposed in the marriage revolt. The Key formula was reminiscent of the Fourierist-Swedenborg-Spiritualist approval of men and women finding their affinities, even after marriage, "as the relentless force of nature's will." Freedom of divorce was also part of the scheme.

Joined with Ellen Key in the literary rebellion were Havelock Ellis, the English socialist Edward Carpenter, the American intellectual Floyd Dell, and, of course, the Irish dramatist, George Bernard Shaw. Dell represented the cult of expressionists whose pleasure-bent philosophy helped place the geographical center of moral laxness in the Greenwich Village section of New York City. It was Dell who left a blueprint of the new morality in his *Outline of Marriage,* and described the failure of the plan in operation in his *Intellectual Vagabondage.* All did not go well in the village paradise built by Dell's impecunious writer friends. Many an idealistic male, freely joined to a "new" woman, discovered that the element of experimentalism in their relationship frequently left the woman the loser.

While Dell was a feminist close to the Ibsen variety, Shaw was a thorough going critic of the unreasonableness of social institutions. The characters in his plays flung defiance at Victorian marriage ideals, while his prefaces reasoned facetiously about them. His clever though questionable logic often reached odd conclusions. The introductory remarks to *Getting Married,* for instance, predicated divorce as the condition for the maintenance of marriage rather than for its destruction. A thousand indissoluble marriages, he explained, meant nor more nor less than a thousand marital units, whereas a thousand divorces could result in up to two thousand remarriages. Strangely enough, our contemporary statisticians have shown, without evaluating the moral desirability of the fact, that divorcées have a greater chance at marriage than their single sisters.

This latest wave of criticism of the marriage institution was a result of the strengthening of woman's position in the overall power

relationship. However, it provoked an answering masculinist movement, arising out of protest against feminist presumption. Having
added economic power to their other traditional influences in society,
women were too great a threat for husbands to counteract each in
his own home. Accordingly, while the men never organized formally,
they had their spokesmen in many fields of intellectual endeavor.
The most violent of the campaigning anti-feminists were the young
German philosopher, Otto Weininger, whose *Sex and Character* was
first translated here in 1906, and the playwright, August Strindberg,
whose works became popular in America about a half-dozen years
later.

Weininger dealt with both the physiological and psychological
phase of his subject without finding anything favorable to say about
women under either heading. As far as he was concerned, they were
heartless, shameless, and amoral. "Women," he concluded, "have no
existence; and no essence; they are not, they are nothing." It surprised
no one that the possessor of such a morbid philosophy committed
suicide at the age of twenty-three. Yet many discriminating readers
found parts of his work brilliant. Much of it was admitted by the
same readers to be below the standard of a college boy's theme for
clarity and logic.

Strindberg was almost as morbid and far more convincing. His
meaning was clear to misunderstood husbands and thinking citizens
who were legitimately worried about the increasing incidence of
divorce in American life. Himself thrice caught in the web of jealousy,
shrewishness, and marital conflict, Strindberg was rendered incapable of finding the true roots of incompatibility. Yet he was keenly
sensitive to subtle and elusive springs of human action and was
therefore able, in his plays, to present personalities and situations
with which his audiences could identify themselves. Sex, he indicated, was an overpowering magnet which drew together two well-
armed antagonists. The woman, an inferior combatant, was in this
case the stronger because she was more realistic and less scrupulous.
The world, said he, contained but one disagreeable woman: pity 'twas
that each man drew her for his own lot!

The essential masculinist criticism of Ibsen's position was that
women were dangerously near winning a complete but functionless
independence. The Strindberg view on this question reached America
before Strindberg's plays did. It arrived through Robert Herrick's
novels, which depicted the confusion attending the transitional phase
in the change of sexual power relationships. To Herrick, the new
woman was vicious and parasitic. This complaint about American
middle-class women was not a complete novelty. In the early part
of the preceding century, the British traveler J. R. D. Beste had denounced them as indolent, slovenly, and affected; men, he said,

worked late and hard to lavish their money on wives. But where Beste observed that it was nothing for the women he saw to pick up their belongings—dropping their "whining, pining, helpless, lacka-daisical affectation of fine ladyism"—and willingly endure the hard-ships of life in the West, Herrick found them marrying the country over in order to become queens with all rule and no work.

BATTLE OF THE SEXES

The entire range of imaginative literature, both partisan and dis-interested, was altered in its basic framework by the ideological assault of marriage iconoclasts. Only a generation before it had been usual for a story to start with the meeting of a boy and girl who passed through a stage of careless romance and then were happily married. The new stories frequently began with a hopeful marriage and proceeded to an account of dissatisfaction and restlessness. The development of a story was as much an exploration of disappoint-ment as the older themes were an avoidance of it.

A few latter-day women feminists with literary skill tried their hands at defense and compromise. Ida Minerva Tarbell, who had delivered a man-sized muckracking blow at the Standard Oil Com-pany in the early years of the century, discussed woman's contradic-tory status in her *Business of Being a Woman* (1912). She blamed women of the world for not staying at home and criticized stay-at-homes for lacking the qualities that came from being out in the world. She wanted women to leave their homes and retain the virtues that went with domesticity. Elinor Glyn wrote novels of flaming youth, offering pointers on how to conquer a man, but finally retired conservatively in *Three Things* to a reaffirmation of the double stand-ard in favor of men. Gertrude Atherton's *Living Present* denied the notion—apparently in the air on the eve of America's entrance into the first World War—that women have an instinctive urge to return to the primeval matriarchate.

But none of the important questions concerning marriage and morals had been answered when the war arrived to aggravate mat-ters. Wartime dispensations were seized with alacrity. The assump-tion of moral freedoms was easy for young women eager to follow the now-or-never impulse side by side with men about to fight and die. Hasty marriages, and even more hasty illicit unions, were at-tributed to the uncertainty and emotional confusion of the times. Moral and religious leaders were known to encourage indiscriminate alliances.

For a while, in the pre-war days and for a short time during the war, feminist leaders preached pacifism, an understandable position for wives and mothers. Their efforts were soon washed away in the surging tide of patriotism. Thereafter women's energies were diverted to nursing, factory work, supply packing, and bandage winding. This may not have helped the cause of peace; it *was* an important adjunct to the military activities in which their men were engaged. It was politic, too, as was proven straightway by President Wilson's shift from anti-suffragism to complete support of women's political rights. The suffrage amendment, he urged, was vital to the winning of the war.

The war settled the ballot question, but in other respects accelerated the deterioration of the sex question. An inventory of post-war woes listed many hardy perennials. The ballot had given women courage to assert themselves not so much on the political platform as in the home and in their place of employment. Relaxed wartime morals remained relaxed, and the youth which had won the war became even more disrespectful of its elders' admonitions. The victorious army brought home unwanted trophies from abroad. Venereal disease propaganda, formerly used in sex-education literature as a deterrent, now implemented the struggle against a real national menace. A successful campaign to drive urban prostitution out of existence directed young men to girls of their own social group.

With the adoption of the suffrage amendment, writers turned their attention to the woman citizen. The many question marks of the initial period of political rights were reflected in voluminous discussion about women at the crossroads. Friends of the ballot remained tentative in their verdict, explaining that the newly enfranchised minority needed time to find its way. Hostile losers in the rights struggle found ample evidence that the crossroads was a blind alley, that inferior womanhood would never find its way out. But reasonable people had to admit that there had not been enough time to prove anything. They preferred to talk about the economic effects of the war on women. Wartime employment had intensified the problems of wages, hours, health, and the general welfare of women workers. Mary Van Kleeck, more deeply analytic than most of her contemporaries, recognized the connection between the ballot and the job when, in 1919, she wrote about *Suffragists and Industrial Democracy*. Not enough thought had been given to problems created by the recent substitution of woman-power for manpower in industry, Miss Van Kleeck declared, and not enough attention to the implications of the tremendous influx of women into government service. Women had new but still undefined rights in our industrial democracy; the men would be needing their jobs. Luckily years of high employment were ahead; the competition between the sexes was to be postponed until the depression thirties.

In the meantime masculine fears grew in proportion to the number of women entering better paid commercial jobs. Professional men also felt the threat to their quasimonopolistic position. Still in a position to interpret femininity for public consumption, the men worked their pictorial and literary stereotypes overtime. The American girl had gone through a radical transformation but she still retained her old look on magazine covers. As one woman free-lance writer put it, a cover girl still held a mirror, a fan, a flower, and—in the Christmas season—a baby. She was neither active nor individual. The literary world, with W. L. George and H. L. Mencken setting the example, had it that women's best use for their freedom was to give it up as fast as they could in marriage. The career to which most women aspired, the most lucrative, said Mencken, was that of a wife. The majority of firebrands in the birth control and feminine hygiene movement were, according to his *In Defense of Women* (a poor defense at that) those whose efforts to ensnare a man had failed. No matter to this essayist that the Sangers and Dennetts were all married women.

The stereotype was useful as a propaganda weapon which might be expected to retard social currents a little. However, something more substantial was obviously needed if there was to be any hope of putting woman back in her place. The retreating male asked for a master plan of attack, and the answer came from England. It was supplied by the self-appointed health and civilization expert, Anthony M. Ludovici. Shouting at the top of his literary voice, this herald of the masculine renaissance poured forth his stock of apriorisms and non-sequiturs to fill the widening breach between men and women. Puritanism, now aided by feminism, had, he declared, for too long subverted the strength of the race. Puritanism had championed the soul while encouraging the body to degenerate. The placid acceptance of false teeth, eyeglasses, and constipation were symbolic of a race-destroying perversion of values. The choice of mates was being made on the basis of moral and personal characteristics, in complete disregard of physical factors. If people learned to despise factory-made parts in themselves as well as in others, complicated eugenics programs would not be necessary.

Unknown to the participants, so said Ludovici's *Lysistrata*, imperfect bodies had meant imperfect unions of bodies. Now the disillusioned married women, who had become negative to love and marriage, were helping the Puritans and feminist spinsters to work their vengeance against the tottering male. For their own part, the men had done their own rolling downhill without the push of insidious feminine forces. After years of overwork and neglect of their bodies, they found themselves so depleted of masculinity that they were no longer the masters of the world. Women were seizing industrial power and were expressing their disaffection in celibacy. The male was conceivably in danger of becoming superfluous—a most unnatural state of affairs because historically Old England had always had an oversupply of women.

Ludovici's new breed of masculine men did not intend to avenge themselves on England's extra women. They would, in the course of regenerating society, also overcome Puritanism; and, having done so, they would reestablish the ancient custom of honorable concubinage. Every body was entitled to full physical employment; half a husband was infinitely better than none at all. Men were going to be full-time men and women the positive (feminine) type. All of the "instinctive" virtues and vices of positive womanhood were to come back into their pristine glory with a sneer at "weak idealism" which hoped to make woman honest, upright, straightforward, and scrupulous. Back to the petty powers over children and household industries for her! She would love it, and she would love *him* the more for it. There were other things the revived male would accomplish in his strength: he would expose "the shallowness, the impracticability, and danger to national survival of Democracy as we now understand it, and therefore the evanescence of democratic forms of government."

These thunderous sounds frightened the British feminist camp into reconsidering their plan of action. Dora Russell, wife of Bertrand Russell, delivered a militant, yet hesitant, counterblast with her *Hypatia; or Woman and Knowledge*. Mrs. Russell admitted the existence of a sex war and also conceded that women had started it. Women had indeed made errors through presumptuousness in the early stages of the conflict; but men had imposed their will ruthlessly, and the conditions of settlement would have to embody compromises on both sides. The intelligence of Hypatia—symbolizing the wisdom of martyred woman in a changing civilization—was called upon to settle the quarrel. Following her own wise estimate of the conflict, Mrs. Russell advised her followers to accept sex and to proclaim it from the housetops. The offer to compromise was meant to be a start in the direction of sexual amity, but *Hypatia* was generally understood to be a call to promiscuity without any social aim to justify it.

In the United States, the feminists seemed confident. They saw no immediate threat to their recent gains in politics and economics. Perhaps the prosperity of the mid-twenties tended to soften whatever latent antagonism existed between male and female. Women had to solve their own dilemma of career and/or children without immediate reference to opposing males. Disregarding Ludovici's gospel of the perfect body, their sense of imminent difficulties dwelt rather on broad aspects of individual freedom, the labor problem, the problem of economic stability, and the beat of distant war drums.

THE JAZZ AGE

The new woman did not represent as much of a menace to her male contemporaries as she did to the framework of morals prized by the entire older generation. In the eyes of young men of the time, girls were veering toward masculinity but in a pleasing way: By acting like "one of the boys," the "flapper" of the twenties made real boys feel more comfortable in her presence. Slender, saucy, and smartly insolent, the boyish girl of this era considered it proper to pursue the young man of her choice. Candid, confident, trim, and gay, this New Woman really knew what she wanted and set about unabashedly to get it.

The feminists of yesteryear had cut their hair, dressed in mannish clothes, and avoided men except in intellectual contacts. The new feminist bobbed her hair and shortened her skirt to make herself not less but more noticeable to men. The shortened hair of feminist "Pantsy" Walker was a challenge to the enemy sex; the mannish bob, made stylish by actresses in the last thirty years, has been designed to attract an opposite but friendly sex.

Minorities which gain a measure of equality with their erstwhile oppressors are wont to take on the habits of the majority in an exaggerated way. A liberated sectarian group imposes its own sectarianism where it can. The economically oppressed engage in ostentatious consumption when money comes their way. Women adopted men's drinking and smoking habits to show that they were able; and then they attempted to imitate his sexual standards.

The age which sloughed its sex inhibitions—of which the women no longer wished to be honored guardians—was the so-called "jazz age." One fourth of radio time in 1928 was devoted to torrid tunes like "Baby Face, I Need Lovin'," "Hot Mama," "I Gotta Have You," and "Hot Lips." Motion picture production in this decade joined the party when two German directors arrived on American soil and immediately capitalized on a satirization of native taboos. Ernst Lubitch and Erich von Stroheim exploited the casual infidelities of the socially elect in films like "Blind Husbands," "Kiss Me Again," and "Forbidden Paradise." Contemporary movie titles included "Is Matrimony a Failure?" "Why Be Good?" "Flaming Youth," and "Mad Love." The Lynds, checking Middletown's cinema offerings for one week in 1925, listed "The Daring Years," "Sinners in Silk," "Women Who Give," and "The Price She Paid." Movie culture, the authors commented, is what people have always wanted to do but never dared.

Novelists and poets had begun practicing sexual freedom and writing about it in the pre-war days (the writing phase could indeed be traced back to Hawthorne's novels of passion and adultery), and they enlarged their scope after the all-too-liberating war had produced an entire generation which wanted to live like the literary folk. The best selling works of Dreiser, Dos Passos, and Hemingway were packed with suggestions of a less restricted moral code. The literature of sex—both solid and sensational, highbrow and lowbrow, factual and fictional, naturalistic and romantic—raced through the presses of printers of books, magazines, and lurid tabloid newspapers. Only romantic love and crime films outdistanced portrayals of biological sex in movie popularity.

PSYCHOLOGY REVIVED

Part of the impetus which brought sex out into the front yard was furnished by an infiltration of psychological knowledge into the minds of literary intellectuals who promptly translated it, though not always accurately, for their readers. The Freudian psychology fit the openness of that age well. It happily confirmed the spirit of revelation as opposed to concealment. It championed expression over repression. What generations of social dissidents had striven to accomplish was at last to become the order of the day: the old bogey was finally receiving diplomatic recognition. The sociologists finally admitted psychoanalysis to their court and were influenced by its testimony. A few accepted its offerings uncritically; others tried to test the theories and integrate them with the findings of sociology. Many rejected them but nevertheless found themselves using terms like "sublimation," "repression," and "inferiority complex." John B. Watson's behaviorist psychology rejected psychoanalysis because of its complex unverifiable presuppositions. Promising to provide means of studying and influencing behavior by laboratory methods, behaviorism replaced vaguely understood Freudianism in popular thought. Economic prosperity in the mid-twenties produced the illusion that, as a people, we had the means of bringing the social environment under control. Watson's psychology suited the confident mood engendered by material success.

Sexology failed to take its cue from the shift in psychological preferences, but it did experience a parallel change of emphasis. The fight for the right to love had been won for women equally with men. Now it was time to look into ways and means of deriving the maximum benefits from this right. The sexologists therefore set about to rediscover the territory that the Roman poet Ovid had surveyed two thousand years before. They reasoned that if instinct had done its job well, widespread dissatisfaction would not be marring the sexual scene. The professionals therefore considered it their obligation to teach techniques for implementing desire—the art of love came into its own once more. So prominent a place did it occupy in the public mind that the critic Joseph Wood Krutch predicted that fiction in the succeeding quarter-century would be heavily concerned with the success or failure of individuals in the practice of this art.

Various new editions and new works of Freud, Sandor Ferenczi, and Wilhelm Stekel were appearing during this period, discussing the implications of psychoanalysis for sex in general, explaining the

devious routes taken by repressed sexual drives in manifesting themselves, and translating the language of dreams into real meanings.
For avid converts, these translations were inspired scripture. The
public at large looked for technical inspiration to Doctors Long,
Stopes, Robie, and Van de Velde.

THE ART OF LOVE

The works of all but the last of this group became available to
American readers at about the same time. The Boston publisher
R. G. Badger issued Long's and Robie's books in his Rational Sex
Series, while Critic and Guide, which still distributed Dr. William
Robinson's extensive sex-education library, handled Mrs. Stopes'
Married Love. The literature of amatory technique, in large measure
a distillation of physicians' office notes and reading, was circulated
surreptitiously. Among the booksellers there was a great deal of
uncertainty as to when some local Comstock, with or without legal
authority, might swoop down on a victim chosen at random. Among
readers, a mixture of excitement and shame condemned this kind of
reading to *sub rosa* consumption.

Privileged readers who had some acquaintance with the long
history of this literary genre probably saw in the current change of
emphasis a natural development that had come with the accumulation of knowledge. Most readers, however, started their sex education after Freud had drawn the curtains aside, and were somewhat
agreeably surprised to see how much and what kind of reading matter was available. As someone observed, the moment civilized man
began to be interested in his own reproduction to the extent of experi-
menting on it and trying to control it, it was certain that there would
be great competition "to lay bare all the phenomena of the sexual
relations which precede and the obstetrical results which follow
cohabitation."

Walter Franklin Robie's *Rational Sex Ethics* appeared, the first
of the new genre, in 1916. Based on a physiological and psychological
study of sex behavior of normal men and women, it offered suggestions for rational, hygienic living. During the war, Robie wrote a
twenty-five cent pamphlet on *Rational Sex Ethics for Men in the
Army and Navy.* His next work was *Sex and Life,* purporting to tell
"what the experienced should teach and what the inexperienced
should learn." His popular technician's handbook, *The Art of Love,*
came in 1921.

The public found the Robie offerings overweighted, both in
knowledge and price. The intelligentsia with long purses could afford
to absorb upwards of three hundred pages at upwards of six dollars.
Publisher Badger met the mass market with a work that was cheaper
and more to the point. This book, Harland William Long's *Sane Sex
Life and Sane Sex Living,* provided the outlines of necessary knowl-

edge. Readers came away with a comforting sense that correctness and conformity were by no means synonymous in matters of love. How they obtained their copies was a mystery referred to by knowing smiles. If we are to believe the title page of the 1922 printing, eleven editions had been issued between 1919 and that date.

England, which had already shared her Wollstonecrafts, Wrights, and Besants with America, now made available a woman's ideas of as wide a range as any in the past. Marie Charlotte Carmichael Stopes—Mrs. Reginald Gates to her friends and Erica Fay to the very young readers of her fairy tales—was as versatile as anyone could hope to be. A fellow and lecturer in palaeobotany at University College, London, she was responsible for *The Study of Plant Life* and collaborated in a study of fuel science and practice called *Spontaneous Combustion of Coal.* Among her non-scientific writings were *A Journal from Japan,* a travel book; *Love's Creation,* a novel; *Love Songs for Young Lovers,* a book of verse; *A Road to Fairy Land* for children, and a number of plays.

Her interest in birth control, the medical aspects of marriage, and eugenics (the matter of bearing better babies weighed heavily in most twentieth-century sexology) seemed to have matured in the course of her activities as a member of the British National Birth Rate Commission. Mrs. Stopes' eugenics ideas combined nineteenth-century emphases on the circumstances attending conception, gestation, and parturition, with some of the newer notions about the influence of birth trauma on later personality traits of the child. She very much resembled Dr. Foote and others in the central theme of her *Radiant Motherhood,* namely, that the creation of the next generation must be the deliberate enterprise of a healthy couple, with the focus placed on the expectant mother's well-being, happy thoughts, and easy childbirth. Convinced of the power of prenatal influence, she built her "new and irradiated race" on assumptions which contemporary scientists generally denied. Her pleasant romanticising of the nine-month process had its merits, even though the poetic rendering was often unreliable as fact. It helped to overshadow and perhaps to eliminate many of those maternal anxieties which actually do influence the child in infancy and early childhood.

The most popular of Mrs. Stopes' books was *Married Love,* which made its first appearance in the United States in 1918 and has been kept in print ever since. *Married Love* had much to say about the physiological aspects of the wedded state and added something about the spiritual side of the relationship. It was critical of current moral tenets and conditions, but offended no one with radical suggestions for change. Theoretically, its interest was in the quality of progeny. There is no way of telling how well *Married Love* has done its work. No doubt those who abided by its instructions did not heed the author's word of advice on the best time of life to have children. The Stopes formula for a man who wanted to breed a potential mastermind—and what father did not?—was to mate with a long-young, late-maturing type of woman and have her bear the child somewhere between the ages of thirty-five and forty-five. One reviewer reminded his readers that at that age muscular rigidity overtook the "gateway of pain" (as Mrs. Stopes called it), and the mastermind might very well be stillborn.

The translations from the Dutch of Theodoor Hendrick Van de Velde came in the early thirties and were in the expensive class, for distribution to physicians and lawyers only. But naturally they found their way into the hands of non-professionals just as had the Robie books. Seven dollars and fifty cents was, however, a considerable sum in depression years, a factor which somewhat diminished the zeal of the most ardent amateurs of erotica. The *Marriage Manual,* by Hannah and Abraham Stone, filled the need of the many in its own day as had Long's contribution before it. These and large numbers of less widely known manuals were read and discussed and translated into experience.

THE NEW MORALITY

The amount of talk about sex in the twenties created the impression that it was *the* social problem of the day. Actually, the big issue was not between virtue and license. The question centered rather around which sex was to create the standard of sexual morality. Among those free to reason about the imminent change, there was one point of general agreement. Everyone recognized that there existed a working relationship between changing standards of behavior and the increasing freedom of women. This was a certainty, although one could not be sure if women were forcing the change, or if freedom itself made change inevitable. There were those who, influenced by currents of psychoanalytic thought, declared that sexuality and its expression in society were woman's peculiar province, that it was women who were chiefly responsible for the disintegration of old standards. As events proved, the single standard was soon to become a fact, but the rule adopted was not women's accustomed conception of virtue, but men's.

For their own part, men had long had a guilt complex about their dominant position and were struggling valiantly to free themselves. Their need to escape from exaggerated sensuality had made them feel inferior and ashamed, as was illustrated in barbershop conversation and humor. Resentment against hair bobbing was taken both as fear of symbolic incursion on the masculine domain, and as a reaction to female intrusion on men's private sublimations. Two decades later, when psychoanalysis had plumbed greater depths in the process of charting the sea of human personality, one canny doctor was able to show how the sense of gutter verbs was generally demeaning to women. Minority psychology apparently exhibited itself once more when "liberated" women began to use these selfsame verbs in describing sexual relations.

∽ ∽

Those who saw life mostly on the surface concluded that the whip had merely changed hands now that men and marriage had to compete with income and property for women's favor. Sexual selection under these circumstances took on a highly complex cultural definition, and women became the selectors. If raw statistics were proof of anything, they showed (up to the census of 1950) an excess of two million males. This should have resulted automatically in a raised status for women because of the increased "buyer" competition for their society as wives. Again, if marriage involved positive selection, divorce was a form of negative selection; and two-thirds of all divorces were being granted to women. This could mean that the male was still gentleman enough to accept the onus for adultery and other demeaning grounds for divorce. It could also mean that women were availing themselves of newly acquired independence to impose a standard of marital behavior that husbands were not yet trained to meet. There may also have been a backlog of unresolved grievances which could be settled only while economic conditions were favorable.

Experts in social diagnosis accepted as the explanation for moral chaos women's changing role in economic and political life. Anthropology had demonstrated that the division of labor between men and women was closely associated with their power relations in society. In ancient societies, where men dominated, women were relegated to the lower status at home. In the few instances where women held power, the opposite was the case. As formulated by M. Vaerting, the German author of *The Dominant Sex*, the ruling sex always put the domestic duties on the subordinate sex. In 1927, John Langdon-Davies boldly summarized this view in his *Short History of Woman*, saying that real differences between the sexes had not so much determined the history of woman as had the fictions invented to explain the differences.

Here lay the crux of unrest. But there was a host of contributing factors that intensified it, and these were examined to round out the explanation for moral upheaval. Among the unsettling phenomena of the times was the post-war disillusionment of youth, especially with regard to the ability of the older generation to set conditions for a harmonious world. The popularity of Freudian excuses entered the accounting. Prohibition seems to have made drinking a favorite pastime; the automobile put youngsters out of range of parental eyes; technological progress had left too little for womenfolk to do at home.

379

With less work to occupy idle hands, encouragement to engage in sexual experimentation was provided by pulp fiction, popular songs, and motion pictures attuned to erotic values.

With this host of convincing explanations before them, it was surprising to find some people still blaming Havelock Ellis and Bertrand Russell for their difficulties in controlling the younger generation. It is hardly conceivable that Russell, who let slip a few ultra-anarchistic ideas in the course of his visits to America in 1924 and 1929, could have been instrumental in causing what was already a fact. He must, however, have made a deep and disagreeable impression on social leaders who remembered in 1940 what Russell had said and written for the record in his *Marriage and Morals*. In that year old sins returned to plague him, and his appointment to teach philosophy at City College, New York, was cancelled by the city fathers upon complaint of a city mother who urged that this monster was unfit to teach her children. The case was fought unsuccessfully on grounds of academic freedom. The fact that Professor Russell had been engaged to teach philosophy courses which had nothing to do with marriage and morals failed to move the court in his favor.

Strong arguments were of little avail when quotations from the philosopher's subversive pen were exhumed to recreate the malodorous memory of the twenties. No one wished to defend Russell's disquieting views on marriage, but fellow educators and philosophers deemed such quotations irrelevant to mathematical logic, the subject which Russell had been hired to expound. The city councilors who might accept limited prostitution as the condition of monogamy, or even Shaw's half-truth about the benefits of divorce to the marriage institution, were, however, unwilling to countenance a foreigner's advocacy of adultery. And no one could deny, in the face of the quoted text, that Russell had preached the irrelevance of fidelity to matrimony. A couple's duty, he had declared, was to nurture children; the only claim they had upon one another was cooperation in this one enterprise. Occasional adultery should have no effect on lasting affection. Jealousy was a form of immature behavior.

Rational people, he said, should be aware of the scientifically verified hypothesis of cultural relativity. The intelligent American should by this time have read the works of Edward Alexander Westermarck, whose *History of Human Marriage* and *Origin and Development of Moral Ideas* had long been available in numerous editions. If Westermarck—and F. C. Muller-Lyer whose *Evolution of Modern Marriage* was published here in 1930—had proven anything, it was that customs change, and that there was no reason to expect harm to come from change. Had Russell's opponents been intellectually inclined, they could have cited the findings of anthropologists, which indicated that monogamy had been the most consistently successful marriage form in the long history of organized society.

ELEVEN

From Lindsey to Kinsey

That change in the conventions of marriage was inevitable was accepted by all who thought about it, but hardly change in the direction of institutionalized adultery. Progressive lawyers like Arthur Garfield Hays, civil liberties defender and manager of the New York State La Follette campaign in 1924, could see modern society moving toward freedom of contract in marriage. Obviously sexual and social compatibility could not be determined in advance, and society, these thinkers indicated, was responding to its belated realization of the fact by slowly and unobtrusively modifying its divorce laws. Revolutionary changes were taking place quietly without upsetting people's conscious conservatism.

This was the consensus among marriage "liberals" who refused to be frightened by the current radicalism in morals. There was more bark than bite in the radicals, they felt sure; or, in more formal terms, the loosening of verbal taboo made change look more drastic than the facts warranted.

Not so, said Judge Ben B. Lindsey of the Denver Juvenile Court. Things were worse, not better, than talk attested. A quarter of a century of dealing with juvenile delinquency from the bench gave him more than verbal evidence of alarming change. He and his collaborator, Wainwright Evans, presented the evidence in their *Revolt of Modern Youth* (1925), a book which was less than a tonic for complacent minds.

COMPANIONATE MARRIAGE

Arguing from his case materials, Lindsey demanded that society provide a wider educational preparation for youth. The judge recommended rational rather than restrictive legislation. At first he advocated trial marriage, but upon reconsidering, he observed the resemblance of trial marriage to objectionable free love practices and proposed "companionate" marriage instead. Lindsey's special meaning for the term had little in common with its use in sociology, where it signified a childless relationship as opposed to the more common one designed for regulating reproduction, child care, property inheritance, and related matters. Such was the interest created by the Lindsey proposal that in common parlance the word has kept Lindsey's meaning.

Before proceeding with his own definition, Judge Lindsey wanted it understood that he was doing little more, in the main features of his marriage reform, than giving a name to practices already widespread. The first of these features was birth control information, legalized and made accessible. The second was divorce by mutual consent for childless couples who were incompatible. Mutual consent in this scheme was not of the Hollywood variety, invoked on short notice to satisfy periodic whims. The application submitted by both parties—or by one aggrieved party—was to come before a House of Human Welfare composed of psychiatrists and other specialists.[1]

A further feature of the new program, reminiscent of one offered a generation before, was the element of state education of the young (before and after marriage) in the art of love and successful marriage. "Marriage is an art," Lindsey declared, confident of being supported by contemporary thought, "and as such it should be taught in the schools." Another idea, which the jurist urged his readers to consider although it was not central to the program, was the desirability of having the state add to its licensing requirements qualifications pertaining to health and parenthood. Those who were familiar with the history of thought on marriage in the late nineteenth century would remember this too.

The fourth major feature of the proposed system—after birth control, divorce by mutual consent, and education for marriage— was the reform of laws regulating alimony. Advances in sexual equality had already placed a huge question mark over the laws which automatically awarded alimony to a divorced wife regardless of her economic status or her husband's. The Lindsey courts would award alimony only where the circumstances justified it. One of the lessons learned in the judge's court contact with delinquent girls was that women's hands should be idle no more than men's. Able-bodied divorcées would therefore be expected to earn their own keep.

From a review of the acrimonious debate which followed the announcement of Lindsey's program, it is clear that the most vulnerable spot in it was the *sina qua non* position occupied by birth control. However much the supporters of companionate marriage

[1] It is surprising that no commentator on the Lindsey proposal, which was debated from the cracker barrel to the lecture hall, recognized the resemblance of Houses of Human Welfare to Dr. Foote's boards of physiologists. To those familiar with both, the companionate marriage courts must have appeared a reconstruction from memory of Foote's expert bodies of scientific inquiry, arbitration, and award. The structural description of both was the same, except for language changes born of a quarter-century of advancement in the social sciences. The duty of reconciling the parties if possible was to be assumed by both. Both were intended to supplant divorce courts.

might cite authorities to bolster their contention, the opposition could quote physicians of even more imposing reputation. The revered neurologist, Dr. Joseph Collins, whose book *The Doctor Looks at Love and Life* was pleasant but not instructive, was one among many medical authors who took it upon themselves to refute Judge Lindsey. Collins' psychological observations were glaringly faulty. Lindseyites were prepared to argue and refute, but honest debate before the tribune of a mass audience was not feasible.

Few people read reliable descriptions of the program; everybody took sides in the argument. Lindsey's tribulations reminded one of the Owen and Wright experience. As a sincere proponent of a new idea, he wanted to think things through with reasonable opponents. Instead they shouted him down in the forum, and treated him with silence in the press. They called his proposed scheme "free love," "trial marriage," and "promiscuity"—and then stuffed their ears against further argument. One group which listened with interest and sympathy, however, was the college student population. On campus, in corridors, and in classroom debates, an affirmative attitude toward companionate marriage was common. Youngsters at school were especially receptive to the prospect of early marriage. Less amenable to certain forms of prestige persuasion than their brothers and sisters at home, they frequently won the day by citing the advanced age of anticompanionate authorities. Whether or not birth control was completely successful, they were eager to try it.

The one powerful point on the negative side, a point probably of greater weight in women's colleges than in men's, was that biology and society persisted in favoring men. The impermanence which characterized the idea of companionate marriage, argue as Lindsey did for the erroneousness of this attitude, promised to leave many a woman with neither a firm economic foundation nor youthful attractiveness in the event of an unsuccessful venture. All of the arguments against making divorce easily available to the ruthless male were pertinent here. Moreover, social habit would need to undergo a great change before a once married woman would be accepted at her virgin value.

LOVE WITHOUT MONEY

A strong feeling was rising among those deeply concerned with sex equality that, now that the campaign was almost over, the weary victors may have fought for vain objectives. The correctness of Mary Wollstonecraft's guess was becoming evident. *Equal* rights, she had said in essence, might turn out to be something other than the *same* rights. Experience would tell. Experience seemed to be telling in the twentieth century that women might have to be granted special or extra rights in order to arrive at equality.

It was at this point in American history, when pragmatic minds were preparing to try new formulae toward a more balanced equation, that the entire social equilibrium was upset by an economic depression. The quarrelsome intellectuals who had devoted their strength to the war of the sexes were drafted into the war against poverty. What matter masculinism or feminism when families had insufficient income for food, clothing, and shelter? The problem of preserving moral standards seemed unimportant in the face of general family demoralization.

This did not mean, to be sure, that the social processes involved in the sex struggle ceased their operations. What actually happened was that full-scale ideological war was suspended while positions were realigned perforce by economic circumstances. In the early years of the depression men suffered more in the employment market because they worked in heavy—or capital—industries which reacted first and most violently to lowered demand for goods. Partial employment and unemployment of men forced more women into the labor market because family subsistence had somehow to be maintained. Then, when conditions deteriorated further, enormous pressure was exerted to drive married women out of the employment market. Beyond the fact of their harmful competition (women accepted lower wages because their earnings were merely supplementary to the family income) society still harbored powerful prejudices as to the normal functions of male and female. A woman's place was still in the home. She was to be permitted to leave the kitchen in large numbers only when the nation had more work than workers.

Naturally women workers were discriminated against most in those employments where competition for desirable jobs was at its highest. Women white-collar workers bore the brunt of discrimination. The National Education Association found in its study of 1500 city school systems undertaken 1930-1931 that 77 per cent of these refused to hire married women as school teachers, while 63 per cent had adopted the policy of firing single women teachers who married. Nor did single women escape entirely the onus of their sex membership. It was "males preferred" when equally skilled applicants of both sexes applied for employment. Women in general were treated like members of racial minority groups—last to be employed and first to be discharged in periods of diminished business activity.

If any describable effect on the balance of household power arose out of the employment situation, no responsible sociologist was able to identify it. Theoretically, hungry wives should have set upon their nonproviding husbands. The presence of unemployed husbands in the home increased the opportunity for friction. For themselves, the men were unhappy about their own helplessness, and gave vent to their guilt feelings by grumbling about burdensome families. Again, wives who went out to win the family bread might easily come to the decision that their husbands should be discarded for not performing their expected economic functions.

All of these things happened in thousands upon thousands of homes, but statisticians found themselves unable to describe the results numerically. The only measuring rod available to them was the number of divorces reported in official tabulations, and these always show a downward trend during depression years. On the one hand, conditions of life, especially when young couples had to double up with parents in crowded living quarters, were conducive to conflict. On the other, many a pair must have weathered their marital storms successfully merely because they could not pay the price of a divorce.

When the experts gathered up their case study data to get a more accurate picture of family love under economic stress, they found that the ultimate fate of domestic unity depended on factors other than the state of the stomach. An examination of how the depression changed the attitude of women toward their unemployed husbands showed a marked loss of affection only where hard times accentuated unwholesome feelings already existing in dormant form. Trouble was more likely to occur where women had married for selfish gain, or had been accepting their husband's authority in the past because of fear. If the husband's power derived instead from emotions such as love and deep respect, family disturbances were infrequent.

There were many peripheral forces which also favored or hindered happy husband and wife relationships in the dark thirties. The prevalence of unemployment in a given social circle might prevent the loss of a man's prestige at home. If, in a given community, work was relatively more available to women than to men, a woman was readier to sever relations when irritated by home life. A man who spent his time looking for a job—even though by common knowledge his chances of finding one were slim—had a better chance of preserving his marriage than the one who, having lost confidence in himself and in the world, sat sulking at home, listening to his wife outsulk him. Nevertheless, consequences refused to follow set formulae. The identical circumstances which promised ruin for some unions were a source of strength for others. For example, husbands and wives whose pre-depression rapport had been deep and strong might even gain by spending more time together in inexpensive forms of recreation.

The net measurable result, as we have seen, was a lowered divorce rate. It may well have been that the separation count taken during the depression failed to tell the whole story. Since four out of five divorces are known to occur in the first few years of marriage, statistics needed more careful interpretation than social science was in a position to offer. Marriage itself suffered a sharp decline in the early thirties, and it would therefore seem correct to count some of the divorces in the recovery period as depression-bred.

However that may be, the decline of marriage was obvious to all. Young people at first postponed marriage in order to await the turn of the economic tide. They later decided against marriage because they concluded that the tide would never turn. Many quietly agreed upon a kind of companionate marriage without Lindsey's legal safeguards. The exigencies of the times made birth control more acceptable to all. Newspapers and magazines waxed candid in their articles. Roman Catholic leaders recognized a *fait accompli* among their followers (whose birth rate had become noticeably lower since the World War) and began to advertise the Ogino-Knaus "safe period" theory. In 1930 there were only forty medically directed birth control clinics in the United States; by 1936 there were 288 of these spread over forty States of the union.

The institution of marriage took on features directly attributable to the general confusion of the day. The number of marriages for biological convenience increased. The intention of permanence and children was absent from many of these so-called impulsive marriages. Pre-marital pregnancies also became more frequent. Expectant parents were often forced into marriage because they could not afford an illegal abortion. Others went through the wedding ceremony because relief agencies were known to finance such couples when apprised of their predicament.

One would guess from known facts of behavior that postponement of marriage in the context of shaken standards would produce a further sagging of the morals front. Idleness and lowered barriers would in normal times have produced a turn to sexual activities. They should have had a more visible effect in a decade which is aptly characterized by the slogan "So what?" To add to the task of the elders, prohibition was repealed in the very depths of the depression.

Counterbalancing these discouraging tendencies, however, one large inhibition was placed on erring youth: Sex freedom cost money, and money was scarce. The fact that young men, especially of the middle class, were limited in their ability to provide the usual program of dining, dancing, and the theatre, must have reduced their contacts with the other sex. At lower income levels, where the standards of entertainment had never been high, the "adjustment" was probably smoother.

❧　❧

Historical certainty with regard to these surmises is difficult for lack of sufficient documentary and statistical evidence. In other periods discussions centered about a leading idea, or pointed to some consistent trend. The thirties had its movements and schools of criticism, but no one of them dominated the field. The decade started with behaviorism still popular as a philosophy of individual and social conduct. Men and women were confident that adjustment would come with improved skill in conditioning everybody's responses along lines which experience had shown to be desirable. Sexual happiness, they thought, was going to be a logical outgrowth of controlled behavior. When social stability itself was disrupted, confidence in the ability to control personal relations went with it.

At this point, the Marxists moved into the lead. Using behavioristic terminology, they told the public that its troubles—down to domestic incompatibility—derived from the unworkable capitalist system. All behavior was conditioned by existing property arrangements and inevitably reflected the distortions thereof.

In confirmation of this view that morality depended largely on man-owned private property, the New Zealand anthropologist and surgeon, Robert Briffault, was present on the scene with weighty scholarship behind his contentions. Briffault had given needed confidence to the feminists in 1927 when his three-volume *Mothers* came forth to prove that the maternal instinct rather than the sexual instinct was the guarantee of race preservation. In 1931 he supplemented his matriarchal theory of social evolution with an anti-Puritan broadside called *Sin and Sex*. Once more the idea of primitive promiscuity had found a champion to challenge the formidable Westermarck, whose scholarly writings had denied the prevalence of promiscuity at any time in man's long history. Briffault not only reasserted this obsolete anthropological finding, but also failed to challenge its logical extension—that if people were promiscuous when still living close to nature, then perhaps this was nature's prescription for human conduct. Such, at any rate was the thought that suggested itself to many of his readers.

Actually Briffault made no such recommendation. He merely insisted that the emancipation of women must be a determining factor in the alteration of unjust, male-conceived moral codes. The economic value of virginity was tied to systems under which women were sold into marriage, or else where men wanted to maintain rigid property inheritance lines. Where women owned their own property, things could be different.

SEX AND PSYCHOANALYSIS

As long as the worst years of the depression were with us, Marxism stood well in the lead of competing philosophies. As long as every other woe could be blamed on "the system," difficulties in men's and women's relations with each other could also be blamed on "the system." Almost everybody admitted that there was something wrong with our way of life, but not everybody was prepared for social revolution. Among the dissident reformists were those who had a blind spot for mass social solutions. They preferred their personal therapy on an individual basis.

Freudian theory throve among those who preferred the dictatorship of the psychoanalyst to that of the proletariat. The subject of sex was still as important as ever, and in this connection the language of Freud was far richer for purposes of discussion than that of Marx. The afflicted found the revolution not imminent enough for their needs, which demanded immediate attention. The analyst, for all his lengthy and expensive interviews, held forth more promising results than the vague paradise of the proletariat. Those who could afford to pay for the more personal therapy of a doctor were not eager for social upheaval in any case. And as economic stringency relaxed, greater numbers abandoned the impersonal materialism of Marx for the more personal philosophy of the Freudians. They found it convenient to contemplate their emotional disturbances in relation to an attached mother, a rival father, or a jealous sibling. The dialectic which connected inner personal conflict with class conflict was for the political specialist. Nevertheless, the marriage of psychoanalysis with dialectical materialism actually did take place in the minds of a few thinkers. In many instances of such union, especially when it occurred during recovery years, the Freudian elements dominated.

Back in the days when psychology first invaded literature on a grand scale, only the select few fully appreciated the themes exploited by writers like Maxwell Anderson, Eugene O'Neill, and Robinson Jeffers. Readers had to go through a period of psychological instruction before they could readily see through the subtleties of Freudian meaning. Frustration, for example, could be sensed by anyone, but the detection of its causes required special knowledge. By the thirties, there was a fairly large body of people who felt prepared to understand and discuss stories of incest, intra-family rape, and other abnormal sexual attachments. No family entanglement portrayed in play, novel, or poem was shocking to sophisticates. The boundaries of the "natural" were extended to infinity.

When applied to the marriage problem, all of this seemed to give the superficially informed a feeling of utter helplessness in the face of forces too immense to conquer. What hope was there for ever adjusting in marriage with a mate whose motivations stemmed from events in early childhood and for whom change in adult life was at best highly problematic? The old marriage manuals had established a set of rules for marital behavior; conformity with these carried the promise of wedded bliss. In the new psychology, a multitude of acceptable variations in conduct were advertised. Standard patterns were out of the question. The doctor invited each one to come for individual analysis toward a solution of his peculiar problem. No wonder people accepted their petty incompatibilities as matters of ultimate fact and preferred the easier road of divorce. It was certainly simpler to put aside a mate than a neurosis.

SEX AND THE SCHOOLS

There was one group of investigators who would not accept defeat so easily. While others were retreating before human irrationalism, the sociologists insisted that the situation could be brought under reasonable control through a system of information and education. The new program of finding joy through knowledge was conducted partly through books and articles, and partly in the classroom. At first only the colleges undertook education for family life. After a decade of experience at this level, the new subject-matter area began to move down into the secondary schools.

Outside of the classroom, the field continued to be exploited by free-lance writers with or without benefit of up-to-date information. A few who came with specialized training in one or more pertinent fields gained prominence for themselves as marriage advisers both in print and in freshly organized enterprises called family clinics. Paul Bowman Popenoe arrived at his position as an authority on the marriage question through the biological gateway. When his *Modern Marriage* was published in 1925, it carried with it the author's reputation as a well-known eugenist and former editor of the *Journal of Heredity*. He had, in addition, gained much experience working on the social disease problem for the United States Army.

Popenoe stressed two factors in his study of marriage. The first was its physiological basis, and the second, those personal qualifications which, by experience, husbands and wives found most satisfactory in one another. In drawing up his list of qualifications, he worked not from casual observation, as his predecessors in the field had done, but from a sample poll of married subjects. At the time *Modern Marriage* made its appearance, the interested public had been so harried by psychoanalytic words like "complex," "suppressed desires," and "neurotic emotionalism," that it received Popenoe's conventional terminology with a sigh of relief. Nevertheless some thought that this eugenist's suggestions on courtship etiquette were ludicrous and subject to improvement by any bright sixteen-year-old. Other aspects of his teachings were also regarded as highly questionable. Popenoe, for instance, advocated government bonuses in proportion to family size, because, he said, divorce became less and less likely as the number of children born to a couple got larger.

Popenoe must have learned a good deal between 1925 and 1930, the year in which he founded and became director of the American Institute of Family Relations at Los Angeles. In the first eight years of its operation, there was not a single divorce among the thousands of couples to whom the Institute had given premarital advice. The science of marriage seemed to have matured in the hands of a biologist after approximately a century of speculation by self-styled social scientists. Popenoe's belief that family education in the schools, communities, courts, and homes would reduce the divorce rate was justified by its apparent success in practice. It may have been that the Institute drew on young men and women so conscientiously bent on making a correct mating selection as to make them an unrepresentative group. In any case, the Institute's reputation as a prep school for marriage grew. The reputation of its director grew with it. He has written prolifically, lectured in over a hundred and fifty colleges and universities, and has been a strong influence in inducing educational institutions of every variety to introduce material on marriage and sex into their courses of study.

America's faith that any problem, however serious or difficult, can be solved in the classroom and lecture hall, was about to receive the acid test. Educational institutions were asked to solve one of the most perplexing enigmas the world could offer. Higher education had committed itself to protecting every human value through specialized instruction. It was also offering specialized training for a great variety of vocations. Marriage education qualified under both headings. The majority of college students were destined to pursue the family avocation on a lifetime basis. Many of them would be professionally engaged (in the roles of teacher, lawyer, clergyman, social worker, or doctor) in guiding the moral behavior of clients and pupils.

The informal lecture to students on family life dates, as we have noted, back to the latter years of the eighteenth century, when Princeton's president, John Witherspoon, spoke to his graduating class on marriage. More formal classroom instruction on family customs and problems arrived with the introduction of sociology and anthropology into the college course of study. During those recitation hours devoted to marriage and sex practices, the probability is that academic objectivity was lost despite all efforts of teachers to keep discussion on an impersonal level. A good deal of intellectual effort was expended—as it is now in similar courses—in examining the pertinence of the customs of primitives to our own highly complex society. When marriage finally attained to the dignity of being treated as a separate study unit, the historical study of familiar society and family disorganization received increasing emphasis.[2]

[2] Despite the widespread historical interest, there were few texts to feed it. At the beginning of the century, Professor George Elliott Howard met the need

After World War I, there was a shift of interest away from history to aspects of family life of more practical importance. One such matter was an enquiry into the why's and wherefore's of family disruption. The professional motive was to train social workers, with the hope of some day' eliminating unwholesome conditions or, at least, of minimizing their effects. The students who clamored for new marriage courses in the thirties were motivated personally rather than professionally. Professors of sociology were eager to inaugurate such courses too, for, beyond the very plausible arguments made by others for such teaching and training, the scarcity of teaching posts —in a period when academic unemployment ran industrial unemployment a close race—caused much enthusiasm for any innovation which would stimulate registration in colleges.

The clothing and feeding of college teachers' families was, however, incidental. The rationale of family life education had been enlarged and developed in the previous decade as a response to the marriage crisis in America. Since 1926, when Professor Ernest Rutherford Groves' elective course on marriage attracted wide attention among students and teachers, between six and seven hundred institutions have listed courses dealing with preparation for family living. Judging from the variety of departments which teach the subject, it is not yet apparent whether the biologists, psychologists, home economists, or sociologists are thought most competent to teach it. Nor is there agreement as to why the subject is being taught. A large number of teachers prefer to think of their work as a scientific study of the family from the historical, sociological, and psychological points of view. Almost as many others indicate that they lean toward the practical job of helping both the married and the unmarried make more satisfactory adjustments to everyday life. More women's and coeducational colleges than men's have introduced the practical type of course. Practical content ranges from dating and courting— with homework exercises—to laboratory demonstrations of birth control methods (reported in 1948 by a woman's college of high standing).[3]

---

with his somewhat pedantic, lengthy *History of Matrimonial Institutions.* Howard summarized conflicting ideas on matrimony briefly, devoting almost the whole of his three-volume work to the development of institutional law and practice in England and the United States. Divorce received the full measure of his attention along with marriage. Willystine Goodsell's *History of the Family as a Social and Educational Institution* (1915) was sufficiently brief and simple to be broadly accepted as a text. The most quoted work on the subject, Arthur Wallace Calhoun's *Social History of the American Family,* appeared in three volumes during the war years 1917 to 1919. This book remains a standard in the field despite its lack of thoroughness and integration.

[3] When called upon to pass judgment on the "credit" value of some of these practical studies, administrators and philosophers of education have had

MARRIAGE, MORALS AND SEX IN AMERICA

The Groves school started with the assumption that *all* education is education for marriage, ·inasmuch as many marriages, beginning with the necessary sexual attraction, soon fall apart for want of permanent common interests. As for sexual incompatibility, the Groves faction was confident that knowledge would dispel the fear of physiological unknowns; the danger, declared Professor Groves in *The Marriage Crisis* (1928), lay not in the lack of experience but in the lack of reliable, specific information about the sexual aspect of married life. Candor, and the ability to discuss what each had learned would add to the probability of male-female adjustment within the permanent marriage contract.

If students came out of marriage courses having absorbed only a part of the materials contained in Professor Groves' sound text on marriage, they did well. For in it the author succeeded in epitomizing the best that had been thought and said on that all-embracing matter. The student was carried from the purposes of marriage through the possible solution of mismatched marriage in divorce. Problems of sex appeal, courtship, engagement, and honeymoon and postmarital adjustment were tackled without lowered eyelids. The facts of reproduction, eugenics, infertility, contraception, and abortion were faced squarely. Parturition and child care received due attention. The delicate social situation of women, the dark area of female ambitions and frustrations, the contradiction of career and children—all of these tensions and trouble-makers were accorded the unbiased exploration that is their due.

A course of study as extensive as this would seem to have fulfilled the responsibility of the colleges toward breaking the marriage crisis. But, sensitive to the needs of youth, the marriage educators were not yet satisfied. They urged the schools to develop, with the assistance of other moulders of public opinion, a program wherein youth would not have to postpone marriage in order to go to college. They recommended material aid and moral understanding for married students; false social standards regarding home and furniture had to be discarded by the youngsters themselves. The colleges were to shorten their courses by abandoning the rigid credit system. An accelerated course, Groves felt, would work successfully for genuine students; those who went to college to have sugar-coated intellectual fare fed them by the spoon must fall by the wayside.

---

to reshape their standards lest they be labeled "unprogressive" or "reactionary." If schools are to comply with their stated purpose of educating for life, the foundations of marriage may be said to rate with the fundamentals of mathematics. A few ultra-moderns may find that their experimental approaches have overshot the mark. It may well be that the broad, carefully developed concepts taught by sociologists like Groves, are capable of delivering insights of longer lasting practical value than laboratory exercises.

Although only minor changes have occurred in the public treatment of college students who are married or want to marry, those responsible for marriage education within the colleges have done their part well. Building upon students' questions, they have used the data of psychology, psychiatry, biology, and sociology to design courses worthy of their place beside other studies on the college level. Researches into the ways of predicting success or failure in marriage have added much to the store of solid subject matter. The literature of practical techniques for dealing with marriage problems has been incorporated judiciously, while detailed statistical reports like Robert L. Dickinson and Lura Beam's *Thousand Marriages* and Katherine B. Davis' *Factors in the Sex Life of 2200 Women* have supplied concrete factual materials.

MARRIAGE REVIVED

The dozens of books written for classroom use are good reading for literate adults also. On many points they confirm the teachings of the traditional "advice" literature, lending it the weight of professional authority. These texts resemble the old common-sense manuals in the important sense that they aim to make marriage work. The constructive emphasis has been characteristic of marriage literature from the depression era onward. The reaction against those who would undermine the whole marriage structure and invent a new system of relationships has been unmistakable. The sex radicals have either been driven underground in the counter-revolution or have been converted to the moderate side. Many of them were disillusioned by such events as the unsavory proceedings incident to Bertrand Russell's divorce in 1933, and Havelock Ellis' confession (in his autobiography) that his "Semi-Detached Marriage" had not been all he and his novelist wife had led people to believe. This couple's separate interests, friendships, and separate residences looked, upon reexamination, like a description of one of the abnormal case studies out of Ellis' own books.[4]

The decade of the thirties was an unproductive one from the point of view of human inventiveness. Perhaps the time was due for intellectuals to take stock of the knowledge they already had accumulated. Reduced activity on the economic front was accommodatingly providing the relaxed environment in which newer ideas got their chance to take a suitable place among the old. Conservatism had lost its influence all along the line; reformers could break through almost at will, but seemed unwilling to bear the full weight of responsibility.

[4] The English sociologist's lifelong opponents also took occasion to point out that Ellis had never been a father. This fact, they averred, must severely circumscribe the validity of much that he had said in his writings.

The big lesson of the era penetrated the minds of willing learners imperceptibly. The lesson was in effect that sex was indivisible; that all matters having to do with sex morals, sex education, marriage, divorce, woman's rights, birth control, and censorship were necessarily connected and chronologically continuous. A mental portrait of the age revealed that the Freudians had quietly succeeded in teaching that total behavior was connected with sex behavior and that the complete preparation for marriage had best be started in infancy.

Energized by the climate of the times, educators, who had previously dared to introduce sex education only in ultra-progressive private schools, openly urged its adoption by large public school systems. They must have thought the need very urgent. Educators went ahead with such programs in many localities despite the opposition of parents and school board members whose religious and moral convictions automatically damned any form of sex instruction. The experience of the second World War succeeded in breaking down some of this opposition. The teen-age problem—a new name for the uncontrollability of adolescents in wartime—was far more convincing to parents of the old school than were the learned arguments of educators.

By the end of the war parents acquiesced in the necessity for sex education. It was generally thought that parents should take over a good portion of such instruction, but, being themselves products of the back-fence and curbstone schools, fathers and mothers, pleading incompetence, waived the privilege. Official recognition was accorded this state of affairs when the Oregon legislature made the subject of sex education compulsory in the junior and senior high schools. The State education department, in carrying out the law, made use of pamphlets, lectures, and slides as teaching materials. Observing that error and embarrassment on the part of teachers (who had been reared under the same system of miseducation as the parents) stood in the way of desirable results, the Oregon educators prepared and released in the spring of 1948 a film called "Human Growth."

"Human Growth" was designed by its producers to teach the elementary facts of life to youngsters between the ages of twelve and fifteen. ("Human Beginnings," a film for six-year-olds, was released in 1950). The central theme of "Human Growth" was the development of glands and organs in preparation for the reproductive process. Animated diagrams illustrated the functioning of the organs of both sexes and explained the changes that accompany adolescence. Experience has established the fact that this film did none of the things the elder statesmen said it would. It neither focused undue attention on sex nor stimulated a wave of sex experimentation. It stimulated rather the framing of wholesome questions which led to matter-of-fact discussions with teachers and parents. As one editorial writer put it, the film "is as lurid as a table of logarithms." It seemed mighty peculiar to this writer that anyone should approve an explicit description of the horrible consequences of a possible atomic attack while hiding the simple knowledge of how a human individual comes into being.

CENSORSHIP CENSORED

To old hands in the struggle against sex censorship, the controversy about "Human Growth" was not nearly as exciting as events in the early thirties when the courts rendered a series of decisions reversing convictions under the Comstock laws. The case of Mary Ware Dennett's *The Sex Side of Life: An Explanation for Young People* marked the turning of the tide. Mrs. Dennett, long active in the feminist and birth control movements, had written this short compilation in 1918 for her own two adolescent sons. It was first published in the *Medical Review of Reviews* and later in pamphlet form. In 1928 the author mailed a copy in reply to the usual decoy letter and found herself indicted on criminal charges in the following year. A jury found her guilty after forty minutes of deliberation. In 1930 the Circuit Court of Appeals unanimously reversed the decision.

Mrs. Stopes' books were, at about the same time, experiencing obstruction at the customs house rather than in the post office. *Married Love* had been printed and circulated in the hundreds of thousands within the United States, but the customs officials branded it "obscene" and therefore forbade its importation. The exclusion of *Married Love* came to an end when Federal Judge Woolsey gave it a clean bill of health. Finding its language correct and unprovocative of salacious thoughts when read by normal people, this jurist ruled out charges on all counts. He had not only heard expert witnesses with judicial impartiality but had apparently himself given the book a careful reading. The decision did more than curb the nation's censors. Judge Woolsey also touched upon what underlay their censoring proclivities when in describing *Married Love* he said:

> It makes some apparently justified criticisms of the inopportune exercize by the man in the marriage relation of what are often referred to as his conjugal or marital rights, and it pleads with seriousness, and not without some eloquence, for a better understanding by husbands of the physical and emotional side of the sex life of their wives.

The Woolsey decision had at long last given status to the efforts of anarchists and their eugenist friends to expose unreasonable exercise of the "male perogative." The next step was to remove customs censorship of birth control literature. Success in this field came when Judge Galston ruled against a government seizure in 1937 and was upheld in the Circuit Court of Appeals.

Another form of censorship, that imposed upon university scholars in search of scientific data on sex attitudes and behavior, has been making its rapid exit in these latter years. There is a dramatic difference between the penalties incurred by Professors De Graff and Meyer at the University of Missouri in 1930 and the current celebration of Dr. Alfred Kinsey and his associates at Indiana University. Dr. De Graff, a zoologist, was dismissed from his post for collaborating in the preparation of a questionnaire whose purpose it was to collect data toward devising a system of practical sex ethics. Dr. Max Meyer, his co-worker in the university's department of psychology, was suspended without salary. Missouri University's President Brooks denounced the questionnaire as "sewer sociology" and stood solidly with his Board of Curators against the offending professors. The technique employed by these two faculty members, they charged, was not only scientifically unsound but was also productive of immorality among the students. The victimized teachers were vigorously supported by the American Association of University Professors, but to no avail. The wholehearted backing given by university authorities to the Kinsey questionnaire technique—to say nothing of the handsome financial assistance provided by the Rockefeller Foundation—needs no elaboration here. Apart from the possible merits or deficiencies of the Kinsey studies, there is remarkable unity of feeling among thoughtful readers about the benefits of the mere publication of results. Science seems at last to be devising a method of objectively examining and describing human sexual behavior. And more: Out of its traditional respect for scientific accomplishment, American popular feeling tacitly agrees to cooperate toward eliminating the vestiges of censorship in this area of human affairs.

THE SECOND WORLD WAR

At the very time when Professor Kinsey and his colleagues were questioning their first subjects on the details of their individual sex history, historical events on a worldwide scale were operating to affect the character of his data. Under the aegis of war conditions, the complexion of sexual and marriage relations accommodated itself to the demands of national emergency. The expected loosening of moral restraints came with the war. Months before the war, as if young men and women were responding to foreknowledge, the parade toward the altar began.

The social experts recalled the occurrence of this phenomenon in Europe before the first great war and studied it with renewed interest. Some of the old explanations still applied and were mentioned. The analysts supposed, for example, that men, fearing conscription, hastened to regularize the status of their children already conceived out of wedlock. Social science in the early forties was, however, more precise. It noted that men found themselves in a better position to enter marriage as industry expanded in preparation for war and wages rose. There was, too, the factor of self-protection: governments were wont to defer married men, especially where children entered the picture. Nor could the now-or-never philosophy, which normally accompanies periods of uncertainty, be overlooked.

Women, customarily observing greater caution in their sex contacts, responded to the war with increased courage and daring. It was said of those who married in seeming haste that they were sublimating their patriotic urge to serve by having a husband in the army. Less charitable analysts explained that many had taken advantage of the acceleration and confusion of the times to get a husband and have children in order to insure their future social status—one never could tell but that the war might last beyond the age of female attractiveness and create a generation of forgotten women. Nor did eligible women overlook the inducement of soldiers'—and widows'—allowances and pensions. Sociologists could only speculate on such motivations. They could, however, describe with certainty a social change which brought young women into frequent company with the fittest of American young men—those in uniform. Meetings were frequent and comparatively unrestricted; on the other hand, there were no standards by which to judge people of different backgrounds from one's own. Romance moved swiftly and marriage followed close upon.

And so it came to pass that statisticians reported a sizeable decline in the proportion of single persons from 1940 to 1947. The backlog of depression bachelors of both sexes was so well erased in these years that a marked decline in marriage rates from 1948 onward was not difficult to explain. Theoretically, the unsettled international situation in 1949 and 1950 should have produced an upward swing on the marriage graph. The fact that it did not may indicate that power politics have become so erratic that the supposed intuition of young people no longer moves them to marry in advance of a war. The suddenness of the Korean crisis in June 1950 apparently caught young people's intuitions napping. But they awakened with a start and plotted a swift upward curve on the marriage graph in the succeeding years.

❧   ❧

The elder romantics rejoiced at the popularity of marriage in the early forties. But as they settled back to praise the younger generation for finally recognizing its obligations to society, they were rudely jolted by the mounting divorce rate of this same generation. It was a case of marry in war and repent in peace. The war, far from turning the tide toward marital permanence, added its own disturbances to the list of factors to which sociologists attributed the alarming breakdown of family life. The historical trend of divorce statistics was in itself disturbing to those who held union for life to be the ideal. For, aside from wars, depressions, and other unusual situations that affect interpersonal relationships, the probability of divorce showed a chronic upward movement with no peak in view. The school of experts which was more influenced by social facts than by traditional ideals began to suggest that perhaps divorce was a positive contribution to the total happiness of individuals and societies.

But for those who believed that society operated at its smoothest when families were most cohesive, there was cause indeed for loud Jeremiads. Of the many functions and powers which belonged to the family in rural America at the beginning of the nineteenth century, few remained in the family's hands by the middle of the twentieth. In days gone by the family unit produced its own economic goods and consumed them. Now, with rare exceptions, food, clothing, and other household needs are made in factories and bought in stores. Formerly, education, religion, recreation, and medical and even legal needs were satisfied by members of the family group under the leadership and control of the head of the family; now the schools, churches, doctors, lawyers, social agencies, and commercial purveyors of amusement offer their specialized services. The only areas in which the contemporary family still performs as it did of old are those of reproduction and emotional satisfaction.

The good old family, called "domestic" by those who prefer it to the newer forms, is certainly disappearing; and there are few who look forward to its return. Professor Carle Zimmerman is chief among those (excluding the representatives of the churches who feel the same way) who would have the family resist passive adaptation to social forces. The democratic family, he insists, "weakens fundamental value systems and natural infinite beliefs upon which society is built." Recognizing that you can no longer force people to cling tenaciously to old family loyalties and fashions, he suggests putting familism and childbearing in the category of duties that are expected of all good citizens. He advocates offering monetary inducement in the form of tax relief or subsidies to increase the chances of citizens volunteering to perform their voluntary duties.

Supporters of the democratic family use words like "companionship" and expressions like "consensus of its members" to describe the same thing which opponents depreciatingly call "atomistic." This figure of speech conveys the impression of a group of unrelated particles which fall apart easily. The "companion" symbol celebrates the freedom to remain together by choice. The idea of a person-centered family within a society which is person-centered too is based upon a faith just as much as is the opposing faith in "natural infinite beliefs." It rests upon a belief that the right people will mate to have the right size of family under favorable conditions. Under auspicious circumstances, it is urged, parents will stay together and have enough children to insure race survival, at the same time enjoying pleasant leisure and opportunities for self-development.

While embattled sociologists argue their favorite solutions, social change continues to produce family change without guidance from either school of sages. The facts are that people can no longer be chained to their families by threats of economic sanctions or moral censure. Matters of marriage and children are now largely questions of private choice. If bachelorhood is at all frowned upon at present it is because that state carries with it a faint suspicion of homosexuality. The traditional complaint against single people for not fulfilling their obligations to society has practically disappeared. Likewise are childless couples no longer chided for selfishness.

Quite apart from the conflict of the companionates and conservatives, a new school of thought has appeared with the argument, not yet as vociferous as that of the other two, that there cannot be a correct school of thought. Learning much from anthropologists and psychoanalysts, the adherents of this belief demonstrate that family habits actually do differ so widely among groups and individuals that no one pattern of behavior can ever be found to apply satisfactorily to all. The dramatic description of human variability supplied by the Kinsey studies so fully supports this claim, they say, that never again should any custom or majority decision attempt to enforce a uniform system of family morality. One may not, from this new point of view, speak of divorce as a symptom of a sick society. For divorce may very well be the safety valve for the release of unwholesome social and psychological tensions; and a sporadic escape of steam may be preventing a major explosion.

Granting that morals should be geared to harmonize with the society in which they function—a point which has been pushed vigorously from New Harmony days to the present—the partisans of the "functional" sociology position have their own internal differences in the realm of marriage thought. There are a few who seem ready to undertake an active campaign to do away with sexual prohibitions and taboos. As far as this handful of theorists is concerned, the attempt to stifle sexual independence is a known failure. Why then, they say, should we perpetuate a struggle of which only undesirable frustration can be the outcome?

There are, however, other proposals for applying the principles of "functionalism." One of these is to get family relationships to assume a form which will agree with the social structure as a whole. Herein the wary see the use of anthropological studies in an effort to assign separate roles to male and female. Once more, in this proposal, the male is awarded the exclusive agency for economic activity while his wife is relegated to home and motherhood. No matter that American industry is employing myriads of married women; according to some of the professors campaigning under the banner of functionalism, the social system cannot work well if women work. Feminists might have predicted in this connection that some day ingenious democrats would deprive them of their hard-earned freedom the democratic way.

∾ ∾

Either the professors are making their observations upon women and work on some distant planet or they are speaking only of women in the American middle class. For women have for more than a century occupied positions in front of machines and behind office desks without reducing the male-built social structure to ruin. Were they not acceptable, and even important, to their employers, they would have been sent home long before this. The nuisance capacity of woman, intimated by functional sociologists, must consist rather in her potentialities for social power and family power. The greatest threat in both these spheres actually comes from the middle class woman educated for better things; but since mass psychology habitually takes its cue from the middle class in America, woman-pressure is felt throughout the social structure.

As sensitive writers assayed the balance in the decade just behind us, they decided that the woman scare was completely unfounded. If the men hoped to improve their relations with their women by this maneuver, they were in for a rude disappointment according to David L. Cohn's *Love in America*. And the fault lay more heavily with the men than with the women they were wont to accuse of disruptive tactics. Woman's alleged status was high; her actual status, low. Her influence both at home and in the affairs of society was weak. Susan B. Anthony, grandniece of the feminist pioneer, was doubly indignant in her *Out of the Kitchen and into the War* as she observed that women failed to receive equal treatment in industry even during the critical wartime period.

The novelist Pearl S. Buck was inclined to render a similar judgment on woman's social rating. Miss Buck's dissatisfaction with man's treatment of woman, as well as with woman's treatment of herself, was strongly indicated in both *Men and Women* (1941) and *American Argument* (1949). What perturbed her most was the width of the chasm which separated the actualities from the potentialities of American womanhood. On a matter as deeply important to their welfare as war, the women eagerly joined with male patrioteers lustily crying for bloody combat. Such an utter lack of consonance between human need and human action—cited numberless times in the earlier history of American social thought—was to Miss Buck but one irregular piece in the designless mosaic called American society. This lack of statement or understanding concerning ends and means, said Miss Buck, was characteristic of American family life itself. Where expectations were not set, they could not be realized. Hence the grievous misunderstandings between husbands and wives, and between parents and children. Adjustment was difficult without a well-defined group behavior pattern to adjust to. Family organization in China, though unsatisfactory to America in several ways, did provide its participants with the rewards of conformity with an accepted social pattern.

Several informal commentaries on the advances of womanhood in politics from the time of the ratification of the suffrage amendment through the second great war were in substantial accord on the broad findings of writers like Pearl Buck: Women had not achieved political power in any way commensurate with their numbers, but had gone far considering that they had had only a quarter of a century to prove themselves. There was considerable disappointment that their voting strength had not forced any improvement upon the morality of men and nations. The fact that the women now had to share with men responsibility for moral chaos, despite the fact that their political influence was still weak, made a few thoughtful ones express the wish to go back to the happy voteless days of their grandmothers.

〜 〜

For the most part, however, people were not as much concerned with the realities of political inequality as they were with unconcealed prejudices against women in economic life. Strength in politics seemed assured with the passing of time; but the outlook in business and finance was not as hopeful. Much time had passed since women had first enrolled in the army of producers and distributors of man's earthly goods. Whether they had volunteered because of shrinking home duties, or had been conscripted for factory and office posts in an economic organization whose needs grew faster than the male population, was of little importance. Women by the million were in business and had been in long enough to have got farther than they had.

When the Women's Bureau of the United States Department of Labor made a survey of women in positions of responsibility in a selected group of businesses and industries, it reported that some women had advanced into work areas formerly reserved for men only, but that women did not hold higher-level jobs in proportion to their number employed in a given enterprise. Several interesting sidelights made women's prospects look the more discouraging: Men were monopolizing the posts of top-level responsibility, leaving middle or lower administrative and executive work for the women. Male directors were making the decisions and then turning them over to women executives for routine execution. Men were, on the average, receiving higher salaries than women in equivalent positions. Men were favored for promotion as against women of equal ability and education. Business offices, in short, could still very appropriately be described as hives humming with female workers, ruled by a king bee or two.

The disposition to ascribe such a state of affairs to the deliberate tyranny of men seemed absent in the postwar years. Recent writers have described it rather as social lag, or the drag of tradition on men and women alike. It is possible that men intentionally slowed up the social process, but it was unscientific to say so. Evidence there was that men discriminated against women; but either they did not mean to, or they had good reasons. The good reasons were that women's work attendance was not as good as men's. They tended to stay with a given job for a shorter period of time, leaving jobs suddenly to follow their husbands to distant parts, to have babies, or to take care of sick relatives. These things could not, to be sure, be helped; but they did create problems for management to solve. There were things that women could help and did not. Many firms pointed out that, on the average, women did not possess the educational and experience qualifications for higher-level positions, and that, when offered equal opportunity with men for in-service training, they failed to take advantage of it.

The women, on their side, could prove that it was the habit of firms to favor men even in the in-service training offerings. Experience, moreover, taught women that it was a waste of energy to take additional training. They could not expect fair treatment with the best of added qualifications. This attitude could be illustrated by showing that women were frequently deeply interested in beginning courses but were less likely to take the advanced ones. Intelligent people rarely repeat an error of judgment under identical circumstance.

Women leaders, nevertheless, were still hopeful. The more exceptionally successful were the most hopeful. Having learned much from experience, they were prepared to advise their sisters on the lower rungs of the success ladder against their alleged weaknesses. Some of their formulas were: "Strive for recognition as individuals.

Do not ask for favors as women or on a feminist basis." "Be more gracious and cooperative." Learn to "live and let live." "Forget your importance—too many women believe they are all important and can't be replaced." And, "Overcome the tendency toward an emotional and personal approach to all problems."

Extensive researches of the Women's Bureau sort did little more than confirm what observers could see on the surface. Equality existed only in a very limited sense in the upper reaches of the career world. Moreover, the war emergency of the forties had failed to advance the cause of women in the way that previous wars had—this despite the obvious fact that causes which had exalted women's role in society in former wars, operated in World War II more powerfully than ever. This time women were actually admitted to the fighting branches of the armed forces, if not to handle weapons, at least to perform functions like those of male soldiers on "limited service." Women were needed urgently in civilian posts as well. So many men were in uniform that highly attractive wage incentives had to be set up for women. Vast government spending made generosity easier. In industry, mechanization proceeded to a point where women could be taught skills quickly. Work shifts were arranged so that mothers could look after both their children and their jobs. Nursery schools were organized for the same reason. Men still got preferred status in industry during the war; but it would have been captious to protest when women were faring so well in the economic sense.

∽ ∽

By all the old criteria of judging profit and loss in the matter of women's status, the gain at the end of the war was considerable. But, in reality, the nation's victory brought women's defeat. When servicemen returned to civilian life, the normal reaction set in. In comparable situations of an earlier time, the women resisted social pressures and eventually came off with a net gain. In 1946, the retreat was a rout. Resistance was spotty and weak. The female aggressors returned speedily to their prewar boundaries and beyond. Some of them, it was discovered, had joined the enemy and were leading the attack to drive their "buddies" back to kitchen and nursery. Those who observed the trend wondered if the conquered Nazis had not sent their conquerors home with a dose of *Kinder, Küche und Kirche* virus.

Actually it was no foreign ideology that sent the women scurrying home to dependent status. Rather it should be said that an interplay of personal and social factors—some old and some new—made it plainer than ever that women had best make their bid for equality through passive resistance and watchful waiting. Chronically fatigued as a result of their double burden of homekeeping and job-keeping, uncertain of the future of an unsure world, and already nominally in possession of sixty-five percent of the nation's property, American women apparently decided to entrench themselves as strongly as possible in their position as wives and mothers. Perhaps this was a decision of intelligent choice. More likely, the tribulations of house-hold management determined the decision.

The tribulations looked something like this: The demand of middle-class feminists for equality of participation in worldly affairs had from the beginning been contingent on an unlimited supply of cheap, willing household labor. As homes shrank in size and function, the demand for full-time domestic help also dwindled and made conditions of employment unsatisfactory from the point of view of employer and employed. The relationship between housewife and housekeeper was not a happy one. The war in the forties, because it demanded a fresh supply of female factory workers, turned the tide in favor of the domestics. Offering better salaries, an impersonal boss (always preferable to the personal interest which enslaves), better defined and shorter hours, and social security benefits to boot, in-dustry caused the nearly complete disappearance of domestics from American households. It was no longer feasible for women to hold moderate salaried jobs the income from which was to be transferred almost *in toto* to belligerent houseworkers. Gone were the profes-sional housekeepers who had been happy to exchange room, board, and being a "part of the family" for a large portion of their full earn-ings for services rendered. Hard realities drew women inexorably away from business careers and returned them to their traditional household roles.

The unhappy male rejoiced at the turn of events because he had always considered himself a martyr to sexual democracy. Outside of the home he had had to face and forestall feminine competition for money and recognition. Within the confines of his family he had found his own opportunities for self-development lessened by his wife's career activities. His share of household operations was larger when his was a working wife; and the clatter of the dishes he washed was never completely offset by the jingling of coins in his wife's pay envelope. Worst of all, this wife's energies, never abundant enough to give him all the comfort, security, care, and affection to which he felt entitled, were further depleted by the day's work away from home. Thoughts like these, always potent stimuli in the masculine drive to discriminate against women, rushed into play as soon as women admitted that they, too, were tired of their experience with equal opportunity.

Nor were psychological and sociological theorists of both sexes slow to justify and strengthen the trend. In 1943, Amram Scheinfeld demonstrated that nature had decreed woman's inequality. His

Women and Men summarized the biological differences of the sexes and cited analogies among various animal species in support of the male dogma about male superiority in everything but parenthood. It seemed that woman's handicaps were insurmountable. Her child-bearing activity, the one place where her superiority went unchallenged, proved to be the supreme handicap inasmuch as it interfered with continuity of effort demanded by modern life. Handicaps inherent in the conventional division of labor and power merely exaggerated her basic liability. Scheinfeld, writing in a popular, entertaining manner, impressed lay readers with his apparent scientific soundness. Sociologists like Ernest Rutherford Groves, however, were not convinced. They wanted to know why society had not tried harder to make adjustments and compensations for women. They wanted to know what in the nature of things had incapacitated men for the job of taking care of a house and children. The culture had made woman a housekeeper and then condemned her for her supposed inability to compete with men. And was it not true that every time America tested women's capacity to do men's work, male superiority proved to be an illusion?

The psychiatrists, whose business it is to make people happier, were not interested in the question of which sex was superior to the other in its ability to do things. It was of more consequence to them to decide whether a career outside of the home made a woman a better or worse *woman*. On this point, a flock of Freudians and neo-Freudians testified with certainty—and wrote voluminously on the subject for public consumption—that when a woman worked, it was bad for her, for her husband, and, most of all, for her children. The emotional security of the young ones was to their mind completely jeopardized by the absence of the female parent from the home for part of the day. Since it was believed that all sex and other mental troubles suffered by adults were a result of earlier parental coldness and rejection, the female parent was urged to stay at home and give her child the human warmth which the nursery school could not provide.

Moreover, what was bad for the child was worse for the mother. For, said the psychiatrists: woman's prime attribute, her femininity, was at stake. Two prominent women doctors, Helene Deutsch and Marynia F. Farnham, made this the essence of their message to American women. Dr. Deutsch declared unreservedly in her *Psychology of Women; a Psychoanalytic Interpretation:*

> Woman's intellectuality is to a large extent paid for by the loss of valuable feminine qualities: it feeds on the sap of effective life and results in impoverishment of this life either as a whole or in specific emotional qualities. . . . All observa-

tions point to the fact that the intellectual woman is mas-
culinized. . . .

A woman could, of course, stay home with her children and also be
ruined by intellectuality. Conversely, she could go out into the big
world without ever aspiring to intellectuality. But the distinguishing
marks of femininity go deeper. Dr. Deutsch's clinical experience told
her that "femininity is largely associated with passivity and masoch-
ism." In other words, women had a fundamental need to be kept
under the iron heel of men.

Dr. Farnham was in complete agreement with these sentiments
both in her popular articles and in *Modern Woman: the Lost Sex,*
a book in which she collaborated with the social historian, Ferdinand
Lundberg. The authors admonished women to return to their traditional feminine functions—mostly those of motherhood—unless they
wished to aggravate their own unhappiness and spread havoc among
both young and old in American society. Mother Nature had designed
the entire life of woman around motherhood and was to be challenged
only on penalty of universal misery. The special genius of woman
was for nurture.

The pattern, viewed as a whole, resembled those patterns of
national insecurity exhibited in the lives of America's totalitarian
enemies of World War II: A paternalistic state would direct a paternalistic male, who would in turn exercise authority over a subordinate
female and still more subordinate children. The program of Lundberg
and Farnham did in fact presuppose that the government would let
loose a flood of propaganda to persuade the public to alter its ways.
The contemplated alteration entailed a throwback to the days when
notions of democracy in the family and equality between parents
were considered dangerous. Women were to be re-established in
their socially recognized maternal role and were to cease their efforts
to invade masculine pursuits. In short, the aims of the long-fought,
uphill struggle of the feminist movement were ordered into the discard. And, quite logically, efforts to achieve a single standard of
morality must be abandoned too. A double standard was actively
advocated on the grounds that only men need and can have satisfactory casual sex relationships.

So then, women, according to one variety of popular psychiatric
literature (strong supported by religious influence and authoritarian
political propaganda) have wandered far from their accustomed
positions at home plate. The coaches shout to them to run back to
safety. But, either because they have lost their sense of direction, or
because their accustomed position is no longer what it used to be,
women find it impossible to resume where they left off a few decades
ago. It is as if they are in a continuing insecurity dream, trying one

after another the familiar hiding places of childhood days, always to find these exposed to the all-seeing eyes of their playmate adversaries. Fortunately women are receiving some ideological assistance in their search for safety from a friendly school of psychiatrists. The experts in this camp deny that the difficulty lies in women's having gone too far in demanding fulfillment. They censure society for not going far enough in furthering women's aspirations.

COUNTER-ATTACK

This group, trading under the sign of the Association for the Advancement of Psychoanalysis and its Auxiliary Council, is highly critical of the unscientific haste with which scientists rush to conclusions anent the distinctions between male and female behavior. No attempt, it is claimed, has ever made to determine how much of masculinity and femininity is shaped by culture and how much is inherent in physiology. There is cause for thought as one discovers, by way of illustration, that masculine behavior in some societies is feminine behavior in others. Nature's original distinguishing marks may be very few. Moreover, declares the psychiatrist Harold Kelman, "what is called masculine or feminine in our society . . . can be changed or dissipated in the short course of analysis, or by the longer course of history." The possibility lies before us that what so many psychologists note as basic sexual differences are actually, in large part, social infiltrations into the personality of such subtlety and long standing—so pervasive of the perceptions of the doctors themselves —that they look as if they have been irrevocably fixed by nature. Dr. Kelman has demonstrated that all the platitudes about "women in general" and "men in general" have flowed from the roles each has been assigned in our particular form of society. In the final accounting, to be a complete person, whether male or female, is to exhibit a balance of dependence and independence, softness and hardness. No quality or trait is the exclusive property of either sex.

When applied to the question of whether children gain or lose in emotional security when their mothers pursue careers outside the home, the theory of this school runs counter to keeping mothers in the nursery and fathers in the shop. In brief, only in social strata where motherhood is celebrated as a full-fledged career are full-time mothers capable of transmitting the feeling of completeness and fulfillment to their children. Everywhere else, which means practically everywhere in our society, the frustrations of the mothers are visited upon the children. Always under the weight of emotional conflict, the nursery-chained mother is the one who imposes her mental burdens upon her children, possesses them, and drives them to realize her own unrealized ambitions. Fathers do this to some extent too; but, inasmuch as they have a sporting chance at fulfillment, they are not as likely to transmit as many personality distortions to their children. Again, they have much less contact with their children—a matter of little consolation to children, who are the more exposed to their conflict-ridden mothers.

The mother best equipped to provide for a child's emotional security, according to this sociological school of psychiatry, is one who feels she has some measure of control over the environment in which her child lives. She is the human being who feels well integrated with her society and equal with others in the direction of its affairs. She is the one who believes in her own importance. In the words of Dr. Antonia Wenkart:

> Free access to any kind of human organization is a prerogative to development. In this sense a mother's career contributes toward the enrichment and depth of her relationship with her child, since a woman not restricted in her interest and activities is a happier and freer human being than one who attributes only one function to herself and literally stands sentinel at the child's cradle and watches anxiously her baby's development. . . . Not the quantity of time or affection offered to the child is the determining factor, but the quality.

The psychiatrists had their ways—contradictory ways—of describing the conflict between feminism and female-ism. The anthropologists had theirs. The task of writing an anthropological apologia for American women fell quite naturally to Margaret Mead, whose on-the-spot investigations of contemporary primitives gave her authority to speak of the cultural origins of sexuality. Anthropology, as conceived by Dr. Mead in her *Male and Female,* had a job to do for readers in English-speaking civilizations. By using examples of behavior of uncivilized peoples in far-off places, it could teach sex-shy Americans and Englishmen the things which made them grow up to be what they were as members of one sex faction or the other.

Writing when the feminist cause was weathering a dangerous crisis, Margaret Mead seemed oversensitive to the fact that, for equal recognition she had to be more than equal in scholarship *because* she was a woman. *As* a woman, she leaned backward from making a *prima facie* case for sexual equality. Instead she pleaded for a reexamination of the facts—in agreement with the recommendation of a few psychoanalysts—to determine how much of sexual behavior is learned in the school of the mother's lap, and, again, how much is patterned by the social group so as to perpetuate its time-worn assumptions. Granted the biological differences existing for procreative functions, the question still remained as to how much, or how little, of "femininity" or of "masculinity" is physiologically determined.

Psychoanalysis helped anthropology bolster feminist arguments save in a few instances. There was one Freudian point in particular which would have shattered Dr. Mead's case had she accepted it. This was the castration theory, the foundation on which Freudians had placed their prefabricated structure of male superiority. Dr. Mead found no such thing in the rituals of her primitive societies. Instead she found a precisely contrary manifestation. The men, in their initiation ceremonies, had used symbols which exposed a deep-seated envy on their part of the woman's childbearing mechanism.

In the eyes of a pro-feminist sociologist like Lester Frank Ward, or of the aggressive feminist movement of the first quarter of our century, these ritualistic symbols would have argued the superiority of women. When the obviously defensive Margaret Mead divulged the existence of womb-envy to her contemporaries, she did it so subtly that the threat was not felt. Dr. Mead boasted no competitive strength; she merely asked for a compromise familiar to pioneer feminists whose writings were published more than a hundred years before. She asked that women be permitted to work out their vocational ambitions without being encumbered by the extra weight of being a member of a sexual minority. Most emphatically she was opposed to women being treated on the job like men; she wished them to be permitted to bring their special feminine qualities—culturally produced or otherwise—to their activities. The feminine East and the masculine West were urged to unite in a world where complementary characteristics would enmesh to set in motion one harmonious operation. As in all the other fields of intercultural cooperation, the fusion of peoples in simulated sameness was no longer to be prized. Each of the two sexualities—male and female—was to be celebrated for its own contributions to the working world.

∽ ∽

The changed complexion of the woman question is best revealed when we examine the line-up of political forces on the question of the Equal Rights Amendment to the Constitution. Instead of finding all the "liberals" in politics and religion on the side of the amendment, we find most of them against it. Eleanor Roosevelt, who consistently represents the cause of women's rights from her vantage point in the upper regions of public affairs, is against it. So also is the Women's Bureau of the U. S. Department of Labor. The "anti" group includes as well the National League of Women Voters, the National Consumers' League, the Y. W. C. A., and the women of the American Federation of Labor and the Congress of Industrial Organizations. Numerous "virile" women's organizations have, in fact, opposed the amendment since it was first presented for consideration in 1923.

This lack of gratitude has always been a source of shock and disgust to the leaders of the National Woman's Party, the organization behind the twenty-seven year campaign to make absolute equality of the sexes a constitutional right. The very women for the winning of whose franchise the old-line feminist militants had served jail sentences, were now using political influence to defeat the ultimate goal of egalitarian feminism—an amendment which would erase all laws that discriminate. On the face of it, the supporters of the amendment had excellent grounds for indignation. It seemed unreasonable for anyone to oppose the principle that "Equality of rights under the law shall not be denied or abridged by the United States or by any State on account of sex."

But when the other side was heard it became apparent that all was not *equal* that was *uniform* in application. There was a question as to whether woman's lot would improve if all "discriminatory" legislation were erased from the books. Did women, for example, want to give up their right to maternity leaves from their jobs? Did they want to be sued by estranged husbands for adequate support? Would they give up legislative protection against unilateral divorce proceedings on the grounds of insanity? Again, as Senator Kefauver pointed out, the amendment might eliminate rape as a crime because, by definition, it involved an act of aggression on the part of one sex only, the male. And what would happen in that case to the Mann Act? Again, if the principle of equal treatment applied to military conscription, it was conceivable that the United States might have an army in which the women outnumbered the men. Suppose both mother and father were drafted at the same time: poor kiddies!

While each side sought to dramatize its appeal by adding a few such absurdities to the records of Congressional proceedings, there was no mistaking the essentials of the argument. The opposition, composed of senators generally described as progressives, was genuinely interested in preserving for women the benefits of protective measures in the common law as well as in the statutes of State and Nation. They had in mind, for example, widows' allowances, the inviolate concept of primary duty (of a husband to support his wife and family), laws governing the age of majority and the age of consent, minimum wages and maximum hour legislation designed to protect women workers, and the right of annulment of marriages.

A statement, drawn up by Professor Paul Freund of the Harvard Law School and signed by a host of leading jurists, testified that the whole body of jurisprudence which dealt benignly with woman in her social context was placed in jeopardy by the amendment. Every piece of special legislation would be subject to attack on Constitutional grounds if the new idea of absolute equality were to become a part of the primary law of the land. Equality held forth more dangers than rights. The prospect of innumerable controversies and confusions was a fearsome one. The future of woman's rights looked particularly somber when practical-minded legislators reminded their listeners of the likelihood that courts, as now constituted, would be inclined to favor the men in judging cases which came before them.

The protagonists of equal rights, for their part, pointed convincingly to examples of irrational family and labor legislation which operated to the disadvantage of women. They could show how the army had discriminated against women physicians. They could ask their adversaries to name one woman who had served on a draft board in either World War I or World War II. There were, in fact, many such pieces of legislative chivalry which kept women out of work which they desired very much to enter. The women crusaders at mid-century claimed that they were overprotected. The guard rails which had been set up for their safety were actually keeping them from reaching things they wanted and needed. They were altogether cynical about the gallantry of lawmakers who forbade them to work where they would be required to lift ten pounds or more up five steps or more. Was any husband, they asked, ever called away from his office at midday to help carry the baby up a flight of steps?

All agreed that both law and custom were working hardships on women both as regards their family life and their economic welfare. But, said Senator Lehman of New York, you cannot legislate custom and tradition out of existence in one fell swoop. Time and tide, would, he said, wear away the stubborn wall of social habit. You could not, for example, force an employer to hire a woman instead of a man. Another point, contributed by Senator Russell of Georgia, had to do with the danger of such an amendment to the principle of States' rights as well as to the right of local councils to legislate in behalf of women. Upon which, the progressives were aptly reminded that similar arguments had been used against Fair Employment Practices legislation, which adherents of the New Deal and the Fair Deal had always supported. If the position of other oppressed population sectors demanded Federal intervention to curb the inequities of traditional practice, why was the case of a sexual minority to be treated differently?

The answer to this question was provided in communications from national labor union bodies in opposition to the Equal Rights Amendment. The essential weakness of the amendment, according to official spokesmen of both the A. F. of L. and the C. I. O., was that it was designed to protect only the wealthier part of our female population. It left defenseless the countless women who held industrial and commercial jobs. Women were not sufficiently organized to bargain for their own wage and hour rights. And therefore they needed special legislative assistance. The unions preferred specific ameliorative laws to a blanket Constitutional amendment.

When the amendment finally came up for a vote, the reasoning of neither side was influential in shaping the outcome. The enormous party power which resided in Mrs. India Edwards, head of the Women's Division of the National Democratic Committee, weighed more heavily in the balance than did the force of experience and principle. President Truman had warned his party not long before that fifty-two per cent of the votes are women's votes. Both major party platforms had endorsed the amendment in recognition of this fact. Political promises had to be honored, especially when dealing with polling strength based not on changeable political opinion but on permanent sex membership.

Opponents of the amendment were fully aware of the danger of political reprisals. They therefore combined principle with politics in an attempt to substitute legislation for the Constitutional amendment. Their bill proposed the establishment of a Commission on the Legal Status of Women. This Commission was to study discriminatory legislation and to encourage the modernization of legal codes. It was to investigate discrimination in government employment and to foster a revamping of administrative practices in this respect. It was also to act in an advisory capacity for and in conjunction with State and private bodies. The bill—designed to write into official American policy the idea "that in law and its administration no distinctions on the basis of sex shall be made except such as are reasonably justified by differences in physical structure or by maternal function"—was defeated by sixty-five votes to eighteen.

At this point it occurred to a few astute legislators that a qualifying statement added to the amendment might swing the votes of a number of progressives. Senator Hayden of Arizona offered an amending clause which said that "the provisions of this article shall not be construed to impair any rights, benefits, or exemptions now or hereafter conferred by law upon persons of the female sex." The party commitment was thereby satisfied, at the same time negating the force of the amendment as originally drawn up. This promoted the greatest good for the greatest number in the Senate. It was preeminently satisfactory to one lawmaker who was greatly distressed by the fact that Russia was using our existing sexual inequality as grist for its propaganda mill in Far Eastern countries. The amendment, as thus amended, won by a vote of sixty-three to nineteen. Gloom descended upon the victorious camp and representatives of the National Woman's Party immediately declared their intention of fighting this form of the joint resolution when it appeared on the floor of the House of Representatives. The battle has not yet been resumed.

Short though it was, the Senate debate on equal rights was built on firmer foundations than were discussions on the same subject in other American forums and media of communication. At the present moment, writing on the education of women is oriented away from the idea of equality. The questions of greatest concern are those dealing with schooling girls for domestic proficiency and preparing them to be happy with their appointed lot. The reason for this emphasis is a belief that twentieth-century women are not as well prepared for household management and child management as nineteenth-century women were. The proposed solution is to devote a block of the high-school and college curricula to this form of education for life. Male writers holding this view are doubtless reasoning in this way out of irritation over the increase of their own participation in kitchen and nursery. Women writers are also subject to the current addiction of educated women to home and family. The ruthless world has made no provision to ease their double burden of career and children. They avenge themselves by withdrawing from the extra-familial tasks of society.

Script writers for the motion picture, radio, and stage have joined in the general retreat. They created the stereotype of the female physician whose practice interferes with her marriage. Interrupted on her nuptial night and every night thereafter by the demands of patients, she finally is forced to adjust either her career or her husband to the exigencies of a doctor's married life. Another stock character is the female executive who is so proficient in giving orders to her subordinates that the male hero fears and fails to make the overtures which inwardly—in her role of woman—she so ardently desires. The executive, after some minor crisis, bursts into tears, thereby revealing that she is just a woman, and really wants a man more than she wants a career.

On the musical comedy stage, the theme is developed along lighter lines. In "Love Life," we witness a vaudeville act in which a woman is being sawed in half as a symbol of her divided attentions in modern life. As the story unfolds we are presented with a situation in which married life deteriorates in proportion as feminism thrives. The heroine of "Annie Get Your Gun," to provide an example in which apparent nonsense makes itself amply clear, sings "Anything You Can Do, I Can Do Better" until she learns her sad lesson: when she excels in a shooting contest, the losing male is unhappy and becomes visibly cool. Her solution is to withdraw from competition in male activities so that her erstwhile competitor—and cause of her heartsickness—will respond to her latent feminine attractions.

The subtlety prevailing on stage and screen pays a certain deference to an existing sector of feminist opinion. Seldom is the yearning to go back to the days "when men were men and women were womeny" expressed as it is in Ogden Nash's piece of absurdity which appeared in *Flair's* All Male Issue of July 1950. Said Mr. Nash:

> I attribute much of our modern tension
> To a misguided striving for intersexual comprehension.
> It's about time to realize, brethren, as best we can,
> That a woman is not just a female man.

In literature, only the novel did not respond significantly to the reaction against women of the world. Perhaps it was because so many women were eminently successful in the novelist's calling that it did not occur to women or men writers of fiction to use their medium for transmitting so contradictory an idea. Femininity *was* celebrated, but in the tradition of equality. To some women novelists, true equality meant the creation of a heroine who in her exaggerated sexuality would correspond to the overworked Don Juan hero of novels past and present. The species *Forever Amber* rose to the occasion and met with immediate public approval. If thousands upon thousands of American readers failed to perceive that a frankly promiscuous heroine was staging male heroics in the struggle for sexual power, perhaps it was because they were too absorbed in erotic details to notice the analogy.

More adept in transmitting psychological subtleties to readers was the novelist who insinuated a living psychiatrist into the structure of his tale. This one all-purpose character could readily explain near-miraculous solutions to sexual and sexually connected problems. Conscientious humanitarians were overjoyed at having the people's writers explain intricate linkages between troublesome adult behavior and the distortions of human personality which start in the cradle. They were satisfied that such distortions were frequently connected with the repression or misdirection of sexual emotions. The humane scientists were, however, rarely convinced that writers were presenting reliable psychological data about the characters they created. One sympathizes with these doubts when reading, in Philip Wylie's novel, *Opus* 21, about a marriage which is rescued *ipso facto* when a young wife comes to realize and accept her husband's bisexuality as well as her own.

ANALYSTS-IN-LAW

It is to the credit of the psychologists and psychiatrists that they favored more demonstrable conceptions in their dealings with the marriage problem. They sensed that too strong a dose of psychotechnicalities would find either a resentful audience or no audience.

A book like Dr. Edmund Bergler's *Unhappy Marriage and Divorce* (1946) failed to have widespread influence because it more than implied that marriage failed only because one or both parties were neurotic. The layman could not accept this unless, in view of the prevalence of divorce, he also accepted the universality of neurosis. Also beyond his understanding was the idea that marriage, as Dr. Bergler had it, was a patent medicine which people took in the hope that it would help them attain unconscious infantile goals. Educators, psychologists, and sociologists, for their part, were suspicious of the analyst's intent to build up his own trade. The analyst had closed the roads around marital trouble by way of sex and marriage education, and had conspired to funnel all traffic through the doctor's office.

An interpretation which the uninitiated accept more readily is that marital failure can occur if one or both mates respond neurotically to the responsibility entailed in marriage. Responsibility in this sense has a broad definition. It includes an honest estimation of one's own worth as well as a genuine respect for the dignity of his partner. It provides for the one's maximum self-realization insofar as it is consonant with the self-realization of the other. Each partner obviously does come to his mate harboring a lifelong accumulation of sensitivities, unresolved mental conflicts, and non-rationally shaped goals. In the case of individuals who are hopelessly overloaded with such excess mental baggage, marital failure is certain, unless, by chance, persons with compensating disturbances join with them in the family enterprise. In the case of less disturbed people, who are laden with only a normal complement of quirks, the explosive potential is there, but in a lesser degree.

What this amounts to (notwithstanding the frightening labels which parlor analysts tend to pin on their helpless friends) is that many husbands and many wives cannot readily achieve a satisfactory balance between their own inner needs and the legitimate psychological demands of their marriage partners. A mistaken or distorted attitude toward one's own privileges and deserts seriously impairs the possibility of cooperation in the two-sided process of married life. The professionals call this a neurotic response. Laymen make the same kind of distinction between a "considerate" mate and an "inconsiderate" one. The use of epithets like "demanding," "aggressive," and "selfish" reflects an understanding of the psychologists' diagnosis. This understanding, however, rarely carries with it either boundless sympathy with the unfortunate behavior of a spouse or acceptance of a psychotherapeutic program.

The complaint of a woman correspondent in the *Nation* of August 26, 1950, is an apt example of popular negativism with regard to psychoanalysis. The woman in question and her husband had been divorced a short time before at the suggestion, she claimed, of his psychoanalyst. None of the usual causes were applicable to their case. There had been no competing male or female on the scene to alienate their reciprocal affection; no mother-in-law, no father fixation or other family complex to hinder their free exchange of love. Always it was his psychiatrist who helped him nurture petty, ancient grievances into big present impediments. Always the spirit of the psychiatrist hovered about the home and infringed upon its privacy. The problems a husband should have shared with his wife he took instead to his psychiatrist. The energies which a man should have expended on making two hearts beat in unison were concentrated on examining his own emotional pulse. Analytic interviews should theoretically have helped to socialize the husband; instead they made him morbidly egocentric.

Two psychiatrists who were invited to comment on this complaint—entitled "The Psychoanalytic Joyride"—were at odds as to the validity of the bill of particulars presented. Dr. Frederic Wertham thought the case a typical one, and coined the hyphenate, "analyst-in-law" to epitomize his criticism of medical meddling in other people's marital business. In Dr. Gregory Zilboorg's opinion, the charges of the lady, Dr. Wertham, and for that matter of Monsignor Sheean (who was currently heading the Catholic Church's attack on psychiatry) were entirely misdirected. It was not psychoanalysis that was immoral and disruptive of family life, but the misuse and abuse of psychoanalysis. The critics, he said, were all of a piece in mistaking "Freud for the ghost which so many people in their amateurish and professional ignorance make of him."

∽ ∽

Disregarding the internecine intellectual wars of the psychiatrists, the American layman continues to be suspicious of the claims of psychiatry with respect to its ability to calm the troubled waters of marital relations. The layman has many reasons for his mistrust. As far as he can determine, there is little objective evidence of the workability of the new cure. Again, the dependence of the analyzed on a totally strange analyst does not suit the layman's illusions of self-reliance. Furthermore, he is repelled by the fear of what might come to the surface. Finally, the ideas and language he meets in connection with this newest mental science are at once strange, technical, and full of uncomfortable implications.

The manner in which the reading public seized upon Lafayette Ronald Hubbard's *Dianetics* demonstrates the eagerness with which the layman receives an unknown quantity (of highly questionable quality) provided it gives promise of curing people with homey words in the privacy of their own abodes. *Dianetics* reached the best-seller lists quickly by establishing and defining its own verbal conventions for use in a procedure which may be called "companionate catharsis." The object of the operation is to accomplish a mutual "clearing" of "aberrations." An "aberration," it is understood, is anything that is not "clear." So then, two friends—each having read in and absorbed the science of dianetics—have a series of conversations in the course of which they help each other reconstruct a mental autobiography starting as far back as their womb experiences.

Marriage too, says Hubbard, can be saved by clearing the partners of their aberrations. The minds which show most aberrations are the "reactive" ones which have subconscious motivations of guilt. The clearing operations start with a mutual friend and continue with the marriage partner. In marriages so cleared, it seems, "it was discovered that the partners, beneath the dirty cloth of aberration, loved each other well." Substitute "aberration" for "neurotic behavior," "reactive" for "repressed," "clearing" for "analytic therapy," eliminate the drain of a psychiatrist's fees on the family budget—and you have translated a science of great social usefulness into a public menace. The only remaining consolation is that whatever harm is done will be accomplished voluntarily by and to the individual participants. Conceivably, too, little ill should come of the wide reading of a book which few, if any, can actually comprehend. Only some things learned previously from the Freudian emphasis will be confirmed and therefore better remembered. An example in point is the principle that (in Dianetic language) "nearly all marital discontent has its major factor aberration on the second dynamic, sex."

SEX AND THE CALCULATING MACHINE

The popularity of *Dianetics* is one further symptom, to those who measure intellectual trends, that Americans are yielding to antiscientific tendencies in current social thought. This or its opposite are both plausible suppositions. It may be that book-buyers are acting out of their customary faith in the powers of science when they embrace *Dianetics*—whose subtitle is "The Modern Science of Mental Health." However that may be, but a short time before the appearance of *Dianetics*, the same public reaffirmed its "belief" in the scientific approach to human problems by elevating to the status of a common noun the name of the scientist scholar, Professor Kinsey. Alfred C. Kinsey and his co-workers offered no direct solutions to domestic problems. They did, through carefully prepared charts and tables, provide the foundations on which others will some day erect a science of the "major factor aberration" which is, according to Hubbard—and according to an impressive number of serious students who preceded him—sex. If, then, "nearly all marital discontent" is associated with sexual behavior, Professor Kinsey's multitude of readers—plus additional multitudes who learn about *the report* through watered-down versions and hearsay—are justified in their revived hope for the long-awaited rapprochement between biology and our social codes.

This rapprochement may not take place. Western civilization may not soon achieve a working arrangement like that of the ancient Hebrews, who solved their underpopulation problem by making sex without procreation a sin; or like that of the ancient Greeks who solved their overpopulation by encouraging hetaerism and homosexuality when infant exposure failed to limit the number of hungry Greeklings. The immediate promise of reports on the sexual behavior of the human animal in the United States—and elsewhere, as the Kinsey fashion is exported—is that, through hundreds of thousands of open discussions, criticisms, and even jokes, progress in the task of improving sexual adjustment will be accelerated. Talk, in and of itself, is expected to help "clear" society and the individuals who comprise it of much of their aberration in the "second dynamic."

Sexual Behavior in the Human Male, the first of a series of volumes to publish data gathered by the Kinsey pollsters, finds its greatest audience outside the groups of professional workers for whom it was intended. Caution was exercised by reporting in such a way as to avoid sensationalism and unjustified conclusions. But this laudable intention does not guide the typewriters of interpreting journalists or the mouths of public speakers. In more instances than one would want to count, people translate the carefully gathered, non-opinionated materials of the report into a release for their own repressed drives. And indeed, statistics are most useful when they justify their interpreter's purposes; sociologists see in the distant wake of the Kinsey Report a radical overhauling of human institutions. Nature may once more have its say in the adjustment of society; at any rate, the world's conception of the unnatural, inasmuch as it is a product of social definition, is seen to be in need of reconsideration.

Despite all the verbal fences erected around the first volume to forestall hasty demands for changes in social standards, such demands are forthcoming in the guise of prognosis of change. Some say, for example, that if individual differences in sexual capacity present the enormous variability revealed in the Kinsey Report, perhaps moral codes are the sublime contradiction of the civilized world. Or, if they are necessary to society, should they not be as elastic as conduct is variable? The desirability of polygyny and polyandry has occurred to some. The ancient practice of having men marry women younger than themselves may be reversed by the knowledge that men reach their sexual activity peak in adolescence, and women theirs in the late twenties.

The experts in mental hygiene aspects of sex education are cheered by the report for their own reasons. The addition of data on the sexual maturation of youth assists the efforts of parents and teachers in creating sex education programs. Again, many a morbid misconception about adolescent behavior may disappear after a healthy airing. The Report seems to indicate that precocious exercise of the libido does not invite early death. Moreover, there is no statistical support for the somber warning that the solitary and social vices cause impotence, insanity, or that disease vaguely called "degeneracy." One Kinsey commentator, highly critical of the Report as a whole, praised it for freeing sexuality from science itself. The doctors, he explained, had always been the leaders in enforcing religious and moral prohibitions. More than physical injunction would in the future be necessary to curb sexuality, if curbing were socially desirable.

Bachelors, young and old, also find comfort in the Report. Having suffered long from gnawing guilt and inferiority feelings about their way of life, they discovered that the differences in behavior between married and unmarried men hinge only on the factor of opportunity. Perhaps the innuendoes, stories, and jokes that made the bachelor an object of ridicule throughout some three hundred years of American life will some day disappear from conversation and popular literature.

The implications of the report for persons about to marry and for married people themselves are less clear than for children, adolescents, and bachelors. The statistics on male sexual activity outside the marriage bonds have as yet not touched off a concerted movement by the women to hold their husbands to account. Possibly the imminence of a report on the American female makes it impolitic to cast the first aspersion. The optimists forecast an improvement in the adjustability of brides by virtue of their wide foreknowledge of male behavior. Another bright hope is that divorce will decrease when wives learn to tolerate the not-so-different behavior of husbands, and when husbands are no longer so upset by their own misbehavior that they cannot live normally at home. Some have it that it is the obsession of guilt about misconduct, and not misconduct itself, that leads to divorce. This is one kind of logic. Another view is that of the sociologists of the traditional-family school who deplore the destructive effect of the Kinsey Report on the American family.

Coursing through the troubled minds of those who criticize the Report on moral grounds is a worry engendered by the assumption, based on belief in Godly design, that "whatever is is right." Projecting their own beliefs onto the Indiana scientists, these people charge that the investigators have morally accepted, condoned, or favored the behavior described in their statistical analyses. One count in the indictment is that the first Kinsey volume has been over-lenient in its "judgment" of human sexual expression through animal contact. Another is that homosexualism got a boost from the Report. The statistics, allegedly, also give the nod to other forms of extra-marital sexual activity. Speakers and organizations publicly express their state of shock, a state brought about by the Kinsey Report's implication that our moral standards must be in need of revision if people consistently violate them. The next step in this kind of criticism is to concentrate all the blame for the moral deviations of the young on Kinsey and his associates.

Having imposed many of their own constructions on the Report, the denouncers overlook one of its stated conclusions, to wit, that neither events nor suggestions in print seem to change thè pattern of sexual behavior from one generation to another. Moreover, the setting of the pattern depends infinitely more on one's social class, educational accomplishments, traditions, and family group habits than on his immediate associations and cultural milieu. *Reading materials are among the less influential determinants.* Furthermore, no responsible observer has as yet sensed or measured a perceptible change in attitudes or their behavior correlates since the publication of the Report. In fact, the excitement attending the initial publicity has left a residue of academic interest chiefly. Doubtless, public interest will be revived with the report on the sexual behavior of women. The flash generated by a *Redbook* article in 1950 on the forthcoming "female" volume may be a forewarning of the thunder to be expected with the actual publication of the book. The matured state of the American mind may be inferred from the fact that only one loud voice, that of a Canadian church group, has called for the suppression of the second Kinsey Report.

The conciliatory attitude of clergymen in general has its measure in the casualness of their discussions of the first volume. "You look at it your way," they seem to say, "We'll look at it our way. We think you are wrong." Such a philosophic acceptance, however, has not been exhibited as uniformly by other professional groups. Public opinion experts question Kinsey's sampling techniques, indicating, for example, that he has too heavy a representation of educated groups, of personality types who volunteer readily for this particular kind of survey, and of people from Indiana and New York. Pollsters also object to the use of non-standardized interviewing techniques. A few statisticians have joined the opinion measurers in pointing out what they consider to be limitations arising out of the source and type of data, as well as distortions due to carelessness in the presentation of data.

The group most vociferous in its rejection of certain aspects of the report is that practicing the medical science of psychiatry. This reaction is understandable as one notes the number of passages in the Report which are critical of psychiatry and psychiatrists. But, beyond this, the specific differences between Kinsey and the psychiatrists are many and real. The psychiatrists take exception, to cite a fundamental difference, to the device of direct questioning as used in the Kinsey investigations. They assert that, however skillfully applied, this method will not elicit accurate information about sexual behavior, inasmuch as the respondents, in recalling their own past behavior, are certain to confuse fact with fantasy. Repressions, wishful forgetting, and similar psychic mechanisms are likely to defeat the best interviewee's intentions. Moreover, events such as the Report claims to record are known to be recalled best in context—a context which as often as not is forgotten or repressed because it once incurred social disapproval. The psychologists also insist that the mind does not work like a calculating machine which records latest totals in properly tabulated categories.

The psychiatrists are at sword's point with the Report on key questions like that of the relationship of neurosis with sex behavior and the characteristics of pregenital sexuality. The Report asserts that neurosis is the result of sexual misbehavior *via* the guilt obsession. The doctors say deviant behavior is a symptom of underlying neurosis. The Report finds that sexual experience in childhood results from curiosity and that it is a matter of accident which kind of experience occurs first and what sequence ensues. The psychiatrists —particularly the Freudians—consider "curiosity" a euphemism and identify sexuality as one of the primal drives of animal life. They are firm believers in a fixed order of developmental stages, such as the anal, the oral, and the genital. Within these zonal units of sexual maturation they describe another order of movement from narcissism to homosexualism, and thence to ultimate heterosexuality. Inasmuch as much psychoanalytic diagnosis depends on locating the precise stage at which a given patient's personality was "arrested," the opposition of the psychiatrists to Kinsey's thesis of "curiosity and response to sufficient stimulus" is natural. Kinsey and his biologist partisans, for their part, maintain that their analysis of causation and response fits better with the expectations of natural science than does the analysts' assertion of a mystic *id* having properties independent of the rest of living things.

Many of these criticisms and counter-criticisms never reach the minds of laymen. One objection, however, is made by both sensitive citizens and specially trained professionals: The Kinsey unit of "outlet" failed to interpret the full spirit of sexual experience. Based entirely on physiological manifestations, the Report admittedly has no interest in psychological involvements, or in the origins and consequences of sexual feeling. It caters in a sense to the values of brute man, man who is concerned with numbers rather than with depths and qualities. Moreover, it falls in with a badly misdirected tendency—a tendency deplored by scientists and moralists alike—to separate sex from man's other activities. One partisan may believe that sexual behavior is patterned after the total personality; another may argue that the pattern of personality traits is cut along lines of an individual's sexual habits; a great many may not be able to draw lines of cause and effect but are nevertheless convinced that non-sexual thoughts and emotions are intimately meshed with sexual ones in the same person. The Kinsey investigators have stated their awareness of their limitations in this respect. When asked why they did not try to penetrate the subtler layers of feeling and experience, they reply rather convincingly that to do so would be to obtain inaccurate replies and distorted statistics. They imply that the field for deeper probing has not been preempted; instead, easier access has been provided into what should have been declared common territory a long time ago. Before the Kinsey Report, the outer gates to the guarded terrain of sexual research were more heavily bolted than the inner ones.

Granting that the Kinsey Report of 1948 struck a telling blow at censorship it is easy to exaggerate immediate results as well as probable future consequences. It is also easy to underrate efforts of some one hundred and fifty years standing to break through customary and legal restrictions on public discussions of matters concerning sex. It is surely more rhetoric than truth to say, as have Morris Ernst and David Loth in their *American Sexual Behavior and the Kinsey Report*, that "The Kinsey Report has done for sex what Columbus did for geography. It makes a successful scientific voyage to explore an unknown world which had been open only to speculation and suspicion —the sex life of human beings." But, then again, perhaps there is no thought too grandiose to be appropriate with regard to a text which, more than any other in our time, has cleared the approaches to candor among people. It is even conceivable that when the report on women's sex habits makes its appearance, the contemporary movement back to feminine fragility will be reversed in favor of equality. If the male has counted his superiority by his extra-moral privileges, the "paper doll he wants to call his own" may demonstrate her equality in terms of having exercised *his* sexual privileges. Out of much that is considered unwholesome by present standards, time may fashion a wholesome solution. Male and female may reach a lasting peace. "There even may be among men and women," as Harrison Smith editorialized in the *Saturday Review of Literature*, "more love and less loving."

But this is rather more than may be hoped for in the immediate future. Old definitions of social offenses and crimes do not disappear automatically merely because they are in opposition to reality. Discussions of the Kinsey Report itself are still characterized by averted glances, augmented pulse rate, and other psycho-physiological symptoms of discomfort. One of the genuine changes in attitude and interest to come to notice is that of the yellow journals and magazines of high circulation. Now that lurid descriptions of youthful escapades, divorce scandals, and such have lost some of their salacious quality by virtue of having been reduced to statistics in the Kinsey Report, reporters and free-lance writers have seized upon homosexualism as a replacement item. The dens of iniquity where boys used to visit evil women now house evil men. Books like "The Well of Loneliness" —unique for its treatment of lesbianism in 1928, and read only *sub rosa* at the time—are guaranteed a more placid reception in the future.

NEW DIRECTIONS

Obviously the distinctions between yesterday and today are not sharp ones. The past is and is not with us in a number of ways. An inventory at the middle of the twentieth century shows that part of the current stock of ideas on sex and marriage is well over a hundred years old. A good deal is quite new. And distinctions between the new and the old are not always easy to make. For ideas intermingle more easily than people, and many breeds come to have common characteristics.

There is, however, a characteristic feature of present ideas on sex and marriage that is notably new. The trade of counseling is now formalized. While the trade is old, there is novelty in its transfer out of the hands of amateur practitioners and into those of professional sex and marriage experts. The new marriage technicians have borrowed as they pleased from sociology, religion, law, medicine, and psychology to produce a fresh and aggressive science. There is as yet no claim that the old professions are completely unfit to counsel individuals in distress. On the other hand the sex scientists are not reticent about notifying doctors, lawyers, ministers and such that they cannot consider themselves qualified unless they fulfill specified requirements with regard to academic training, scientific knowledge and attitudes, and diagnostic skills. It seems at the moment that, measured by instruments available to social scientists, ninety per cent of the ministry is not qualified to perform the job of marriage counseling.

The sociologists specializing in marriage problems are, in short, making their bid for the position of sole guide to church, state, and community in matters which pertain to marriage stability and family relationships. They are insinuating their influence into newspapers and popular magazines, as well as into the "advice" operations of other mass media of communication. Free-lance writers and amateur moralists still, on occasion, serve up their own recipes for solving sexual and marital problems. The pulps, the slicks, and the pocket magazines continue to warm over stale fare for anxious adolescents and adults. For the most part, the personal-problem books and articles are popular translations from sociologese by psychologist counselors and by college professors who teach marriage courses.

The moralist's lament about unhappy marriage and increasing divorce is disappearing. Gone also is the old reliance on choosing the right husband or wife; the psychological sciences have proved interpersonal relationships to be too complicated for reliance on the initial momentum of an accidentally or "scientifically" fashioned choice of mate. The once-upon-a-time, fairy-tale land of love, inhabited by perfectly matched pairs, is surrendering to the realities of human behavior. The new world of love is one in which domestic harmony is to be conscientiously cultivated by the parties concerned. And, as the guidance experts indicate, the responsibility for this cultivation devolves first upon the individual, and only secondarily upon his mate. What the counselors are in essence saying to all the self-righteous who choose to listen is: "Look inward, angel."

Shifting the blame from the "other" to the "self" could, if successfully engineered, promote family stability to a considerable extent in a community of self-contained, well-informed, emotionally and economically secure selves. But, since such individual selves are few and far between, the sociologists are presently engaged in marshaling forces that will strengthen and perpetuate the family unit of social organization. To this end they encourage welfare services which lighten those burdens under which family units may crumble. They promote security programs which help families carry the strains of ill-health, accident, unemployment, and old age. Included as well in the framework of family engineering are things like nutrition research and education, clinics and printed information concerning child care, mental hygiene facilities, and guidance programs in school systems. The promotion of housing developments ranks high on the list of activities; for it is indicated that when too many particles are compressed into too small a chamber, the result may be a bursting out on all sides, the particles flying in separate directions.

These are matters in which the marriage experts are collaborators but not prime movers. Theirs primarily is the assigned task of counseling the disturbed and of educating to forestall disturbance. America's abiding faith in education as a solution for human ills applies now as much to domestic personal relations as it does to political and social relations on the grand one-world scale. Moreover, the task of marriage education is now conceived to extend from the cradle to the grave. What started as an educational frill in a few colleges now pervades entire school systems as well as agencies of adult education.

The sequence begins with parent education in behalf of children's better adjustment, special emphasis being placed on sex education beginning with the child's earliest consciousness of the family situation—this because of the firm belief that from childhood misdirections arise the divorce statistics of the next generation. The continuation of the educational process on the elementary school level is much discussed, but little is undertaken in this area beyond incidental material which is woven into instruction in the social sciences, literature, biology, or nature study. Alert teachers make the most of the lessons to be learned from pairs of pet rabbits or families of white mice. Lessons drawn directly from the activities of human beings are at the moment confined to the showing of available films on biological aspects of reproduction, and this only where parents, teachers, supervisors, and school board members have been educated to the point of permitting it.

High school marriage education takes the shape of reading and a large dose of free classroom discussion. Discussion, which requires intelligent guidance in direct proportion to the teacher's knowledge and skill, revolves about boy-girl relationships in general, the etiquette proper to specific heterosexual situations, the relationship between a teen-ager and his parents, and the comparison of life in the movies or on the radio with real-life conditions. The matter of "dating," a pre-courtship institution indigenous to America, is discussed in the classroom and an attempt is made to relate it to later married life. The emphasis in all these discussions bears on the point that two people must work and work hard to make the marriage enterprise a success. Marriage courses on the college level also make much of the mutual character of marriages that keep.

Outside the walls of the school, marriage experts pursue their specialty in women's and men's clubs, parent-teacher associations, and wherever else adults meet for discussion purposes. Recently, in recognition of the popularity of public library forums, sociologists have urged upon librarians the need to sponsor and promote family education through books and group talks. The librarians are not rushing to heed the call. Their reticence is not grounded, as may be thought, in personal inadequacies generally portrayed in occupational stereotypes. Backwardness in this respect is traceable rather to fear of reprisals from puritanical trustees. The librarians' response to the urgings of marriage information promoters is to publish—as they have always done to implement discussions of current social importance—lists of books on mate selection, wedding plans, the family, sex in marriage, and other related subjects.

As often in the past enterprising publishers have printed books to teach what teachers fail to teach, so in the present do producers of educational films fill the gaps where readers fail to read. Hence over seventy separate motion pictures, in black and white and in color, to present to young and old the gamut of family relations from youth to old age. For the very young there are "Human Growth," "Human Reproduction," and the "Story of Menstruation;" for adolescents, "Are You Popular," "Dating: Do's and Don'ts," "You and Your Friends," "Body Care and Grooming," and "Shy Guy;" on youth and the drinking problem, "It's the Brain that Counts" and "Alcohol and the Human Body." Those of an age to marry are shown "Choosing for Happiness," "It Takes All Kinds," "This Charming Couple," and "Who's Boss?" "Marriage and Divorce" takes a fifteen minute glance at the problems young couples must face in building and preserving their families intact. "Life with Grandpa" concerns itself with the economic and emotional problems of aged Americans.

∽ ∽

Despite the effort and wisdom placed on the side of solving the problem of the sexes in and out of the family context, the struggle is still a losing one. Elements of an outworn romantic tradition still persist in most stories printed, filmed, and broadcast; and these outweigh by sheer volume the best our experts have to offer. The aspect of love and life presented in commercial movies is that of a perpetual man-hunt or woman-hunt. The males vary from the hunting type, which is middle-aged, balding, and well-financed, to the hunted he-male of brawny form and symmetrical feature. (Recent concessions of sexual equality have reduced the hero's biceps or, on occasion, have endowed him with a girlish charm.) The females are almost invariably the unsubtly alluring kind. Marriage in Hollywood art rarely changes the quality and tempo of life for the married. The hunt continues—under cover, in order to elude the wary censors.

Radio broadcasting, deprived of visual properties, relies somewhat more on the element of romantic suffering for its representations of love life. The shape of sexual affection, especially in the daytime serial, or "soap-opera," is normally triangular. The villains, or the villainesses, are no longer evil-intentioned as of old. They are essentially virtuous but subject to error. Error, however, keeps everyone in a state of sentimental suffering. This somber picture, further darkened by daily illness, accident, and sleeping pills "to end it all," is the daily diet for listeners by the million. The idea of love and its culmination in family life probably vacillates in unsophisticated minds between the carefree sexual contact of the movies and the beautiful torment of the radio.

The sophisticated chide their less fortunate compatriots for a certain lack of discernment. They do so with bad grace; for they themselves are in no less confusion. Marriage among the intellectuals is, if anything, less stable than among their untutored contemporaries. The love experts themselves suffer frequent affectional dislocations; the marriage counselors too have their divorces. And whose is wisdom in the matter of divorce? Who can arbitrate between the contradictory values involved in solving family difficulties? Family stability seems desirable; but unhappiness in marriage is a crime against reason. Personal freedom is a most laudable goal; but destroying a family in order to insure freedom is evil. Separation and divorce are destructive of children's morals and morale; life in an unhappy home may be more so.

The statement that "Love is America's Problem No. 1" is not made by the facetious. The search for a rationally based marriage ethic is matched in seriousness only by the search for a rationally based sex ethic. With the advent of efficient birth control methods and of effective drugs for combatting venereal disease, some of the old motives for conforming with established moral codes are gone. For those who find it possible to adhere to the rules laid down by the Creator and interpreted by the clergy, there is no problem. For the rest—and there are multitudes if the Kinsey percentages hold proportionately for the entire population—a new definition of what is acceptable in sexual behavior is needed, and along with it, a revised set of reasons for compliance.

Ultra-rationalists lean toward the anarchist rule of for each his own ideals; traditional taboos and conceptions of chastity are categorically rejected; the individual has the disposal of his own body. Practitioners of the social sciences, especially the anthropologists, have their own rationale: they find that many a taboo, itself originating in myth and superstition, is necessary for the scientific regulation of society to the end that everyone may achieve maximum fulfillment during his life span. As a writer for *Harper's* has phrased it, "Hypocrisy is the lubricant of society."

∽ ∽

Countless words have been expended on sexual problems over the past three centuries. It may appear to some as though the American mind has concentrated more on these problems than the results warrant. Nevertheless, for an area of life so fundamental, no effort is too great and no achievement too small. Fortunately the mind does not wear with exercise; likewise the supply of printer's ink and electronic communications seems inexhaustible. At the moment of writing, the manufacture and exchange of ideas show no signs of weakening in their perennial striving to adjust the balance of the sexes.

TWELVE

A Continuing American Dilemma

HISTORICAL PRESENTISM

What is altogether clear about the sexual aspect of American thought and behavior is that ideas tend to surface before corresponding actualities become widespread. Frequently, those who have been perceptive about the processes of change, or who themselves were advance actors in the pragmatic play, were also advocates and heralds of the Newness. The pressures for sexual justice—and sexual expression —exhibit rises and declines which sometimes correspond to spurts and relaxations in the general social ferment.

Historians have written much about the feminist factor of freedom's upsurge before the Civil War; but only recently have they worked the mines of sexual unrest in the Progressive Era of early twentieth century America. It had long been assumed by social historians and commentators that a sexual revolution of sorts took place in the Roaring Twenties; hence few scholars thought to investigate the real seedtime of change—the decade or so which preceded World War I. Recent historians have shown considerable interest in the subject either because of presentism in their choice of research problems or because the culture has recently accorded academic respectability to sexual history. What seems clear now is that the period of political and social Progressivism (1900-1915) was also one of incipient sexual assertiveness and feminist participation in some of the joys and privileges of the American male. A close look at this period[1] shows not only that women were liberating themselves in the matter of manners and morals but that numerous perceptive contemporaries were well aware of what was occurring. Observers in this early period noted—as the Kinsey studies have confirmed—the breaking down of conventional sexual standards for the female and the adoption of other traditionally masculine styles and attitudes. What apparently has made the 1920's seem so dramatic was the extension of earlier urban upper-class leadership behavior to smaller places and lower classes.

The struggle for a sexual balance of power stimulated the beginnings of a relevant historical scholarship during the Progressive period itself.[2] If the output of scholarly books is at all indicative of public interest, the period of the 1950's and 60's has been a time of high sexual tension and attention.[3] There were also numerous scholarly articles to confirm the newly established respectability of hitherto sensitive topics.[4] Most significant in terms of academic attitudes was the run of doctoral dissertations undertaken in history and literature departments of American universities. Among the titles were studies dealing with *The Beginnings of the Women's Rights Movement in the United States, 1800-1840; Some Ethnographic Aspects of Pregnancy, Parturition and Infancy in 18th Century Anglo-American Civilization; Magaret Sanger and the Birth Control Movement; Revolution in Manners and Morals: The Treatment of Adultery in American Drama between the Wars; Attrition of the Male Image during the Great Depression;* and *Images of Women in American Magazine Fiction, 1905-1955.*

However impressive this accumulation of recent serious study and writing, it has not yielded a precise explanation of what has been exciting, plaguing, agitating and, in some circles, consuming the minds of men and women for the last quarter of a century. This does not minimize its values. The best of the histories do indeed collectively comprehend most of the factors of feminist dissatisfaction. Eleanor Flexner's *Century of Struggle*[5] was a paean to the suffragists which hailed the courage of women's rights stalwarts who fought to realize the equality principles of the American Revolution. Andrew Sinclair's more comprehensive treatment of *The Emancipation of American Women*[6] seized upon some of the prime motivations of the feminist cause. He found among the leading subverters of historic female dependence: the city with its ample supply of contacts, services and opportunities; the available immigrant servants, later supplemented by technologic aids to the much denigrated housekeeper, wife and mother; and the upward sights set by educational opportunity and accomplishment. These were some of the social developments which stirred some women to work in the feminist context towards capturing solid self-esteem.

But for all the care of social and intellectual historianship, the full portrait of social, intellectual and personal "causation" has yet to emerge in clear delineation. Despite the wit and wisdom that pervades American expression of all sorts (the humor, spoof, satire, and irony in print and the arts betray an unrelieved anxiety), the core of the problem has not been extricated from the complications of psyche and society. There are always new avenues and insights. A few minds, for example, have recently come to see that feminism is at least fifty per cent a male problem. The 'hominists', comprising under fifty per cent of the American population, feel threatened with the loss of their exploitative position.

MARRIAGE, MORALS AND SEX IN AMERICA

Recent dimensions of the power struggle were clearly reflected by the manner in which best selling books captured the imagination of American women and, for that matter, of a large number of men. Two items, together with their militant lecturer authors, were doubtless the strongest stimuli (and appropriately drew the greater popular response) for the feminist cause of the past two decades. The first, a blast from abroad, was Simone de Beauvoir's *The Second Sex*, published in the United States in 1953. *The Feminine Mystique*, a native eruption, came from the pen of Betty Friedan in 1963 out of some twenty years of study and simmering. Both bore the marks of the personal and social scenes in which these authors lived and worked. Both were buttressed by a scholarly apparatus but were designed for mass appeal. Both spoke for assertive middle-class women.

Despite its universal character, there is a strong temptation to doubt whether the Beauvoir book would have won its wide audience without the huge publicity assist of its publisher, without the author's charisma and lecture tours, without critical and clarifying comment in mass circulation newspapers and news weeklies, and without the penchant of the American press for exploiting the author's "association" with the existentialist Jean Paul Sartre. For here was a famous literary liaison in which a woman asserted both her sex and her independence, in the manner of the Wollstonecraft-Godwin relationship a century and a half earlier, by eschewing marriage. What identification did the mass of American womanhood find in the mass of shrewdly selected scholarship which Mlle de Beauvoir drew from all areas of scientific and humanistic scholarship? What in elements of her argument and exhortation which ranged from the complex to the simple, from the abstruse to the superficial? It would seem that the popularity process started with public relations, was enhanced by the central message of the book, and was sealed with much confirming supportive evidence compressed into an overlong book. Was it the lofty, often soaring, poeticism of the work, or its prosaic paranoia, which impressed American readers? Was it the unaccustomed candor of a woman (a Frenchwoman at that)? Or the overwhelming case made against female Uncle Tomism—that chronic internalization of social and personal subordination, causing self-hatred? Surely the most telling contact Mlle de Beauvoir made with American women's perceptions was: Woman is always considered in relationship to man; she is the Other, possessing a mained selfhood; locked into her subordinate position, she is alienated and alienation is contagious to the whole society. In its special purpose, *The Second Sex* was an argument and a demand for yielding to women their existential equality, the right and opportunity for self-actualization, for establishing and pursuing their own goals. In its general impact, this was a book which anticipated the cry for defeating widespread alienation through each—male and female—doing his or her own "thing".

The Feminine Mystique gains in immediacy more than it loses in universal value. American women—also Frenchwomen, as an examination of French media shows[7]—have been brainwashed by male dominated magazines, radio and television to believe themselves best served by sequestered, pedestrian, household preoccupations. Mrs. Friedan's women, as Mlle de Beauvoir's, are suffering from an identity crisis in which their individual boundaries and self-awareness are obscured or lost. The French literary-philosopher delivered her analysis in broadly humanistic terms; her American counterpart, socio-psychological in professional orientation, made her diagnosis and complaint in terms of the contemporary environment. Women, Mrs. Friedan insisted, are taught by male prejudiced psychiatry and its Madison Avenue applications to accept as "natural" the intellectual, aesthetic and emotional satisfactions of a well-decorated home and a maximally beautified body.[8] Happiness is passive; it is bounded by the household shell. With such severe limitations on self-fulfillment, boredom follows, reflecting immediately on the psyches of husband and children. As women break into or are enlisted in male occupations, their role and their rewards tend to be on a lesser scale than that of men performing similar functions. Result: revolt.

Mrs. Friedan's feminine profile, obtained from extensive review of responsible studies and supplemented by questionnairing middle-class women, is fair enough. It would seem to apply with even greater sadness to blue-collar wives[9] whose entire upbringing and subsequent married life is geared toward housework, family service and husband service. With little of the education and egalitarian tradition that leads to self-assertiveness among their middle-class sisters, this class is doomed to greater dependency, insecurity, and concomitant anxiety. Shared activity with husbands is minimal. Assertiveness of any small degree tempts to reprisal (often physical punishment) or desertion; in any case, the threat of accentuated loneliness keeps self-expression in check. If the feminine mystique has produced a quiescent generation of middle-class women, their silence was considerably more audible than that of women of the working class, except where opportunities for independent earnings begin to break the spell of complete dependence.

But the fact of shared subordination merely adds vividness to the picture of sexual inequality and its consequences. The condition is there despite disagreements concerning elements of causation. One might, for example, object to Mrs. Friedan's blaming the mass media for inducing this oppressive feminine mystique. Magazine editors and their counterparts in other communications production do, after all, reflect—and possibly accentuate—existing audience needs whether aesthetic, social or sexual. Whether or not Mrs. Friedan was correct in assessing blame, American women—and women world-wide—have been receiving minority group treatment in business, the professions and other forms of institutional life,[10] and this the author of *The Feminine Mystique* has placed in sharp focus.

How then does America assess its dilemma? Much of its political, cultural and social history has led to a belief in socio-sexual equality. But equality seems as distant as ever. Assuming what only a handful of serious minded male supremacists deny, that there exists an equality of intelligence and talent, why has this not produced the realization of equal accomplishment? There are, to be sure, no visible restrictions on employment; but unemployment rates are higher for women, wages for comparable performance are lower, and acceptance into high-paid prestigious employment is severely limited. Many professional and academic women leaders,[11] accepting historic male values, are using pecuniary and status yardsticks of success. They demand a share in forms of human involvement now monopolized by men. This is not always true, as will be seen, of young women radicals who, side by side with like-minded males, would do their own "thing" rather than the "establishment thing".

Sexual democracy has failed for known reasons. For one matter, in human affairs of this nature, social and personal attitudes change even more slowly than the sanction of law. Majority power groups, "male" in this case, have yielded slowly. In a highly competitive society as prevails in the United States, differences (including sex differences) are defended stoutly in order to maintain the superiority they have signified. Secondly, the less powerful group has been disarmed by the established power by force of generally satisfactory affectional and social relationships. Women find it hard to fight against men when they share so many common goals. Finally, the producers of sexual wisdom have belonged to or have supported the male establishment. For example, social scientists study the ways of the present and the past, and tend therefore to confirm a laggard society by reporting it as it was and is. Feminist critics maintain with a high degree of conviction that psychiatry and psychoanalysis are male dominated. Such being the case, the psychological professions emphasize role differentiation in the family of the present, which differs only a little from the family of the past. Convinced by these overpowering repositories of knowledge and therapy, women beat a retreat to the bedroom and kitchen. This distortion of women's capacities carries over into the human organization in general and corrupts the masterclass in particular.

The current scene, none too quiescent, is rich with proposed remedies, experiments and tactics. There are proposals for compensatory assistance and institutional levers as, for example, child care centers located strategically close to places of employment and higher education. America's abounding faith in cure-all education has suggested the retreading of both sexes for changed role relationships. In view of general institutional sluggishness, there may be, for the time being, a *private* step to be taken by self-aware, forward looking couples (or families): as part of a general reaction to competitive materialism, male members of families will moderate their exaggerated (often leading to frustration) aspirations sufficiently to make possible an equal measure of self-realization for their women. In the calculus of competitive achievement, families might rate themselves—and ask to be rated—as teams.

THE POLITICS OF CONTEMPORARY FEMINISM

Among several plausible explanations for the post-World War II recession of American feminism is that which points up the absence of reform movements with which women could ally themselves in mutual assistance pacts. The study of history would indicate that such alliances have in the past yielded enhancement in the shape of training and organizational discipline rather than of reciprocal support. Whatever may be true of the past, the current resurgence of militant feminism does indeed show marks of overlapping left-liberal and radical programs, albeit the women participants are already accusing the males of using them for clerical chores only. Both the feeling and the rhetoric of recent movements—more or less organized—exhibit a philosophy of struggle between the exploiters and the exploited that works equally well with class and racial agitations.

The National Organization for Women (NOW), formed in 1966 and led by the redoubtable author of *The Feminine Mystique,* is the least radical of new feminist organizations in its programs of ends and means. NOW's members are largely youngish career women whose campaigns are generally directed toward career equality. They would, for example, invoke Title VII of the 1964 Civil Rights Act for the purpose of forcing newspapers to desegregate their male and female 'want ad' listings. Some success has already attended this demand. In line with American feminist thinking from the early nineteenth century onward, NOW would increase women's control over their own destinies by strengthening their decision-making power in the matter of childbirth. NOW asks for the repeal of abortion laws.[12]

Whereas the moderate National Organization for Women accepts the cooperation of sympathetic males, the loosely woven Women's Liberation Movement (or Front) insists on its sexual exclusiveness in much the fashion that black militant organizations exclude white participants. WLM (or WLF) advertises a new leftist abhorrence of ideological fences erected by rigid organizations. It follows the tactic of attempting to raze accepted behavioral structures by means of disruption, but occasionally joins moderate campaigns for equal rights. The movement has graced the scene of 'want ad' and pro-abortion agitations. It was the moving spirit of a beauty contest disruption claiming that men had made sex objects of women, thereby rendering them less than autonomous human beings. WITCH (Women's International Terrorist Conspiracy from Hell) is farther out on the radical line. Somehow connected with WLM, it carried out the bra-burning protest at a Miss American contest. Its acronym describes bizarre (disruption by antic) hexing activities which serve to dramatize the Movement. The Women's Radical Action Project (WRAP) is the movement's academic arm which resists condescending attitudes toward women students and demands a more equitable sexual distribution of Ph.D's. The disturbing fact is that when student couples are making joint career decisions, the male partner has been accorded the favored position for reasons both biological and logical. For, in the nature of family breeding, the risks of an interrupted, or disrupted, academic career are fewer for a husband than for a wife, other things like intellectual capacity being equal.

SEX IS INDIVISIBLE

There are several paths of reasoning that have led, and continue to lead, from the thrust for sexual equality to a drive for woman's right to a bounding sex life. Historically, equality with men has meant to both threatened males and very aggressive females the right to practice a single sex standard. For many, this has translated itself into varietism and infidelity; that is, traditional male privilege in a double standard system. One notes, indeed, a certain correspondence between militancy and promiscuity in the lives of a few old-time "far out" feminists. Again, there is a current brand of sexologic thinking which claims that generally assertive behavior will carry over into sexually assertive behavior. Whether the assertive female has an emasculative effect or achieves a happy compatibility of sexual drives provides a set of alternatives for experts who seem to be deciding the question more as a matter of individual taste than in accordance with ground rules of science.

Mrs. Friedan reports a number of effusive suburban housewives whose repressed ego-expression leads them to various gradations of sexual and marital irregularity. In her small sample of women who answered questions they were not asked, we observe dammed streams of social and personal energy diverted into marital unhappiness and extramarital sexual activities. The feminine mystique of passivity and inadequacy has spilled over into reservoirs of sexual exercise. Mothers of four and five children reported unsatisfied states of being that ranged from mild dissatisfaction with a spouse's intercourse performance to thoughts of infidelity, to thoughts of divorce or departure, to an actual liaison or two, to a nymphomaniacal search for some Orgastic Grail. How these cases of 'wanderlust' relate to career frustrations and other subordinations is still to be investigated on sounder scientific grounds. It may occur to speculative minds that such frantic sex seeking has long been characteristic of husbands who participated richly in shaping their own destinies as well as the projects of their society. We may be witnessing an upward adjustment of women's status rating. In suburban and 'exurban' scenes of sex seeking, the folks are reputedly engaging in wife-swapping, a sport which indeed offers husbands and wives equal opportunity.

The flurry of excitement in women's magazines and other media of idea exchange occasioned by the Masters-Johnson report on *Human Sexual Response*[13] revealed some of the intertwining of physical with social-sexual questions. Writers of both sexes took exception to the cold scientific approach—the study and measurement of physiological sex—to a relationship complicated by so many interpersonal nuances of socially conditioned people. Only a few commentators appreciated the fact that behaviors first studied and learned on a conscious and sometimes mechanistic level later became integrated in 'spontaneous' responses. To be sure, sex manuals had long been primers for those embarking on the great mating adventure although the profits and losses of such remain debatable. Further criticisms of Master's methodology and selection of subjects—certainly a hardy breed which performed before an audience an act which still is almost universally considered private—are worth considering and doubtless merit extended exploration.

By bringing sex into the laboratory, Masters and Johnson intensified the legitimate fear that the "objectifying forces of our culture [would] prevail over against the longing for truly human relations." But more immediately, their attention to enhancing the possibilities for female orgasm exposed an area of inequality which had but infrequently surfaced in the long drama of women's rights agitation. With so great a volume of current literature implying that orgasm is an open door to identity or self-realization, no wonder that alert sexual democrats should make special note of this aspect of human sexual response. No wonder the vigorous exchange of ideas provoked by a psychiatrist[14] who hinted that women fared very well before modern sexology instructed them to demand more of life. As one penetrating correspondent wrote: "But for the analyst to conclude that the problem lies with unrealistic expectations is an indication of how profoundly it is a man's world, and how widespread is the corruption." In political terms, the attitude of threatened male superiority was reactionary and counterrevolutionary. The tables of power were turning from an old definition of being pleasured to a new one of pleasuring. To fearsome males this was the sexual equivalent of an imminent reversal in social class position.

Having been made public property by reviewers and commentators, the scientific team of Masters and Johnson felt constrained to explain themselves in mass circulation magazines. Of course love and morality were paramount. Naturally sex discussions and sex instruction must elaborate more than parts and mechanics. Youth needs more object lessons within family life itself, and more school instruction on mutual honoring and loving, in contradistinction to mutual sexual exploitation by male and female. This emphasis becomes the more urgent in the face of improved contraception, with one of the consequences being an exaggerated tendency to physical sexual exploitation.[15]

EDUCATION—FOR WHAT?

Doubtful as it is that schools can inculcate ethical-social behavior patterns in a social environment that glorifies the. Darwinian struggle for individual power, the national faith in education would have it so. Sex instruction has expanded considerably in the era of the feminine mystique but without any relationship to it. Under the aegis of a general liberalization of sex attitudes in the United States, educators and their allies have succeeded in obtaining the widespread consent of community and state educational authorities for comprehensive sex instruction. Parents and teachers have assumed the idea that physical aspects of sexuality are altogether bound up with the perennial interest in moral questions.

But America in 1969 was undergoing a reaction to all things deemed liberal or dissident. Tolerance of greater sexual candor and freedom, gradually increasing since the beginning of the twentieth century, became in some quarters an acceptance of flaunted sexual expression. During the same period, a comparatively quiescent generation had been replaced by one seemingly in open revolt. Following an historic pattern, the moral indignation of conservative leaders has tended to fuse matters sexual with matters political. For them, sex education was surely a lever of subversive communism and both were attacked with comparable vigor. This conflict over sex education was complicated by non-political, reasoned complaints about bungling in the classroom. There was very little common ground among overambitious and under-sex-educated teachers, overanxious and part-ready parents, and students who arrived at their studies with a background of parental and peer group distortions.

Citizen groups brought vast and often successful pressures to bear on state and local legislatures to circumscribe the curriculum or forbid sex instruction altogether. The Boston rally of Conservative Americans gathered on July 4, 1969 to deplore the moral decay of the nation. The impeachment of sex education replaced the impeachment of Chief Justice Warren as a battle cry of conservative reaction. Said the leader of the Christian Crusade, the Reverend Billy James Hargis: "I don't want any kid under 12 to hear about lesbians, homosexuals and sexual intercourse. They should be concerned with tops, yo-yos and hide and seek."[16] Sex education was deemed a plot to sap the American moral fiber, thus exposing the nation to foreign conquest. SIECUS (the Sex Information and Education Council of the United States) was communism's fifth column.[17]

THE BREAKDOWN OF TRADITIONAL CONTROLS

Without denying the consistency of rebellion among certain types of rebel, the historian of twentieth century sexual behavior can hardly speak of sudden revolt in any one year or decade. Americans have been extricating themselves from Victorian morality slowly. The impatient drive of youth toward change has met with retarding social influences in the shape of family, social class, religious and other community counterpressures. The big change in sexual freedom took shape at the beginning of the century. Contrary to the popular habit of blaming socialism for the liberalization of sexual morality, this aspect of social evolution would seem to be more a product of accentuated individualism. It has represented more an unshackling of social restraint than a socialization of behavior.

If American sex life has seemed to some observers[18] to have gone wild suddenly, apparently they had been inattentive to change until some temporary acceleration jolted them into realization. The process of attitude liberalization has been speeding up gradually for decades. During the past few years the media of stage, screen and print have capitalized on the phenomenon. Even so expert an observer as Betty Friedan felt that an era of licentiousness had come upon us, noting that:

> Instead of fulfilling the promise of infinite orgastic bliss, sex in the America of the feminine mystique is becoming a strangely joyless national compulsion, if not a contemptuous mockery. The sex-glutted novels become increasingly explicit and increasingly dull; the sex kick of the women's magazines has a sickly sadness; the endless flow of manuals describing new sex techniques hint at an endless lack of excitement.[19]

One could substantially accept this observation without subscribing to its author's argument that the mystique which confines women's worthiness to household and sex functions is somehow responsible for American 'sexhibitionism'. The causes run deeper in the mechanisms of American society and thought. A penchant for the erotic is ancient; even Victorian America had its supplies of sluicy literature.[20] The twentieth century process of slow maturation, with its urban sophistication and libertarian ideals, has produced a climate in which neither law nor social sanction is yet capable of separating liberty and art from license and pornography. Literary *avant guardism* and commercial exploitation of the sexual stimulus met in the same tavern and drank to common success. The *Playboy* philosophy of high male status consisting of cool, confident and complete sexuality sat on a bar stool next to low cult magazines with crude "girlie" appeal without excessive problems of communication.[21] Sex for sophisticated males, with coy magazine counterparts for women (Kinsey reported that women responded far less to visual stimuli), was properly set on a platter garnished with the names of prestigious literary figures. It was in many ways a wholesome thing for high cultural talent to bed with the mass mind, but the offspring could be ambiguous creatures.[22] The law had *its* criteria. Critics of literature, drama and the cinema had *theirs*. But the lack of consistency of judgment in the courts and among the critics produced fuzzy pronouncements everywhere.

The dicta of critics and courts, however, were perhaps unrelated to the responses of large consumers of popular art—the people. Sex in America has been the consequence of neither of the country's creative industries nor of subversive foreign importations. People, after all, play a strong if not commanding role in selecting their entertainment stimuli. When the Motion Picture Association of America rated pictures from G (for general audiences) to X (for adults only) it was protecting profits against the potential censor rather than viewers against moral deterioration. Audiences which queued up for blocks to attend a well-publicized cinematic sex stimulator were eager for more than art. Writers of semi-obscure plays on the whole fared better with both critics and audiences in proportion to their sexual implicitness or explicitness. Playwrights may have intended worthy social and philosophic messages, but their sexual transmission apparatus was more easily understood.

Sexual realism, never a resounding success in the American novel, was intensified in the high cult novels of Norman Mailer, Jeremy Larner, Ken Kesey, Leonard Cohen, Philip Roth and others.[23] This literary phenomenon was more than a market response, although these authors have reaped a fair harvest. Fictional reassertion of high male sexuality could be a caricature of America's preoccupation with gonadal existence. Literary Don Juanism, promising identity, existential meaning and keys to Utopia *via* sexercise, may conceivably have been a creative response to a depolarization of sexual roles in America life.[24] Nor was there a lack for sex-bent heroines such as were to be found in the pages of lesser fiction like *Peyton Place* and *Valley of the Dolls*.

To what precise extent writing, the arts and the general public candor reflected norms of sexual and sex associated behavior cannot be measured because of the subtlety of distinctions and the inaccessibility of data. But many things can be known without ultimate precision. For example, the novel and the theatre exploited the homosexual theme, and homosexuals flaunted the deviance they formerly concealed without, to our knowledge, appreciably increasing the incidence of homosexual tendencies; public attitudes were merely more casual and tolerant. Nor has the observed depolarization of sexual roles in America perceptibly affected—except possibly to add slightly to normal maladjustments—sexual behavior as such.[25] This blurring of traditionally masculine and feminine tastes, clothes, coiffures, sports activities and such probably did not diminish the search for sexual union any more than has the gradual though very incomplete leveling of the male-female status struggle in American society.[26]

Did widespread expression of social permissiveness carry over into permissive sexual behavior? Did unblushing discussion correlate with a startling increase of premarital or extramarital intercourse? The evidence is most incomplete. On summarizing numerous studies, Charles Winick found an "inverse relationship between sexual attitudes and behavior. . . . In sex, it seems relatively easy to 'go away a little closer' and adapt to an incompatibility between attitudes and behavior: those who do, say they don't; those who don't, say they do. Those who coo don't bill and those who bill, coo less."[27] Increases of illegitimacy which have been reported were for women over twenty; teenagers have shown a rate decrease. A minority of college girls (about a quarter) were non-virgins; some two to three per cent were promiscuous. The incidence of equal sexual privilege has grown slowly since the 1920's but, as a knowledgeable wag has expressed it, only because those who have lost their virginity have lost it many times. Such estimates do not deny surprisingly higher scores for some college campuses; they do provide the basis for a national estimate, averaging more traditional young people with their more adventurous sisters. They say too little of older populations (the Kinsey studies need updating). They say nothing of a galloping potential in the last several years by dint of the popularization of oral contraceptives.

One should not, however, proceed to hasty projections. There has, indeed, been a connection between the relative safety of contraception and the relative incidence of unsanctioned intercourse. However, as long as doubt remains concerning the safety factor and side effects, larger social considerations have retarded the movement toward permissiveness. Sociological studies have given little solace to parents who —and this seems an almost universal statement—have always wanted their children to be more restricted in their sexual behavior than they themselves were a generation earlier. But recent professional findings should provide some comfort for worries of cataclysmic proportion.

If lower class parents of daughters are more anxious than middle-class parents, this is a just apportionment of anxiety. For among the poor, women tend more to carry on their own family lines, mating serially (for short periods) and non-maritally. There are fewer factors of property and family status to restrain them. Available husbands offer meager material security; relief payments are preferable. Illegitimacy often runs, as if by inheritance, from mother to daughter and so on down the line.

But among the white collar and middle classes generally,[28] the risks of pregnancy and bastardy score seriously against family honor and status. The firmness of such class oriented barriers to premarital intercourse was illustrated in the Kinsey studies of women born after 1900. The 1920's showed some increase but with future husbands. An apparent trend, which can be expected to develop further, is the permissibility of intercourse for betrothed couples, a practice which some other cultures have long since placed within the bounds of acceptability. American society decades ago made the transition from total rejection of breaches of intactness to an acceptance of "technical" virginity, allowing petting to climax. The promise of contraceptive perfection may move moral guardians in the direction of permitting cohabitation with a loved one. Immediate marriage would be automatic in the case of pregnancy; a wedding would be intended at some time in every case. What may be expected is a gradual and incomplete yielding of forces which protect traditional morality to forces which foster a new morality. An increase in heterosexual meetings in commerce, industry and education; a dating system which removes girls from familial and community supervision; a continual thrust for women's rights; an efficient contraceptive technology—such forces toward permissiveness may well result in social acceptance of an ethic already on the way to change in widespread practice.

The family institution doubtless gained strength in the past from its legal monopoly on sex. The limited loss of this monopoly has not endangered the institution. Free love advocates, who proposed sex without marriage, have all but disappeared from the American scene —partly because social controls have been relaxed so that those who would avoid marriage are permitted to practice quietly what sex radicals in the past preached from the rooftops. Anti-marriage feminists have made similarly small inroads on historic marriage and family customs. However, the possibility of increased resort to divorce for the solution of marital problems remains a threat to institutional stability.

FAMILY STABILITY

Radical feminists of the nineteenth and twentieth centuries, when confronted by an incorrigible male-favoring society, hit upon the simple logic of liberating oppressed wives by increasing the possibilities for divorce. Sympathetic—and many chronically restless—males concurred. The idea of equality came to include an equal right to secede from an unsatisfactory relationship. By another line of reasoning, the *feminine mystique* nexus of ideas would lay the blame for family instability at the door of exaggerated female dependence. To quote Mrs. Friedan: "There are, of course, many reasons for divorce, but chief among them seems to be the growing aversion and hostility that men have for the feminine millstones hanging around their necks, a hostility that is not always directed at their wives, but at their mothers, the women they work with—in fact, women in general."[29]. On the distaff side of the mystique complex, unfulfilled millstones become rolling stones which move about in search of new necks to hang onto. The nuances of the divorce question have been numerous and the millstone syndrome has not been a chief source of trouble.

As social and legal restraints on the availability of divorce slowly corroded in the United States, the divorce rate did indeed rise; but the "causes" of increase were neither divorce availability, militant feminism nor the exclusion of women from ego-bolstering activities. The root causes of the problem were present before Europeans began settling in North America. America's divorce plant became visible in post-Civil War decades, budded in the period of waning national innocence—the years before World War 1[30]—and came to full bloom in the aftermath of World War II. Observers of this last period seemed to see a revolution by family dissolution. But what they witnessed was the culmination of a gradual evolution somewhat accelerated by second thoughts on thoughtless wartime marriages. The divorce rate had ascended very gradually from 1900 to 1940, soared in the mid'forties (the peak year was 1946) and then dropped, but never back to the pre-1940's level.

Divorce, as recent social historians have viewed it, became an increasing necessity as husbands, wives and their families moved from relaxed community interdependence in village societies into a suffocatingly close interpersonal dependence of larger community life. This occurred in sixteenth and seventeenth century Europe. The compression of the family was both social and spatial. The older mode had offered numerous social and affectional alternatives to marital irritations so as to relieve them and to minimize the need for dissolving families. Coming up to our own time and place: Divorce was difficult to contemplate in sparsely settled America where mutual need drove people toward rather than away from each other. Urbanizing America, however, not only pressed couples and offspring into small living spaces; it also offered a cloak of anonymity—an effect city life invariably has had— for men and women to seek and find, or just encounter, alternative sources of personal and sexual gratification. These facts of life, earlier felt and vaguely understood in the Progressive Era, have stimulated leaders of thought and thoughtful leaders to seek suitable modifications of divorce law and, at the same time, a lessening of social sanctions against divorced people.

Public interest in the divorce "boom" of the past quarter century exhibited a period of high excitement during the half-dozen years following World War II and then tapered off to a mood of acceptance of conditions as they existed. The graph line of this vaguely national attitude seemed to follow the leveling off of divorce rates. For despite periodic exclamations of alarm about rising divorce incidence, the peak (already noted) had been reached immediately after the war. Divorce has apparently not been the dissolving, destructive force as it had appeared to family 'conservatives' of an earlier time. Moreover, remarriages have provided assurance of the viability of American family life.

Factors which tend to unglue marriages have frequently been as discernible by observant laymen as they have been by trained psychologists and sociologists. The function which professionals may be expected to perform is that of approximating equations of personal and social forces which portend relative permanence or impermanence of family units. The promise has been altogether discouraging. A review[31] of major studies leads to the unpromising conclusion that the balance of elements that account for divorce makes marriage counseling a problematic endeavor. Especially intractable are personality factors. Future marriage mates should, in theory, take a close look at each other for a sufficient time in a realistic setting; yet they are also enjoined by custom to engage in romantic courtship games while at a respectable distance from each other. What seems auspicious for upper-class couples is inauspicious for lower orders; but mating crosses class lines frequently, especially from higher male to lower female class position. Rural families dissolve at lower rates than urban families. Yet the population drive has always been toward the city. It is also on the urban scene that family compression engenders irritations and economic opportunity decreases dependence. There are indications that suburban life, where the watchfulness of social circles is respected by their members, has a positive effect on family solidity; but still other observations report that suburban loneliness leads to a search for alternative attachments. Among the strong restraints against family dissolution has been a strong commitment to "strict" religions; but such religious ties are weakening, and proscriptive religions are undergoing change in the direction of permissive modernization.

The American democratic ethos, with its stress on individualism and equality—especially in the context of feminism—has complicated the problem of family cohesion. The male-female power balance is at best a delicate one. Males, educated to believe in democratic principles but nurtured in an environment of sexual inequality, have been taxed considerably in their adjustment to equality-minded wives. In aggravation of this tension, rebellious youth has recently been accenting anarchistic dimensions of democratic individualism. Self-expression, carried to an extreme by way of striving always to "do one's thing," would seem to be antipathetic to the cooperative merger of wills required by marriage. A successful outcome may be possible in unions of complementary personalities; but the prognosis cannot be optimistic in view of the complex of drives and ambivalences that two people, having met largely by chance, bring to each other. Divorce may have to remain the surgery for accidents of marriage.

THE ROAD AHEAD

All of which leaves us with a formulation of our problem in which the issues have remained substantially unchanged in the couple of centuries since the American nation fought its revolution for the principle of human equality. Of the many conditions and circumstances that complicate the problem of sexual peace, the factor most amenable to mastery would seem to involve a balance of esteem, independence, power, and mutual respect between the sexes. A more general and generous appreciation of the nature of the other's needs, plus a deeper awareness of self and its drives, may mitigate the irritations of close living. Certainly it does not breed self-confidence for women to read—this time from the pen of Norman Mailer, a first-rate grasper of behavioral essences: "The fact of the matter is that the prime responsibility of a woman probably is to be on earth long enough to find the best mate possible for herself, and conceive children who will improve the species."

Such dicta may be designed for shock value. They may also represent a relief, through humor, from male anxiety. For the problems which beset marriage, morals and sex in America are at least equally, if not 'more than equally', male problems despite the fact that the master sex has been blaming women for them. Women leaders have long suspected an unwillingness on the part of males to identify problems whose solution may harm their status advantage. They have also intimated their belief that male intellectuals have a tendency to accentuate difference in sexual character and capacity in order to confirm a belief in female inferiority. But feminist militance may prove to be as mistaken about its insistence on sharing of roles and goals as male chauvinism is about sexual exclusiveness.

Recently the writings of Charles Winick[32] and Erik Erikson[33] have directed our attention to a better appreciation of the essential character and role differences of male and female. Admittedly, the capabilities and aspirations of men and women overlap a great deal; but equality need not be sameness. Winick hypothesized that balance and complementarity are in danger of being lost when men and women try to assume common roles and behaviors. Erikson's observations of personality development have demonstrated a distinctive unity of female behavior that somehow is related to biological structure. Whatever woman's personality uniqueness, this femaleness promises, if honored by general acceptance, to provide selfhood and worldly roles that can be both appropriate and satisfying. Nor need distinctive femininity dam up women's desires to participate in many traditionally male activities. Moreover, the recognition of separate but equal identity may help to reduce competition that sharpens the ongoing struggle.

Were not sexual behavior in its broadest sense inextricably bound up with numerous social structures and circumstances, the intervention of educational agencies and the responsible use of social scientific knowledge by communications media might be expected to produce an improved *modus vivendi*. But education and communications are themselves restrained by fears of diminished male dominance. If some women leaders have in recent times been waging a limited campaign of social disruption, they have merely been sampling the tactics of other groups which consider available mechanisms for redress to be inadequate and frustrating. The fact is of little consequence that an historical view would prove the women's rights movement to have had substantial successes. Rarely has an upward pressing social movement been deterred from agitation by the knowledge that the class or group position was worse in the past. Revolt accelerates in times of rising expectation. Feminist aggression is also nourished by frustrating obstacles in the way of realizing historic principles and promises. In the manner of most privileged groups, maledom resists what it perceives to be a status threat.

We are, in the final analysis, dealing with a struggle which possesses both public and private phases. At the public front, the struggle is vigorous, and retreat is infrequent and limited. Behind the lines, the sides in conflict would seem to have arrived at an accommodation of objectives. The public rebuffs of American women have been offset, for married women at least, by private victories. For middle class homes have in general worked out their problems of personal dignity and equality, and this accounts for the largest number of American families. Of course, much remains to be achieved for equality in social and public life; but surely the pacifist slogan "Make love not war" can be seen to apply also to our internal, ambivalent war of the sexes.

NOTES

1. James R. McGovern, "The American Woman's Pre-World War I Freedom in Manners and Morals," *The Journal of American History* LV (September 1968), p. 315-333.

2. e.g. George E. Howard, *A History of Matrimonial Institutions* (3 vols. 1904); Arthur W. Calhoun, *A Social History of the American Family* (3 vols. 1917-19).

3. John Sirjamaki, *The American Family in the Twentieth Century* (Harvard University Press, 1953), a sociological and historical analysis; Sidney Ditzion, *Marriage, Morals and Sex in America* (Bookman, 1953), a history of ideas from colonial times; Eleanor Flexner, *Century of Struggle* (Harvard University Press, 1959), emphasizes political aspects of the women's rights movement; Andrew Sinclair, *The Emancipation of American Woman* (Harper, 1965), American feminist history from a variety of viewpoints; Aileen S. Kraditor, *The Ideas of the Woman Suffrage Movement, 1890-1920* (Columbia University Press, 1965); also A. S. Kraditor, ed., *Up from the Pedestal: Selected Writings in the History of American Feminism* (Quadrangle, 1968); Robert E. Riegel, *American Feminists* (University of Kansas Press, 1963), a psychosocial history of American feminists; Gerda Lerner, *The Grimké Sisters from South Carolina* (Houghton Mifflin, 1968), a biographical study of two early anti-slavery and women's rights agitators; Charles Winick, *The New People: Desexualization in American Life* (Pegasus, 1968), on the blurring and depolarization of sexual roles since World War II; for a central repository of all branches of learning, see Albert Ellis and Albert Abarbanel, eds., *The Encyclopedia of Sexual Behavior* (2 vols., Hawthorne, 1961).

4. *The American Quarterly* (Organ of the American Studies Association) has been alert to the possibilities of an interdisciplinary approach to the subjects of woman, sex, etc. Among its articles have been those by Robert Riegel on "Women's Clothes and Women's Rights"; by Carl Bode on "Columbia's Carnal Bed;" by William Bridges on "Family Patterns and Social Values in America, 1825-1875"; by William O'Neill on "Divorce in the Progressive Era"; by Carol Brooks on "The Early History of the Anti-Contraceptive Laws in Massachusetts and Connecticut"; by Kenneth A. Yellis on "Prosperity's Child: Some Thoughts on the Flapper."

5. Flexner, loc. cit.

6. Sinclair, loc. cit.

7. H. A. Bouraoui, "La Femme Revoltée: A Contrastive Cultural Study," *Journal of Popular Culture* II (Spring 1969), pp. 593-614.

8. Albert Ellis, in the *American Sexual Tragedy* (Twayne, 1954), has emphasized the frustrating disparity between the promise of commercial aids to beautification and the actual possibilities of achieving what is considered to be standard sexual attractiveness.

9. Lee Rainwater, Richard P. Coleman and Gerald Handel, *Working-man's Wife: Her Personality, World and Life Style* (Oceana Publications, 1959.)

10. Among recent works are: Caroline Bird, *Born Female: The High Cost of Keeping Women Down* (McKay, 1968), an impassioned but humorless account of the facts of inequality which scores a valid point on the social inefficiency of subordinating womanpower; Mary Daly, *The Church and the Second Sex* (Harpers, 1968), on historic misogynistic tendencies of the Church; Mary Ellmann, *Thinking about Women* (Harcourt, 1968), argues that matters are in better balance than they seem; also Eli Ginzberg, *Educated American Women* (Columbia University Press, 1966); Eli Ginzberg, *Self-Portraits and Life Styles of Educated Women* (Columbia University Press, 1966).

11. Most of the views developed in this portion of the text are found in essays by several contributors to Robert J. Lifton, ed., *The Woman in America* (Houghton Mifflin, 1965), previously published in large part as *Daedalus* XCIII (Spring 1964), pp. 579-808.

12. Jo Freeman, "The New Feminists," *Nation* CCVIII (Feb. 24, 1969), pp. 241-44; Paula Stern, "When's It Going to be Ladies' Day?" *New Republic* CLXI (July 5, 1969), pp. 14-16.

13. William H. Masters and Virginia E. Johnson, *Human Sexual Response* (Little Brown, 1966).

14. Leslie H. Farber, "I'm Sorry Dear," *Commentary* XXXVIII (November 1964), pp. 47-54; *Same*, XXXIX (April 1965), pp. 14, 16, 18, 20, 22, 24, 26-27; and (May 1965), pp. 8, 10, 12, 14, 16.

15. W. H. Masters and V. E. Johnson, "Defense of Love and Morality," *McCalls* XCIV (November 1966), pp. 102-103; also "Sex and Sexuality: The Crucial Difference," *Readers Digest* XC (February 1967), pp.123-126.

16. John H. Fenton, "At Conservative Rally, the Tone is Moral," *New York Times*, July 7, 1969, p. 37, col. 1-4.

17. Richard M. Cohen, "Teaching Sex in the School," *New Republic* CLX (June 28, 1969), pp. 11-12.

18. e.g. Vance Packard, *The Sexual Wilderness: The Contemporary Upheaval in Male-Female Relationships* (McKay, 1968).

19. Betty Friedan, *The Feminine Mystique* (Dell, 1963), p. 250.

20. Carl Bode, "Columbia's Carnal Bed," *American Quarterly* XV (Spring 1963), pp. 52-64.

21. Walter M. Gerson and Sander H. Lund, "Playboy Magazine: Sophisticated Smut or Social Revolution?" *Journal of Popular Culture* I (Winter 1967), pp. 218-227.

22. Bernard Weinraub, "Obscenity or Art? A Stubborn Issue," *New York Times*, July 7, 1969, p. 20 col. 1-4.

23. Robert Boyers, "Attitudes toward Sex in American 'High Culture,'" *The Annals of the American Academy of Political and Social Science* CCCLXXVI (March 1968), pp. 36-52.

24. Winick, pp. 45-52.

25. *Ibid., passim*

26. Sidney Ditzion [review article] *American Quarterly* XXI (Spring 1969), pp. 130-132.

27. Winick, p. 306.

28. This section draws heavily upon Hallowell Pope and Dean D. Knudsen, "Premarital Sexual Norms, the Family, and Social Change," *Journal of Marriage and the Family*, XXVII (August 1965), pp. 314-323.

29. Friedan, p. 261.

30. William L. O'Neill, *Divorce in the Progressive Era* (Yale University Press, 1967).

31. George Levinger, "Marital Cohesiveness and Dissolution: an Integrative Review," *Journal of Marriage and the Family* XXVII (February 1965), pp. 19-28.

32. Winick, pp. 350-357 and *passim*.

33. Erik H. Erikson, "Inner and Outer Space: Reflections on Womanhood," in R. J. Lifton, ed., *The Woman in America*, pp. 1-26.

A NOTE ON SOURCES

A conscientious effort was made in the writing of this book to avoid belaboring the general reader, for whom it was written, with hundreds of documentary footnotes. The author has, however, woven into the text the names of literary sources out of which his contribution to historical knowledge was fabricated. In a real sense the book is itself a bibliographical essay.

Moreover, much has been drawn from the works of previous scholars who have dealt with, or touched upon the persons, movements and historical trends which fall within the scope of interest of *Marriage, Morals, and Sex in America*. In all but a few instances the indebtedness is slight. But where such existing works have provided connecting links among seemingly unrelated particles of the present author's research, no expression of gratitude is large enough.

The only extensive work which is devoted exclusively to the past of the American family and related subjects is Arthur W. Calhoun, *A Social History of the American Family from Colonial Times to the Present* (3 vols., 1917-19; reprinted in one vol., 1945). Bernhard J. Stern, in *The Family, Past and Present* (1938), has edited with excellent introductory notes selected passages illustrating change in the structure and functions of the American family. The historical portions of Joseph K. Folsom, *The Family and Democratic Society* (1943), provide a brief summary.

George E. Howard, *A History of Matrimonial Institutions Chiefly in England and the United States* (3 vols., 1904), is irreplaceable in its treatment of the legal roots of Anglo-Saxon family evolution. The task of supplementing it adequately for the last half century is a project for a team of family historians. Illustrations of briefer treatments covering a broad geographical range are Willystine Goodsell, *History of Marriage and the Family* (1934), and Carle C. Zimmerman, *Family and Civilization* (1947).

The above constitute but the edges of a vast field, rich in scholarship and source materials. For those seeking to penetrate more deeply, there are the lengthy, suggestive lists provided by the books already mentioned as well as by several syllabus-bibliographies for students and other interested members of the adult population. The most recent work in this category is William L. Ludlow, *A Syllabus and a Bibliography of Marriage and the Family* (1951). Older, but still useful, are *A Bibliography on Family Relationships* (National Council of Parent Education, 1932), and George E. Howard, *The Family and Marriage; an Analytical Reference Syllabus* (University of Nebraska, 1914).

A NOTE ON SOURCES

Notable recent attempts to keep family sociologists up to date are those of Ernest R. Groves in the periodical *Social Forces* for December 1940, March 1942, October 1943, and May 1946, and of Albert Ellis *et al.* in *Marriage and Family Living* for Summer 1950, Spring 1951, and May 1952. The last of these, containing a list of some five hundred items from professional and welfare sources alone, is an indication of how much attention the sex problem receives annually. A comparable figure for popular and semi-popular imprints would by itself be a staggering one. Also to be noted in the *Marriage and Family Living* bibliography is an obvious recognition that the sociosexual problem is an all-embracing one. The coverage of the Ellis lists includes (in addition to recent lists offered by other compilers) subject divisions as follows: Abortion; Artificial Insemination; Birth Control; Childbirth and Maternity; Courtship and Love; Divorce and Separation; Fertility and Sterility; Genetics and Population Problems; Illegitimacy; Intermarriage; Marriage and Family Counseling and Psychotherapy; Marriage and Family Law; Marriage and Family Life Education; Marriage and Family Statistics; Marriage Customs and Ceremonies; Menstruation and Menopause; Parent-Child Relations; Prostitution; Religion and Marriage and Family Relations; Sex Attitudes and Behavior; Sex Censorship; Sex Deviations; Sex, Love, and Marriage in Literature; Sex, Marriage and Family Adjustment; Sex Offenses; Sterilization; Venereal Disease; Women.

In addition to the inevitable attention accorded problems of womanhood in works devoted to marriage and the family, the woman question has had its own extensive literature on the social, economic, and family status of the feminine sex. The outstanding current bibliographical compilation in this field is that of the Women's College Library at the University of North Carolina. Inasmuch as this bibliography of materials in the Woman's Collection purports to list only those items added since 1937, the materials of interest to historians of past centuries are not too plentiful. The subjects covered by this list are: The Child, The Family, The Home, Costume, Women in Education, Women's Personal Problems, Women's Cultural Interests, Avocations, Women in the World's Work, Interesting Women, Women in History, Social History of Women, Women and War.

The histories of the needs and deeds of American women are so numerous that it is possible to name only a few here. The literary monument to the feminist movement is the *History of Woman Suffrage,* edited by Elizabeth C. Stanton, Susan B. Anthony, and Matilda J. Gage (6 vols., 1881-1922). Among the shorter comprehensive works are Ernest R. Groves, *The American Woman; The Feminine Side of a Masculine Civilization* (revised and enlarged 1944); Eugene A. Hecker, *A Short History of Women's Rights from the Days of Augustus to the Present Time* (1914); Belle Squire, *The Woman Movement in America*

(1911); and Abbie Graham, *Ladies in Revolt* (1934). Mary R. Beard, *Women as a Force in History* (1946), is valuable for its historical depth and insight as well as for its illustrative bibliography. The serious student of ideas and their history must also read Viola Klein, *The Feminine Character; History of an Ideology* (1946; first American edition, 1949), which is an eclectic sociological study of the results of researches in biology, philosophy, history, anthropology and other fields.

Also deserving of attention are some of the better specialized studies which deal with early stages of American history. The social position of women is explored extraordinarily well in Mary S. Benson, *Women in Eighteenth-Century America* (1935) as is their legal status in Richard B. Morris, *Studies in the History of American Law* (1930). Elisabeth A. Dexter has provided invaluable studies in *Colonial Women of Affairs* (1924) and in *Career Women of America, 1776-1840* (1950).

Inasmuch as the feminist movement of the nineteenth and twentieth centuries is closely identified with the lives of a few women leaders, biographical works contribute a great deal toward our understanding of its history. To cite a suggestive handful, there are Ida H. Harper, *The Life and Work of Susan B. Anthony* (3 vols., 1898-1908); Theodore Stanton and Harriot Stanton Blatch, editors, *Elizabeth Cady Stanton as Revealed in Her Letters, Diary and Reminiscences* (2 vols., 1922); Lloyd C. M. Hare, *The Greatest American Woman, Lucretia Mott* (1937); Alice Stone Blackwell, *Lucy Stone, Pioneer of Woman's Rights* (1930). The later political phase of the suffrage movement is treated in Mary G. Peck, *Carrie Chapman Catt* (1944).

The most comprehensive work on birth control thought and progress in America—and also in the world at large from ancient times onward—is Norman E. Himes, *Medical History of Contraception* (1936). For those interested in popular and professional aspects of American medical history, Richard H. Shryock, *The Development of Modern Medicine* (1936) will prove helpful.

The reader seeking further knowledge of the intellectual, social and religious movements touched upon in *Marriage, Morals, and Sex in America*, will find his most advantageous starting point in Merle Curti, *The Growth of American Thought* (1943; second edition, 1951). Professor Curti's Bibliographical Note of some sixty pages is sufficient for the pursuit of information on a multitude of ideas and their place in history. For general background materials, there are also the standard Vernon L. Parrington, *Main Currents in American Thought* (3 vols., 1927-30; also one volume editions in 1930 and 1939), and Ralph H. Gabriel, *The Course of American Democratic Thought* (1940). Harvey Wish, *Society and Thought in America*, (2 vols., 1950-1952) is a welcome addition to the literature of social and intellectual history. Oscar Cargill, *Intellectual America; Ideas on the March* (1941), and Frank L. Mott, *Golden Multitudes* (1947) are recommended for the contribution they make to the history of ideas in literature as well as to our knowledge of the literary preferences of American readers.

The richest treatise on movements of social dissent in America before 1860—and also the most helpful to the present author in tracing the origins and history of various religious and communitarian settlements—is Alice Felt Tyler, *Freedom's Ferment* (1944). Along similar lines, but covering longer time spans, are Lillian Symes and Travers Clement, *Rebel America* (1934), and Victor F. ·Calverton, *Where Angels Dared to Tread* (1941).

Not to be neglected in any expedition into social history are the 'period' and 'decade' works which, because of their limited time scope, traverse the ground of social habit in more leisurely fashion. The thirteen volumes of the History of American Life series (Macmillan, 1927-1948) are most comprehensive in this respect. The 'period' works of special pertinence to the writing of *Marriage, Morals, and Sex in America* are: Thomas L. Nichols, *Forty Years of American Life,* 1821-1861 (1937; first published in 1864), Edward D. Branch, *The Sentimental Years,* 1836-1860 (1934), Robert E. Riegel, *Young America,* 1830-1840 (1949). Grace K. Adams and Edward Hutter, *The Mad Forties* (1942), Fred L. Pattee, *The Feminine Fifties* (1940), Henry Seidel Canby, *The Age of Confidence; Life in the Nineties* (1934).

Readers who so desire may gain entrance into a vast and intricate network of historical trends and relationships by following out the lists of references contained in a few of the scholarly social histories already cited. The present Note on Sources does not name individually the long list of works consulted by the author. Suffice it to say that an immense and fascinating literature awaits readers who are interested in community experiments of all sorts, in Shakerism, Mormonism, Noyesism, Spiritual Wifery, Freethought, and other special kinds of intellectual innovation. Nor can one afford to overlook biography's horn of plenty which any decently stocked public or institutional library can offer. For, ideas divorced from the lives of persons who expressed and interpreted them, cannot possibly be portrayed in their full meaning. The writing of our chapter on the Free Enquirers, for example, was substantially aided by Richard W. Leopold's *Robert Dale Owen* (1940), William R. Waterman's *Frances Wright* (1924), and A. J. G. Perkins' and Theresa Wolfson's *Frances Wright: Free Enquirer* (1939).

Among the many other research studies drawn upon, the following merit special mention: Osborne Earle, *The Reputation and Influence of William Godwin in America* (unpublished Ph.D. dissertation, Harvard University, 1938); Julia Power, *Shelley in America in the Nineteenth Century* (University of Nebraska studies, vol. 40 no. 2,

1940); Ellen Ransom, *Utopus Discovers America; or, Critical Realism in American Utopian Fiction,* 1798-1900 (unpublished Ph.D. dissertation, Vanderbilt University, 1946); Eunice M. Schuster, *Native American Anarchism* (Smith College Studies in History no. 17, 1931-32).

Acknowledgments to previous assemblers and interpreters of historical data are customary, necessary and proper. But too often authors accept without comment or gratitude, or, at best, with mechanical acknowledgment, the uncopyrighted labors of those anonymous compilers, organizers, and preservers of knowledge—the members of the library profession. A grand salute, therefore, to those colleagues past and present who selected, arranged, and preserved the raw materials for this book.

[CHAPTER TWELVE IS NOT INCLUDED IN THIS INDEX]

NINETEENTH AND TWENTIETH CENTURY
AMERICAN HISTORY IN THE NORTON LIBRARY